WHERE TO EAT
PIZZA

WHERE TO EAT
PIZZA

—

DANIEL YOUNG

**THE EXPERTS' GUIDE
TO THE BEST PIZZA
PLACES IN THE WORLD**

CONTENTS

Preface 6
The Regional Experts 9
Introduction 20

OCEANIA
Australia   **32**
     Sydney   38
     Melbourne   44
     Perth   52
New Zealand   **56**

ASIA
Southwest Asia   **68**
South & Southeast Asia   **76**
     Singapore   82
China, Hong Kong &
     South Korea   **90**
     Hong Kong   96
Japan   **102**
     Tokyo   110

EUROPE
Norway, Sweden,
     Denmark & Finland   **122**
UK & Republic of Ireland   **136**
     London   144
The Netherlands, Belgium
     & Luxembourg   **156**
     Amsterdam   160
France & Monaco   **170**
     Paris   180
Spain, Portugal & Malta   **188**
Germany & Switzerland   **196**
     Munich   204
     Hamburg   208
Austria, the Czech Republic
     & Slovenia   **218**
The Russian Federation   **224**
Italy   **230**
     Naples   278
     Rome   288
     Milan   298
     Turin   302
     Florence   306
Croatia, Serbia & Greece   **316**

AFRICA
South Africa   **328**

NORTH AMERICA
Canada   **336**
     Toronto   348
USA West   **354**
     Los Angeles   376
     San Francisco   384
USA Midwest   **392**
     Chicago   422
USA South   **434**
USA Northeast   **460**
     New York City   484
     Philadelphia   500
Central America   **508**

SOUTH AMERICA
South America North   **514**
South America South   **520**
     Rio de Janeiro   530
     São Paulo   536
     Buenos Aires   546

PIZZA ESSAYS
Neapolitan Pizza's Soft Spot 64
The *Pizzaiolo* in the Home
     Stretch 88
Japan's Neapolitan Pizza
     Obsession 118
Christian Puglisi Masters
     Mozzarella 134
The Original Pizza Truck
     Movement 186
The Neapolitan Pizza
     Renaissance 216
In Rome and New York, Some
     Like it Crisp 312
Neapolitan Pizza Ovens: As Hot
     as Ever 314
The Art of the Pizza Box 390
Pizza Tours 430
The Secret of Detroit Pizza Gets
     Out 432
Small-Batch Pizza in Small Town,
     USA 458
The Ways of the Pizza Fold 506
A Visit to Castelões 552

The Contributors 554
Index by Restaurant 558
Index by Country 565

PREFACE

Knowing where to eat pizza—near home, on the road, or on the other side of the world—isn't getting easier. It's only getting better.

Where To Eat Pizza is a comprehensive insider's guide to the best pizza places in the world: 1,705 selections in 48 countries chosen by 121 regional experts and 956 pizza informants. The guide's vast scope suits a food of such universal popularity and emotional power: we argue about which is the best with the same ardor, conviction, and love that we devote to every bite of it. In the best hands pizza is the world's fastest slow food: the dough can rest for 24 hours or longer, then bakes into a pizza crust in minutes. It is an impulse food that instantly melts the resistance of two groups of diners more petulant and difficult to please than any other: famous chefs and six-year-olds.

How do you like your pizza? Thick-crust or thin-crust? Round or square? Crisp or forgiving? Pan-baked or stone-baked? Creative or old school? Lightly dressed or piled on? Wholesome or trashy? In *Where To Eat Pizza* every side in the raging pizza wars has its champions.

The standout pizza places in the guide are organized by continent, then by country, region, or city. Basic information about each venue is augmented by the opinionated insights of the contributors. My topical essays dispersed throughout the guide focus on pizza passions and obsessions, among them custom-crafted brick ovens, repurposed Citroën trucks, house-made mozzarella, pizza boxes, and pizza folding.

None of the featured pizzerias has been awarded stars or assigned a ranking in the pizza charts. No tasting geniuses, not even our distinguished regional experts, are so astute they can fairly compare and rate pizzas of different styles across continents without having actually tried them. So instead of a top ten or top thousand we offer, in no particular order, our list of the top 1,705 pizza places in the world. This total can be broken down by country, by region, and by city—top 569 in the USA, top 333 in Italy, top 66 in Brazil, and so on. Ultimately, over one thousand pizza critics cannot put an end to one big international pizza discussion. Their collected experience, wisdom, and recommendations can only be the beginning of one.

This is an auspicious moment to be leading a global conversation about first-rate pizza. Pizza now has its own flourishing craft, gourmet, organic, locavore, and food truck movements. Real Neapolitan pizza is all the rage in North America, Japan, and Australia. The original classic that, with Italian immigrants leading the way, inspired more robust and daring pizza styles in the USA, Argentina, and Brazil, is fast winning converts in the food capitals of Europe and Asia. The audience for sensational American regional pizza keeps growing and so do expectations: you can now find better New York-, New Haven-, or Detroit-style pizza outside their hometowns than ever before.

The question of *Where To Eat Pizza* has never been more challenging, nor its answers more rewarding.

DANIEL YOUNG

THE REGIONAL EXPERTS

NOMI ABELIOVICH
Regional expert for Israel
An architect turned food writer, consultant, and editor, Nomi Abeliovich is the founder of Gastronomi. Her work includes research and writing on *Jerusalem: A Cookbook* by Yotam Ottolenghi and Sami Tamimi, articles featured on "The Atlantic" online food channel, food consultation on the BBC's *Jerusalem on a Plate* documentary and the "Jerusalem" episode of Anthony Bourdain's " *Parts Unknown*.
www.gastronomi.co.il

GIUSEPPE ALDÈ
Regional expert for Friuli-Venezia Giulia, Italy and Slovenia
Giuseppe Aldè is a winemaker and the co-owner of Valter Sirk Vini del Collio Sloveno. He studies wine and cooking on a regular basis due to his work in many types of restaurants and wine bars at all levels.
www.valtersirk.com

AILIN ALEIXO
Regional expert for São Paulo, Brazil
A food journalist for more than a decade, Ailin Aleixo was editor of some of the most important magazines in Brazil. She acts as a judge in cocktail and food contests, such as Diageo World Class, and also as a consultant for large advertising agencies, assisting in product launches. Since August 2009, Ailin dedicates each bite to Gastrolândia.
www.gastrolandia.com.br

BRETT ANDERSON
Regional expert for New Orleans, USA
Brett Anderson is the restaurant critic and features writer at Nola. com, *The Times-Picayune*, in New Orleans. He is a former Harvard Nieman Fellow and has won two James Beard Awards.

SILVANA AZEVEDO
Regional expert for Brasilia, Brazil
A journalist and food critic, Silvana Azevedo researches Italian culture and cuisine on behalf of the University of São Paulo. She helped to coordinate the Cozinhas da Itália (Italian cuisine) book series and contributes to some of Brazil's major magazines, including *Veja* São Paulo.

LIZ BARRETT
Regional expert for the USA-at-large
Liz Barrett is the author of *Pizza, A Slice of American History* and editor-at-large at *PMQ Pizza Magazine*, where she's been covering pizza—and the industry—since 2007.
bestpizzabook.com

JUAREZ BECOZA
Regional expert for Rio de Janeiro, Brazil
A journalist and researcher of the Rio de Janeiro food and drink scene, Juarez Becoza has written a column on local bars for *Jornal O Globo* (Brazil's main newspaper) for the last 15 years and has reviewed and photographed over 1,500 bars in Brazil and abroad. He also coordinated the Época—O Melhor do Rio (Era—The Best of Rio) gastronomy award from 2011 to 2014. He consults on the annual Boni & Amaral gastronomy guide, providing information on bars and pubs, and is a judge for the city's main culinary competitions.

SABINO BERARDINO
Regional expert for Tuscany, Italy
A gourmet and pizza lover, Sabino Berardino organizes gastronomic evenings, writes for lucianopignataro.it, and contributes to the restaurant guide *I Cento di Firenze* (EDT/Lonely Planet).
www.berardino.info

FRANCESCO BIASI
Regional expert for Apulia, Italy
Passionate about wine and food, Francesco Biasi is national councilor for Slow Food and the president of the association Quelli della Bombetta. He is the guardian and supporter of his own land and products and of the various producers of Murgia and of the Itria Valley.

LESLIE BRENNER
Regional expert for Texas, USA

Leslie Brenner is restaurant critic and dining editor at the *Dallas Morning News* and founding editor of *Palate*, the *Morning News*'s annual food and wine magazine. Previously Leslie served as editor of the *Los Angeles Times*'s award-winning food section.

DARA BUNJON
Regional expert for Maryland, USA

From public relations, food writing, and restaurant promotions to social media, cookbooks, and food styling, Dara Bunjon has the strategic and tactical expertise to get restaurants, brands, and products noticed. Her passion for food—its origins, preparation, and enjoyment—provides the foundation for highly successful culinary promotions.
www.dara-does-it.com

DONNIE BURTLESS
Regional expert for western New York, USA

Food blogger Donnie Burtless is one of the co-founders of Buffaloeats.org, a leading food blog in "The Queen City" (Buffalo, USA). Over the last six years he's reviewed over 600 restaurants and has worked with Visit Buffalo Niagara, Buffalo Spree, and Chowzter.com.
www.buffaloeats.org

ANNA MARLENA BUSCEMI
Regional expert for Aosta and Piedmont, Italy

A gastronome principally involved in educative culinary projects, Anna Marlena Buscemi sneaks into every (interesting) kitchen that lets her do so in order to observe and then attempt to pass on what she has learned.

COLIN M. CAPLAN
Regional expert for Connecticut, USA

An author, historian, architect, and tour guide, Colin M. Caplan operates Taste of New Haven, which provides culinary tours and events. He writes about local pizza history and establishments and helps produce both pizza and other culinary related events.
www.tasteofnewhaven.com

AMANDA CLARK
Regional expert for North Carolina, USA

When she is not doing her day job in the world of theater, food blogger Amanda Clark writes about local restaurants and movies. She loves to travel and has been known to plan vacations around food.
www.cuisineandscreen.com

MARCO COLOGNESE
Regional expert for Veneto and Emilia-Romagna, Italy

Marco Colognese has written about food for over 20 years, both for a great Italian guide and online. Food criticism is his greatest passion.
viaggiandonelgusto.volvotv.it

SASHA CORREA
Regional expert for Mexico

A Venezuelan journalist specializing in food writing, Sasha Correa is the author of the cookbook *Nuestra Comida a la Manera de Caracas* (2014) and writes for magazines including *Bienmesabe* (Venezuela), in which she has a regular column called "Al Dente," *Avianca* and *Cocina Semana* (Colombia), *Uva* (Chile), and *Hoja Santa* (Mexico). She is Director of the Mesamérica Conference, Mexico, and a member of the Venezuelan Academy of Gastronomy.

MAURIZIO CORTESE
Regional expert for Campania, Italy

Maurizio Cortese owes his culinary expertise to Alfonso Iaccarino, chef and owner of the famous restaurant Don Alfonso 1890, attending his cooking from a young age and learning all his secrets. Maurizio went on to work with Stefano Bonilli, the most important Italian food journalist, with whom he founded the web project Gazzetta Gastronomica. He also writes for other major magazines, including *Fool*.

SEVERIN CORTI
Regional expert for Austria

Severin Corti was the London correspondent for German, Austrian, and Swiss newspapers before he opened a restaurant in Vienna, where he was also the chef. Over the past 10 years he has specialized in food journalism, penning the weekly restaurant reviews in the newspaper *Der Standard* and writing in the current affairs magazine *News* about everything to do with food and drink.

SARAH CROWTHER
Regional expert for The Russian Federation

A Canadian copy-editor living in Moscow, Sarah Crowther has edited art guides, articles, recipes, and even a dating book. She is currently working on a book of Russian baked goods.
www.russianbakingblog.com

DAVID DADEKIAN
Regional expert for Rhode Island, USA

According to the *Providence Phoenix*, David Dadekian is "Rhode Island's unofficial Food Laureate" and "a mastermind of the food news website and event-organizing operation, Eat Drink RI, who seems to know every chef, restaurant, farm stand, and manufactured food product within state lines."
www.eatdrinkri.com

MASSIMO D'ALMA
Regional expert for Lombardy, Italy

Gastronomic consultant Massimo D'Alma is passionate about food, and especially about pizza.
www.enotecheamilano.it

MIREIA DE LA TORRE
Regional expert for Catalonia, Spain

Mireia de la Torre is a journalist from Barcelona with a special contemporary view about food trends. She specializes in gastronomy and enology communication, working for several media outlets, including the fashion magazines Spanish *V Magazine* and *Woman Madame Figaro* and radio and TV programs *Cuines* (TV3), *Directe 4.0* (RTVE), and Tendencias TV. Mireia also edits her own website, mireiadelatorre.com, and designs communication projects for enterprises focused on the food and beverage sector.
mireiadelatorre.com

VINCENT DELMAS
Regional expert for Nice and the Côte d'Azur, France

A writer, blogger, and former radio journalist, Vincent Delmas lives in Paris and Nice. He writes for the *Guide Petits Futés* and *City Guide Paris* and is a contributor to Atlantico.fr.
www.critiquegastronomique.com

CAROL DEPTOLLA
Regional expert for Wisconsin, USA

Carol Deptolla is the dining critic for the *Milwaukee Journal Sentinel*. She writes about restaurants, bars, and other food- and drink-related businesses.

ISIDORA DÍAZ
Regional expert for Chile

Isidora Díaz is a food writer, cook, and researcher and promoter of traditional Chilean food culture. She writes about food, beer, and Chilean food culture for *UVA* magazine, the Nirvino website, *La Cav* magazine, and several other Chilean publications. She is also the co-author of the cookbook *Todo a la Parrilla*, which she created with co-author Carolina Carriel and photographer Araceli Paz. Currently based in Columbus, Ohio, Isidora spends her time writing for *Stock & Barrel* magazine and organizing pop-up dinners and cooking classes.

FIONA DONNELLY
Regional expert for Queensland, Australia

A former food editor and respected restaurant reviewer, Fiona Donnelly is *Gourmet Traveller*'s Queensland editor and a weekly columnist for Brisbane's daily newspaper, the *Courier-Mail*. She writes mainly on food and travel topics and her byline appears in many national publications.

TOM DOORLEY
Regional expert for Ireland

Tom Doorley has been Ireland's foremost restaurant critic for over 20 years, formerly with the *Irish Times*, now with the *Irish Daily Mail*. He is a presenter of the long-running TV series *The Restaurant*.
www.tomdoorley.com

SURESH DOSS
Regional expert for Ontario, Canada

A food and drink writer based in Toronto, Canada, Suresh Doss is the publisher of SpotlightToronto.com and has contributed to a variety of online and print outlets. He has been a pioneer for the Street Food movement in Toronto and is the founder of the Food Truck Eats movement. Suresh is also the global editor for Whitecap's StreetEats series of travel guides, which focus on the best street food across North America.

JIM DUNCAN
Regional expert for Iowa, USA

Jim Duncan has been writing about food in Iowa for 25 years and for numerous publications. He is the Cityview Food Dude.

VICTORIA PESCE ELLIOT
Regional expert for Florida, USA

A graduate of the Columbia School of Journalism, Victoria Pesce Elliott has been writing about food, wine, and travel for three decades. Her Italian parents taught her lots but a dozen years of "research" in New York City helped, too.
mondaydinner.com

DIEGO FABRIS
Regional expert for southern Brazil

Diego Fabris is the co-creator, with Diogo Carvalho and Lela Zaniol, of Destemperados, a multi-platform publisher devoted to gastronomy in all its senses. In 2015 the organization, based in Porto Alegre, Brazil, opened Casa Destemperados, a culinary center with a library, grocery store, bar, cafe, and rooms for a full schedule of tastings, classes, and lectures throughout the year. Destemperados also operates a food truck for its events.
www.destemperados.com.br

GIOVANNI FARINELLA
Regional expert for Luxembourg
Born in Sicily, Giovanni Farinella is a management consultant who moved to Luxembourg, after having experienced life across Italy and France. He has a passion for food in all its expressions: ingredients, culture heritage, craft, sensory experience, and memories.

RACHEL FORREST
Regional expert for New Hampshire, USA
Rachel Forrest writes two food and restaurant columns for the *Portsmouth Herald* in Portsmouth, New Hampshire, and about food, cocktails, and beer for magazines and online publications. She is also a cookbook author and is co-author of *Maine Classics: More Than 150 Delicious Recipes from Down East* (Running Press) with James Beard Award-winning chefs Mark Gaier and Clark Frasier.
www.rachelforrest.com

IAN FROEB
Regional expert for Missouri, USA
Ian Froeb has been a restaurant critic in St. Louis since 2006, first at the weekly *Riverfront Times* and since 2013 at the daily *St. Louis Post-Dispatch*.
www.stltoday.com/stl100

JENNY GAO
Regional expert for China
Born in Chengdu, a UNESCO World City of Food, Jenny Gao is an expert on Chinese food culture. Her blog Jing Theory has been featured in *New York Magazine*, *Epicure*, CNN, BBC, and Vice. She is currently launching China's first fast-casual chain restaurant concept focused on transparently sourced ingredients at an affordable price.
www.jingtheory.com

FIONA GAZE
Regional expert for the Czech Republic
Fiona Gaze is a travel writer, food critic, and editor based in Prague. She has written a Michelin guidebook to Prague and reviewed restaurants for the *Prague Post*, and she is a regular contributor to the *International New York Times*.

PETER GENOVESE
Regional expert for New Jersey, USA
Peter Genovese is the author of 10 books, including *Pizza City: The Ultimate Guide to New York's Favorite Food*, *A Slice of Jersey: Your Ultimate Guide to Pizza in the Garden State*, *Food Lovers Guide to New Jersey*, and *Jersey Diners*. He is chief food writer for nj.com and the *Star-Ledger*.

HANS GERLACH
Regional expert for Munich, Germany
Hans Gerlach trained and worked as a chef in two- and three-star restaurants, including with Gaultiero Marchesi in Italy's first three-star restaurant, and in a very good Sicilian restaurant on a cliff overlooking the sea. Later he studied architecture and at the same time began working as a food writer, food photographer, and kitchen coach. He is a regular columnist for the magazine of the *Süddeutsche Zeitung* and for *Gault Millau* magazine and is the author of many cookbooks, including some award-winning works.
www.food-und-text.de

ED GILBERT
Regional expert for Wales, UK
A Cardiff-based Geordie, Ed Gilbert's blog, Gourmet Gorro, won best food and drink blog at the Wales Blog Awards 2012. His interests range from doner kebabs to Michelin-starred meals.
www.gourmetgorro.blogspot.co.uk

JOHN GILCHRIST
Regional expert for Alberta, Canada
John Gilchrist reviews restaurants for CBC Radio and the *Calgary Herald* and has written 11 national bestselling books on restaurants in Southern Alberta. He writes for numerous Canadian magazines and is the Calgary judge for the Canadian Culinary Championships.

TORE GJESTELAND & CRAIG WHITSON
Regional experts for Norway
Co-authors of *Passion for Pizza* (Agate Publishing, 2015), Tore Gjesteland owns the Jonas B. Gundersen pizza restaurants in Norway and Craig Whitson works with product development, cooking classes, and food writing.
www.pizzaangels.com

BARBARA GOERLICH
Regional expert for Frankfurt, Germany
A freelance journalist and author, Barbara Goerlich writes about food and drink, gastronomy, and lifestyle and design for magazines and trade publications. She is editor-in-chief of the Citysential Guides and author of numerous books on travel, gastronomy, lifestyle, and business admin.
www.tafelspitzen.de

TORSTEN GOFFIN
Regional expert for Cologne, Germany
An author, journalist, and university lecturer, Torsten Goffin has been telling stories about food, wine, and related stuff in print and online for almost 50 years.
www.allemanfang.tumblr.com

JOHN GOLDEN
Regional expert for Maine, USA
John Golden has written about food, dining, and lifestyle subjects for the *Portland Press Herald*, as the dining critic and blogger for *MaineToday*, as well as for *Downeast* magazine, the *Boston Globe*, *Cottages and Gardens* magazine, *Gourmet* magazine, *Cuisine* magazine, the *New York Times*, and the *New York Post*. In his highly opinionated blog, John reports on his experiences dining out all over Maine and his visits with food personalities, farmers, and farmers' markets throughout the state.

DANIEL GRAY
Regional expert for South Korea
Daniel Gray is a Korean-American adoptee who returned to Korea in 2005 to rediscover his roots. A Korean food expert, he has worked on and appeared on *Bizarre Foods with Andrew Zimmern*, *Parts Unknown* with Anthony Bourdain, *Kimchi Chronicles*, *Gourmet's Diary of a Foodie*, *Unravel Travel*, and much more. He is currently the tour and events director of Delectable Travels. In his free time, he writes about and photographs food, culture, and travel topics. He writes on his blog Seoul Eats and he has an upcoming book on his adoptee experiences.
www.seouleats.com

SARAH BAKER HANSEN
Regional expert for Nebraska, USA
Sarah Baker Hansen is the restaurant critic for the *Omaha World-Herald*. She also writes food trend stories and a "best of" series called Food Prowl where she builds teams of tasters and explores the city in search of the best dishes in different categories. An Omaha native, she graduated from the University of Nebraska-Lincoln with a bachelor's degree in News Editorial Journalism. She loves eating, cooking, travel, and fashion.
omavore.omaha.com

IAN HARRISON
Regional expert for Quebec, Canada
Ian Harrison is the editor of *Eater Montreal* and a freelance writer. His articles have appeared in the *Montreal Gazette*, *Hotelier*, and *Foodservice and Hospitality*, among others. He was the field coordinator and fixer for the "Quebec" episode of *Anthony Bourdain: No Reservations*. For nine memorable months in 2007, he shucked a lot of oysters, and made a lot of Bloody Caesars, at Montreal's Joe Beef restaurant.

JANICE LEUNG HAYES
Regional expert for Hong Kong
Janice Leung Hayes is a Hong Kong-based food writer and farmers' market organizer. Her written work can be found in publications such as the *South China Morning Post*, the *New York Times*, *Monocle*, *Wall Street Journal*, *Australian Gourmet Traveller*, *Discovery Magazine* (Cathay Pacific), eater.com, LUXE City Guides, and more.
www.janiceleung.net

SAKURA HORI
Regional expert for Switzerland
Based in Geneva, Sakura Hori has been writing her culinary blog, Le Petit Chou, since 2012. She's always looking for new restaurants and wants to share her experience with all epicureans.
www.le-petitchou.com

TOBIAS HÜBERLI
Regional expert for Switzerland
Tobias Hüberli is a Swiss journalist living in Zurich. Since 2007 he has worked as editor-in-chief of *Salz&Pfeffer*. In this role he takes responsibility for the gastronomic magazine *Salz&Pfeffer* and the smoker magazine *Cigar*.

LUCA IACCARINO
Regional expert for Liguria, Italy
A food editor at Edizioni di Torinol, Luca Iaccarino travels and eats thanks to Lonely Planet, *La Repubblica*, Osterie d'Italia, Vanityfair.it, and Mondadori.

MARJAN IPPEL
Regional expert for The Netherlands
Food trend analyst cum food writer cum indie publishing house, Marjan Ippel is the author of *Foodlingo Bijbel*, a culinary dictionary. She is also editor-in-chief of indie food magazine *My Beautiful Mayonnaise* and initiator of Underground Boerenmarkt, the first Dutch food market for micro producers.
www.talkinfood.nl

DANIELLE ISSA
Regional expert for Beirut, Lebanon
An engineer by education, a management consultant by training, a banking strategist by profession, and a food writer by passion, Danielle Issa is Beirut's resident foodie expert, dishing up her latest finds and favorites in Lebanon's capital city. She writes for her food and lifestyle blog Beirutista.
www.beirutista.blogspot.com

MIKE IVES
Regional expert for Vietnam
Vietnam-based journalist Mike Ives is a regular contributor to the *New York Times*, the *Economist*, and other publications.
www.mikeivesetc.com

DENNY KALLIVOKA
Regional expert for Greece
Denny Kallivoka studied Marketing Management in Athens and did an MA in Media Communications at City University London. Since 2003 she has been a restaurant and cocktail critic and writes about food, wine, spirits, and travel for newspapers and magazines in Greece and for *TimeOut London*.

JOLENE KETZENBERGER
Regional expert for Indiana, USA
Food writer Jolene Ketzenberger is the founder and editor of EatDrinkIndy.com, where she covers the local food scene in central Indiana. She also hosts Eat Drink Indiana Radio on National Public Radio affiliate WFYI and is the co-author of *Cafe Indiana Cookbook*.

TODD KLIMAN
Regional expert for Washington, DC, USA
Todd Kliman is a James Beard Award-winning food critic at the *Washingtonian*.

MATTIAS KROON
Regional expert for Sweden
An editor, writer, columnist, and traveler, Mattias Kroon produces the Skanör Falsterbo Matfestival, the leading food festival in the Nordic region. He lives in Paris, France.
www.skanorfalsterbomatfestival.com

MANUELA LAIACONA
Regional expert for Sicily, Italy
Manuela Laiacona writes for industry publications that specialize in wine and food, such as Agrodolce.it and Winenews.it. She is also a video maker and has a feature called "Storie di Terra" (stories from the earth) for the daily newspaper *La Repubblica*. She is the creator and founder of Cooking Soon, a format to promote the local territory that brings together young Calabrian chefs.

CHRISTIANE LAUTERBACH
Regional expert for southeastern USA
Born in Paris, Christiane Lauterbach discovered pizza in Italy and then refined her taste in New York. She lives in Atlanta and has been reviewing restaurants for more than 30 years.

DREW LAZOR
Regional expert for eastern Pennsylvania, USA
Drew Lazor writes about food, drink, movies, and music both locally and nationally. He's contributed to *Bon Appétit*, *Condé Nast Traveler*, *First We Feast*, *Food Network*, *Food Republic*, *Lucky Peach*, *Punch*, *Saveur*, *Serious Eats*, and the *Wall Street Journal*.
www.drewlazor.com

JUSTIN LEE
Regional expert for Arizona and New Mexico, USA
Based in Phoenix, Arizona, Justin Lee is a freelance food and travel writer, hospitality industry professional, and imperfect home cook who is pulled by experiences that taste good. Justin's work has appeared in *Phoenix Magazine*, *Bite Magazine*, and *Downtown Phoenix Journal*, and he is the reserved personality behind the local award-winning food blog Justin Eats.
www.justineats.com

RACHEL LEVIN
Regional expert for northern California, USA
Rachel Levin is a San Francisco-based writer and editor who has written for the *New Yorker*, the *New York Times*, *Food & Wine*, *Outside*, *San Francisco Magazine* (where she was a regular restaurant critic), and *Sunset* magazine (where she was a senior travel editor). A presenter at *Pop-Up Magazine*'s "Dinner" issue, her work has also appeared in *Best Food Writing*. And yes, her favorite food is pizza.
www.byrachellevin.com

ALICE LEVITT
Regional expert for Vermont, USA
The award-winning senior food writer at *Seven Days*, Vermont's alternative newsweekly, Alice Levitt is also co-author of *Explorer's Guide Vermont*. You can also see her on Vermont news magazine program *The :30*, or hear her on WVMT radio in the morning.
www.alicelevitt.com

STEPHANIE MARCH
Regional expert for Minnesota, USA
Stephanie March is the senior editor for the Eat + Drink section of *Mpls.St.Paul Magazine* in Minneapolis. She is always hungry.
www.mspmag.com

JULIE MAUTNER
Regional expert for Provence, France
A career journalist with over 30 years' experience writing about food and travel, Julie Mautner now lives most of the year in the south of France, arranging amazing vacations and activities in Provence and on the Côte d'Azur for clients from all over the world.
www.provencepost.com

MELISSA MCCART
Regional expert for western Pennsylvania, USA
Melissa McCart is the dining critic for the *Pittsburgh Post-Gazette*. Her favorite pizzas are true Neapolitan-style and *pizza al taglio*. She maintains there's a distinct Pittsburgh-style pizza with a thin, yet spongy crust, and a three-cheese blanket of dry mozzarella and two types of provolone.
www.post-gazette.com

LEAH MENNIES
Regional expert for Massachusetts, USA
In addition to eating pizza over the course of her entire lifetime by choice, Leah Mennies also had the opportunity to do so professionally throughout the Boston region as the food editor of *Boston* magazine. Now working as editor for John Brown Media in Boston, she's looking to up her at-home pizza skills, too.

NIKHIL MERCHANT
Regional expert for India
A food writer and chef, Nikhil Merchant channels his expertise as Chef-de-Cuisine from his restaurant Imli in Los Angeles, USA.
www.nonchalantgourmand.com

MASAYUKI MINEZAKI
Regional expert for Japan
Masayuki Minezaki is a photographer and blogger who knows the pizzerias in Japan really well, having eaten at over 200 pizzerias all over the country.
pizza.hatenadiary.jp

JAMES MIRABELLI
Regional expert for northern Pennsylvania, USA
Owner of NEPApizzareview.com and longtime professional pizza maker, James Mirabelli is a blogger who visits pizzerias "secret-shopper style" and reports his findings online. He is a supporter of small business.
www.nepapizzareview.com

ANDREW MORRISON
Regional expert for British Columbia, Canada
A restaurant-industry veteran turned restaurant critic and cookbook author, Andrew Morrison is also the co-founder of *Scout Magazine*, Vancouver's leading food and culture publication. He is the National Referee at the Canadian Culinary Championships, the country's largest cooking competition.

CRISTINA MOSCA
Regional expert for Abruzzo, Italy
Specializing in wine and food culture from the Abruzzo region of Italy, Cristina Mosca founded the free food and wine magazine *C Come Magazine* in 2007. Today she is still its managing director and is often chosen for projects, tests, or conferences in the field of food and wine culture.
www.ccomemagazine.it

SILVIJA MUNDA & TOMISLAV STIPLOŠEK
Regional experts for Croatia
Silvija Munda and Tomislav Stiplošek are editors of *GET Report*, the online magazine for Gastronomy, (o)Enology, Tourism (GET), a culture association from Zagreb, Croatia. They also organize Panorama Pizza Expo in Prelog, Croatia, which is held at the end of September.
www.get4u.hr

KENNETH NARS
Regional expert for Finland
Kenneth Nars is a food writer and publisher based in Helsinki. He has written for several magazines, including *Gourmet Sweden*, *Lucky Peach*, and *Monocle*, and he has also published and written seven cookbooks. Occasionally, he sells pulled pork from his pop-up restaurant.

FRANCESCA NEGRI
Regional expert for Trentino-Alto Adige, Italy
Francesca Negri is a journalist, writer, blogger, and wine expert for *Detto Fatto* on Rai 2.
www.geishagourmet.com

SARAH NICHOLSON
Regional expert for New Zealand
Award-winning editor Sarah Nicholson has worked on food magazines for 14 years. After editing *delicious*, and *Vogue Entertaining + Travel* in Australia, she returned to her home country, New Zealand, to take the helm of *Cuisine*.

REBECCA THANDI NORMAN
Regional expert for Denmark
Rebecca Thandi Norman is the co-founder and editorial director of the Scandinavian lifestyle website Scandinavia Standard. She lives in Copenhagen, Denmark.
www.scandinaviastandard.com

PAT NOURSE
Regional expert for New South Wales, Australia
Pat Nourse is the chief restaurant critic and deputy editor of *Gourmet Traveller*. He lives in Sydney, and shuns all who eat pizza with anything other than their hands.

TAKESHI OZAWA
Regional expert for Japan
A photographer with a special interest in Italian food, Takeshi Ozawa has eaten hundreds of Neapolitan pizzas over the past 15 years, both in Naples and Japan.
www.facebook.com/
TakeshiOzawaOfficial

KATIE PARLA
Regional expert for Lazio, Italy
Katie Parla is a Rome-based food and beverage journalist, Italian craft beer expert, and certified sommelier. She is the author of the blog Parla Food and the mobile apps Katie Parla's Rome and Katie Parla's Istanbul.
www.katieparla.com

BRUNO PETRONILLI
Regional expert for Umbria, Italy
Born in Milan, Bruno Petronilli is a wine and food journalist. He works with major national newspapers and is a judge at the international wine competitions Concours Mondial de Vins Bruxelles and International Wine and Spirits Competition, London.

ALBA PEZONE
Regional expert for Paris, France
Alba Pezone is also a food journalist and cookbook writer. She spent the first part of her professional life in the world of marketing and consulting. After studying for a CAP in cookery and a CAP in pastry-making, and working in some prestigious institutions, she decided to turn her passion for cooking into her job. In April 2004 she founded the Parole in Cucina (an Italian cooking school) in Paris.

LOREDANA PIETRONIRO
Regional expert for Molise, Italy
Loredana Pietroniro has a degree in Agricultural Science from the University of Bologna. Since 1995 she has worked at the Agenzia Regionale per lo Sviluppo Agricolo, Rurale e della Pesca (Regional Agency for Agricultural Development, Rural and Fisheries). She is also a sommelier, an official taster of olive oil and cheese, and lectures for Slow Food Italy.

MIGUEL PIRES
Regional expert for Portugal
Miguel Pires is a food writer. He is the author of *Lisboa à Mesa - Guia Onde Comer*. *Onde Comprar* and co-author of the blog Mesa Marcada. He writes for various publications, including *Essência do Vinho* and *NauXXI*.

PENNY POLLACK
Regional expert for Illinois, USA
Penny Pollack has been the dining editor of *Chicago* magazine since 1994. Under her direction, the dining department produced "Through Thick and Thin," the magazine's comprehensive 1998 pizza feature, which was nominated for a James Beard Award and won a gold from the City and Regional Magazine Association. An avid traveler, Pollack has explored the cuisines of five continents—but her favorite food is still pizza.
www.chicagomag.com

WILLIAM PORTER
Regional expert for Colorado, USA
A native of North Carolina, William Porter has spent 35 years in the newspaper business, writing for such publications as the *Phoenix Gazette*, *Arizona Republic*, and the *Denver Post*. He has been the *Denver Post*'s dining critic since 2010.
www.denverpost.com

FABIO GÁNDARA PUMAR & SUSANA LÓPEZ-URRUTIA
Regional experts for Madrid, Spain
Bloggers Fabio Gándara Pumar and Susana López-Urrutia are a foodie couple who seek out the most amazing, unique, and delicious restaurants in Madrid. They want to have fun and live special moments, all the while enjoying food and life in their beloved city. They always try to recommend places and experiences that fulfill the "three Bs"—*bueno, bonito, y barado* (good, nice, and cheap).
eatandlovemadrid.es

SYLVIA RECTOR
Regional expert for Michigan, USA
Sylvia Rector has been combining her twin passions for journalism and food since 1999 as the *Detroit Free Press* restaurant critic. She dines at places both highbrow and humble and is always on the lookout for the next great restaurant.
www.freep.com/sylviarector

JEAN-PIERRE ROSSOUW
Regional expert for South Africa
Jean-Pierre Rossouw founded *Rossouw's Restaurants Guide* in 2004. This independent guide to dining out in South Africa went on to become the leading "tell it like it is" guide, and in 2015 it was acquired by Diners Club. Jean-Pierre now publishes both the restaurant guide and the internationally respected *Platter's Wine Guide*.

VIJAY SAPRE
Regional expert for Hamburg, Germany
Vijay Sapre worked as a taxi driver, waiter, and copywriter before becoming a successful internet entrepreneur and founding the German food magazine *Effilee* in 2008. He cooks a decent pizza at home, for which he never uses more than 10 g of yeast per 2.2 lb (1 kg) of flour.

ALLISON SCHEFF
Regional expert for Washington, USA
A freelance food and wine writer, Allison Scheff's work has been featured in *InStyle*, *Wine and Spirits*, *Northwest Palate*, *Sunset* magazine, and more. She was food and dining editor at *Seattle* magazine for seven years and prior to that she worked as a restaurant critic in New York and Seattle.
allisonscheff.com

SCOTT FROM BACON ON THE BEECH
Regional expert for northern England, UK
Scott is a food photographer, illustrator, and designer and he runs the food website Bacon on the Beech. He works with restaurants, mainly in Manchester, England, and his photographs have appeared in magazines like the *Guardian*'s *The Guide*, *Olive*, and *Waitrose Food*.
www.bacononthebeech.com

RENÉ SÉPUL
Regional expert for Belgium
René Sépul is food specialist and gastronomic journalist at *Journal Le Soir*, Brussels. He owns Sh-op Editions and is the author of *Mange Bruxelles Remet le Couvert*, *Mange Wallonie*, and *La Belgique, Le Vin*.
www.sh-opeditions.com

PIETRO SORBA
Regional expert for Argentina
Pietro Sorba has lived in Buenos Aires since 1992. He is the author of 13 food books and guides published with Editorial Planeta, including *Pizzerie Di Buenos Aires*. He writes editorials for *Viva*, the *Clarín* Sunday magazine, and works on several programs for radio and television. He is the content manager and organizer of the Semana de los Bodegones Porteños (a weekly culinary celebration of the traditional restaurants of the city of Buenos Aires) and he also acts as a gastronomical consultant to help public institutions develop gastronomical strategies.

GABY SOUTAR
Regional expert for Scotland, UK
Gaby Soutar has been a lifestyle editor at Scotland's national newspaper, the *Scotsman*, since 2002 and has been responsible for the weekly restaurant review in its Saturday supplement since 2007. She's lucky enough to live in Edinburgh, Scotland—a city with the highest concentration of Michelin-starred restaurants outside London. However, sometimes fine dining won't cut it and, like the Teenage Mutant Ninja Turtles, she has a weakness for good pizza.

SUSAN STAPLETON
Regional expert for Las Vegas, USA
Susan Stapleton is the editor of Eater Vegas.
vegas.eater.com

JEN STEVENSON
Regional expert for Oregon, USA
Portland-based food writer
Jen Stevenson is the author of
*Portland's 100 Best Places to Stuff
Your Faces* and the website Under
The Table With Jen. She is partial
to picnics, pretty places, and,
obviously, pizza.
www.underthetablewithjen.com

ZOJA STOJANOVIC
Regional expert for Serbia
Zoja Stojanovic is a genuine food
lover and adventurous traveler with
a great sense for good taste and
well-made wine.

NORA SUGOBONO
Regional expert for Peru
Nora Sugobono is a food journalist
and culinary adventurer from Peru.
She has worked for El Comercio
media group since 2008, writes
articles related to gastronomy, and
publishes a weekly restaurant page
in *Somos* magazine. She also has a
recipe blog, and she loves to eat.

ROBBIE SWINNERTON
Regional expert for Tokyo, Japan
Robbie Swinnerton is a food writer
and freelance journalist who has
been based in Tokyo for over 30
years. Besides his long-standing
Japan Times restaurant column,
"Tokyo Food File," he writes for
leading publications in Asia,
Europe, and North America.

MARCOS TARDIN
Regional expert for northern Brazil
Marcos Tardin is a journalist. He
is general director of Fundação
Demócrito Rocha and also
operations director of TV O POVO.
He is a native of Rio and lives
in Fortaleza.

DANI VALENT
**Regional expert for Victoria,
Australia**
Dani Valent has been writing
about food for more than 15 years,
including as a restaurant critic
and cookbook author. She lives
in Melbourne, but is happy to eat
pizza anywhere in the world.
www.danivalent.com

MAURIZIO VALERIANI
Regional expert for Sardinia, Italy
Maurizio Valeriani is the author
of *Guida I Ristoranti d'Italia
de L'Espresso* and writes for
magazines and blogs, such as
lucianopignataro.it, epulae.it, and
thespaghettijunction.com. He
is also responsible for Sardinia's
regional commission for the Italian
Slow Wine Guide, is a teacher
on sommelier courses for the
Federazione Italiana Sommelier
Albergtaori Ristoratori (FISAR),
and is a taster of Italian and
international extra virgin olive oil
(Guida Flos Olei).

FEDERICO VALICENTI
**Regional expert for Calabria and
Basilicata, Italy**
Federico Valicenti is a gourmet
taster and temporary chef manager,
and has been chef patron of the
Ristorante Luna Rossa since 1981.
www.federicovalicenti.it

S. IRENE VIRBILA
**Regional expert for southern
California, USA**
S. Irene Virbila has written about
wine and food for the *Los Angeles
Times* for more than 20 years. For
18 years she was the chief
restaurant critic for the paper and
won a James Beard Foundation
Award and American Food
Journalists Award for her reviews.
Before joining the newspaper in
1993, she wrote about food, wine,
and travel from Europe and Asia,
trained as a sommelier in Paris,
edited cookbooks, and was part of
the culinary scene in Berkeley when
Chez Panisse changed everything.

SARAH WALI
Regional expert for Kuwait
An international journalist with
experience covering all issues
from social taboos to breaking
news, Sarah Wali is currently the
Digital Content Manager for *Bazaar*
magazine, Kuwait's leading lifestyle
magazine with a focus on food.
www.bazaar.town

MELANIE M. WARD
**Regional expert for Mississippi,
USA**
Melanie M. Ward has been the
editor of *Mississippi Magazine*
since March 2008. She is also
the former editor of *Tattler* and
Mistletoe Tidings magazines
and was the publisher for the
publications of the Junior League
of Jackson.

LUISA WEISS
Regional expert for Berlin, Germany
A food writer based in Berlin, Luisa Weiss is the food columnist for *Harper's Bazaar Germany*, maintains the acclaimed food blog The Wednesday Chef, and is currently at work on a book about German baking for Ten Speed Press.
www.thewednesdaychef.com

SCOTT WIENER
Regional expert for New York City, USA
Scott Wiener is the founder of Scott's Pizza Tours in NYC, columnist for *Pizza Today Magazine*, competition pizza judge, and author of *Viva La Pizza!: The Art of the Pizza Box*, a book about his Guinness World Record collection of pizza boxes.
www.scottspizzatours.com

GAIL WILLIAMS
Regional expert for Western Australia, Australia
Gail Williams is an award-winning food writer based in Perth. She has written restaurant reviews and food stories for over 30 years.

SAMANTHA WOOD
Regional expert for United Arab Emirates
A Dubai resident for the last 16 years, Greek-Cypriot-British Samantha Wood is the publisher of the impartial award-winning restaurant review website FooDiva and the curator of dine around experiences. She is also a freelance food writer and regular speaker, presenter, and awards judge on her favorite subjects—food, restaurants, hotels, travel, and social media.
www.foodiva.net

BETHIA WOOLF
Regional expert for Ohio, USA
A British transplant, Bethia Woolf is the co-owner of Columbus Food Adventures and Columbus Brew Adventures. In addition, she blogs, writes for *Crave Magazine*, and sits on the boards of Slow Food Columbus and Dine Originals Columbus.
www.columbusfoodadventures.com

DEBBIE YONG
Regional expert for Singapore
Debbie Yong is a bilingual journalist who specializes in features and food writing. She has written for national publications the *Straits Times* and the *Business Times* in Singapore and contributed to leading luxury magazines such as the *Robb Report*, the *Peak* and *ZbBz*. In late 2014, she started Batch, a digital farmers' market for artisanal food and kitchenware by small-batch makers.
www.debbieyong.com

DANIEL YOUNG
Regional expert for southern England, UK
Food critic Daniel Young is the London pop-up pioneer behind youngandfoodish.com and its PizzaTuesday event series. He established himself as a pizza authority while restaurant critic of the *New York Daily News*. "He has," wrote Ed Levine, the creator of Serious Eats, "perfect pizza pitch."
www.youngandfoodish.com

EZÉCHIEL ZÉRAH
Regional expert for Marseille, Aix-en-Provence, and Bouches-du-Rhône, France
A food writer living between Paris and Marseille, Ezéchiel Zérah is a graduate of ESSEC business school. It was after seeing a documentary on Michel and Sébastien Bras and their move into cooking that he decided to change tack, choosing a career that would mean unfolding his napkin at almost 200 restaurants every year. He is currently writing a book on Marseille's culinary renaissance.
atabula.com

STEFANIA ZOLOTTI
Regional expert for Marche, Italy
A journalist and professional sommelier, Stefania Zolotti is the author of *Vino a Doppio Senso* and has worked with Il *Sole 24 Ore*, Il *Corriere Vinicolo*, and *Artù*. Since 2015, she is the director in charge of the digital magazine *Senza Filtro*. A law graduate who didn't choose the legal profession, she has spent several years providing legal advice on the food industry for consumer associations.
www.stefaniazolotti.it

INTRODUCTION

There is this incredible place, a kind of bespoke bakery restaurant with remarkably sane prices, where you can walk in any time of day or night, tell them exactly what you want and how you want it, down to the last ingredient. Your customized order is quickly assembled by hand and baked for you on the spot, by a practiced craftsman, before your eyes. In a matter of minutes you're served a finished product fresh from the oven— a shallow, savory, open-faced pie of sorts that's too hot to touch, much less eat right away, yet too tantalizing to wait for it to cool some.

It is called a pizzeria.

Where To Eat Pizza chases our shared passion for this remarkable institution, in all sizes and shapes, and this beloved Italian specialty, in all styles and variations, to 1,705 locations in 48 countries. In this guide there is no tiptoeing around a food obsession. We are in the thick— and thin—of it. The pizzerias have been handpicked by 121 regional experts and the 956 knowledgeable, strategically placed critics they recruited as pizza informants. They've revealed not only the identities of the pizzas closest to their hearts, but also what makes them, as well as the people and venues behind them, so special.

The contributors did not limit consideration to pizzerias or pizza-only enterprises. They could designate any restaurant, bar, cafe, bakery, pub, food truck, market stall, street vendor, deli, farmhouse eatery, or grocery store that bakes its own pizza with its own dough. Oddly, they overlooked the most popular pizza-eating venue of all: the living room couch.

The omission likely stems from the conviction that good pizza must be consumed fresh and hot, as near as possible to the oven in which it was baked. If off-site consumption is dictated either by personal circumstance, habit, or the lack of available seating in the pizzeria itself then the pickup and takeout options have important advantages over delivery. It's far better to wait an hour for your pizza to be made and then a minute for it to reach your hands than the reverse. Plus, when you get to the head of the line you can watch the agile pizza showman as he preps and bakes your order and gets your juices flowing in tandem with those of the pizza. Then you can devour it fresh and close to the source, sometimes in your car or right on the sidewalk, long before you get to where you're going. This too heightens pleasure in untold ways.

In the best of hands pizza is fast food but it is not fast-food: an artisan *pizzaiolo*, Italian for "pizza maker," allows his dough up to a day or longer to gradually ferment, only to flatten, stretch, dress, and bake it in a matter of minutes. In the hottest of wood-fired brick ovens the pizza can bake in as little as 60–90 seconds. The base layers of tomato and cheese form a molten pool on the lunar-like surface of the browned crust, achieving an ethereal ideal of structural abandon. This volcanic valley and its floating vegetation, cheeses, meats, or seafood are contained only by the ridge around it—a puffy, chewy, air-pocketed border Italians call the *cornicione* (cornice). And sometimes even that is not enough to contain the topping.

In the worst of hands, typically belonging to global fast-food giants or independent junk-food joints, pizza is a salty, fatty, greasy, denatured heap of processed food thickly piled onto rubbery, spongy, or cardboardy rafts of absorbent bread substance. It is an addictive food that instantly dupes six-year-old salt fiends as it encourages their older siblings and parents not only to eat ugly and cheaply but to do too much of it as often as possible.

There's no denying that really good trashy pizza has its satisfactions, and its place in *Where To Eat Pizza*. We haven't ruled out any style of shallow bread-with-toppings that is called pizza and was inspired, even indirectly, by the Italian original. We haven't taken sides in any pizza debates. We haven't told the contributors what we're looking for. As a group, they don't agree on many things, except that the best pizza is handmade with fresh, first-rate ingredients by proud and practiced craftsmen.

How the Contributors Were Chosen

Selecting the selectors was a painstaking process that started with one discerning pizza lover in London and, in five months, grew to a community of over a thousand on six continents. The enormous scale of the undertaking was a persuasive selling point, second only to the topic itself, pizza. Qualified food people were immediately curious, if at first hesitant. The more they heard, the more they wanted to be involved. If they were really serious about pizza they didn't wish to leave the enormous responsibility of choosing the best pizzerias in their respective areas to someone else.

At the core of *Where To Eat Pizza* are 121 trusted food writers, editors, critics, bloggers, chefs, and culinary professionals who are the guide's regional experts. They were chosen and corralled by me, or, every so often, by each other, for their pizza perceptiveness as well as their impressive networks of sources and contacts who could bring diverse perspectives to the project. Each named respected colleagues, restaurateurs, chefs, bakers, food producers, wine producers, culinary professionals, or pizza bakers to vote with them for the best pizza places.

It might at first seem inappropriate to have given *pizzaioli* the opportunity to vote for themselves or against fierce rivals. But if their pizzerias were more or less guaranteed to get in the guide anyway, there was little they could do to help themselves. And since the guide would not rank pizzerias or award them scores, they could do little to harm the prospects of a competitor, other than not vote for it. We welcomed their insiders' insights but left it to the regional experts to resolve this ethical dilemma: many invited the most acclaimed *pizzaioli* in their regions to participate. Others thought it best not to.

The regional experts recruited between three and thirty-three contributors from their respective regions, the number depending on the size of the regions and their relative importance as pizza strongholds. Not surprisingly the southern Italian region of Campania, encompassing Naples, the world capital of pizza, had twenty-nine voters, compared to eight for the city of Montreal and four for the Republic of South Korea. Each regional expert and contributor was asked to nominate up to three pizza places in the locality and as many as three more outside their home region, yet clearly worth a detour across the country or to the other side of the world. They were asked to tell us what was special about each pizza place and to choose a favorite pizza.

The Story of Pizza As We Know It

The Neapolitans didn't cook up the idea of pizza out of air, even if their crusts are sometimes so light they give that impression. Flat breads date back to Neolithic times. For millennia civilizations throughout the Mediterranean have developed their own versions. The ancient Greeks may have brought *plakous*, their flat and round cheese pie, to southern Italy when they colonized the region's coastal areas between the eighth and fifth centuries BCE. *Pita* (or *pitta*), which means "pie" in modern Greek and refers to a leavened flatbread, might be a precursor to "pizza" the word and "pizza" the food. In Calabria, *pitta* refers to various breads, cakes, and pies, including *pitta pizzulata*, a deep-dish tomato pie.

In the Mediterranean Basin the notion of a flat yeast bread covered with baked-in toppings is hardly unique to Italy. Across the French-Italian border Nice has *pissaladière*, garnished with caramelized onions, anchovies, olives, and garlic. Catalonia adorns its *coca* with the likes of red bell pepper, olives, tuna, sardines, and onions. The Turkish version of *lahmacun*, from the Arabic for "meat and bread," is slathered with a lamb and tomato mixture and is often characterized as Turkish pizza.

But the story of pizza, as understood in this guide— and by much of the modern world—begins either in the sixteenth century, when the term was introduced in Naples, the eighteenth century, when Neapolitans tried it with tomato, or the nineteenth century, when a Neapolitan discovered the perfect pizza pairing of tomato and mozzarella.

Neapolitan peasants were among the first in this part of the world to take their chances with tomatoes. Many Europeans feared this exotic fruit, brought to the continent from the New World by the Spanish, was poisonous. According to University of Naples's Professor Carlo Mangoni, tomatoes were introduced to pizza in 1760. It is said that Ferdinand IV, King of Naples from 1759 to 1825, was an early admirer of the red pizza *all'olio e pomodoro*—topped with "olive oil," "tomato," garlic, and oregano. This, the classic pizza better known as Marinara (in the mariner's style, though there's no fish), was sold during the period of Ferdinand's reign by street vendors and peddlers who sourced their pizza from the city's *laboratori* (workshops), as wholesale bakeries were known. It wasn't until 1830 that one such *laboratorio di pizza* opened Antica Pizzeria Port'Alba, the first pizzeria in Naples, and probably the world, with tables, chairs, and, naturally, tomatoes. Port'Alba is still serving its pizza in the historic center of the city, both inside the pizzeria and outside to passersby on the busy Via Port'Alba.

On a royal tour of Naples in 1889 Queen Margherita of Savoy, consort of Umberto I, observed many peasants enjoying the local specialty, which they folded like a *libretto* (booklet) and ate with great relish. The street scene was, in this respect, much as it is today, and so it is *this* part of *this* version of the story that casts the least doubt: you go to Naples. You see people eating pizza on the street. You want some. An official from the Royal Palace summoned Raffaele Esposito, certainly now, if not also then, the most famous *pizzaiolo* of the day, to make pizza for the Queen. Esposito seized the moment. He created a new pizza in the colors of the Italian flag: tomato red, mozzarella white, and basil green. She liked it. He christened this tricolore sensation the Margherita.

Apocryphal or not the tale holds important truths. If this was not the first tomato and mozzarella pizza ever made, by this *pizzaiolo* or another, so what? It is through the retelling of this story and the remaking of this humble culinary masterpiece that Esposito and his successors at Pizzeria Brandi, the "Antica Pizzeria Della Regina d'Italia," changed history. The invention that made Margherita Maria Teresa Giovanna an enduring first-name-only celebrity marks the inception of what the world recognizes and loves as pizza.

The Dough

The life of pizza begins with four ingredients: flour, water, salt, and yeast. A key variable with any flour, from the pizza baker's point of view, is its quantity of gluten-producing protein. The sticky gluten that develops in the dough gives it its strength and elasticity. These structural properties are essential when stretching it into thin rounds for pizza. Many *pizzaioli* source flours with a gluten content of 12 percent or more. Too little gluten can yield a stubborn dough that's not easy to handle. Too much gluten can make the dough too flexible and the resulting crust too chewy.

Italian pizza dough is traditionally made from type "00" flour, a highly refined bread flour from which virtually all the bran and germ found in wholewheat flours have been removed. "00" flours milled specially for pizza come from hard wheat, which has more protein than a soft flour better suited to cake flours. Long rising times at warm, ambient temperatures let the dough develop and help yield a lighter, chewier "crumb," to use the baker's term for the internal structure of a bread crust with the desired hole structure. This network of air pockets in varying sizes compresses under pressure. This crunch, whether in crisp fortissimo or yielding pianissimo, is one of the great pleasures of pizza eating.

Many artisan pizza bakers replace some, most, or all of the refined flour in their dough with stone-ground wholewheat flours and wholegrain flours. Heirloom wheat varieties and ancient grains, such as spelt, einkorn, and kamut, are increasingly in demand and in vogue, reflecting trends in artisanal bread baking. These give crusts more substance, fiber, and micronutrients, and a complex, nutty flavor. The challenge for pizza bakers is that these healthy and flavorful flours, especially those lower in gluten, can produce a less elastic, more fragile dough that is more difficult to stretch out and manipulate.

With pizza flours, the selection may only be as good as the purpose behind it. When *pizzaiolo* and baking guru Massimo Bosco enters a pizzeria for the first time he is curious to hear what the pizza maker has to say about his flour. "Many *pizzaioli* do not know what flour they're using," says the owner of Pizzeria Panetteria Bosco in the town of Tempio Pausania in northern Sardinia. "And if they do know they are unfamiliar with its characteristics."

As a rising agent for pizza dough, a natural sourdough starter yeast is an artisanal alternative to a dry yeast or commercial baker's yeast. A sourdough starter is itself a dough or, more precisely, a "mother dough"—*madre lievito* in Italian. It originates from a blend of wheat flour and water that is periodically fed more flour and water as it rises and ferments. When a small quantity of this mother dough is worked into the master pizza dough the bubbles get trapped and perform their levitation act, all the while delivering a unique flavor. The unused portion of the mother dough is continually refreshed and regenerated, to give life to more dough and more pizza.

The Tomatoes

When tomatoes are employed as the base layer of a pizza, which is not always but close enough to it, they are usually canned peeled tomatoes, often the elongated plum variety. Fresh tomatoes are used infrequently and applied more as a topping than a sauce or background color. The thinking goes if you are lucky enough to have really good, peak-season tomatoes you don't want to lose their delicate character, or beautiful shape, to a sauce.

Canned whole tomatoes, drained and then cut, chopped, or crushed, can go on the dough right away, as they typically do for a classic Margherita or Marinara.

The canning process involves heating and effectively par-cooks the tomatoes. Any pizza oven can finish the job, transforming the tomatoes, the olive oil, the seasonings, and any flavors rendered from various toppings into a sauce. Several pizza styles do call for tomato sauces, both cooked and uncooked, and these too are mostly made from canned tomatoes, either peeled whole tomatoes, crushed tomatoes, tomato purée (*passata*) or tomato concentrate, also known as tomato paste.

The world's most prized pizza tomato is the Pomodoro San Marzano dell'Agro Sarnese-Nocerino or, more simply, the San Marzano. The tomato originates in the town of San Marzano sul Sarno, where it was cultivated in volcanic soil on the slopes of Mount Vesuvius. Today it is produced in the expanded Argo Sarnese-Nocerino area between Salerno and Naples. The warm terrain produces an exceptionally full-bodied and sweet plum tomato with low acidity. The tomato has many imitators, including "San Marzano" varieties grown in other parts of the world. But only San Marzanos from Argo Sarnese-Nocerino can carry the DOP seal. DOP stands for Denominazione Di Origine Controllata (controlled designation of origin).

Dozens of pizza places in this guide bear the extra expense of San Marzano tomatoes and make no secret about it. The name San Marzano evokes Naples and, printed on a menu hung in a pizzeria window, could be perceived as an indicator of high standard in any pizzeria. It's a pizza snob's buzzword: if your tomatoes are genuine San Marzano that can only mean that everything else is top-shelf quality, too. Other pizzerias don't get too caught up about it. They manage to get good results with the best Roma tomatoes, a standard variety of plum tomato found in canned products.

Mozzarella

Mozzarella is hardly the only cheese used on pizza but it is the one most closely associated with it. The undisputed king of pizza cheeses can be made with buffalo milk or cow's milk. In Italy the two have different names, at least officially. The cheese made with the milk of water buffalo is supposed to be called mozzarella or, more descriptively, *mozzarella di bufala*, which, like all dairy bovines, is in the feminine form. It's *bufala*, not *bufalo*. The one made with cow's milk is denominated in either three words, *fior di latte,* or one, *fiordilatte*, both meaning "flower of milk." The reality is that when most

Italians say "mozzarella" they, like everyone else, mean the kind made with cow juice. To distinguish buffalo mozzarella they spell it out—*mozzarella di bufala*.

Fresh buffalo mozzarella, with a sweet, lightly tangy flavor and divine, milky core, is widely regarded as the superior of the two. It's springy, not rubbery. Its higher fat content makes it creamier. And, crucially, it's more expensive to buy and a lot harder to get. Cow's milk mozzarella is almost too easy to find. Processed versions produced on an industrial scale and widely available in supermarkets taste mostly of nothing. It is not a cheese many eat on its own, at room temperature or lightly chilled, as a delicacy prized for its leaden blandness.

Certified buffalo mozzarella produced in the southern Italian provinces of Caserta and Salerno, near Naples, bears the trademark *Mozzarella di Bufala* Campana DOP. A rustic example of this beloved cheese from Campania, the heartland of pizza, was certainly the mozzarella laid on the first Margherita served to its namesake, the Italian queen, in 1889. A strict traditionalist will accept no other mozzarella on his pizza.

The irony is that fresh, high-quality cow's milk mozzarella, with its supreme melting capacities, might now be the more appropriate cheese to cook on a pizza. Fresh buffalo mozzarella, hardly a peasant's cheese anymore, gets leaky when it melts over a pizza in the oven, releasing milky juices that can run off its sides. Many will drain the cheese first, resolving the issue by removing a cherished characteristic. Cheese purists may prefer their buffalo mozzarella undrained and uncooked, eaten as a finger food, in a salad, or applied to a pizza only after it's been baked. Several *pizzaioli* whose places are featured in this guide are suggesting exactly that.

Then there are the questions of availability and accessibility. The overwhelming majority of pizza bakers cannot get their hands on day-fresh buffalo mozzarella from Campania or other producing regions in Italy and other countries, including the USA, the UK, Australia, New Zealand, Brazil, and Argentina. Some who can get it can't afford it. In most areas of the world cow's milk is more accessible to cheese makers and therefore fresh mozzarella made with it is more readily available to pizza makers. Few should regard the "newer" mozzarella as somehow not genuine. The cow's milk kind has been used by *pizzaioli* in the Naples area for over 65 years and has the blessing for use on Margheritas by the VPN association, the official arbiter of Neapolitan authenticity.

Pizza Ovens

The type of oven dictates the style of the pizza, which subsequently dictates the type of oven. Or something like that. It's pretty much all one big circle, as it usually is with pizza, even when it's square.

Most pizza ovens are first defined by their heating source—wood, coal, gas, and electric. The old-style brick ovens tend to be fired with wood or coal, although gas may be used, too. The newer commercial ovens—convection, deck, or conveyor—are powered by gas or electricity. In convection ovens heat is circulated by a fan. This blowing will cook the pizza evenly and may also dry it a bit, which may or may not be a desired effect. Deck ovens employ conduction, cooking the crust through direct contact between the pizza's underskirt or undercarriage, to use the parlance for its bottom surface, and the stone or ceramic base of the oven chamber. Heat in a deck oven also radiates from gas or electric burners positioned either above or below the baking chamber. In conveyor ovens a conveyor belt carries the pizza from one end of the oven to the other, heating the pizza through forced-air convection, infrared heat, or radiation. In all ovens conduction heat can be applied directly to the crust from heat absorbed by a pan, as in the pan pizzas of Detroit, Rome, and Argentina.

Oven temperature affects the character and color of the pizza. A wood-fired oven heated above 900°F (482°C) can char and blacken a crust even before its crumb is fully dry and cooked through. The pizza is typically done in 90 seconds or fewer. A gas oven heated to 700°F (370°F) will brown more gradually, cooking in approximately 5 minutes, depending on the thickness of the crust and the desired crispness.

Coal is used primarily in the earliest pizzerias of New York and New Haven. Like wood, it is thought to impart a smoky char and old-world character, revealed in the leopard-spotting on both the *cornicione* and undercarriage of the crust. The high temperatures transform the flavors of the toppings in magical ways, too.

The Obsession

Today we eat in a world of food obsessions populated by food obsessives. In the twentieth century sharing a pizza meant dividing it among friends, not posting lascivious photos of it for strangers on social media. "Viral" meant dangerous, not desirable. Chefs were not so single-minded as the monogamous food geeks of today. Married to only one food, these zealots lock themselves in garages with only the essential ingredients and equipment required for their task and don't see the light of the day until, eight months later, they've perfected the object of their obsession.

This is a hospitable environment for pizza and, in particular, the health and happiness of fanatics who stop thinking about pizza only when they're eating it. That's to be applauded. You don't have to share their fixations to appreciate how these enhance the pizza landscape. The obsessives make this a better place to live, especially if you don't have to share an apartment with one.

To celebrate, rather than hide, wonderful pizza obsessions my tributes to them are dispersed throughout the guide. The titles of these essays will give you some indication of their gist: The Art of the Pizza Box. The Original Pizza Truck Movement. Japan's Neapolitan Pizza Obsession. Christian Puglisi Masters Mozzarella. The Secret of Detroit Pizza Gets Out. The Ways of the Pizza Fold.

You don't have to be a pizza obsessive, or become one, to get a lot of pleasure from *Where To Eat Pizza*. If you only use this guide to discover new pizza places near you, or compare its contributor views to yours, or those you've seen or heard elsewhere, that's already fabulous. But if you let the exhaustive range of the 1,705 recommendations and the persuasive opinions of the contributors sweep over you then get ready to hit the road.

Take this as a hint from the contributors: in our minds, the full title of this guide is....

Where You Have To *Go To Eat Pizza*

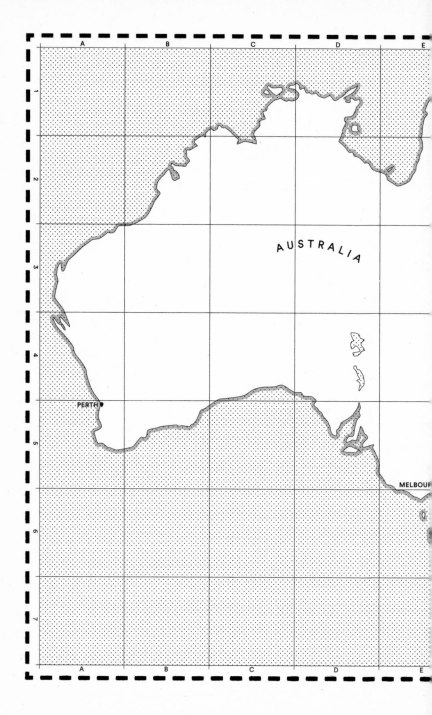

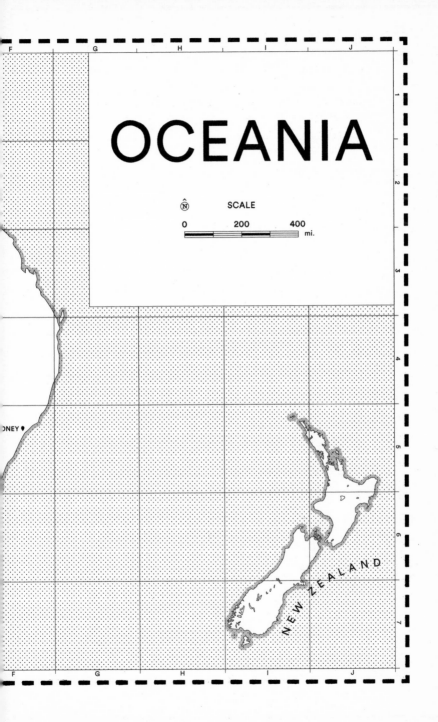

OCEANIA

SCALE

0   200   400 mi.

NEW ZEALAND

"IT'S ALWAYS PACKED, WITH A LOUD, BUSTLING ATMOSPHERE."

CORDELL KHOURY P.34

"THIS PLACE ROCKS."

PAT NOURSE P.34

AUSTRALIA

"IT'S EVERYTHING THAT TYPIFIES ITS FREMANTLE HOME: LAID-BACK, FULL OF FLAVOR, AND A BIT OFF THE WALL."

MAX BREARLEY P.37

"IT'S LIKE A LITTLE SLICE OF MILAN, BOXED UP AND TRANSPORTED TO BRISBANE, WITH ITS ITALIAN WOOD-FIRED OVEN AND ITALIAN-SPEAKING STAFF."

MORAG KOBEZ P.34

"YOU CAN ENJOY YOUR PIZZA WITH A SELECTION OF GREAT BOUTIQUE BEERS MADE AT OCCY'S OFFSITE BREWERY."

DARREN HAUNOLD P.36

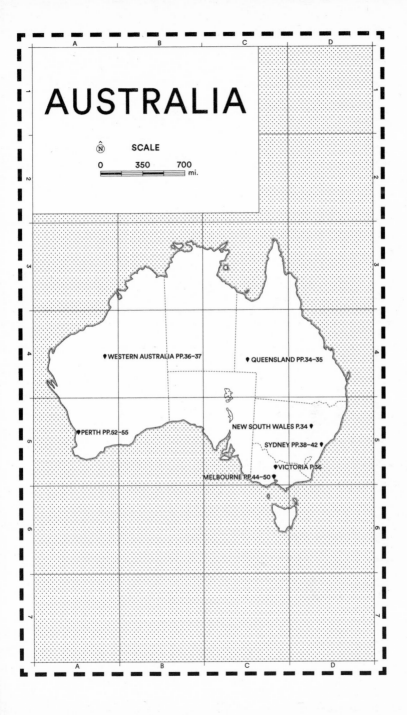

AUSTRALIA

N

SCALE

0   350   700
mi.

WESTERN AUSTRALIA PP.36–37

QUEENSLAND PP.34–35

PERTH PP.52–55

NEW SOUTH WALES P.34

SYDNEY PP.38–42

VICTORIA P.36

MELBOURNE PP.44–50

MILK AND HONEY

Shop 5/59A Station Street
Mullumbimby
New South Wales 2842
Australia
+61 266841422
www.milkandhoneymullumbimby.com.au

Opening hours..........................Closed Sunday and Monday
Credit cards.....................................Accepted but not AMEX
Style of pizza..Modern Australian
Recommended pizza..............Hot Salami, Bottarga, Olives,
Chile, Garlic, Tomato, and Mozzarella

"It nails the classics, but chef Timmy Brebner
(an alumnus of Tetsuya's and several other high-
falutin' fine diners in the big city) also freestyles
with confidence, making the most of the abundant
produce surrounding this tiny country town,
whether it's bottarga made from locally caught
mullet or sausage from the nearby Salumi Australia
operation—the best coldcuts in the state. A short,
smart, natural-leaning wine list doesn't hurt, nor does
the charm of the local surfie kids who run the floor.
This place rocks."—Pat Nourse

BECCOFINO

10 Vernon Terrace
Brisbane
Queensland 4005
Australia
+61 736660207
www.beccofino.com.au

Opening hours...Closed Monday
Credit cards...Accepted
Style of pizza...Traditional Italian
Recommended pizza.....................................Marinara Deluxe;
Mushroom; Prosciutto

"Long-ferment doughs properly treated, passionate
pizzaioli, flirty waiters—what's not to like?"
—Fiona Donnelly

"It's always packed, with a loud, bustling
atmosphere."—Cordell Khoury

JULIUS PIZZERIA

77 Grey Street
Brisbane
Queensland 4101
Australia
+61 738442655
www.juliuspizzeria.com.au

Opening hours...Closed Monday
Credit cards...Accepted
Style of pizza...Neapolitan
Recommended pizza.............................Number 1; Prosciutto

"Pizzas are full of flavor, have the right amount
of cheese, and the crust is not too chewy."
—Jocelyn Hancock

PIZZERIA VIOLETTA

10 Wongabel Street
Brisbane
Queensland 4069
Australia
+61 733782533
www.pizzeriavioletta.com.au

Opening hours...Open 7 days
Credit cards....................................Accepted but not AMEX
Style of pizza...Neapolitan
Recommended pizza.................Diavola; Maiala; Margherita

"Every suburb could do with a pizzeria like this
one. A small but elegantly sufficient menu using
good-quality ingredients and cooked with skill."
—Michael Dalton

"It's like a little slice of Milan, boxed up and
transported to Brisbane, with its Italian wood-fired
oven and Italian-speaking staff. Pizzas are authentic
with lovely thin bases, charred, bubbly-edged crust,
and sparingly applied quality toppings. And they take
only minutes to cook."—Morag Kobez

SORELLINA

31 Logan Road
Brisbane
Queensland 4102
Australia
+61 733918459
www.sorellinapizzeria.com

Opening hours.........................Closed Monday and Tuesday
Credit cards......................................Accepted but not AMEX
Style of pizza..Traditional wood-fired
Recommended pizza.............Mozzarella, Tomato, and Basil;
Pork Sausage, Squid, Caramelized Onion, and Mozzarella

"Amazing bases—the dough is cold-risen for three
days and pizzas are cooked in a wood-fired oven.
None of the pizzas have more than five toppings."
—Morag Kobez

"Any restaurant that has a ninja turtle mural is worth
a look!"—Ben Devlin

SUGO MI

3/190 Oxford Street
Brisbane
Queensland 4171
Australia
+61 733956327
www.sugomi.com.au

Opening hours...Closed Monday
Credit cards..Accepted
Style of pizza...........................Traditional Italian wood-fired
Recommended pizza...Margherita

"Despite its unfortunate name (particularly if one is
Sicilian), this pizzeria goes to great lengths to ensure
the pizza is as close to tradition as possible and it's
a good thing too. It always uses extremely fresh
ingredients along with an excellent dough."
—Cav. Alessandro Sorbello

TARTUFO

1000 Anne Street
Brisbane
Queensland 4006
Australia
+61 738521500
www.tartufo.com.au

Opening hours...Open 7 days
Credit cards..Accepted
Style of pizza..Neapolitan
Recommended pizza.............Diavola; Margherita; Mimosa;
Rustica alla Noel Staunton

"Classic Napoli all the way. Puffy chewy crust
and sparsely topped pizzas cooked in a Stefano
Ferrara oven."—Cordell Khoury

"I live in both Australia and Italy and Tony Percuoco's
pizza is as close as it gets to being in my village in
Tuscany. The *pizzaioli* are serious about the art of
making pizza and thus the results are excellent and,
above all else, consistent, which is challenging to
do day in and day out."—Cav. Alessandro Sorbello

Most viewed La Belle Époque restaurant in the suburb of
Fortitude Valley as a Brisbane version of a New York imitation
of a classic Parisian brasserie. For Tony Percuoco, however,
it was a reminder of a grand galleria restaurant in his native
Naples. So he recast La Belle Époque, located in the
Emporium complex, as Tartufo, a restaurant for fine Italian
dining, with a more informal area reserved for pizza. Once
a Stefano Ferrara wood-fired pizza oven was installed by the
entrance the place really did feel like Naples. The soft and
chewy pizza crust is resolutely Neapolitan, with minimal
concession to Australian tastes.

TINDERBOX

7/31 James Street
Brisbane
Queensland 4006
Australia
+61 738523744
www.thetinderbox.com.au

Opening hours...Closed Monday
Credit cards..Accepted
Style of pizza..Neapolitan
Recommended pizza...............................El Greco; Tinderbox

"I would not often order a seafood pizza but the
Tinderbox, made with local shrimp (prawns),
a little chile, zucchini (courgette), and mozzarella,
is perfect."—Michael Dalton

BANK STREET

5 Bank Street
Avenel
Victoria 3664
Australia
+61 357962522
www.bankstreet.com.au

Opening hours.........................Closed Monday–Wednesday
(don't serve pizza on Thursday)
Credit cards...Accepted
Style of pizza...Wood-fired
Recommended pizza..Scotty

"It's worth the hour and a bit drive north out of
Melbourne and up the Hume highway to Avenel to
discover this gem. Summer is spent in the garden and
winters find diners tucked inside in the cozy warmth.
Local produce and wines are part of the charm."
—Sharlee Gibb

VOLPINO

2/42 Lochiel Avenue
Mount Martha
Victoria 3934
Australia
+61 359744435
www.volpino.com.au

Opening hours...Open 7 days
Credit cards.......................................Accepted but not AMEX
Style of pizza...Wood-fired
Recommended pizza..Our Favourite

"Volpino is across the road from the beach, so
a beach walk followed by pizza and wine is a treat.
Plus it has a lovely wooden deck, AND offers a mean
Negroni."—Liz Egan

CENA PIZZERIA

59 Queen Street
Busselton
Western Australia 6280
Australia
+61 897542066
www.cenapizzeria.com.au

Opening hours...Open 7 days
Credit cards...Accepted
Style of pizza...Traditional thin-crust
Recommended pizza....................................Bacon Deluxe

"A great local pizzeria. Excellent traditional bases,
well executed with great mix of ingredients."
—Darren Haunold

AL FORNO

1/19 Bussell Highway
Busselton
Western Australia 6280
Australia
+61 897513775
www.al-forno.com.au

Opening hours...Open 7 days
Credit cards.......................................Accepted but not AMEX
Style of pizza...Traditional thin-crust
Recommended pizza....................................Quattro Stagioni

"Hans van Diest makes a fantastic pizza, well
prepared with only the freshest ingredients."
—Darren Haunold

OCCY'S

12/34 Dunn Bay Road
Dunsborough
Western Australia 6281
Australia
+61 897567777
www.occys.com.au

Opening hours...Open 7 days
Credit cards.......................................Accepted but not AMEX
Style of pizza..............Traditional with modern ingredients
Recommended pizza...The Carbunup

"You can enjoy your pizza with a selection of great
boutique beers made at Occy's offsite brewery."
—Darren Haunold

THE POUR HOUSE

26 Dunn Bay Road
Dunsborough
Western Australia 6281
Australia
+61 897591720
www.pourhouse.com.au

Opening hours...Open 7 days
Credit cards.....................................Accepted but not AMEX
Style of pizza...Wood-fired
Recommended pizza............................4 Cheese; Portobello
Mushroom, Thyme, and Goat Cheese

"The Pour House has a really nice range of pizzas that combine some lovely high-quality ingredients with a cool vibe and a great drinks list."
—Darren Haunold

LITTLE CREATURES

40 Mews Road
Fremantle
Western Australia 6160
Australia
+61 862151000
www.littlecreatures.com.au

Opening hours...Open 7 days
Credit cards.....................................Accepted but not AMEX
Style of pizza...Wood-fired
Recommended pizza............................Harissa Spiced Lamb,
Melanzane (eggplant/aubergine), and Feta

"Not your traditional pizzeria, but a beer and a wood-fired pizza at Little Creatures harborside brewery is not just an iconic Freo experience but a Western Australian one. It's everything that typifies its Fremantle home: laid-back, full of flavor, and a bit off the wall."—Max Brearley

LITTLE CAESARS PIZZERIA

7125 Great Eastern Highway
Mundaring
Western Australia 6073
Australia
+61 892956611
www.littlecaesarspizzeria.com.au

Opening hours...Closed Tuesday
Credit cards.....................................Accepted but not AMEX
Style of pizza...Modern
Recommended pizza......................Greek Lamb; Mudhoney;
Vegetarian

"Award-winning pizza chef Theo Kalogeracos makes a fantastic pizza and there are always new releases to try."—Catherine Natale

"AMAZING THIN PIZZAS WITH BEAUTIFUL INGREDIENTS."

LARA CARATURO P.40

SYDNEY

"I ALWAYS HAVE TO HAVE THE LUCIO—ONE HALF IS A TRADITIONAL MARGHERITA TOPPED WITH MOZZARELLA, BASIL, AND TOMATO WHILE THE OTHER IS A FOLDED-OVER CALZONE FILLED WITH HAM AND RICOTTA." FLAVIO CARNEVALE P.41

"THE SERVICE IS WORLD CLASS AND OFTEN THERE IS A LINE TO THE FRONT DOOR TO GET IN— THAT'S WHEN YOU KNOW IT'S GOOD."

PETE DILLON P.42

"IT'S ALL ABOUT THE BASE OF THE PIZZA— PUFFY, A LITTLE SCORCHED, BUT WITH PLENTY OF FLAVOR."

PAT NOURSE P.42

"THIS IS MY FAVORITE PIZZA BAR IN HABERFIELD, ONE OF THE BETTER ITALIAN AREAS OF SYDNEY."

ANDREW LEVINS P.41

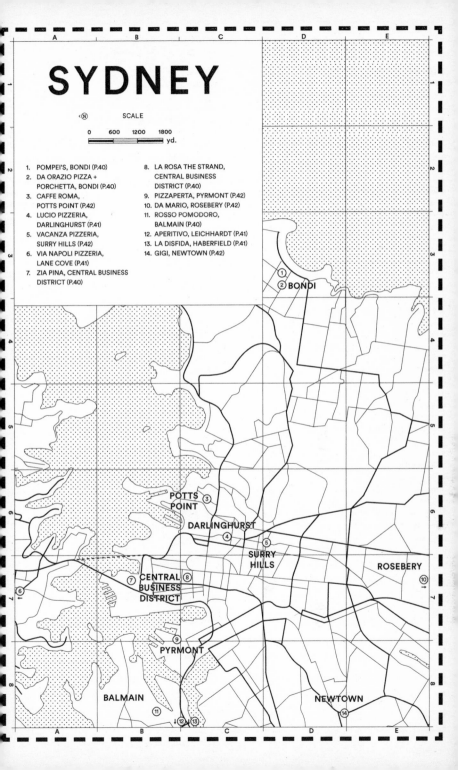

SYDNEY

‹Ⓝ›   SCALE

0   600   1200   1800
                        yd.

1. POMPEI'S, BONDI (P.40)
2. DA ORAZIO PIZZA + PORCHETTA, BONDI (P.40)
3. CAFFE ROMA, POTTS POINT (P.42)
4. LUCIO PIZZERIA, DARLINGHURST (P.41)
5. VACANZA PIZZERIA, SURRY HILLS (P.42)
6. VIA NAPOLI PIZZERIA, LANE COVE (P.41)
7. ZIA PINA, CENTRAL BUSINESS DISTRICT (P.40)
8. LA ROSA THE STRAND, CENTRAL BUSINESS DISTRICT (P.40)
9. PIZZAPERTA, PYRMONT (P.42)
10. DA MARIO, ROSEBERY (P.42)
11. ROSSO POMODORO, BALMAIN (P.40)
12. APERITIVO, LEICHHARDT (P.41)
13. LA DISFIDA, HABERFIELD (P.41)
14. GIGI, NEWTOWN (P.42)

BONDI

POTTS POINT

DARLINGHURST

SURRY HILLS

ROSEBERY

CENTRAL BUSINESS DISTRICT

PYRMONT

BALMAIN

NEWTOWN

ROSSO POMODORO

20–24 Buchanan Street
Balmain
Sydney
New South Wales 2041
Australia
+61 295555924
www.rossopomodoro.com.au

Opening hours..Closed Monday
Credit cards....................................Accepted but not AMEX
Style of pizza..Classic
Recommended pizza.............Anything with Italian sausage
on it and a Margherita on the side

"These guys use an electric oven but you can't tell.
The crust comes out perfectly charred and chewy,
and it may be my favorite pizza base in Sydney. The
stuff on top of that base is very decent too. I once ate
three pizzas from here by myself and didn't even feel
that horrible."—Andrew Levins

DA ORAZIO PIZZA + PORCHETTA

75–79 Hall Street
Bondi
Sydney
New South Wales 2026
Australia
+61 280906969
www.daorazio.com

Opening hours..Open 7 days
Credit cards..Accepted
Style of pizza..Neapolitan
Recommended pizza..Diavoletta

"The focaccia stuffed with porchetta is amazing."
—Cordell Khoury

POMPEI'S

126–130 Roscoe Street
Bondi
Sydney
New South Wales 2026
Australia
+61 293651233
www.pompeis.com.au

Opening hours..Closed Monday
Credit cards..Accepted
Style of pizza..Traditional wood-fired
Recommended pizza..................Bufala; Spinach and Ricotta

"Amazing thin pizzas with beautiful ingredients."
—Lara Caraturo

"Great atmosphere here—very buzzy."
—Fiona Donnelly

LA ROSA THE STRAND

The Strand Arcade
193 Pitt Street
Central Business District
Sydney
New South Wales 2000
Australia
+61 292231674
www.larosathestrand.com.au

Opening hours..Closed Sunday
Credit cards..Accepted
Style of pizza..Roman
Recommended pizza..Mushroom

ZIA PINA

93 George Street
Central Business District
Sydney
New South Wales 2000
Australia
+61 292472255
www.ziapinatherocks.com.au

Opening hours..Open 7 days
Credit cards..Accepted
Style of pizza..Italian
Recommended pizza..Four Seasons

"Tasty pizzas with a crispy base. I love the typical
Italian atmosphere."—Renata Diem

LUCIO PIZZERIA

248 Palmer Street
Darlinghurst
Sydney
New South Wales 2010
Australia
+61 293323766
www.luciopizzeria.com.au

Opening hours	Closed Tuesday
Credit cards	Accepted
Style of pizza	Neapolitan
Recommended pizza	Carrettiera; Lucio

"I always have to have the Lucio—one half is a traditional Margherita topped with mozzarella, basil, and tomato while the other is a folded-over calzone filled with ham and ricotta."—Flavio Carnevale

LA DISFIDA

109 Ramsay Street
Haberfield
Sydney
New South Wales 2045
Australia
+61 297988299
www.ladisfida.com.au

Opening hours	Closed Monday and Tuesday
Credit cards	Accepted but not AMEX
Style of pizza	Classic Italian wood-fired
Recommended pizza	Diavola

"This is my favorite pizza bar in Haberfield, one of the better Italian areas of Sydney. There are a handful of pizzerias in the area and after eating at all of them at least 10 times, my wife and I decided this was the best. It definitely has the most atmosphere of all Sydney's pizza bars, very dark and warm. The pizzas come out quick and crispy and the specials are always worth ordering."—Andrew Levins

VIA NAPOLI PIZZERIA

141 Longueville Road
Lane Cove
Sydney
New South Wales 2066
Australia
+61 294283297
www.vianapolipizzeria.com.au

Opening hours	Open 7 days
Credit cards	Accepted
Style of pizza	Neapolitan
Recommended pizza	Margherita; Napoletana

"The pizze are excellent, textbook, but there's also a real family feeling to the place that's easy to get wrapped up in."—Pat Nourse

"The pizzas that come out of the oven at Via Napoli are the closest thing to the pizza I ate in Naples—to taste that is, not so much to look at as it serves huge rectangles of pizza instead of round ones."
—Andrew Levins

APERITIVO

163 Norton Street
Leichhardt
Sydney
New South Wales 2040
Australia
+61 295640003
www.aperitivo.com.au

Opening hours	Closed Monday
Credit cards	Accepted
Style of pizza	Neapolitan
Recommended pizza	Margherita Bufala STG

"Awesome pizza."—Lara Caraturo

GIGI

379 King Street
Newtown
Sydney
New South Wales 2042
Australia
+61 295572224
www.gigipizzeria.com.au

Opening hours...Open 7 days
Credit cards...............................Accepted but not AMEX
Style of pizza...Neapolitan
Recommended pizza...................Gorgonzola and Radicchio;
Three Types of Mushroom and Stracchino Cheese

"The service is world class and often there is a line
to the front door to get in—that's when you know
it's good."—Pete Dillon

PIZZAPERTA

The Star, Harbourside Ground Floor
Pirrama Road
Pyrmont
Sydney
New South Wales 2009
Australia
+61 297779000
www.star.com.au

Opening hours...Open 7 days
Credit cards...Accepted
Style of pizza...Gourmet
Recommended pizza...........Quattro Formaggi and Walnuts

CAFFE ROMA

9 Kellet Street
Potts Point
Sydney
New South Wales 2011
Australia
+61 293583578
www.cafferoma.com.au

Opening hours...Open 7 days
Credit cards...Accepted
Style of pizza...Standard

DA MARIO

36 Morley Avenue
Rosebery
Sydney
New South Wales 2018
Australia
+61 296692242
www.damario.com.au

Opening hours...Closed Monday
Credit cards...Accepted
Style of pizza...Neapolitan
Recommended pizza...............................Partenopea; Sausage
with Broccoli Raab

"It's all about the base of the pizza—puffy, a little
scorched, but with plenty of flavor. The place has
a nice sunny outlook as well, amid the warehouses
and wide streets of semi-industrial Rosebery."
—Pat Nourse

VACANZA PIZZERIA

414 Bourke Street
Surry Hills
Sydney
New South Wales 2010
Australia
+61 286946414
www.vacanza.com.au

Opening hours...Closed Monday
Credit cards............................Accepted but not AMEX
Style of pizza...Classic Italian
Recommended pizza................"Brandi" Bufalina Margherita

"Vacanza makes a light classic Italian pizza—not
as big as the Neapolitan-style or as thin as the
Roman-style. The edges are a bit bigger than a
Roman-style pizza and it is very easy to pick up
a slice and fold it in two and eat with your hands."
—Flavio Carnevale

"LADRO CREATES FABULOUS WOOD-FIRED PIZZAS THAT TOY WITH THE CHAR AND HAVE THE PUFFIEST, AIRIEST CRUSTS GOING—LIKE CHEWING CRISP AIR."
LARISSA DUBECKI P.47

"THE MOOR'S HEAD SERVES A FINE EXAMPLE OF A TRADITIONAL LEBANESE PIZZA CALLED A 'MANOUSHE.'"
INGRID LANGTRY P.49

MELBOURNE

"JOHNNY'S PIZZA IS FIERCELY NEAPOLITAN: A THIN CHEWY CRUST, A SCATTERING OF INGREDIENTS, AND 90 SECONDS IN THE OVEN. BOOM."
SHARLEE GIBB P.46

"GREAT PIZZA IN AN OLD-SCHOOL COMFORTING ENVIRONMENT WITH REAL ITALIAN ATMOSPHERE."
ELIZABETH RODRIGUEZ P.48

"LAZERPIG DOESN'T JUST ROCK THE BEST NAME IN THE GAME, BUT BACKS UP THE MODERN ATTITUDE WITH SOME SERIOUSLY EXCELLENT WOOD-FIRED PIZZAS." DAN STOCK P.47

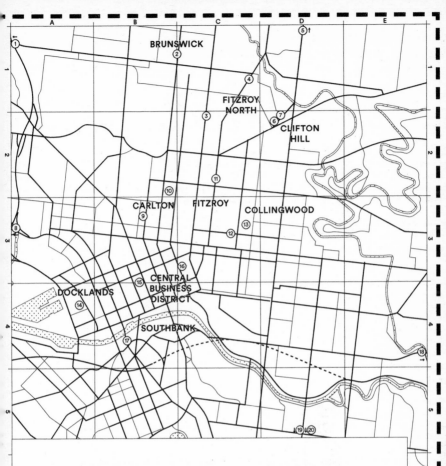

MELBOURNE

N̂   SCALE

0   500   1000   1500
                            yd.

1. SCOOZI, ASCOT VALE (P.46)
2. 400 GRADI, BRUNSWICK (P.46)
3. WOODSTOCK, FITZROY NORTH (P.48)
4. SUPERMAXI, FITZROY NORTH (P.48)
5. MOOR'S HEAD, THORNBURY (P.49)
6. QUEEN MARGARET, FITZROY NORTH (P.48)
7. TUTTI I SAPORI, CLIFTON HILL (P.47)

8. OVEST, WEST FOOTSCRAY (P.50)
9. KAPRICA, CARLTON (P.46)
10. D.O.C., CARLTON (P.46)
11. SHAWCROSS PIZZA, FITZROY (P.48)
12. LADRO, FITZROY (P.47)
13. LAZERPIG, COLLINGWOOD (P.47)
14. 90 SECONDI, DOCKLANDS (P.47)
15. +39, CENTRAL BUSINESS DISTRICT (P.47)
16. OMBRA, CENTRAL BUSINESS DISTRICT (P.46)

17. GRADI AT CROWN, SOUTHBANK (P.49)
18. PIZZA RELIGION, HAWTHORNE EAST (P.49)
19. LADRO, PRAHRAN (P.49)
20. GROSVENOR HOTEL, ST KILDA EAST (P.49)

SCOOZI

136 Union Road
Ascot Vale
Melbourne
Victoria 3032
Australia
+61 393700100
www.scoozi.net

Opening hours	Closed Monday
Credit cards	Accepted
Style of pizza	Neapolitan
Recommended pizza	Margherita; Sausage

"The Margherita is the classic Neapolitan pizza and the Scoozi version is exemplary."—Dan Stock

400 GRADI

99 Lygon Street
Brunswick
Melbourne
Victoria 3057
Australia
+61 393802320
www.400gradi.com.au

Opening hours	Open 7 days
Credit cards	Accepted
Style of pizza	Neapolitan
Recommended pizza	Caserta; Margherita Verace; Sausage and Broccoli Raab

"Manning the wood-fired oven is 2014 World Pizza Champion Johnny Di Francesco (much to the Italians protest of course). Johnny's pizza is fiercely Neapolitan: a thin chewy crust, a scattering of ingredients, and 90 seconds in the oven. Boom."
—Sharlee Gibb

"You won't find better pizza in Naples, in Italy, or, for that matter, anywhere else."—Richard Klein

Ordinarily it's impossible to say for sure who makes the best pizza in Melbourne, Naples, or anywhere. But in mid-April 2014 those who dared argue 400 Gradi's Margherita Verace (San Marzano tomato, buffalo mozzarella, basil) was the world's best had something to back them up: Johnny Di Francesco, the Australian-born, Naples-trained owner and *pizzaiolo* of that resplendent pizzeria in Brunswick, a suburb of Melbourne, had just been named World Pizza Champion at the Campionato Mondiale della Pizza in Parma, Italy. He won the prestigious prize by preparing the same pizza he makes in Brunswick every day. "I didn't do anything extraordinary," said Di Francesco, not grasping the tantalizing irony of his assertion.

D.O.C.

295 Drummond Street
Carlton
Melbourne
Victoria 3053
Australia
+61 393472298
www.docgroup.net

Opening hours	Open 7 days
Credit cards	Accepted
Style of pizza	Neapolitan
Recommended pizza	Abruzzio; San Daniele; Speck

"It is no wonder the crowds keep coming—crisp but with a nice chewiness, the bases hold a range of authentic toppings and are created with care."
—Dan Stock

KAPRICA

19 Lincoln Square
Carlton
Melbourne
Victoria 3053
Australia
+61 393471138

Opening hours	Open 7 days
Credit cards	Not accepted
Style of pizza	Electric Neapolitan
Recommended pizza	Capricciosa

"Kaprica is a bit of romance—a hard-to-find gem, quirkily fitted out with hints of Italian-ness without going overboard about it, and the pizza being made by owner Pietro Barbagello is part of the show."
—Larissa Dubecki

OMBRA

76 Bourke Street
Central Business District
Melbourne
Victoria 3000
Australia
+61 396391927
www.ombrabar.com.au

Opening hours	Open 7 days
Credit cards	Accepted
Style of pizza	Traditional
Recommended pizza	Bianca; Margherita; Prosciutto

"Ombra is passionate about all things Italian. It's run by a big Italian family who've had restaurants in

Melbourne for generations. They are passionate about everything, the right flour, cheeses, they make their own salumi for the pizzas, and their crusts are always perfect."—Liz Egan

from a 5-year-old living yeast culture, the dough—proven for at least 72 hours—makes for a crisp base that's chewy and charred and eat-every-crust good." —Dan Stock

+39
362 Little Bourke Street
Central Business District
Melbourne
Victoria 3000
Australia
+61 396420440
www.plus39.com.au

Opening hours	Open 7 days
Credit cards	Accepted
Style of pizza	Neapolitan thin-crust
Recommended pizza	Tirolese

"A great minimalist but stylish modern pizzeria." —Nino Zoccali

TUTTI I SAPORI
398 Queens Parade
Clifton Hill
Melbourne
Victoria 3068
Australia
+61 394810745
www.tuttiisapori.net

Opening hours	Closed Sunday
Credit cards	Accepted
Style of pizza	Italian
Recommended pizza	Calabrese

LAZERPIG
9 Peel Street
Collingwood
Melbourne
Victoria 3066
Australia
+61 394171177
www.lazerpig.com.au

Opening hours	Open 7 days
Credit cards	Accepted but not AMEX
Style of pizza	Wood-fired
Recommended pizza	The Fun Guy

"Lazerpig doesn't just rock the best name in the game, but backs up the modern attitude with some seriously excellent wood-fired pizzas. The ingredients on top are almost as good as the base itself. Made

90 SECONDI
1/700 Bourke Street
Docklands
Melbourne
Victoria 3000
Australia
+61 396002841
www.90secondi.com.au

Opening hours	Closed Sunday
Credit cards	Accepted
Style of pizza	Neapolitan

LADRO
224 Gertrude Street
Fitzroy
Melbourne
Victoria 3065
Australia
+61 394157575
www.ladro.com.au

Opening hours	Open 7 days
Credit cards	Accepted
Style of pizza	Roman
Recommended pizza	Badabing; Lazio; Otto; Puttanesca

"Arguably the first pizzeria to bring the real artisanal thing to Melbourne. Ladro creates fabulous wood-fired pizzas that toy with the char and have the puffiest, airiest crusts going—like chewing crisp air." —Larissa Dubecki

"Elbows may knock and conversations overlap in the busy, popular dining room with a classic black-and- white fit-out, but the quality of the pizza is consistently excellent."—Veda Gilbert

When, in 2003, Ingrid Langtry and her husband Sean Kierce opened Ladro in Fitzroy, an inner city suburb of Melbourne, everything about it was on the early side of up and coming: the location on bohemian Gertrude Street. The industrial chic design. The emphasis on local sourcing and sustainability. The very notion of artisanal pizza. Stylistically, the wood-fired pizza has always leaned toward Rome and away from Naples. Ladro now serves gluten-free pizza, both here and at its second location on 162 Greville Street in the Melbourne suburb of Prahran.

SHAWCROSS PIZZA

324 Brunswick Street
Fitzroy
Melbourne
Victoria 3065
Australia
+61 394199596
www.shawcrosspizza.com.au

Opening hours..Open 7 days
Credit cards..Accepted
Style of pizza..............................Traditional hand-stretched
with a modern take
Recommended pizza...........Durkah Durkah; Mexicutioner;
Notorious PIG; Shawcross 22"

"The best (and largest) pizza in Australia."
—Darren Haunold

QUEEN MARGARET

356 Queens Parade
Fitzroy North
Melbourne
Victoria 3068
Australia
+61 394825988
www.queenmargaret.com.au

Opening hours...Closed Monday
Credit cards......................................Accepted but not AMEX
Style of pizza...Italian
Recommended pizza..QM II

"Named after Queen Margherita of Savoy, this local
pizzeria serves up 18 varieties of Italian-style 24-hour
fermented thin-crust pizza, three of which are
devoted to the noble Margherita."—Veda Gilbert

SUPERMAXI

305 St Georges Road
Fitzroy North
Melbourne
Victoria 3068
Australia
+61 394822828
www.supermaxi.com.au

Opening hours...Closed Monday
Credit cards..Accepted
Style of pizza...Electric Neapolitan
Recommended pizza.........................Badabing; Strada Nova

"Supermaxi is warm and generous, a place for
families, friends, and food fans. It is proud to keep it
simple, which makes it easy to relax and enjoy. The
seasonal specials are glorious; if there's anything with
figs it's essential to try it."—Dani Valent

"The pizza bases are perfect—chef Rita Macali
always nails the thin, crisp yet pliable bases that are
charry on the bottom and puffy around the edges.
The toppings are judiciously composed—top-notch
ingredients with an eye for minimalism without
making diners feel they're missing out."
—Larissa Dubecki

WOODSTOCK

612 Nicholson Street
Fitzroy North
Melbourne
Victoria 3068
Australia
+61 394818122
www.woodstockpizza.com.au

Opening hours...Closed Monday
Credit cards..Accepted
Style of pizza..Traditional

"Great pizza in an old-school comforting environment
with real Italian atmosphere."—Elizabeth Rodriguez

PIZZA RELIGION

493 Tooronga Road
Hawthorne East
Melbourne
Victoria 3123
Australia
+61 398822555
www.pizzareligion.com.au

Opening hours..Open 7 days
Credit cards...............................Accepted but not AMEX
Style of pizza..................................Non-traditional toppings
Recommended pizza...Beef

LADRO

162 Greville Street
Prahran
Melbourne
Victoria 3181
Australia
+61 395102233
www.ladro.com.au

Opening hours..Open 7 days
Credit cards...Accepted
Style of pizza..Roman
Recommended pizza...............................Porcini Mushrooms
and Gorgonzola

"Great-tasting pizza, gutsy flavors, and quality
ingredients."—Jocelyn Hancock

GRADI AT CROWN

8 Whiteman Street
Southbank
Melbourne
Victoria 3006
Australia
+61 396969888
www.gradicrown.com.au

Opening hours..Open 7 days
Credit cards...Accepted
Style of pizza..Neapolitan
Recommended pizza...............................Margherita Verace

GROSVENOR HOTEL

10 Brighton Road
St Kilda East
Melbourne
Victoria 3183
Australia
+61 395311542
www.grosvenorhotel.com.au

Opening hours..Open 7 days
Credit cards...Accepted
Style of pizza..Roman
Recommended pizza...Capricciosa

"The Grosvenor is a local pub with a strong focus on
excellent food and wine. Wood-fired pizza is only
part of what it does, but it takes it very seriously.
Dedicated Italian pizza cooks prepare pizze in full
view in the glowing heat of the furnace and pizze
are baked on stone. The dough is long-rested and
gluten-free bases are available for no extra charge."
—Dani Valent

MOOR'S HEAD

Rear 774 High Street
Thornbury
Melbourne
Victoria 3071
Australia
+61 394840173
www.themoorshead.com

Opening hours..Open 7 days
Credit cards...............................Accepted but not AMEX
Style of pizza...Middle Eastern
Recommended pizza.......................Beiruti; Fred the Deaf;
Shams of Tabriz

"Owner Joseph Abboud plays with a cool mix of
Middle Eastern flavors in his inauthentic pizzas; sujuk
(spicy sausage), tahini, and soused onions all have
a role. Manoushe are the round pizzas and pide are
the boa-shape ones. In our family everyone has a
favorite."—Sharlee Gibb

"The Moor's Head serves a fine example of a
traditional Lebanese pizza called a 'manoushe.'
The dough is slightly sweeter and is often topped
with fresh ingredients after it is has been cooked in
a wood-fired oven."—Ingrid Langtry

OVEST

572 Barkly Street
West Footscray
Melbourne
Victoria 3012
Australia
+61 396877766
www.ovestwest.com.au

Opening hours	Closed Monday
Credit cards	Accepted but not AMEX
Style of pizza	Traditional Italian
Recommended pizza	Parma Prosciutto

"Ovest always has a special, which is usually the best I can order."—Pete Dillon

"GINO IS THE GRANDFATHER ('NONNO') OF PIZZA IN WESTERN AUSTRALIA AND HAS BEEN MAKING PIZZA FOR OVER 40 YEARS."

CATHERINE NATALE P.55

PERTH

"IT'S PIZZA BY THE SLICE WITH AMAZING COMBINATIONS."

THEO KALOGERACOS P.55

"THE PLACE IS RUN BY A WARM-HEARTED FAMILY FROM NAPLES AND THE PASSION SHOWS."

GAIL WILLIAMS P.55

"THE BEST TAKEOUT PIZZA IN PERTH!"

TRISTRAM FINI P.54

"IN LINE WITH ITS ROMAN ROOTS, STUZZICO IS AN UNASSUMING BY-THE-SLICE PIZZERIA."

MAX BREARLEY P.54

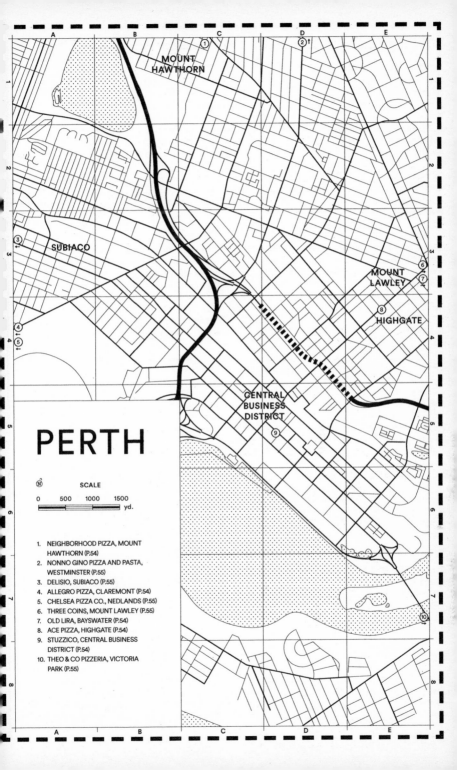

PERTH

N

SCALE

0   500   1000   1500
                        yd.

1. NEIGHBORHOOD PIZZA, MOUNT
   HAWTHORN (P.54)
2. NONNO GINO PIZZA AND PASTA,
   WESTMINSTER (P.55)
3. DELISIO, SUBIACO (P.55)
4. ALLEGRO PIZZA, CLAREMONT (P.54)
5. CHELSEA PIZZA CO., NEDLANDS (P.55)
6. THREE COINS, MOUNT LAWLEY (P.55)
7. OLD LIRA, BAYSWATER (P.54)
8. ACE PIZZA, HIGHGATE (P.54)
9. STUZZICO, CENTRAL BUSINESS
   DISTRICT (P.54)
10. THEO & CO PIZZERIA, VICTORIA
    PARK (P.55)

MOUNT
HAWTHORN

SUBIACO

MOUNT
LAWLEY

HIGHGATE

CENTRAL
BUSINESS
DISTRICT

OLD LIRA

395B Guildford Road
Bayswater
Perth
Western Australia 6053
Australia
+61 861611789
www.oldlira.com.au

Opening hours	Closed Monday–Wednesday
Credit cards	Accepted but not AMEX
Style of pizza	New Age
Recommended pizza	Prosciutto, Arugula (rocket), Parmesan, Mayo, and Red Sauce

"Great, crisp bases—extensive pizza offering across *calde* (hot), *freschi* (room temperature), and *dolci* (sweet). The best takeout pizza in Perth!"
—Tristram Fini

STUZZICO

556 Hay Street
Central Business District
Perth
Western Australia 6000
Australia
+61 892210199
www.stuzzico.com.au

Opening hours	Closed Saturday and Sunday
Credit cards	Accepted but not AMEX
Style of pizza	Roman
Recommended pizza	Salami

"In line with its Roman roots, Stuzzico is an unassuming by-the-slice pizzeria. No hype. No claims of greatness. Just smashing out slices to hungry office workers and tradesmen. It's pizza on the go in the best way."—Max Brearley

ALLEGRO PIZZA

231A Stirling Highway
Claremont
Perth
Western Australia 6009
Australia
+61 893831347
www.allegropizza.com.au

Opening hours	Open 7 days
Credit cards	Accepted
Style of pizza	Traditional
Recommended pizza	Martino

ACE PIZZA

448 Beaufort Street
Highgate
Perth
Western Australia 6003
Australia
+61 499448000
www.acepizza.com.au

Opening hours	Closed Monday and Tuesday
Credit cards	Accepted
Style of pizza	New York
Recommended pizza	Cheeky Pumpkin; Godfather; Nuclear Pig; The OP

"Is it a New York speakeasy? Is it a Roman pizzeria? Is it just a nice place to hang out and drink beer and eat top-quality pizza? Yes, it's all of the above with the added bonus of friendly staff and a great drink selection."—Gail Williams

"A funky atmospheric place with freshly cut meats, wood-fired pizzas, and great salads."—Sophie Budd

Ace, in Highgate, an inner suburb of Perth, is cherished for its friendly staff, its even friendlier cocktails, and top-quality pizza baked in a wood-fired oven. Those who want San Marzano tomatoes on their pizza must take on the OP (basically a Margherita), the Godfather (a Margherita with San Daniele prosciutto) or the Rosso Grantico, a red number (no cheese) with tomato, capers, olives, anchovies, garlic, and basil. The name comes from Rosso Antico, an Italian vermouth.

NEIGHBORHOOD PIZZA

Anvil Lane
Mount Hawthorn
Perth
Western Australia 6016
Australia
+61 419507432
www.neighborhoodpizzabar.com

Opening hours	Closed Monday and Tuesday
Credit cards	Accepted but not AMEX
Style of pizza	Wood-fired
Recommended pizza	Fennel Sausage, Roasted Tomato, Parmesan, Fresh Arugula (rocket), Pine Nuts, Red Base; Pumpkin, Feta, Chile, Almonds, Fresh Mint, Balsamic Glaze, Bianca Base

"Located in an old warehouse, this pizza bar is a great place for a casual catch-up with old and new friends. The menu is small with only 12 options, but simple ingredients and a thin-crust base make this pizza joint a winner. No bookings are required, just walk

in—and it is BYO drinks, which makes it a very
affordable night out!"—Sophie Budd

THREE COINS

2/776 Beaufort Street
Mount Lawley
Perth
Western Australia 6050
Australia
+61 892716033
www.threecoins.com.au

Opening hours	Closed Monday
Credit cards	Accepted but not AMEX
Style of pizza	Traditional southern Italian
Recommended pizza	Caprese

"The place is run by a warm-hearted family from
Naples and the passion shows."—Gail Williams

CHELSEA PIZZA CO.

145 Stirling Highway
Nedlands
Perth
Western Australia 6009
Australia
+61 893867833
www.chelseapizza.com.au

Opening hours	Open 7 days
Credit cards	Accepted
Style of pizza	Traditional yeast-free
Recommended pizza	Portofino

DELISIO

94 Rokeby Road
Subiaco
Perth
Western Australia 6008
Australia
+61 893817796
www.delisio.com.au

Opening hours	Closed Sunday
Credit cards	Accepted but not AMEX
Style of pizza	Roman
Recommended pizza	Mushroom

"It's pizza by the slice with amazing combinations."
—Theo Kalogeracos

THEO & CO PIZZERIA

838 Albany Highway
Victoria Park
Perth
Western Australia 6100
Australia
+61 893616776
www.theoandcopizzeria.com.au

Opening hours	Open 7 days
Credit cards	Accepted but not AMEX
Style of pizza	Contemporary
Recommended pizza	Jane's Addiction

NONNO GINO PIZZA AND PASTA

386 Wanneroo Road
Westminster
Perth
Western Australia 6061
Australia
+61 894406463

Opening hours	Closed Tuesday
Credit cards	Accepted
Style of pizza	Traditional
Recommended pizza	Gino's Special

"Gino is the grandfather ('nonno') of pizza in Western
Australia and has been making pizza for over 40
years. Honest, tasty, great value for money."
—Catherine Natale

"NEAPOLITAN PIZZAS RULE SUPREME HERE."

SARAH NICHOLSON P.58

NEW ZEALAND

"TUCKED SMARTLY AWAY FROM THE TOURIST THRONGS, VKNOW IS WHERE THE LOCALS GO TO FOR GENEROUSLY TOPPED PLAYFUL PIZZAS THAT ARE A THROWBACK TO THE GOURMET DAYS OF THE 1980S."

DARREN LOVELL P.60

"NEVER MIND THE MYTHICAL SUNSHINE OF NELSON; IT'S WORTH MAKING A TRIP THERE FOR STEFANO'S PIZZA ALONE."

RICHARD KLEIN P.59

"YOU CAN GET THIS PIZZA DELIVERED BY RED VESPA OR SIT IN NEIGHBORING DIVE BAR GOLDING'S FREE DIVE AND ENJOY A LOCAL DELICIOUS CRAFT BEER WITH YOUR PIZZA THERE."

DELANEY MES P.62

AUCKLAND PP.58-59 ♦

♦WELLINGTON P.P.61-62

NELSON P.59 ♦

♦CANTERBURY P.59

♦OTAGO PP.59-61

NEW
ZEALAND

(N̂)   SCALE

0   80   160
                         mi.

IL BUCO

113 Ponsonby Road
Auckland
Auckland 1011
New Zealand
+64 93604414
www.ilbuco.co.nz

Opening hours	Open 7 days
Credit cards	Accepted but not AMEX
Style of pizza	Roman *pizza al taglio*
Recommended pizza	Spinach and Mushroom

DANTES PIZZERIA NAPOLETANA

Ponsonby Central
136 Ponsonby Road
Auckland
Auckland 1011
New Zealand
+64 93784443
www.dantespizzeria.co.nz

Opening hours	Open 7 days
Credit cards	Not accepted
Style of pizza	Neapolitan
Recommended pizza	Regina Margherita DOC

"Kevin Morris is said to describe himself as 'a British chassis with an Italian motor.' Don't let the red hair or accent mislead you; this man has pizza in his blood. He is one of the two pizza chefs in the country and 472 pizzerias in the world to be certified by the VPN Association. Kevin's pizzas tick all the boxes for authenticity and quality."—Richard Klein

"Neapolitan pizzas rule supreme here. This is the place to be a purist and stick with Dantes' benchmark Regina Margherita DOC."—Sarah Nicholson

At his snug pizzeria in the Ponsonby Central Market, Kevin Morris limits his selection of pizzas to six. Few in Ponsonby, an inner city suburb of Auckland particularly hospitable to passionate food geeks, are complaining. In fact most of the habitués the British-born *pizzaiolo* has converted into Neapolitan pizza devotees would be perfectly content with a choice of one: the Regina Margherita DOC—tomato, fresh basil, *mozzarella di bufala*.

SETTEBELLO

3/1 Rata Street
Auckland
Auckland 0600
New Zealand
+64 98260777
www.settebello.co.nz

Opening hours	Closed Monday
Credit cards	Accepted but not AMEX
Style of pizza	Neapolitan
Recommended pizza	Rossa SetteBello

"Admittedly, Settebello is in an unlikely location in the suburbs with a pretty sparse interior, but the red-and-white checkered tablecloths and twee Italian music set the scene for some very good Neapolitan pizza."
—Sarah Nicholson

TONINO'S

35 Tamaki Drive
Auckland
Auckland 1071
New Zealand
+64 95288935

Opening hours	Open 7 days
Credit cards	Accepted
Style of pizza	*Pizza al taglio*
Recommended pizza	Calabria

"Traditional, authentic, and consistent."
—Antonio Cacace

TOTO PIZZA

53 Nelson Street
Auckland
Auckland 1010
New Zealand
+64 212868674
www.totopizza.co.nz

Opening hours	Closed Sunday and Monday
Credit cards	Accepted
Style of pizza	*Pizza al metro*
Recommended pizza	Toto' by the Metre

"It is a meter of pizza! It has a thick crust with a delicious tomato salsa and really good mozzarella."
—Giulio Sturla

AL VOLO PIZZERIA

27 Mount Eden Road
Auckland
Auckland 1023
New Zealand
+64 93022500
www.alvolo.co.nz

Opening hours	Closed Monday
Credit cards	Accepted but not AMEX
Style of pizza	Neapolitan
Recommended pizza	Al Volo

"Eat in or takeout, the guys here have personality and spunk, and the pizzas are consistently great. The bases are puffy and light but have a good amount of chew, too."—Sarah Nicholson

FREEMANS

47 London Street
Lyttelton
Canterbury 8082
New Zealand
+64 33287517
www.freemansdiningroom.co.nz

Opening hours	Closed Monday and Tuesday
Credit cards	Accepted but not AMEX
Style of pizza	Traditional
Recommended pizza	Margherita with Prosciutto

"Freemans always has an offering of specials pizzas with seasonal ingredients."—Giulio Sturla

STEFANO'S

Upstairs at State Cinema
91 Trafalgar Street
Nelson
Nelson 7010
New Zealand
+64 35467530
www.pizzeria.co.nz

Opening hours	Open 7 days
Credit cards	Accepted
Style of pizza	Classic Italian
Recommended pizza	La Greca; Margherita; Roaring Stag

"Orginally from the Veneto region, Stefano Bonazza has made his home in Nelson where he is the undisputed 'King of Pizza.' Even if this is essentially small-town New Zealand, Stefano manages to turn out and sell more pizzas per day (averaging 350+) than just about any pizzeria you'll find in Auckland or Wellington. Above all, he makes superb use of that quintessential Italian ingredient: generosity. Never mind the mythical sunshine of Nelson; it's worth making a trip there for Stefano's pizza alone."
—Richard Klein

ESPLANADE

2 Esplanade
Dunedin
Otago 9012
New Zealand
+64 34562544
www.esplanade.co

Opening hours	Open 7 days
Credit cards	Accepted but not AMEX
Style of pizza	Traditional
Recommended pizza	Quattro Formaggi; Sausage

"Like any good pizzeria, it has its oven stoked up, thus its pizzas come fast, hot, and perfectly cooked. I have had a scorching hot pizza in front of me in less than 5 minutes before. I like that. Pizza as it should be."—Bevan Smith

CUCINA 1871

1 Tees Street
Oamaru
Otago 9400
New Zealand
+64 34345696
www.cucina1871.co.nz

Opening hours	Closed Sunday
Credit cards	Accepted
Style of pizza	Modern meets traditional
Recommended pizza	Capricciosa

"Oamaru will always be better known for its penguins than its pizza but this smart Italian restaurant punches above its weight delivering top-notch pizzas that showcase the bountiful local produce."
—Darren Lovell

SCOTTS BREWING CO.

Oamaru Waterfront
1 Wansbeck Street
Oamaru
Otago 9400
New Zealand
+64 34342244
www.scottsbrewing.co.nz

Opening hours	Open 7 days
Credit cards	Accepted
Style of pizza	Good basic pizza with a regional twist
Recommended pizza	Meat Worker (ask for extra jalapeños); Red Bandit

"Scotts is a local brewery just opposite the historic precinct, with views to the sea and a outdoor deck to enjoy the weather. The beer is good and so is the pizza."—Bevan Smith

THE COW PIZZA AND SPAGHETTI HOUSE

Cow Lane
Queenstown
Otago 9300
New Zealand
+64 34428558
www.thecowrestaurant.co.nz

Opening hours	Open 7 days
Credit cards	Accepted
Style of pizza	Homely
Recommended pizza	Pepperoni

"Housed in Queenstown's oldest building, this atmospheric pizza and pasta house, an institution since 1976, serves up hot bubbling cheesy pizzas that are the perfect foil to a southern wintery blast."
—Darren Lovell

SASSO

14–16 Church Street
Queenstown
Otago 9300
New Zealand
+64 34090994
www.sasso.co.nz

Opening hours	Open 7 days
Credit cards	Accepted
Style of pizza	High end
Recommended pizza	Buffalo Mozzarella, Tomato, Arugula (rocket), Parmesan, and Duck Prosciutto

"When a wine list is as important as a larder of traditional Italian toppings, Sasso delivers with chefy pizzas taking center stage in this classy Italian restaurant."—Darren Lovell

VKNOW

Corner Fernhill Road and Richards Park Lane
Queenstown
Otago 9300
New Zealand
+64 34425444
www.vknow.co.nz

Opening hours	Open 7 days
Credit cards	Accepted but not AMEX
Style of pizza	The local's secret
Recommended pizza	Kumara (sweet potato), Pumpkin, Olives, Feta, Zucchini (courgette), Tomato, and Mushrooms

"Tucked smartly away from the tourist throngs, VKnow is where the locals go to for generously topped playful pizzas that are a throwback to the gourmet days of the 1980s. Favorite Kiwi ingredients, blue cod, smoked chicken, kumara (sweet potato), and their Italian counterparts are piled high on thin, crispy crusts. The real attractions here, however, are hosts Danny and Liz: it's just like having pizza with family."—Darren Lovell

FRANCESCA'S ITALIAN KITCHEN

93 Ardmore Street
Wanaka
Otago 9305
New Zealand
+64 34435599
www.fransitalian.co.nz

Opening hours	Open 7 days
Credit cards	Accepted
Style of pizza	Traditional wood-fired
Recommended pizza	Margherita; Nick's pizza of the week

"Tucked back from the main street in a gorgeous space with service to match, Francesca's Italian Kitchen makes great wood-fired pizza."
—Bevan Smith

LA BELLA ITALIA

10 Nevis Street
Wellington
Wellington 5012
New Zealand
+64 045669303
www.labellaitalia.co.nz

Opening hours	Open 7 days
Credit cards	Accepted
Style of pizza	Traditional Italian
Recommended pizza	Quattro Stagioni; Romana

FRATELLI

15 Blair Street
Courtenay Place
Wellington
Wellington 6011
New Zealand
+64 48016615
www.fratelli.net.nz

Opening hours	Closed Sunday
Credit cards	Accepted
Style of pizza	Neapolitan
Recommended pizza	Pizza del Nino

"The base is thin, soft, pliable, puffy at the edges, and crisp only on the very outside. You can pick up a whole slice, but you have to hold it in a shallow U to eat it. In effect, this was perfect Neapolitan-style pizza."—David Burton

LORETTA

181 Cuba Street
Wellington
Wellington 6011
New Zealand
+64 43842213
www.loretta.net.nz

Opening hours	Closed Monday
Credit cards	Accepted
Style of pizza	Modern wood-fired
Recommended pizza	Tomato

"Loretta is not a pizzeria, it is a chic, casual eatery in Wellington's hipster-central Cuba Street. On its large, healthy-leaning menu there are always half a dozen wood-fired pizzas on offer with modern toppings, such as smoked fish, black olive tapenade, watercress, and lemon. The generous-sized pizzas have crisp, puffy bases, are presented on smart wooden boards, and have generous amounts of fresh herbs scattered over the top."
—Sarah Nicholson

PIZZA POMODORO

13 Leeds Street
Wellington
Wellington 6011
New Zealand
+64 43812929
www.pizzapomodoro.co.nz

Opening hours	Open 7 days
Credit cards	Accepted but not AMEX
Style of pizza	Neapolitan
Recommended pizza	Margherita; Margherita DOC; Marinara DOC; Pomodorina

"The owner, Massimo Tolve, is a real artisan and is passionate about introducing New Zealanders to Naples-style pizza."—Leonardo Bresolin

"It's down a little lane, surrounded by inner-city boutique factories. You can get this pizza delivered by red Vespa or sit in neighboring dive bar Golding's Free Dive and enjoy a local delicious craft beer with your pizza there. A fantastic Wellington experience." —Delaney Mes

"Apart from his world- or Naples-class pizza, Massimo is as nice a man as you could ever hope to meet. Anywhere. His smile is guaranteed to warm your heart as much as his pizzas will tantalize your palate."—Richard Klein

Naples native Massimo Tolve bakes Neapolitan pizza according to guidelines as tight as his two-table, hole-in-the-wall shop. The cognoscenti who order takeout don't dare give their Margheritas much of a chance to cool. They carry their pizza boxes to Golding's Free Bar, at 14 Leeds Street, to pair the craft pizza with craft beer. Along with Dantes in Auckland, Pizza Pomodoro is one of only two pizzerias in New Zealand with VPN certification.

PIZZERIA NAPOLI

30 Courtenay Place
Wellington
Wellington 6011
New Zealand
+64 48025908
www.pizzerianapoli.co.nz

Opening hours	Open 7 days
Credit cards	Accepted but not AMEX
Style of pizza	Neapolitan
Recommended pizza	Margherita; Pescatore

"This is how pizza Napoli ought to be!"
—David Burton

SCOPA

Corner Ghuznee and Cuba Street
Wellington
Wellington 6011
New Zealand
+64 43846020
www.scopa.co.nz

Opening hours	Open 7 days
Credit cards	Accepted
Style of pizza	Traditional Italian
Recommended pizza	Pizzaiolo (pizza of the week)

TOMMY MILLIONS

Corner Courtenay Place and Taranaki Street
Wellington
Wellington 6011
New Zealand
+64 43828866
www.tommymillions.co.nz

Opening hours	Open 7 days
Credit cards	Accepted but not AMEX
Style of pizza	New York
Recommended pizza	Mushroom; Pepperoni

"Tommy Millions is the first pizzeria in Wellington to serve New York-style pizza by the slice. It's great any time of the day, but the locals will tell you it's best enjoyed at 3 a.m.—it stays open very late! The pizzas are hand tossed and stone baked and the dough is fermented for 48 hours—this is real NYC meets NZ pizza."—Leonardo Bresolin

"Tom Kirton, a.k.a. Tommy Millions, is a former lawyer who traveled to New York and Montreal and learned how to make pizza properly. He now occupies a windy corner of Wellington, in a former public toilet building, and makes incredibly simple pizza by the slice."—Delaney Mes

NEAPOLITAN PIZZA'S
SOFT SPOT

Naples shared its love for pizza and dry pasta with the world many years ago but something got lost in translation. Rather than eat pasta firm and pizza soft, in the Neapolitan way, foreigners learned to do the opposite. Non-Italians at last discovered the pleasures of *al dente* pasta in the last quarter of the twentieth century. But only recently have crisp-crust devotees in the pizza diaspora unstiffened their opposition to a pliable pizza with an inflated *cornicione* around it.

Breakthroughs aside, there lingers, outside of Naples and the province of Campania in southern Italy, more initial resistance toward traditional Neapolitan pizza than there is within a Neapolitan's crust. This is as true in Milan as it is in Miami. It is a clash between competing notions of authenticity: "real" can mean a pizza faithful to its origins or a pizza exactly like the one you grew up with. A Brazilian won't be fiercely loyal to the style of soccer played by the English national team just because the modern-day game was invented in Britain. Brazilians, or people of any nationality with its own strong pizza culture, may find the Neapolitan model soggy and floppy. It doesn't hold its shape. It looks burnt on the leopard-spotted undercarriage and undercooked in the steamy middle. The characteristic *cornicione* is doughy and bloated. The end pieces are almost begging to be discarded, like chicken bones.

And, oh yeah, one more thing: Neapolitan pizza is not crisp. It's this detail that most frustrates brave pizza missionaries who set sail from the Bay of Naples to distant shores to convert nonbelievers. When Giovanni Santarpia brought classic Neapolitan pizza north to Tuscany the locals did not express their gratitude by leaving bottles of their finest wine at his doorstep. Mostly they complained, telling him their preference was for, as he tells it, thin pizza as crisp as *biscotti*. The proud *pizzaiolo* refused to make his crust as hard as twice-baked Italian cookies, but did end up baking it a little longer.

The rustic look and ethereal texture of Neapolitan pizza is partly a function of its being cooked in a 900°F (482°C) wood-fired oven. The crust chars and blisters before the interior crumb has dried out and crisped. But the dough itself is built to be elastic and the crust baked from it pliable, reflecting pizza's humble origins as a Naples street food. To be eaten on the go pizza had to be soft enough to be folded twice *a portafoglio* (like a wallet), gathering and protecting its tomato sauce in the folds. "I was born selling pizzas on the *banco* [street counter]," says *maestro pizzaiolo* Enzo Coccia of Pizzaria La Notizia in Naples. "It has to be soft and light. There is no other way."

Purists like Coccia insist on soft pizza even when it is served in a restaurant, where diners presumably have access to knives and forks, if they want them, and double folding is not essential. "You can eat pizza in many ways," says Santarpia, "but the sensations you get from tasting a soft and well-leavened pizza are different. You feel all the flavors in one bite."

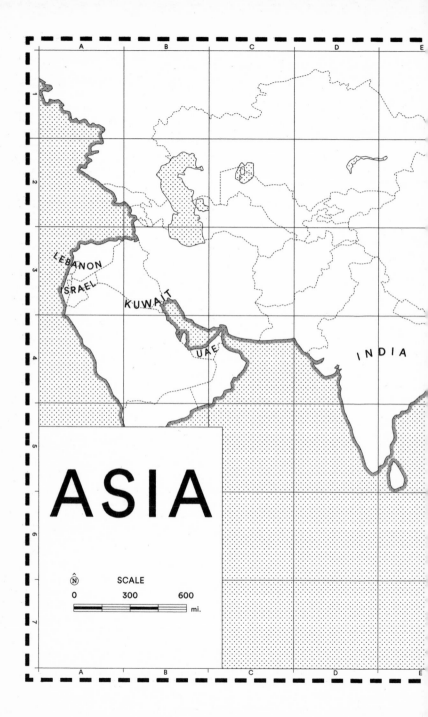

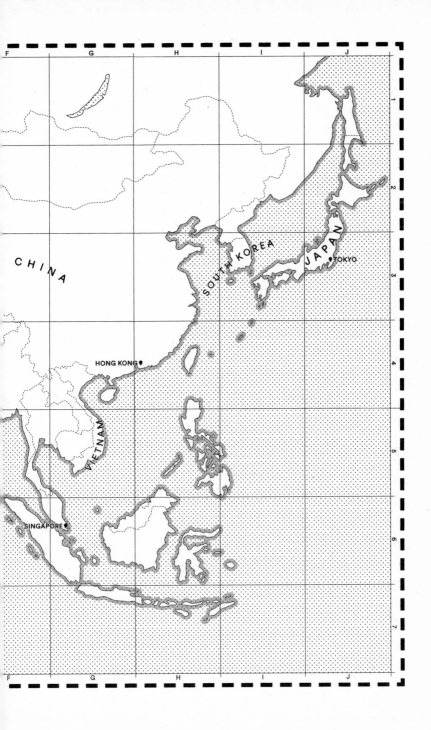

"A MUST-TRY PIZZERIA IN BEIRUT, THE CHARM OF THE INGREDIENTS IS SOULFUL!"

BADEEH ABLA P.74

"THIS IS ONE OF ISRAEL'S FINEST BAKERIES. IN ADDITION IT IS ALSO A COFFEE SHOP AND MAKES GREAT PIZZAS."

NURIT KARIV P.71

SOUTHWEST ASIA

"PLANT YOURSELF ON THE PIZZA BAR-STOOL, AND LET THE EXPERT PIZZAIOLO HASSAN AKKARY TREAT YOU TO ONE OF HIS SPECIALTIES."

DANIELLE ISSA P.74

"EVERYTHING ABOUT AMAMI'S PIZZA IS INCREDIBLE."

SARAH WALI P.73

"THE CRISPY, CHEWY DOUGH DRENCHED IN OLIVE OIL IS THE PERFECT BITE ON A LATE NIGHT OUT."

NOMI ABELIOVICH P.72

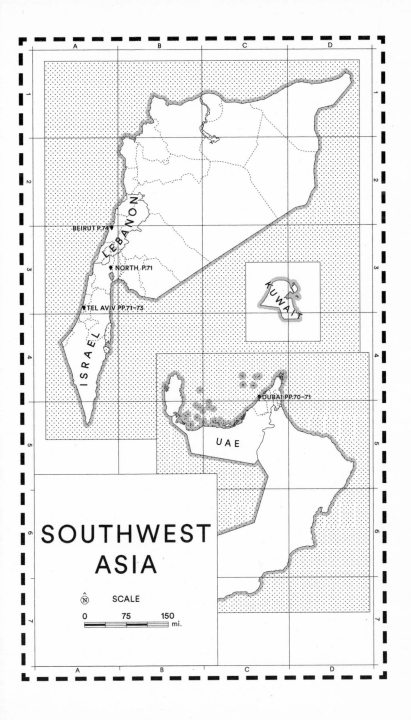

SOUTHWEST
ASIA

N SCALE

0   75   150 mi.

800 PIZZA

Dubai Marina Walk
Dubai
United Arab Emirates
+971 80074992
www.800pizza.com

Opening hours	Open 7 days
Credit cards	Accepted
Style of pizza	Italian

"800 Pizza makes authentic thin-crust pizzas, using fresh, high-quality ingredients. It was one of the first brands in the region to offer gluten-free pizzas."
—Sudeshna Ghosh

BRANDI PIZZERIA

The Dubai Mall
Dubai
United Arab Emirates
+971 43253336
www.ginzaretail.com/restaurants/brandi-pizzeria

Opening hours	Open 7 days
Credit cards	Accepted
Style of pizza	Neapolitan
Recommended pizza	Margherita; Romana

"Here you can eat a classic Neapolitan pizza. High edges, very fluffy dough, little mozzarella, and the sweetness of San Marzano peeled tomatoes. It's a place for purists."—Stefano

"The pizza arrives with a thick *cornicione* crust, while slightly soft in the middle. It's true to the traditional recipe from Naples—tender, elastic, and easily foldable into four."—Samantha Wood

CASA MIA

Le Méridien Dubai Hotel & Conference Centre
Airport Road
Dubai
United Arab Emirates
+971 42170000
www.casamia-dubai.com

Opening hours	Open 7 days
Credit cards	Accepted
Style of pizza	Roman
Recommended pizza	Margherita

EATALY

The Dubai Mall
Dubai
United Arab Emirates
+971 43308899
www.eataly.ae

Opening hours	Open 7 days
Credit cards	Accepted
Style of pizza	Italian
Recommended pizza	Sausage and Mushroom

"Eataly pays tribute to the quality of every single ingredient. Every component of its pizzas is carefully selected, and this attention can be felt in the final product."—Stefano

FRATELLI LA BUFALA

The Beach Mall
Jumeirah Beach Residence
Dubai
United Arab Emirates
+971 44303497
www.fratellilabufala.com

Opening hours	Open 7 days
Credit cards	Accepted but not AMEX
Style of pizza	Neapolitan
Recommended pizza	Napoletana

ROSSOVIVO

Block A, Office Park Building
Internet City
Dubai
United Arab Emirates
+971 44272477
www.rossovivo.ae

Opening hours	Open 7 days
Credit cards	Accepted but not AMEX
Style of pizza	Neapolitan
Recommended pizza	Bufalina; Napoli; Raffaelo

"Rossovivo is run by two Romans with a pizza chef from Naples. The clay brick-oven wood-fired pizzas are as authentic as those in Naples. The hot air rolls over the top of the pizza, while the bricks seal the base immediately to make it firm and crispy. Free of artificial additives and preservatives, the dough is leavened for 24 hours, which also helps makes it light, fluffy, and crispy."—Samantha Wood

RUSSO'S NEW YORK PIZZERIA

Jumeirah Centre
Jumeirah Beach Road
Dubai
United Arab Emirates
+971 43856549
www.nypizzeria.com

Opening hours	Open 7 days
Credit cards	Accepted
Style of pizza	New York
Recommended pizza	Margherita

"A New York spin on traditional Italian pizza with richer toppings and a slightly denser base."
—Samantha Wood

FRESCA

Kibbutz Massada
Jordan Valley
North 15140
Israel
+972 46657266
www.frescapizzeria.co.il

Opening hours	Closed Sunday
Credit cards	Accepted
Style of pizza	Neapolitan
Recommended pizza	Bianca; Carbonara

"Fresca is located in northern Israel in a small kibbutz. It isn't near a big city and yet it is one of the best pizzerias in the country and is run by a very good *pizzaiolo*."—Mena Strum

PIZZA SLICE

72 Sokolov Street
Ramat Hasharon
Tel Aviv 4723701
Israel
+972 35409239

Opening hours	Open 7 days
Credit cards	Accepted
Style of pizza	Local

"Pizza Slice is a neighborhood-style place with a loyal fan base. The tomato sauce contains a lot of carrot, which gives it its unique color and flavor, and the garlic sauce is marvelous. This pizza is the perfect comfort food."—Nurit Kariv

ABRAXES NORTH

40 Lilienblum Street
Tel Aviv
Tel Aviv 65133
Israel
+972 35104435
www.abraxas.co.il

Opening hours	Open 7 days
Credit cards	Accepted
Style of pizza	Local
Recommended pizza	The daily pizza

"Chef Eyal Shan is a local culinary superstar and new Israeli cuisine pioneer. The menu changes daily. There's a small fluffy pizza for an appetizer that is dusted with black pepper and topped with crème fraîche and a drizzle of olive oil and tomato, and depending on the day one can find a sardine pizza, a zucchini (courgette) pizza, and other local delicacies."
—Nomi Abeliovich

BAR LEHEM

7 Kehilat Saloniki Street
Tel Aviv
Tel Aviv 69513
Israel
+972 36480055

Opening hours	Closed Saturday
Credit cards	Accepted
Style of pizza	Focaccia
Recommended pizza	Buffalo; Market; Quattro Formaggi; Tomato Focaccia; Truffle, Crème Fraîche, and Black Pepper

"Located in a northern suburb of Tel Aviv, this is one of Israel's finest bakeries. In addition it is also a coffee shop and makes great pizzas. The pizza is not your 'classic' pizza; they use focaccia dough for the crust and complement it with superb ingredients for the choice of toppings."—Nurit Kariv

CAMPANELLO CAFFÈ DELICATESSEN

230 Ben Yehuda Street
Tel Aviv
Tel Aviv 63473
Israel
+972 35445558

Opening hours	Open 7 days
Credit cards	Accepted
Style of pizza	Gourmet Neapolitan
Recommended pizza	Puttanesca

"Mena Strum, the owner of Campanello, is known in Israel as Mr. Pizza. He bakes the flavors of Napoli in a beautiful brick oven that dominates the small restaurant."—Ofer Vardi

HAPIZZA

51 Bograshov Street
Tel Aviv
Tel Aviv 63145
Israel
+972 35281077
www.hapizza.com/hapizza.html

Opening hours	Open 7 days
Credit cards	Accepted
Style of pizza	Neapolitan
Recommended pizza	Classic

DA PEPPE PIZZERIA NAPOLETANA

334 Dizengoff Street
Tel Aviv
Tel Aviv 62593
Israel
+972 35539980

Opening hours	Open 7 days
Credit cards	Accepted
Style of pizza	Neapolitan
Recommended pizza	Margherita

"Da Peppe is the only pizzeria in Tel Aviv that makes the real Neapolitan pizza. It is delicious!"
—Mena Strum

SANTA KATARINA

2 Har Sinai Street
Tel Aviv
Tel Aviv 6581602
Israel
+972 587820292

Opening hours	Open 7 days
Credit cards	Accepted
Style of pizza	Neapolitan
Recommended pizza	Lahmajun (Turkish spiced meat pizza); Salami

"Located in a hidden courtyard behind the great Tel Aviv synagogue, the centerpiece of Santa Katarina is the wood-fired oven brought over from Florence. Almost all of the dishes on the menu are prepared in the oven and inspired by various Mediterranean cuisines, including a small but meticulous selection of freshly baked pizzas."—Nomi Abeliovich

TONY VESPA

267 Dizengoff Street
Tel Aviv
Tel Aviv 6311629
Israel
+972 35460000

Opening hours	Open 7 days
Credit cards	Accepted
Style of pizza	*Pizza al taglio*
Recommended pizza	Artichoke; Bacon; Spicy Pepperoni

"The *pizza al taglio* is freshly made throughout the day with a variety of toppings. The crispy, chewy dough drenched in olive oil is the perfect bite on a late night out."—Nomi Abeliovich

TONY VESPA

140 Rothschild Boulevard
Tel Aviv
Tel Aviv 6527216
Israel
+972 36858888

Opening hours	Open 7 days
Credit cards	Accepted
Style of pizza	*Pizza al taglio*
Recommended pizza	The last one to come out from the oven

"Open almost 24 hours a day, this cool chain serves one of the most tasty pizzas in town to say good night (or good morning) with after a great party. Here you can buy your pizza according to weight, sliced into squares with varying toppings like bacon, feta cheese, or mushrooms."—Ofer Vardi

UPPER CRUST

The Village
Abu Hasaneah
Kuwait
+965 23907087
www.uppercrustpizzeriakuwait.com

Opening hours..Open 7 days
Credit cards...............................Accepted but not AMEX
Style of pizza...Boston-Neapolitan
Recommended pizza..........................Margherita, Swellesley

"Upper Crust is one of the very few pizzerias that offer huge slices that are dripping with cheese. It uses all the freshest vegetables and meats for the delicious pizza and it has an incredible sauce that isn't too thick or too much on the thin crust. However, it's the loads of cheese that keeps me coming back for more. I love biting into a cheese pizza and having it stretch out as I pull the slice away. With the perfect amount of oregano and awesome olive oil, Upper Crust in Kuwait is a top contender for best pizza."
—Sarah Wali

DOPPIO

The Salhia Complex
Mohammad Thunayan Al-Ghanim Street
Kuwait City
Kuwait
+965 22451511
www.doppio.pizza

Opening hours..Open 7 days
Credit cards...............................Accepted but not AMEX
Style of pizza...Neapolitan
Recommended pizza.................Montanara al Forno; Napoli

MARGHERITA

The Arabella Complex
Al Ta'awn Street
Kuwait City
Kuwait
+965 1888848
www.pizzeriamargherita.com

Opening hours..Open 7 days
Credit cards...Accepted
Style of pizza...Traditional
Recommended pizza...Margherita

"Your everyday pizza with flavorful ingredients."
—Alia Al Ramli

SOLO PIZZA NAPULITANA

Behind Omar Ben Al Khattab Street
Kuwait City
Kuwait
+965 22474741
www.solopn.com

Opening hours..Closed Friday
Credit cards...Accepted
Style of pizza...Neapolitan
Recommended pizza.....................Margherita; Mushroom;
Ring of Fayaaa

"I am a personal fan of the thin-crust pizza, just out of the oven and a crunch with every bite. At Solo Pizza, this is the kind of pizza I get every time. Besides having the freshest ingredients around, it truly tastes authentic. The sauce is incredible but not overwhelming, the cheese is dairy and not oil based. Most important, it's cooked in a wood-fired oven that was made in Napoli. The sweet dough browns just right, and is so good it's one of the few times I eat the pizza backward, crust first."—Sarah Wali

PIZZERIA AMAMI

The Symphony Complex
Salem Al Mubarak Street
Salmiya
Kuwait
+965 25770733

Opening hours..Open 7 days
Credit cards...............................Accepted but not AMEX
Style of pizza...Italian
Recommended pizza...Amami

"Everyone at this pizzeria is Italian, from the servers and the management to the chef. Each of these people gives their own input into the pizza and how it is prepared so your pizza at Amami is a unified voice of Italy. Everything about Amami's pizza is incredible."—Sarah Wali

MARGHERITA
Gouraud Street
Beirut
Beirut 00961
Lebanon
+961 1560480
www.pizzeriamargherita.com

Opening hours	Open 7 days
Credit cards	Accepted
Style of pizza	Neapolitan
Recommended pizza	Bresaola; Diavola; Rustica

"This is the classic Neapolitan-style pizza that you would find in the heart of Naples. Margherita's crust is unlike any other I've seen in Lebanon. Made of wheat flour, brewer's yeast, salt, and water, the dough is baked to perfection, extremely thin at the center, and rather thick and crispy at the outer rim."
—Danielle Issa

"Fresh and consistently delicious."
—Nadim Safieddine

PZZA.CO
Patriarch Howayek Street
Beirut
Beirut 00961
Lebanon
+961 1999838
www.thepzza.co

Opening hours	Open 7 days
Credit cards	Accepted
Style of pizza	Neapolitan
Recommended pizza	Marinara; Verde

"I loved its pizzas so very much that I can tell you confidently to go and try one of the best pizzas in Lebanon."—Anthony Rahayel

TAVOLINA
Camille Youssef Chamoun Street
Beirut
Beirut 00961
Lebanon
+961 1442244

Opening hours	Open 7 days
Credit cards	Accepted
Style of pizza	Italian
Recommended pizza	Bresaola; Buffalo Mozzarella; Diavola; Margherita

"The most consistent and delicious pizza in town by far. The freshest ingredients with the best dough and the most flavorful toppings!"—Nadim Safieddine

"The Tavolina is the spark of the town, it takes the first rank in my heart and belly. A must-try pizzeria in Beirut, the charm of the ingredients is soulful!"
—Badeeh Abla

TOTÒ
Armenia Street
Beirut
Beirut 00961
Lebanon
+961 1566991
www.totocucina.com

Opening hours	Open 7 days
Credit cards	Accepted
Style of pizza	Gourmet
Recommended pizza	Bolognaise; Tartufona

"The pizza dough is balanced (not too fluffy or too crispy) and the sauce is perfect (just the right amount). I would go to Totò for a business lunch or a sparkling dinner, it is the perfect chic and glamorous pizza in Beirut."—Badeeh Abla

TSC SIGNATURE
Weygand Street
Beirut Souks
Beirut
Beirut 00961
Lebanon
+961 1993170
www.beirutsouks.com.lb/fnb/tsc-signature

Opening hours	Open 7 days
Credit cards	Accepted
Style of pizza	Gourmet Neapolitan
Recommended pizza	The chef's special

"Plant yourself on the pizza bar-stool, and let the expert *pizzaiolo* Hassan Akkary treat you to one of his specialties. Don't even reach for the menu or bother leafing through its offerings—his creations are not in print, their blueprints are only etched loosely in his mind."—Danielle Issa

"ONE OF THE MOST AUTHENTIC-TASTING PIES IN MUMBAI."
SHILARNA VAZE P.79

"EVERY SINGLE PIZZA IS A WORK OF ART."
FRANCESCO PATELLA P.81

"THIS IS ONE OF THOSE PLACES THAT'S OFF THE BEATEN TRACK. YOU WOULD BE SURPRISED THAT A PLACE LIKE DHARAMSALA IN HIMACHAL PRADESH (FLOCKED TO BY TOURISTS NONETHELESS) HAS A RESTAURANT LIKE THIS."
NIKHIL MERCHANT P.78

SOUTH & SOUTHEAST ASIA

"YOU CAN'T GO TO RAY'S AND BE DISAPPOINTED."
ROSHINI BAJAJ SANGHVI P.80

"THE PIZZA TOPPINGS ARE GENEROUS AND THE TOMATO-BASED FRESH SAUCE IS TO DIE FOR."
SARANSH GOILA P.79

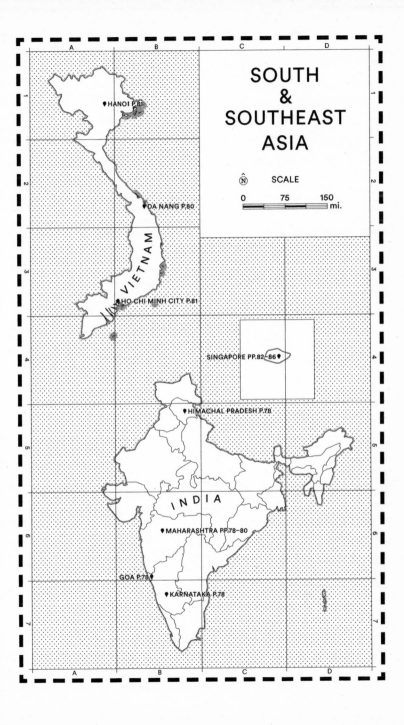

SOUTH
&
SOUTHEAST
ASIA

N̂   SCALE

0   75   150
▬▬▬▬▬▬▬ mi.

♦ HANOI P.81

♦ DA NANG P.80

V I E T N A M

♦ HO CHI MINH CITY P.81

♦ SINGAPORE PP.82-86

♦ HIMACHAL PRADESH P.78

I N D I A

♦ MAHARASHTRA PP.78-80

GOA P.78 ♦

♦ KARNATAKA P.78

FELLINI'S

Arambol Beach
Arambol
Goa 403524
India
+91 9881461224

Opening hours	Open 7 days (Closed May–September)
Credit cards	Not accepted
Style of pizza	Wood-fired
Recommended pizza	Seafood

"Neither deep dish nor thin-crust, the pizza at Fellini's is made in front of you in a wood-fired oven, with the *pizzaiolo* spinning dough disks in the air. It's the perfect pizza base, with just enough tomato sauce and toppings."—Shilarna Vaze

DA TITA

Nuvem-Majorda Road
Majorda
Goa 403713
India
+91 8322791885

Opening hours	Open 7 days
Credit cards	Not accepted
Style of pizza	Local
Recommended pizza	Goan Sausage

"With Italian influences but local flavors, this pizzeria is a hole-in-the-wall in one of India's most popular holiday destinations—Goa. The pizzas dished out here are gorged on by locals as well as tourists."—Nikhil Merchant

PICCOLA ROMA

Chapora Road (Near Petrol Pump)
Vagator
Goa 403509
India
+91 7507806821

Opening hours	Open 7 days
Credit cards	Not accepted
Style of pizza	Wood-fired
Recommended pizza	Goan Sausage

FAMILY PIZZERIA

Dharamkot
Himachal Pradesh 176219
India
+91 9418121474

Opening hours	Closed Tuesday
Credit cards	Not accepted
Style of pizza	Wood-fired
Recommended pizza	Machli

"This is one of those places that's off the beaten track. You would be surprised that a place like Dharamsala in Himachal Pradesh (flocked to by tourists nonetheless) has a restaurant like this. The pizza is made using locally sourced ingredients, excellent flour made with local grains, and a special sauce made with an Indian spice called ajwain. Ajwain is a close cousin to oregano and it has a power-packed flavor profile that makes the pizzas engaging and soul satisfying."
—Nikhil Merchant

CHEZ MARIANNICK

1A Anjanappa Building
Varthur Main Road
Bangalore
Karnataka 560066
India
+91 9739406536

Opening hours	Closed Sunday
Credit cards	Not accepted
Style of pizza	Wood-fired
Recommended pizza	La Bergere

"Set up by an Indo-French couple, Chez Mariannick has a rustic look about it and it is serious about its pizzas."—Nandita Iyer

CELINI

Grand Hyatt Mumbai
Off Western Express Highway
Mumbai
Maharashtra 400055
India
+91 2266761149
www.mumbai.grand.hyatt.com

Opening hours	Open 7 days
Credit cards	Accepted
Style of pizza	Thin-crust
Recommended pizza	Capricciosa

"The crust is fab."—Vicky Ratnani

FRANCESCO'S PIZZERIA

Shop No.3, Chinoy Mansion, Ground Floor
Warden Road
Mumbai
Maharashtra 400026
India
+91 2267527000
www.francescospizzeria.com

Opening hours...Open 7 days
Credit cards.....................................Accepted but not AMEX
Style of pizza..Gourmet
Recommended pizza.........................Breakfast Pizza All Day

"Reasonably priced authentic pizzas are hard to come by. To experience a great pizza you have to either rely on expensive outlets or five-star hotels that have the capacity and the resources to churn out good pizzas. With Francesco's you get quality pizzas at prices lower than most pizza chains with good-quality ingredients and quick service. It is one of the only places where I have seen a breakfast pizza complete with a whole sunny-side-up fried egg—the yolk runny and mixing in with the sauce and cheese is a heady palate-gratifying experience."—Nikhil Merchant

INDIGO DELICATESSEN

Clifton Trishul CHS, Off Link Road
Oshiwara Village
Mumbai
Maharashtra 400053
India
+91 2266326262
www.indigodeli.com

Opening hours...Open 7 days
Credit cards..Accepted
Style of pizza..Thin-crust
Recommended pizza.........................Chorizo and Scamorza;
Tomato, Pesto, and Fresh Mozzarella

"This chain of diners has created its own unique version of ultra-thin, barely-there pizza crust that's quick to crumble. To be enjoyable, the pizza has to be devoured within minutes of it being served, which is an easy task since it's 90 percent cheese and sauce toppings and 10 percent crust that flakes quickly."
—Purva Mehra

INDIGO DELICATESSEN

Palladium Mall
Senapati Bapat Marg
Mumbai
Maharashtra 400013
India
+91 2243666666
www.indigodeli.com

Opening hours...Open 7 days
Credit cards..Accepted
Style of pizza..Thin-crust
Recommended pizza.........................Spinach and Mushroom

"The crust is the real winner here, it is extra thin and crispy."—Saransh Goila

JOEY'S PIZZA

6/7 Upvan Building
DN Nagar Road
Mumbai
Maharashtra 400053
India
+91 2226304809

Opening hours...Open 7 days
Credit cards.....................................Accepted but not AMEX
Style of pizza..Deep-dish
Recommended pizza...Meat Ultimo

"The pizza toppings are generous and the tomato-based fresh sauce is to die for."—Saransh Goila

PIZZA METRO PIZZA

Jharna Apartments
Dr BR Ambedkar Road
Mumbai
Maharashtra 400050
India
+91 2226485697

Opening hours...Open 7 days
Credit cards..Accepted
Style of pizza..Neapolitan
Recommended pizza...............Capricciosa; Portobello with
Truffle Oil; Arugula (rocket) and Parma Ham

"Large rectangular pies are served on massive wooden platters. The tomato sauce and the thin-crust base make this pizza one of the most authentic-tasting pies in Mumbai."—Shilarna Vaze

RAY'S CAFE & PIZZERIA

133 Hill Road
Mumbai
Maharashtra 400050
India
+91 2226451414
www.rayscafeandpizzeria.com

Opening hours	Open 7 days
Credit cards	Accepted
Style of pizza	New York
Recommended pizza	Californian; Fire and Smoke

"Ray's is small, delightful, and cramped, with a small open kitchen that dishes out great pizzas."
—Nikhil Merchant

"You can't go to Ray's and be disappointed."
—Roshini Bajaj Sanghvi

TRATTORIA

Vivanta by Taj - President
90 Cuffe Parade
Mumbai
Maharashtra 400005
India
+91 2266650808
www.vivantabytaj.com

Opening hours	Open 7 days
Credit cards	Accepted
Style of pizza	Italian thin-crust
Recommended pizza	Fiamma

"Trattoria is the hotel's all-day coffee shop with a menu focused on Italian fare. It has perfected the pizza base, which is desirably crisp, crunchy, and charred at the edges. The base holds up under the simple but effective garnish of lightly caramelized crisp onions and a heaping of chili flakes."
—Purva Mehra

"One of my go-to places for pizza cravings at any time of the day."—Nikhil Merchant

WOODSIDE INN

Wodehouse Road
Mumbai
Maharashtra 400005
India
+91 2222875752

Opening hours	Open 7 days
Credit cards	Accepted
Style of pizza	Thin-crust
Recommended pizza	Goat Cheese Pizza with Scallions (spring onions), Olives, and Basil; Pickled Goan Chorizo Pizza with Fresh Onions

"This popular pub peddles thin-crust pies with rich toppings that are ideal fodder for post-bender binges."
—Purva Mehra

"The base and sauce are perfectly balanced, and the toppings are inventively tweaked for local tastes, without letting us forget that it is a damn fine pizza even with just cheese."—Roshini Bajaj Sanghvi

BREAD OF LIFE

4 Dong Da
Da Nang
Da Nang 511000
Vietnam
+84 5113565185
www.breadoflifedanang.com

Opening hours	Open 7 days
Credit cards	Not accepted
Style of pizza	Multiple

"Bread of Life is a non-governmental organization that supports the local deaf community. The deaf staff are well trained to make pizzas, serve, and even deliver."
—Le Ha Uyen

NHÀ LÉO PIZZA & CAKES

11 Ha Chuong
Da Nang
Da Nang 511000
Vietnam
+84 935019443

Opening hours	Closed Monday
Credit cards	Not accepted
Style of pizza	French-Italian

"These are truly European-style pizzas, which are hard to come across anywhere else in Vietnam."
—Le Ha Uyen

DA PAOLO WESTLAKE
18, Lane 50/59/17
Dang Thai Mai Street
Hanoi
Hanoi 10000
Vietnam
+84 437186317
www.dapaolo.vn

Opening hours..Open 7 days
Credit cards...Accepted
Style of pizza..Classic
Recommended pizza.........................Speck and Brie

"Very good quality of pizza. The main ingredients,
ham, bacon, mozzarella, and ricotta, are all homemade by the owner."—Francesco Patella

THE LONG @ TIMES SQUARE
57–69F Dong Khoi Street
Ho Chi Minh City
Ho Chi Minh City 700000
Vietnam
+84 838236688
www.thelong.timessquare.vn

Opening hours..Open 7 days
Credit cards...Accepted
Style of pizza...Neapolitan

"The quality of the pizza makes The Long worth
a visit."—Francesco Patella

PIZZA 4P'S
8/15 Lê Thánh Tôn
Ho Chi Minh City
Ho Chi Minh City 700000
Vietnam
+84 1207894444
www.pizza4ps.com

Opening hours..Open 7 days
Credit cards.....................................Accepted but not AMEX
Style of pizza...Neapolitan
Recommended pizza...........4 Cheese (with some honey on
                              top); Burrata Prosciutto

"Every single pizza is a work of art."
—Francesco Patella

"THE QUINTA HAS BEEN MY FAVORITE PIZZA FOR NEARLY 13 YEARS. IT CONTAINS AN UMAMI BOMB OF TRUFFLE PASTE AND IS TOPPED WITH A FRESHLY CRACKED EGG JUST BEFORE IT GOES INTO THE WOOD-FIRED OVEN."

SULYN TAN P.85

"TIMBRE IS MORE WIDELY KNOWN AS A LIVE MUSIC VENUE BUT FOODIES KNOW THAT IT FLIPS SOME OF THE BEST PIZZAS IN TOWN."

DEBBIE YONG P.84

"IT DOES NOT GET MORE ITALIAN THAN THIS HERE IN SINGAPORE."

MARCO GUCCIO P.84

SINGAPORE

"ABSOLUTELY THE BEST AND MOST ORIGINAL INTERPRETATION OF THE NEAPOLITAN STYLE IN SINGAPORE."

BEPPE DE VITO P.85

"EVERY BITE IS A CULINARY DELIGHT."

DOLORES TAY P.85

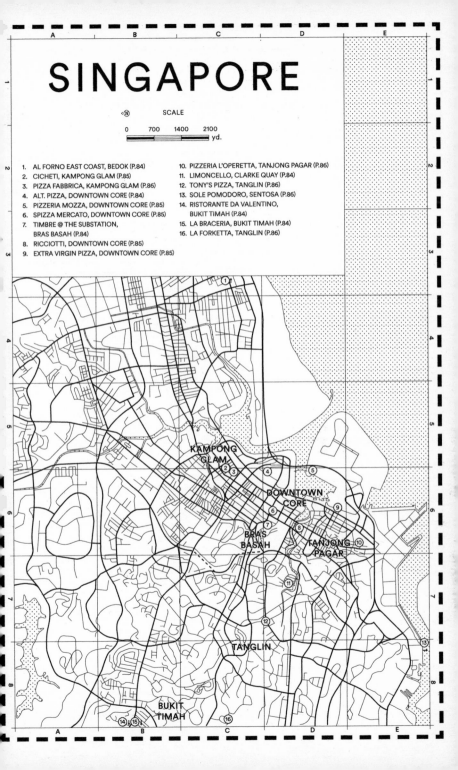

SINGAPORE

SCALE

0   700   1400   2100
                    yd.

1. AL FORNO EAST COAST, BEDOK (P.84)
2. CICHETI, KAMPONG GLAM (P.85)
3. PIZZA FABBRICA, KAMPONG GLAM (P.86)
4. ALT. PIZZA, DOWNTOWN CORE (P.84)
5. PIZZERIA MOZZA, DOWNTOWN CORE (P.85)
6. SPIZZA MERCATO, DOWNTOWN CORE (P.85)
7. TIMBRE @ THE SUBSTATION, BRAS BASAH (P.84)
8. RICCIOTTI, DOWNTOWN CORE (P.85)
9. EXTRA VIRGIN PIZZA, DOWNTOWN CORE (P.85)
10. PIZZERIA L'OPERETTA, TANJONG PAGAR (P.86)
11. LIMONCELLO, CLARKE QUAY (P.84)
12. TONY'S PIZZA, TANGLIN (P.86)
13. SOLE POMODORO, SENTOSA (P.86)
14. RISTORANTE DA VALENTINO, BUKIT TIMAH (P.84)
15. LA BRACERIA, BUKIT TIMAH (P.84)
16. LA FORKETTA, TANGLIN (P.86)

KAMPONG GLAM

DOWNTOWN CORE

BRAS BASAH

TANJONG PAGAR

TANGLIN

BUKIT TIMAH

AL FORNO EAST COAST

400 East Coast Road
Bedok
Singapore
428996
+65 63488781
www.alfornoeastcoast.sg

Opening hours	Open 7 days
Credit cards	Accepted
Style of pizza	Neapolitan
Recommended pizza	Bufala

"Very hearty and rustic—you can taste the home-cooked goodness."—Marco Guccio

TIMBRE @ THE SUBSTATION

45 Armenian Street
Bras Basah
Singapore
179936
+65 63388030
www.timbregroup.asia

Opening hours	Open 7 days
Credit cards	Accepted
Style of pizza	Modern
Recommended pizza	Lamb Meatballs of Fire

"Timbre is more widely known as a live music venue but foodies know that it flips some of the best pizzas in town. Extremely good value for money—and it stays open until late too."—Debbie Yong

LA BRACERIA

5 Greendale Avenue
Bukit Timah
Singapore
289501
+65 64655918
www.labraceria.com.sg

Opening hours	Closed Monday
Credit cards	Accepted
Style of pizza	Neapolitan
Recommended pizza	Gorgonzola, Porcini Mushrooms, and Zucchini (courgette)

"A homey environment, good service, and great pizza."—Michel Lu

RISTORANTE DA VALENTINO

200 Turf Club Road, #01-19
Bukit Timah
Singapore
287994
+65 64620555
www.ristorante-da-valentino.com

Opening hours	Closed Monday
Credit cards	Accepted
Style of pizza	Neapolitan
Recommended pizza	Napoletana

"There are 15 different pizzas on the menu and most of them are winners in their own rights. Ingredients are always fresh and the crust is typically thin and soft with a nicely charred outer layer that lends an oomph to every bite."—Dolores Tay

LIMONCELLO

95 Robertson Quay #01–19/20
Clarke Quay
Singapore
235256
+65 66345117
www.limoncello.sg

Opening hours	Open 7 days
Credit cards	Accepted
Style of pizza	Amalfi
Recommended pizza	Ham and Mushroom

"It does not get more Italian than this here in Singapore."—Marco Guccio

ALT. PIZZA

Suntec City Tower 4, #01-602
Downtown Core
Singapore
038983
+65 68369207
www.altpizza.com.sg

Opening hours	Open 7 days
Credit cards	Accepted
Style of pizza	Neapolitan with modern American-inspired toppings
Recommended pizza	Crabby Ninja; Lean and Green; Krazy for Kale

"The crust is perfectly Neapolitan, and while I'm usually a stickler for traditional ingredients, the combinations put together—whether a tribute to the Philly cheese steak or northeast Atlantic crab—

work astoundingly. The vibe is fun, the craft beer is delicious, and it's an oasis in a slightly off-city center location that's a great place to hang out at."
—Desiree Koh

EXTRA VIRGIN PIZZA

8 Marina View, #01–04, Asia Square Tower 1
Downtown Core
Singapore
018960
+65 62475757
www.extravirginpizza.com/evp

Opening hours	Closed Saturday and Sunday
Credit cards	Accepted
Style of pizza	Neapolitan
Recommended pizza	Margherita; Pistachio Pesto

"It's a joy to sink your teeth into the chewy, pillowy crust while admiring the crispy bubbles all around."
—Desiree Koh

PIZZERIA MOZZA

10 Bayfront Avenue
Downtown Core
Singapore
018956
+65 66888522
www.singapore.pizzeriamozza.com

Opening hours	Open 7 days
Credit cards	Accepted
Style of pizza	Italian-American
Recommended pizza	Bianca; Burocotta; Burrata; Prosciutto di Parma; Squash Blossoms, Tomato, and Burrata

"Every bite is a culinary delight."—Dolores Tay

"Great energy, great service, and fabulous pizzas."
—Michel Lu

"The crust is the best in town."—Bjorn Shen

RICCIOTTI

20 Upper Circular Road
B1-49/50 The Riverwalk
Downtown Core
Singapore
058416
+65 65339060
www.ricciotti.co

Opening hours	Open 7 days
Credit cards	Accepted
Style of pizza	Neapolitan
Recommended pizza	Quattro Stagioni

"This Riverwalk outlet provides a great atmosphere to enjoy the food."—Marco Guccio

SPIZZA MERCATO

13 Stamford Road, Capitol Piazza #B2-52
Downtown Core
Singapore
178905
+65 67021835
www.spizza.sg/pages/mercato

Opening hours	Open 7 days
Credit cards	Accepted
Style of pizza	Neapolitan thin-crust
Recommended pizza	Quinta

"The Quinta has been my favorite pizza for nearly 13 years. It contains an umami bomb of truffle paste and is topped with a freshly cracked egg just before it goes into the wood-fired oven."—Sulyn Tan

CICHETI

52 Kandahar Street
Kampong Glam
Singapore
198901
+65 62925012
www.cicheti.com

Opening hours	Closed Sunday
Credit cards	Accepted
Style of pizza	Neapolitan
Recommended pizza	Napoletana

"Absolutely the best and most original interpretation of the Neapolitan style in Singapore."
—Beppe De Vito

PIZZA FABBRICA

69–70 Bussorah Street
Kampong Glam
Singapore
199482
+65 62910434
www.pizzafabbrica.sg

Opening hours	Closed Monday
Credit cards	Accepted
Style of pizza	Neapolitan
Recommended pizza	Cream of Pumpkin and Broccolini; Margherita; Pears Cooked in Chianti, Radicchio, and Fontina

"Possibly the best and most technically sound dough in Singapore, with lusciously fresh and extraordinarily inspired ingredient combinations on top. I'm always pleasantly surprised and delighted by new surprises atop the pizzas, and they always work."—Desiree Koh

SOLE POMODORO

#01–14 Quayside Isle
Sentosa
Singapore
098375
+65 63394778
www.solepomodoro.com

Opening hours	Open 7 days
Credit cards	Accepted
Style of pizza	Italian
Recommended pizza	Capricciosa

"Run by two Italian cousins who have lived in Singapore for over a decade, Sole Pomodoro's pizzas are as Italian as they get. You can always rely on them to churn out classic wood-fired pizzas with deliciously thin crusts and cheese so runny that you have to eat the pizza folded up just like the Italians do."
—Debbie Yong

LA FORKETTA

9 Dempsey Road
Tanglin
Singapore
247697
+65 64752298
www.laforketta.com.sg

Opening hours	Open 7 days
Credit cards	Accepted
Style of pizza	Neapolitan
Recommended pizza	Margherita

"La Forketta has been producing some of the best pizzas in Singapore for more than 20 years."
—Beppe De Vito

TONY'S PIZZA

397 River Valley Road
Tanglin
Singapore
248292
+65 67774992
www.tonyspizza.sg

Opening hours	Open 7 days
Credit cards	Accepted
Style of pizza	New York
Recommended pizza	Cheese

"This is true blue New York-style pizza in all it's hearty, cheesy glory."—Dolores Tay

PIZZERIA L'OPERETTA

12 Gopeng Street, #01-78-81 Icon Village
Tanjong Pagar
Singapore
078877
+65 62229487
www.operetta.sg

Opening hours	Open 7 days
Credit cards	Accepted
Style of pizza	Neapolitan
Recommended pizza	Margherita

"Great-tasting pizzas with wonderful tasty dough."
—Michel Lu

THE PIZZAIOLO IN THE HOME STRETCH

When an accomplished *pizzaiolo* works a ball of dough with his hands into the shape of a pizza, he owns it. No matter his nationality, his training, or preferred style of pizza, if he knows his craft the dough will be putty in his hands. With a master *pizzaiolo* it is less a case of owning the dough than it is of becoming one with it. It goes where he tells it to go. He does what it tells him to do.

Sometimes the accomplished *pizzaiolo*'s spellbinding feats of manual dexterity are an act. It can be a performance, a show of dough. This is not necessarily a bad thing. Pizza making *is* live entertainment.

The *pizzaiolo* transfers the ball of dough from its storage box, tray, or drawer onto a lightly floured bench. The dusting flour is usually exactly that, flour, but occasionally something coarser is used, like semolina or cornmeal. The bench, from the Italian *banco*, is actually a work counter, traditionally made of marble, not something you sit on.

If he's preparing a round pizza the *pizzaiolo* flattens and stretches the dough into a flat, uniform circle in a variety of ways, according to the end shape and texture he desires. He may apply pressure to the dough with his fingertips just inside the rim, building up and defining the *cornicione* and delineating the flat valley framed by it. Or he may press his fingertips closer to the middle, flattening and stretching the dough and pushing the bubbles outward to become part of the *cornicione*. These will expand in the oven. Others may draw out the dough over raised knuckles, rotating it with their hands.

The dough may be tossed or slapped back and forth from hand to hand, which helps it expand. It's almost like taming the dough. If the dough is soft this only needs to be done a few times. If it's a bit stiff additional slaps may be necessary. When the dough reaches the desired diameter and thickness and the bubbles have either been popped or strategically relocated to the outskirts, it's ready to be adorned with tomato sauce, cheese, and other wonderful things.

If the *pizzaiolo* spanks the disk of dough as he tosses it from hand to hand, throws it down on the bench, or flips it high into the air, with flour flying everywhere, this may be where the theatrics have kicked in. Kneading takes time. The shaping stage can be completed in seconds. "Unless the dough is too hard it should be treated gently," advises Francesco Salvo of Pizzeria Salvo in San Giorgio a Cremano, near Naples. "The movements must be short and decisive."

As for the cloud of flour around the *pizzaiolo* it's all just smoke and then more smoke. Only a little is needed to dust the bench to keep the dough from sticking to it. Otherwise the excess flour sticks to the pizza and can burn in the oven, making the crust taste bitter.

"SIMPLY THE BEST CRUST IN SEOUL."

TIM MITCHELL P.101

"CAPO IS DESIGNED TO LOOK LIKE A CHURCH, WHICH ISN'T A BAD THING WHEN YOU'RE WORSHIPPING GOOD EATS THE WAY MY FRIENDS AND I DO." AUSTIN HU P.93

CHINA, HONG KONG & SOUTH KOREA

"GREAT ITALIAN PIZZA WITH FRESH INGREDIENTS AND SIMPLE FLAVORS."

IAIN SHAW P.92

"PIZZAS ARE THE RAISON D'ÊTRE TO DINE IN THE BAMBOO HOUSE KNOWN AS CALYPSO."

JAMIE BARYS P.93

"NEW YORKERS IN SEOUL CLAIM THIS IS THE CLOSEST SEOUL HAS GOTTEN TO AUTHENTIC NEW YORK PIZZA."

JOE MCPHERSON P.100

CHINA, HONG KONG & SOUTH KOREA

SCALE

0   100   200 mi.

BEIJING PP.92–93

SEOUL PP.100–101

SHANGHAI PP.93–94

HONG KONG PP.96–100

SOUTH KOREA

CHINA

HONG KONG

BOTTEGA

18 Sanlitun Lu
Beijing
Beijing Shi 100027
China
+86 1064161752
www.bottegacn.com

Opening hours...Open 7 days
Credit cards...Not accepted
Style of pizza...Neapolitan
Recommended pizza..................................Calzone al Salame

"If there's any pizzeria serving decent Neapolitan-style pizzas in Beijing, it's likely that brothers Daniele and Paolo Salvo have been involved. Having previously consulted for La Pizza and Matta, the Salvos recently opened their first own venture, Bottega. The crusts are insanely flavorful, chewy in the best of ways and perfectly charred in the wood-burning MG Forni oven that they imported from Naples. Toppings are of the highest quality—burrata cheese that oozes cream when you cut it; salty, peppercorn-studded salami. It's truly unforgettable pizza."—Cat Nelson

GREAT LEAP BREWING #45 BREWPUB

45 Xinyuan Jie
Beijing
Beijing Shi 100027
China
+86 1059476984
www.greatleapbrewing.com

Opening hours...Open 7 days
Credit cards...Accepted
Style of pizza...New York
Recommended pizza.......................................Green Machine

"In a city without any pizza tradition to call its own, the development of truly great American-style pizza has taken a backseat to Italian styles. Great Leap brought in a pizza consultant from Philadelphia's Pizza Brain and has put a lot of effort into making a truly great, pillowy crust. At 16 inches (40 cm), these pies are a force to be reckoned with, loaded with everything from kale, roasted garlic, and black pepper ricotta to mushrooms and arugula (rocket) with lemon-honey ricotta. With sleek dark wood and a polished industrial feel, the brewpub itself has fantastic atmosphere; it's the kind of place you'll spend hours in without ever realizing the time passing."—Cat Nelson

PIE SQUARED

Cathay View Place
2A Xiang Jiang Bei Lu
Beijing
Beijing Shi 100102
China
+86 4000314743
www.piesquaredchina.com

Opening hours...Open 7 days
Credit cards...Accepted
Style of pizza...Detroit
Recommended pizza................................."MO"town Meatball

"Chicago-style deep dish is nonexistent in Beijing, and most places vary between a thin Italian-style crust and a still-thin New York-style crust. Given the above, I'm happy to accept Pie Squared's 'Detroit' alternative—square pizzas, deep and chewy, served in metal baking tins. The pizza is great, it does some equally hearty sides, and if the one downside is that it's a bit of a trek from downtown Beijing, it makes the trip all the more memorable."—Iain Shaw

LA PIZZA NAPOLI

3.3 Shopping Mall
33 Sanlitun Lu
Beijing
Beijing Shi 100600
China
+86 1051365990
www.lapizzanapoli.com

Opening hours...Open 7 days
Credit cards.................................Accepted but not AMEX
Style of pizza...Neapolitan
Recommended pizza...............................Pulcinella Ventaglio

"If you want a great crust and a huge array of topping combinations, La Pizza Napoli's got you covered."
—Cat Nelson

"Great Italian pizza with fresh ingredients and simple flavors."—Iain Shaw

LA PIZZA NAPOLI

1112 SOHO Shangdu
8 Dongdaqiao Lu
Beijing
Beijing Shi 100020
China
+86 1059003112
www.lapizzanapoli.com

Opening hours...Open 7 days
Credit cards..............................Accepted but not AMEX
Style of pizza..Neapolitan
Recommended pizza..Bufalina

PIZZA+

112–115 Bojinghaoting
8 Shizipo Jie
Beijing
Beijing Shi 100027
China
+86 1064130991
www.pizzaplus.com.cn

Opening hours...Open 7 days
Credit cards..............................Accepted but not AMEX
Style of pizza...Italian
Recommended pizza.................................Sweet Beijing

"Interesting topping combinations, with a few locally inspired creations. The distinction between white pizzas (with no sauce) and traditional tomato sauce-based pizzas is rare for Beijing."—Iain Shaw

CALYPSO RESTAURANT & LOUNGE

Jing'an Shangri-La
1218 Middle Yan'an Road
Shanghai
Shanghai Shi 200040
China
+86 2122038889
www.calypsoshanghai.com

Opening hours...Open 7 days
Credit cards...Accepted
Style of pizza..Neapolitan
Recommended pizza..................................San Daniele

"Pizzas are the raison d'être to dine in the bamboo house known as Calypso."—Jamie Barys

CAPO

Yifeng Galleria, 5/F
99 Beijing Dong Lu
Shanghai
Shanghai Shi 200001
China
+86 2153088332
www.capoatrockbund.com

Opening hours...Open 7 days
Credit cards...Accepted
Style of pizza..Neapolitan
Recommended pizza..Diavola

"Classic wood-fired pizza in a handmade oven shipped over from Italy. The pizza is but a small component of what Capo does, but it does it very well. Capo is designed to look like a church, which isn't a bad thing when you're worshipping good eats the way my friends and I do."—Austin Hu

D.O.C.

5 Dongping Lu
Shanghai
Shanghai Shi 200031
China
+86 2164739394
www.docitalian.com

Opening hours...Open 7 days
Credit cards...Accepted
Style of pizza..Neapolitan
Recommended pizza..................Lamb and Fennel Sausage; Pear and Gorgonzola; Sausage

"D.O.C. has an always-buzzing, super-sexy ambience and it does a more-than-passible pie, even for a New Yorker like me."—Camden Hauge

LIQUID LAUNDRY

Kwah Centre
1028 Huaihai Middle Road
Shanghai
Shanghai Shi 200031
China
+86 2164459589
www.theliquidlaundry.com

Opening hours	Open 7 days
Credit cards	Accepted
Style of pizza	American
Recommended pizza	The Beast

"With a great selection of home-brewed and imported beers, Liquid Laundry is Shanghai's first real gastro-pub, providing a raucous environment in which to get steadily sloshed while eating solid food."
—Camden Hauge

MERCATO

Three on the Bund
6/F, 3 Zhongshan Dong Yi Lu
Shanghai
Shanghai Shi 200030
China
+86 2163219922
www.threeonthebund.com

Opening hours	Open 7 days
Credit cards	Accepted
Style of pizza	Neapolitan
Recommended pizza	Pancetta, Spring Greens, Homemade Ricotta, and Herbs; Spicy Pork Sausage, Kale, and Fresh Cheeses; Spicy Salami, Broccolini, and Homemade Ricotta; Wild Mushroom, Three Cheeses, and Farm Egg

"It's hard to go wrong with a Jean-Georges Vongerichten establishment. The gorgeous space, designed by local star architects Neri&Hu, makes this an amazing and relatively affordable option for its quality compared to all others with Shanghai's famous Bund view. A great date spot."
—Camden Hauge

"Excellent pizzas with non-traditional toppings that are well sourced."—Jamie Barys

SEVE

600 Huashan Lu
Shanghai
Shanghai Shi 200040
China
+86 2162493638
www.seveshanghai.com

Opening hours	Open 7 days
Credit cards	Accepted but not AMEX
Style of pizza	Northeastern Italian
Recommended pizza	Briosa; Diavola

"The appeal starts with the crust, a slightly charred crackle of dough that barely supports the generous application of toppings."—Jamie Barys

"IT'S A QUICK PLACE FOR TAKEOUT OR A BITE ON THE GO IN TSIM SHA TSUI."

DARIO MULINO P.100

"GAIA OFFERS A GOOD SELECTION OF ROMAN-STYLE PIZZAS."

WILSON FOK P.98

HONG KONG

"A FRIENDLY NEIGHBORHOOD JOINT WITH A GREAT AMBIENCE AND PIZZA MADE WITH GOOD-QUALITY INGREDIENTS."

GARY SUEN P.99

"NEW YORK-STYLE PIZZA SERVED BY THE SLICE ON WEEKENDS."

RACHEL BALOTA P.98

"NOTHING TASTES BETTER THAN PAISANO'S PIZZA WHEN THOSE HUNGER PANGS STRIKE AT MIDNIGHT!"

RACHEL READ P.98

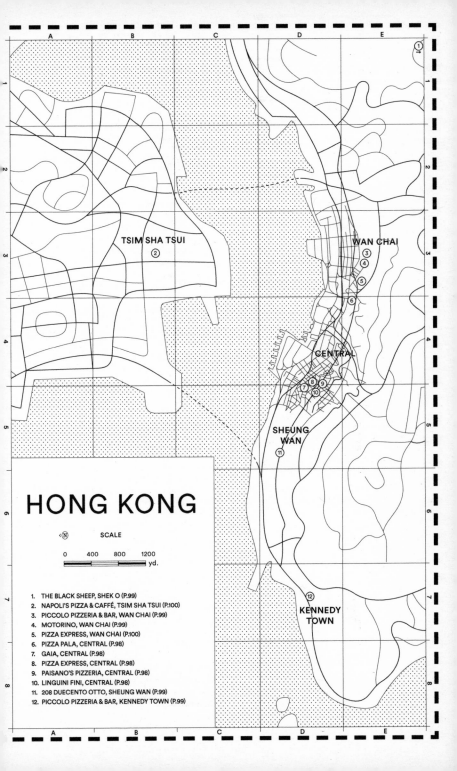

HONG KONG

<N> SCALE

0   400   800   1200
|___|___|___|___| yd.

1. THE BLACK SHEEP, SHEK O (P.99)
2. NAPOLI'S PIZZA & CAFFÉ, TSIM SHA TSUI (P.100)
3. PICCOLO PIZZERIA & BAR, WAN CHAI (P.99)
4. MOTORINO, WAN CHAI (P.99)
5. PIZZA EXPRESS, WAN CHAI (P.100)
6. PIZZA PALA, CENTRAL (P.98)
7. GAIA, CENTRAL (P.98)
8. PIZZA EXPRESS, CENTRAL (P.98)
9. PAISANO'S PIZZERIA, CENTRAL (P.98)
10. LINGUINI FINI, CENTRAL (P.98)
11. 208 DUECENTO OTTO, SHEUNG WAN (P.99)
12. PICCOLO PIZZERIA & BAR, KENNEDY TOWN (P.99)

GAIA

Grand Millennium Plaza
181 Queen's Road
Central
Hong Kong Island
Hong Kong S.A.R., China
+852 21678200
www.gaiagroup.com.hk/gaia

Opening hours	Open 7 days
Credit cards	Accepted
Style of pizza	Roman
Recommended pizza	Five Melted Cheeses, Asparagus and Fava (broad) Beans

"Don't be fooled by the fine-dining decor and the popular alfresco dining set-up, Gaia offers a good selection of Roman-style pizzas. The toppings are secondary to the extra-crisp thin crust, which is consistent on every visit."—Wilson Fok

LINGUINI FINI

49 Elgin Street
Central
Hong Kong Island
Hong Kong S.A.R., China
+852 23876338
www.linguinifini.com

Opening hours	Open 7 days
Credit cards	Accepted
Style of pizza	New York
Recommended pizza	Bronx; Pepperoni

"New York-style pizza served by the slice on weekends. It's the best I've found outside of NYC!"
—Rachel Balota

PAISANO'S PIZZERIA

23 Hollywood Road
Central
Hong Kong Island
Hong Kong S.A.R., China
+852 25444445
www.paisanos.com.hk

Opening hours	Open 7 days
Credit cards	Accepted but not AMEX
Style of pizza	New York
Recommended pizza	Pepperoni

"Nothing tastes better than Paisano's pizza when those hunger pangs strike at midnight! Pro tip: although it does sell giant slices separately, order a whole pizza so it's made fresh."
—Rachel Read

PIZZA EXPRESS

Soho Square
21 Lynhurst Terrace
Central
Hong Kong Island
Hong Kong S.A.R., China
+852 25621088
www.pizzaexpress.com.hk

Opening hours	Open 7 days
Credit cards	Accepted
Style of pizza	Neapolitan
Recommended pizza	Pomodoro Pesto Pizza

PIZZA PALA

Great Food Hall, Pacific Place Mall
88 Queensway
Central
Hong Kong Island
Hong Kong S.A.R., China
+852 61656549
www.pizzapala.com

Opening hours	Open 7 days
Credit cards	Accepted
Style of pizza	*Pizza al taglio*
Recommended pizza	Margherita; Mushroom and Truffle; Potato and Pesto

"Started by Slow Food advocates and graduates of the Slow Food University, all the ingredients are carefully sourced and the pizzas are meticulously made. The incredibly high hydration of the dough gives it a great texture—and yet these slices are affordable for all."—Janice Leung Hayes

"Pizza Pala is a takeout food counter that makes square pizzas by the slice. It's tasty and there's a lot of choices."—Dario Mulino

PICCOLO PIZZERIA & BAR
Shop 1E, Davis Street
Kennedy Town
Hong Kong Island
Hong Kong S.A.R., China
+852 28243000

Opening hours	Open 7 days
Credit cards	Accepted
Style of pizza	Thin-crust
Recommended pizza	Bianca

"A friendly neighborhood joint with a great ambience and pizza made with good-quality ingredients."
—Gary Suen

THE BLACK SHEEP
Shek O Village
330 Shek O Village Road
Shek O
Hong Kong Island
Hong Kong S.A.R., China
+852 28092021

Opening hours	Open 7 days
Credit cards	Accepted
Style of pizza	Wood-fired thin-crust
Recommended pizza	Merguez; Planet Cheese

208 DUECENTO OTTO
208 Hollywood Road
Sheung Wan
Hong Kong Island
Hong Kong S.A.R., China
+852 25490208
www.208.com.hk

Opening hours	Open 7 days
Credit cards	Accepted
Style of pizza	Neapolitan
Recommended pizza	Diavola; Margherita

"Made using a custom-designed pizza oven shipped over from Naples, these are gourmet pizzas. The quality of the ingredients that 208 uses really shines through."—Rachel Read

"The two-story restaurant comprises a bar downstairs and a bigger dining space above. Neapolitan-style pizzas are turned out from a wood-fired oven for a thin, crisp crust. The pizzeria doubles as an Italian restaurant featuring a good selection of pasta dishes and mains. Lunch deals are value for money and pizzas are made to order."—Wilson Fok

MOTORINO
15 Ship Street
Wan Chai
Hong Kong Island
Hong Kong S.A.R., China
+852 25200690
www.motorinopizza.com/hong_kong

Opening hours	Open 7 days
Credit cards	Accepted but not AMEX
Style of pizza	Neapolitan
Recommended pizza	Brussels Sprout; Margherita; Meatball; Soppressata Piccante

"An American import made famous by owner and chef Mathieu Palombino, Motorino delivers hand-turned pizza dough that is slow-fermented, and the pizza itself is soft and chewy to the bite. Pre-set pizzas feature great combinations of ingredients from the simple Margherita, to the Soppressata Piccante (fiery hot to some) and the awesome Brussels Sprout pizza with pancetta and mozzarella."—Wilson Fok

"Debate has raged in Hong Kong about whether the pizzas from this Brooklyn import are nicely charred or just burnt—but whenever I've had them, they've been pretty perfect."—Rachel Read

PICCOLO PIZZERIA & BAR
Shop 4/5, 22 Tai Wong Street East
Wan Chai
Hong Kong Island
Hong Kong S.A.R., China
+852 28243002

Opening hours	Open 7 days
Credit cards	Accepted
Style of pizza	Thin-crust
Recommended pizza	Pancetta

PIZZA EXPRESS

23 Wing Fung Street
Wan Chai
Hong Kong Island
Hong Kong S.A.R., China
+852 35280541
www.pizzaexpress.com.hk

Opening hours..Open 7 days
Credit cards...Accepted
Style of pizza..Neapolitan
Recommended pizza...American Hot

NAPOLI'S PIZZA & CAFFÉ

44 Carnarvon Road
Tsim Sha Tsui
Kowloon
Hong Kong S.A.R., China
+852 23688842
www.napolisjapan.com

Opening hours..Open 7 days
Credit cards...Accepted
Style of pizza..Japanese
Recommended pizza.................Sausage and Broccoli Raab

"This is a Japanese cafe that makes small, round
pizzas. It's a quick place for takeout or a bite on the
go in Tsim Sha Tsui."—Dario Mulino

BRICK OVEN NEW YORK PIZZERIA

617–4 Yeoksam-dong
Seoul
Seoul 135-907
South Korea
+82 25081325

Opening hours..Open 7 days
Credit cards...Accepted
Style of pizza..New York
Recommended pizza..Pepperoni

"The owner was one of the first Koreans to take a
serious course on making New York-style pizza in
New York. He imported almost everything from the
USA, including his oven. New Yorkers in Seoul claim
this is the closest Seoul has gotten to authentic New
York pizza."—Joe McPherson

DAEJANGJANGI FABBRO

202–1 Gahoe-dong
Seoul
Seoul 110-260
South Korea
+82 27644297

Opening hours..Open 7 days
Credit cards...Accepted
Style of pizza..Neapolitan
Recommended pizza..............Arugula (rocket); Capricciosa

"The setting is a Korean traditional-style house or
hanok so eating pizza and Italian food here is fun and
unique."—Daniel Gray

THE KITCHEN SALVATORE CUOMO

Gangnam-gu Sinsa-dong 646-2
Seoul
Seoul 135-896
South Korea
+82 234470071
www.kitchensalvatore.kr

Opening hours..Open 7 days
Credit cards...Accepted
Style of pizza..Neapolitan
Recommended pizza..DOC; Salumeria

"The restaurant sticks to tradition and doesn't bend
to the opinionated patrons that might demand less
salt or a side of pickles to come with the pizza.
It's classic Neapolitan pizza made with the finest
ingredients."—Daniel Gray

MADDUX PIZZA

26 Itaewon-ro, 26 Gil
Seoul
Seoul 140-200
South Korea
+82 27922420

Opening hours..Open 7 days
Credit cards...Accepted
Style of pizza..New York
Recommended pizza..Margherita

"Maddux Pizza is the new darling of the expat crowd,
selling pizza by the slice. Many pizza devotees claim
that it is the new king of pizzas in Seoul."
—Joe McPherson

AL MATTO

38-11 Yongsan-dong 2-GA
Seoul
Seoul 140-021
South Korea
+82 27944616

Opening hours	Open 7 days
Credit cards	Accepted
Style of pizza	Neapolitan
Recommended pizza	Margherita

"Al Matto has a great variety of toppings and styles that aren't found in other places. It's fairly affordable compared to similar quality pizzerias."
—Joe McPherson

PIZZERIA D'BUZZA

743-33 Hannam-dong
Seoul
Seoul 140-893
South Korea
+82 27929474
www.buzzapizza.com

Opening hours	Open 7 days
Credit cards	Not accepted
Style of pizza	Neapolitan
Recommended pizza	Napoletana

"The dough is crisp outside and has a soft interior. It's like eating hot August wind. The staff are dedicated to the art and each pizza is made with precision. It's the love, passion, and attention to detail that makes this pizzeria great."—Daniel Gray

TREVIA

557 Itaewon-dong
Seoul
Seoul 140-861
South Korea
+82 27946003

Opening hours	Open 7 days
Credit cards	Accepted
Style of pizza	Roman-Neapolitan
Recommended pizza	Four Cheese

"Simply the best crust in Seoul. The dough is mixed the day before, and rises very slowly. Then it's hand-stretched, dressed, and baked in a very hot oven. Sublime."—Tim Mitchell

"THIS IS TRUE JAPANESE-STYLE PIZZA."

NAO FUKUMURA P.108

"SAKURAGUMI IS THE PIZZERIA WITH THE BEST VIEW IN ALL OF JAPAN."

SACHI AKIMOTO P.105

"IF YOU FANCY DELICIOUS NEAPOLITAN PIZZA IN KYOTO, THIS IS THE PLACE."

TSUGUO KONISHI P.106

JAPAN

"TO WATCH A JAPANESE PIZZA CHEF WHO IS AS GOOD AS THE BEST NEAPOLITAN CHEFS IS PRICELESS."

ANTONIO BARBA P.106

"WITH ONLY 15 SEATS, A LITTLE FORWARD PLANNING IS NEEDED FOR THIS LITTLE GEM THAT'S LOCATED IN THE SMALL SKI VILLAGE OF ANNUPURI IN HOKKAIDO, JAPAN."

KATHERINE BONT P.105

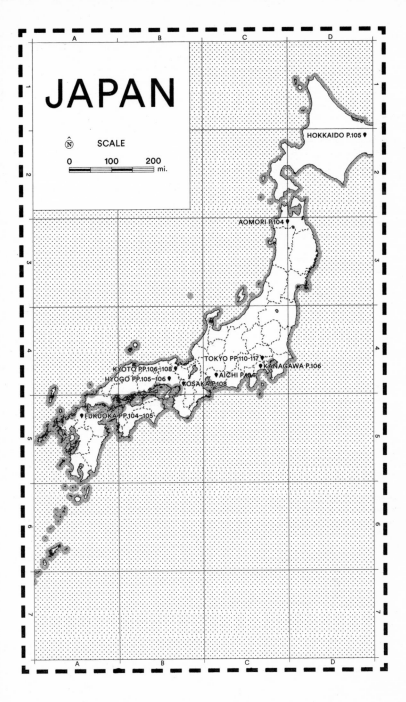

JAPAN

N

SCALE

0   100   200
mi.

HOKKAIDO P.105

AOMORI P.104

TOKYO PP.110-117
KYOTO PP.106-108
KANAGAWA P.106
HYOGO PP.105-106
AICHI P.104
OSAKA P.108
FUKUOKA PP.104-105

PIZZERIA TRATTORIA CESARI

3-36-44 Naka-ku Oosu
Nagoya
Aichi 460-0011
Japan
+81 522380372
www.cesari.jp

Opening hours..................Closed Tuesday and Wednesday
Credit cards..Accepted
Style of pizza..Neapolitan
Recommended pizza..Marinara

"Not only is the owner and *pizzaiolo*, Akinari Pasquale Makishima, one of the world's top Neapolitan *pizzaioli* (having won the World Pizza Championships in Naples), but he is a wonderful person, putting his heart and soul into training up young pizza chefs. Whenever you go to Cesari, you will enjoy wonderful Neapolitan pizzas and other authentic Neapolitan cuisine. Even if Mr Makishima himself is away in Italy, you will enjoy wonderful customer service and top-class cooking."—Hirofumi Jaffa Morita

SOLO PIZZA NAPOLETANA

3-32-8 Sakae Naka-ku
Nagoya
Aichi 460-0008
Japan
+81 522381200
www.solopizza.jp

Opening hours..Open 7 days
Credit cards..Not accepted
Style of pizza..Neapolitan
Recommended pizza................................Margherita Extra

"I chose this branch rather than the main branch. The main branch is good, of course, but I personally prefer this one. If you can get there, the pizzas fired by Mr Ota are truly wonderful."—Ohata Katsutoshi

PIZZERIA DA SASINO

62-1 Dotemachi
Hirosaki
Aomori 036-8182
Japan
+81 172332139

Opening hours..Closed Monday
Credit cards..Not accepted
Style of pizza..Neapolitan
Recommended pizza..Sasino

"The mozzarella is all homemade from local milk."
—Michiaki Sasamori

PIZZA AR TAIO

Maison de Mars 1F
1-5-16 Sawara-ku Yayoi
Fukuoka
Fukuoka 814-0014
Japan
+81 924077405
www.artaio-shop.com

Opening hours..Closed Monday
Credit cards..Accepted
Style of pizza..Roman

"This was the first restaurant in Japan to sell pizza by weight. The special bases make these pizzas really delicious, served as they come, at room temperature, or reheated. This is pizza just like in Rome!"
—Sachi Akimoto

PIZZA WORLD & M

1-6-7 Chuou-Ku Shirogane
Fukuoka
Fukuoka 810-0012
Japan
+81 925235279

Opening hours..Closed Thursday
Credit cards..Not accepted
Style of pizza..Neapolitan
Recommended pizza..........................Pane with Parmesan
and Rosemary Oil

"The bases are delicious and wonderful."
—Sachi Akimoto

PIZZERIA DA CIRUZZO

1-9-8 Imajuku Ekimae Nishi-ku
Fukuoka
Fukuoka 819-0167
Japan
+81 928051770

Opening hours................................Closed Tuesday
Credit cards..................................Not accepted
Style of pizza................................Neapolitan
Recommended pizza........................Margherita

"The pizzas are really well balanced. They are as
good, or even better, than the ones I have eaten
in Naples."—Sachi Akimoto

VELONA

Chuo Ward
4-8-28 Watanabedoori
Fukuoka
Fukuoka 810-0004
Japan
+81 927210057

Opening hours..............................Closed Wednesday
Credit cards..................................Not accepted
Style of pizza................................Roman
Recommended pizza........................Anchovy

DEL SOLE

483-1 Niseko-cho Niseko
Abuta-gun
Hokkaido 048-1511
Japan
+81 136583535
www.pizza-delsole.com

Opening hours..............Closed Wednesday and Thursday
Credit cards..................................Accepted
Style of pizza........................Neapolitan thin-crust
Recommended pizza........................Bianca with Garlic,
Chile, and Baby Fish

"With only 15 seats, a little forward planning is needed
for this little gem that's located in the small ski village
of Annupuri in Hokkaido, Japan. The delicate touch
and finesse of a Japanese chef is felt with each and
every bite of the pizza."—Katherine Bont

TRATTORIA PIZZERIA CIRO

Urban Life 213
2-4-1 Nakazaki
Akashi
Hyogo 673-0883
Japan
+81 789129400

Opening hours................................Closed Monday
Credit cards..................................Not accepted
Style of pizza................................Neapolitan
Recommended pizza........................Marinara; Octopus

"This unique Neapolitan-style pizza is extraordinarily
light and easy to eat. It has good flavor and makes
great use of local ingredients and home-grown
vegetables."—Akio Nishikawa

SAKURAGUMI

2-1 Misaki
Ako
Hyogo 678-0215⬚
Japan
+81 791423545
www.vera-pizza-sakuragumi.co.jp

Opening hours........................Closed Tuesday and the first
Wednesday and third Monday of the month
Credit cards..................................Accepted but not AMEX
Style of pizza................................Neapolitan
Recommended pizza............Conger Eel; Margherita DOP;
Pesce Bandiera

"Sakuragumi is the pizzeria with the best view in all
of Japan. The pizzas are delicious, of course, but you
cannot find a better location than this!"
—Sachi Akimoto

"It is worth visiting this area just to go to Sakuragumi.
There are lots of guesthouses nearby, so you can relax
and stay overnight."—Taijiro Mori

Misaki, a tiny peninsula in the southwestern Hyogo Prefecture,
gets its reputation as the Naples of Japan from the striking
views inside and outside Sakuragumi. With a "Vera Pizza
Napoletana" sign as your beacon it is nearly possible to confuse
the cobalt blue Seto Inland Sea for the azure blue Tyrrhenian.
But it gets far easier to suspend disbelief the closer you get
to one of Akio Nishikawa's pizzas. Though he recommends
a seasonal pizza with a fresh seafood topping, the truth
is it would be unthinkable to come here and not have the
Margherita DOP Japan's great Neapolitan pizza pioneer has
been fine-tuning for 25-plus years. Eating a second pizza is the
only way out of a dilemma such as this.

PIZZERIA AZZURRI

Utopiatoa 1F
3-7-3 Chuo-ku Yamamoto-dori
Kobe
Hyogo 650-0003
Japan
+81 782416036
www.azzurri-p.com

Opening hours..Closed Thursday
Credit cards...Not accepted
Style of pizza...Neapolitan
Recommended pizza..................Braccio di Ferro; Marinara;
Mushroom with Special Cheese

"Located in the Kitano area of Kobe, this restaurant is packed day and night with people wanting delicious pizza."—Tsuguo Konishi

"The large, piping hot bases are cooked to perfection with a wonderful aroma of flour. Then pizzas are so soft and light that you can wolf them down despite their size. And they are wonderfully balanced with the other ingredients."—Hitomi Nakano

DA RICKNYO

2-27 Koshien Abiki-cho
Nishinomiya
Hyogo 663-8156
Japan
+81 798461430

Opening hours.......................................Closed Wednesday
Credit cards...Not accepted
Style of pizza...Neapolitan

PIZZERIA E TRATTORIA DA MASANIELLO

Crescent Sakaswgawa 1F
1-8-20 Isoshi
Takarazuka
Hyogo 665-0033
Japan
+81 797715971
www.masaniello-p.com

Opening hours..Closed Monday
Credit cards...Not accepted
Style of pizza...Neapolitan
Recommended pizza..Pizza DOC

"Cooked to perfection in the homemade wood-fired oven, the pizzas smell delicious, the bases are cooked perfectly with a good texture, and they are so light you want to have another."—Akio Nishikawa

PIZZERIA GG KAMAKURA

2-9-62 Yuigahama
Kamakura
Kanagawa 248-0014
Japan
+81 467335286

Opening hours...Open 7 days
Credit cards...Not accepted
Style of pizza...Neapolitan
Recommended pizza.............Margherita, Marinara, Popolo

"Enjoy Neapolitan pizza from an authentic wood-fired oven in the ancient capital of Kamakura."
—Takeshi Ozawa

SISILIYA

Wadou Building 1F
1-7 Aioi-cho
Yokohama
Kanagawa 231-0012
Japan
+81 456710465
www.sisiliya.com

Opening hours..Closed Sunday
Credit cards...Not accepted
Style of pizza...Neapolitan
Recommended pizza......................................Marinara Special

"To watch a Japanese pizza chef who is as good as the best Neapolitan chefs is priceless."
—Antonio Barba

PIZZA MERCATO

KYOCA Hall 105
1-1 Shimogyo-ku Sujakushokaicho
Kyoto
Kyoto 600-8841
Japan
+81 753534777
www.pizza-mercato.net

Opening hours.......................................Closed Wednesday
Credit cards...Not accepted
Style of pizza...Neapolitan
Recommended pizza............................Don Cicco; Mercato;
Neghinara

"If you fancy delicious Neapolitan pizza in Kyoto, this is the place. It has a large range of pizzas, many of which feature vegetables from Kyoto, and all of which are delicious."—Tsuguo Konishi

PIZZA PAZZA ITALIANA

Kita-ku
12-1 Kamigamo Asatsuyugahara-cho
Kyoto
Kyoto 603-8035
Japan
+81 752003708
www.kyoto.zaq.ne.jp/pizzapazza

Opening hours	Closed Monday
Credit cards	Not accepted
Style of pizza	Italian

"These are pizzas made by an Italian chef in Kyoto.
It's a bit of a journey to get there, but worth it.
You'll feel like you've left Kyoto and landed in Italy."
—Yukari Sakamoto

PIZZERIA NAPOLETANA DA YUKI

Sakyou-ku
36-3 Okazaki Enshoji-cho
Kyoto
Kyoto 606-8344
Japan
+81 757616765

Opening hours	Closed Monday
Credit cards	Not accepted
Style of pizza	Neapolitan
Recommended pizza	Marinara

"It's a small restaurant, but it's so good I have to go
there every time I visit Kyoto."
—Hirofumi Jaffa Morita

PIZZERIA SOLONO

Nakagyou-ku
90-3 Machigashira-cho
Kyoto
Kyoto 604-8206
Japan
+81 757082729
www.pizzeria-solono.net

Opening hours	Closed Monday
Credit cards	Not accepted
Style of pizza	Neapolitan
Recommended pizza	Margherita

"Pizzeria Solono serves delicious traditional pizzas."
—Nao Fukumura

TRATTORIA PIZZERIA AMORE KIYAMACHI

Shimokyou-ku
161 Kiyamachi Izumiyacho
Kyoto
Kyoto 600-8014
Japan
+81 757087791

Opening hours	Open 7 days
Credit cards	Accepted
Style of pizza	Neapolitan
Recommended pizza	Margherita

"The Japanese have a special skill for mastering
a foreign cuisine and then adding their own
quintessentially Japanese inflection to it so that
the result is even better than the original. I love
the overall menu at Amore, it uses the very best
seafood and the finest seasonal ingredients. Its
pizzas are flawlessly prepared in a wood-fired
oven, with crusts that are neither too thin, nor too
doughy. Add to this the fact that Amore enjoys
picturesque views of the Kamo river, you have
pizzeria perfection."—Sulyn Tan

FRITZ K

1-9-105 Jyurakumawari-Minamimachi
Nakagyo-ku
Kyoto 604-8411
Japan
+81 758019978☐
www.fritz-k.com

Opening hours	Closed Tuesday and the first Saturday of the month
Credit cards	Not accepted
Style of pizza	*Pizza fritta*
Recommended pizza	Margherita

"Fritz K is unusual in that it specializes in deep-fried
pizza. The portions are modest and at a reasonable
price, so you can try a variety of pizzas."
—Nao Fukumura

TAMPOPO

Wazuka-Chou
8 Owaza Kamatsuka Koaza Kawahara
Souraku-gun
Kyoto 619-1212
Japan
+81 774782445

Opening hours	Closed Monday
Credit cards	Not accepted
Style of pizza	Okonomiyaki
Recommended pizza	Margherita

"The pizzas are served on an okonomiyaki hotplate,
so the cheese oozes as it is heated constantly,
producing a great aroma. This is true Japanese-style
pizza."—Nao Fukumura

LA PIZZA NAPOLETANA REGALO

Horino Building 1F
1-5-2 Fukushima-ku Fukushima
Osaka
Osaka 553-0003
Japan
+81 647962215

Opening hours	Closed Tuesday
Credit cards	Not accepted
Style of pizza	Neapolitan
Recommended pizza	Diavola; Margherita

"This is a truly Osaka-style pizzeria, where people
of all ages can enjoy delicious Neapolitan pizzas."
—Tsuguo Konishi

IL SOLE TEN-3

3-5-16 Kitaku-Tenjinbashi
Osaka
Osaka 530-0041
Japan
+81 668092767
www.ilsole.jp/ten3

Opening hours	Open 7 days
Credit cards	Accepted
Style of pizza	Neapolitan
Recommended pizza	Marinara

"The Neapolitan pizza bases are wonderful; they are
cooked well and go perfectly with the tomato sauce.
The *pizzaioli* are young and full of energy, creating
an enjoyable atmosphere."—Hitomi Nakano

> **"THE PIZZA WAS SO GOOD I ACTUALLY CRIED."**
> JOE BEDDIA P.115

> **"IN A CITY OBSESSED WITH NEAPOLITAN PIZZA, IL PENTITO STANDS OUT AS A RARE STANDARD-BEARER FOR THE ROMAN STYLE."**
> ROBBIE SWINNERTON P.116

TOKYO

> **"THIS PIZZERIA HAS A SUPERB LOCATION IN TOKYO MIDTOWN, WHERE YOU CAN ENJOY THE CHERRY BLOSSOMS FROM THE WINDOWS OR FROM THE SEATS ON THE TERRACE."**
> TAKESHI OZAWA P.114

> **"LUCCANALU'S CASUAL STYLE MAKES IT A GREAT PLACE FOR PIZZA AND WINE."**
> TAKANORI NAKAMURA P.116

> **"THE AMBIENCE AND THE ATMOSPHERE ARE WONDERFUL."**
> OHATA KATSUTOSHI P.117

TOKYO

SCALE

0 700 1400 2100 yd.

1. PIZZERIA IL TAMBURELLO, CHUOU-KU (P.112)
2. PIZZERIA DA PEPPE NAPOLI STA' CA", MINATO-KU (P.114)
3. FREY'S FAMOUS PIZZERIA, MINATO-KU (P.113)
4. PIZZERIA TRATTORIA NAPULE, MINATO-KU (P.114)
5. SAVOY, MINATO-KU (P.115)
6. PIZZERIA ROMANA GIANICOLO, MINATO-KU (P.114)
7. PIZZA STRADA, MINATO-KU (P.113)
8. PIZZERIA SABATINI AOYAMA, MINATO-KU (P.114)
9. PIZZERIA TRATTORIA PARTENOPE EBISU, SHIBUYA (P.116)
10. LA TRIPLETTA, SHINAGAWA (P.116)
11. PIZZERIA ROMANA IL PENTITO, SHIBUYA (P.116)
12. DOMANI, SHIBUYA (P.115)
13. LUCCANALU, SHIBUYA (P.116)
14. PIZZERIA E TRATTORIA DA ISA, MEGURO (P.113)
15. SEIRINKAN, MEGURO (P.113)
16. IL LUPONE, MEGURO (P.112)
17. GALEONE, MEGURO (P.112)
18. PIZZERIA VINCERE, KOKUBUNJI (P.112)
19. MANA RICCO, KOKUBUNJI (P.112)
20. LA PICCOLA TAVOLA, SUGINAMI (P.117)
21. MASSIMOTTAVIO, SUGINAMI (P.116)
22. PIZZERIA DINO, SETAGAYA (P.115)
23. DA OGGI, SETAGAYA (P.115)
24. L'ARTE, SETAGAYA (P.115)
25. PIZZERIA GG KICHIJYOUJI, MUSASHINO (P.115)
26. PIZZERIA YUICIRO & A, TACHIKAWA (P.117)

PIZZERIA IL TAMBURELLO
DIG DUG 1F
1-2-9 Nihonbashi Horidome-chou
Chuou-Ku
Tokyo 103-0012
Japan
+81 366616628
www.il-tamburello.com

Opening hours	Closed Sunday
Credit cards	Accepted
Style of pizza	Neapolitan
Recommended pizza	Calzone; Margherita

"This pizzerias is exactly as you would expect from someone who learned their craft living in Naples for three years."—Kiyoshi Ciccio Nakamura

MANA RICCO
1-38-28 Hikari-chou
Kokubunji
Tokyo 185-0034
Japan
+81 425730160

Opening hours	Closed Sunday
Credit cards	Not accepted
Style of pizza	Neapolitan
Recommended pizza	Margherita

"The uncompromising pizza is quite masterful. The pizza chef is really dedicated to his craft, and takes special care when he's baking the pizza, keeping a constant eye on the wood-fired oven."
—Ohata Katsutoshi

PIZZERIA VINCERE
3-22-12 Minami-chou
Kokubunji
Tokyo 185-0021
Japan
+81 423120422

Opening hours	Closed Monday
Credit cards	Accepted
Style of pizza	Neapolitan
Recommended pizza	Margherita

"This pizzeria is special due to the wonderfully harmonious combination of the care taken over the dough by the talented pizza chef and the way the pizza is baked with great attention to the pizza bases."
—Ohata Katsutoshi

GALEONE
Office Toritsudai Building 1F
1-7-3 Nakane
Meguro
Tokyo 152-0031
Japan
+81 364595739
www.galeone2014.jimdo.com

Opening hours	Closed Monday
Credit cards	Accepted
Style of pizza	Neapolitan
Recommended pizza	Galeone; Quattro Formaggi

"The pizza bases are light and delicious, while the toppings are so well thought out that you could come back every day without getting bored."
—Hirofumi Jaffa Morita

IL LUPONE
2-10-19 Nakameguro
Meguro
Tokyo 153-0061
Japan
+81 357226789
www.il-lupone.jp

Opening hours	Closed Monday
Credit cards	Accepted
Style of pizza	Neapolitan

"Located in Nakameguro in a lovely detached building between Yamate-dori and the Meguro River, Il Lupone offers cuisine from the Campania region of southern Italy. It uses ingredients such as cheese from Hokkaido to produce mild pizzas that suit the Japanese taste. It's a bit far from the station, but I would travel even further to get there."—Yuri Nomura

PIZZERIA E TRATTORIA DA ISA

1-28-9 Aobadai
Meguro
Tokyo 153-0042
Japan
+81 357683739
www.da-isa.jp

Opening hours	Closed Monday
Credit cards	Accepted
Style of pizza	Neapolitan
Recommended pizza	Margherita; Marinara; Pizza Fritta; Prosciutto and Arugula (rocket)

"A slice of Naples in the middle of Tokyo's ever-happening Nakameguro district."
—Robbie Swinnerton

"The flavors and atmosphere are absolutely wonderful. The restaurant has a boisterous, noisy atmosphere, but it's very jolly. The huge, unusually shaped pizzas are impressive."—Hitomi Nakano

Pizzeria E Trattoria da ISA may be in Tokyo's Nakameguro district but everything you see conspires to make you think you're elsewhere: the Roman lettering on the awning. The word *entrada*—Italian for entrance—on the sliding-door entrance. The bottle of Ferrarelli Italian mineral water on the table. But what really makes this bustling recreation of a classic Naples pizzeria work, more so than even the World Pizza Cups won by superstar *pizzaiolo* Hisanori Yamamoto at the Campionato Internazionale per Pizzaioli, is the pizza. The Italian trappings and Neapolitan souvenirs don't produce a beautifully rustic Margherita with over-bubbled hills and under-sauced valleys. Yamamoto does.

SEIRINKAN

2-6-4 Kamimeguro
Meguro
Tokyo 153-0051
Japan
+81 337145160

Opening hours	Open 7 days
Credit cards	Accepted
Style of pizza	Neapolitan
Recommended pizza	Margherita; Marinara

"Owner and pizza chef Susumu Kakinuma has created his pizzeria in his own image. Having fallen in love with the culture, colors, people, and Neapolitan pizza, Kakinuma expresses his respect for the fantastic city of Naples with the spirit and the passion that is in his pizza."—Ivo Virgilio

"Kakinuma-san is one of the most revered *pizzaioli* in Tokyo, and for good reason. His dough has a bit more salt than is traditional, making the crust delicious on its own. There are only two pizzas on the menu: Marinara and Margherita. Simple is best."
—Yukari Sakamoto

FREY'S FAMOUS PIZZERIA

4-5-15 Roppongi
Minato-Ku
Tokyo 106-6108
Japan
+81 334978820

Opening hours	Closed Monday
Credit cards	Accepted
Style of pizza	Neapolitan
Recommended pizza	Margherita

PIZZA STRADA

Azabu-Jyuban Building 1F
3-6-2 Azabu-Jyuban
Minato-Ku
Tokyo 106-0045
Japan
+81 364351944
www.pizzastrada.jp

Opening hours	Open 7 days
Credit cards	Accepted but not AMEX
Style of pizza	Roman
Recommended pizza	Margherita

"To find a high-level pizzeria outside Italy is very difficult. Pizza Strada offers consistency and excellent produce resulting in a light, high-quality pizza."—Luca Fantin

PIZZERIA DA PEPPE NAPOLI STA' CA"

1-11-4 Azabudai
Minato-Ku
Tokyo 106-0041
Japan
+81 364591846

Opening hours	Closed Monday
Credit cards	Accepted
Style of pizza	Neapolitan
Recommended pizza	Don Salvo

"Neapolitan owner Peppe Errichiello has a passion for pizza as well as pride in his city (Naples). The restaurant is adorned with Neapolitan curios and ornaments and the atmosphere is youthful and welcoming."
—Ivo Virgilio

"A slice of Naples in Tokyo run by two Neapolitan brothers in a central area of the city with a glimpse of the Tokyo tower."—Rossella Ceccarini

PIZZERIA ROMANA GIANICOLO

Watanabe Building B1F
2-8-8 Azabujyuban
Minato-Ku
Tokyo 106-0045
Japan
+81 364352080
www.gianicolo.jp

Opening hours	Closed Monday
Credit cards	Accepted
Style of pizza	Roman
Recommended pizza	Margherita

"The chef, Taku Uchino, won an overwhelming victory at the Italian cuisine contest Gran Concorso di Cucina 2014 that was held recently at Tokyo Gas Studio + G Ginza by the Italian Chamber of Commerce in Japan."—Masayuki Minezaki

PIZZERIA SABATINI AOYAMA

Suncrest Building B1F
2-13-15 Kita-Aoyama
Minato-Ku
Tokyo 107-0061
Japan
+81 334022027
www.sabatini.co.jp

Opening hours	Open 7 days
Credit cards	Accepted
Style of pizza	Roman
Recommended pizza	Bella Italia

"The atmosphere of this pizzeria is one of the best in Tokyo: warm, friendly, and not too expensive. The open stone oven with flames sometimes flaring out makes for a very nicely cooked thin-crust pizza."
—Michael Kleindl

PIZZERIA TRATTORIA NAPULE

Tokyo Midtown Garden Terrace 1F
9-7-4 Akasaka
Minato-Ku
Tokyo 107-0052
Japan
+81 354130711
www.bellavita.co.jp/napule/tmt

Opening hours	Open 7 days
Credit cards	Accepted
Style of pizza	Neapolitan
Recommended pizza	Margherita; Marinara; Quattro Formaggi

"This pizzeria has a superb location in Tokyo Midtown, where you can enjoy the cherry blossoms from the windows or from the seats on the terrace. You will love the authentic Neapolitan pizza and local southern Italian dishes."—Takeshi Ozawa

SAVOY

Nakaoka Building 201
3-10-1 Motoazabu
Minato-Ku
Tokyo 106-0046
Japan
+81 357707899
www.savoy.vc/4_azabu/azabu1_top.html

Opening hours..Open 7 days
Credit cards...Accepted
Style of pizza..Neapolitan
Recommended pizza..Marinara

"Savoy only has two kinds of pizza: Marinara and
Margherita. The pizza was so good I actually cried."
—Joe Beddia

PIZZERIA GG KICHIJYOUJI

Plaisir B1F
1-17-1 Kichijyouji Minami-cho
Musashino
Tokyo 180-0003
Japan
+81 422265024

Opening hours..Open 7 days
Credit cards..Not accepted
Style of pizza..Neapolitan
Recommended pizza..................................Margherita; Popolo

"Pizzeria GG Kichijyouji has talented young chefs
who learnt their craft in Naples. The flavor and price
of the pizzas and the menu choices are just like those
seen in the city of Naples."
—Kiyoshi Ciccio Nakamura

L'ARTE

1-35-17 Sangenjyaya
Setagaya
Tokyo 154-0024
Japan
+81 334243003
www.larte.jp

Opening hours..Closed Tuesday
Credit cards...Accepted
Style of pizza..Neapolitan
Recommended pizza...Bianca Ciccioli

"These are truly great pizzas, their size, flavor, and
seasoning are all perfectly suited to the Japanese
taste."—Taijiro Mori

DA OGGI

MART Shimokitazawa 1F
2-29-2 Daizawa
Setagaya
Tokyo 155-0032
Japan
+81 357798577

Opening hours..Closed Tuesday
Credit cards..Not accepted
Style of pizza..Neapolitan
Recommended pizza..Margherita

PIZZERIA DINO

5-11-3 Minami-Karasuyama
Setagaya
Tokyo 157-0062
Japan
+81 353843339
www.pizzeriadino.jp

Opening hours..Open 7 days
Credit cards...............................Accepted but not AMEX
Style of pizza..Neapolitan
Recommended pizza..Margherita

"Authentic Neapolitan pizza cooked in a wood-fired
oven. All the ingredients are strictly imported from
Italy."—Antonio Barba

DOMANI

3–4 Sakuragaoka-cho
Shibuya
Tokyo 150-0031
Japan
+81 334961112
www.mydomani.jp/cafedomani

Opening hours..Closed Monday
Credit cards...Accepted
Style of pizza...Italian
Recommended pizza..Daily special

"Being able to eat an Italian pizza on the other side
of the world in the most animated district of Tokyo,
but in a calm and relaxing street, in a very Italian and
cozy setting, while looking at the chef getting the
pizzas out of the wood-fired oven...it was magical!
And it was just as magical in the mouth...the dough
is incredibly good."—Priscilla Davigny

LUCCANALU

1F
1-7-2 Uehara
Shibuya
Tokyo 151-0064
Japan
+81 368049367
www.luccanalu.jp

Opening hours	Open 7 days
Credit cards	Accepted
Style of pizza	Neapolitan wood-fired
Recommended pizza	Marinara

"Luccanalu's casual style makes it a great place for pizza and wine."—Takanori Nakamura

PIZZERIA ROMANA IL PENTITO

Axis Bldg. 1F
3-1-3 Yoyogi
Shibuya
Tokyo 151-0053
Japan
+81 333205699
www.pentito.jp

Opening hours	Closed Sunday and Monday
Credit cards	Not accepted
Style of pizza	Roman
Recommended pizza	Margherita; Pentito

"In a city obsessed with Neapolitan pizza, Il Pentito stands out as a rare standard-bearer for the Roman style. Simple, honest, and uncompromising, it does not aspire to gourmet status. But the pizza is crisp and excellent. And so is the setting, with its obsessive retro decor."—Robbie Swinnerton

"Restaurants like this don't even exist in Rome any more!"—Yumiko Inukai

PIZZERIA TRATTORIA PARTENOPE EBISU

Ebisu Kouwa Building
1-22-20 Ebisu
Shibuya
Tokyo 150-0013
Japan
+81 357915663
www.partenope.jp/shop/ebisu.html

Opening hours	Open 7 days
Credit cards	Accepted
Style of pizza	Neapolitan
Recommended pizza	Partenope

"The Neapolitan pizzas are consistently delicious at this restaurant approved by the VPN Association."
—Hirofumi Jaffa Morita

LA TRIPLETTA

3-13-12 Koyama
Shinagawa
Tokyo 142-0062
Japan
+81 364513537

Opening hours	Closed Tuesday
Credit cards	Accepted
Style of pizza	Neapolitan
Recommended pizza	Margherita

"The pizzas are delicious, and the service and atmosphere are fantastic. The pizzas are big, but soft and chewy and so light that you can just wolf them down."—Hitomi Nakano

MASSIMOTTAVIO

4-4-4 Eifuku
Suginami
Tokyo 168-0064
Japan
+81 368027648
www.massimottavio.com

Opening hours	Closed Wednesday
Credit cards	Accepted
Style of pizza	Neapolitan
Recommended pizza	Bollicine; Margherita

"Chef Massimottavio Minicucci struck out on his own to open this place. He hand-built the stone oven, which bakes his Neapolitan-style pizzas to perfection. What I like about his pizzas is the crust: soft, pillowy, and perfectly spot-charred around the edges."
—Michael Kleindl

LA PICCOLA TAVOLA

4-2-4 Eifuku
Suginami
Tokyo 168-0064
Japan
+81 359300008
www.piccolatavola.com

Opening hours...Closed Monday
Credit cards...Accepted
Style of pizza.......................................Thin-crust Neapolitan
Recommended pizza................Margherita with Parma Ham
and Arugula (rocket)

"This was the first pizzeria in Tokyo to be granted
the VPN license. The crusts are thin and crisp, and
cooked to perfection in the large stone oven at the
front of the charming restaurant."—Michael Kleindl

"The ambience and the atmosphere are wonderful."
—Ohata Katsutoshi

PIZZERIA YUICIRO & A

1F Tachikawa Inoue Building
1-30-21 Akebono-cho
Tachikawa
Tokyo 190-0012
Japan
+81 425129570
www.yuiciro-a.com

Opening hours...Closed Monday
Credit cards...Accepted
Style of pizza...Neapolitan
Recommended pizza...Marinara

JAPAN'S NEAPOLITAN PIZZA OBSESSION

According to regulations set by the VPN Association the dough for true Neapolitan pizza must be made with flour highly refined to the *doppio zero* ("00") grade. It should have a final pH level of 5.8 and density of 0.79 grams per cubic centimeter. Once shaped by hand into a base no thicker in the middle than 0.4 centimeters (less than $1/6$ inch), and garnished with only approved ingredients, the pizza has to be baked in a wood-fired oven at a minimum temperature of 905°F (485°C). The finished Margherita pizza is soft and elastic, its mozzarella appearing over the tomato in evenly spread white patches.

In Japan the number of pizza places proudly displaying the VPN seal of approval is 54, placing them third among pizza-loving nations, behind only Italy, with 200, and the USA, with 77. France, Germany, and the UK each have one. The artisans in those countries attempting pizza the Neapolitan way either can't make the grade or can't be bothered to try. "The Japanese pizza makers need something to show they've achieved a very high standard," explains Rossella Ceccarini, who holds a PhD in global studies from Sophia University in Tokyo and is author of *Pizza and Pizza Chefs in Japan: A Case of Culinary Globalization*. "This certifies the authenticity of what they're doing."

Often the Japanese are pursuing a made-in-Naples look, too. Though Neapolitan pizza does not require a Neapolitan-made oven, hundreds of custom-built, wood-fired pizza *forni* have been imported to Japan from Naples. Akio Nishikawa, the Japanese pizza pioneer who apprenticed in Campania under Neapolitan pizza masters Gaetano Esposito and Gaetano Fazio, took home more than lessons learned to Sakuragumi, his Neapolitan pizza shrine in the Hyogo Prefecture. He ordered a custom-built oven by master craftsman Gianni Acunto to bake pizzas made with imported Caputo "00" flour, San Marzano tomatoes, and *Mozzarella di Bufala* Campana DOP. "You have to preserve the tradition if you wish Neapolitans to be moved when they eat your pizza," says Nishikawa.

It is the prize-winning Japanese *pizzaioli* trained in Naples who appear most regularly on Japanese television. But recognition from their Italian masters some 6,000 miles (9,656 km) away is valued more. "They learn from the masters," says Antimo Caputo of Molino Caputo. "They follow everything. They try to be perfect." Akinari "Pasquale" Makishima of Pizzeria Trattoria Cesari in Nagoya adopted his middle name to honor Pasquale Parziale, the first of his Neapolitan mentors. "It is common among Japanese pizza makers who have lived in Italy to be linked to a *maestro pizzaiolo*," notes Ceccarini. "Apprenticeship is highly valued in Japanese society. The disciple copies the *sensei* [teacher]. Only when he has mastered the art is some innovation is allowed."

Years after winning the best *pizzaiolo* prize at the 2010 International Pizza Championship in Naples, Makishima still refuses to modify the instructions of his Neapolitan pizza *sensei*. He won't even cut back on salt to suit prevailing Japanese tastes. "If you reduce the formulation of salt," insists Makishima, "it's no longer pizza Napoletana."

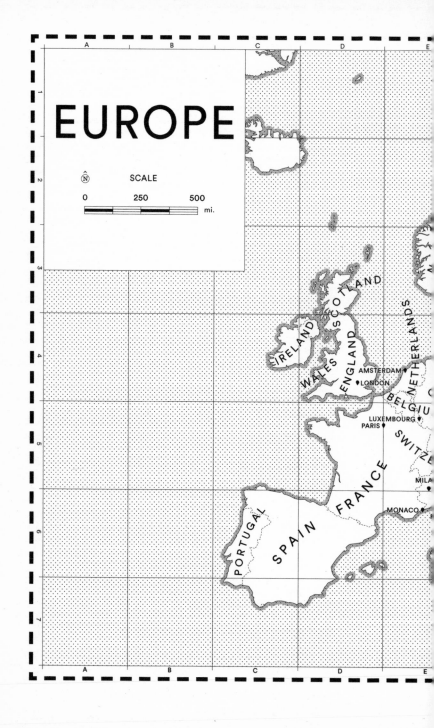

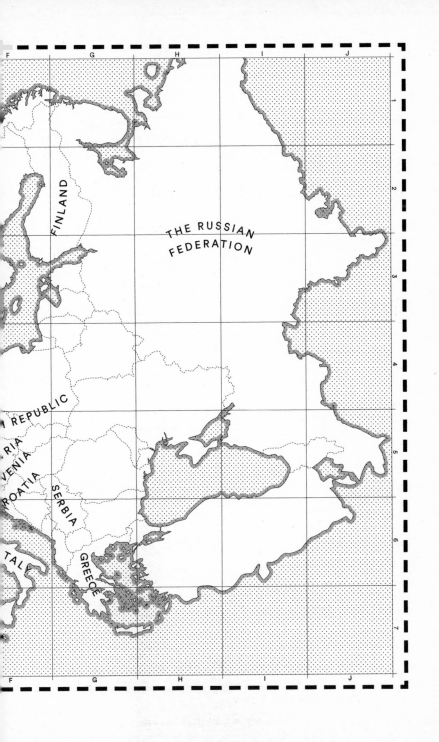

"THE FOOD IS A DARING ATTEMPT TO ASK WHAT PIZZA WOULD HAVE BEEN, HAD IT BEEN INVENTED BY NORWEGIANS." ANDREAS VIESTAD P.124

"FRIDEN GÅRDSKROG IS FRIENDLY, ECCENTRIC, FUN, AND UNUSUAL." MATTIAS KROON P.126

NORWAY, SWEDEN, DENMARK & FINLAND

"IT'S A GREAT PLACE TO SIT AND ENJOY THE LONG SCANDINAVIAN SUMMER NIGHTS." SIKKE SUMARI P.133

"IT'S THE ABSOLUTE BEST PIZZA I HAVE HAD IN DENMARK, IF NOT IN NORTHERN EUROPE." SOFIE WOCHNER P.128

"ON TOP OF THE PIZZAS YOU MAY FIND A WHOLE FISH OR EVEN SOME STRAWBERRIES BUT FUNNILY ENOUGH EVERYTHING TASTES GREAT." MIKKO TAKALA P.133

NORWAY, SWEDEN, DENMARK & FINLAND

SCALE

0   90   180 mi.

NORWAY

SWEDEN

FINLAND

DENMARK

PIRKANMAA P.131

SOUTHWEST FINLAND P.131

UUSIMAA PP.132–133

OSLO PP.124–125

ROGALAND P.125

STOCKHOLM PP.126–128

VASTRA GOTALAND P.128

JÖNKÖPING P.125

HALLAND P.125

HOVEDSTADEN PP.128–131

SCANIA P.126

BALTAZAR

Dronningensgate 27
Oslo
Oslo 0154
Norway
+47 23357060
www.baltazar.no

Opening hours	Closed Sunday
Credit cards	Accepted
Style of pizza	Roman

"Baltazar is a small piece of Italy in Oslo."
—Hector G. Guardia

BRUNELLO PIZZERIA AND RISTORANTE

Stenersgata 10
Oslo
Oslo 0184
Norway
+47 22178880
www.brunellopizzeria.no

Opening hours	Closed Sunday
Credit cards	Accepted but not AMEX
Style of pizza	Neapolitan
Recommended pizza	Bottarga

"Brunello produces a fantastic pizza dough. The crust and acidity of its pizzas are really good."
—Hector G. Guardia

HELL'S KITCHEN

Møllergata 23
Oslo
Oslo 0179
Norway
+47 22112000

Opening hours	Open 7 days
Credit cards	Accepted but not AMEX
Style of pizza	Straight-up
Recommended pizza	Meatballs, Jalapeños, Red Onion, and Cherry Tomatoes

"Noisy and crowded at night, friendly and welcoming from 2 p.m. until around 9 p.m., when the bar crowds arrive. I have eaten here dozens of times and never had, or heard of, a disappointing pizza. There's also a great selection of drinks made by skinny hipster bartenders."—Andreas Viestad

LOFTHUS SAMVIRKELAG

Åsengata 42
Oslo
Oslo 0480
Norway
+47 22600666
www.lofthussamvirkelag.no

Opening hours	Closed Monday and Tuesday
Credit cards	Accepted
Style of pizza	Italian with a Nordic twist
Recommended pizza	Five-cheese; Porcini Mushrooms; Reindeer

"The combinations of ingredients are the most exciting in Norway—truly original."
—Tore Gjesteland & Craig Whitson

Øyvind Lofthus and Emmanuel Rang know about dough. They opened this pizzeria at a branch of Åpent Bakeri, their outstanding Oslo bakery. A second location is at Kongsveien 94 in Oslo's Nordstrand district. "The food is a daring attempt," says Andreas Viestad, "to ask what pizza would have been like had it been invented by Norwegians." The signature pizza, the Reinsdyr, is layered with reindeer carpaccio, pomegranate, and red onion. Other pizzas employ classic Italian toppings. The Fem Oster is a five-cheese pizza with English farmhouse Cheddar, *mozzarella di bufala*, Gouda, Kraftkar (a well-aged Norwegian blue cheese), and a cheese of the day.

MASCHMANNS MATMARKED

Karenslyst Allè 51
Oslo
Oslo 0279
Norway
+47 22553344
www.maschmanns.no

Opening hours	Open 7 days
Credit cards	Accepted
Style of pizza	Classic Italian
Recommended pizza	Margherita

PIZZA DA MIMMO

Behrens' Gate 2
Oslo
Oslo 0257
Norway
+47 22444020
www.pizzadamimmo.no

Opening hours...Open 7 days
Credit cards.................................Accepted but not AMEX
Style of pizza...Italian
Recommended pizza.................................Calabrisella

SKUR 33

Akershusstranda 11
Oslo
Oslo 0150
Norway
+47 23357060
www.skur33.no

Opening hours...Closed Sunday
Credit cards..Accepted
Style of pizza.............................Italian-inspired seafood
Recommended pizza...............Norwegian Lobster and Cod
Cheeks; Seafood

"Dag Tjersland has long been the best Italian chef in Norway. In his newest venture, in a converted warehouse on the waterfront in Oslo harbor, he serves the best seafood pizza in the country—by far. It is a successful blend of quality local ingredients and deep respect for Italian cooking."
—Andreas Viestad

VILLA PARADISO

Olav Ryes Plass 8
Oslo
Oslo 0552
Norway
+47 22354060
www.villaparadiso.no

Opening hours...Open 7 days
Credit cards.................................Accepted but not AMEX
Style of pizza...Italian
Recommended pizza.......................................Cheese

"Authentic Italian-style pizza."—Hilde Gulbrandsen

RENAA XPRESS

Breitorget 6
Stavanger
Rogaland 4006
Norway
+47 51551111
www.restaurantrenaa.no

Opening hours...Open 7 days
Credit cards.................................Accepted but not AMEX
Style of pizza...Italian
Recommended pizza...............................The daily special

"Beniamino Bilala is making different types of Italian pizza, all based on dough using *lieveto madre* (mother dough). His pizzas are the best in Norway and represent the true spirit of Italian pizza."
—Tore Gjesteland & Craig Whitson

PROSTENS PIZZA

Skrea 203
Gamla Prästgården
Falkenberg
Halland 311 97
Sweden
+46 705271873
www.prostenspizza.se

Opening hours.............................Variable (check website)
Credit cards.................................Accepted but not AMEX
Style of pizza.............................Imaginative Swedish hillbilly
Recommended pizza..........New Potato, Vendace Roe, and
Smoked Bone Marrow; Vendace Roe, Sour
Cream, and Dill

"This wood-fired hillbilly pizza joint by celebrity chef Lisa Lemke is open occasionally in the winter and most days in the summer. All the pizzas are named after Iron Maiden songs!"—Olle T. Cellton

SHALOM

Falkgatan 7
Tranås
Jönköping 577 33
Sweden
+46 14010833

Opening hours...Open 7 days
Credit cards...Not accepted
Style of pizza...Tranås
Recommended pizza...................................Mamma Mia

"Order takeout and eat it straight from the box."
—Rasmus Ragnarsson

FRIDEN GÅRDSKROG

Mellby 267
Kivik
Scania 277 35
Sweden
+46 41421036
www.friden.nu

Opening hours.........................Open 7 days (summer); open
weekends (February–December)
Credit cards....................................Accepted but not AMEX
Style of pizza...Italian

"Friden Gårdskrog is friendly, eccentric, fun, and
unusual."—Mattias Kroon

SÖDERBERG & SARA

Örumsvägen 119
Löderup
Scania 271 76
Sweden
+46 411556688
www.soderbergsara.se

Opening hours.........Open 7 days (end June–mid-August);
Closed Monday–Thursday (March–mid-June and end
August–October)
Credit cards....................................Accepted but not AMEX
Style of pizza...Sourdough
Recommended pizza.................................Mushroom

"Söderberg & Sara puts a lot of effort into sourcing
some incredible local ingredients and spends plenty
of time preparing them before they´re ready to put on
the pizza, like the slow- cooked pig."
—Peter Ljungquist

DI PENCO

Roskildevägen 3
Malmö
Scania 211 47
Sweden
+46 40396655
www.penco.se

Opening hours........................Closed Saturday and Sunday
Credit cards....................................Accepted but not AMEX
Style of pizza...Italian

DA ALDO

Mellangatan 47
Skanör
Scania 239 30
Sweden
+46 40474026
www.aldo.se

Opening hours...Open 7 days
Credit cards....................................Accepted but not AMEX
Style of pizza.................................Southern Italian

"Italian Aldo and his Swedish wife Annika run this
place with love and charm. The pizzas are as good as
they can get, very authentic southern Italian style."
—Mattias Kroon

800 GRADER

Sigtunagatan 17
Stockholm
Stockholm 113 22
Sweden
www.800grader.se

Opening hours...Closed Monday
Credit cards..Accepted
Style of pizza...New

THE ARTISAN

Odengatan 78
Stockholm
Stockholm 113 22
Sweden
+46 8316525

Opening hours...Closed Monday
Credit cards....................................Accepted but not AMEX
Style of pizza..Roman

"Here, thick, Roman 'pan-style' pizzas reign. They
have a focaccia-like consistency with fresh seasonal
toppings."—David Lundin

BABETTE
Roslagsgatan 6
Stockholm
Stockholm 113 55
Sweden
+46 850902224
www.babette.se

Opening hours...Open 7 days
Credit cards...Accepted
Style of pizza...Classic artisanal
Recommended pizza.................Ask the chef for his choice
of the day

"Great honest dough, cooked until blistering and then topped with quality toppings. The cheese or meat toppings are often classic Italian, but they often bring in some 'foreign' twists, like harissa, mint, etc." —David Lundin

"Lovely place and people, always packed." —Rasmus Ragnarsson

FORNO AUTO
Food truck—check website, Facebook, and Instagram for upcoming locations
Stockholm
Stockholm
Sweden
+46 704802701
www.fornoauto.se

Opening hours...Closed Monday
Credit cards...Accepted
Style of pizza..Neapolitan
Recommended pizza........................Bianca with Cauliflower

"Amazing and super-fresh pizzas made with great produce."—Zvonko Sokcic

GIRO
Sveavägen 46
Stockholm
Stockholm 111 34
Sweden
+46 84406767
www.giropizzeria.com

Opening hours...Open 7 days
Credit cards...Accepted
Style of pizza..Neapolitan
Recommended pizza...Margherita

"The pizza is fantastic. Celebrity chef Stefano Catenacci flew in a few *pizzaioli* from Naples and built a massive wood-fired oven."—Olle T. Cellton

OMNIPOLLOS HATT
Hökens Gata 3
Stockholm
Stockholm 116 46
Sweden
www.omnipolloshatt.com

Opening hours...Open 7 days
Credit cards...Accepted
Style of pizza.......................................Swedish wood-fired
Recommended pizza................Bacon, Gruyère, and Chervil

"This bar serves excellent wood-fired pizzas and fantastic craft beer to go with them." —Olle T. Cellton

SPECERIET
Artillerigatan 14
Stockholm
Stockholm 114 51
Sweden
+46 86623060
www.speceriet.se

Opening hours..........................Closed Sunday and Monday
Credit cards...Accepted
Style of pizza...Alsatian

TAVERNA BRILLO

Sturegatan 6
Stockholm
Stockholm 114 35
Sweden
+46 851977800
www.tavernabrillo.se/sv

Opening hours...Open 7 days
Credit cards..Accepted
Style of pizza..................................New Neapolitan-Roman
Recommended pizza..............................Porcini Mushrooms,
Prosciutto, Figs, Parmesan, and Tomato

"A nice and busy pizzeria-bistro with a wood -fired oven. The pizzas have a nice char on the edges and new-style toppings."—Kenneth Nars

CYRANO

Prinsgatan 7
Gothenburg
Vastra Gotaland 413 05
Sweden
+46 31143110
www.cyrano.se

Opening hours...Open 7 days
Credit cards..Accepted
Style of pizza...French
Recommended pizza...Roxanne

TRATTORIA ALBEROBELLO

Doterödsvägen 3
Stenungsund
Vastra Gotaland 444 40
Sweden
+46 30380722
www.alberobello.se

Opening hours...Closed Monday
Credit cards.................................Accepted but not AMEX
Style of pizza..Traditional
Recommended pizza...Napoli

"It is not so easy to find a good pizza on the west coast of Sweden. In this scene, Alberobello stands out as the best."—Andrea Consonni

BÆST

Guldbergsgade 29
Copenhagen
Hovedstaden 2200
Denmark
+45 35350463
www.baest.dk

Opening hours...Closed Monday
Credit cards..Accepted
Style of pizza...Neapolitan
Recommended pizza..................Bæst Burrata, Fresh Herbs, and New Garlic; Bæst Mozzarella, Pine Nuts, Potato, and Blue Cornflower; Bæst Mozzarella, Semi-dried Tomatoes, and Parma Ham; Bæst Mozzarella, Ramson, Bæst Ricotta, and Crispy Pork; Pecorino, Pancetta, Leek, and Black Chanterelle; Tomato, Bæst Mozzarella, and Basil

"The crust is particularly spectacular—it's sourdough and baked to perfection, with just enough crunch on the outside and a beautiful bready-softness inside. The ingredients are excellent as well; unusual combinations, all organic, and seasonal. Bæst also makes its own mozzarella. You can tell these pizzas are made with love and attention to detail verging on obsessive. The interior is lovely—kind of a rustic Scandinavian vibe—and the place is always packed."—Rebecca Thandi Norman

"It's the absolute best pizza I have had in Denmark, if not in northern Europe."—Sofie Wochner

"Christian Puglisi (the man behind Manfreds and Relæ) goes back to his Sicilian roots with this lively pizza joint."—Katherine Bont

Bæst is not, chef Christian Puglisi is quick to tell you, a pizzeria. It's a restaurant with a heavy focus on organic meats and produce that just happens to bake world-class pizza. Puglisi suggests diners have a few bites of pizza as part of American chef Kris Schram's nine-dish tasting menu. But if a group of friends is coming in only for pizza he recommends they order one at a time, sharing a Margherita first, a white pizza—perhaps the one with Bæst burrata, fresh herbs and spring garlic—second, and so on. In this way the thin-crusted pizza is enjoyed at its hottest, freshest best. For another kind of pizza, Mirabelle, Bæst's adjoining bakery, has rafts of Roman-style *pizza al taglio* ready to go.

LA FIORITA

Charlotte Ammundsens Plads 2, kld.
Copenhagen
Hovedstaden 1359
Denmark
+45 33339960
www.pizzalafiorita.com

Opening hours...Open 7 days
Credit cards.................................Accepted but not AMEX
Style of pizza...Traditional Italian
Recommended pizza....................................Margherita

"Don't be fooled by the simple appearance of this pizzeria—it is one of the best ones in Copenhagen. A local favorite, this small place only has a couple of seatings inside, but on a warm summer evening, the outdoor tables make for a perfect low-key dinner. Its homemade tomato sauce is the best I've ever tasted."—Nana Hagel

GORM'S

Magstræde 16
Copenhagen
Hovedstaden 1204
Denmark
+45 33161292
www.gormspizza.dk

Opening hours...Open 7 days
Credit cards...Accepted
Style of pizza...Nordic
Recommended pizza...........................Gorm's Hottie

"One of the best pizzas I have ever eaten was at Gorm's. This young chef can be considered the inventor of a new Nordic-style gastronomic pizza." —Vincent Delmas

LAGANO

Dronningens Tværgade 22
Copenhagen
Hovedstaden 1302
Denmark
+45 33130814
www.lagano.dk

Opening hours...Open 7 days
Credit cards...Not accepted
Style of pizza...Thick base
Recommended pizza....................................Officiale

"It's small but always bustling and offers a variety of pizzas with simple but thoughtful topping combinations."—Katherine Bont

MEYERS BAGERI

Gammel Kongevej 103
Copenhagen
Hovedstaden 1850
Denmark
+45 35301512
www.meyersmad.dk

Opening hours...Open 7 days
Credit cards...Accepted
Style of pizza...Neapolitan
Recommended pizza.............Air-dried Pork Cheeks, Green
Asparagus, and Ramsons

"Pizzas are made with organic flour and 10 percent stone-milled wholegrain Ølands wheat, giving it a distinct flavor. Choose pizzas with Scandinavian ingredients—they change along with the seasons." —Jonas Astrup

MOTHER

Høkerboderne 9–15
Copenhagen
Hovedstaden 1712
Denmark
+45 22275898
www.mother.dk

Opening hours...Open 7 days
Credit cards................................Accepted but not AMEX
Style of pizza.....................................Neapolitan sourdough
Recommended pizza............Burning Love; Gorgonzola and
'Nduja; Porcella; Zuccone

"Located in the buzzing Meatpacking district, Mother offers Naples-style sourdough pizza from wood-fired ovens. Expect pizzas with distinct bread-flavor and classic combination toppings of organic ingredients."
—Jonas Astrup

"I love the touch of a little pot of basil on the table that you can pick fresh for your pizza."
—Desiree Koh

"This was really the first gourmet pizzeria in Copenhagen, paving the way for all the restaurants that cropped up after. The fact that it's still popular speaks volumes. I've gotten the same pizza from here for years and am not planning on changing any time soon."—Rebecca Thandi Norman

In Copenhagen, the mother of gourmet pizza and sourcing of A-list Italian ingredients is David Biffani. The chef-proprietor at Mother, a stylish pizzeria-plus in the Meatpacking district, has Rome in his blood but Naples in his organic sourdough pizzas. Sixteen pizza combinations feature on the menu, including one called David Says It's Even Better, with tomato, mozzarella, spicy spring broccoli, and soft salami from the Marche region of Italy. But some can't stray very far from the potent Gorgonzola and 'Nduja pairing, with tomato and mozzarella as well as Gorgonzola and 'nduja, the spicy, spreadable salami from Calabria.

NEIGHBOURHOOD

Istedgade 27
Copenhagen
Hovedstaden 1656
Denmark
+45 32122212
www.neighbourhood.dk

Opening hours...Open 7 days
Credit cards................................Accepted but not AMEX
Style of pizza...Thin-crust
Recommended pizza....................................Pumpkin Sausage

"This is really innovative pizza—served on a board so big and wide it looks like you're getting a salad. The crust is very thin; it's really just a satisfying crunch to go with your pile of seasonal, organic, and local vegetables, meats, and cheeses."
—Rebecca Thandi Norman

PIZZA HUSET

Gothersgade 21
Copenhagen
Hovedstaden 1123
Denmark
+45 33153510
www.pizzahuset.dk

Opening hours...Open 7 days
Credit cards................................Accepted but not AMEX
Style of pizza.....................Late night pizza and sandwiches
Recommended pizza....................................Contadina; Roma

"Located on the busy Gothersgade, Pizza Huset can get pretty hectic on the weekends. Bust through the crowds into the tiny shop and choose from its range of pizzas, with some monthly specials like porchetta pizza. It is also renowned for its pizza sandwiches, where a small ball of pizza dough is baked into a soft square bun and filled with anything your heart desires."—Katherine Bont

MEYERS SPISEHUS

Lyngby Hovedgade 49
Kongens Lyngby
Hovedstaden 2800
Denmark
+45 72301331
www.meyersmad.dk

Opening hours...Open 7 days
Credit cards...Accepted
Style of pizza...Nordic
Recommended pizza.................Mozzarella, New Potatoes,
       Rosemary, Salted Bacon, and Smoked Cheese

"The pizzas are made with seasonal ingredients and homemade charcuterie."—Claus Meyer

PIZZERIA NAPOLI

Aleksanterinkatu 31
Tampere
Pirkanmaa 33100
Finland
+358 32238887
www.pizzerianapoli.fi

Opening hours.....................................Closed Sunday
Credit cards...Accepted
Style of pizza...Roman
Recommended pizza.......................................Verona

"Pizzeria Napoli has 100 pizzas on the menu."
—Alex Nieminen

OSTERIA OVO

Linnankatu 1
Turku
Southwest Finland 20100
Finland
+358 469222488
www.osteriaovo.fi

Opening hours....................................Closed Monday
Credit cards.....................................Accepted but not AMEX
Style of pizza...Neapolitan
Recommended pizza....................................The tasting menu

"The best Neapolitan pizzas in Finland."
—Saku Tuominen

PIZZARIUM

Hansakortteli, Kultatalo 3rd Floor
Aurakatu 12A
Turku
Southwest Finland 20100
Finland
+358 504105920
www.pizzarium.fi

Opening hours...Open 7 days
Credit cards...Accepted
Style of pizza...*Pizza al taglio*
Recommended pizza..............Amatriciana; Napoli; Tasting
            menu of small slices from the daily selection

"The food court of a shopping mall is hardly a place where you'd expect to find the best pizza in Finland. Yet, Pizzarium has a huge loyal fan base. Luca, the *pizzaiolo*, is originally from Rome and he has brought Roman-style *pizza al taglio* to pizza fans in Finland. The dough is proofed for a minimum of 48 hours and the toppings—whether classic or modern—always take your breath away."—Alex Nieminen

TINTÅ

Läntinen Rantakatu 9
Turku
Southwest Finland 20100
Finland
+358 22307023
www.tinta.fi

Opening hours...Open 7 days
Credit cards...Accepted
Style of pizza.............Oval thin pizza with luxury toppings
Recommended pizza...........Pear and Peltolan Blue Cheese

"Tintå is a very popular wine bar in the center of Turku that overlooks the river Aura."
—Mariaana Nelimarkka

ALFONS' PIZZA

Vuorimiehenkatu 35
Helsinki
Uusimaa 00150
Finland
+358 9626707
www.alfonspizza.fi

Opening hours	Open 7 days
Credit cards	Accepted
Style of pizza	Finnish-Italian thin-crust
Recommended pizza	Alfons' Margherita; Alichino; Capricciosa; Pulcino

"Pizza fans flock to Alfons' Pizza from all around Helsinki."—Alex Nieminen

"An unpretentious place with a neighborhood feel. Simple pizzas but tasty."—Tony Ilmoni

"This is a fresh venue on Helsinki's pizza scene that works really nicely. The tasty pizza has spelt in the crust, making it crunchy and healthy, too."
—Mariaana Nelimarkka

Anywhere else in Helsinki, Alfons, with its bare brick walls, narrow French oak tables, whitewashed floor, and blackboard messages, would be a hipster coffee shop. But only here in the Ullanlinna district is it a small, cozy, groovy neighborhood pizza shop with a loyal, city-wide following. The big draw is the organic spelt in the dough, which gives the thin, sourdough crust a mildly sweet, almost nutty flavor. The Alfons' Margherita adds sun-dried tomato and red onion to the traditional tricolore. The Pulcino blends Gorgonzola and mozzarella with walnuts and marinated pizza.

FORNITALY

Jollaksentie 54B
Helsinki
Uusimaa 00850
Finland
+358 404692258

Opening hours	Closed Sunday–Thursday
Credit cards	Accepted but not AMEX
Style of pizza	Traditional Italian
Recommended pizza	Diavola

"Fornitaly is open only Friday and Saturday but it is worth waiting the whole week for a good thing! Three Italian pizza professionals prepare authentic Italian pizzas in an old barn and you can either take the pizza away or eat it sitting somewhere on the cliffs around the barn."—Sikke Sumari

PJAZZA

Yrjönkatu 18B
Helsinki
Uusimaa 00120
Finland
+358 105812883
www.pjazza.fi

Opening hours	Open 7 days
Credit cards	Accepted but not AMEX
Style of pizza	Roman
Recommended pizza	Diavola; Margherita; Napoli

"The pizzas are thin and crisp, garnished with quality toppings. They are easy to digest because the dough is made of top-quality ingredients, and they leave it to rise for a minimum of 72 hours, and even up to 96 hours. This way, once the food reaches your stomach it's no longer fermenting."—Arto Koskelo

"During the evenings some serious jazz bands take to the stage."—Kenneth Nars

PUTTE'S

Kalevankatu 6
Helsinki
Uusimaa 00100
Finland
+358 102818243
www.puttes.fi

Opening hours	Open 7 days
Credit cards	Accepted
Style of pizza	Helsinki underground
Recommended pizza	Cold-smoked Pike with Raisins and Capers; Margherita; Puttanesca; Salami; Silence of the Lambs

"Well-made classic pizzas as well as some new versions, like smoked pike pizza. The venue, run by chef-artist Antto Melasniemi, is a cool bar that turns into a DJ-club downstairs after midnight."
—Kenneth Nars

The name of this hot spot in central Helsinki puts the bar first and pizza second, crediting its arty, East Berlin-inspired vibe ahead of the crisp-on-the-outside, soft-on-the-inside pizza crust. Putte's is the brainchild of Antto Melasniemi, the celebrity chef behind the restaurants Atelje Finne and Kuurna. He says the dough matures for two to three days. Slight exaggeration or not, the proof is in the pleasant chewiness of the pizzas. The combinations are classic Italian, with a couple of new-Nordic exceptions. Melasniemi is especially proud to have introduced cold-smoked pike and foraged greens as toppings, with the option of a gluten-free base.

RIVOLETTO

Albertinkatu 38
Helsinki
Uusimaa 00180
Finland
+358 9607455
www.rivoletto.fi

Opening hours..Open 7 days
Credit cards...Accepted
Style of pizza....................................Helsinki-Mediterranean
Recommended pizza................................Pescatore; Rivoletto

"Rivoletto is a true Helsinki classic, one of the first better-quality pizzerias in Finland running since the 1970s. Its pizzas have a light crispy base and fillings are used in modest amounts, enabling the thin dough to rise properly. It also serves a nice selection of antipasti and desserts."—Antto Melasniemi

SKIFFER

Erottaja 11
Helsinki
Uusimaa 00100
Finland
+358 453445351
www.skiffer.fi

Opening hours..Open 7 days
Credit cards...Accepted
Style of pizza..Innovative
Recommended pizza..................CCCP; Buffalo Mozzarella

"The most important thing in a pizza is the dough and Skiffer nails it. Its pizzas are rustic in appearance, like a pizza should be, but come with creative toppings that often use locally sourced ingredients."—Arto Koskelo

"On top of the pizzas you may find a whole fish or even some strawberries but funnily enough every-thing tastes great."—Mikko Takala

SKIFFER

Liuskaluoto
Helsinki
Uusimaa 00140
Finland
+358 451868933
www.skiffer.fi

Opening hours..Open 7 days
Credit cards....................................Accepted but not AMEX
Style of pizza...............................Trendy, inventive thin-crust
Recommended pizza..................................Tomato; Soignon

"Skiffer Liuskaluoto is situated on a small island in front of Helsinki. It opens only during the summer-time for alfresco dining. The five minutes you spend on a boat to get there make a great difference, and the oval-shaped pizzas with some unusual toppings are tastier here than anywhere else. For me, a perfect summer day means a pizza with chèvre, strawberries, basil, and pine nuts enjoyed with a craft beer."—Mariaana Nelimarkka

"It's a great place to sit and enjoy the long Scandinavian summer nights. The pizzas are thin and the toppings are fun and inventive like strawberries and goat cheese."—Sikke Sumari

CHRISTIAN PUGLISI
MASTERS MOZZARELLA

Christian Puglisi had an epiphany on a vacation visit to Tenuta Vannulo, a producer of organic *mozzarella di bufala* in the mozzarella mecca of Paestum in the Campania region of southern Italy. The acclaimed chef at Relæ in Copenhagen gave a ball of mozzarella a playful squeeze. White juice squirted out. "This was so different than anything I ever expected," recalls Puglisi. "It was juicy and bouncy, not soft and creamy. It wasn't falling apart. It had many layers inside the curd."

Until then Puglisi had been perfectly happy with organic *mozzarella di bufala* imported to Denmark from Italy. It too was from Campania. It too had DOP (Denominazione d'Origine Protetta) certification. Now he could not imagine laying it over the pizzas at Bæst, the Italian-inspired restaurant taking shape in his mind, if not yet on the ground. The only way to share the experience of buffalo mozzarella consumed within meters and minutes from where it was made was to produce his own, even if that required his substituting cow's milk for buffalo milk. If he succeeded, Bæst would join Pizzeria Bianco in Phoenix, Arizona, and Kesté in New York in a small but growing club of pizza restaurants making their own mozzarella.

The first batches made in the small dairy installed directly above the eventual site of the Bæst dining room and kitchen were, recalls Puglisi, "bad, bad, bad." Returning in desperation to Campania and Caseificio Il Casolare, a producer of both *mozzarella di bufala* and *fior di latte*, as cow's milk mozzarella is known in Italy, he made a discovery. The two cheeses were handled differently. For his *fior di latte*, master cheesemaker Mimmo La Vecchia, a supplier to several top pizzerias in the region, sought a firmer product, with less juice.

Puglisi adopted Mimmo's cow's milk mozzarella as a model for his own, but only to a point. He never tried to duplicate it. This is not the chef's way. He prefers to examine the tradition and craft of classic foods and then make them new, exciting, personal. Years ago Puglisi assumed pizza should be crispy. Then he fell for soft Neapolitan pizza. For the pizza at Bæst, crisp spots with a bit of burn would contrast with the softness of a crust. The *cornicione* crafted by *pizzaiolo* Giuseppe Oliva would not swell as much as those brought to life in the Naples style. The bubbles would be smaller. "Some say pizza should be crispy," says Puglisi. "Some say it should be soft. No, pizza should be how you want it to be."

Puglisi decided his pizza cheese would have more fat and cream than was typically found in *fior di latte*. Back in his dairy to test yet another trial run, he squeezed a fresh ball and, eureka, white juice squirted out. Two years after he'd embarked on his mozzarella mission the Danish chef was finally ready to open Bæst.

> "THE DOUGH IS A THING OF WONDER."
> LEE BURNS P.141

> "THE VIEWS OUT TO SEA FROM NEWQUAY'S FISTRAL RESTAURANT ARE STUNNING."
> ELLIE MICHELL P.138

UK & REPUBLIC OF IRELAND

> "PETER'S YARD PIZZAS HAVE A THIN AND YEASTY SOURDOUGH BASE WITH CRISPY, BUBBLY FLOUR-DUSTED EDGES."
> GABY SOUTAR P.150

> "LOOKING FOR ALL THE WORLD LIKE A SMALL NEIGHBORHOOD CAFE, THERE'S NOTHING ON ENTERING CALABRISELLA THAT PREPARES YOU FOR THE FOOD IT IS CAPABLE OF SERVING."
> KIRSTIE MCCRUM P.151

> "THE TASTIEST PIZZA I'VE EVER EATEN."
> BEN DAVY P.142

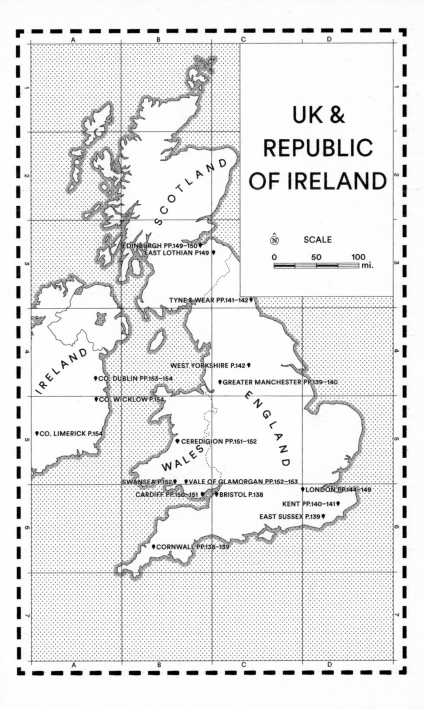

UK &
REPUBLIC
OF IRELAND

N̂   SCALE

0   50   100
━━━━━━━━━━━━ mi.

SCOTLAND

EDINBURGH PP.149–150♥
EAST LOTHIAN P.149 ♥

TYNE & WEAR PP.141–142 ♥

IRELAND

WEST YORKSHIRE P.142 ♥

♥CO. DUBLIN PP.153–154   ♥GREATER MANCHESTER PP.139–140 ♥

♥CO. WICKLOW P.154

ENGLAND

♥CO. LIMERICK P.154

♥CEREDIGION PP.151–152

WALES

SWANSEA P.152♥   ♥VALE OF GLAMORGAN PP.152–153
CARDIFF PP.150–151 ♥   ♥BRISTOL P.138   ♥LONDON PP.144–149 ♥
                                                KENT PP.140–141♥
                                                EAST SUSSEX P.139 ♥

♥CORNWALL PP.138–139

BERTHA'S PIZZA

Food truck—check website, Facebook, and Twitter for
upcoming locations
Bristol
England
+44 7917752853
www.berthas.co.uk

Opening hours...Variable
Credit cards...Not accepted
Style of pizza...Sourdough
Recommended pizza........................Fennel Fest; Margherita

"Great sourdough pizza served from a bright yellow
Land Rover. These hand-stretched pizzas have been
pleasing hoards of Bristolians for the past two years."
—Samantha Evans

KERNOWFORNO

Pop-up pizzeria—check website, Facebook, and
Twitter for upcoming locations
Lostwithiel
Cornwall
England
+44 7824325633
www.kernowforno.co.uk

Opening hours...Variable
Credit cards...Not accepted
Style of pizza...Wood-fired
Recommended pizza..............Middle Eastern Lamb Ragout
Topped with Crumbled Feta Cheese

"The bases of Kernowforno's wood-fired pizzas
are thin and crispy; the toppings are generous and
full of flavor. Simon and Sarah Pryce's mobile pizza
company appears at regular pitches in Cornwall,
as well as at festivals and events across the West
Country. Simon makes all the bases and tomato sauce
to authentic Italian recipes, and it takes just two
minutes to cook each pizza in the wood-fired pizza
oven."—Ellie Michell

THE STABLE

Fistral Beach
Headland Road
Newquay
Cornwall
TR7 1HY
England
+44 1637878311
www. stablepizza.com/locations/the-stable-fistral-
beach

Opening hours...Open 7 days
Credit cards.....................................Accepted but not AMEX
Style of pizza...Organic sourdough
Recommended pizza...Billy the Kid

"The Stable has eight restaurants across the West
Country and the views out to sea from Newquay's
Fistral restaurant are stunning. The organic sourdough
pizza bases are heaped with brilliant combinations of
locally sourced ingredients and accompanied by
a wide range of ciders."—Ellie Michell

ROJANO'S IN THE SQUARE

9 Mill Square
Padstow
Cornwall
PL28 8AE
England
+44 1841532796
www.rojanos.co.uk

Opening hours...Open 7 days
Credit cards.....................................Accepted but not AMEX
Style of pizza.....................................Stone-baked sourdough
Recommended pizza..............Spicy Sausage; White Shrimp

"Dubbed by Heston Blumenthal as 'the best pizzas
outside Italy,' Rojano's stone-baked sourdough pizza
bases are charred and crisp, topped with homemade
pomodoro tomato sauce and mozzarella, and heaped
with super-fresh ingredients."—Ellie Michell

WILDBAKE

Mobile pizzeria—check website, Facebook, and Twitter
for upcoming locations
Wadebridge
Cornwall
England
+44 7707082415
www.wildbake.co.uk

Opening hours...Variable
Credit cards..Not accepted
Style of pizza..Wood-fired
Recommended pizza.....................................Weekly special

"Lewis and Claire Cole run their pizza restaurant,
Wildbake, from a converted horse trailer, which pops
up at regular spots in towns and campsites, and at
festivals and events across Cornwall. The dough
bases are all handmade before being cooked to order
in the mobile wood-fired oven, and customers can
pre-order their pizzas in advance to avoid missing
out. The menu features weekly specials, many of
which include foraged ingredients, and their sweet
dessert pizzas are inspired."—Ellie Michell

PIZZAFACE

35 Saint George's Road
Brighton
East Sussex
BN2 1ED
England
+44 1273699082
www. pizzafacepizza.co.uk

Opening hours...Open 7 days
Credit cards..............................Accepted but not AMEX
Style of pizza..Wood-fired
Recommended pizza...Albore

"Pizzaface has a fun and contemporary feel and the
ingredients are great, really high quality and well
considered."—Emma Wilcox

THE HEARTH PIZZERIA

Eastgate
Lewes
East Sussex
BN7 2LP
England
+44 1273470755
www.thehearth.co

Opening hours...Closed Sunday
Credit cards..Accepted
Style of pizza...Neapolitan
Recommended pizza..Holy Grail

"The Hearth Pizzeria is all about the dough with
third-generation baker Michael Hanson at the helm.
Local produce features heavily and even the dough
starter contains some of the town brewer's (Harvey's)
barm. There's also a lot of heart and charm about
the place. It's not glossy or stylized in any way, but
somehow it feels the right sort of place in which to
enjoy the rustic and authentic Neapolitan pizza."
—Fran Villani

HONEST CRUST

Market House
Greenwood Street
Altrincham
Greater Manchester
WA14 1SA
England
+44 7717725980
www.honestcrustpizza.co.uk

Opening hours...Closed Monday
Credit cards..Accepted
Style of pizza...Sourdough
Recommended pizza..............Bianca; Margherita; Smoked
Pig's Cheek

"Two guys who really love pizza and deliver a
consistently excellent product. Their passion shines
through their food."—Ben Davy

RUDY'S NEAPOLITAN PIZZA

9 Cotton Street
Manchester
Greater Manchester
M4 5DH
England
+44 7940577932

Opening hours..Closed Monday
Credit cards...Accepted
Style of pizza...Neapolitan
Recommended pizza..Margherita

"Great dough, lovely flavor combinations."
—Richard Carver

POSILLIPO

14 Albion Street
Broadstairs
Kent
CT10 1LU
England
+44 1843601133
www.posillipo.co.uk

Opening hours..Open 7 days
Credit cards...Accepted
Style of pizza...Neapolitan
Recommended pizza...............Marinara; Posillipo; Romana;
Sausage

"The service is great and the pizzas are very tasty—
the menu has lots of other Neapolitan dishes too so
masses of choice including plenty of fish to reflect
the seaside location. All of the portions are generous
and the focaccia is delicious. It has a good kids'
menu, too, with all of the crowd-pleasers at a sensible
size."—Emma Wilcox

POSILLIPO

Provender Mill
Belvedere Road
Faversham
Kent
ME13 7LD
England
+44 1795590580
www.posillipo.co.uk

Opening hours..Open 7 days
Credit cards...Accepted
Style of pizza...Neapolitan
Recommended pizza...San Martino

"Posillipo has three branches in Kent and the
Faversham one is my favorite. The pizzas have
good-quality toppings with a good char on top and
more underneath, and the welcoming and attentive
staff and variety of seating overlooking the river all
go toward making Posillipo a great experience."
—Bruno Breillet

IL PADRINO

23 Stone Street
Gravesend
Kent
DA11 0NP
England
+44 1474320066
www.ilpadrino-restaurant.com

Opening hours..Closed Monday
Credit cards.................................Accepted but not AMEX
Style of pizza...Traditional Italian
Recommended pizza..........................Anchovies and Capers

"The restaurant is an oasis in the middle of Gravesend
and a good place to start the Kent pizza trail right
outside London."—Bruno Breillet

A CASA MIA

160 High Street
Herne Bay
Kent
CT6 5AJ
England
+44 1227372947
www.acasamia.co.uk

Opening hours	Open 7 days
Credit cards	Accepted but not AMEX
Style of pizza	Neapolitan
Recommended pizza	Casa Mia; Diavola; Margherita

"This little seaside pizzeria has been rewarded accreditation from the VPN Association, whose aim is to protect the 'true Neapolitan pizza.' It's the only pizzeria in the UK to have been granted this coveted certification."—Laura Nickoll

"It's the kind of Italian restaurant where I genuinely want to try everything on the menu."—Bruno Breillet

GB PIZZA CO.

14A Marine Drive
Margate
Kent
CT9 1DH
England
+44 1843297700
www.greatbritishpizza.com

Opening hours	Open 7 days
Credit cards	Accepted
Style of pizza	Wood-fired thin-crust
Recommended pizza	Chorizo and Chile; Margaterita

"Set on the seafront in Margate with views over the beach and sea, GB Pizza Co. has a really laid-back vibe, great music, wonderful staff, and superb pizza. It has a short list of regular pizzas as well as seasonal specials and uses British charcuterie too."
—Emma Wilcox

SCREAM FOR PIZZA

Food truck—check Facebook and Twitter for upcoming locations
Gateshead
Tyne and Wear
England
+44 7944715714

Opening hours	Variable
Credit cards	Not accepted
Style of pizza	Neapolitan
Recommended pizza	The Mountie

"Two girls, one oven. Excellent toppings and flavor combos."—Ben Davy

CAL'S OWN

207 Chillingham Road
Newcastle upon Tyne
Tyne and Wear
NE6 5LJ
England
+44 1912765298
www.calsown.co.uk

Opening hours	Closed on Monday
Credit cards	Accepted
Style of pizza	Brooklyn
Recommended pizza	White Pie

"Run by Calvin Kitchin, Cal's Own (geddit?) does by miles the best pizza I've had in Newcastle. The dough is a thing of wonder, the slow proving process resulting in something crisp and chewy all at once. There are four basic pizzas available, which can be added to with extra toppings, all extremely high quality. Calvin is clearly fanatical about good pizza and it shows in the product. Go during the week— you've more chance of getting a table."—Lee Burns

"As far as I know, Cal is the only person in Newcastle making proper Brooklyn pizzas. They are truly fabulous. And his white pizza is best of all."
—Secret Diner

SLICE

Aisle 4
Grainger Market
Newcastle upon Tyne
Tyne and Wear
NE1 5QG
England

Opening hours	Closed Sunday
Credit cards	Not accepted
Style of pizza	Neapolitan
Recommended pizza	Italian Meatball

"It's cheap and it tastes great, which is what most good pizza should aspire to I think. Expect a line at lunchtime."—Lee Burns

DOUGH BOYS

Belgrave Music Hall and Canteen
1–1A Cross Belgrave Street
Leeds
West Yorkshire
LS2 8JP
England
+44 1132346160
www.doughboyspizza.co.uk

Opening hours	Open 7 days
Credit cards	Accepted
Style of pizza	Neapolitan
Recommended pizza	Baa No More

"Forward-thinking and imaginative toppings with nods to some of the classics. Literally the tastiest pizza I've ever eaten."—Ben Davy

FRIZZA

Pop-up pizzeria—check website for upcoming locations
Leeds
West Yorkshire
England
+44 7870241825
www.frizza.uk

Opening hours	Variable
Credit cards	Not accepted
Style of pizza	*Pizza fritta*
Recommended pizza	Panzerotti

"It's great to see classic Neapolitan street food being recreated in the UK. Fried pizza really is a wonderful thing."—Ben Davy

SALVO'S

115 & 107 Otley Road
Leeds
West Yorkshire
LS6 3PX
England
+44 1132752752
www.salvos.co.uk

Opening hours	Open 7 days
Credit cards	Accepted but not AMEX
Style of pizza	Traditional Italian
Recommended pizza	Buongiorno

"Just straight-up pizza heroes. Good flavor, good dough, great pizza."—Ben Davy

"THIS IS A HIP PIZZA TAKEOUT SPOT (IT ALSO DELIVERS) THAT KEEPS IT SIMPLE, WITH JUST FIVE PIZZAS ON OFFER, AND TWO SIZES."

LAURA NICKOLL P.147

"KNOCKOUT NEAPOLITAN-INSPIRED PIZZAS ARE COOKED AT THIS INFORMAL SOHO EATERY."

ED GILBERT P.149

LONDON

"THE MARINARA IS THE SILKIEST PIECE OF HEAVEN YOU'LL EVER EAT."

HELEN GRAVES P.149

"THIS TRULY IS A LOCAL SECRET THAT YOU ONLY TELL TO VERY GOOD FRIENDS."

BRUNO BREILLET P.148

"L'ANTICA PIZZERIA LIVES UP TO ITS REP: IT'S LONDON'S NUMBER ONE!"

MERRY WHITE P.148

LONDON

Ⓝ SCALE

0   500   1000   1500
                        yd.

1. SANTA MARIA, EALING (P.147)
2. SAPORITALIA, NOTTING HILL (P.148)
3. SACRO CUORE, KENSAL RISE (P.148)
4. L'ANTICA PIZZERIA, HAMPSTEAD (P.148)
5. ROSSOPOMODORO, CAMDEN (P.146)
6. PIZZA PILGRIMS, SOHO (P.149)
7. HOMESLICE, COVENT GARDEN (P.146)
8. ADDOMMÉ PIZZERIA AND
   TRATTORIA, STREATHAM HILL (P.149)
9. BRAVI RAGAZZI, STREATHAM (P.149)
10. FRANCO MANCA, BRIXTON (P.146)
11. SAPORE ITALIANO, LIMEHOUSE (P.148)
12. PIZZA EAST, SHOREDITCH (P.148)
13. STORY, BETHNAL GREEN (P.146)
14. SODO, HACKNEY (P.147)
15. LORD MORPETH, BOW (P.146)
16. YARD SALE PIZZA, HACKNEY (P.147)
17. LARDO, HACKNEY (P.147)

KENSAL
RISE

NOTTING
HILL

CAMDEN

SOHO

COVENT
GARDEN

SHOREDITCH

BETHNAL GREEN

STORY

123 Bethnal Green Road
Bethnal Green
London
E2 7DG
England
+44 7918197352
www.storydeli.com

Opening hours...Open 7 days
Credit cards...Not accepted
Style of pizza...Flatbread
Recommended pizza...........................Fast Eddie; Fico

"It sources the best local ingredients possible and
then top its incredibly thin-crust pizza, which is more
like a flatbread. The toppings are what makes this
pizza amazing and they are a potpourri of veggies,
meats, and cheeses that just mingle perfectly in the
oven and into your stomach."—Daniel Gray

LORD MORPETH

402 Old Ford Road
Bow
London
E3 5NR
England
+44 2089803012
www.lordmorpeth.co.uk

Opening hours...Open 7 days
Credit cards...........................Accepted but not AMEX
Style of pizza...Neapolitan
Recommended pizza...Morpeth

"The Lord Morpeth is a pretty cool little hipster pub
that dishes out beautiful Neapolitan-style pizzas."
—Dan Clapson

FRANCO MANCA

Unit 4, Market Row
Brixton
London
SW9 8LD
England
+44 2077383021
www.francomanca.co.uk

Opening hours...Open 7 days
Credit cards...Accepted
Style of pizza.......................................Italian sourdough
Recommended pizza.......................Tomato, Cured Organic
Chorizo, and Mozzarella

"A London institution, and with good reason.
No bookings, only great pizza to eat in or take away.
It's not showy, but it's damn good."—Ailbhe Malone

ROSSOPOMODORO

10 Jamestown Road
Camden
London
NW1 7BY
England
+44 2074249900
www.rossopomodoro.co.uk

Opening hours...Open 7 days
Credit cards...Accepted
Style of pizza...Neapolitan
Recommended pizza...................................Quattro Formaggi

"Good dough and good-quality ingredients, quick
service, and good presentation of food with nice
fresh burrata."—Alessandro Betti

HOMESLICE

13 Neal's Yard
Covent Garden
London
WC2H 9DP
England
+44 2031517488
www.homeslicepizza.co.uk

Opening hours...Open 7 days
Credit cards.............................Accepted but not AMEX
Style of pizza...Neapolitan

"Homeslice combines technical proficiency with daring
ingredients and bold flavors to create delicious,
salty bases with unusual toppings. Most of the
combinations don't look like they will work when

you read them on the menu, but without exception once on the table they prove themselves to be tasty, interesting, cleverly thought out, and well balanced. The atmosphere is great, service is friendly and attentive, and the pizzas are unlike anything you will find elsewhere in London."—Julian Rea

SANTA MARIA

15 Saint Mary's Road
Ealing
London
W5 5RA
England
+44 2085791462
www.santamariapizzeria.com

Opening hours	Open 7 days
Credit cards	Accepted but not AMEX
Style of pizza	Neapolitan
Recommended pizza	Margherita; San Giuseppe; Santa Bufalina

"Santa Maria is one for the traditionalists. Small and somewhat out of the way in south Ealing, this team take their pizza very seriously indeed with spectacular results; it is certainly worth the pilgrimage. An absolute must for anyone in London looking for a top-class slice."—Julian Rea

"I always benchmark pizza against the best in Naples and Rome and find this establishment has the best package in the UK in terms of oven, dough, top-quality mozzarella (very rare in the UK) and San Marzano tomatoes—all the essentials for a well-executed Margherita."—Dino Joannides

A recent facelift of this west London pizzeria featured a new Carrara marble counter and a new pizza oven hand-built by a Neapolitan craftsman with *biscotto di Sorrento* clay bricks. But one thing did not change at Santa Maria: you can still see the reflection of the divine in the Margherita's shimmering pools of milky, oozy, salty mozzarella floating over its surface. This pizza, like its demanding co-owners Pasquale Chionchio and Angelo Ambrosio, is Neapolitan to the core, its soft, delicate yet resilient crust holding up to pressure from the beautiful San Marzano DOP tomato sauce as well as from your eager fingers.

LARDO

197–201 Richmond Road
Hackney
London
E8 3NJ
England
+44 2089852683
www.lardo.co.uk

Opening hours	Open 7 days
Credit cards	Accepted but not AMEX
Style of pizza	Hackney

SODO

126 Upper Clapton Road
Hackney
London
E5 9JY
England
+44 2088065626
www.sodopizza.co.uk

Opening hours	Closed Monday
Credit cards	Accepted but not AMEX
Style of pizza	Sourdough
Recommended pizza	Margherita

"Wonderfully chewy sourdough base, with truly delicious tomato sauce (made with canned tomatoes imported from Italy) and melting mozzarella. It doesn't scrimp on sides either—a side salad is made with local leaves, and its affogato is to die for." —Ailbhe Malone

YARD SALE PIZZA

105 Lower Clapton Road
Hackney
London
E5 0NP
England
+44 2036029090
www.yardsalepizza.com

Opening hours	Open 7 days
Credit cards	Accepted
Style of pizza	Stone-baked sourdough
Recommended pizza	Pastrami Half-moon Calzone

"This is a hip pizza takeout spot (it also delivers) that keeps it simple, with just five pizzas on offer, and two sizes. No toppings overload here, just proper mozzarella, the perfect proportion of topping, and a supple wood-fired crust with a pillowy soft center." —Laura Nickoll

L'ANTICA PIZZERIA

66 Heath Street
Hampstead
London
NW3 1DN
England
+44 2074318516
www.anticapizzeria.co.uk

Opening hours	Open 7 days
Credit cards	Accepted
Style of pizza	Neapolitan
Recommended pizza	Dante Alighieri; Ferdinando di Borbone; Giuseppe Garibaldi

"L'Antica's dough is slow-fermented for over 24 hours. The result is an aesthetically pleasing and stunning flavored pizza."—Ed Gilbert

"L'Antica Pizzeria lives up to its rep: it's London's number one!"—Merry White

Luca de Vita and Alessandro Betti have always managed to find capable *pizzaioli* for their little Neapolitan pizzeria in London's Hampstead. None have surpassed Giacomo Guido, from the island of Ischia, near Naples. His crust is divinely light and airy, in the Neapolitan fashion. The only things keeping the weightless Margherita from levitating above the table are its tomato sauce and dreamy mozzarella. Rather than traditional names, the pizzas are named after great Italians in history: Dante Alighieri, Michelangelo, Marcello Mastroianni, etc. But who minds when the pizza is this good? Happily, if you put the menu down and simply ask for a Margherita or a Marinara these people know better than most what you're talking about.

SACRO CUORE

45 Chamberlayne Road
Kensal Rise
London
NW10 3NB
England
+44 2089608558
www.sacrocuore.co.uk

Opening hours	Open 7 days
Credit cards	Accepted but not AMEX
Style of pizza	Neapolitan
Recommended pizza	Margherita; Marinara

"I like the nice dough, fresh ingredients, and relaxed atmosphere."—Alessandro Betti

SAPORE ITALIANO

106 Salmon Lane
Limehouse
London
E14 7PQ
England
+44 2075317492
www.saporeitaliano.co.uk

Opening hours	Open 7 days
Credit cards	Not accepted
Style of pizza	Italian thin-crust
Recommended pizza	Parma and Porcini Mushrooms

"I stumbled upon Sapore Italiano while walking in the area. It's set in an old kebab joint and has only two tables, but all the offerings are absolutely delicious for what is essentially a takeout Italian place. It's unexpected to find such gourmet pizza in such a backstreet area. This truly is a local secret that you only tell to very good friends."—Bruno Breillet

SAPORITALIA

222 Portobello Road
Notting Hill
London
W11 1LJ
England
+44 2072433257
www.saporitalialondon.co.uk

Opening hours	Open 7 days
Credit cards	Accepted but not AMEX
Style of pizza	Neapolitan
Recommended pizza	Saporita

"The islets of mozzarella melt into one another, keeping soft and fluid even minutes after the pizza has been pulled from the wood-fired oven."
—Daniel Young

PIZZA EAST

56 Shoreditch Hight Street
Shoreditch
London
E1 6JJ
England
+44 2077291888
www.pizzaeast.com/shoreditch

Opening hours	Open 7 days
Credit cards	Accepted
Style of pizza	Italian-American
Recommended pizza	Cream, Ricotta, and Sausage

"The dough is amazing. It's just cooked until perfection with a few simple and classic toppings—a perfect pizza in my mind."—David Lundin

PIZZA PILGRIMS

11 Dean Street
Soho
London
W1D 3RP
England
+44 2072878964
www.pizzapilgrims.co.uk

Opening hours	Open 7 days
Credit cards	Accepted
Style of pizza	Neapolitan sourdough
Recommended pizza	'Nduja

"Originally sold out of a truck, Pizza Pilgrims are grassroots pizza lovers. The pizzas are small but perfectly formed, with a just-chewy-enough crust and generous, inventive toppings. The 'Nduja pizza (their signature) is a delight."—Ailbhe Malone

"Knockout Neapolitan-inspired pizzas are cooked at this informal Soho eatery."—Ed Gilbert

BRAVI RAGAZZI

2A Sunnyhill Road
Streatham
London
SW16 2UH
England
+44 2087694966
www.braviragazzi.co.uk

Opening hours	Open 7 days
Credit cards	Accepted but not AMEX
Style of pizza	Neapolitan
Recommended pizza	Maradona; Napoli

"An easily missed hidden gem out in Streatham, Bravi Ragazzi aims to represent a new generation of Neapolitan pizza. It uses traditional methods and flavors but isn't afraid to introduce ingredients you wouldn't necessarily expect to find in an old-school Neapolitan pizzeria, such as tuna, cream, and corn. All the classics are well represented here, so the purists won't feel left out, but a few more adventurous options provide some nice variety. Underpinning all this, however, is a focus on the methods and attention to detail typical of all hardcore Neapolitan pizzerias."—Julian Rea

ADDOMMÉ PIZZERIA AND TRATTORIA

17–21 Sternhold Avenue
Streatham Hill
London
SW2 4PA
England
+44 2086788496
www.addomme.co.uk

Opening hours	Closed Monday
Credit cards	Accepted but not AMEX
Style of pizza	Neapolitan
Recommended pizza	Marinara

"You can almost taste the wood (from the wood-fired oven) in that base. I don't know how they get such an incredible flavor in there. The Marinara is the silkiest piece of heaven you'll ever eat."—Helen Graves

THE BIG BLU

Food truck—check website, Facebook, and Twitter for upcoming locations
Dunbar
East Lothian
Scotland
+44 7790003572
www.thebigblu.co.uk

Opening hours	Variable
Credit cards	Accepted
Style of pizza	Wood-fired
Recommended pizza	Margherita

"It's special because it's a street food truck with a wood-fired oven. The truck travels around various locations and street food events."—Hilary Sturzaker

CIVERINOS

5 Hunter Square
Edinburgh
EH1 1QW
Scotland
+44 1312200851
www.civerinos.com

Opening hours	Open 7 days
Credit cards	Accepted but not AMEX
Style of pizza	Classic Neapolitan street food
Recommended pizza	Parma Ham, Ricotta, and Honey

"Authentic Italian street food, shared tables, great atmosphere, cool interior, exposed brick walls, drinks served in jam jars—good fun."—Hilary Sturzaker

LA FAVORITA DELIVERED

321 Leith Walk
Edinburgh
EH6 8SA
Scotland
+44 1315555564
www.lafavoritadelivered.com

Opening hours...Open 7 days
Credit cards..................................Accepted but not AMEX
Style of pizza...Delivered to you
Recommended pizza.................................Giro d'Italia

"It's all about choice at this pizza outlet, it even does vegan (with rice milk mozzarella) and gluten-free options."—Gaby Soutar

ORIGANO

236 Leith Walk
Edinburgh
EH6 8DB
Scotland
+44 1315546539
www.origano-leith.co.uk

Opening hours...Open 7 days
Credit cards...Accepted
Style of pizza..................................Traditional Italian
Recommended pizza.................................Capricciosa

"This unassuming restaurant halfway down Leith Walk makes better pizza than all the other contenders that line this street (and there are quite a few). The pizza menu is short but effective and it does an especially good Capricciosa."—Gaby Soutar

PETER'S YARD CAFÉ

3 Deanhaugh Street
Edinburgh
EH4 1LU
Scotland
+44 1313322901
www.petersyard.com

Opening hours...Open 7 days
Credit cards...Accepted
Style of pizza...Sourdough
Recommended pizza.................................The Meaty One

"Peter's Yard pizzas have a thin and yeasty sourdough base with crispy, bubbly flour-dusted edges. They are created in the Edinburgh bakery, Söderberg, then baked in the cafe. Each pizza comes with a palate cleansing 'salad' of pickled cabbage."—Gaby Soutar

SÖDERBERG BAKERY

Quartermile
27 Simpson Loan
Edinburgh
EH3 9GG
Scotland
+44 1312281905
www.soderberg.uk/pizza-at-the-bakery

Opening hours...Open 7 days
Credit cards..................................Accepted but not AMEX
Style of pizza...Sourdough
Recommended pizza.................................Anchovies

ANATONI'S

25 Clearwater Way
Cardiff
CF23 6DL
Wales
+44 2920765419

Opening hours...Closed Monday
Credit cards...Accepted
Style of pizza...Neapolitan
Recommended pizza.................................Quattro Stagioni

"The Neapolitan-style wood-fired oven at this Cardiff-based Italian restaurant can belch out a Margherita every 90 seconds."—Ed Gilbert

CAFE CITTA

4 Church Street
Cardiff
CF10 1BG
Wales
+44 2920224040

Opening hours.........................Closed Sunday and Monday
Credit cards...Accepted
Style of pizza...Wood-fired
Recommended pizza.................................Goat Cheese, Wild
Mushrooms, and Sausage

"A name known and loved by true pizza aficionados in Cardiff, Cafe Citta is as underplayed as its food is mouthwatering. The cozy but minimalist surroundings are always boosted by legions of happy diners tucking into a laundry list of perfect Italian specials, but the pizza is above and beyond the Citta specialty."—Kirstie McCrum

CALABRISELLA

154 Cowbridge Road East
Cardiff
CF11 9ND
Wales
+44 2920225839

Opening hours..Open 7 days
Credit cards...Accepted
Style of pizza...Calabrian
Recommended pizza.................Calabrisella; Milano; Parma
Ham and Arugula (rocket)

"Looking for all the world like a small neighborhood cafe, there's nothing on entering Calabrisella that prepares you for the food it is capable of serving. Brightly lit and busy, it's not a romance hot spot—but it is a go-to for excellent pizza, well made and cooked to crisp perfection with an array of simple but delicious toppings to suit all tastes. One visit will never be enough."—Kirstie McCrum

"Calabrisella's gargantuan pizzas are comprised of a golden crust and a millimeter-thin base topped with perky tomato sauce."—Ed Gilbert

"In my opinion the most authentic Italian pizza in Wales. No-frills brilliant homemade Italian cooking. It does a range of other Italian dishes and sweet treats too, but the pizza is knockout, and nowhere in Cardiff comes close."—Owen Morgan

CIBO

83 Pontcanna Street
Cardiff
CF11 9HS
Wales
+44 2920232226
www.cibodelivery.com

Opening hours..Open 7 days
Credit cards.................................Accepted but not AMEX
Style of pizza...Traditional Italian
Recommended pizza..Mediterranea

"With a true flavor of Italy, this bustling little family pizzeria is a real treat indeed. Inside, the covers are quite close together, allowing for a garrulous atmosphere and a holiday vibe."—Kirstie McCrum

DUSTY KNUCKLE PIZZA COMPANY

Pop-up pizzeria—check website, Facebook, and Twitter for upcoming locations
Cardiff
Wales
+44 7807038690
www.dustyknucklepizzacompany.co.uk

Opening hours..Variable
Credit cards...Not accepted
Style of pizza..Wood-fired
Recommended pizza...........................Welsh Laverbread and
Cockle Pizza

"As a street food pizza offering, this husband-and-wife team serve up Welsh ingredients on great sourdough pizza. They bake them to perfection using interesting and collaborative ingredients."—Samantha Evans

BARAVIN

1 Llys y Brenin
Aberystwyth
Ceredigion
SY23 2AP
Wales
+44 1970611189
www.baravin.co.uk

Opening hours..Closed Sunday
Credit cards...Accepted
Style of pizza...Gourmet Neapolitan
Recommended pizza......................Pulled Penlan Belly Pork,
Caramelized Onions, and Perl Las Cheese

"The food is delicious, the service is excellent without being pretentious, and the views are truly amazing. It is all-round fantastic! This is the place I take all my friends when they visit, mostly just so I get another excuse to go."—Paul Grimwood & Shauna Guinn

PIZZATIPI
Cambrian Quay
Cardigan
Ceredigion
SA43 1EZ
Wales
+44 1239623633
www.pizzatipi.co.uk

Opening hours..........................Closed Sunday and Monday
Credit cards...Accepted
Style of pizza..Gourmet

"Although this pizzeria is only open during the summer months its fantastic food and unusual setting mean that it has a small army of loyal customers. It is based on the quay next to the river Teifi in Cardigan and has loads of outdoor seating so its customers can enjoy the beautiful views. The pizzas themselves are beautifully prepared. They are a little rustic looking but scrumptious every time."
—Paul Grimwood & Shauna Guinn

PIZZERIA VESUVIO
200–201 Neath Road
Swansea
SA1 2JT
Wales
+44 1792648346
www.vesuvioswansea.co.uk

Opening hours..Open 7 days
Credit cards...Accepted
Style of pizza..Wood-fired
Recommended pizza..............................Mushroom and Ham

"A great place for a pre- or post-soccer or rugby meal as it's just across the road from the Liberty Stadium, home of Swansea City FC and Ospreys Rugby."—Victoria Trott

CASTELLAMARE
Bracelet Bay
Mumbles
Swansea
SA3 4JT
Wales
+44 1792369408
www.castellamare.co.uk

Opening hours..Open 7 days
Credit cards...Accepted
Style of pizza..Traditional
Recommended pizza ....Calzone

VERDI'S
Knab Rock
Mumbles
Swansea
SA3 4EN
Wales
+44 1792369135
www.verdis-cafe.co.uk

Opening hours..Open 7 days
Credit cards...................................Accepted but not AMEX
Style of pizza..Traditional
Recommended pizza..........................Margherita (with added
mushrooms)

"Located at the water's edge in Mumbles, a charming former fishing village just outside Swansea, this light and airy Italian cafe offers fast service and reasonable prices."—Victoria Trott

PIZZA PRONTO
The Kiosk
Stanwell Road
Penarth
Vale of Glamorgan
CF64 3EU
Wales
www.pizzaprontopenarth.co.uk

Opening hours..........................Closed Sunday and Monday
Credit cards...Not accepted
Style of pizza.................................Neapolitan-New York
Recommended pizza..........................Margherita; Tuna and
Anchovies

"These guys operate out of a shack that only holds two people! They make superb homemade artisan pizza with excellent ingredients, putting thought and time into their dough and sauce. Due to its location and size the pizza is takeout, but boy it's good."
—Owen Morgan

THE ARTISAN COOK

Food truck—check website, Facebook, and Twitter for
upcoming locations
Sully
Vale of Glamorgan
Wales
+44 7895092875
www.theartisancook.co.uk

Opening hours	Variable
Credit cards	Not accepted
Style of pizza	Thin and crispy
Recommended pizza	Primavera

"A wood-fired brick oven in a truck? Yes please. What
incredible pizza. Authenticity driven from an oven
that reaches the temperature needed for great pizza,
coupled with simple flavor combinations."
—Owen Morgan

DIFONTAINE'S

22 Parliament Street
Dublin 2
County Dublin
Republic of Ireland
+353 16745485

Opening hours	Open 7 days
Credit cards	Accepted
Style of pizza	New York
Recommended pizza	Pepperoni

"DiFontaine's is a New York-style, by the slice, place.
Swing by after a couple of drinks in the city center for
some soakage. It's not flashy, but the slices are giant
and it stays open late, and after hours the music is
turned up."—Ailbhe Malone

GOTHAM CAFÉ

8 South Anne Street
Dublin 2
County Dublin
Republic of Ireland
+353 16795266
www.gothamcafe.ie

Opening hours	Open 7 days
Credit cards	Accepted
Style of pizza	New York
Recommended pizza	Chinatown

"Gotham Café is always busy and bustling. Its sourcing of
ingredients (many local) is outstandingly selective. Good
value and highly consistent—since 1993."—Tom Doorley

OSTERIA LUCIO

The Malting Tower, Clanwilliam Terrace
Grand Canal Quay
Dublin 2
County Dublin
Republic of Ireland
+353 16624199
www.osterialucio.com

Opening hours	Open 7 days
Credit cards	Accepted
Style of pizza	Neapolitan
Recommended pizza	Quattro Formaggi; Smoked Speck and Chile

"Osteria Lucio's simplicity of approach lets excellent
raw materials speak for themselves."—Tom Doorley

SKINFLINT

19 Crane Lane
Dublin 2
County Dublin
Republic of Ireland
+353 16709719
www.joburger.ie/skinflint

Opening hours	Open 7 days
Credit cards	Accepted but not AMEX
Style of pizza	Flatbread with an Irish take on toppings
Recommended pizza	Eithne

"Few have done more to democratize Dublin's
restaurant scene than Joe Macken, and at Skinflint
he serves up good-quality, flatbread-style pizzas that
won't break the bank."—Gillian Nelis

PAULIE'S PIZZA

58 Upper Grand Canal Street
Dublin 4
County Dublin
Republic of Ireland
+353 16643658
www.juniors.ie/paulies-pizza.php

Opening hours	Open 7 days
Credit cards	Accepted but not AMEX
Style of pizza	Neapolitan
Recommended pizza	Margherita; Meat Special

"Great wood-fired oven and friendly staff."
—Niall Harbison

MANIFESTO

208 Lower Rathmines Road
Dublin 6
County Dublin
Republic of Ireland
+353 14968096
www.manifestorestaurant.ie

Opening hours..Open 7 days
Credit cards..Accepted but not Amex
Style of pizza....................................Italian thin-crust
Recommended pizza..Don Corleone

"They don't take themselves seriously at Manifesto
—the staff are super-friendly, and the pizza chef
has been known to put on a dough-spinning display
accompanied by disco tunes—but they do take their
food seriously, and the pizzas are as good as you will
find in Dublin. They can also make any of their pizzas
gluten free for a small extra charge."—Gillian Nelis

CAMPO DE' FIORI

1 Albert Avenue
Bray
County Wicklow
Republic of Ireland
+353 12764257
www.campodefiori.ie

Opening hours......Closed Monday (except Bank Holidays)
Credit cards..Accepted
Style of pizza............................Traditional Italian thin-crust
Recommended pizza..Napoli

"I love everything about this little gem of an Italian
restaurant just off the promenade in Bray: the
charming Italian waiting staff, the chatter of the
groups of Italians who frequent it, and the superb
attention to detail shown by the chef, Marco
Roccasalvo. The pizza is made to Marco's mother's
recipe."—Gillian Nelis

LA CUCINA

University Court
Castletroy
County Limerick
Republic of Ireland
+353 61333980
www.realitalianfoodies.com/la-cucina

Opening hours..Open 7 days
Credit cards..Accepted
Style of pizza....................................Italian thin-crust
Recommended pizza..Atina

"Lorraine Fanneran and Bruno Coppola's small
restaurant just outside Limerick doesn't try to be all
things to all people: instead it offers great-quality
Italian food and coffee at a very reasonable price. The
pizzas are as good as you will find along the western
seaboard."—Gillian Nelis

"A PIZZERIA THAT NEVER NEGLECTS THE BASICS, BUT ALSO RETHINKS THE ART OF MAKING PIZZA WITH BOTH VERY LOCAL AND EXOTIC INGREDIENTS." JEHAN DELBRUYÈRE P.166

THE NETHERLANDS, BELGIUM & LUXEMBOURG

"THE CRUST IS JUST MAGICAL— VERY THIN, CRISPY, AND LIGHT!"
NICOLA DE SIMONE & MASSIMO CINQUINA P.165

"THE PLACE IS ALWAYS PACKED AT WEEKENDS."
MIRIAM BUNNIK P.158

"THIS IS THE IDEAL SPOT IN BRUSSELS IF YOU LIKE *PIZZA AL TAGLIO*."
LAURA CENTRELLA P.164

"ASK THE *PIZZAIOLO* TO COMBINE THE REGULAR APPETIZER SCAMPI FORNO WITH A PIZZA. MAN, THAT'S HEAVEN!"
MARCO ZANDER P.159

THE NETHERLANDS, BELGIUM & LUXEMBOURG

N

SCALE

0   250   500 mi.

NORTH HOLLAND PP.160–164

AMSTERDAM PP.160–164

SOUTH HOLLAND PP.158–159

THE NETHERLANDS

WEST FLANDERS P.166

BRUSSELS-CAPITAL P.164

WALLOON BRABANT P.166

HAINAUT P.165

LIÈGE PP.165–166

BELGIUM

LUXEMBOURG

LUXEMBOURG P.166

ANGELO BETTI

Schiekade 6B
Rotterdam
South Holland 3032 AJ
Netherlands
+31 104658174
www.angelobetti.nl

Opening hours	Open 7 days
Credit cards	Not accepted
Style of pizza	Tuscan
Recommended pizza	Pirata

BIRD

Raampoortstraat 24–28
Rotterdam
South Holland 3032 AH
Netherlands
+31 107371154
www.bird-rotterdam.nl

Opening hours	Closed Sunday–Tuesday
Credit cards	Accepted
Style of pizza	Neapolitan
Recommended pizza	Margherita

"A Neapolitan pizzeria combined with a jazz club and poppodium. It has a very young and urban crowd."
—Marco Zander

CIAO CIAO

Bergweg 94A
Rotterdam
South Holland 3036 BE
Netherlands
+31 102655045
www.ciao-ciao.nl

Opening hours	Closed Monday
Credit cards	Not accepted
Style of pizza	Sicilian
Recommended pizza	Ciao Ciao

O'PAZZO

Mariniersweg 90
Rotterdam
South Holland 3011 NV
Netherlands
+31 102827107
www.opazzo.nl

Opening hours	Closed Monday
Credit cards	Accepted
Style of pizza	Neapolitan
Recommended pizza	O'Pazzo; Sapori d'Estate

"It has one of the most insane wood-fired ovens I have ever seen—it is shaped like an octopus."
—Marco Zander

"The place is always packed at weekends."
—Miriam Bunnik

LA PIZZA

Scheepstimmermanslaan 21
Rotterdam
South Holland 3016 AD
Netherlands
+31 102417797
www.lapizza.nl

Opening hours	Closed Sunday
Credit cards	Accepted but not AMEX
Style of pizza	Roman wood-fired
Recommended pizza	Ham and Mozzarella; Sausage

"The most luxurious pizzeria in town."
—Marco Zander

SUGO

Aert van Nesstraat 20
Rotterdam
South Holland 3012 CA
Netherlands
+31 102374520
www.sugopizza.nl

Opening hours	Open 7 days
Credit cards	Accepted but not AMEX
Style of pizza	*Pizza al taglio*
Recommended pizza	Parma Ham, Potato, Mozzarella, and Fresh Basil

"Nice Roman-style *pizza al taglio*—small pieces cut off large rectangular pizzas on oven plates. The menu changes from day to day and depends on the chef's choice."—Miriam Bunnik

LA SICILIA

Emmastraat 76
Rozenburg
South Holland 3181 GC
Netherlands
+31 181214634
www.lasicilia.nl

Opening hours	Closed Monday
Credit cards	Accepted but not AMEX
Style of pizza	Mixed influences
Recommended pizza	Chicken

"Ask the *pizzaiolo* to combine the regular appetizer Scampi Forno with a pizza. Man, that's heaven!"
—Marco Zander

"**YAMYAM IS ONE OF THE MOST HISTORIC PIZZERIAS IN AMSTERDAM.**"

GESSICA & GIANNI BORDINI P.164

"**IT'S THE ONLY PIZZERIA I KNOW THAT HAS SOURDOUGH PIZZAS, AND THE DOUGH IS FANTASTIC.**"

MARJAN IPPEL P.163

AMSTERDAM

"LA PERLA IS A POPULAR AMSTERDAM GO-TO SPOT FOR WOOD-FIRED, CHEWY PIZZAS TOPPED MAINLY WITH INGREDIENTS IMPORTED FROM ITALY."

DEBORAH MULLIN & CLAUDIA KRIJGER P.162

"**IT'S THE REAL THING.**"

MICK SONNENFELD P.163

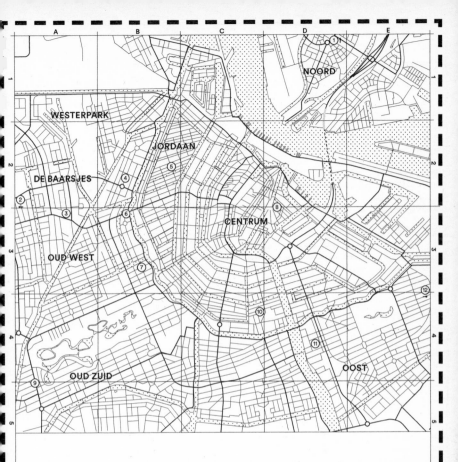

AMSTERDAM

SCALE

0   500   1000   1500
yd.

1. KEBEC MICRO BAKERY,
   NOORD (P.163)
2. EETWINKEL BUURMAN &
   BUURMAN, BOS EN LOMMER (P.162)
3. FAAM, DE BAARSJES (P.162)

4. YAMYAM, WESTERPARK (P.164)
5. LA PERLA, JORDAAN (P.162)
6. FUOCO VIVO, OUD WEST (P.163)
7. DE ITALIAAN, OUD WEST (P.163)
8. IL SOGNO, CENTRUM (P.162)

9. SOTTO, OUD ZUID (P.163)
10. PISTACHE, CENTRUM (P.162)
11. MANGIASSAI, OOST (P.163)
12. LA FUCINA, OOST (P.163)

EETWINKEL BUURMAN & BUURMAN

Mercatorstraat 171
Bos en Lommer
Amsterdam
North Holland 1056 RE
Netherlands
+31 202628262
www.eetwinkelbuurmanenbuurman.nl

Opening hours	Closed Monday
Credit cards	Not accepted
Style of pizza	Wood-fired thin-crust
Recommended pizza	4 Cheese

"This pizza spot is owned by two really nice guys, the service is personal and attentive, the atmosphere is jovial and warm, and the tasty pizzas are made with respect for wholesome, healthy, and unique ingredients."—Deborah Mullin & Claudia Krijger

PISTACHE

Frederiksplein 6–8
Centrum
Amsterdam
North Holland 1017 XM
Netherlands
+31 634093123
www.pistachepizza.nl

Opening hours	Closed Monday and Tuesday
Credit cards	Not accepted
Style of pizza	Wood-fired
Recommended pizza	Burrata and 'Nduja

"The wood-fired oven is maybe the coolest I've ever seen: it's a completely rusted all-iron oven (with stones on the inside)."—Marjan Ippel

IL SOGNO

Koningsstraat 19
Centrum
Amsterdam
North Holland 1011 ET
Netherlands
+31 203200611
www.ilsogno.eu

Opening hours	Open 7 days
Credit cards	Not accepted
Style of pizza	Roman
Recommended pizza	Margherita

FAAM

Reinier Claezenstraat 10
De Baarsjes
Amsterdam
North Holland 1056 WJ
Netherlands
+31 203702354
www.restaurantfaam.nl

Opening hours	Open 7 days
Credit cards	Accepted but not AMEX
Style of pizza	Neapolitan
Recommended pizza	Margherita

"We enjoy this pizzeria, located on a tree-lined corner in Amsterdam's hip De Baarsjes neighborhood, because it is run by really nice people making really good, plump-crusted pizzas served up with an appetizing selection of antipasti choices and a tasty beer and wine list."
—Deborah Mullin & Claudia Krijger

LA PERLA

Tweede Tuindwarsstraat 14 & 53
Jordaan
Amsterdam
North Holland 1015 RZ
Netherlands
+31 206248828
www.pizzaperla.nl

Opening hours	Open 7 days
Credit cards	Accepted
Style of pizza	Neapolitan wood-fired
Recommended pizza	Stracchino and Buffalo Mozzarella

"La Perla is a popular Amsterdam go-to spot for wood-fired, chewy pizzas topped mainly with ingredients imported from Italy. What we like about La Perla is the concise, but quality-oriented, Italian-centric wine list...perfect for pairing with what we would say is the most Neapolitan-style pizza in town."—Deborah Mullin & Claudia Krijger

KEBEC MICRO BAKERY

TT Melaniaweg 12
Noord
Amsterdam
North Holland 1033 ST
Netherlands
+31 646483643
www.kebec.nl

Opening hours...............................Closed Saturday–Monday
Credit cards..Not accepted
Style of pizza...Wood-fired
Recommended pizza..Margherita

"A quirky micro bakery with a giant wood-fired oven and great pizzas in a very hip neighborhood full of festivals."—Marjan Ippel

LA FUCINA

Javastraat 99H
Oost
Amsterdam
North Holland 1094 HC
Netherlands
+31 611236108

Opening hours...Open 7 days
Credit cards..Not accepted
Style of pizza...Roman
Recommended pizza..................Pizza with Smoked Provola
delle Madonie

MANGIASSAI

Ruyschstraat 42
Oost
Amsterdam
North Holland 1091 CD
Netherlands
+31 206655967
www.mangiassai.nl

Opening hours..Closed Monday
Credit cards..Not accepted
Style of pizza...Neapolitan
Recommended pizza..Margherita

"It's the real thing."—Mick Sonnenfeld

FUOCO VIVO

De Clercqstraat 12
Oud West
Amsterdam
North Holland 1052 NC
Netherlands
+31 206124309
www.fuocovivo.nl

Opening hours...Open 7 days
Credit cards..Not accepted
Style of pizza.......................................Wood-fired sourdough
Recommended pizza..Sausage

"It's the only pizzeria I know that has sourdough pizzas, and the dough is fantastic."—Marjan Ippel

DE ITALIAAN

Bosboom Toussaintstraat 29
Oud West
Amsterdam
North Holland 1054 AN
Netherlands
+31 206836854
www.deitaliaan.com

Opening hours...Open 7 days
Credit cards..............................Accepted but not AMEX
Style of pizza...Roman wood-fired
Recommended pizza......................Pizza of the day; Potato

"A real hidden gem."—Marjan Ippel

SOTTO

Amstelveenseweg 89
Oud Zuid
Amsterdam
North Holland 1075 VW
Netherlands
+31 202239000
www.sottopizza.nl

Opening hours...Open 7 days
Credit cards..............................Accepted but not AMEX
Style of pizza...Neapolitan
Recommended pizza................................Margherita; Tartufo

YAMYAM

Frederik Henrikstraat 90
Westerpark
Amsterdam
North Holland 1052 HZ
Netherlands
+31 206815097
www.yamyam.nl

Opening hours...Closed Monday
Credit cards...Accepted
Style of pizza..Neapolitan
Recommended pizza.............................Finocchiona; YamYam

"YamYam is one of the most historic pizzerias in
Amsterdam."—Gessica & Gianni Bordini

"It has a nice and friendly ambience."
—Jannet van der Ree & Maurice Pilet

LA BOTTEGA DELLA PIZZA

Avenue Ducpétiaux 39
Brussels
Brussels-Capital 1060
Belgium
+32 487780052

Opening hours...Closed Tuesday
Credit cards...Not accepted
Style of pizza..Authentic
Recommended pizza.............................Barbary Fog; Buffalo
Mozzarella and Fresh Basil; Marinara DOC;
Octopus Sashimi

"This place is all about freshness, creativity, respect
for produce, savoir-faire, and ambience. The flavor
developed on the crust allows the chef to play around
with bold toppings, like surprising vegetables with
pancetta, or broccolini with spicy sausage. The chef
is from Sardinia and imports his produce from there."
—René Sépul

SALE PEPE ROSMARINO

Rue Berckmans 98
Brussels
Brussels-Capital 1060
Belgium
+32 25389063

Opening hours...Open 7 days
Credit cards......................................Accepted but not Amex
Style of pizza...Rustic

"An emblematic Italian restaurant in Brussels where
you eat well and with no fuss."—Boris Beaucarne

ECCOME NO!

Rue Ernest Solvay 10
Ixelles
Brussels-Capital 1050
Belgium
+32 25021611

Opening hours...Open 7 days
Credit cards...................................Accepted but not AMEX
Style of pizza..Roman
Recommended pizza..Margherita

"This is the ideal spot in Brussels if you like *pizza al
taglio*. You can choose between a dozen varieties and
after a few snips of the scissors you can enjoy pizza
slices with a light, crusty, and oil-free dough."
—Laura Centrella

POSTO AL SOLE

Chaussée de Forest 122
Saint-Gilles
Brussels-Capital 1060
Belgium
+32 484708958

Opening hours...Closed Monday
Credit cards...Not accepted
Style of pizza...Neapolitan
Recommended pizza.............................Margherita; Pulcinella

"Better known under the name of its owner 'Momo,'
Posto al Sole is one of the best pizzerias in Brussels.
You can choose a classic, round pizza or a half-meter
if you prefer to share with friends."—Laura Centrella

LE MARCO POLO

Rue Ferrer 104B
Frameries
Hainaut 7080
Belgium
+32 65662038
www.marcopoloframeries.be

Opening hours	Closed Monday
Credit cards	Accepted
Style of pizza	Traditional
Recommended pizza	Siciliana

"Le Marco Polo is very special. It advocates the use of an electric oven as a gustatory choice. The pizzas are small and topped with fresh ingredients."
—Philippe Genion

MULINO BIANCO

Chaussée de Soignies 26
Le Roeulx
Hainaut 7070
Belgium
+32 64678081
www.mulinobianco.be

Opening hours	Open 7 days
Credit cards	Accepted
Style of pizza	Wood-fired focaccia
Recommended pizza	Bresaola

"It has the atmosphere of a chic Italian restaurant."
—Stéphanie Candidoflore

SERENO

Rue Georges Tourneur 116
Marchienne au Pont
Hainaut 6030
Belgium
+32 71517489

Opening hours	Closed Monday and Tuesday
Credit cards	Accepted but not AMEX
Style of pizza	Classic
Recommended pizza	Napoletana

"A young team has taken over this restaurant and their work is excellent. The pizza is in the classic style but with a high-quality dough."—Philippe Genion

IL TRULETTO

Place Louis Delhaize 15
Ransart
Hainaut 6043
Belgium
+32 71354418
www.iltrulletto.com

Opening hours	Closed Monday
Credit cards	Accepted
Style of pizza	Wood-fired
Recommended pizza	Prosciutto, Mushrooms, and Spinach

"Excellent!"—Philippe Genion

L'ARTE PIZZERIA

Rue Walter Jamar 205
Ans
Liège 4430
Belgium
+32 42260093
www.lartepizzeria.be

Opening hours	Open 7 days
Credit cards	Not accepted
Style of pizza	Classic
Recommended pizza	Buffala

"A little family-run pizzeria where the freshness of the products is a requirement. The owner is knowledgeable about mushrooms and in the past I've had the chance to eat an excellent pizza with the daily harvest."
—Jehan Delbruyère

LA BAMBOLA

En Feronstrée 99
Liège
Liège 4000
Belgium
+32 42230323

Opening hours	Open 7 days
Credit cards	Accepted
Style of pizza	Thin-crust
Recommended pizza	Three Cheese

"The crust is just magical—very thin, crispy, and light!"—Nicola de Simone & Massimo Cinquina

PIZZERIA PUGLIESE

Boulevard de la Souvenière 129
Liège
Liège 4000
Belgium
+32 42221479

Opening hours	Closed Thursday
Credit cards	Accepted
Style of pizza	Southern Italian
Recommended pizza	Parmigiana

"The pizza is great and affordable."
—Nicola de Simone & Massimo Cinquina

IL VIOLINO

Rue de la Baume 267
Seraing
Liège 4100
Belgium
+32 43369088
www.il-violino.be

Opening hours	Closed Monday
Credit cards	Not accepted
Style of pizza	Creative
Recommended pizza	Vesuvio

"A pizzeria that never neglects the basics, but also rethinks the art of making pizza with both very local and exotic ingredients."—Jehan Delbruyère

CASA & GUSTO "DA NATALE"

Avenue de la Résistance 528
Soumagne
Liège 4603
Belgium
+32 43773811

Opening hours	Closed Monday
Credit cards	Accepted but not AMEX
Style of pizza	Wood-fired
Recommended pizza	Ripiena

LA CARRETTA

Rue de la Vallée 3
Hotton
Luxembourg 6990
Belgium
+32 84467690

Opening hours	Open 7 days
Credit cards	Accepted but not AMEX
Style of pizza	Wood-fired
Recommended pizza	Salmon

"Well-topped pizza with generous toppings and a spongy crust."
—Nicola de Simone & Massimo Cinquina

TRATTORIA DEL PARCO

Avenue Léon-Jeuniaux 2
Nivelles
Walloon Brabant 1400
Belgium
+32 67219898

Opening hours	Open 7 days
Credit cards	Accepted but not AMEX
Style of pizza	Wood-fired
Recommended pizza	Flavio

"This pretty trattoria has a nice terrace and serves simple food. Its wood-fired pizzas are delicious."
—Stéphanie Candidoflore

IN DE WULF

Wulvestraat 1
Dranouter
West Flanders 8950
Belgium
+32 57445567
www.indewulf.be

Opening hours	Closed Monday and Tuesday
Credit cards	Accepted
Style of pizza	Gastronomic
Recommended pizza	Vieux Lille

"In the menu of chef Kobe Desramaults, certainly the most significant chef in Belgium to this day, there is a small cheese pizza that fits nicely in the hand. It is a work of great simplicity and yet on the verge of culinary goldsmithery, an object of perfection in every way."—Boris Beaucarne

VALLELUNGA BEACH

57 Rue de Luxembourg
Bridel
Luxembourg 8140
+352 26331594
www.vallelungabeach.lu

Opening hours	Open 7 days
Credit cards	Accepted but not AMEX
Style of pizza	Mediterranean thin-crust
Recommended pizza	Diavola

"This is a pizzeria managed by Calabrians. The pizza is crispy with delicate ingredients. The atmosphere is informal with with absolutely no frills."
—Isabella Sardo

RESTAURANT GIOVANNI RANA

18–22 Rue du Brill
Foetz
Luxembourg 3898
+352 26550191
www.dagiovannirana.com/lu

Opening hours	Open 7 days
Credit cards	Accepted
Style of pizza	Neapolitan
Recommended pizza	Parma

"Attentive service and a nice setting."
—Francesco Malvezzi

RESTAURANT BEIM ABRUZZEBIER

21 Rue d'Arlon
Grosbous
Luxembourg 9155
+352 26881125
www.beimabruzzebier.lu

Opening hours	Closed Tuesday and Wednesday
Credit cards	Accepted but not AMEX
Style of pizza	Italian
Recommended pizza	Abruzzebier

"High-quality pizza in a neat and tidy restaurant. The ingredients are carefully chosen, the dough is well made and with a good rise, and the young couple who own the pizzeria are very friendly hosts."
—Gianfranco Aiello

BELLA NAPOLI

4 Rue de Strasbourg
Luxembourg City
Luxembourg 2560
+352 493367
www.bellanapoli.lu

Opening hours	Open 7 days
Credit cards	Accepted but not AMEX
Style of pizza	Rustic wood-fired
Recommended pizza	Bella Napoli; Calzone; Sausage and Spinach; Trentina

"Excellent value for money."—Giovanni Farinella

"The pizza is cooked in a wood-fired oven and is subtle and crispy."—Francesco Malvezzi

RESTAURANT NOTARO

149 Rue de la Tour Jacob
Luxembourg City
Luxembourg 1831
+352 423070
www.notaro.lu

Opening hours	Open 7 days
Credit cards	Accepted
Style of pizza	Neapolitan
Recommended pizza	Mushroom

"A very cute and convivial venue, suitable for a dinner with friends or a date. It has a large selection of pizzas that respect Italian gastronomic traditions and an excellent wine list."—Giovanni Farinella

"A restaurant out of the ordinary in Luxembourg thanks to the quality of its food and wine."
—Gianfranco Aiello

RISTORANTE PIZZERIA ONESTO

11 Rue du Nord
Luxembourg City
Luxembourg 2229
+352 223818
www.resto-onesto.lu

Opening hours...Closed Sunday
Credit cards..Accepted
Style of pizza...Neapolitan
Recommended pizza..............................Maestro; Margherita

"Simple with a slightly international feel, this is probably the pizza most similar to Neapolitan style to be found in Luxembourg."—Isabella Sardo

LA TORRE

82 Avenue du Bois
Luxembourg City
Luxembourg 1250
+352 471871
www.pizzerialatorre.lu

Opening hours...Open 7 days
Credit cards...Accepted
Style of pizza..Traditional
Recommended pizza..............................Calzone; Margherita

"La Torre gives you the impression of being in a really good pizzeria in Italy."—Isabella Sardo

"A CULT ADDRESS FOR ANYONE WHO LOVES PIZZAS, FOCACCIAS, AND PISSALADIÈRES."

PIERRE PSALTIS P.178

"MY LOVE AFFAIR WITH PIZZA STARTED WITH PIZZA FROM PIZZA CAPRI."

ADAM BARU P.173

"LA GROTTE IS A PLACE NOT TO BE MISSED IN MARSEILLE."

PRISCILLA DAVIGNY P.176

FRANCE & MONACO

"THE SETTING IS MAGNIFICENT, WITH LOTS OF COLOR AND THE SEA PROVIDING THE BACKGROUND NOISE."

LUDOVIC TURAC P.176

"ANY PIZZA MADE BY FRANCE'S INFAMOUS EDOUARD LOUBET IS BOUND TO BE DELICIOUS."

LISA PEPIN P.174

"COLETTE AND BRUNO WELCOME LOCALS AND TOURISTS ALIKE WITH HUGE SMILES AND THE DELECTABLE AROMAS FROM THEIR PROVENÇAL-INSPIRED PIZZA CREATIONS."

STEPHANIE FRAY P.177

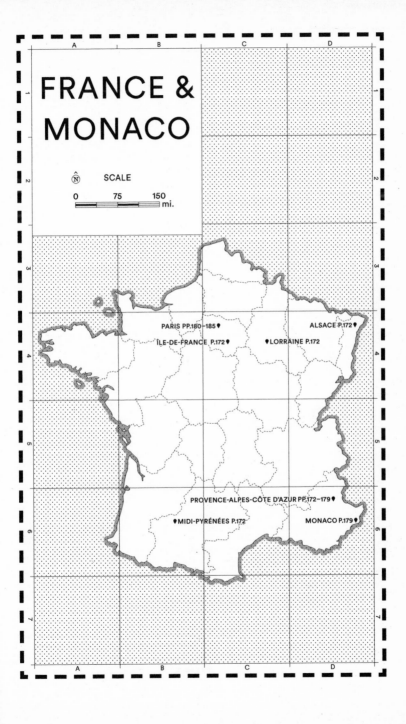

FRANCE & MONACO

N̂ SCALE

0   75   150
—————————— mi.

PARIS PP.180–185 ♥

ÎLE-DE-FRANCE P.172 ♥

ALSACE P.172 ♥

♥ LORRAINE P.172

PROVENCE-ALPES-CÔTE D'AZUR PP.172–179 ♥

♥ MIDI-PYRÉNÉES P.172

MONACO P.179 ♥

COME A ROMA

7 Rue de la Chaîne
Strasbourg
Alsace 67000
France
+33 388327321
www.comearoma.com

Opening hours	Open 7 days
Credit cards	Accepted
Style of pizza	By the slice
Recommended pizza	Fresh Tomato and Basil

"If you're looking for a good pizza to eat on the go, this is definitely the right place to go in Strasbourg." —Gianfranco Aiello

L'ATELIER PIZZA

7 Avenue de la Pointe Ringale
Saint-Germain-lès-Corbeil
Île-de-France 91250
France
+33 164988399
www.latelierpizza.fr

Opening hours	Closed Sunday and Monday
Credit cards	Accepted but not AMEX
Style of pizza	Classic
Recommended pizza	Margherita

LA TOSCANE

12 Rue Dupont des Loges
Metz
Lorraine 57000
France
+33 387756073

Opening hours	Closed Sunday
Credit cards	Accepted but not AMEX
Style of pizza	Classic
Recommended pizza	La Toscane

"The whole of Metz comes here on the sly for their favorite pizza, cooked over a wood fire in front of the whole room."—Gilles Pudlowski

PIZZA MONGELLI

Impasse Max Baylac
Tournefeuille
Midi-Pyrénées 31170
France
+33 562489104
www.pizza-mongelli.com

Opening hours	Closed Sunday and Monday
Credit cards	Accepted but not AMEX
Style of pizza	Neapolitan
Recommended pizza	Botticelli

"A minuscule pizzeria that serves hundreds of pizzas every evening (eat in or takeout) in a convivial, lively setting. The journey is worth it for the quality and flavor of the pizzas."—Romain Clavel-Millo

LA GRANGE

2 Bis Rue Nazareth
Aix-en-Provence
Provence-Alpes-Côte d'Azur 13100
France
+33 442261985

Opening hours	Open 7 days
Credit cards	Accepted
Style of pizza	Thin-crust
Recommended pizza	Royale

"A pizzeria in an upscale university town where students and locals alike give it rave reviews is quite an accomplishment, especially when it has maintained that status since the mid-1990s."—Lisa Pepin

LA PIZZA

3 Rue Aude
Aix-en-Provence
Provence-Alpes-Côte d'Azur 13100
France
+33 442262217

Opening hours	Closed Monday
Credit cards	Accepted
Style of pizza	Traditional
Recommended pizza	Classique Royale

"Always served in halves, the crust is extremely thin and crunchy, and reasonably burnt on the edges for a woody aroma. The tomato sauce is tangy, never sour nor acidic."—Pierre Psaltis

PIZZA CAPRI

1 Rue Fabrot
Aix-en-Provence
Provence-Alpes-Côte d'Azur 13100
France
+33 442385543
www.pizza-capri.fr

Opening hours	Open 7 days
Credit cards	Not accepted
Style of pizza	Traditional
Recommended pizza	Cheese

"Located on a small side street, this kiosk turns out fantastic pizzas with ingredients from the region. It has been 20 years since I had pizza from Capri, but it lives on in my memory as one of the highlights of my year in Aix-en-Provence. My love affair with pizza started with pizza from Pizza Capri."
—Adam Baru

MICHELANGELO MAMO

2 Rue des Cordiers
Antibes
Provence-Alpes-Côte d'Azur 06600
France
+33 493340447
www.michelangelo-mamo.com

Opening hours	Open 7 days
Credit cards	Accepted
Style of pizza	Mediterranean
Recommended pizza	Truffle

LA PIZZA D'OR

10 Rue Lacan
Antibes
Provence-Alpes-Côte d'Azur 06600
France
+33 492954668

Opening hours	Closed Monday and Tuesday
Credit cards	Not accepted
Style of pizza	Thin-crust
Recommended pizza	Napolitaine

"It's a small place with only a few covers, and the quality is fabulous."—Romain Clavel-Millo

LA MAMMA

20 Rue Amphithéâtre
Arles
Provence-Alpes-Côte d'Azur 13200
France
+33 490961160
www.lamammaarles.com

Opening hours	Closed Sunday and Monday
Credit cards	Accepted but not AMEX
Style of pizza	Neapolitan
Recommended pizza	Margherita

"La Mamma is the perfect respite from a day of shopping at the Arles market. It's a favorite with locals."—Stephanie Fray

VEZZO PIZZA

71 Rue Guillaume Puy
Avignon
Provence-Alpes-Côte d'Azur 84000
France
+33 432762317
www.vezzo-pizza.com

Opening hours	Closed Monday
Credit cards	Accepted but not AMEX
Style of pizza	Artisan
Recommended pizza	Di Parma

"A beautiful thin crust is executed in a very make-shift oven. The products are king here; top-quality hams and vegetables are all bought from Les Halles central market in Avignon."—Jon Chiri

AFRICAN QUEEN

Port de Plaisance
Beaulieu-sur-Mer
Provence-Alpes-Côte d'Azur 06310
France
+33 493011085
www.africanqueen.fr

Opening hours	Open 7 days
Credit cards	Accepted but not AMEX
Style of pizza	Italian-Provençal
Recommended pizza	La Toscane; Truffle

"African Queen is the most elegant and the most popular restaurant in Beaulieu harbor."
—Vincent Delmas

FAVOLSA PIZZA

27 Rue Marche aux Raisins
Bédoin
Provence-Alpes-Côte d'Azur 84410
France
+33 490621505

Opening hours	Closed Wednesday
Credit cards	Not accepted
Style of pizza	Wood-fired thin-crust
Recommended pizza	Juliette

"Chef Rudy Solomon makes his custom pizza dough every day from a flour mix created just for him. He tops his pizzas with fresh seasonal ingredients from the agricultural producers in the Mont Ventoux region of Provence, and cooks them to order in a wood-fired oven. Solomon was a chef at a Michelin-star restaurant in Avignon, and brings this creativity and experience to his pizzas. Rather than trying to imitate an Italian pizza, he creates pizzas that represent the flavors of France and especially Provence. The special menu changes regularly, and is based on the seasonal ingredients available from the local producers."—Ken Wallace

LA BERGERIE

Les Claparèdes
Chemin des Cabanes
Bonnieux
Provence-Alpes-Côte d'Azur 84480
France
+33 490758978
www.capelongue.com

Opening hours	Closed Monday
Credit cards	Accepted
Style of pizza	Gourmet thin-crust
Recommended pizza	Truffle

"Any pizza made by France's infamous Edouard Loubet is bound to be delicious. But when you add fresh Provençal truffles and a gorgeous bistro with magnificent views surrounded by manicured gardens full of modern sculptures, then you have a real gastronomic experience that all your senses will savor."—Lisa Pepin

PIZZERIA LE CASTELLAR

9 Place Mirabeau
Cadenet
Provence-Alpes-Côte d'Azur 84160
France
+33 490682053

Opening hours	Closed Thursday
Credit cards	Accepted
Style of pizza	Thin-crust

"It's not on the menu, but if you ask, they'll make you a white pizza with mushrooms that's absolutely divine, especially for takeout, as you can take it home and drizzle it with truffle oil for a real gourmet treat."—Lisa Pepin

LA PIZZA CRESCI

3 Quai Saint Pierre
Cannes
Provence-Alpes-Côte d'Azur 06400
France
+33 493392256
www.maison-cresci.fr

Opening hours	Open 7 days
Credit cards	Accepted
Style of pizza	Italian wood-fired
Recommended pizza	Aubergine

LES CHINEURS

18 Rue Hoche
Carcès
Provence-Alpes-Côte d'Azur 83570
France
+33 494043199

Opening hours	Closed Sunday and Monday
Credit cards	Not accepted
Style of pizza	Wood-fired thin-crust
Recommended pizza	Margherita

"The atmosphere is busy and friendly and the pizzas are best washed down by a glass of fresh rosé. You may need to make a reservation though, this place gets busy!"—Stephen Cronk

CAFÉ DU COURS

27 Cours Gambetta
Cotignac
Provence-Alpes-Côte d'Azur 83570
France
+33 494046014

Opening hours	Closed Monday
Credit cards	Accepted
Style of pizza	Thick-crust
Recommended pizza	Truffle

"Café du Cours is situated on the main square in Cotignac, one of the most charming villages in Provence. The service is prompt and friendly and the pizzas have interesting toppings on ultra-thick bread."—Stephen Cronk

LA GOUTTE BLEUE

171 Chemin Louise Michel
Courthézon
Provence-Alpes-Côte d'Azur 84350
France
+33 490300965

Opening hours	Open 7 days
Credit cards	Accepted but not AMEX
Style of pizza	Italian

"Good quality, good prices, large portions."
—Michel Blanc

GILLES

Place Marcel Bonnein
Eygalières
Provence-Alpes-Côte d'Azur 13810
France
+33 490260328

Opening hours	Open 7 days
Credit cards	Accepted but not AMEX
Style of pizza	Neapolitan
Recommended pizza	Vegetable

"Situated in one of the most beautiful villages of the region, this is the place to dine when you are looking for a leisurely afternoon lunch of spritzes, pizza, lambrusco, and espressos in the quintessential Provençal outdoor garden setting."—Stephanie Fray

LA PINÈDE

Quartier Roque-Rousse
Route Nationale 7
Les Arcs sur Argens
Provence-Alpes-Côte d'Azur 83460
France
+33 494459192
www.pizzerialapinede.fr

Opening hours	Open 7 days
Credit cards	Accepted
Style of pizza	Thin-crust
Recommended pizza	Three Cheeses

"The traditional wood-burning oven gives the pizzas a genuine smoky flavor."—Stephen Cronk

LA BARONNE

Route Nationale 113
Les Pennes-Mirabeau
Provence-Alpes-Côte d'Azur 13170
France
+33 442465385
www.labaronnejohnbergh.com

Opening hours	Closed Monday
Credit cards	Accepted
Style of pizza	Thin-crust
Recommended pizza	Artichoke Cream

"John Bergh is a real character, with a thick local accent, a real love of produce, and above all boundless love for his pizza bases (from the leavening to the cooking). He's a pizza master, creating perfect crispiness and air bubbles."—Julia Sammut

CHEZ ETIENNE

43 Rue de Lorette
Marseille
Provence-Alpes-Côte d'Azur 13000
France

Opening hours..Closed Sunday
Credit cards..Not accepted
Style of pizza..Provençal
Recommended pizza...Regina

"Chez Etienne is a clubby little hole-in-the-wall in the Le Panier district of Marseille run by the Cassaro family. It has a lot of atmosphere and offers a fascinating on-the-plate introduction to life in Marseille. No credit cards, no reservations, no phone number, but always packed to the rafters with local regulars."—Alexander Lobrano

CHEZ NOËL

174 La Canebière
Marseille
Provence-Alpes-Côte d'Azur 13001
France
+33 491421722

Opening hours...Closed Monday
Credit cards............................Accepted but not AMEX
Style of pizza..Marseille
Recommended pizza.....................Daily special; Mozzarella

"A popular pizzeria among the people of Marseille, who come regularly en famille to celebrate some good news or to enjoy a catch-up. Booking is recommended."—Ezéchiel Zérah

CHEZ SAUVEUR

10 Rue d'Aubagne
Marseille
Provence-Alpes-Côte d'Azur 13001
France
+33 491543396
www.chezsauveur.fr

Opening hours........................Closed Sunday and Monday
Credit cards..Accepted
Style of pizza..Marseille-Neapolitan
Recommended pizza..........Half Cheese and Half Anchovy;
    Mozzarella and Figatelli; Mozzarella and Sausage;
    Piemontaise

"Sauveur di Paola was the first person to bring Neapolitan-style pizza to Marseille. By the same token, he created the 'moitié moitié' pizza: half tomato and anchovy; half tomato and Emmental cheese. Fabrice Giacalone has taken over the business and is keeping the secret alive, always choosing the best produce to pay tribute to Sauveur."—Julia Sammut

Hidden amid the West Asian, African, and Vietnamese markets in the Marseille quarter of Noailles is this wonderful relic from a time when Italian merchants crowded the quarter, too. Sauveur di Paola was one of them. He opened the pizzeria that bears his name in 1943. Its pizza is classic Marseille-Neapolitan, which dictates an uninterrupted blanket of molten mozzarella or Emmental over a thin, crisp, blistered crust. The menu is itself a Mediterranean melting pot, with *frigatelli* (a Corsican sausage), *pastourma* (Armenian or Turkish air-dried beef), and *brousse* (a Provençal goat cheese) among the options.

L'EAU À LA BOUCHE

120 Corniche Président John Fitzgerald Kennedy
Marseille
Provence-Alpes-Côte d'Azur 13007
France
+33 491521616
www.pizzerialeaualabouche.fr

Opening hours........................Closed Monday and Tuesday
Credit cards..Not accepted
Style of pizza..Gourmet
Recommended pizza........................Angelina; Arménienne;
    Capucine

"The setting is magnificent, with lots of color and the sea providing the background noise. The pizzas respect tradition and the quality of the produce is excellent."—Ludovic Turac

"This is no ordinary pizza: thin, delicious, and appetizing, it makes you want to take your time without getting tired."—Gilles Pudlowski

LA GROTTE

1 Avenue des Pebrons
Marseille
Provence-Alpes-Côte d'Azur 13008
France
+33 491731779
www.lagrotte-13.com

Opening hours..Open 7 days
Credit cards..................................Accepted but not AMEX
Style of pizza..Marseille

"La Grotte is a place not to be missed in Marseille."
—Priscilla Davigny

PIZZA PIERROT

1 Rue du 10 Août
Marseille
Provence-Alpes-Côte d'Azur 13011
France
+33 491898939
www.pizza-pierrot-marseille.fr

Opening hours..Open 7 days
Credit cards...Not accepted
Style of pizza...Neapolitan
Recommended pizza...Noah

"The pizza has a thin crust that is slightly crispy at the bottom and flexible on top, and it is well topped without being too loaded up."—Daniel Luperini

PIZZÉRIA LA BONNE MÈRE

16 Rue Fort du Sanctuaire
Marseille
Provence-Alpes-Côte d'Azur 13006
France
+33 491582205

Opening hours...Closed Monday
Credit cards...Not accepted
Style of pizza...Neapolitan
Recommended pizza..............Buffalo Mozzarella and Basil;
L'Italienne; La Marius

"The dough is prepared 24 hours in advance and is subjected to the notorious 'boule-boule' technique. Jérémy does everything by hand and the pizzas are cooked twice, which makes them crustier and ensures a better distribution of the heat while respecting the ingredients. The result is disconcertingly delightful."—Pierre Psaltis

"It's all about sourcing great quality: great tomatoes, house-pulled mozzarella, and a puffy, chewy crust made with fantastic flour."—René Sépul

LA SERENATA

37 Avenue de la Pointe Rouge
Marseille
Provence-Alpes-Côte d'Azur 13008
France
+33 491757905
www.laserenata.fr

Opening hours..Open 7 days
Credit cards.................................Accepted but not AMEX
Style of pizza...Italian
Recommended pizza..San Daniele

"La Serenata is a prettily decorated restaurant with views overlooking the Iles du Friol."
—Ludovic Turac

"An authentic Italian place where the chef dishes out Tuscan and Neapolitan food."—Florence Bianchi

PIZZA BRUN

1 Rue Edouard Foscalina
Maussane
Provence-Alpes-Côte d'Azur 13520
France
+33 490544073

Opening hours... Closed Monday
Credit cards...Not accepted
Style of pizza...Wood-fired
Recommended pizza.................Try combinations of savory
and sweet

"Colette and Bruno welcome locals and tourists alike with huge smiles and the delectable aromas from their Provençal-inspired pizza creations. Dine *sur place* picnic-style on colorful tables in a small garden or order *a emporter* to eat at home or pool-side. Either way, call ahead. They book up days in advance during the high season (even for to go orders)."
—Stephanie Fray

SINI

7 Rue des Marins
Menton
Provence-Alpes-Côte d'Azur 06500
France
+33 489987177

Opening hours	Closed Monday
Credit cards	Accepted
Style of pizza	*Pizza al taglio*

"A cult address for anyone who loves pizzas, focaccias, and pissaladières. A man from Corsica and his wife work with Italian organic flours. Why Italian? Because Italian wheat varieties have a less pronounced taste than French types of wheat. As a result these pizzas can be enjoyed like a little treat at any time of the day."—Pierre Psaltis

LES AMOREUX

46 Boulevard Stalingrad
Nice
Provence-Alpes-Côte d'Azur 06300
France
+33 493075973

Opening hours	Closed Sunday and Monday
Credit cards	Accepted but not AMEX
Style of pizza	Neapolitan
Recommended pizza	Nanninella

ATTIMI

10 Place Masséna
Nice
Provence-Alpes-Côte d'Azur 06000
France
+33 493620022
www.attimi.fr

Opening hours	Open 7 days
Credit cards	Accepted but not AMEX
Style of pizza	Italian
Recommended pizza	Autumn; Domenica

"It serves both pizzas and attimi, another version of pizza with crescenza cheese and a different shape."
—Romain Clavel-Millo

"Attimi makes its very light dough using Evian water and organic flour."—Kevin Hin

AUBERGE DE THÉO

52 Avenue Cap-de-Croix
Nice
Provence-Alpes-Côte d'Azur 06100
France
+33 493812619
www.auberge-de-theo.com

Opening hours	Closed Sunday and Monday
Credit cards	Accepted but not AMEX
Style of pizza	Provençal
Recommended pizza	Margherita; Shrimp (prawn)

PIZZA COCO

38 Boulevard Risso
Nice
Provence-Alpes-Côte d'Azur 06300
France
+33 493269293

Opening hours	Closed Sunday
Credit cards	Not accepted
Style of pizza	Italian
Recommended pizza	Pirata

"The moment you enter the pizzeria you feel like you're in Italy. Careful: there aren't many tables, so think about booking."—Isabelle Battarel

LA PIZZA CRESCI

43 Rue Masséna
Nice
Provence-Alpes-Côte d'Azur 06000
France
+33 493877029
www.maison-cresci.fr

Opening hours	Open 7 days
Credit cards	Accepted
Style of pizza	Italian
Recommended pizza	Neptune

"These pizzas are easy to eat since they are served by the half, but they're still big."—Isabelle Battarel

SAFARI

1 Cours Saleya
Nice
Provence-Alpes-Côte d'Azur 06300
France
+33 493801844
www.restaurantsafari.fr

Opening hours	Open 7 days
Credit cards	Accepted
Style of pizza	Wood-fired thin-crust
Recommended pizza	Provençal

"Safari offers a selection of wood-fired pizzas that are very good value for money."—Vincent Delmas

CHEZ HENRI

738 Route de la Madrague
Saint-Cyr-sur-Mer
Provence-Alpes-Côte d'Azur 83270
France
+33 494264615

Opening hours	Open 7 days
Credit cards	Accepted
Style of pizza	Thin-crust
Recommended pizza	La Madrague

"The ambience is cozy in this well-known neighborhood pizzeria (established 30 years ago), which also serves the fresh catch from the adjacent port. In the late spring and summer, you can sit out on the little terrace and see across the bay to La Ciotat."—Kristin Espinasse

PIZZA DU SUD

66 Boulevard Jean Juarès
Saint-Cyr-sur-Mer
Provence-Alpes-Côte d'Azur 83270
France
+33 494322222

Opening hours	Open 7 days
Credit cards	Accepted
Style of pizza	Thin-crust
Recommended pizza	La Provençale

"A few steps from the old train station in Saint-Cyr-sur-Mer, and facing the tabac, where locals buy their weekly lottery ticket, this pizzeria is relaxed, young, and convivial. The waiters are charming and welcome you with a warm smile. Its modestly priced pizzas can be eaten *sur place* (on picnic tables where you can watch local traffic file by) or delivered to you."
—Kristin Espinasse

BASTA COSI

7 Impasse du Pont
Villeneuve-les-Avignon
Provence-Alpes-Côte d'Azur 30400
France
+33 469001331
www.bastacosi.fr

Opening hours	Open 7 days
Credit cards	Accepted but not AMEX
Style of pizza	Italian
Recommended pizza	Calzone

LA TRATTORIA SPORTING MONTE-CARLO

Avenue Princesse Grace
Monte Carlo 98000
Monaco
+377 98067171
www.alain-ducasse.com/fr/restaurants

Opening hours	Open 7 days
Credit cards	Accepted
Style of pizza	Tuscan
Recommended pizza	Margherita

"This chic address is the place to eat a Tuscany-inspired pizza, made with exceptional products, in a contemporary setting with an incredible view of the Mediterranean sea."—Vincent Delmas

"SALVATORE HAS REVOLUTIONIZED PIZZA IN PARIS! YOU GET THE FEELING THAT PROPER PIZZA HAS FINALLY LANDED IN THE CAPITAL."

JULIA SAMMUT P.185

"THE AMBIENCE IS PURE 1950S BISTRO IN A CHARMING, RETRO SPACE."

GILLES PUDLOWSKI P.184

PARIS

"THE FIRST SQUARE-SLICE PIZZERIA IN PARIS."

COLETTE MONSAT P.184

"A TRUE TASTE OF SOUTHERN ITALY WITH WONDERFUL SUN-DRENCHED INGREDIENTS."

NATHALIE CHIVA P.182

"A TINY LITTLE PIZZERIA IN THE MARAIS DISTRICT OF THE CITY WITH DELICIOUS, CAREFULLY MADE PIZZAS AND HIGH-QUALITY GARNISHES." ALEXANDER LOBRANO P.182

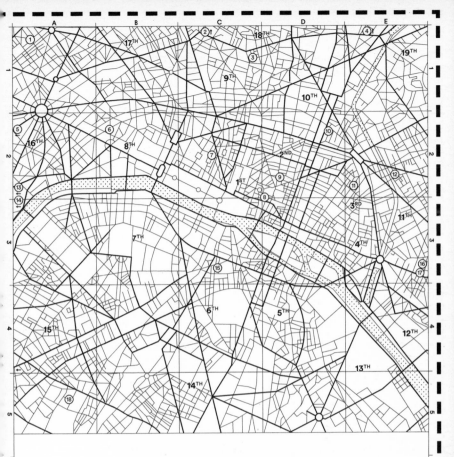

PARIS

N

SCALE

0   500   1000   1500

yd.

1. ROCO, 17TH ARRONDISSEMENT (P.185)
2. IL BRIGANTE, 18TH ARRONDISSEMENT (P.185)
3. LA PIZZETTA, 9TH ARRONDISSEMENT (P.183)
4. LE CAMION À PIZZA DU 104, 19TH ARRONDISSEMENT (P.185)
5. LA PIZZERIA DI REBELLATO, 16TH ARRONDISSEMENT (P.185)
6. LE BISTROT NAPOLITAIN, 8TH ARRONDISSEMENT (P.183)
7. MIPI, 1ST ARRONDISSEMENT (P.182)
8. LA FAMIGLIA DI REBELLATO, 1ST ARRONDISSEMENT (P.182)
9. O'SCIÀ, 2ND ARRONDISSEMENT (P.182)
10. ALLEGRA, 10TH ARRONDISSEMENT (P.183)
11. LA BRICIOLA, 3RD ARRONDISSEMENT (P.182)
12. AL TAGLIO, 11TH ARRONDISSEMENT (P.184)
13. GENIO, 16TH ARRONDISSEMENT (P.184)
14. PIZZERIA D'AUTEUIL, 16TH ARRONDISSEMENT (P.184)
15. CHEZ BARTOLO, 6TH ARRONDISSEMENT (P.182)
16. PIZZA DEI CIOPPI, 11TH ARRONDISSEMENT (P.184)
17. EAST MAMMA, 11TH ARRONDISSEMENT (P.183)
18. GREEN PIZZ, 15TH ARRONDISSEMENT (P.184)

LA FAMIGLIA DI REBELLATO

37 Rue Berger
1st Arrondissement
Paris
Île-de-France 75001
France
+33 140390640
www.rebellato.fr

Opening hours	Open 7 days
Credit cards	Accepted but not AMEX
Style of pizza	Neapolitan
Recommended pizza	Foie Gras

"A great Neapolitan pizza outside of Italy."
—Salvatore Salvo & Francesco Salvo

MIPI

11 Rue Danielle Casanova
1st Arrondissement
Paris
Île-de-France 75001
France
+33 142868080
www.mipi.pizza/fr

Opening hours	Closed Sunday
Credit cards	Accepted but not AMEX
Style of pizza	Neapolitan
Recommended pizza	Margherita; Napule

"The pizzas are small but very good, with a well-raised, moist base and good-quality ingredients. The restaurant's wine list exclusively contains wines from the Naples region."—Stefano Palombari

O'SCIÀ

44 Rue Tiquetonne
2nd Arrondissement
Paris
Île-de-France 75002
France
+33 175772318
www.pizzeriaoscia.fr

Opening hours	Open 7 days
Credit cards	Accepted but not AMEX
Style of pizza	Neapolitan
Recommended pizza	Broccoli Raab and Sausage; Focaccia Amalfitana; Pizza Fritta; Quattro Stagioni

"One of the most generous and tasty pizzas I've eaten in Paris."—Tina Meyer

"Sublime base, beautiful toppings…a true taste of southern Italy with wonderful sun-drenched ingredients."—Nathalie Chiva

LA BRICIOLA

64 Rue Charlot
3rd Arrondissement
Paris
Île-de-France 75003
France
+33 142773410

Opening hours	Closed Sunday
Credit cards	Accepted
Style of pizza	Neapolitan
Recommended pizza	Sausage

"A tiny little pizzeria in the Marais district of the city with delicious, carefully made pizzas and high-quality garnishes."—Alexander Lobrano

CHEZ BARTOLO

7 Rue des Canettes
6th Arrondissement
Paris
Île-de-France 75006
France
+33 143262708
www.chezbartolo.fr

Opening hours	Closed Sunday and Monday
Credit cards	Accepted but not AMEX
Style of pizza	Classic
Recommended pizza	Bartolo; Reine

"In the heart of the Saint-Germain area, Chez Bartolo was the first Neapolitan pizzeria to open in Paris in 1950."—Myriam Darmoni

LE BISTROT NAPOLITAIN

18 Avenue Franklin Delano Roosevelt
8th Arrondissement
Paris
Île-de-France 75008
France
+33 145620837

Opening hours..Open 7 days
Credit cards......................................Accepted but not AMEX
Style of pizza..Italian
Recommended pizza...Calzone

"Proper Neapolitan-style, wood-fired pizza with perfect
ingredients. The atmosphere is a bit overcharged and
has a real Golden Triangle feel, but you're sure to eat
very good pizza here."—Colette Monsat

LA PIZZETTA

22 Avenue Trudaine
9th Arrondissement
Paris
Île-de-France 75009
France
+33 173202120
www.restaurant-lapizzetta.fr

Opening hours..Open 7 days
Credit cards...Accepted
Style of pizza..Italian
Recommended pizza.................................Wholewheat Pizza
with Vegetables

"This place doesn't go with the trends. Ever since it
opened, it's served up thin, crispy-based pizza made
with wholewheat flour, using quality ingredients, and
it's open every day."—Gilles Pudlowski

ALLEGRA

70 Rue du Faubourg Saint-Martin
10th Arrondissement
Paris
Île-de-France 75010
France
+33 142081681

Opening hours..Open 7 days
Credit cards......................................Accepted but not AMEX
Style of pizza...Neapolitan
Recommended pizza...Fior di Latte

"Allegra uses first-rate produce, first and foremost
organic flour. The base is slightly more crispy than
a classic Neapolitan-style pizza."—Stefano Palombari

EAST MAMMA

133 Rue du Faubourg Saint-Antoine
11th Arrondissement
Paris
Île-de-France 75011
France
+33 143413215
www.bigmammagroup.com/east-mamma

Opening hours..Open 7 days
Credit cards...Accepted
Style of pizza...Wood-fired
Recommended pizza............Bufala; Fresh; Hot; Margherita;
Marinara

"The pizzas are made by a master pizza chef from
Naples, under the watchful eye of the young
Neapolitan head chef Ciro Cristiano. You feel like
you're in Italy!"—Clotilde Roux

"East Mamma is fun, lively, and tasty, with a joyful
atmosphere and decent prices."—Gilles Pudlowski

Parisians pining for real Neapolitan pizza made with sublime
ingredients had a *coup de coeur* for East Mamma. Still some
were more wait-and-see toward the modish trattoria. Would
the high standards last? Alba Pezone, our regional expert in
Paris, was concerned the clever owners Victor Lugger and
Tigrane Seydoux came from a business background, not a food
one. But soon her tune changed. The dough was supple and
well raised. The crust had its charred marks and soft spots in
the right places. "It doesn't bother me if the owners are
entrepreneurs," Pezone now reasoned. "If their project is
economically viable that's all for the better."

PIZZA DEI CIOPPI

44 Rue Trousseau
11th Arrondissement
Paris
Île-de-France 75011
France
+33 984481458

Opening hours	Open 7 days
Credit cards	Accepted but not AMEX
Style of pizza	Roman
Recommended pizza	Scarmoza and Artichoke; Scarmoza, Zucchini (courgette), and Calabrese Sausage

"First up, this Roman-style pizza is cut into squares. Surprisingly, the base is thicker than in most pizzerias, but it's ultra-moist on the inside and crispy on the outside, like a cake! It's a great change, and you can eat in or takeout."—Clotilde Roux

AL TAGLIO

2 Bis Rue Neuve-Popincourt
11th Arrondissement
Paris
Île-de-France 75011
France
+33 143381200
www.altaglio.fr

Opening hours	Open 7 days
Credit cards	Accepted but not AMEX
Style of pizza	Square
Recommended pizza	Potato and Truffle

"The first square-slice pizzeria in Paris. I love the concept, since it lets you try small amounts of several types, then pay by weight. I also love the little terrace outside—it's charming."—Colette Monsat

GREEN PIZZ

32 Rue Dantzig
15th Arrondissement
Paris
Île-de-France 75015
France
+33 966943748
www.greenpizz.com

Opening hours	Closed Monday
Credit cards	Not accepted
Style of pizza	Organic and eco-friendly
Recommended pizza	All Green; Euskadi; Fondue; Reine d'un Jour

"At Green Pizz, everything is homemade and organic, including the flour—a special spelt-based mix developed by the chef and a miller from Anjou. The shape of the pizza is oval and not round for a better cooking—in a wood-fired oven of course!"
—Myriam Darmoni

GENIO

3 Avenue Théophile Gauthier
16th Arrondissement
Paris
Île-de-France 75016
France
+33 173202439
www.geniotrattoria.fr

Opening hours	Closed Sunday
Credit cards	Accepted
Style of pizza	Roman and piadina
Recommended pizza	Genio Piadina

"Tucked away in the 16th arrondissement of Paris, it's definitely worth traveling to Genio for its authentic, delicious Italian pizza, not to mention the piadina (flatbreads), which are a house specialty."
—Clotilde Roux

PIZZERIA D'AUTEUIL

81 Rue Jean de la Fontaine
16th Arrondissement
Paris
Île-de-France 75016
France
+33 142880086
www.pizzeriadauteuil.com

Opening hours	Open 7 days
Credit cards	Accepted
Style of pizza	Classic
Recommended pizza	Margherita

"The ambience is pure 1950s bistro in a charming, retro space. Don't worry about the no-booking policy and the up-and-down service, because the prices are decent and the Neapolitan-style pizzas, with thick, crispy bases, are delightful."—Gilles Pudlowski

LA PIZZERIA DI REBELLATO

138 Rue de la Pompe
16th Arrondissement
Paris
Île-de-France 75016
France
+33 144050808
www.rebellato.fr

Opening hours...Open 7 days
Credit cards...Accepted
Style of pizza...Neapolitan
Recommended pizza.............................Foie Gras; Margherita

"Gennaro Nasti, a great and creative Neapolitan *pizzaiolo*, managed to bring to Paris a pizza that is every bit as good as those you can find today in Naples, the birthplace of pizza."—Antonio Lucisano

ROCO

1 Rue Guillaume Tell
17th Arrondissement
Paris
Île-de-France 75017
France
+33 147644939
www.rocoparis.com

Opening hours.........................Closed Sunday and Monday
Credit cards...........................Accepted but not AMEX
Style of pizza...Neapolitan
Recommended pizza...................Formagissima; Margherita;
Parigi

IL BRIGANTE

14 Rue du Ruisseau
18th Arrondissement
Paris
Île-de-France 75018
France
+33 144927215

Opening hours...Closed Sunday
Credit cards...Not accepted
Style of pizza...Neapolitan
Recommended pizza..........Carbonara; Margherita; 'Nduja;
Ronzatti; San Nicola

"Salvatore, the *pizzaiolo*, makes pizzas with a very thin base, well cooked and well topped with beautiful, characteristic products. The toppings are original and always tasty. You eat at a communal table in a small, crowded room. The clients love it."
—Alba Pezone

"Salvatore has revolutionized pizza in Paris! You get the feeling that proper pizza has finally landed in the capital."—Julia Sammut

Salvatore Rototori, Il Brigante's owner and chef, is the most loved *pizzaiolo* in Paris. It helps that the cramped kitchen and crammed dining area in his 18th-arrondissement trattoria are one and the same. The 20-odd diners have no choice but to get to know the bearded Calabrian and he them. They're adopted into his family. But it's his super-thin, ultra-crisp crust that wins hearts, along with his nose for the best Italian cheeses and salumi. Their quality and freshness are most apparent in the Carbonara pizza topped with mozzarella, Pecorino, Parmesan, *guanciale*, runny egg, and cracked black pepper.

LE CAMION À PIZZA DU 104

Food truck
Le Centquatre-Paris
5 Rue Curial
19th Arrondissement
Paris
Île-de-France 75019
France
+33 153355000
www.104.fr/les_espaces/restauration/camion-pizza.html

Opening hours...Closed Monday
Credit cards...Not accepted
Style of pizza...Neapolitan
Recommended pizza...Margherita

"This truck offers pizzas cooked in a wood-fired oven at any time of the year. You write your choice of pizza and your name on a piece of paper, then you wait to be called when it comes out of the oven to enjoy it piping hot, on the spot or to take away. I like this place for its conviviality, the good mood, the good scents it generates, and the fact that you eat on the fly, like in Naples."—Alba Pezone

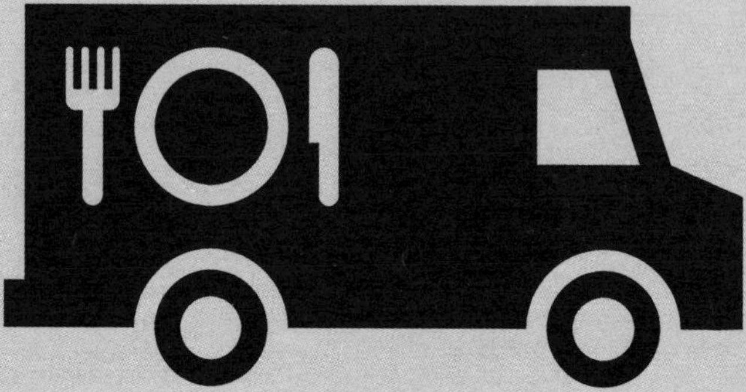

THE ORIGINAL
PIZZA TRUCK MOVEMENT

Silvestro Morlando bakes Neapolitan pizza for Londoners in the wood-fired oven fitted into a vintage blue Citroën Type H truck. Very cool. Yet the millennial geek behind the rolling pizzeria he named Sud Italia can hardly be called pioneer of the pizza truck. The movement, like their Citroën, traces back to France and a time when hipsters made movies and music, not Margheritas. In 1962, Marseille ferry steward Jean Meritan loaded a wood-burning oven onto a trailer, hooked it to a pickup truck and changed the eating habits of a city.

In Meritan's day many Marseille homes still had no telephones, no freezers. Pizza delivery and frozen pizzas were off the table. The low-cost convenience of street pizza proved irresistible. Soon there were over 200 pizza trucks, the majority of them Citroën "tubes," as the Type Hs were known, filling the air with the aromas of charred pizza crusts and melted Emmental, the domestic stand-in for Italian mozzarella.

In 1973 a pizza trucker's union, the Syndicat des Marchands Ambulants de Pizza et Similaires de la Ville de Marseille (Union of Mobile Merchants of Pizza and Related Products of the City of Marseille), was established to regulate, so to speak, the industry. To this day the man—if not every pizza baker—on the street sees the union as a shady group dictating who gets to park his pizzeria on the busiest boulevards. "I know the charge," says Francis Sposito, the union's honorary president. "We are not the mafia."

When Sposito began selling pizza out of a Citroën tube a half-century ago, lawless pizza truckers ruled the streets. "It was anarchy," recalls Sposito. The new union helped transfer the power over parking-space allocation to city hall, presumably a less corrupt authority, but did little to address the stifling work conditions. Come summer temperatures inside the pizza trucks could exceed 122°F (50°C).

As the trade spread beyond Marseille the union followed, ultimately adopting the name Fédération Nationale des Artisans Pizza en Camion Magasin (National Federation of Pizza Artisans in Food Trucks). Why artisans instead of merchants? From their trucks, the *pizzaioli* heard the buzz of pizza delivery scooters. Supermarkets were selling frozen pizza. Aware they could no longer compete on convenience and cost, the union doubled down on quality, urging its members not to shortcut the dough and its maturation.

Will the union's new catchphrase, "slow food *ambulante,*" be effective? Will the original pizza truck movement endure? Marseille still has its roadside artisans who craft delicately crisp pizzas topped with thin layers of good-quality ingredients. The exploits of hipster pizza trucks in London, Stockholm, and Geneva give new hope to Sposito. Now in his eighties, his dream is to live long enough to see his union change its name once more, from Fédération Nationale to Fédération Européenne des Artisans Pizza en Camion Magasin.

"YOU CAN GUARANTEE THAT THE PIZZA WILL BE GREAT AND THAT THE WAITERS WILL PUT ON A SHOW."
MIREIA DE LA TORRE P.190

"THE BEST ARGENTINIAN-STYLE PIZZA IN MADRID."
CATHRIN BRANDES P.192

SPAIN, PORTUGAL & MALTA

"THIS IS THE BEST PIZZERIA IN LISBON."
ALEXANDRA PRADO COELHO P.192

"IT HAS A GOOD SELECTION OF ITALIAN CRAFT BEERS."
MIGUEL PIRES P.193

"THOUGH THE ULTRA-HOT WOOD OVEN PROMISES NEAPOLITAN PIES, CHEF CLAUDE CAMILLERI'S PIZZA IS MALTESE TO THE CORE."
ALICE LEVITT P.195

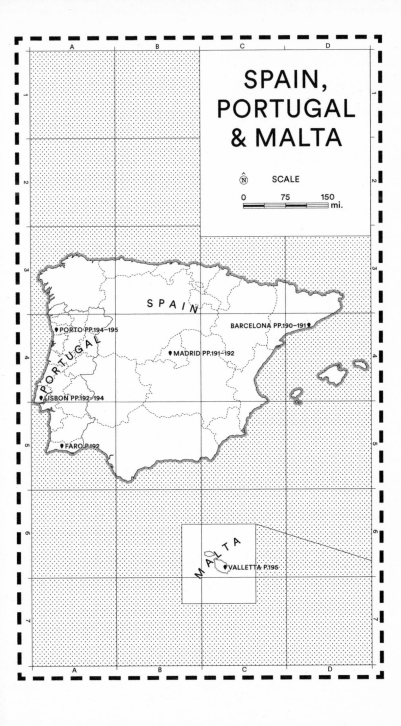

SPAIN, PORTUGAL & MALTA

SCALE

0   75   150 mi.

SPAIN

PORTUGAL

PORTO PP.194–195

BARCELONA PP.190–191

MADRID PP.191–192

LISBON PP.192–194

FARO P.192

MALTA

VALLETTA P.195

LA BELLA NAPOLI
Villarroel 101
Barcelona
Barcelona 08011
Spain
+34 934547056
www.labellanapoli.es

Opening hours	Open 7 days
Credit cards	Accepted but not AMEX
Style of pizza	Neapolitan
Recommended pizza	Napoletana

"La Bella Napoli is a classic that never disappoints. The authentic trattoria is run by Rafaelle Iannone who has been serving up traditional Neapolitan dishes for over 10 years. His wonderful pizzas are a particular standout. There's always a line, but it's worth the wait! You can guarantee that the pizza will be great and that the waiters will put on a show."—Mireia de la Torre

LA BRICIOLA
Carrer d'Olzinelles 19
Barcelona
Barcelona 08014
Spain
+34 934321933
www.pizzerialabriciola.com

Opening hours	Closed Sunday
Credit cards	Accepted
Style of pizza	Italian
Recommended pizza	Campione

"Italians Pino Prestanizzi and Patricio Sodano were among the first to open a trattoria in Barcelona, over 20 years ago. They are the kings of pizza, and their secret lies in making very thin bases, a change from the Neapolitan style we're used to."
—Mireia de la Torre

N.A.P. (NEAPOLITAN AUTHENTIC PIZZA)
Avenue Francesc Cambó 30
Barcelona
Barcelona 08003
Spain
+34 686192690

Opening hours	Open 7 days
Credit cards	Accepted but not AMEX
Style of pizza	Neapolitan
Recommended pizza	Regina

"I really like the fact that you can see the wood-fired oven, where generous-sized pizzas are cooked to perfection, filling the room with their characteristic aroma."—Mireia de la Torre

O'PRINCIPE
Carrer de Pujades 209
Barcelona
Barcelona 08019
Spain
+34 931805994
www.oprincipe.com

Opening hours	Open 7 days
Credit cards	Accepted but not AMEX
Style of pizza	Wood-fired
Recommended pizza	Fresca

"One of the most authentic Italian restaurants to be found anywhere in the world, O'Principe impressed us so much with its perfect pizza dough that we ate there three times during a week in Barcelona. Poblenou is a pleasant suburb away from the tourist center of the city but easily reached by metro (the restaurant is across the road from the metro stop)."
—Sue de Groot

AL PASSATORE
Pla Palau 8
Barcelona
Barcelona 08003
Spain
+34 933197851
www.alpassatore.com

Opening hours	Open 7 days
Credit cards	Accepted but not AMEX
Style of pizza	Roman
Recommended pizza	The Bismark

"The best crusts in the world, ultra-crispy, very thin, and full of flavor."—Marissa Chiappe Lanatta

LA PIZZA DEL BORN

Passeig del Born 22
Barcelona
Barcelona 08003
Spain
+34 933106246
www.lapizzadelborn.com

Opening hours...Open 7 days
Credit cards..Not accepted
Style of pizza...Argentinian

"Amazing choices baked all night."—Jeffrey Finkelstein

LA CÚPULA

Calle Goya 25
Madrid
Madrid 28290
Spain
+34 916309147
www.pizzerialacupula.es

Opening hours...Open 7 days
Credit cards..............................Accepted but not AMEX
Style of pizza...Neapolitan
Recommended pizza..Siciliano

"Simplicity at its best, subscribing to the motto 'less is more.'"—Javier Marca

DON LISANDER

Calle de la Infanta Mercedes 17
Madrid
Madrid 28020
Spain
+34 915709290

Opening hours...Closed Monday
Credit cards...Accepted
Style of pizza...Neapolitan
Recommended pizza.....................Margherita; Sardagnola

"Don Lisander is an authentic trattoria with an extensive menu. Over 30 different pizzas are on offer, including some very original flavor combinations, all of which are exquisite."—David Maldonado

"Elegant oval-shaped pizzas with a perfect thin crust and good crust to topping ratio, served in sophisticated surroundings. The pizzas have an extremely thin, paper-like crust and crispy *cornicione*."—Javier Marca

KILÓMETROS DE PIZZA

Avenida de Brasil 6
Madrid
Madrid 28020
Spain
+34 917557232
www.kilometrosdepizza.com

Opening hours...Open 7 days
Credit cards..............................Accepted but not AMEX
Style of pizza...Roman
Recommended pizza..........Diabolo; Matador; San Danielle

"This is a Spanish restaurant concept created by former World Pizza Champion Jesús Marquina, from La Mancha. It uses a very special oven and Italian flour to create a wide range of oval pizzas."
—Marta Fernández Guadaño

"Very thin and crispy Italian-style pizza served by the meter. It's perfect for groups."—Pablo Giudice

OUH BABBO

Calle de Caños del Peral 2
Madrid
Madrid 28013
Spain
+34 915476581

Opening hours...Open 7 days
Credit cards...Accepted
Style of pizza...Roman
Recommended pizza...Gourmet

"An enormous wood-fired oven made from volcanic rock is the main reason that pizza bases here come out very thin, nicely browned, and crispy. The authentic flavor is turned up a notch every Thursday when the owner, actor Bruno Squarcia, treats his customers to a live serenade."—David Maldonado

PICSA

Calle de Ponzano 76
Madrid
Madrid 28003
Spain
+34 915341009
www.casapicsa.com

Opening hours...Open 7 days
Credit cards...............................Accepted but not AMEX
Style of pizza...............................Argentinian wood-fired
Recommended pizza................Aladino; Calabrese; Chorizo
Criollo; Fugazza with Cheese;
Peppers with Arugula (rocket)

"The best Argentinian-style pizza in Madrid.
Big, thick, chewy, and with lots of cheese!"
—Cathrin Brandes

Picsa is a sleek laboratory for Argentine pizza from Estanis
Carenzo and Pablo Giudice, the architects of the restaurant
Sudestada and its modern *madrileño* take on Southeast Asian.
For Picsa the chefs reached back to Buenos Aires and its
thicker, fluffier, cheesier *picsa* ("pizza" in a local dialect) for
inspiration. Seated at the counter, you can view the entire
assembly of the light, fluffy, spongy pizza, from its construction
in the pan to its exit from the oak-fired oven. Each pizza, though
sized for per capita consumption, is meant to be shared—an
especially difficult proposition when confronting the Fugazza
Con Queso, with sweet onion, red onion, house cheese,
rosemary, and Spanish black olives.

PIZZA AL CUADRADO

Calle Ballesta 10
Madrid
Madrid 28004
Spain
+34 915213515
www.pizzalcuadrado.com

Opening hours...Open 7 days
Credit cards...............................Accepted but not AMEX
Style of pizza...*Pizza al taglio*
Recommended pizza............Conference Pear, Gorgonzola,
and Walnut; Eggplant (aubergine), Chicory, and
Gorgonzola; Zucca Gialla

"Pizza al Cuadrado offers high-quality *pizza al taglio*
with excellent combinations of toppings and perfectly
textured thick-crust dough. The pizzas are ready on
display, but a blast in the oven just before serving
gives them that freshly baked taste. The decor is
simple but inviting, making this the ideal place to
get together with friends for beers and pizza."
—Ignacio Barrios Jacobs

LUNA ROSSA

Rua Marina de Vilamoura
Vilamoura
Faro 8125-401
Portugal
+351 289302245
www.lunarossa.pt

Opening hours...Open 7 days
Credit cards...Accepted
Style of pizza...Neapolitan
Recommended pizza...San Daniele

"Luna Rossa is situated in a delightful location
next to Vilamoura Marina. Its excellent pizzas are
produced with creative flair."
—Luís Américo Aguiar de Moura Rodrigues Teixeira

CASANOVA

Avenue Infante Dom Henrique
Cais da Pedra, Armazém 7, Loja B
Lisbon
Lisbon 1900-264
Portugal
+351 218877532
www.pizzeriacasanova.pai.pt

Opening hours...Open 7 days
Credit cards...Accepted
Style of pizza...Italian thin-crust
Recommended pizza................Boscaiola; Pesto; Prosciutto
and Fig; Rustica

"This is the best pizzeria in Lisbon, in my opinion.
High-quality ingredients, a wood-fired oven, efficient
service (although you normally have to wait for a table,
as it gets very busy), and a charming and relaxed
atmosphere right next to the river Tejo. What more
could you want?"—Alexandra Prado Coelho

"The thin-crust bases perfectly showcase the
toppings, which are never excessive."
—Suzana Parreira

LA FINESTRA

Avenida Conde de Valbom, Nº 52-A
Lisbon
Lisbon 1050-069
Portugal
+351 217613580
www.lafinestra.pt

Opening hours................................Open 7 days
Credit cards........................Accepted but not AMEX
Style of pizza...................................Thin-crust
Recommended pizza.................................Calabria

FORNO D'ORO

Rua Artilharia 1 16B
Lisbon
Lisbon 1250-039
Portugal
+351 213879944
www.fornodoro.pt

Opening hours................................Open 7 days
Credit cards...................................Accepted
Style of pizza..................................Neapolitan
Recommended pizza...........Diavola; Formosa; Napoletana;
Transumância

"The combination of traditional Portuguese flavors
and dough that is well fermented and nicely raised
(in classic Neapolitan style) produces pizzas that
emerge from the oven with a golden glow, making
chef Tanka Spakota's creations unique."
—Suzana Parreira

"It has a good selection of Italian craft beers."
—Miguel Pires

IN BOCCA AL LUPO

Rua Manuel Bernardes 5
Lisbon
Lisbon 1200-250
Portugal
+351 213900582
www.inboccaallupo.pt

Opening hours.................Closed Monday and Tuesday
Credit cards........................Accepted but not AMEX
Style of pizza...................................Thin-crust
Recommended pizza................................Caprese; Ortolana

"Each pizza is lovingly made with the utmost respect
for the ingredients, producing fresh and simple
flavors. The thin-crust pizza dough is cooked in
a wood-fired oven, making it crispy and very tasty."
—Suzana Parreira

PIZZA À PEZZI

Rua Dom Pedro V 84
Lisbon
Lisbon 1250-001
Portugal
+351 934563170
www.restaurantecasanostra.com

Opening hours................................Open 7 days
Credit cards..................................Not accepted
Style of pizza......................................Roman
Recommended pizza.........................Rosemary, Mozzarella,
and Potato

"Pizza a Pezzi offers traditional Roman-style thin and
crispy pizza. You can also try different types of pizza,
which is an added bonus."—Tanka Sapkota

PIZZARIA DO BAIRRO

Rua da Cintura do Porto de Lisboa
Armazém A, Nº 18
Lisbon
Lisbon 1200-450
Portugal
+351 218066584
www.pizzariadobairro.com.pt

Opening hours..Closed Monday
Credit cards..Not accepted
Style of pizza..Italian
Recommended pizza.............................Maria; Portugal

"Pizzaria do Bairro's aim is to produce Italian-style
pizza but with Portuguese ingredients such as salt
cod, peppers, oregano, or traditional Portuguese
cheese. The place is very small—it's good for a quick
bite and you can also buy takeout pizza and enjoy
it as you wander around Lisbon."
—Alexandra Prado Coelho

PIZZARIA LISBOA

Rua dos Duques de Bragança 5H
Lisbon
Lisbon 1200-166
Portugal
+351 211554945
www.pizzarialisboa.pt

Opening hours..Open 7 days
Credit cards...Accepted
Style of pizza...Thin-crust
Recommended pizza..Graça

BH FOZ

Avenida Brasil 498
Porto
Porto 4150-153
Portugal
+351 910993040
www.bhfoz.pt

Opening hours..Open 7 days
Credit cards...Accepted
Style of pizza..Italian
Recommended pizza...Pepperoni

"This is a young and modern restaurant near the
beach, which also serves pizza. The Neapolitan pizza
chef produces thin-crust pizzas that are both soft and
crispy and uses high-quality ingredients, such as the
spicy pepperoni featured on the menu."
—Susana Ribeiro

CASADORO

Rua do Ouro 797
Porto
Porto 4150-555
Portugal
+351 226106012
www.restaurantecasanostra.com

Opening hours..Open 7 days
Credit cards...Accepted
Style of pizza...Roman
Recommended pizza.........................Margherita; Tartufo

"These are thin and crispy wood-fired pizzas made
with fresh authentic Mediterranean ingredients."
—Fátima Iken

D'OLIVA

Rua Brito e Cunha 354
4450 Matosinhos
Porto
Porto 4450-087
Portugal
+351 229351005

Opening hours..Closed Monday
Credit cards...Accepted
Style of pizza...Thin and crispy
Recommended pizza...Tuna

"These are made by a Neapolitan chef who really
knows how to stretch pizza dough and all the
ingredients are very fresh."—Fátima Iken

PIZZERIA PULCINELLA

Avenida Menéres 390
Matosinhos
Porto
Porto 4450-189
Portugal
+351 229382806

Opening hours..Closed Monday
Credit cards...................................Accepted but not AMEX
Style of pizza..Neapolitan
Recommended pizza.........................Il Padrino; Margherita

"This was the first place in Portugal to serve authentic
Neapolitan pizza. The pizza chef, a genuine
Neapolitan, makes thin-crust pizzas with fresh and
tasty ingredients. It is a veritable foray into the
flavors of Italy."—Susana Ribeiro

PORTAROSSA

Rua Côrte Real 289
Porto
Porto 4150-235
Portugal
+351 226175286
www.portarossa.pt

Opening hours..Open 7 days
Credit cards.................................Accepted but not AMEX
Style of pizza...Roman
Recommended pizza...Diavola; Rustica

"Located in the most prestigious part of the city
of Porto—Foz do Douro—this pizzeria, although
informal, has a cosmopolitan feel with plenty
of outside space. Pizzas are made in a traditional
wood-fired oven."
—Luís Américo Aguiar de Moura Rodrigues Teixeira

RESTAURANT AL FORNO

Rua Adro da Foz 4
Porto
Porto 4150-013
Portugal
+351 226173549

Opening hours..Closed Sunday
Credit cards.................................Accepted but not AMEX
Style of pizza...Wood-fired
Recommended pizza...Capricciosa

FORNERIA DE SÃO PEDRO

Rua Eduardo de Matos 84
Vila Nova de Gaia
Porto 4400-434
Portugal
+351 227722736
www.forneria.pt/a-forneria-de-sao-pedro

Opening hours..Open 7 days
Credit cards.................................Accepted but not AMEX
Style of pizza...Roman
Recommended pizza..............Capricciosa; Wild Mushroom
and Truffle

"All the pizzas are made in a wood-fired oven, which
gives them a very distinct flavor. There are plenty of
pizzas to choose from with various toppings, so you
can try something different each time. One of the
pizzas has also been adapted to taste like a typical
Porto-style dish (Francesinha) with spicy sauce."
—Susana Ribeiro

MARGO'S

63 Republic Street
Valletta 1117
Malta
+356 27627467
www.margosmalta.com

Opening hours..Open 7 days
Credit cards...Not accepted
Style of pizza...Neapolitan
Recommended pizza.......................................L'Affumicata

"Though the ultra-hot wood oven promises Neapolitan
pies, chef Claude Camilleri's pizza is Maltese to
the core. The team hand-mills its own flour for its
naturally leavened crust and smokes and cures
its own meat."—Alice Levitt

NENU THE ARTISAN BAKER

143 Saint Dominic Street
Valletta 1605
Malta
+356 22581535
www.nenuthebaker.com

Opening hours.........................Closed Sunday and Monday
Credit cards.................................Accepted but not AMEX
Style of pizza...Maltese ftira
Recommended pizza.....................................Ta' Ġorġ ir-Raġel

"*Ftira* is an ultra-buttery savory pastry that splits the
difference between Middle Eastern breads and pizza.
This is the place for the best preparation you'll find."
—Alice Levitt

"WHO WOULD EXPECT TO FIND ONE OF THE BEST PIZZAS IN THE COUNTRY IN A PLACE LIKE THIS?" TORSTEN GOFFIN P.198

"MONTANA IS MODERN AND TRENDY, AND TOTALLY WACKY."
GIUSEPPE ABBATE P.200

"ONE OF BERLIN'S BEST BREAD BAKERIES, SIRONI ALSO TURNS OUT SOME MEAN PIZZA SLICES."
JOE DILIBERTO P.199

GERMANY & SWITZERLAND

"IT HAS A RELAXED TRADITIONAL ALPINE ATMOSPHERE, A PLEASANT OUTDOOR GARDEN, AND A SMALL BOWLING ALLEY DOWNSTAIRS." CATHRIN BRANDES P.198

"ONCE YOU KNOW WHERE TO FIND THIS FOOD TRUCK YOU'LL NEVER BE ABLE TO PASS IT BY."
SAKURA HORI P.212

"IT'S THE IDEAL PLACE FOR NIGHT OWLS."
CHRISTIAN MOOK P.200

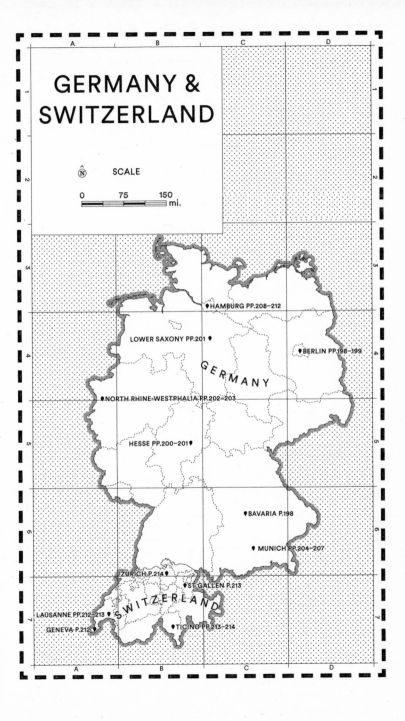

GERMANY &
SWITZERLAND

N

SCALE

0   75   150
‗‗‗‗‗‗‗‗ mi.

♥HAMBURG PP.208–212

LOWER SAXONY PP.201 ♥

♥BERLIN PP.198–199

G E R M A N Y

♥NORTH RHINE-WESTPHALIA PP.202–203

HESSE PP.200–201♥

♥BAVARIA P.198

♥MUNICH PP.204–207

ZURICH P.214♥

♥ST GALLEN P.213

S W I T Z E R L A N D

LAUSANNE PP.212–213 ♥

♥TICINO PP.213–214

GENEVA P.212♥

BELLA ITALIA IM KAUFLAND

Äussere Münchener Strasse 100
Rosenheim
Bavaria 83026
Germany
+49 80314082079

Opening hours	Closed Sunday
Credit cards	Not accepted
Style of pizza	Neapolitan
Recommended pizza	Pupatella

"The combination of absolutely first-class, authentic, Neapolitan pizza on the one hand and the location in a simple shopping center on the other is bizarre and endearing in equal measure. Who would expect to find one of the best pizzas in the country in a place like this?"—Torsten Goffin

PIZZERIA JOLLY

Waldhauserstrasse 18
Schönau am Königssee
Bavaria 83471
Germany
+49 865264500
www.pizzeria-jolly.de

Opening hours	Open 7 days
Credit cards	Not accepted
Style of pizza	Classic
Recommended pizza	Orchidea

"Thanks to the long rise, the wood-fired oven, and the expert way in which the dough is stretched and baked, Pizzeria Jolly means that you can eat a pizza that is 100 percent Italian even in Germany. Head *pizzaiolo* Andrea Antoccia offers a great variety of toppings and types of pizza. He was also one of the first in Germany to provide a diverse gourmet menu for vegetarians and vegans."—Valerio Valle

LA PIAZZETTA

Büttnerstrasse 7–9
Würzburg
Bavaria 97070
Germany
+49 93199136810
www.la-piazzetta-würzburg.com

Opening hours	Closed Monday
Credit cards	Not accepted
Style of pizza	Neapolitan
Recommended pizza	Margherita; Napoletana

"La Piazzetta is a six-table pizzeria that is very cozy and warm. It is very popular so reservations are necessary."—Tilen Konte

CAFÉ AROMA

Hochkirchstrasse 8
Berlin
Berlin 10829
Germany
+49 307825821
www.cafe-aroma.de

Opening hours	Open 7 days
Credit cards	Accepted
Style of pizza	Traditional
Recommended pizza	Zio Pepé

"Café Aroma is a long-time institution for trattoria-style food in Berlin. The owners are early Slow Food promoters and use really good products from small Italian producers. The pizzas are thin, tasty, and quite big, and you smell and taste the excellent ingredients like really good mozzarella, ham, and sausages."
—Cathrin Brandes

GASTHAUS FIGL

Urbanstrasse 24
Berlin
Berlin 10967
Germany
+49 3072290850
www.gasthaus-figl.de

Opening hours	Closed Monday
Credit cards	Not accepted
Style of pizza	North Italian
Recommended pizza	Alsace; Tyrolean Cheese; Tyrolean Special

"For thin-crust Tyrolean-style pizza with alpine mountain cheese, speck, and herbs, head to Gasthaus Figl. It has a relaxed traditional alpine atmosphere, a pleasant outdoor garden, and a small bowling alley downstairs."—Cathrin Brandes

"The Alsace pizza with blood sausage (black pudding) is truly amazing."—Joe Diliberto

I DUE FORNI

Schönhauser Allee 12
Berlin
Berlin 10119
Germany
+49 3044017333

Opening hours	Open 7 days
Credit cards	Not accepted
Style of pizza	Italian
Recommended pizza	Buon Gustaio

"What I love about this pizzeria is its wild and bustling atmosphere in a messy surrounding."—Malin Elmlid

MASANIELLO

Hasenheide 20
Berlin
Berlin 10967
Germany
+49 306926657
www.befo.de/masaniello

Opening hours	Open 7 days
Credit cards	Accepted but not AMEX
Style of pizza	Neapolitan
Recommended pizza	Verace Rosa Margherita

"This is the only place I have been to outside of Naples that really does authentic Neapolitan-style pizza. It's truly amazing."—Joe Diliberto

"From the outside it looks like a terribly cheap trattoria, but inside it's a kitsch Neapolitan dream: Napoli scarves, portraits of politicians, and faux-wooden furniture. It has great service and a lovely outdoor terrace."—Tommy Tannock

RON TELESKY CANADIAN PIZZA

Dieffenbachstrasse 62
Berlin
Berlin 10967
Germany
+49 3061621111
www.ron-telesky.de

Opening hours	Open 7 days
Credit cards	Not accepted
Style of pizza	Canadian

"I love the enormous slices of pizza with really eccentric toppings."—Cathrin Brandes

SIRONI (IL PANE DI MILANO)

Eisenbahnstrasse 42/43
Berlin
Berlin 10997
Germany

Opening hours	Closed Sunday
Credit cards	Not accepted
Style of pizza	Italian

"One of Berlin's best bread bakeries, Sironi also turns out some mean pizza slices."—Joe Diliberto

STANDARD PIZZA

Templiner Strasse 7
Berlin
Berlin 10119
Germany
+49 3048625614
www.standard-berlin.de

Opening hours	Closed Monday
Credit cards	Not accepted
Style of pizza	Neapolitan
Recommended pizza	Margherita; Parma; Taste of Brandenburg

"Simplicity and high-quality ingredients make this pizzeria your best bet in Prenzlauer Berg."
—Malin Elmlid

ZOLA

Erster Innenhof, Paul-Lincke-Ufer 39–40
Berlin
Berlin 10999
Germany
+49 17670798442

Opening hours	Closed Saturday and Sunday
Credit cards	Not accepted
Style of pizza	Neapolitan
Recommended pizza	Margherita

LORENZO
Homburger Strasse 3
Bad Vilbel
Hesse 61118
Germany
+49 61019539596
www.lorenzo-pizza.de

Opening hours	Closed Tuesday
Credit cards	Not accepted
Style of pizza	Wood-fired
Recommended pizza	Parma

"This pizzeria may have limited seating space but it offers a fantastic taste experience, and not just because of the size of the pizzas (which wouldn't fit on any plate). Crisp yet delicate, the dough has the sweet fragrance of fresh ingredients and intoxicates the senses and the palate."—Giuseppe Abbate

A TAVOLA! PIZZA & PASTA
Diesterwegstrasse 4
Frankfurt
Hesse 60594
Germany
+49 6966124477
www.atavola.kitchen

Opening hours	Open 7 days
Credit cards	Not accepted
Style of pizza	Classic
Recommended pizza	Bresaola; Porcini Mushrooms

DAS LEBEN IST SCHÖN
Hanauer Landstrasse 198
Frankfurt
Hesse 60314
Germany
+49 6943057870
www.daslebenistschoen.de

Opening hours	Open 7 days
Credit cards	Accepted
Style of pizza	Thin and crispy
Recommended pizza	Celentano

"Imagination is the name of the game here, so the pizzas are not called Margherita or Capricciosa, but Rossi, Benigni, Pavarotti, or Briatore (very spicy!), to name just a few."—Giuseppe Abbate

MONTANA
Weserstrasse 14
Frankfurt
Hesse 60329
Germany
+49 6921998627
www.montana-pizzeria.de

Opening hours	Open 7 days
Credit cards	Accepted
Style of pizza	Neapolitan
Recommended pizza	Mushroom White; Queen Margherita

"Montana is modern and trendy, and totally wacky."
—Giuseppe Abbate

"The Stefano Ferrara pizza oven is designed to look like a bright yellow Pac-Man."—Christian Mook

PANINOTECA NO. 1
Bleidenstrasse 13
Frankfurt
Hesse 60311
Germany
+49 69284487
www.paninoteca.co

Opening hours	Open 7 days
Credit cards	Accepted but not AMEX
Style of pizza	Classic
Recommended pizza	Surf and Turf

"Paninoteca No. 1 has a very elegant atmosphere. It's located in the heart of Frankfurt, close to the Zeil shopping street. That only 10 pizzas are on the menu suggests a focus on quality, not quantity."
—Giuseppe Abbate

PIZZA PETRO
Paradiesgasse 38
Frankfurt
Hesse 60594
Germany
+49 69611576

Opening hours	Open 7 days
Credit cards	Not accepted
Style of pizza	Snack bar
Recommended pizza	Salami

"Pizza Petro stays open very late. It's the ideal place for night owls."—Christian Mook

PIZZERIA DA CIMINO

Adalbertstrasse 29
Frankfurt
Hesse 60486
Germany
+49 69771142
www.pizzeria-cimino.de

Opening hours	Open 7 days
Credit cards	Not accepted
Style of pizza	Wood-fired
Recommended pizza	Arugula (rocket) with Parma Ham; Hawaii; Quattro Formaggi

"For me, this is the best pizza in the city, and has been for decades. It has a very lively, student clientele and is lots of fun."—Hans Petersen

PIZZERIA DICK & DOOF

Berger Strasse 248
Frankfurt
Hesse 60385
Germany
+49 69457317
www.dickunddoofonline.de

Opening hours	Open 7 days
Credit cards	Not accepted
Style of pizza	Snack bar
Recommended pizza	Margherita

"Dick & Doof is a takeout pizzeria and snack bar with a couple of high tables. It's a perennial favorite in the Bornheim district of Frankfurt."—Barbara Goerlich

PIZZERIA OLBIA

Glauburgstrasse 14
Frankfurt
Hesse 60318
Germany
+49 695972925
www.pizzeriaolbia.de

Opening hours	Open 7 days
Credit cards	Not accepted
Style of pizza	Italian
Recommended pizza	Margherita

"This is a stand-up pizzeria with a few chairs. The service is quick and the pizza is consistently good."
—Barbara Goerlich

LA VELA

Wittelsbacherallee 65
Frankfurt
Hesse 60385
Germany
+49 6913826402
www.lavela-frankfurt.de

Opening hours	Closed Monday
Credit cards	Not accepted
Style of pizza	Rustic
Recommended pizza	Caligula Imperatore

"La Vela has a really nice atmosphere. The pizza is made in a charcoal oven and tastes far better than average."—Christian Mook

BUONA SERA

Rosenstrasse 4
Lüneburg
Lower Saxony 21335
Germany
+49 413137275
www.buona-sera.de

Opening hours	Closed Tuesday
Credit cards	Not accepted
Style of pizza	Italian thin-crust

LA ROMA

Stöteroggestrasse 71
Lüneburg
Lower Saxony 21339
Germany
+49 413131393
www.la-roma.de

Opening hours	Open 7 days
Credit cards	Not accepted
Style of pizza	Thick-crust
Recommended pizza	Diavola

AMALFI

Gerberstrasse 2
Bochum
North Rhine-Westphalia 44787
Germany
+49 2348936253

Opening hours	Closed Tuesday
Credit cards	Not accepted
Style of pizza	Neapolitan
Recommended pizza	Caprese; Leone; Margherita

"Sergio Naclerio, who has been manning a pizza oven since he was a boy, now makes probably the best pizzas in the entire Ruhr district in a nondescript, rather cold building from the 1990s in a side street in Bochum's city center."—Sebastian Enste

"Sergio Naclerio is almost unrivaled in the art of making pizzas."—Herwig Niggemann

485 GRAD

Kyffhäuserstrasse 44
Cologne
North Rhine-Westphalia 50674
Germany
+49 22139753330
www.485grad.de

Opening hours	Open 7 days
Credit cards	Not accepted
Style of pizza	Neapolitan
Recommended pizza	Bloody Napoli; Green-White-Red; Hellboy; Margherita; Parma Power; Rocky Balboa's Speckbirne; Speckenwolf with Bacon

"Here you get pure pizza with a dash of tomato sauce, one of the best mozzarella cheeses in Italy, and some basil. Just 60 seconds in the 905°F (485°C) oven and it's ready to enjoy. Perfect. It doesn't get any better than this, even in Italy."
—Fritz Zickuhr

"The best, most exceptional, and authentic pizzeria in Cologne!"—Beatrix Eichbaum

485 Grad is Neapolitan pizza by the numbers: 36 hours for the dough to rest, 905°F (485°C) for the Stefano Ferrara brick oven to heat, 60–90 seconds for the pizza to cook. Co-owner Lars Zöllner is a great Neapolitan pizza enthusiast if not quite a purist: his menu is a 50–50 split between classics like the Marinara de Luxe and brilliant innovations (or abominations) like the Reuben Pastrami pizza, with pastrami, Gruyére, caramelized onions, and coleslaw. Co-owner Sebastian Georgi, formerly a three-star sommelier, chooses the wines, brews, and soft drinks. "Not just good pizza but also adequate drinks," says our Cologne regional expert Torsten Goffin, summing up the 485 Grad experience with 90 percent understatement.

LA GUSTOSA

Sudermanplatz 6
Cologne
North Rhine-Westphalia 50670
Germany
+49 22137998577

Opening hours	Closed Monday
Credit cards	Not accepted
Style of pizza	Sicilian
Recommended pizza	Brontese

"I only have to hear the name Brontese for my mouth to start watering. Instead of tomato sauce, the base is covered with a delicious pistachio cream, with arugula (rocket), Parma ham, Parmesan, and crunchy pistachios rounding off the appeal."
—Beatrix Eichbaum

OSTERIA IL NIDO

Weisser Strasse 71
Cologne
North Rhine-Westphalia 50996
Germany
+49 22182821660
www.ilnido.de

Opening hours	Closed Tuesday
Credit cards	Not accepted
Style of pizza	Italian
Recommended pizza	Bell'Italia; Emiliana

"I really like the Bell'Italia, made with Parma ham, arugula (rocket), and Parmesan, and the Emiliana, a *pizza bianca* made with pears, caramelized walnuts, and Gorgonzola cheese. These are the two pizzas that epitomize the honest, creative, and high-quality Italian cuisine of Il Nido."
—Beatrix Eichbaum

SALUTE

Lindenthalgürtel 51
Cologne
North Rhine-Westphalia 50935
Germany
+49 2214069099

Opening hours..Open 7 days
Credit cards...Not accepted
Style of pizza..Classic
Recommended pizza...Rustica

"What looks from the outside like a fast-food joint from the 1950s soon reveals itself to be the pizza paradise of Lindenthal. You have to book a table, and even if you order your takeout pizza in good time over the phone you may still have a few minutes' wait at peak times. But the wait is worthwhile."
—Fritz Zickuhr

TOSCANINI

Jakobstrasse 22
Cologne
North Rhine-Westphalia 50678
Germany
+49 2213109990
www.toscanini-koeln.com

Opening hours..Open 7 days
Credit cards...Not accepted
Style of pizza...Italian
Recommended pizza.....................................Calzone; Rustica

WACKES

Beneisisstrasse 59
Cologne
North Rhine-Westphalia 50672
Germany
+49 2212573456
www.wackes-weinstube.de

Opening hours..Open 7 days
Credit cards.....................................Accepted but not AMEX
Style of pizza..........Flammkuchen (Alsatian tarte flambée)

MUNICH

"H'UGO'S HAS BECOME PART OF THE MUNICH SCENE."

HANS-JÜRGEN HARTAUER P.206

"THERE ARE FEW SUMMER TERRACES AS ATTRACTIVE AS THAT OF RIVA SCHWABING."

MICHAELA BOGNER P.207

"THIS IS MUNICH'S LIFESTYLE PIZZERIA CREATED BY THE EXCELLENT GASTRONOMIC DUO OF RUDI KULL AND KURT WEINZIERL."

CLAUDIA EILERS P.206

"AN AUGUSTINER LAGER IS THE ESSENTIAL ACCOMPANIMENT!"

JOSSI LOIBL P.206

MUNICH

N⟩

SCALE

0   500   1000   1500
yd.

1. LOCANDA BUSENTO, SENDLING-WESTPARK (P.207)
2. NEUHAUSER, NEUHAUSEN-NYMPHENBURG (P.207)
3. OH JULIA, ALTSTADT (P.206)
4. H'UGO'S, ALTSTADT (P.206)
5. FABBRICA, MAXVORSTADT (P.206)
6. NERO PIZZA & GRILL, GLOCKENBACHVIERTEL (P.206)
7. RIVA TAL, ALTSTADT (P.206)
8. SALÒ, SCHWABING (P.207)
9. PIZZERIA PASSAPAROLA ENOTECA, SCHWABING (P.207)
10. RIVA SCHWABING, SCHWABING (P.207)
11. L'ANGOLO DELLA PIZZA, HAIDHAUSEN (P.206)

MAXVORSTADT

ALTSTADT

SCHWABING

GLOCKENBACHVIERTEL

H'UGO'S

Promenadeplatz 1–3
Altstadt
Munich
Bavaria 80333
Germany
+49 89221270
www.hugos-pizza.de

Opening hours	Open 7 days
Credit cards	Accepted
Style of pizza	Stone-baked
Recommended pizza	Truffle; Tuna II

"H'ugo's has become part of the Munich scene.
It's a place to see and be seen."—Hans-Jürgen Hartauer

OH JULIA

Sendlinger Strasse 12A
Altstadt
Munich
Bavaria 80331
Germany
+49 89215524620
www.ohjulia.de

Opening hours	Open 7 days
Credit cards	Accepted
Style of pizza	Classic
Recommended pizza	Margherita

"The pizzas always taste fresh and they are crispy on
the outside, softer on the inside. An Augustiner lager
is the essential accompaniment!"—Jossi Loibl

RIVA TAL

Tal 44
Altstadt
Munich
Bavaria 80331
Germany
+49 89220240
www.riva-tal.de

Opening hours	Open 7 days
Credit cards	Accepted
Style of pizza	Wood-fired
Recommended pizza	Carne Salada; Chicken Curry; Margherita; Salmon; Vitello Tonnato

"This is Munich's lifestyle pizzeria created by the
excellent gastronomic duo of Rudi Kull and Kurt
Weinzierl. There's another branch in the Schwabing
district."—Claudia Eilers

NERO PIZZA & GRILL

Rumfordstrasse 34
Glockenbachviertel
Munich
Bavaria 80469
Germany
+49 8921019060
www.nero-muenchen.de

Opening hours	Open 7 days
Credit cards	Accepted
Style of pizza	Stone-baked
Recommended pizza	Crudo; Norcina; Truffle

"This pizzeria in Munich has nothing to envy from the
best Italian pizzerias."—Michaela Bogner

L'ANGOLO DELLA PIZZA

Breisacher Strasse 30
Haidhausen
Munich
Bavaria 81667
Germany
+49 894488979
www.langolo-della-pizza.de

Opening hours	Open 7 days
Credit cards	Accepted but not AMEX
Style of pizza	Wood-fired
Recommended pizza	L'Angolo

FABBRICA

Katharina-von-Bora-Strasse 8A
Maxvorstadt
Munich
Bavaria 80333
Germany
+49 15171204000
www.fabbrica-muenchen.com

Opening hours	Closed Sunday
Credit cards	Not accepted
Style of pizza	*Pizza al metro*
Recommended pizza	Pizza in Pala Deluxe

"Fabbrica is located on the site of a former power
station, which has been released for temporary use.
The menu is not huge but has been well thought
out—the specialty is the *pizza alla pala* (meter-long
pizza) with various toppings for several people."
—Claudia Eilers

NEUHAUSER

Schulstrasse 28
Neuhausen-Nymphenburg
Munich
Bavaria 80634
Germany
+49 8920208857
www.cafeneuhauser.de

Opening hours...Open 7 days
Credit cards...Accepted
Style of pizza..Neapolitan
Recommended pizza..Neuhauser

LOCANDA BUSENTO

Fürstenrieder Strasse 277
Sendling-Westpark
Munich
Bavaria 81241
Germany
+49 8978576070
www.locanda-busento.de

Opening hours...Open 7 days
Credit cards...............................Accepted but not AMEX
Style of pizza..Neapolitan
Recommended pizza..Calibrese

"Locanda Busento serves pizzas made from unusual
flours, such as the so-called Pinsa Romana, and some
gluten-free versions—all of which taste really good.
Even the 'normal' dough is light and aromatic."
—Hans Gerlach

PIZZERIA PASSAPAROLA ENOTECA

Kaiserstrasse 47
Schwabing
Munich
Bavaria 80801
Germany
+49 8938889590
www.passaparola-muenchen.de

Opening hours..Closed Saturday
Credit cards..Not accepted
Style of pizza..Wood-fired
Recommended pizza.............................Bufala; Trevisana

"In summer the terrace in the backyard is a pleasant
place to sit."—Michaela Bogner

"For years this small, compact, often hectic, and very
Italian restaurant has been a real favorite for Munich
pizza fans. The waiting times are never too long and

are spent watching the *pizzaiolo* whirling around
in front of the wood-fired oven. It's not a place for
romantic dinners or long lingering evenings—at a
certain point the waiter will just bring you the bill!"
—Claudia Eilers

RIVA SCHWABING

Feilitzschstrasse 4
Schwabing
Munich
Bavaria 80802
Germany
+49 89309051808
www.riva-schwabing.de

Opening hours...Open 7 days
Credit cards...Accepted
Style of pizza.............................Neapolitan sourdough
Recommended pizza..................................Bianca; Caprese;
Carpaccio of Potato

"The slow, natural sourdough process gives the pizza
a particular aroma and makes it very easy to digest.
The toppings are modern or classics at their best,
and the Margherita is sensational."—Hans Gerlach

"A stone's throw from the Münchner Freiheit in the
middle of Schwabing, there are few summer terraces
as attractive as that of Riva Schwabing."
—Michaela Bogner

SALÒ

Schraudolphstrasse 44
Schwabing
Munich
Bavaria 80799
Germany
+49 8927374000
www.salomuenchen.de

Opening hours...Open 7 days
Credit cards...Accepted
Style of pizza...Roman piadina
Recommended pizza...Bufala

"DAS MEHL IN HAMBURG IS ONE OF THE MOST INNOVATIVE PIZZERIAS IN THE WORLD. IT EXPERIMENTS WITH NEW INGREDIENTS, USES SPECIAL DOUGHS, AND MAKES COLORFUL BREAD."

HANS-JÜRGEN HARTAUER P.210

"THE REALLY RELAXED ATMOSPHERE AND THE EXCEPTIONALLY CRISPY BASE MAKE THIS SNACK BAR A TOP CHOICE WHEN YOU DON'T FEEL LIKE GOING TO A CLASSIC PIZZERIA."

ANDREA THODE P.211

HAMBURG

"UTTERLY HARMONIOUS PIZZA THAT'S MADE WITH OUTSTANDING DOUGH."

TORBEN BONHÖFT P.211

"CLASSIC NEAPOLITAN-STYLE PIZZA IN AN AUTHENTIC PIZZERIA."

ANDREA THODE P.211

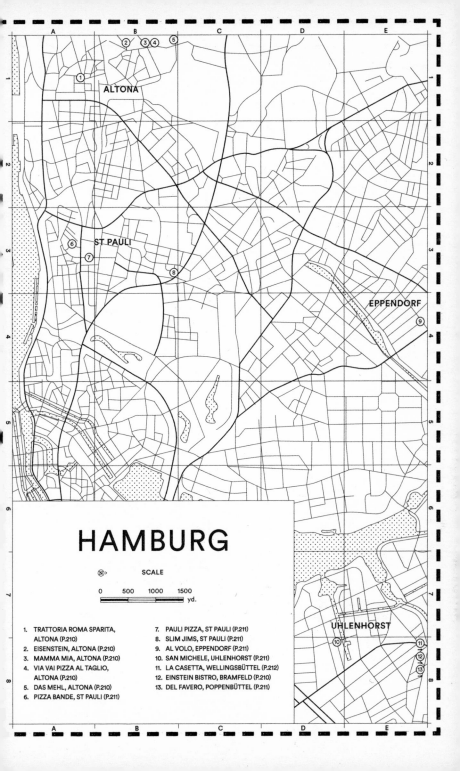

HAMBURG

SCALE

0   500   1000   1500
yd.

1. TRATTORIA ROMA SPARITA,
   ALTONA (P.210)
2. EISENSTEIN, ALTONA (P.210)
3. MAMMA MIA, ALTONA (P.210)
4. VIA VAI PIZZA AL TAGLIO,
   ALTONA (P.210)
5. DAS MEHL, ALTONA (P.210)
6. PIZZA BANDE, ST PAULI (P.211)

7. PAULI PIZZA, ST PAULI (P.211)
8. SLIM JIMS, ST PAULI (P.211)
9. AL VOLO, EPPENDORF (P.211)
10. SAN MICHELE, UHLENHORST (P.211)
11. LA CASETTA, WELLINGSBÜTTEL (P.212)
12. EINSTEIN BISTRO, BRAMFELD (P.210)
13. DEL FAVERO, POPPENBÜTTEL (P.211)

EISENSTEIN

Friedensallee 9
Altona
Hamburg
Hamburg 22765
Germany
+49 403904606
www.restaurant-eisenstein.de

Opening hours..Open 7 days
Credit cards..Not accepted
Style of pizza..Classic
Recommended pizza..Blöde Ziege

MAMMA MIA

Barnerstrasse 42
Altona
Hamburg
Hamburg 22765
Germany
+49 403900386

Opening hours..Closed Tuesday
Credit cards..Accepted
Style of pizza..Classic
Recommended pizza..Neapolitan

DAS MEHL

Gaussstrasse 190
Altona
Hamburg
Hamburg 22765
Germany
+49 4073449969
www.dasmehl.com

Opening hours..Open 7 days
Credit cards..Accepted
Style of pizza..Experimental
Recommended pizza..Dark Side of Power

"Das Mehl in Hamburg is one of the most innovative pizzerias in the world. It experiments with new ingredients, uses special doughs, and makes colorful bread. This pizzeria never stands still and always keeps its finger on the pulse."
—Hans-Jürgen Hartauer

TRATTORIA ROMA SPARITA

Lobuschstrasse 24
Altona
Hamburg
Hamburg 22765
Germany
+49 4025777495
www.roma-sparita.de

Opening hours..Closed Wednesday
Credit cards..Accepted
Style of pizza..Roman
Recommended pizza..Cesare; Luca with Scampi

VIA VAI PIZZA AL TAGLIO

Bahrenfelder Strasse 223
Altona
Hamburg
Hamburg 22765
Germany
+49 4079692626

Opening hours..Closed Sunday
Credit cards..Not accepted
Style of pizza..*Pizza al taglio*

EINSTEIN BISTRO

Bramfelder Chaussee 361
Bramfeld
Hamburg
Hamburg 22175
Germany
+49 4063683770
www.einstein-bistro.de

Opening hours..Open 7 days
Credit cards..Accepted but not AMEX
Style of pizza..Classic
Recommended pizza..Pizza Bruschetta

"Even though this restaurant is part of a chain, the pizza here is also unbelievably good. It looks just as you would imagine a classic Italian pizza to be and tastes amazing. The only difference is that the base is noticeably harder."—Marius Schöttler

AL VOLO

Eppendorfer Weg 211
Eppendorf
Hamburg
Hamburg 20253
Germany
+49 4043275924
www.alvolo.de

Opening hours	Open 7 days
Credit cards	Accepted but not AMEX
Style of pizza	Neapolitan
Recommended pizza	Contadina; Margherita; Ortolana

"Classic Neapolitan-style pizza in an authentic pizzeria."—Andrea Thode

DEL FAVERO

Heegbarg 30
Poppenbüttel
Hamburg
Hamburg 22391
Germany
+49 406061075
www.delfavero.de

Opening hours	Open 7 days
Credit cards	Accepted
Style of pizza	Classic

PAULI PIZZA

Talstrasse 22
St Pauli
Hamburg
Hamburg 20359
Germany
+49 4067303046

Opening hours	Closed Wednesday and Saturday
Credit cards	Not accepted
Style of pizza	Classic

"Customers watch their pizzas being baked in a tiny space measuring just 160 square feet (15 square meters). The pizzas are then eaten at home, on the steps, or on the folding benches outside the door. The pizzas have a slightly thicker base with juicy toppings."—Rabea Ganz

PIZZA BANDE

Lincolnstrasse 10
St Pauli
Hamburg
Hamburg 20359
Germany
www.pizza-bande.de

Opening hours	Closed Monday
Credit cards	Not accepted
Style of pizza	Thin and crispy
Recommended pizza	The chef's special

SLIM JIMS

Bei der Schilleroper 1–3
St Pauli
Hamburg
Hamburg 20359
Germany
www.slim-jims.com

Opening hours	Open 7 days
Credit cards	Not accepted
Style of pizza	Classic
Recommended pizza	Anchovy; The chef's special

"The really relaxed atmosphere and the exceptionally crispy base make this snack bar a top choice when you don't feel like going to a classic pizzeria. Delicate souls may be put off by the crude biker furnishings and the tattooed pizza chef."—Andrea Thode

SAN MICHELE

Kanalstrasse 22
Uhlenhorst
Hamburg
Hamburg 22085
Germany
+49 40371127
www.san-michele.de

Opening hours	Closed Sunday
Credit cards	Accepted but not AMEX
Style of pizza	Italian
Recommended pizza	Parma Ham and Arugula (rocket)

"Utterly harmonious pizza that's made with outstanding dough."—Torben Bonhöft

LA CASETTA
Rolfinckstrasse 19
Wellingsbüttel
Hamburg
Hamburg 22391
Germany
+49 405362149
www.restaurant-lacasetta.de

Opening hours...Open 7 days
Credit cards...Accepted
Style of pizza...Classic

GIARDINO ROMANO
Rue de Saint-Jean 30A
Geneva
Geneva 1203
Switzerland
+41 223402627
www.giardino-romano.ch

Opening hours..Closed Sunday
Credit cards...Accepted
Style of pizza...Classic
Recommended pizza.......................................Giardino; Truffle

"This is a restaurant where the truffle takes center stage. The place is a bit kitsch, but that's part of its charm. It serves excellent pizzas that stay great right up to the last mouthful, and it also does gluten-free pizza."—Sakura Hori

LUIGIA
Rue Adrien Lachenal 24A
Geneva
Geneva 1207
Switzerland
+41 228401515
www.luigia.ch

Opening hours...Open 7 days
Credit cards...................................Accepted but not AMEX
Style of pizza...Neapolitan
Recommended pizza...................................Margherita Bufala,
Miracolata DOP

"Luigia serves the best Neapolitan-style pizza in Geneva."—Max Fisher

NERO'S PIZZA
Food truck—check website, Facebook, Instagram, and Twitter for upcoming locations
Geneva
Geneva
Switzerland
+41 791717523
www.nerospizza.ch

Opening hours...Variable
Credit cards...................................Accepted but not AMEX
Style of pizza...Roman
Recommended pizza.....................Parmigiana; Spicy Salami

"Once you know where to find this food truck you'll never be able to pass it by. You buy the pizza by the slice, which means you can try several different types. So there's no excuse for only choosing one!"—Sakura Hori

"The dough is thick but fluffy and extremely crunchy, a style of pizza not very developed in Switzerland. The toppings are a mixture of classics and more playful combinations such as zucchini (courgette) flowers with anchovies or pumpkin cream with pancetta."—Max Fisher

GIARDINI D'ITALIA
Rue du Valentin 12
Lausanne
Lausanne 1004
Switzerland
+41 215464400
www.restaurant-giardini-italia.ch

Opening hours..Closed Sunday
Credit cards...................................Accepted but not AMEX
Style of pizza...Sicilian
Recommended pizza...Norma

"I recommend pizza Norma. The base is cooked by itself and then scattered with cubes of fried eggplant (aubergine) and raw tomato, salted ricotta, and basil."—Nathalie Chiva

GIGIO'S

Avenue Mon-Repos 14
Lausanne
Lausanne 1005
Switzerland
+41 213234313
www.gigiosrestaurant.com

Opening hours	Open 7 days
Credit cards	Accepted
Style of pizza	Neapolitan
Recommended pizza	Montanara

"The base is incredibly good, and the toppings are all appetizing and interesting—a homage to Italian tradition."—Nathalie Chiva

LA MOLISANA

Avenue de Tivoli 68
Lausanne
Lausanne 1007
Switzerland
+41 216248300
www.molisana.ch

Opening hours	Closed Sunday
Credit cards	Accepted but not AMEX
Style of pizza	Thin-crust
Recommended pizza	Roberto; Truffle

"La Molisana serves excellent pizzas with great garnishes. The rest of the menu is also worth trying."
—Nathalie Chiva

DIECI AL LAGO

Fischmarktplatz 1
Rapperswil
St. Gallen 8640
Switzerland
+41 552109020
www.dieci.ch

Opening hours	Open 7 days
Credit cards	Accepted
Style of pizza	Classic
Recommended pizza	Vegetable

PIZZERIA GRÜTLI

Piazzetta Fontana 3
Mendrisio
Ticino 6850
Switzerland
+41 916463144

Opening hours	Closed Sunday
Credit cards	Accepted
Style of pizza	Neapolitan
Recommended pizza	Ciociara

"The staff are friendly and the pizza is superb thanks to the use of fresh, high-quality produce. The pizzeria also has a wide range of regional beers that go well with the extensive variety of pizzas that the restaurant offers."—Laura Righettoni & Gabriele Merlo

PIZZERIA STELLA

Via Stella 13
Mendrisio
Ticino 6850
Switzerland
+41 916467228
www.ristorantestella.ch

Opening hours	Open 7 days
Credit cards	Accepted but not AMEX
Style of pizza	Traditional
Recommended pizza	Ciclista

"Pizzeria Stella has a lovely terrace in the courtyard of an old house where one can enjoy the cool evening air in summer."—Laura Righettoni & Gabriele Merlo

ANEMA E CORE

Via Capelli 2
Viganello
Ticino 6962
Switzerland
+41 919712436
www.anema-e-core.ch

Opening hours...Closed Sunday
Credit cards...Accepted
Style of pizza...Neapolitan
Recommended pizza...Margherita

"As soon as you walk through the door of this
restaurant, you feel like you are in Naples. The colors,
the smells, and the atmosphere carry you off to the
Amalfi Coast—all this just a few steps from the center
of Lugano. The pizzas are classic but the pizza chef
always has a small selection of seasonal offerings."
—Laura Righettoni & Gabriele Merlo

AZZURRO

Hohlstrasse 451
Zurich
Zurich 8048
Switzerland
+41 444924808
www.ristoranteazzurro.ch

Opening hours...Closed Sunday
Credit cards...Accepted
Style of pizza...Thin-crust
Recommended pizza..................Broccoli Raab and Sausage

RISTORANTE CUCINA

Luisenstrasse 40
Zurich
Zurich 8005
Switzerland
+41 442713740
www.cucinarestaurant.ch

Opening hours..Open 7 days
Credit cards...Accepted
Style of pizza..Classic
Recommended pizza...Tommaso

RISTORANTE DON LEONE

Bäckerstrasse 31
Zurich
Zurich 8004
Switzerland
+41 442410101
www.donleone.ch

Opening hours...Closed Sunday
Credit cards...Accepted
Style of pizza...Italian
Recommended pizza...Regina

"This pizzeria is friendly and informal. Don't be put
off by the sheer size of the pizza as it'll disappear in
no time. Making a reservation in advance is highly
recommended as the restaurant is small and always
very busy—you may well end up eating at a table
with other diners."
—Laura Righettoni & Gabriele Merlo

ROSSO

Geroldstrasse 31
Zurich
Zurich 8005
Switzerland
+41 438182254
www.restaurant-rosso.ch

Opening hours..Open 7 days
Credit cards...Accepted
Style of pizza...Italian-New York
Recommended pizza...Bresaola

SANTA LUCIA OERLIKON

Schafhauserstrasse 345
Zurich
Zurich 8050
Switzerland
+41 443124858
www.bindella.ch

Opening hours..Open 7 days
Credit cards..Not accepted
Style of pizza...Neapolitan
Recommended pizza..Napoli

THE NEAPOLITAN PIZZA RENAISSANCE

If, by opening Lombardi's in New York's Little Italy back in 1905, Gennaro Lombardi was the first to etch the words "Pizzeria Napoletana" on an American shop window, Anthony Mangieri, a tattooed pizza fundamentalist from New Jersey, was arguably the first to apply those words in their purest, most literal sense in 1996. The first pizzerias in the United States may have had Neapolitan names over their doors but the proud immigrants behind them lacked the experience or ingredients of *pizzaioli* back home. They somehow managed with whatever they could get their hands on—American bread flour, for example, in place of the Italian pizza flour. The pizzas they baked in coal-fired bread ovens, not wood-fired pizza ovens, were crisper, larger adaptations of the originals in Naples.

Mangieri cultivated his soft spot for softer pizza on visits to Naples. In 1996 he opened Una Pizza Napoletana, a pizzeria on the New Jersey shore and a beachhead, though he didn't know it then, for the Neapolitan pizza renaissance. He relocated his one-man pizza show to New York in 2004 and to San Francisco in 2010, winning fame and notoriety on both coasts for his fanatical focus on the minutiae of classic Naples–Neapolitan pizza baking. Meanwhile, other pizza pilgrims were spreading the true Neapolitan gospel as surely as dough over a lightly floured work surface. Jonathan Goldsmith of Spacca Napoli in Chicago, Hisanori Yamamoto of Pizzeria e Trattoria da ISA in Tokyo, and André Guidón of Leggera Pizza Napoletana in São Paulo shaped ethereal crusts with soft, almost floppy, midsections encircled by charred, pillowy borders.

A new wave of *pizzaioli* from Naples or thereabouts joined their ranks, among them Roberto Caporuscio of Kesté in New York, Massimo Tolve of Pizza Pomodoro in Wellington, New Zealand, Giuseppe Mascoli of Franco Manca in London, and Romualdo Rizzuti of Sud Pizzeria in Florence. By that point, the revival of pizza Napoletana had reached Milan, Turin, Rome, and even the birthplace of one Gennaro Lombardi.

Today the streets of Naples are abuzz with *pizzaiolo*-mania. Pizza protégés more obsessive than Anthony Mangieri practically follow master *pizzaioli* into men's rest rooms, so eager are they to observe their every gesture. A new generation of pizza maestros brings superior ingredients, exacting methods, and a chef's mindset to pizza making, leavening the image of their trade. The most accomplished (and maybe also most media savvy)—Franco Pepe, Enzo Coccia, Ciro Salvo, Gino Sorbillo—have achieved celebrity status. On the slowest Tuesdays of the year their pizzerias draw opening-night crowds. Not every local in the industry is thrilled to see these pizza bakers getting the movie-star treatment. "It's not Gino that made pizza famous," says Antimo Caputo of Molino Caputo, the leading producer of pizza flour. "It's the other way around."

"AVIO IS A NICE PIZZERIA IN THE STYLE OF AN OLD IRISH PUB. IT HAS GOOD PIZZAS AND A GREAT SELECTION OF BEERS." IGOR PERESSON P.223

"PICERIJA ETNA IS THE BEST PIZZERIA IN SLOVENIA—NO DOUBT!"

BOŠTJAN NAPOTNIK P.223

AUSTRIA, THE CZECH REPUBLIC & SLOVENIA

"THE PIZZA IS WONDERFUL AND THE STAFF ARE YOUNG AND DEDICATED— A GREAT MIX."

KONSTANTIN FILIPPOU P.220

"DISCO VOLANTE HAS A WOOD-FIRED OVEN IN THE SHAPE OF A MIRROR BALL."

SEVERIN CORTI P.220

"PIZZA NUOVA HAS A WONDERFUL WINE LIST FOCUSED ON NATURAL WINES FROM CENTRAL EUROPE." MARTIN KUCIEL P.221

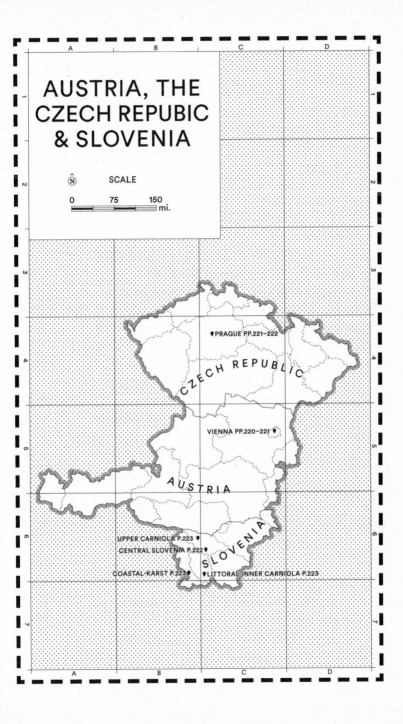

AUSTRIA, THE CZECH REPUBIC & SLOVENIA

N̂ SCALE

0   75   150 mi.

♥PRAGUE PP.221-222

CZECH REPUBLIC

VIENNA PP.220-221 ♥

AUSTRIA

UPPER CARNIOLA P.223 ♥
CENTRAL SLOVENIA P.222 ♥
SLOVENIA
COASTAL-KARST P.223 ♥   ♥ LITTORAL-INNER CARNIOLA P.223

DISCO VOLANTE

Gumpendorferdorferstrasse 98
Vienna
Vienna 1060
Austria
+43 6641952545
www.disco-volante.at

Opening hours	Open 7 days
Credit cards	Not accepted
Style of pizza	Neapolitan
Recommended pizza	Disco; Potato; Sausage and Fennel

"Disco Volante has a wood-fired oven in the shape of a mirror ball."—Severin Corti

IL MARE

Zieglergasse 15
Vienna
Vienna 1070
Austria
+43 15237494
www.ilmare.at

Opening hours	Closed Sunday
Credit cards	Accepted
Style of pizza	Wood-fired
Recommended pizza	Gran Paradiso; Ischitana

PIZZA MARGARETA

Margaretenplatz 2
Vienna
Vienna 1050
Austria
+43 15440722
www.margareta.at

Opening hours	Open 7 days
Credit cards	Accepted but not AMEX
Style of pizza	Thin and crispy
Recommended pizza	Bufala

"This restaurant is located in a really attractive location, on Margaretenplatz. The pizza is wonderfully thin and crispy and the establishment radiates Italian flair."—Konstantin Filippou

PIZZA MARI

Leopoldsgasse 23A
Vienna
Vienna 1020
Austria
+43 6766874994
www.pizzamari.at/home.html

Opening hours	Closed Monday
Credit cards	Not accepted
Style of pizza	Stone-baked
Recommended pizza	Sausage

PIZZA QUARTIER

Karmelitermarkt 96
Vienna
Vienna 1020
Austria
+43 12124994

Opening hours	Closed Sunday
Credit cards	Accepted but not AMEX
Style of pizza	Neapolitan
Recommended pizza	Margherita; Pizza Fritta; Sausage and Broccoli Raab

RIVA

Schlickgasse 2
Vienna
Vienna 1090
Austria
+43 13102088
www.pizzariva.at

Opening hours	Open 7 days
Credit cards	Not accepted
Style of pizza	Neapolitan
Recommended pizza	Margherita with Anchovies and Capers; O'Figlio do Scarparo; Scugnizzo

"Riva is the only place in Vienna to hold certification from the VPN Association. It uses ingredients from Campania, ranging from coppa ham, mozzarella, and Caciocavallo to Gaeta olives."—Severin Corti

"The pizza is wonderful and the staff are young and dedicated—a great mix."—Konstantin Filippou

The business of Alessandro d'Ambrosio, like that of his Neapolitan father, was shoes but despair over the state of pizza in Vienna got him into the boardwalk pizza trade. On a two-week trip to Naples he found all he needed to open Riva, a May-through-September pizza stand at Summer Stage, by the Danube Canal. Every element, from flour and mozzarella through San Marzano tomatoes and *pizzaiolo* Donato Santoro, came with a Naples birthmark. The success of the true Margherita, as well as the classic duo of *salsiccia e friarielli* (sausage and broccoli raab) pushed D'Ambrosio to open this, his first brick-oven-and-mortar pizza place, with reclaimed oak tables, craft beers, and an actual ceiling from which to hang copper lamps.

RIVA SUMMER STAGE

Summer Stage, Rossauer Lände
Vienna
Vienna 1090
Austria
+43 13102088
www.pizzariva.at/summer-stage

Opening hours...................Open 7 days (May–September),
Closed October–April
Credit cards...Accepted
Style of pizza...Neapolitan
Recommended pizza.............................Barbie; Sofia Loren

IL SESTANTE

Piaristengasse 50
Vienna
Vienna 1080
Austria
+43 14029894
www.sestante.at

Opening hours..Open 7 days
Credit cards...Not accepted
Style of pizza..Wood-fired
Recommended pizza...Bufalina

"Il Sestante is located on the beautiful Maria Treu-Platz."
—Konstantin Filippou

PEPE NERO

Bílkova 132/4
Prague
Prague 11000
Czech Republic
+420 222315543
www.en.pepenero.cz

Opening hours..Open 7 days
Credit cards...Accepted
Style of pizza..Neapolitan
Recommended pizza..Amalfi

PIZZA NUOVA

Revoluční 1
Prague
Prague 11000
Czech Republic
+420 221803308
www.pizzanuova.ambi.cz

Opening hours..Open 7 days
Credit cards...Accepted
Style of pizza..Neapolitan
Recommended pizza..............Burrata; Margherita Classica

"Pizza Nuova has a wonderful wine list focused on natural wines from Central Europe."—Martin Kuciel

LE PIZZE DI FRANKIE

Pop-up pizzeria—check Facebook for upcoming locations
Prague
Prague
Czech Republic
+420 776467198

Opening hours...Variable
Credit cards...Not accepted
Style of pizza..Neapolitan
Recommended pizza..Marinara

PIZZERIA FIAT

Vinohradská 83
Prague
Prague 12000
Czech Republic
+420 608645424
www.pizzeriafiat.cz

Opening hours..Open 7 days
Credit cards...Accepted
Style of pizza...Thin and crispy
Recommended pizza.................................Quattro Formaggi

"Good pizza, great ingredients, and excellent service."
—Andrea Crippa

RESTAURANT SAN CARLO

La Ballerina Hotel
Dittrichova 20
Prague
Prague 12000
Czech Republic
+420 221511100
www.ballerinahotel.com

Opening hours...Open 7 days
Credit cards..Accepted
Style of pizza...Neapolitan
Recommended pizza................Broccoli Raab and Sausage;
Margherita with Buffalo Mozzarella

"Restaurant San Carlo offers original Neapolitan
pizzas, great service, and a very merry atmosphere."
—Andrea Crippa

RUGANTINO

Dušní 4
Prague
Prague 11000
Czech Republic
+420 222318172
www.rugantino.cz

Opening hours...Open 7 days
Credit cards..Accepted
Style of pizza...Neapolitan

RUGANTINO 2

Klimentská 40
Prague
Prague 11000
Czech Republic
+420 224815192
www.rugantino.cz

Opening hours...Open 7 days
Credit cards..Accepted
Style of pizza.....................................Roman and Neapolitan
Recommended pizza..Bufalina

"Rugantino 2 is child-friendly. It serves excellent
pizzas and it's possible for children to make pizza by
themselves."—Andrea Crippa

DOBRA VILA PIZZERIA

Vodnikova 8
Ljubljana
Central Slovenia 1000
Slovenia
+386 15051212
www.dobravilapizzeria.si

Opening hours...Open 7 days
Credit cards..Accepted
Style of pizza..Wood-fired thin-crust
Recommended pizza...Hannah Biz

"Dobra Vila Pizzeria is hugely popular for its pizza
delivery in Ljubljana, but it also has a few tables
on location."—Boštjan Napotnik

PIZZERIA PARMA

Trg Republike 2
Ljubljana
Central Slovenia 1000
Slovenia
+386 14268222
www.picerija.net/parma.htm

Opening hours...Closed Sunday
Credit cards..Accepted
Style of pizza.......................................Electric thick-crust
Recommended pizza...Kmečka

"This was the first pizzeria in former Yugoslavia. It is
very retro and reminds everybody how pizzas here
were made in the Seventies: small pizzas with a thick
dough and rich topping. Parma's main attraction is
its unique ancient conveyor-belt electric oven."
—Boštjan Napotnik

PIZZERIA TRTA

Grudnovo Nabrežje 21
Ljubljana
Central Slovenia 1000
Slovenia
+386 14265066
www.trta.si

Opening hours...Closed Sunday
Credit cards.................................Accepted but not AMEX
Style of pizza...Wood-fired
Recommended pizza..........Bianco; Gorgonzola; Mexicana;
Radicchio and Pancetta

PICERIJA ETNA

Kolodvorska Ulica 3A
Divača
Coastal–Karst 6215
Slovenia
+386 57630052
www.etna.si

Opening hours	Closed Monday
Credit cards	Accepted
Style of pizza	Gourmet
Recommended pizza	Autunno; Brkinska; Carbonara; Estate; Etna; Inverno; Primavera; Radicchio; Toscana

"Picerija Etna is the best pizzeria in Slovenia—no doubt!" –Boštjan Napotnik

"Etna offers a unique sensory experience with a tasting menu of six different types of pizza." —Giuseppe Cordioli

Igor Peresson speaks perfect Italian but it's his fluency in pizza, learned at the Università della Pizza in Padua, that draws Italians to Etna. From dough made with wholegrain flour and allowed 48 hours to rise, he fashions divinely crisp pizzas with inventive combinations, some dedicated to the seasons. The winter pizza is topped with tomato, mozzarella, smoked duck breast, and orange-infused olive oil. The Brkinska, with tomato, mozzarella, grilled porcini, coppa ham, and horseradish, is folded at the edges into an eight-point star. The shape is more foreign than the combination to diners crossing the border to Slovenia from northeast Italy, where it's common to eat horseradish with cooked ham.

GOSTILNA-PIZZERIJA AMBASADOR

Lokev 164
Lokev
Coastal–Karst 6219
Slovenia
+386 40740532

Opening hours	Open 7 days
Credit cards	Accepted but not AMEX
Style of pizza	Classic Italian
Recommended pizza	Lokavska

GOSTILNA-PIZZERIA ŠKORPION

Rečica 1A
Ilirska Bistrica
Littoral–Inner Carniola 6250
Slovenia
+386 57141332
www.skorpion.si

Opening hours	Closed Tuesday
Credit cards	Accepted
Style of pizza	Classic
Recommended pizza	Prosciutto

"This family-run restaurant has a long tradition and is renowned among local people."—Igor Peresson

AVIO PUB

Rakitnik 1A
Prestranek
Littoral–Inner Carniola 6258
Slovenia
+386 57201310
www.aviopub.si

Opening hours	Closed Monday
Credit cards	Accepted but not AMEX
Style of pizza	Classic thin-crust
Recommended pizza	Asparagus

"Avio is a nice pizzeria in the style of an old Irish pub. It has good pizzas and a great selection of beers. It's located near the motorway and is a very popular spot for bikers."—Igor Peresson

DA MATTIA

Kidričeva 10A
Trzin
Upper Carniola 1236
Slovenia
+386 15641707

Opening hours	Closed Monday
Credit cards	Accepted but not AMEX
Style of pizza	Wood-fired
Recommended pizza	Calzone; Three Cheese

THE RUSSIAN FEDERATION

♦MOSCOW OBLAST P.228
♦MOSCOW PP.226-228

THE RUSSIAN
FEDERATION

Ⓝ   SCALE

0   140   280 mi.

BOCCONCINO

Novoslobodskaya Ulitsa 24
Moscow
Moscow 127055
Russia
+7 9269265926
www.bocconcino.ru

Opening hours...Open 7 days
Credit cards...Accepted
Style of pizza..Neapolitan

"It's a subtle, crispy round pizza for classic Italian food lovers. The chef Stefano Viti promises Italian-ness and quality."—Valentino Bontempi

BOCCONCINO

Strastnoy Bulvar 7
Moscow
Moscow 107207
Russia
+7 9269265926
www.bocconcino.ru

Opening hours...Open 7 days
Credit cards...Accepted
Style of pizza..Neapolitan
Recommended pizza....................................Buffalo; Country

"The pizza has abundant toppings and a thin and crispy crust."—Anna Belkina

LA BOTTEGA SICILIANA

Okhotny Ryad 2
Moscow
Moscow 109012
Russia
+7 4956600383
www.semifreddo-group.com/venue/la-bottega-siciliana

Opening hours...Open 7 days
Credit cards...Accepted
Style of pizza...Sicilian

CAFÉ CHOKKOLATTA

Tsvetnoy Bulvar 11/2
Moscow
Moscow 117588
Russia
+7 4956249696
www.chokkolatta.ru

Opening hours...Open 7 days
Credit cards...Accepted but not AMEX
Style of pizza..Neapolitan
Recommended pizza..Caprese

"I love creating my own pizza from the list of ingredients, which includes lots of meats, cheeses, seafood, leafy greens, and veggies."—Anna Belkina

CANTINETTA ANTINORI

Denezhny Pereulok 20
Moscow
Moscow 119002
Russia
+7 4992413325
www.cantinettaantinori.ru

Opening hours...Open 7 days
Credit cards...Accepted
Style of pizza...Wood-fired
Recommended pizza..Margherita

"Located in a converted nineteenth-century mansion, this restaurant has everything going for it: it's right off a main street while being extremely quiet, the quality is excellent, and prices are reasonable. Everything on the menu here is good, not just the pizzas!"
—Sarah Crowther

FORNETTO

Timur Frunze 11, Bld 2
Moscow
Moscow 107207
Russia
+7 4957884084
www.ilfornetto.ru

Opening hours...Open 7 days
Credit cards...Accepted
Style of pizza..Neapolitan
Recommended pizza............Pomodorini; Mafia with Bacon

"Quality Italian classics in Moscow."—Anna Belkina

IL FORNO

Neglinnaya Ulitsa 8–10
Moscow
Moscow 107031
Russia
+7 4956219080
www.ilforno.ru

Opening hours..Open 7 days
Credit cards...Accepted
Style of pizza...Italian
Recommended pizza.........................Gorgonzola with Pears
and Figs

"A surprise detour from the Kamchatka bar across the street resulted in a trip to this pizzeria, one of Moscow's many pizza chains. But this chain is different because the pizza is proper good, the wine surprisingly nice."—Sarah Crowther

MONTALTO

Sadovaya-Kudrinskaya 20
Moscow
Moscow 123001
Russia
+7 4952343487
www.montalto.ru

Opening hours..Open 7 days
Credit cards.................................Accepted but not AMEX
Style of pizza................................Brooklyn and Sicilian
Recommended pizza........................Four Cheese; Montalto

"The interior is fashionably stark, pizzas are creative (seafood, barbecue, kimchi) and satisfyingly, authentically wood-fired without being super expensive. Plus, the restaurant is located in the Patriarch's Ponds neighborhood, arguably the loveliest in Moscow."—Sarah Crowther

"Montalto offers freshly made dough, delicious sauces, and artisan toppings that are carefully selected and combined in an eloquent way by the chef."
—Eva Mala

PASTA I BASTA

Sretenskiy Bulvar 4
Moscow
Moscow 10745
Russia
+7 4956245252
www.pastandbasta.ru

Opening hours..Open 7 days
Credit cards...Accepted
Style of pizza...Sicilian
Recommended pizza...Diablo

"A cozy interior, friendly staff, excellent Italian dishes, and good prices in one of the most expensive cities in the world are the right reasons for every single person to visit this restaurant of the I Love Cafe network. The pies are a good size, have nice thin dough, and are presented with flawless toppings. It makes one keep dreaming about pizza for many a night to come."—Eva Mala

PINZERIA BY BONTEMPI

Bolshoi Znamensky Pereulok 2/3
Moscow
Moscow 119019
Russia
+7 4996783009

Opening hours..Open 7 days
Credit cards...Accepted
Style of pizza...Italian
Recommended pizza.........................Bresaola and Taleggio;
Margherita

"The pizza is served on a wooden board with a pizza cutter and it's easy to share with friends."
—Giuseppe Todisco

"What makes this pizza special is the dough. It is a very balanced mix of different flours and there is no rush in the leavening process, which creates a very crispy and light but delicious crust. I can sit here and describe the sensation you get when eating it but you will only understand what I mean if you taste it. It's difficult to find this quality of pizza even in Italy."—Gabrio Marchetti

U. GIUSEPPE

Samotechnaya Ulita 13
Moscow
Moscow 127473
Russia
+7 4956811326
www.ugiuseppe.ru

Opening hours...Open 7 days
Credit cards....................................Accepted but not AMEX
Style of pizza...Thin-crust
Recommended pizza............Broccoli Raab and Homemade
                                        Sausage with Truffle

"U. Giuseppe has a wide choice of pizzas, a cozy
atmosphere, and very friendly staff."
—Giuseppe Todisco

BASHNYA

Sovetskaya Ulitsa 14B
Reutov
Moscow Oblast 143960
Russia
+7 4955280160

Opening hours...Open 7 days
Credit cards..Not accepted
Style of pizza...Khachapuri
Recommended pizza...Mingrelian

"If khachapuris haven't been considered a kind of
pizza yet, it's time to change that! These goddess
Georgian pies are usually stuffed with spiced meat,
sulugini cheese, or vegetables and topped with more
cheese and/or a raw egg yolk. Bashnya restaurant,
owned by a very energetic and friendly Georgian
family, offers the best of the best."—Eva Mala

"AT THE ENTRANCE TO VENICE YOU WILL FIND A TEMPLE TO DOUGH AND LEAVENING, ALL TOPPED WITH INGREDIENTS OF THE HIGHEST QUALITY." ENRICO BONARDO P.274

"FRANCO PEPE IS THE MASTER OF NEAPOLITAN PIZZA. IN THE COLLECTIVE CONSCIOUSNESS, THIS IS PIZZA WITH A CAPITAL P." MARCO LOCATELLI P.241

"THIS IS TRULY A PIZZA PARADISE!" ANDREA CONSONNI P.255

ITALY

"ITS MARGHERITA WAS HANDS DOWN THE BEST PIZZA I'VE HAD IN MY ENTIRE LIFE." EMILY GIOVE P.242

"THIS IS WHERE THE CONCEPT OF GOURMET PIZZA WAS 'INVENTED' AND MADE FAMOUS." ANNA FERRETTI P.275

"NOTHING COULD BE MORE SPECIAL THAN DINING ON TOP-NOTCH PIZZAS IN THE SHADE OF A SAGGING LEMON TREE IN THIS FAMILY-RUN TRATTORIA." DARREN LOVELL P.245

ITALY

SCALE

0   80   160 mi.

TRENTINO-ALTO ADIGE P.270

FRIULI-VENEZIA GIULIA PP.249–252

AOSTA VALLEY PP.233–234

VENETO PP.273–277

MILAN PP.298–301

LOMBARDY PP.254–256

TURIN PP.302–305

PIEDMONT PP.260–262

EMILIA-ROMAGNA PP.245–249

LIGURIA PP.252–253

FLORENCE PP.306–310

MARCHE.256–259

TUSCANY PP.271–272

UMBRIA.272–273

ABRUZZO PP.232–233

LAZIO P.252

ROME PP.288–297

MOLISE P.259

APULIA PP.234–237

CAMPANIA PP.241–245

NAPLES PP.278–286

BASILICATA PP.237–238

SARDINIA PP.262–264

CALABRIA PP.238–240

SICILY PP.264–270

PERCORSI DI GUSTO

Via Leosini
L'Aquila
L'Aquila
Abruzzo 67100
Italy
+39 0862411429
www.percorsidigusto.com

Opening hours	Closed Wednesday
Credit cards	Accepted
Style of pizza	Gourmet
Recommended pizza	Aquilana

"Gourmet pizza from the school of Simone Padoan."
—Cristina Mosca

LO SCARABEO

Corso Mazzini 3
Cupello
Chieti
Abruzzo 66051
Italy
+39 0873316422

Opening hours	Open 7 days
Credit cards	Accepted
Style of pizza	Roman-Neapolitan
Recommended pizza	Cupellese

"Lo Scarabeo has a delicious selection of pizzas and focaccia breads, as well as traditional local dishes. The pizzas are made with a slow-leavened dough and topped with local ingredients, including artichokes from Cupello and Ventricina salami from Vasto."—Carmelita Cianci

LA SORGENTE

Via Antonio Gramsci 9
Guardiagrele
Chieti
Abruzzo 66016
Italy
+39 0871800111

Opening hours	Closed Monday
Credit cards	Accepted but not AMEX
Style of pizza	Gourmet
Recommended pizza	Fior di Latte Mozzarella, Bean Cream, Pancetta, Pomegranate, and Sarawak Black Pepper; Pala alla Romana; Pizz' e Foje

"La Sorgente is the only pizzeria in Abruzzo to have been recognized by the Slow Food movement."
—Cristina Mosca

LE MASCHERE

Via Giuseppe Garibaldi 56
Tollo
Chieti
Abruzzo 66010
Italy
+39 0871961810

Opening hours	Closed Tuesday
Credit cards	Accepted
Style of pizza	Neapolitan
Recommended pizza	Salt Cod

"I like Aldo's flair when it comes to the pizza toppings."
—Eliodoro D'Orazio

LA PERGOLA

Via Adua 6
Vasto
Chieti
Abruzzo 66054
Italy
+39 0873368020

Opening hours	Open 7 days
Credit cards	Accepted
Style of pizza	Neapolitan
Recommended pizza	Margherita

DON FRANCHINO

Via Bologna 14
Castelnuovo Vomano
Teramo
Abruzzo 64020
Italy
+39 0861570596
www.donfranchino.com

Opening hours	Closed Monday
Credit cards	Accepted
Style of pizza	Gourmet
Recommended pizza	Il Volo; Persimmon (kaki fruit); Stella Alpina

"Pizza chef Franco Cardelli, known as Don Franchino, is a role model in Abruzzo, assuring experience, quality, and innovation."—Valerio Valle

RISTORANTE BELLAVISTA

Via Montello 6
Giulianova
Teramo
Abruzzo 64021
Italy
+39 0858003285
www.ristorantebellavista.org

Opening hours	Closed Tuesday, Open 7 days in summer
Credit cards	Accepted
Style of pizza	Traditional wood-fired
Recommended pizza	Bellavista

"Sophisticated and high-quality toppings, in particular the fish-based ones, make Biagio Saccomandi's pizzas one of Abruzzo's gems. There is a choice of different doughs: the classic pizza, pizzas made with kamut, gluten-free pizzas, and wholewheat pizzas."
—Valerio Valle

RISTORANTE PIZZERIA TOTÒ

Via Antonio Gramsci 3
Montorio Al Vomano
Teramo
Abruzzo 64046
Italy
+39 0861598508

Opening hours	Closed Monday
Credit cards	Accepted but not AMEX
Style of pizza	Italian

PIZZERIA FRATELLI VALLE

Via Latini 23
Roseto degli Abruzzi
Teramo
Abruzzo 64026
Italy
+39 3425537512
www.fratellivalle.it

Opening hours	Closed Wednesday
Credit cards	Not accepted
Style of pizza	*Pizza alla pala*
Recommended pizza	Tomato, Stracciatella di Bufala, Confit Cherry Tomatoes, and Artisanal Basil Pesto

"The dough is made exclusively with stone-ground flours, water, unrefined salt, 100 percent Italian yeast, and oil, which gives to the pizza a flavor and a lightness above the average."—Valerio Valle

PIZZERIA BELLA NAPOLI

Via Silvano Lucat 6
Aosta
Aosta Valley 11100
Italy
+39 016540651
www.pizzeriabellanapoli.com

Opening hours	Closed Thursday
Credit cards	Accepted
Style of pizza	Thin-crust
Recommended pizza	Otto Gusti Maxi

"This is a special pizzeria because here you can find real Neapolitan pizza. It's been open for over 30 years and has two wood-fired ovens."—Yves Grange

PIZZERIA GROTTA AZZURRA

Via Croce di Città 97
Aosta
Aosta Valley 11100
Italy
+39 0165262474

Opening hours	Closed Wednesday
Credit cards	Accepted
Style of pizza	Classic

LOCANDA CERVINO

Via Chanoux 31
Chatillon
Aosta
Aosta Valley 11024
Italy
+39 0166563206
www.locandailcervino.it

Opening hours	Open 7 days
Credit cards	Accepted
Style of pizza	Traditional
Recommended pizza	Boscaiola Valdostana

"A very welcoming restaurant in the traditional style of the Aosta Valley, with stone and wood, and lovely colored glass. This is the perfect escape for city dwellers as you really feel like you are in the mountains."—Yves Grange

AVALON

Fraziobe Delliod 4
Introd
Aosta
Aosta Valley 11010
Italy
+39 016595944
www.pizzeriaristoranteavalon.it

Opening hours......................................Closed Tuesday
Credit cards.................................Accepted but not AMEX
Style of pizza...Classic

"You can eat outside and admire the splendid views."
—Fabrizio Gallino

CAVALLO BIANCO

Villaggio Larey 5
Quart
Aosta
Aosta Valley 11100
Italy
+39 0165765358

Opening hours......................................Closed Monday
Credit cards...Not accepted
Style of pizza...Classic

"The pizza is cooked excellently, the pizzeria is never too full, and the service is good."—Fabrizio Gallino

DA DONATO

Via Lattanzio Francesco 59
Bari
Bari
Apulia 70126
Italy
+39 0805542903
www.pizzeriadadonato.com

Opening hours..Open 7 days
Credit cards...Accepted
Style of pizza...Apulian
Recommended pizza.....................................Margherita

"This pizzeria is a symbol of the classic Barese pizza, which is different to Neapolitan and Roman pizzas due to the quantity of dough and cooking time. The choice of ingredients is excellent and there is a very extensive range of craft beers and wine. Private parking for diners in the city center is an added bonus."—Nicola Bove

IL PATRIARCA

Via Beccherie Lisi 15
Bitonto
Bari
Apulia 70032
Italy
+39 3687501700

Opening hours..Open 7 days
Credit cards.................................Accepted but not AMEX
Style of pizza...Neapolitan
Recommended pizza.......................................Artichoke

"One of the best pizzeria in Puglia run by some of the most passionate people in the business."
—Beppe De Vito

LA PAGNOTTELLA

Via Serranova 54
Carovigno
Bari
Apulia 72012
Italy
+39 0831996258

Opening hours..Open 7 days
Credit cards...Not accepted
Style of pizza...Roman
Recommended pizza.......................Culatello di Zibello DOP

I MONELLI PIZZA & CO.

Via Madonna dei Martiri 112
Molfetta
Bari
Apulia 70056
Italy
+39 0809648792
www.pizzeriaimonelli.it

Opening hours......................................Closed Tuesday
Credit cards...Not accepted
Style of pizza...Apulian
Recommended pizza.....................................Margherita

"This pizzeria experiments with using a wide variety of special and exotic types of flour, such as burnt wheat, kamut, spelt, barley, quinoa, and hemp. Gluten-free flour is also available thanks to very careful methods that prevent contamination. This is all done with careful attention to the quality of the raw materials and the leavening processes."—Nicola Bove

OLIVER HARDY
Via Alessandro Volta 3
Noci
Bari
Apulia 70015
Italy
+39 0804974180

Opening hours..Closed Wednesday
Credit cards..Accepted
Style of pizza..Classic
Recommended pizza..Salmon

"Oliver Hardy is a small, cozy restaurant with a pizza menu. The pizzas are cooked in a vast wood-fired oven and are always light and easy to digest thanks to a good leavening of the dough. The staff are young and knowledgeable and it's always packed on a Saturday evening."—Domenico Maraglino

LA CASA DI TOTÒ
Via Conversano
Putignano
Bari
Apulia 70017
Italy
+39 0804057820

Opening hours..Closed Monday
Credit cards..Not accepted
Style of pizza..Classic
Recommended pizza..........Grilled Vegetable with Ricotta-
Stuffed Crust

"If you want to taste a pizza made with traditional Neapolitan dough, this is the place for you. The presentation and ingredients are excellent and the dough is always well risen. There are tables outside in the summer."—Domenico Maraglino

PREMIATA PIZZERIA
Via Carlo Rosselli 32
Putignano
Bari
Apulia 70017
Italy
+39 0804058523

Opening hours..Closed Monday
Credit cards..Accepted
Style of pizza..Neapolitan
Recommended pizza..Strana

DA ZIO PEPPE
Via Padre Arcangelo Gigliola 15
Ceglie Messapico
Brindisi
Apulia 72013
Italy
+39 3355474552

Opening hours..Closed Tuesday
Credit cards..Not accepted
Style of pizza..Neapolitan
Recommended pizza..........Margherita with Mozzarella or
Seasonal Vegetables

LUPPOLO & FARINA
Via Santissimo Crocifisso
Latiano
Brindisi
Apulia 72022
Italy
+39 3924955782

Opening hours..Open 7 days
Credit cards..................................Accepted but not AMEX
Style of pizza..Neapolitan
Recommended pizza..................................Buffalo Mozzarella

"Luppolo & Farina is situated in a beautiful location and offers an excellent selection of beers."
—Angelo Massaro

LE MACÀRE
Via Mariana Albina 140
Alezio
Lecce
Apulia 73011
Italy
+39 0833282192
www.lemacare.it

Opening hours..Closed Tuesday
Credit cards..................................Accepted but not AMEX
Style of pizza..Apulian
Recommended pizza..Capocollo

"Le Macàre is very near the beaches of Gallipoli and the famous Baroque city of Lecce. It has an excellent selection of craft beers and Apulian wines, which it skillfully pairs with the dishes it serves."
—Nicola Bove

CHECCO PIZZA
Via Torquato Tasso 5
Lecce
Lecce
Apulia 73100
Italy
+39 3335993069
www.salentovip.it/checcopizza

Opening hours..Closed Monday
Credit cards...Accepted
Style of pizza...Neapolitan
Recommended pizza.......................Margherita; Scarpariello

"Checco Pizza is a small yet welcoming venue. You
can feel its love of Naples, both in the interior design
and the Neapolitan-style pizzas."
—Laura Gambacorta

PIZZERIA DA ZIO GIACOMO
Via Mariuccia 14
Martina Franca
Taranto
Apulia 74015
Italy
+39 0809673214
www.pizzeriadaziogiacomo.com

Opening hours..Closed Monday
Credit cards..Not accepted
Style of pizza...Neapolitan
Recommended pizza...Margherita

IL PORCOSPINO
Via la Rotonda 34
Massafra
Taranto
Apulia 74016
Italy
+39 0998803517
www.il-porcospino.com

Opening hours..Closed Monday
Credit cards...................................Accepted but not AMEX
Style of pizza...Neapolitan
Recommended pizza...............................Bianca with Walnuts
and Mortadella

MÒMÒ
Viale Trentino 36
Taranto
Taranto
Apulia 74121
Italy
+39 0994005852
www.momotaranto.it

Opening hours..Open 7 days
Credit cards...Accepted
Style of pizza...Traditional
Recommended pizza...Martina

"MòMò is a merry, dynamic, and modern place with
young and very efficient staff who pay great attention
to the needs of the customers."
—Danilo Giaffreda

ROSSO PICCANTE
Via Matteotti 26
Taranto
Taranto
Apulia 74123
Italy
+39 0999461553

Opening hours..Closed Monday
Credit cards..Not accepted
Style of pizza........................Traditional and *pizza alla pala*
Recommended pizza...............................Pizza alla Pala with
Pachino Tomatoes

"The simplicity of the setting contrasts with the large
variety of pizzas on offer."—Danilo Giaffreda

LE VECCHIE CANTINE
Via Girasole 23
Taranto
Taranto
Apulia 74121
Italy
+39 0997772589

Opening hours...Closed Tuesday
Credit cards..Accepted
Style of pizza...Traditional
Recommended pizza...................Pear and Cheese; Smoked
Scamorza Cheese, Raw Amberjack, Herbs and Extra
Virgin Olive Oil

"Le Vecchie Cantine is set in an old wine cellar with a lovely garden. It is a delightful restaurant with a good wine and beer list and a wood-fired oven."
—Antonella Millarte

"It offers a great choice of both white and red pizzas, with a pinch of creativity in the toppings."
—Danilo Giaffreda

AL FALCO GRILLAIO
Via Domenico Ridola 17
Matera
Matera
Basilicata 75100
Italy
+39 0835331128

Opening hours...Closed Tuesday
Credit cards..Accepted
Style of pizza......................................Roman-Neapolitan
Recommended pizza...Murgiana

"Set in a great location on a lovely street in the heart of the buzzing center of Matera, the pizzeria is surrounded by many bars and clubs where customers can continue their evening's revelries. The atmosphere is simple and welcoming, and the pizzas are properly made and baked with a particularly good mozzarella."—Gea De Leonardis

I CAPONI
Via Casalnuovo 39
Matera
Matera
Basilicata 75100
Italy
+39 3891335747

Opening hours...Closed Monday
Credit cards..Accepted
Style of pizza...Neapolitan

"This is great Neapolitan pizza."—Annalucia Festa

OI MARÌ
Via Fiorentini 66
Matera
Matera
Basilicata 75100
Italy
+39 0835346121
www.oimari.it

Opening hours...Open 7 days
Credit cards..............................Accepted but not AMEX
Style of pizza...Neapolitan
Recommended pizza.....................................Pizza Oi Marì

PIZZERIA LA PANCA
Via Giovanni Giolitti 39
Matera
Matera
Basilicata 75100
Italy
+39 3807514616

Opening hours...Closed Monday
Credit cards...Not accepted
Style of pizza...Thin-crust
Recommended pizza..........................Eggplant (aubergine);
The English

"La Panca's pizza is renowned for its lightness and digestibility. The pizza chef has been behind the counter since time immemorial and he takes his time with rhythmic movements in an almost Zen-like ritual."—Gea De Leonardis

LA TALPA RISTORANTE PIZZERIA
Via dei Fiorentini 167
Matera
Matera
Basilicata 75100
Italy
+39 0835335086
www.latalparistorante.it

Opening hours	Closed Tuesday
Credit cards	Accepted
Style of pizza	Thick-crust
Recommended pizza	Crudaiola

"La Talpa is located in the Sassi di Matera [an ancient cave-city where the houses are carved out of the caves and cliffs] and the walls of the pizzeria are partially carved in the calcareous stone."
—Gea De Leonardis

DA MICIONE
Via Eugenio Montale 12
Maschito
Potenza
Basilicata 85020
Italy
+39 3899361661

Opening hours	Closed Wednesday
Credit cards	Not accepted
Style of pizza	Neapolitan

"I like Da Micione's use of natural yeasts, and above all its use of hemp flour."—Federico Valicenti

FANDANGO
Via delle Querce 15
Scalera di Filiano
Potenza
Basilicata 85020
Italy
+39 0971808781
www.fandangopub.it

Opening hours	Open 7 days
Credit cards	Accepted
Style of pizza	Neapolitan
Recommended pizza	Eggplant (aubergine) Parmigiana and Piennolo Tomato; Margherita

"One of the best pizzas I've eaten in the Basilicata region."—Rocco Saracino

OLIVA PIZZAMORE
Via Don Francesco Maria Greco 5
Acri
Cosenza
Calabria 87041
Italy
+39 3297445896

Opening hours	Open 7 days
Credit cards	Not accepted
Style of pizza	*Pizza al taglio*
Recommended pizza	Margherita; Parmesan and Fennel; Pizza of the Day

"The pizza is made with organic stone-ground flour and natural leaven for a slow rise. The ingredients used for the toppings are seasonal so the flavors are always different and the pairings make this a real gourmet pizza."—Concetta Donato

RISTORANTE PIZZERIA MILLELUCI
Via Giovanni Grossi 81
Belvedere Marittimo
Cosenza
Calabria 87021
Italy
+39 098582770
www.millelucibelvedere.it

Opening hours	Open 7 days
Credit cards	Accepted but not AMEX
Style of pizza	Roman
Recommended pizza	Calabrese

IL PICCOLO GHETTO
Viale della Costituzione
Capitano
Cosenza
Calabria 87040
Italy
+39 3458251531

Opening hours	Closed Tuesday
Credit cards	Not accepted
Style of pizza	Calabrian
Recommended pizza	Smoked Scamorza Cheese and Pancetta

"A small but very welcoming family-run pizzeria with polite and friendly service. The pizza is soft and thin and has a raised end crust."—Anna Laura Mattesini

PIZZERIA BLADE RUNNER

Via Papa Giovanni XXIII 110
Castrolibero
Cosenza
Calabria 87040
Italy
+39 0984852859

Opening hours..Open 7 days
Credit cards.............................Accepted but not AMEX
Style of pizza..Neapolitan
Recommended pizza...................................Spicy Salami

"Deep, soft, tasty—this is real Neapolitan pizza."
—Anna Laura Mattesini

RISTORANTE PIZZERIA LA MIMOSA

Contrada Cardame 22
Corigliano Calabro
Cosenza
Calabria 87064
Italy
+39 0983886731

Opening hours..Open 7 days
Credit cards..Not accepted
Style of pizza..Neapolitan
Recommended pizza.........................Bresaola and Truffle Oil

"The pizzeria is simple and unpretentious, but the pizza
is really surprising—subtle, tasty, and well topped,
with a high and fluffy crust."—Concetta Donato

LE MAGNOLIE

Via Donato Bendicenti
Cosenza
Cosenza
Calabria 87100
Italy
+39 0984791683
www.pizzeriamagnolie.altervista.org

Opening hours..Closed Sunday
Credit cards...................................Accepted but not AMEX
Style of pizza..Neapolitan
Recommended pizza..................Campioni del Mondo 2006

PIETRA D'ORO

Via Panoramica 14
Grisolia
Cosenza
Calabria 87020
Italy
+39 098583177
www.pietradoro.com

Opening hours..Open 7 days
Credit cards..Accepted
Style of pizza...Roman
Recommended pizza...Rosemary

PIZZERIA REGINELLA

Via Pantana
Guardia Piemontese
Cosenza
Calabria 87020
Italy
+39 098294049

Opening hours..Open 7 days
Credit cards..Accepted
Style of pizza..Neapolitan

ESCOPOCODISERA

Lungomare Sirimarco
Praia a Mare
Cosenza
Calabria 87028
Italy
+39 0985777623

Opening hours..Open 7 days
Credit cards..Accepted
Style of pizza..Neapolitan
Recommended pizza...Cardinale

"The edges of the pizza have a heavenly texture and
the air pockets, the holes present in the middle of the
dough, are similar to cotton candy."
—Giampiero Valente

8E9

Via Rossini 303
Rende
Cosenza
Calabria 87036
Italy
+39 0984404466
www.8e9fm.it

Opening hours...Open 7 days
Credit cards.....................................Accepted but not AMEX
Style of pizza...Roman
Recommended pizza..................Broccoli Raab and Sausage

"Better known as a restaurant, 8e9 nevertheless offers a very well-made pizza that is thin and crispy. The pizzas with seasonal vegetables are highly commendable."—Anna Laura Mattesini

LA LOCANDA

Via Guglielmo Marconi
Rende
Cosenza
Calabria 87036
Italy
+39 0984402689

Opening hours...Open 7 days
Credit cards..Accepted
Style of pizza..Neapolitan
Recommended pizza.........................Margherita; Salami and
Mushroom

"La Locanda makes superlative Neapolitan pizzas that are baked in a wood-fired oven."
—Miriam Caruso

N'ATA COSA

Via Trieste 19
Rende
Cosenza
Calabria 87036
Italy

Opening hours..Closed Monday
Credit cards...Not accepted
Style of pizza..Neapolitan
Recommended pizza...............Anchovy; Broccoli Raab and
Sausage; Margherita

"From the tomatoes to the mozzarella, everything is delicious and fresh. Every pizza is delivered with a mini mozzarella ball and a fresh basil leaf in the center."—Miriam Caruso

AI PORTICI 2.0

Via Fratelli Salerno 11
Rende
Cosenza
Calabria 87036
Italy
+39 3396061741

Opening hours..Closed Monday
Credit cards...Not accepted
Style of pizza..Roman
Recommended pizza.....................Salami and Broccoli Raab

"The pizzas may be cooked in an electric oven but they are very good. The base is thin and crispy and can be devoured in 5 minutes and the toppings are excellent."—Miriam Caruso

ROSSO POMODORO

Via Guglielmo Marconi
Rende
Cosenza
Calabria 87036
Italy
+39 0984401392
www.pizzeriarossopomodororende.com

Opening hours...Open 7 days
Credit cards..Accepted
Style of pizza..Neapolitan
Recommended pizza..Reginella

PIZZERIA CAPRARO

Via Pietro Nenni
Trebisacce
Cosenza
Calabria 87075
Italy
+39 098158281

Opening hours...Open 7 days
Credit cards.....................................Accepted but not AMEX
Style of pizza..Neapolitan
Recommended pizza....................Francesina; Golosa; Reale

"This pizzeria is in one of the historical spots of Trebisacce. The pizzas are soft with high edges, and you can choose from a huge number of toppings."
—Concetta Donato

ÉLITE

Corso Umberto 168
Alvignano
Caserta
Campania 81012
Italy
+39 0823869092
www.pizzeriaelite.it

Opening hours	Closed Tuesday
Credit cards	Accepted but not AMEX
Style of pizza	Neapolitan
Recommended pizza	Riccia

ANTICA OSTERIA PIZZERIA STEFANO PEPE

Piazza Porta Vetere 4
Caiazzo
Caserta
Campania 81013
Italy
+39 0823868401
www.anticapizzeriapepe.it

Opening hours	Closed Monday
Credit cards	Accepted
Style of pizza	Neapolitan
Recommended pizza	Caiatina; Endive, Anchovies, Capers, and Olives; Marinara

"Pizza to die for."—Paolo Pellegrini

"Authenticity that goes hand in hand with the art of simplicity."—Alessandro Reale

PEPE IN GRANI

Vico San Giovanni Battista 3
Caiazzo
Caserta
Campania 81013
Italy
+39 0823862718
www.pepeingrani.it

Opening hours	Closed Monday (year-round) and Sunday (autumn and winter)
Credit cards	Accepted
Style of pizza	Neapolitan
Recommended pizza	Alifana; Buffalo Mozzarella and Kohlrabi; Calzone with Endive; Calzone with Ricotta; Il Sole nel Piatto; Kilometro Zero; La Pinsa Conciata del '500; La Pizza a Libretto; Margherita; Marinara; Nero Casertano; Tasting Menu; Tuna and Celery

"Lots has been written about pizzerias in Naples but Franco Pepe had the vision to go a bit beyond what's on even the best tables and embrace the local and seasonal for his toppings and create a dough that reflects his family's heritage as grain farmers. Many call it the perfect pizza of its type."—Evan Kleiman

"Franco Pepe is the great artisan of Italian pizza. His hands give life to a fluffy, spongy, and light dough. The texture is a real work of art and the ingredients are of the highest quality. It results in a perfect pizza that's tasty and easy to digest."—Carmelita Cianci

"Franco Pepe is the master of Neapolitan pizza. In the collective consciousness, this is pizza with a capital P."—Marco Locatelli

Naples may be square one of the pizza world but Caiazzo, a hilltop town some 30 miles (50 km) north, has emerged as its ground zero or rather, its kilometer zero. As a proponent of the Kilometro Zero (Km 0) movement, the one and only Franco Pepe is a local hero, in every sense. He sources mostly from nearby producers. It is only people who travel great distances to Pepe in Grani, his stone-walled pizza palazzo. Pepe's mastery covers the three stages of the pizza craft: the before (dough analysis, preparation, and maturation), the during (shaping the dough, arranging toppings, cooking) and the after (finishing touches). From a growing list of destination pizzas comes the Pinsa Conciata del '500—with Conciata Romano cheese, Cilento fig preserves, basil, and Nero Casertano pork fat—and Il Sole nel Piatto (the sun in the plate), with mozzarella di bufala, Piennolo del Vesuvio tomatoes, Cetara anchovies, basil, extra virgin olive oil, and Caiazzo olives.

MORSI & RIMORSI, TERRONI IN PIZZERIA

Viale dei Bersaglieri 14
Caserta
Caserta
Campania 81100
Italy
+39 0823327822
www.morsierimorsi.it

Opening hours	Open 7 days
Credit cards	Accepted
Style of pizza	Neapolitan
Recommended pizza	Calzone

"Excellent pizzas and a charming venue."
—Vincenzo D'Antonio

PIZZA & BABBÀ
Via Fosse Ardeatine
Santa Maria Capua Vetere
Caserta
Campania 81055
Italy
+39 08231711937

Opening hours	Open 7 days
Credit cards	Accepted but not AMEX
Style of pizza	Neapolitan
Recommended pizza	Cetarese

"Pizza & Babbà makes excellent pizzas thanks to the long leavening process and the quality of the ingredients."—Vincenzo D'Antonio

PIZZERIA TOTÒ E I SAPORI
Via San Gioacchino 73–75
Acerra
Naples
Campania 80011
Italy
+39 0815206424

Opening hours	Open 7 days
Credit cards	Accepted but not AMEX
Style of pizza	Neapolitan
Recommended pizza	Mortadella and Pistachio Cream

"The naturally leavened dough, combined with first-choice products, makes Mauro Autolitano's pizza special."—Enrico Di Roberti

AURORA RISTORANTE
Fuorlovado 18
Capri
Naples
Campania 80073
Italy
+39 0818370181
www.auroracapri.com

Opening hours	Open 7 days
Credit cards	Accepted
Style of pizza	Neapolitan
Recommended pizza	Margherita

"Aurora Ristorante is not a pizzeria, but its Margherita was hands down the best pizza I've had in my entire life."—Emily Giove

LO SFIZIO
Via Tiberio 7 E
Capri
Naples
Campania 80073
Italy
+39 0818374128
www.losfiziocapri.com

Opening hours	Closed Tuesday
Credit cards	Accepted
Style of pizza	Traditional
Recommended pizza	Marinara

"At Lo Sfizio you can breathe the air of the Amalfi coast while savoring the best mozzarella in the world."—Ricardo Amaral

LE PARÙLE
Via Benedetto Cozzolino 70
Ercolano
Naples
Campania 80056
Italy
+39 0817396494

Opening hours	Open 7 days
Credit cards	Accepted but not AMEX
Style of pizza	Neapolitan
Recommended pizza	Margherita

IL LIMONETO
Via Baiola II Trav. 94
Forio
Naples
Campania 80075
Italy
+39 0813332009
www.ristorantelimoneto.com

Opening hours	Open 7 days
Credit cards	Accepted
Style of pizza	Neapolitan
Recommended pizza	Limoneto; Tradizione

"Ivano has learnt from the best *pizzaioli* on the mainland, first and foremost Enzo Coccia, and makes a light and digestible Neapolitan dough. In addition to classic pizzas he offers a few pizzas that tell the story of Ischian traditions."—Valentina Scotti

MARIA MARÌ

Via Aviere Mario Pirozzi 63-65
Giugliano in Campania
Naples
Campania 80014
Italy
+39 0815064205

Opening hours.................................Closed Monday
Credit cards..Accepted
Style of pizza..Neapolitan
Recommended pizza..............Burrata; Don Nicola; Mezzini

"Maria Marì offers a warm welcome, very pleasant atmosphere, and high-level pizzas and *pizza fritti*."
—Laura Gambacorta

VILLA GIOVANNA

Via Valle delle Delizie Fine S.P. 159
Ottaviano
Naples
Campania 80044
Italy
+39 0818279014

Opening hours.................................Closed Monday
Credit cards..Accepted
Style of pizza..Neapolitan
Recommended pizza.....................................Margherita

"The choice of flours and the dough-making technique result in particularly good pizzas."
—Vincenzo D'Antonio

LA DEA BENDATA

Corso Umberto I 93
Pozzuoli
Naples
Campania 80078
Italy
+39 08119189636
www.pizzerialadeabendata.it

Opening hours.................................Closed Monday
Credit cards........................Accepted but not AMEX
Style of pizza..Neapolitan
Recommended pizza.................Margherita DOP; Marinara;
Montanara; Pomodorino del Piennolo del Vesuvio;
Ripieno Dea Bendata

"Excellent Neapolitan-style pizzas made according to the tradition, with attention given to the leavening process and to the choice of the ingredients. The *pizza fritti* are delicious."—Luciana Squadrilli

"A solid family tradition rests on Ciro Coccia's shoulders, who honors it without laying back on it. His pizzas are never banal and celebrate the best of the Campanian production."—Lydia Capasso

Whimsically designed with tomato-red walls and mozzarella-white chairs, La Dea Bendata (The Goddess of Justice) sits on the sea coast in Pozzuoli, west of Naples. The resemblance of Ciro Coccia to his older brother Enzo, of Pizzaria La Notizia, shows in his manner and his pizza crust, one more bubbly than the other. In little over a minute in the wood-fired brick oven the *cornicione* develops air holes of significant size, density, and softness. Coccia's *pizza fritta* (deep-fried) and calzone-like *pizza ripiena* (stuffed) possess the same airiness. The Ripieno Dea Bendata is a charred, half-moon fold stuffed with zucchini (courgette), eggplant (aubergine), and sweet peppers and garnished with mozzarella, cherry tomatoes, and arugula (rocket).

PIZZERIA FRATELLI SALVO

Largo Arso 10–16
San Giorgio a Cremano
Naples
Campania 80046
Italy
+39 081275306
www.salvopizzaioli.it

Opening hours	Closed Sunday
Credit cards	Accepted
Style of pizza	Neapolitan
Recommended pizza	Cosacca; Margherita del Vesuvio; Marinara; Montanara Classica; Montanara alla Genovese; 'Nduja and Verzin Cheese; Papacelle e Conciato; Ripieno Fritto

"This is one of the best pizzerias in Italy. The pizzas are made with excellent dough, exceptional care is taken in the choice of the ingredients, and it has a wine, beer, and champagne list worthy of a Michelin-starred restaurant."—Leonardo Ciomei

"Besides having really good pizza featuring a soft pizza crust and top-quality products, the pizzeria is famous for its fried appetizers. Fried pasta with potatoes and fried cod are just two of the specialties on the appetizer menu that clients love."
—Karen Phillips

"The pizza is fluffy, light, and very easy to digest thanks to the 24-hour leavening at room temperature."
—Maria Romano

To serve truly great Neapolitan pizza to 200 people at a time brothers Francesco and Salvatore Salvo procure the best information and ingredients available. When the third-generation *pizzaioli* are not analyzing how flour, yeast, temperature, and maybe 20 other variables affect the dough, they're nurturing lasting relationships with the best suppliers. But sometimes folklore does play a role, too. According to legend, the *cosacca* pizza (cossack's pizza) was created some 180 years ago to honor the visit of Tsar Nicholas I to the Kingdom of Naples. At Pizzeria Salvo, the exquisitely simple *cosacca* is distinguished by the nobility of Corbarì cherry tomatoes from I Sapori di Corbara, Pecorino cheese from the Cooperativa Agricola Pecorino Bagnolese, and organic extra virgin olive oil from Colline Salernitane delle San Salvatore.

RISTORANTE PIZZERIA L'ABATE

Piazza Sant'Antonino 24
Sorrento
Naples
Campania 80067
Italy
+39 0818072304
www.labatesorrento.it

Opening hours	Open 7 days
Credit cards	Accepted
Style of pizza	Neapolitan

"This well-known restaurant is near the harbor. It is aimed at tourists, but still feels local. The restaurant is large with a terrace, and the food is good, making it a must when visiting Sorrento."—Takanori Nakamura

PIZZERIA MASSÈ

Corso Vittorio Emanuele III 429
Torre Annunziata
Naples
Campania 80058
Italy
+39 0815363382
www.pizzeriamasse.it

Opening hours	Open 7 days
Credit cards	Accepted
Style of pizza	Neapolitan
Recommended pizza	Margherita

PALAZZO VIALDO

Via Nazionale 981
Torre del Greco
Naples
Campania 80059
Italy
+39 0818471624
www.palazzovialdo.it

Opening hours	Open 7 days
Credit cards	Accepted
Style of pizza	Gourmet Neapolitan
Recommended pizza	Che Cavolo Vuoi

"The work on the dough and the choice and combinations of toppings are interesting."
—Salvatore Salvo & Francesco Salvo

"I like this pizzeria for the elegance of the venue, the excellent toppings, and the great products from the Vesuvio region."—Giustino Catalano

PIZZA A METRO DA GIGINO

Via Giovanni Nicotera 15
Vico Equense
Naples
Campania 80069
Italy
+39 0818798309
www.pizzametro.it

Opening hours	Open 7 days
Credit cards	Accepted
Style of pizza	*Pizza al metro*
Recommended pizza	Quattro Stagioni; Sausage; Seafood

"Almost half a century ago Luigi D'Amura, a.k.a. Gigino, invented the *pizza al metro*, and to this day this marvelous pizza is still made as it was then with the chance to choose more than one topping on the same pizza."—Concetta Donato

"Gigino may still be in Campania but the pizza is completely different from Neapolitan pizza. It's a sort of hybrid between Neapolitan and deep-pan pizza, with a hard, crunchy base that's considerably deeper than Neapolitan pizza and yet still thinner than deep-dish pizza."—Emidio Mansi

RISTORANTE DA COSTANTINO

Via Corvo 95
Positano
Salerno
Campania 84017
Italy
+39 089875738
www.dacostantino.net

Opening hours	Open 7 days
Credit cards	Accepted
Style of pizza	Classic Italian
Recommended pizza	Margherita

"Anything you order in this charming family restaurant, with its friendly service and breathtaking views of the sea below, will be some of the finest food you'll have in all of Italy, and at the most reasonable price. From beginning to end, Da Costantino is an experience that can't be beat."—Lisa Pepin

SACRACENO D'ORO

Via Pasitea 254
Positano
Salerno
Campania 84017
Italy
+39 089812050
www.saracenodoro.it

Opening hours	Open 7 days
Credit cards	Accepted
Style of pizza	Traditional
Recommended pizza	Margherita

"Nothing could be more special than dining on top-notch pizzas in the shade of a sagging lemon tree in this family-run trattoria."—Darren Lovell

ALCE NERO BERBERÈ

Via Petroni 9C
Bologna
Bologna
Emilia-Romagna 40126
Italy
+39 0512759196
www.alceneroberbere.it

Opening hours	Closed Monday
Credit cards	Accepted
Style of pizza	Gourmet
Recommended pizza	Burrata, Asparagus, Mozzarella, and Chicory with Anchovies and Garlic

OFFICINE DEGLI APULI

Via San Leonardo 4
Bologna
Bologna
Emilia-Romagna 40126
Italy
+39 051236042

Opening hours	Open 7 days
Credit cards	Accepted
Style of pizza	Apulian
Recommended pizza	Faeto Ham and Stracciatella Cheese

PIZZARTIST

Via Marsala 35
Bologna
Bologna
Emilia-Romagna 40126
Italy
+39 0515872755

Opening hours..Closed Sunday
Credit cards...Not accepted
Style of pizza..By the slice

PIZZERIA VECCHIA MALGA

Aeroporto Guglielmo Marconi
Via Triumvirato 84
Bologna
Bologna
Emilia-Romagna 40132
Italy
+39 0516472196
www.vecchiamalganegozi.it

Opening hours...Open 7 days
Credit cards.............................Accepted but not AMEX
Style of pizza..Neapolitan
Recommended pizza....................Mortadella and Parmesan

RANZANI 13

Via Camillo Ranzani 5/12
Bologna
Bologna
Emilia-Romagna 40127
Italy
+39 0518493743
www.ranzani13.it

Opening hours...Open 7 days
Credit cards.............................Accepted but not AMEX
Style of pizza..Gourmet
Recommended pizza..Re Ferdinando

"Ranzani 13 has a great selection of beers to go with
the pizzas."—Giuseppe Aldè

TRATTORIA PIZZERIA BELLE ARTI

Via Belle Arti 14
Bologna
Bologna
Emilia-Romagna 40126
Italy
+39 051225581
www.bellearti-ristorante.com

Opening hours...Open 7 days
Credit cards..Accepted
Style of pizza...Classic
Recommended pizza...Denis

"Natural leavened wholemeal dough gives the pizza
a rustic touch that is perfect for ingredients like
smoked provola cheese, pancetta, porcini mushrooms,
and grilled vegetables."—Marco Paolo Mangiamele

BERBERÈ

Via Pio La Torre 4B
Castel Maggiore
Bologna
Emilia-Romagna 40013
Italy
+39 051705715
www.berberepizza.it

Opening hours...Closed Monday
Credit cards..Accepted
Style of pizza....................................Gourmet Neapolitan
Recommended pizza............Broccoli Raab, Asiago Cheese,
and Mortadella; Mora Romagnola Sausage, Sweet and
Sour Onions, and Mozzarella; San Marzano Tomatoes
DOP, Cetara Anchovies, and Wild Oregano

"This is pizza that borders on perfection. The
perfectly risen dough is light and crispy and the
combination of the toppings and this dough is hard
to find in other pizzas. It is a highly recognizable and
unique product that has been achieved thanks to an
in-depth study. In my opinion, this is currently the
best interpretation of pizza in Italy."
—Marco Locatelli

Brothers Matteo and Salvatore Aloe brought different
experiences to bear at Berberè. Matteo worked as a chef in
Bologna and Milan, interned at Noma in Copenhagen, and
studied pizza for a year with maestro *pizzaiolo* Beniamino Bilali
in Rimini. Salvatore studied business at the University of
Bologna and ate way too much bad street pizza. His motivation
to always surround himself with lighter, healthier, naturally
leavened pizza made with prized ingredients (San Marzano
tomatoes, Mora Romagnola sausage) was nearly as strong
as Matteo's. Incoming students can eat better pizza, now

that the Aloes have opened a Berberè in partnership with Acle Nero, a consortium of organic farmers and producers, in Bologna.

and one without, in two formats, big and small. It also makes chickpea farinata, which is a rarity in the area."—Alberto Rinieri

IL GALEONE

Via Caselle 59
San Lazzaro di Savena
Bologna
Emilia-Romagna 40068
Italy
+39 051464544
www.ristoranteilgaleone.it

Opening hours	Closed Sunday
Credit cards	Accepted but not AMEX
Style of pizza	Neapolitan
Recommended pizza	Galeone

"A slice of Naples conveniently located in Emilia-Romagna."—Marco Tonelli

LA SPARTURA

Via Della Libertà 65
Savigno
Bologna
Emilia-Romagna 40060
Italy
+39 0516708021

Opening hours	Closed Monday
Credit cards	Accepted
Style of pizza	Traditional
Recommended pizza	Porcini Mushrooms

"The pizza is cooked well and seasoned well, and it's made with high-quality ingredients with zero food miles."—Laura Rangoni

PIZZERIA ORSUCCI DA ARMANDO

Via Saraceno 116
Ferrara
Ferrara
Emilia-Romagna 44121
Italy
+39 0532760000
www.pizzeriaorsucciarmando.it

Opening hours	Closed Thursday
Credit cards	Accepted
Style of pizza	Pan-fried
Recommended pizza	Napoli

"This pizzeria is located in a historic venue and it only sells two types of pizza, one with anchovies

LA VECCHIA SCUOLA

Via Nandi 8
Montese
Modena
Emilia-Romagna 41055
Italy
+39 059985285
www.lavecchiascuolamontalto.it

Opening hours	Closed Monday and Tuesday
Credit cards	Accepted
Style of pizza	Traditional
Recommended pizza	Mushroom

LA SMORFIA

Via Roma 52
Nonantola
Modena
Emilia-Romagna 41015
Italy
+39 059545037

Opening hours	Closed Monday
Credit cards	Accepted but not AMEX
Style of pizza	Neapolitan
Recommended pizza	Fried Vegetable; Margherita with Buffalo Mozzarella

"This is a place to relax and eat a good pizza with no fuss nor complicated toppings."—Michela Iorio

IL CASTELLO

Via Ponte Muratori 8
Vignola
Modena
Emilia-Romagna 41058
Italy
+39 059765231
www.castellovignola.it

Opening hours	Open 7 days
Credit cards	Accepted
Style of pizza	Neapolitan
Recommended pizza	Vecchia Modena

"The pizza is made with Neapolitan dough, cooked to perfection with outstanding raw materials, and is excellent value for money."—Laura Rangoni

PIZZERIA RISTORANTE L'AQUILA

Via Mauro Tesi 937
Zocca
Modena
Emilia-Romagna 41059
Italy
+39 059987512

Opening hours	Closed Wednesday
Credit cards	Accepted but not AMEX
Style of pizza	Traditional
Recommended pizza	Prosciutto Crudo

LA DUCHESSA

Piazza Garibaldi 1/BIS
Parma
Parma
Emilia-Romagna 43121
Italy
+39 0521235962
www.laduchessaparma.com

Opening hours	Closed Monday
Credit cards	Accepted
Style of pizza	Neapolitan
Recommended pizza	Margherita

EURIDICE

Strada Rota Ligneres 22/A
Parma
Parma
Emilia-Romagna 43126
Italy
+39 0521603014
www.ristoranteeuridice.it

Opening hours	Open 7 days
Credit cards	Accepted but not AMEX
Style of pizza	Wood-fired

"This restaurant and pizzeria is outside the center of Parma but is well worth a visit. It has a modern relaxed atmosphere and serves thin-crust pizzas that have been cooked in a wood-fired oven. The pizzas are topped with only the best regional ingredients, such as Parma ham and Parmesan cheese."
—Susana Ribeiro

'O FIORE MIO

Via Mura San Marco 4/6
Faenza
Ravenna
Emilia-Romagna 48018
Italy
+39 0546667915
www.ofioremio.it

Opening hours	Closed Monday
Credit cards	Accepted
Style of pizza	Gourmet Neapolitan
Recommended pizza	Endive; 'O Fiore Mio; Romana; Sausage and Broccoli Raab; Via Emilia

"The doughs are the real strong point of the pizzeria. They are made with baker's yeast and various types of cereals using a variety of techniques."
—Matteo Aloe

"The quality of the ingredients, the extraordinarily good bases, and a really special setting are just some of the reasons I'd travel to eat in 'O Fiore Mio. It is, without a doubt, the best pizza I've ever tasted."
—Sasha Correa

"The doughs, the cooking, the venue, the service, the general feel: everything in 'O Fiore Mio is at its best."
—Roberto Bentivegna

Classic pizza is not always ideal for sharing. There's no stopping the tomato sauce and melted mozzarella from running off to places they don't belong. 'O Fiore Mio's gourmet pizzas, pre-cut into eight slices, are guaranteed not to run. Think triangular slices of pizza bread layered with the sublime combinations of most prized cheeses, produce, wild herbs, and salume. The Dall'Appennino al Vesuvio pizza matches prized local ingredients from the Emilia-Romagna region—Parmigiano-Reggiano, the scallions (spring onions) of Romagna, artisan sea salt of Cervia—to Piennolo del Vesuvio tomatoes from Campania. Artisanal doughs are made with a sourdough starter, wholegrain flours, and ancient grains. Not to neglect devotees of wet and potentially messy pizza, 'O Fiore Mio aces its more traditional Neapolitan pizzas, too. At Pizze di Strada (street pizza), 'O Flore Mio's takeout shop in Bologna, a third pizza format is thrown into the mix, Roman *pizza al taglio*.

ZINGARÒ

Via Campidori 11
Faenza
Ravenna
Emilia-Romagna 48018
Italy
+39 054621560
www.ristorantezingaro.com

Opening hours...Closed Sunday
Credit cards...Accepted
Style of pizza...Neapolitan
Recommended pizza............................Ham and Mushrooms

"Zingarò is set in a lovely convent and has
a hard-working *pizzaiolo*. Its pizzas have a tasty,
crispy crust and lush toppings."—John Gilchrist

PICCOLA PIEDIGROTTA

Piazza XXV Aprile 1
Reggio Emilia
Reggio Emilia
Emilia-Romagna 42121
Italy
+039 0522434922
www.piccolapiedigrotta.com

Opening hours..Closed Monday
Credit cards...Accepted
Style of pizza...Neapolitan
Recommended pizza..............1940; Bona; Carbonara Parisi;
Greca; Margherita; Marinara; Montalbano; Napoletana;
Pugliese

"This unpretentious, no-frills pizzeria has an air of
calm, offering a classic pizza with the highest-quality
ingredients such as San Marzano tomatoes, oregano
from the Amalfi Coast, and olives from Gaeta. The
pizza is extremely easy to digest."—Matteo Aloe

When a partisan of puffy Neapolitan pizza meets a clientele
that wants it flat and crisp something's gotta give. Giovanni
Mandara lets diners choose their dough shape. The *tirate e
sottile* (pulled out and thin), one of four options, yields a thin
crust with a high, crisp border. *Tirate e sottile* also characterizes
the stretched slices of lardo, mortadella, and other salume
draped over the pizzas. Mandara's much praised Carbonara
Parisi, with *mozzarella di bufala*, *guanciale*, Conciato Romano
cheese and a Paolo Parisi egg, was probably the world's first—
and maybe the last—pizza named after both a pasta dish and
an egg producer. Some Mandara innovations have proven more
prescient: over 15 years ago he came up with the then crazy
idea of pairing artisanal pizza with craft beers.

PRIMA O POI

Viale Giovanni Pascoli 95
Rimini
Rimini
Emilia-Romagna 47923
Italy
+39 0541386470
www.pizzeriaprimaopoi.it

Opening hours..Closed Monday
Credit cards...Accepted
Style of pizza...Traditional

"The pizza with rice flour is excellent and the staff
are good at recommending the best pairings."
—Luisa Pandolfi

PIZZERIA TRATTORIA EUROPA

Via Terza Armata 98
Fogliano-Redipuglia
Gorizia
Friuli-Venezia Giulia 34070
Italy
+39 0481489030
www.pizzeriaeuropa.it

Opening hours...Closed Wednesday
Credit cards.................................Accepted but not AMEX
Style of pizza...Neapolitan
Recommended pizza...............Radicchio di Treviso and Brie

"The pizzeria uses stone-ground flour, which
makes the pizzas easy to digest. There are hundreds
of pizzas on the menu and the pizza chefs have got
great creativity."—Giuseppe Cordioli

RISTORANTE MEDITERRANEO
Via Pordenone 7
Tamai di Brugnera
Pordenone
Friuli-Venezia Giulia 33070
Italy
+39 0434627775
www.ristorante-mediterraneo.it

Opening hours..Closed Monday
Credit cards...Accepted
Style of pizza...Gourmet
Recommended pizza..Nuvola

"An extremely high standard of pizza."
—Giuseppe Aldè

"The dough is the product of flour from ancient
grains that have been stone-ground, while the
ingredients for the toppings are from seasonal
produce of the highest quality."—Orlando Bortolami

PIZZERIA AL TIGLIO
Center Hotel
Via Srecko Kosovel 3
Basovizza
Trieste
Friuli-Venezia Giulia 34149
Italy
+39 0409220163
www.trattoria.centerhotel.it

Opening hours..Open 7 days
Credit cards...Accepted
Style of pizza..Classic

PIZZERIA & BIRRERIA KARIS
Hotel Pesek
Località Pesek di Grozzana 69
San Dorligo della Valle
Trieste
Friuli-Venezia Giulia 34018
Italy
+39 040226294
www.hotelpesek.it

Opening hours..Open 7 days
Credit cards...Accepted
Style of pizza...Gourmet
Recommended pizza...Asparagus

DI FRONTE AL VERDI
Piazza Verdi 2
Trieste
Trieste
Friuli-Venezia Giulia 34121
Italy
+39 040768864

Opening hours..Open 7 days
Credit cards.............................Accepted but not AMEX
Style of pizza...Wood-fired
Recommended pizza...Ortolana

PEPERINO TRIESTE
Via del Coroneo 19C
Trieste
Trieste
Friuli-Venezia Giulia 34133
Italy
+39 040631234
www.peperinopizza.it/it/trieste

Opening hours..Open 7 days
Credit cards...Accepted
Style of pizza...Neapolitan
Recommended pizza...Bufalina

PIZZERIA DEL NONNO
Via Carlo Combi 13
Trieste
Trieste
Friuli-Venezia Giulia 34123
Italy
+39 0335261700

Opening hours........................Closed Saturday and Sunday
Credit cards...Not accepted
Style of pizza..*Pizza al taglio*
Recommended pizza.................Eggplant (aubergine); White
Focaccia with Mozzarella

"Pizzeria del Nonno sells excellent pizza by the slice
for a quick lunch (it is advised to go in the morning
because it is not open for long in the afternoon and
is closed in the evening)."—Federica Caccamo

PIZZERIA PIEDIGROTTA

Viale XX Settembre 41
Trieste
Trieste
Friuli-Venezia Giulia 34100
Italy
+39 040661300
www.christiang79.altervista.org

Opening hours	Open 7 days
Credit cards	Accepted but not AMEX
Style of pizza	Neapolitan

"Pizzeria Piedigrotta is an old-style pizzeria with
great dough."—Giuseppe Aldè

RISTORANTE PIZZERIA CHICHIBIO

Via Carnia 2
Cervignano del Friuli
Udine
Friuli-Venezia Giulia 33052
Italy
+39 043132704
www.ristorantechichibio.it

Opening hours	Closed Wednesday
Credit cards	Accepted
Style of pizza	Roman

"It also serves gluten-free pizzas."—Catia Gressani

IN TOMASIN

Via Statale
Comeglians
Udine
Friuli-Venezia Giulia 33023
Italy
+39 043360283
www.intomasin.altervista.org

Opening hours	Closed Monday
Credit cards	Accepted
Style of pizza	Roman

"It is never easy to find a good pizza in the mountains
but this pizzeria is really super."—Catia Gressani

LA CATAPECCHIA

Via Trieste 120
Frazione Papariano
Fiumicello
Udine
Friuli-Venezia Giulia 33050
Italy
+39 0431970869
www.lacatapecchia.it

Opening hours	Closed Monday
Credit cards	Accepted
Style of pizza	Classic
Recommended pizza	Diavola

"The dough mixture contains kamut, wheatgerm,
olive extracts, and red grape skins—it's a winning
recipe."—Giuseppe Cordioli

GIOROLDO'S PIZZA

Piazza Vittorio Emanuele 10
Flambro
Udine
Friuli-Venezia Giulia 33050
Italy
+39 3342435656

Opening hours	Closed Monday
Credit cards	Not accepted
Style of pizza	*Pizza al taglio*
Recommended pizza	Frico di Codroip

AL TIGLIO

Via Centa 8
Moruzzo
Udine
Friuli-Venezia Giulia 33030
Italy
+39 0432642024
www.altiglioveg.it

Opening hours	Closed Monday
Credit cards	Accepted
Style of pizza	Vegan
Recommended pizza	Carciofosa

"This is one of the few places where you can eat
vegan pizza. The chef Max Noacco is dedicated to
cooking with the passion and the coherence of his
life philosophy."—Federica Caccamo

GABIN

Via dei Rizzani 19
Udine
Udine
Friuli-Venezia Giulia 33100
Italy
+39 0432294302
www.gabinfood.it

Opening hours	Open 7 days
Credit cards	Accepted but not AMEX
Style of pizza	Pizza by the slice
Recommended pizza	Cantabrico

"Gabin is an informal and welcoming pizzeria that serves pizza by the slice or tastings of pizza on the plate."—Orlando Bortolami

LE DELIZIE DI MARIA

S.S 82
Località Scaffa 84
Arpinio
Frosinone
Lazio 03033
Italy
+39 0776882137
www.ledeliziedimaria.net

Opening hours	Closed Monday
Credit cards	Accepted but not AMEX
Style of pizza	Classic
Recommended pizza	C'era Una Volta

"This is a pastry shop, a store, a restaurant. There is pizza available, though it seems to be hidden in the middle of so many delicacies, but it is worth the trip."—Salvo Gurrieri

SANCHO

Via della Torre Clementina 142
Fiumicino
Rome
Lazio 00054
Italy
+39 3388931807

Opening hours	Closed Sunday
Credit cards	Not accepted
Style of pizza	Pizza al taglio
Recommended pizza	Daily specials; Marinara

FORNO OTTAVIANI

Via Carlo Cattaneo 39
Nettuno
Rome
Lazio 00048
Italy
+39 069881729

Opening hours	Closed Thursday
Credit cards	Not accepted
Style of pizza	Pizza alla pala
Recommended pizza	Bianca; Zucchini (courgette) Flowers

"Pizza with an unforgettable aroma in a location that exudes history."—Pave' Luca Scanni

PIZZERIA RISTORANTE LA MAMA

Via San Bernardo 70
Genoa
Genoa
Liguria 16123
Italy
+39 0102518937
www.lamama.it

Opening hours	Open 7 days
Credit cards	Accepted but not AMEX
Style of pizza	Ligurian
Recommended pizza	Focaccia with Recco Cheese

"La Mama is a cozy restaurant in a dark narrow alley in Genoa with a lot of history. It makes a nice Ligurian-style pizzata and focaccia with cheese."—Miriam Bunnik

SAVÒ

Via al Ponte Calvi 16R
Genoa
Genoa
Liguria 16124
Italy
+39 0108568593
www.pizzeriasavo.it

Opening hours	Closed Saturday and Sunday
Credit cards	Accepted
Style of pizza	Gourmet
Recommended pizza	Camogliese

RISTORANTE LO SCALO

Via XXV Aprile 126
Pieve Ligure
Genoa
Liguria 16030
Italy
+39 0103460342
www.trovavetrine.it/ristorante-lo-scalo

Opening hours..Closed Wednesday
Credit cards...Accepted
Style of pizza...Neapolitan
Recommended pizza.........................Anchovies; Margherita

MANUELINA

Via Roma 296
Recco
Genoa
Liguria 16036
Italy
+39 018574128
www.manuelina.it

Opening hours..Closed Wednesday
Credit cards...Accepted
Style of pizza..Focaccia
Recommended pizza...............Focaccia with Recco Cheese

IL BORGO

Via San Sebastiano 2
Dolceacqua
Imperia
Liguria 18035
Italy
+39 0184206972

Opening hours..Closed Wednesday
Credit cards...Accepted
Style of pizza...Wood-fired
Recommended pizza...................................Porcini Mushrooms

"Il Borgo makes lovely wood-fired pizzas with crispy
crusts. Portions are huge."—Kevin Hin

RIO BARBAIRA

Viale Rimembranze 8
Rocchetta Nervina
Imperia
Liguria 18035
Italy
+39 0184207936

Opening hours...Closed Monday
Credit cards...................................Accepted but not AMEX
Style of pizza...Wood-fired
Recommended pizza...Margherita

MEDITERRANEO

Via Gioberti 20
Sanremo
Imperia
Liguria 18038
Italy
+39 0184501462

Opening hours...Open 7 days
Credit cards...................................Accepted but not AMEX
Style of pizza..Classic

"A traditional family pizzeria that gets better and
better."—Barbara Scabin

BELLA NAPOLI

Via Urbano Rella 11
Savona
Savona
Liguria 17100
Italy
+39 019828727

Opening hours...Closed Sunday
Credit cards...................................Accepted but not AMEX
Style of pizza...Neapolitan
Recommended pizza..Napoletana

"Bella Napoli is a surprisingly good pizzeria. At first
sight it may look just like any other, and yet for years
an entire family—with father Anselmo manning the
oven—has run a simple pizzeria with carefully chosen
ingredients and shrewdness (starting with the oil
added after cooking). Prices are a little higher and
portions a little smaller than average but it is second
to none in the area in terms of satisfaction."
—Luca Iaccarino

PIZZERIA CAPRI DA NASTI
Via Zambonate 25
Bergamo
Bergamo
Lombardy 24122
Italy
+39 035247911
www.danasti.it

Opening hours	Closed Monday
Credit cards	Accepted
Style of pizza	Traditional
Recommended pizza	Alberobello

"With over 250 types of pizza, including gluten-free ones, choices are almost endless at Capri da Nasti."
—Francesca Negri

SIRANI
Via Gramsci 5
Bagnolo Mella
Brescia
Lombardy 25021
Italy
+39 0306821179
www.sirani.com

Opening hours	Closed Sunday
Credit cards	Accepted but not AMEX
Style of pizza	Gourmet
Recommended pizza	Serrano Ham

CARDAMOMO
Via Carloni 2 F/G
Como
Como
Lombardy 22100
Italy
+39 031301919
www.cardamomo.eu

Opening hours	Closed Monday
Credit cards	Accepted but not AMEX
Style of pizza	Classic

NAPULE È
Via Dottesio 22
Como
Como
Lombardy 22100
Italy
+39 031307932
www.napulecomo.it

Opening hours	Open 7 days
Credit cards	Accepted but not AMEX
Style of pizza	Neapolitan
Recommended pizza	Margherita

RIVA CAFÈ
Via Fratelli Cairoli 10
Como
Como
Lombardy 22100
Italy
+39 031264325

Opening hours	Closed Monday
Credit cards	Accepted
Style of pizza	Roman

"Good pizza with a low and crispy base, typical of the round Roman pizza." –Giovanni Tesauro

BISTROT DU PASS
Via Novella 1
Vercurago
Lecco
Lombardy 23808
Italy
+39 0341420429
www.bistrotdupass.it

Opening hours	Closed Monday
Credit cards	Accepted but not AMEX
Style of pizza	Gourmet
Recommended pizza	Da Nord a Sud; Verace

"Among all the other delicacies prepared in his bistro, Luca Dell'Orto produces an excellent pizza. The dough is made with a natural leaven, stone-ground flour, and a long rise. In addition to the excellence of the base, the chef has created toppings that are always well balanced and that use outstanding raw materials."—Marco Locatelli

PIZZERIA LUNA ROSSA

Via Raffaello Sanzio 2
Cormano
Milan
Lombardy 20032
Italy
+39 0289056048

Opening hours	Closed Tuesday
Credit cards	Accepted but not AMEX
Style of pizza	*Pizza al taglio*

"Chef Giorgio, the founder of the pizzeria, is the only person who opens the shop and start the ovens. Should he be sick or on leave, the shop will be closed. The dough for the pizzas is a secret recipe known only to him and an assistant. He uses only the best ingredients and sources them specifically from where they are known to be best, for example porcini mushrooms from Bergamo and fresh buffalo mozzarella from Naples."—Marco Guccio

PIZZERIA MONTEGRIGNA TRIC TRAC

Via Grigna 12
Legnano
Milan
Lombardy 20025
Italy
+39 0331546173
www.pizzeriamontegrigna.com

Opening hours	Closed Monday
Credit cards	Accepted but not AMEX
Style of pizza	Neapolitan
Recommended pizza	Antica Margherita Verace; Enkir; Foresta Nera; Zeus

"Bruno De Rosa has produced a selection of high-quality doughs including flavored ones and ones made with different grains. Each dough is filled with wisdom and flavor, and the raw materials are excellent. This is the tastiest pizza in Lombardy."—Marco Locatelli

The stretched round of raw dough is widely accepted as the white canvas of pizza. The color comes from the toppings applied to it. In Legnano, northwest of Milan, Bruno De Rosa, a master of Neapolitan pizza, sees it differently. His canvases are imbued with an assortment of fragrant wheat and grain flours (rye, buckwheat, spelt, Otto File corn, rye, enkir) and sometimes tastes (walnut, saffron, basil, lemongrass). His pizzeria has a wider assortment of doughs than some gelato shops have flavors. All the mixing and matching is done with purpose: a seven-cereal dough is the novel, but fitting, platform for *salsiccia e friarelli*, the Naples classic of crumbled sausage, broccoli raab, and smoked scamorza.

IL PARADISO DELLA PIZZA

Via Passirano 20
Vimercate
Milan
Lombardy 20059
Italy
+39 0396085894
www.ilparadisodellapizza.it

Opening hours	Closed Monday
Credit cards	Accepted
Style of pizza	Neapolitan
Recommended pizza	Daily special

"This is a gem. The contrast between the location—a very tiny mall in the suburbs of a town north of Milan—and the quality of the groceries and ingredients used in the process is incredible. Everything is top of the line and made by people who are obsessed with quality. This is truly a pizza paradise!"
—Andrea Consonni

ENOSTERIA LIPEN

Via Conte Paolo Taverna 114
Canonica Lambro
Monza and Brianza
Lombardy 20844
Italy
+39 0362919710
www.lipen.it

Opening hours	Closed Tuesday and Saturday morning
Credit cards	Accepted
Style of pizza	Neapolitan
Recommended pizza	Pizza dei Maestri; Quater Stracc

TRATTORIA CAPRESE

Piazza Roma 10
Monza
Monza and Brianza
Lombardy 20052
Italy
+39 039322947
www.trattoriacaprese.it

Opening hours	Open 7 days
Credit cards	Accepted but not AMEX
Style of pizza	Classic
Recommended pizza	Bianca with Prosciutto

PIZZERIA RISTORANTE PIEDIGROTTA

Via Gian Domenico Romagnosi 9
Varese
Varese
Lombardy 21100
Italy
+39 0332287983

Opening hours...Open 7 days
Credit cards..Accepted
Style of pizza..............................Modern Neapolitan
Recommended pizza............Grilled Octopus and Pistachio
Gelato; Margherita

"The creative presentations and great flavors are mind-blowing!"—Emilio Mignucci

ITALIA... AL PEZZO

Via Dell' Industria 8D
Ancona
Ancona
Marche 60127
Italy
+39 3277425492
www.pizzeriaanconaitaliaalpezzo.it

Opening hours...Open 7 days
Credit cards...Not accepted
Style of pizza...................................Pizza alla pala
Recommended pizza.....................................Margherita

"I recommend it absolutely for the quality of the raw materials and ingredients but also for the lightness on the palate from the leavening and the style of cooking. It isn't a thin pizza but rather it is extremely crunchy on the outside and soft on the inside."
—Stefania Zolotti

OSTERIA DELLA PIAZZA

Piazza Ugo Bassi 14B
Ancona
Ancona
Marche 60127
Italy
+39 0712814235
www.osteriadellapiazza.com

Opening hours.................................Closed Saturday
Credit cards........................Accepted but not AMEX
Style of pizza...................................Thin-crust
Recommended pizza.....................................Montanara

PIZZERIA DA FABIO

Corso Amendola 44
Ancona
Ancona
Marche 60123
Italy
+39 0719983173

Opening hours...Open 7 days
Credit cards...Not accepted
Style of pizza...................................Pizza al taglio

PIZZERIA DESIDERIO

Via Maggini 57
Ancona
Ancona
Marche 60127
Italy
+39 07182741
www.pizzeriadesiderio.it

Opening hours.................................Closed Tuesday
Credit cards..Accepted
Style of pizza...................................Thin-crust
Recommended pizza.....................................Stazio

RISTORANTE IL GIARDINO

Via Fabio Filzi 2C
Ancona
Ancona
Marche 60123
Italy
+39 071206847
www.ristorantegiardinoancona.it

Opening hours.................................Closed Monday
Credit cards..Accepted
Style of pizza...................................Neapolitan
Recommended pizza.....................................Margherita

"The dough, the perfect leavening, and the baking in a wood-fired oven fulfill the criteria for a classic Neapolitan pizza. One would expect nothing less given that the owners are Neapolitan by birth."
—Daniele Fava

ROSSOPOMODORO

Via Pietro Filonzi 4
Ancona
Ancona
Marche 60131
Italy
+39 0712916363
www.rossopomodoro.it

Opening hours	Open 7 days
Credit cards	Accepted
Style of pizza	Neapolitan
Recommended pizza	Verace

PIZZERIA CLAUDIO

Piazza Giuseppe Mazzini 12
Chiaravalle
Ancona
Marche 60033
Italy
+39 071741628

Opening hours	Closed Monday
Credit cards	Not accepted
Style of pizza	Roman *pizza stirata*
Recommended pizza	Porchetta

L'ARNIA DEL CUCINIERE

Via Baluffi 12
Falconara Marittima
Ancona
Marche 60015
Italy
+39 0719160055
www.arniadelcuciniere.it

Opening hours	Closed Monday
Credit cards	Accepted
Style of pizza	Deep-crust
Recommended pizza	Margherita

"L'Arnia del Cuciniere produces deep pizza that's soft with a golden end crust. It has great lightness and a very pleasing 'chew' thanks to the quality of the raw materials (local flour or flour from the surrounding territory) and impeccable cooking in a wood-fired oven."—Stefania Zolotti

LIBERO ARBITRIO

Via Gaspare Spontini 42
Maiolati Spontini
Ancona
Marche 60030
Italy
+39 0731776026
www.liberoarbitrio.net

Opening hours	Closed Monday
Credit cards	Accepted but not AMEX
Style of pizza	Traditional
Recommended pizza	Apple and Gorgonzola

LADY GREEN

Via Carducci 8
Moie - Maiolati Spontini
Ancona
Marche 60030
Italy
+39 0731703351
www.ristorantepizzerialadygreenjesian.it

Opening hours	Closed Monday
Credit cards	Accepted but not AMEX
Style of pizza	Traditional
Recommended pizza	Seafood

"Excellent value for money."—Giovanni Elce Fabbretti

ALBERTO BERARDI

Via Lungomare Buglioni 80A
Montemarciano
Ancona
Marche 60018
Italy
+39 0719194218
www.albertoberardi.it

Opening hours	Open 7 days
Credit cards	Accepted
Style of pizza	Traditional
Recommended pizza	Napoli "Slow Food"

"Alberto Berardi uses Slow Food products."
—Francesco Quercetti

MEZZOMETRO

Lungomare Leonardo da Vinci 33
Senigallia
Ancona
Marche 60019
Italy
+39 07160578
www.mezzometro.it

Opening hours...Open 7 days
Credit cards...Accepted
Style of pizza...*Pizza al metro*

MAMMA ROSA

Via Aso 64
Ortezzano
Fermo
Marche 63851
Italy
+39 0734770194
www.pizzeriamammarosa.it

Opening hours.......................................Closed Wednesday
Credit cards...............................Accepted but not AMEX
Style of pizza...Neapolitan
Recommended pizza...................................Pizza Fritta

PIZZERIA MCKENZIE

Piazza Andrea Costa 4
Fano
Pesaro and Urbino
Marche 61032
Italy
+39 0721809380

Opening hours...Open 7 days
Credit cards...............................Accepted but not AMEX
Style of pizza...*Pizza al taglio*
Recommended pizza............Fresh Tomatoes, Spicy Salami,
and Pecorino Cream

"The dough is reminiscent of ciabatta bread made with durum wheat and there are original combinations of excellent toppings."—Luca Leone Zampa

C'ERA UNA VOLTA

Via Carlo Cattaneo 26
Pesaro
Pesaro and Urbino
Marche 61122
Italy
+39 072130911
www.ceraunavolta-ps.com

Opening hours...Closed Monday
Credit cards...Accepted
Style of pizza..Classic
Recommended pizza.......................................Cartoceto

LA CAPANNA

Strada Panoramica Adriatica 189
Pesaro
Pesaro and Urbino
Marche 61121
Italy
+39 072121890

Opening hours...................................Open 7 days in summer
Credit cards...Accepted
Style of pizza..Classic
Recommended pizza...Rossini

PIZZERIA FARINA

Via Leonardo Da Vinci 33
Pesaro
Pesaro and Urbino
Marche 61100
Italy
+39 0721580451
www.pizzeriafarina.it

Opening hours...Open 7 days
Credit cards...............................Accepted but not AMEX
Style of pizza...Gourmet
Recommended pizza................Gennarì l'Artista; Professore

LE 3 PIANTE
Via Voltaccia della Vecchia 1
Urbino
Pesaro and Urbino
Marche 61029
Italy
+39 07224863

Opening hours..Closed Monday
Credit cards..Not accepted
Style of pizza..Neapolitan
Recommended pizza.....................................Quattro Stagioni

"Having been raised on pizza in New York, the rustically elegant individual pies at Le 3 Piante in Urbino were a revelation. One of the few sit-down restaurants in this tiny hillside medieval town in Le Marche, it attracts everyone from businessmen to families and hungry college students. Perhaps they're all drawn in by the smell of smoke that emanates from the wood oven and permeates every winding, narrow street in town."—Michele Parente

PIZZERIA THAT'S AMORE
Via Scardocchia 8H
Campobasso
Campobasso
Molise 86100
Italy
+39 08741961437

Opening hours...Closed Sunday
Credit cards..Accepted
Style of pizza...Neapolitan
Recommended pizza..Truffle

LA REGINA
Via Neri 1/9
Campobasso
Campobasso
Molise 86100
Italy
+39 08741961290
www.pizzerialaregina.it

Opening hours...Closed Monday
Credit cards..Accepted
Style of pizza...Neapolitan
Recommended pizza.........................Margherita; Pizza Fritti

"The pizzas are made with a sourdough starter and double fermentation and then cooked in a wood-fired oven. The ingredients are of excellent quality. After finishing your pizza, you feel light and like you could eat another. The restaurant is spacious and comfortable with extensive outdoor space for the summer months."
—Alfredo Cocchiarella

OSTERIA O' PIZZAIUOLO
Corso Marcelli 214
Isernia
Isernia
Molise 86170
Italy
+39 0865412776

Opening hours...Open 7 days
Credit cards..Accepted
Style of pizza...Thin-crust
Recommended pizza...Marinara

CASCINA LE NOCI
Via Forcella - Borgata Le Noci
Venafro
Isernia
Molise 86079
Italy
+39 3455278954
www.cascinalenoci.it

Opening hours...Closed Tuesday
Credit cards....................................Accepted but not AMEX
Style of pizza...Thin-crust
Recommended pizza...Margherita

PIZZERIA AL VESUVIO
Corso Campano 150
Venafro
Isernia
Molise 86079
Italy
+39 3275511781

Opening hours...Closed Tuesday
Credit cards...Not accepted
Style of pizza...Neapolitan
Recommended pizza...Margherita

IL PIZZ'INO

Via Mondovì 16–18
Alessandria
Alessandria
Piedmont 15121
Italy
+39 0131262085
www.gioilpizzino.it

Opening hours	Closed Tuesday
Credit cards	Not accepted
Style of pizza	Takeout
Recommended pizza	Margherita

"Giuseppe Giordano has patented a new way of cooking pan pizza, the 'pizz'ino,' halfway between the classic way of cooking and frying-pan cooking. It results in a dough that is very soft but crispy at the same time."—Dora Sorrentino

ACQUA E FARINA

Viale Cesare Battisti 2
Biella
Biella
Piedmont 13900
Italy
+39 3339929660

Opening hours	Closed Monday
Credit cards	Accepted but not AMEX
Style of pizza	Takeout
Recommended pizza	Bianca with Endive and Anchovies

"The dough is a natural leaven made with stone-ground Piedmontese flour and the toppings are organic with zero food miles. It's a good pizza, even though it is cooked in an electric oven."—Daniela Acquadro

LA PACE

Via Garibaldi 6
Biella
Biella
Piedmont 13900
Italy
+39 01521930
www.lapacebiella.it

Opening hours	Open 7 days
Credit cards	Accepted
Style of pizza	Neapolitan
Recommended pizza	Moreschina

RISTORANTE PIZZERIA LA LUCCIOLA

Piazza San Paolo 12
Biella
Biella
Piedmont 13900
Italy
+39 0158493801
www.ristorantepizzerialalucciola.net

Opening hours	Open 7 days
Credit cards	Accepted
Style of pizza	Wood-fired
Recommended pizza	Margherita

"A classic pizza, with good execution and without any (unpleasant) surprises."—Daniela Acquadro

PIZZERIA GENNARO ESPOSITO

Piazza XX Settembre 32A
Bra
Cuneo
Piedmont 12042
Italy
+39 01721801796
www.gennaroespositobra.it

Opening hours	Open 7 days
Credit cards	Accepted
Style of pizza	Neapolitan
Recommended pizza	La Gennaro di Bra

"A good Neapolitan pizzeria in the city where the Slow Food movement was born. It is a member of the Alleanza Cuochi Slow Food Italia (Italy's Slow Food Chef Alliance)."—Gessica & Gianni Bordini

PIZZ'ELIA

Via Giacomo Matteotti 10
Fossano
Cuneo
Piedmont 12045
Italy
+39 0172637106

Opening hours	Closed Monday and Tuesday
Credit cards	Accepted but not AMEX
Style of pizza	Wood-fired

"Pizz'Elia is a takeout pizzeria with some tables."
—Federico Molinari

PERBACCO

Via Roma 30
La Morra
Cuneo
Piedmont 12042
Italy
+39 017350609
www.pizzeriaperbacco.com

Opening hours...Closed Monday
Credit cards.......................................Accepted but not AMEX
Style of pizza..Neapolitan
Recommended pizza...............................Buffalo Mozzarella

"The pizzas are very good and so is the vibe."
—Dario Mulino

GUSTO DIVINO

Piazza Cavour 21
Saluzzo
Cuneo
Piedmont 12037
Italy
+39 017542444

Opening hours...Closed Tuesday
Credit cards.......................................Accepted but not AMEX
Style of pizza...Gourmet
Recommended pizza...................Burrata and Iberico Ham;
Burrata and Sicilian Red Shrimp (prawn); Goat Cheese
with Cherry Tomatoes and Capers; Octopus; Parma
Ham and Buffalo Mozzarella

"Massimiliano Prete is without doubt the great
surprise in the province of Cuneo, where traditional
osterias usually win hands down over good
pizzerias. Massimiliano's fortes are the tasting
itinerary and styles that he proposes."
—Enrico Bonardo

"Unlike others, Massimiliano Prete works on
differentiating doughs and not just the toppings.
He is without doubt the greatest—humble and brilliant
at the same time!"—Alessandra Tinozzi

When Massimiliano Prete mixes, kneads, ferments, and bakes
a dough he already knows the sound it will produce when
teeth meet crust. He can hear how certain flavors and textures
will play over it. Gusto Divino's pizza whisperer named one of
his designer doughs Fa Croc!, a phonetic representation of
the snap-crack you hear in your head when the dough's crust is
crushed. The crumb, like those within his other pizza formats—
the croccante (crisp), the thicker and softer pizz'otto, the
classica, the sharing pala (paddle)—is a silent symphony of air
pockets. He applies such prized ingredients as *burrata di Gioia*

del Colle, *mortadella di Prato* and local *prosciutto crudo di
Cuneo* in the same way he speaks: slowly and softly, with
precision, ingenuity, and divine taste.

BUCEFALO

Piazza Cesare Battisti 9
Savigliano
Cuneo
Piedmont 12038
Italy
+39 0172726924

Opening hours.............Open 7 days (April–August), Closed
Wednesday (September–March)
Credit cards..Accepted
Style of pizza...Wood-fired

L'ARROCCO

Piazza San Rocco 14
Rivoli
Turin
Piedmont 10098
Italy
+39 0112767156
www.larrocco.it

Opening hours...Open 7 days
Credit cards.......................................Accepted but not AMEX
Style of pizza...Deep-dish
Recommended pizza.......................Goat Cheese and Leeks;
Gustosa; Regina

POMODORO & BASILICO
Via Martiri della Libertà 103
San Mauro Torinese
Turin
Piedmont 10099
Italy
+39 0118973883
www.pomodoroebasilico.org

Opening hours	Closed Monday
Credit cards	Accepted but not AMEX
Style of pizza	Gourmet
Recommended pizza	Ciociara; Conciata; Daily specials

"Patrick Ricci is an indefatigable researcher of exceptional products. The dough (wheat or spelt) is always made with stone-ground flour and let to rise for 24 to 48 hours. It makes it perfect: fragrant, easy to digest, tasty."—Luca Iaccarino

"The menu represents a real sensory journey, from the pizzas *della memoria* (pizzas of recollection) where we find long-lost flavors, to the extreme pizzas with unique pairings that are of great culinary interest."—Enrico Bonardo

As a proponent of Slow Food in the movement's heartland, *pizzaiolo* Patrick Ricci holds farmers, producers, and craftsmen in the highest esteem. His respect for the land and the seasons is boundless. His regard for some of the more demanding diners at Pomodoro & Basilico, however, is not quite so strong. His "no" to soft drinks and habits he doesn't like as well as to all requests for pizza modifications border on rudeness. But look at it from his point of view: who'd want to change the slightest detail of his Ciociara pizza, with San Marzano tomato sauce, Castelpoto sausage, Tropio red onion, garlic, oregano, and olive oil? And who could object to his reserving all his patience for new materials, new recipes, and great pizza?

AL CONTEGRASSO
Via Marconi 29
Vinovo
Turin
Piedmont 10048
Italy
+39 3319544385
www.alcontegrassovinovo.com

Opening hours	Closed Tuesday
Credit cards	Accepted but not AMEX
Style of pizza	Neapolitan
Recommended pizza	Cicciona

AGO'S PIZZERIA
Via Ludovico Ariosto 3
Cagliari
Cagliari
Sardinia 09129
Italy
+39 0733633327

Opening hours	Open 7 days
Credit cards	Not accepted
Style of pizza	Thin-crust
Recommended pizza	Desulo

"An outstanding pizza! The staff are polite and welcoming and the atmosphere is very pleasant."
—Angelo Concas

MILESTONE PIZZORANTE
Via Corte d'Appello 33
Cagliari
Cagliari
Sardinia 09124
Italy
+39 0707564335
www.milestonepizzorante.it

Opening hours	Open 7 days
Credit cards	Accepted but not AMEX
Style of pizza	Gourmet thin-crust
Recommended pizza	Ricotta, Endive, and Guanciale

"Milestone is a very smart restaurant in a historic building near Cagliari castle. The menu has about 20 pizzas with ingredients that are somewhat different from the usual ones. This can only be described as gourmet pizza."—Angelo Concas

SA TRACCA
Via Carbonia 14
Cagliari
Cagliari
Sardinia 09125
Italy
+39 3347322501

Opening hours	Closed Sunday
Credit cards	Not accepted
Style of pizza	Neapolitan
Recommended pizza	Bottarga and Cherry Tomatoes; Gallurese; Mamothones; Ogliastrina; Sardinian Sausage and Pepper

"Sa Tracca has excellent craft beers and a wide selection of Sardinian wines."—Angelo Concas

RUBIU

Via Bologna SNC
Sant'Antioco
Carbonia-Iglesias
Sardinia 09017
Italy
+39 3467234605
www.rubiubirra.it

Opening hours	Open 7 days
Credit cards	Accepted but not AMEX
Style of pizza	Classic
Recommended pizza	Cabras; Tabarka

"Rubiu is a pub that produces high-quality artisanal beers. On top of that, its pizzas are delicious."
—Giuseppe Carrus

SA VERANDA DI FRA DIAVOLO

Via Roma 30
Pauli Arbarei
Medio Campidano
Sardinia 09020
Italy
+39 070939346

Opening hours	Closed Monday
Credit cards	Not accepted
Style of pizza	Traditional
Recommended pizza	Radicchio and Spicy Salami

"What's special about this pizzeria is the pizza: the dough has a good rise, it's cooked in a wood-fired oven, and the toppings used are often seasonal and locally produced."—Roberto Petza

PIZZERIA S'ARZOLA

Corso Vittorio Emanuele 82
Orotelli
Nuoro
Sardinia 08020
Italy
+39 078479303
www.pizzeriasarzola.com

Opening hours	Closed Monday
Credit cards	Accepted but not AMEX
Style of pizza	Classic
Recommended pizza	Oroteddesa; S'Arzola

DEJAVU

Via Bazzoni Sircana 7
Olbia
Olbia-Tempio
Sardinia 07926
Italy
+39 078967346
www.santeodoropizzerieolbia.it

Opening hours	Open 7 days
Credit cards	Accepted
Style of pizza	Roman
Recommended pizza	Trevigiana

"A welcoming venue with courteous service and a large selection of pizzas, artisanal beers, and small dishes."—Mattia Romano

LA ROSA DEI VENTI

Via Porto Rotondo 64
Porto Rotondo
Olbia-Tempio
Sardinia 07026
Italy
+39 3470823318
www.ristorantelarosadeiventi.org

Opening hours	Open 7 days
Credit cards	Accepted but not AMEX
Style of pizza	Roman
Recommended pizza	Sofia

"A restaurant and pizzeria with a large choice of artisanal beers; regional, national, and natural wines; live music; and creative cooking."—Mattia Romano

TARTARUGHINO

Piazza Quadra
Porto Rotondo
Olbia-Tempio
Sardinia 07026
Italy
+39 0789385004
www.tartarughino.com

Opening hours	Open 7 days
Credit cards	Accepted
Style of pizza	Roman
Recommended pizza	Tartarughino

"Located in a historical venue in the center of Porto Rotondo, this pizzeria and restaurant is a meeting point for the nocturnal life of the village, with a DJ mixset and live music. It also has a nice outdoor terrace."—Mattia Romano

PAPÈ SATAN

Via la Marmora 20–22
Santa Teresa di Gallura
Olbia-Tempio
Sardinia 07028
Italy
+39 0789755048
www.papesatan.it

Opening hours	Open 7 days in summer
Credit cards	Accepted but not AMEX
Style of pizza	Neapolitan
Recommended pizza	Margherita; Marinara

"The Neapolitan owners of Papè Satan have been offering real Neapolitan pizza in this Sardinian paradise for over 25 years. Their excellent pizza is made with products from Campania."
—Laura Gambacorta

BOSCO

Via Vittorio Veneto 4
Tempio Pausania
Olbia-Tempio
Sardinia 07029
Italy
+39 079632494

Opening hours	Closed Monday
Credit cards	Not accepted
Style of pizza	Roman
Recommended pizza	Margherita; Operaia

"Massimo Bosco is a role model to all *pizzaioli*. His dough is crazy, super airy with a very thin crust. In terms of baking he is really the master."
—Max Fisher

SARDASALATA

Via Dogana 9
Licata
Agrigento
Sicily 92027
Italy
+39 09221837195
www.pizzeriasardasalata.it

Opening hours	Closed Tuesday
Credit cards	Accepted but not AMEX
Style of pizza	Classic
Recommended pizza	Robba

LA PIAZZETTA

Via Lampedusa 9
Menfi
Agrigento
Sicily 92013
Italy
+39 092574460

Opening hours	Closed Monday
Credit cards	Accepted
Style of pizza	Sicilian

PIZZERIA CONTE LUNA

Piazza Gerardo Noceto 11A
Sciacca
Agrigento
Sicily 92019
Italy
+39 092527398

Opening hours	Closed Wednesday
Credit cards	Accepted but not AMEX
Style of pizza	Sicilian
Recommended pizza	Saccense

"It has an extensive pizza menu."—Marilena Barbera

RISTORANTE LE GOURMET

Via Monte Kronio 7
Sciacca
Agrigento
Sicily 92019
Italy
+39 092526460
www.legourmet.altervista.org

Opening hours	Closed Tuesday
Credit cards	Accepted
Style of pizza	Sicilian
Recommended pizza	Pecorino Cheese and Pistachios

DIETRO LE MURA

Via Dietro le Mura 26
Aci Castello
Catania
Sicily 95021
Italy
+39 0957111091
www.pizzeriadietrolemura.it

Opening hours	Open 7 days
Credit cards	Accepted
Style of pizza	Thin-crust
Recommended pizza	Dietro le Mura; Margherita

IN UN ANGOLO DI MONDO

Via Nazionale per Catania 180
Acireale
Catania
Sicily 95024
Italy
+39 095877724

Opening hours	Closed Monday–Wednesday
Credit cards	Accepted but not AMEX
Style of pizza	Classic organic
Recommended pizza	Artichokes, Mozzarella, and Ragusano Cheese; Saporita

"It's an organic, vegetarian, and natural pizzeria so a great deal of attention has been paid to the ingredients and to quality."—Antonio Benanti

FUD

Via Santa Filomena 35
Catania
Catania
Sicily 95129
Italy
+39 0957153518
www.fud.it

Opening hours	Open 7 days
Credit cards	Accepted but not AMEX
Style of pizza	Neapolitan
Recommended pizza	Sicilian Focaccia

MIGNEMI MASTRO FORNAIO

Viale Vittorio Veneto 140
Catania
Catania
Sicily 95127
Italy
+39 3454859299
www.mignemimastrofornaio.it

Opening hours	Open 7 days
Credit cards	Accepted
Style of pizza	Round and *pizza al taglio*
Recommended pizza	Timilia Flour Pizza with Eggplant (aubergine)

"Mignemi Mastro Fornaio makes naturally leavened pizzas with flours made of selected grains, including flours made from old Sicilian grains such as Timilia and Kamut."—Cristina Barbera

SAZI E SANI

Via Sisto 46
Catania
Catania
Sicily 95129
Italy
+39 095311203

Opening hours	Open 7 days
Credit cards	Accepted
Style of pizza	Neapolitan

BORGHETTO SANTA CATERINA

Corso Ara di Giove 63
Pedara
Catania
Sicily 95030
Italy
+39 0957807633
www.pizzeriailborghetto.it

Opening hours	Closed Monday
Credit cards	Accepted but not AMEX
Style of pizza	Neapolitan
Recommended pizza	Lasagna di Pizza; Pizzella Fritta; Sgonfiotti

"Classic no-frills Neapolitan pizza of excellent quality and very, very well made. The atmosphere is charming and in the summer you can eat outside."
—Antonio Benanti

ANTICO CAMPANILE

Via Salvatore Mirone 10–12
Viagrande
Catania
Sicily 95029
Italy
+39 0959891173
www.anticocampanile.it

Opening hours	Closed Sunday–Wednesday
Credit cards	Accepted
Style of pizza	Classic

"Viagrande is a very welcoming village and Antico Campanile is very close to the main Piazza San Mauro. It is an elegant, informal restaurant that offers a vast variety of pizzas with very refined ingredients and the chance to build your own pizza by asking for a mixture of two or three varieties."
—Antonio Benanti

TAVOLA CALDA EUROPA

Viale IV Novembre 11
Enna
Enna
Sicily 94100
Italy
+39 093537467
www.tavolacaldaeuropa.it

Opening hours	Closed Monday
Credit cards	Accepted
Style of pizza	*Pizza al taglio*
Recommended pizza	Pepata

"This pizzeria is special because the pizzas are made with simple ingredients, without any added fat: only flour, salt, water, 70 percent baker's yeast and 30 percent brewer's yeast. For the toppings, it uses only Sicilian and Slow Food products. All of this makes the pizza fluffy, natural, and genuine!"
—Cristina Barbera

TRAMINER

Via Enna
Barcellona Pozzo di Gotto
Messina
Sicily 98051
Italy
+39 0909763814
www.traminer.biz

Opening hours	Open 7 days
Credit cards	Accepted but not AMEX
Style of pizza	Classic
Recommended pizza	La Ruota del Carretto Siciliano

PIZZERIA U CUCUNCIO

Via Roma 81
Malfa - Salina
Messina
Sicily 98050
Italy
+39 0909844408

Opening hours	Open 7 days
Credit cards	Accepted but not AMEX
Style of pizza	Classic
Recommended pizza	Tomato and Basil

ESPOSITO

Via Lungomare Garibaldi
Milazzo
Messina
Sicily 98057
Italy
+39 0909222012
www.espositomilazzo.com

Opening hours	Open 7 days
Credit cards	Accepted
Style of pizza	Modern
Recommended pizza	Broccoli Raab

VILLA ZUCCARO

Piazza Carmine 5
Taormina
Messina
Sicily 98039
Italy
+39 0942628018
www.villazuccaro.it

Opening hours	Open 7 days
Credit cards	Accepted
Style of pizza	Sicilian
Recommended pizza	Villa Zuccaro

"I went to Villa Zuccaro while on honeymoon, so it's one of those experiences you don't forget. The food, the setting, the overall holiday, and the location probably all had a part to play, but the pizza was incredible and to this day I have never had a better pizza."—Owen Morgan

ANTICO BAGLIO

Via della Conceria 1
Castelbuono
Palermo
Sicily 90013
Italy
+39 0921679512
www.anticobaglio.it

Opening hours	Open 7 days
Credit cards	Accepted
Style of pizza	Traditional
Recommended pizza	Basil and Ricotta

"Natale Allegra could be defined as a *pizzaiolo* 'obsessed' with slow fermentation. His rule is: it shouldn't last less than 48 hours. It results in a perfectly elastic, fluffy, and light pizza. Allegra personally selects the best produce from the small businesses of the Castelbuono territory. Here the pizza becomes a pretext, or—even better—a tasty postcard to make someone appreciate the high-altitude gastronomic tradition of this Sicilian alpine patch."
—Manuela Laiacona

LA STAZIONE

Stazione FS Cinisi-Terrasini
Cinisi
Palermo
Sicily 90045
Italy
+39 0918665200

Opening hours	Closed Monday
Credit cards	Accepted but not AMEX
Style of pizza	Rustic wood-fired

"Every pizza made at La Stazione is original in the choice of ingredients and flavors (even though there are over 30 types of pizza on the menu). The names of the pizzas refer to place names in the environs."—Giuseppe Russo

LA BUFALACCIA

Via De Cosmi 13
Palermo
Palermo
Sicily 90143
Italy
+39 0915079930
www.labufalaccia.it

Opening hours	Closed Monday
Credit cards	Accepted but not AMEX
Style of pizza	Neapolitan
Recommended pizza	Bufala Regina

CICCIO PASSAMI L'OLIO

Via Castrofilippo 4
Palermo
Palermo
Sicily 90133
Italy
+39 3389095598
www.cicciopassamilolio.it

Opening hours	Open 7 days
Credit cards	Accepted but not AMEX
Style of pizza	Rustic

FRIDA PIZZERIA

Piazza Sant'Onofrio 37
Palermo
Palermo
Sicily 90100
Italy
+39 0915505440
www.fridapizzeria.it

Opening hours...Closed Tuesday
Credit cards.....................................Accepted but not AMEX
Style of pizza..Classic

PERCIASACCHI

Via Del Monte di Pietà 5
Palermo
Palermo
Sicily 90134
Italy
+39 0916123960
www.perciasacchi.it

Opening hours...Closed Sunday
Credit cards...Accepted
Style of pizza..Sicilian
Recommended pizza............Affumicata DOP; Sausage and
    Broccoli Raab; Sfincione; Vastedda in Perciasacchi

"Due to gluten that is hardly firm or elastic, it isn't easy to work with flour from the so-called 'ancient grains.' But Perciasacchi manages to do so, guaranteeing the use of single varieties and starting from a wholemeal product. The result is a rustic, tasty pizza."—Giuseppe Russo

"Perciasacchi is more than a pizzeria: it is a project to promote the resources and traditions of Palermo. In the oldest part of the city, Renata Feruzza and her daughter Laura have created a network of people who produce products par excellence. Each and every ingredient is supplied by Sicilian smallholding farmers and shepherds in the district of Palermo. The pizzas reflect their rural culture, toppings are strictly seasonal, and there is no lack of tributes to local specialties such as the sfincione and the rianata."
—Manuela Laiacona

TONDO

Piazza Ignazio Florio
Palermo
Palermo
Sicily 90139
Italy
+39 091328254

Opening hours...Open 7 days
Credit cards.....................................Accepted but not AMEX
Style of pizza..Neapolitan
Recommended pizza............Sausage and Broccoli Raab; A'
    Sciavata; U' Cudduruni

"In the heart of Palermo, just a few minutes away from the port, you can taste Sicilian pizza and Neapolitan-inspired deep-fried pizza. Tondo pays tribute to what used to be the Kingdom of the Two Sicilies by choosing a slow leavening process, ancient grain flours, and zero-kilometer ingredients. The large menu presents 'folk' pizzas evocative of old-fashioned rural and home specialties, such as U' Pituni, A' Rianata, and U' Cudduruni."
—Manuela Laiacona

IL VECCHIO CORTILE

Via Veneziano 104
Palermo
Palermo
Sicily 90138
Italy
+39 0917099380
www.ilvecchiocortile.com

Opening hours...Closed Tuesday
Credit cards...Accepted
Style of pizza..Classic

VILLA COSTANZA

Via Pietro Bonanno 42
Palermo
Palermo
Sicily 90142
Italy
+39 091547027
www.villacostanza.com

Opening hours...Closed Tuesday
Credit cards.....................................Accepted but not AMEX
Style of pizza..Sicilian
Recommended pizza..........................Piacere Nostro; Robba

LE MAGNOLIE
Via Gianforma 179
Frigentini - Modica
Ragusa
Sicily 97015
Italy
+39 0932908136
www.ristorantelemagnolie.it

Opening hours	Closed Tuesday
Credit cards	Accepted
Style of pizza	Neapolitan and Roman
Recommended pizza	Dei Monti Iblei; Le Magnolie

CASA CIOMOD
Via Nazionale Modica Ispica
Modica
Ragusa
Sicily 97015
Italy
+39 0932455412
www.casaciomod.com

Opening hours	Open 7 days
Credit cards	Accepted but not AMEX
Style of pizza	Neapolitan
Recommended pizza	Quattro Formaggi

"The pizza is soft, fragrant, and most of all light and delicious!"—Cristina Barbera

RISTORANTE DELFINO
Piazza delle Sirene 4
Pozzallo
Ragusa
Sicily 97016
Italy
+39 0932954732
www.ristorantedelfinopozzallo.it

Opening hours	Closed Monday
Credit cards	Accepted
Style of pizza	Traditional
Recommended pizza	Delfino Super

"Carefully selected pairings of surf and turf ingredients make this pizza special."—Giuseppe Barone

CARAVANSERRAGLIO
Via Pietro Nenni 78
Ragusa
Ragusa
Sicily 97100
Italy
+39 0932654342
www.caravanserraglioragusa.com

Opening hours	Closed Monday
Credit cards	Accepted
Style of pizza	Neapolitan
Recommended pizza	Pizza of the day; Ragusano Cheese

"Delectable pizza with well-balanced toppings."
—Francesco Pensovecchio

"One of the best wine lists in Sicily."
—Valerio Capriotti

VILLA FORTUGNO
Km 4 Contrada Fortugno
Ragusa
Ragusa
Sicily 97100
Italy
+39 0932667348
www.villafortugno.it

Opening hours	Closed Monday
Credit cards	Accepted
Style of pizza	*Pizza al metro*
Recommended pizza	Pizza alla Ragusana

"Master pizza chef Salvatore Articolo proposes a very light, fragrant dough with a 72-hour fermentation and seasonal and fresh ingredients that are locally sourced for a pizza that is 100 percent Sicilian."—Giuseppe Barone

LA GIARA
Corso Dei Mille 105
Alcamo
Trapani
Sicily 91011
Italy
+39 0924507979
www.lagiaraalcamo.it

Opening hours	Closed Tuesday
Credit cards	Accepted
Style of pizza	Traditional

DUCA DI CASTELMONTE

Via Salvatore Motisi 3
Frazione di Xitta
Trapani
Trapani
Sicily 91100
Italy
+39 0923526139
www.ducadicastelmonte.it

Opening hours..Closed Tuesday
Credit cards...Accepted
Style of pizza...Neapolitan
Recommended pizza...Vegetarian

"With perfectly risen pizzas and excellent vegetables
from its own garden, Duca di Castelmonte is a typical
trattoria with some rooms if you want to stay overnight."—Francesco Pensovecchio

PIZZERIA EXCELSIOR

Piazza Cesare Battisti 11
Cavalese
Trento
Trentino-Alto Adige 38033
Italy
 +39 0462248421
www.alessandrogilmozzi.it

Opening hours..Closed Tuesday
Credit cards...Accepted
Style of pizza..Gourmet
Recommended pizza...Arctic Char

SMORZA

Via Rimoni 26
Romagnano
Trento
Trentino-Alto Adige 38123
Italy
+39 0461349130
www.smorza.it

Opening hours..Closed Tuesday
Credit cards...Accepted
Style of pizza...Classic
Recommended pizza..Smorza

PIZZERIA OKAY

Corso Verna 78
Rovereto
Trento
Trentino-Alto Adige 38068
Italy
+39 0464436411

Opening hours......................................Closed Wednesday
Credit cards....................................Accepted but not AMEX
Style of pizza...Classic

IL RISTORANTE NOVECENTO DELL' HOTEL ROVERETO

Corso Rosmini 82D
Rovereto
Trento
Trentino-Alto Adige 38068
Italy
+39 0464435222
www.hotelrovereto.it

Opening hours..Closed Sunday
Credit cards...Accepted
Style of pizza..Gourmet
Recommended pizza.......................Baccalà alla Roveretana

PIZZERIA DA ALBERT

Via Bernardino Bomporto 2
Trento
Trento
Trentino-Alto Adige 38122
Italy
+39 0461231712

Opening hours..Closed Sunday
Credit cards....................................Accepted but not AMEX
Style of pizza..Gourmet
Recommended pizza............................Rustichella; Speckale

UVA E MENTA

Via Dietro le Mura A 35
Trento
Trento
Trentino-Alto Adige 38122
Italy
+39 04611903162
www.uvaementa.it

Opening hours..Closed Monday
Credit cards....................................Accepted but not AMEX
Style of pizza..Wood-fired

MENCHETTI

Via Avvocato Fulvio Croce 11
Arezzo
Arezzo
Tuscany 52100
Italy
+39 0575350682
www.menchetti.it

Opening hours	Open 7 days
Credit cards	Accepted but not AMEX
Style of pizza	*Pizza al taglio*
Recommended pizza	Bianca with Sautéed Endive, Tarese Valdarno Pancetta, and Pecorino Cheese; Ciaccia

"The Ciaccia (the local name for white pizza) is topped with extra virgin olive oil from the family business. It must be eaten as soon as it gets out of the oven in order to fully appreciate its fragrance."
—Paola Mencarelli

RISTORANTE PIZZERIA LO STRONCAPANE

Viale Diaz 73
Monte San Savino
Arezzo
Tuscany 52048
Italy
+39 0575849352
www.lostroncapane.com

Opening hours	Closed Tuesday
Credit cards	Accepted but not AMEX
Style of pizza	Tuscan wood-fired
Recommended pizza	Truffle

"Set in the Tuscan countryside overlooking the valley below, this pizzeria is excellent value for money and consistently exciting with a classical approach to the art form along with flair for creativity and diversity."
—Cav. Alessandro Sorbello

LO SPELA

Via Poneta 44
Greve in Chianti
Florence
Tuscany 50022
Italy
+39 055850787
www.lospela.it

Opening hours	Closed Monday
Credit cards	Accepted but not AMEX
Style of pizza	Gourmet
Recommended pizza	Margherita

LA LAMPARA

Via Tito Speri 3
Capoliveri
Livorno
Tuscany 57031
Italy
+39 0565968970
www.ristorantelalampara.net

Opening hours	Open 7 days
Credit cards	Accepted
Style of pizza	*Pizza al metro*

BAR BRANDUZZI

Località Fucina 7
Borgo a Mozzano
Lucca
Tuscany 55023
Italy
+39 0583832016

Opening hours	Closed Monday–Thursday
Credit cards	Accepted
Style of pizza	Tuscan wood-fired
Recommended pizza	Prosciutto and Mushrooms

LA BERSAGLIERA

Via Pisana 2136
Lucca
Lucca
Tuscany 55100
Italy
+39 058351075

Opening hours	Closed Wednesday
Credit cards	Not accepted
Style of pizza	Neapolitan-Calabrian
Recommended pizza	Spicy Sausage and Onions

PIZZERIA LA KAMBUSA

Via Della Torbiera 38
Massarosa
Lucca
Tuscany 55054
Italy
+39 0584631832

Opening hours	Closed Monday
Credit cards	Accepted
Style of pizza	Neapolitan
Recommended pizza	Calzone with Endive; Marinara

PIZZERIA APOGEO

Via Pisanica 136
Pietrasanta
Lucca
Tuscany 55045
Italy
+39 0584793394
www.pizzeriaapogeo.it

Opening hours...Closed Monday
Credit cards.....................................Accepted but not AMEX
Style of pizza...Gourmet
Recommended pizza.........................Burrata and Anchovies;
    Burrata, Beets (beetroot), Artichokes, and Bottarga

PIZZERIA O' SOLE MIO

Via Giuseppe Mazzini 160
Viareggio
Lucca
Tuscany 55049
Italy
+39 0584944850

Opening hours...Open 7 days
Credit cards.....................................Accepted but not AMEX
Style of pizza...Neapolitan
Recommended pizza...Margherita

"Excellent value for money and high-quality ingredients make this pizzeria stand out in an area where there are few Neapolitan-style pizzerias."
—Leonardo Ciomei

DA SIRULICCHIU

Via Nursina 7
Località Sant'Angelo
Norcia
Perugia
Umbria 06046
Italy
+39 33920631

Opening hours...Open 7 days
Credit cards..Accepted
Style of pizza...Classic
Recommended pizza.........................Sirulicchiu with Truffle

LA ROMANTICA

Borgo XX Giugno 9
Perugia
Perugia
Umbria 06121
Italy
+39 0753721406

Opening hours...Closed Monday
Credit cards.....................................Accepted but not AMEX
Style of pizza...Traditional

"It is probably impossible to eat a better pizza in the city."—Jacopo Cossater

PORCELLI TAVERN

Via Farrattini 73
Amelia
Terni
Umbria 05022
Italy
+39 0744983639
www.porcellitavern.it

Opening hours...Open 7 days
Credit cards..Accepted
Style of pizza...Classic
Recommended pizza...................Sausage and Broccoli Raab

CIBUS NOSTER

Via Castello 2
Terni
Terni
Umbria 05100
Italy
+39 0744431077

Opening hours...Open 7 days
Credit cards..Accepted
Style of pizza.............................*Pizza al taglio* and focaccia
Recommended pizza...Famiglia

"I think this is one of the best pizzas that one can currently eat in Terni. The base is excellent and the options are never banal and always well balanced. There's also always a lot of focaccia available—just looking at it makes you want to eat it."
—Marzio Contessa

PIZZERIA STOÀ REALE

Via Gabelletta 190
Terni
Terni
Umbria 05100
Italy
+39 0744241166
www.pizzeriastoareale.it

Opening hours...Closed Monday
Credit cards.....................................Accepted but not AMEX
Style of pizza...Classic
Recommended pizza...Black Pizza

"The pizza is very well made and never too rich. The pizzeria has been using for some time a dough made from vegetable charcoal, which make the pizzas, calzones, and the (rigorously homemade) bread not only special because of its black color, but also appetizing and easy to digest."—Marzio Contessa

LA BUCA

Via Carrera 15C
Belluno
Belluno
Veneto 32100
Italy
+39 0437940191
www.labucabelluno.it

Opening hours...Closed Monday
Credit cards...Accepted
Style of pizza...Classic
Recommended pizza..Margherita

EL GRINGO

Via Mazzini 21
Calalzo di Cadore
Belluno
Veneto 32042
Italy
+39 043531118

Opening hours..Closed Sunday
Credit cards.....................................Accepted but not AMEX
Style of pizza..Neapolitan

AUBERGINE

Via Ghislandi 5
Abano Terme
Padua
Veneto 35031
Italy
+39 0498669910
www.aubergine.it

Opening hours...Closed Tuesday
Credit cards...Accepted
Style of pizza...Neapolitan
Recommended pizza..Margherita

GIGI PIPA

Viale Rimembranze 1
Este
Padua
Veneto 35042
Italy
+39 0429600533
www.pizzeriagigipipa.it

Opening hours...Closed Monday
Credit cards.....................................Accepted but not AMEX
Style of pizza..Gourmet
Recommended pizza......................Broccoli Raab, Pork, and
Vitelotte Potatoes; Margherita

SAPORI A COLORI

Via Aureliana 50
Montegrotto Terme
Padua
Veneto 35036
Italy
+39 3803344166

Opening hours...Open 7 days
Credit cards...Not accepted
Style of pizza...*Pizza al taglio*
Recommended pizza..Margherita

TOMMY - IL CANTIERE DELLA PIZZA

Via Montegrappa 50
Selvazzano Dentro
Padua
Veneto 35030
Italy
+39 0498056572
www.tommypizza.it

Opening hours..Closed Sunday
Credit cards....................................Accepted but not AMEX
Style of pizza...Gourmet
Recommended pizza...Margherita

ARIELE RISTORO E PIZZA BIO

Via San Giuseppe 36
Conegliano
Treviso
Veneto 31015
Italy
+39 0438370642

Opening hours..Closed Sunday
Credit cards....................................Accepted but not AMEX
Style of pizza...Traditional
Recommended pizza.......................................Ariele; Libretto

"The dough is the star attraction at this pizzeria.
Or rather the flour and the ancient grains that
produce it are. There are four different types of
dough, topped according to Italian tradition, but
with organic ingredients from a certified supply
chain."—Orlando Bortolami

SAPOROSO

Via Podgora 13
Conegliano
Treviso
Veneto 31015
Italy
+39 438450220

Opening hours..Closed Monday
Credit cards....................................Accepted but not AMEX
Style of pizza...Classic
Recommended pizza.............Bianca with Cherry Tomatoes
and Anchovies

GRIGORIS

Via Asseggiano 147
Chirignago
Venice
Veneto 30030
Italy
+39 041915501
www.grigoris.it

Opening hours...Open 7 days
Credit cards..Accepted
Style of pizza...Traditional
Recommended pizza....................Ligure; Margherita; Mora
Romagnola; Tuna and Onion

"Lello and Pina Ravagnan are the creators and
owners of Grigoris. It is without doubt one of my
most favorite pizzerias. At the entrance to Venice
you will find a temple to dough and leavening, all
topped with ingredients of the highest quality."
—Enrico Bonardo

"There is so much love in the selection of the
ingredients and in the preparation of the pizza."
—Anna Marlena Buscemi

TRE LEONI LA PIZZERIA CON CICCHETTERIA

Via Piave Vecchio 34
Jesolo
Venice
Veneto 30016
Italy
+39 3311240208

Opening hours...Open 7 days
Credit cards....................................Accepted but not AMEX
Style of pizza..Multiple
Recommended pizza..................Guanciale, Quail Eggs, and
Shrimp (prawn)

"A pizzeria obsessed with the leavening process and
the raw products it uses."—Marco Colognese

TRATTORIA PIZZERIA A CASA VECIA
Via Moniego Centro 90
Moniego di Noale
Venice
Veneto 30033
Italy
+39 041440467

Opening hours...Open 7 days
Credit cards.....................................Accepted but not AMEX
Style of pizza..Gourmet Roman
Recommended pizza.................Mozzarella, Tomato, Angus
  Beef Carpaccio, Raw Asparagus, and Balsamic Vinegar

"There is a great selection of niche beers to go with
the pizzas."—Giuseppe Aldè

DA MAMO
Calle dei Stagneri 5251
Venice
Veneto 30124
Italy
+39 0415236583
www.damamo.it

Opening hours..Open 7 days
Credit cards.....................................Accepted but not AMEX
Style of pizza...Traditional

I TIGLI
Via Camporosolo 11
San Bonifacio
Verona
Veneto 37047
Italy
+39 0456102606
www.pizzeriaitigli.it

Opening hours.......................................Closed Wednesday
Credit cards.....................................Accepted but not AMEX
Style of pizza...Gourmet
Recommended pizza......................ABC; Bufala; Burrata and
  Prosciutto Crudo; Carpaccio of Scallops with Yuzu
  Sauce; Foie Gras; Il Piccione; Liguria; Margherita; Red
  Shrimp (prawn) Sashimi

"This is where the concept of gourmet pizza was
'invented' and made famous."—Anna Ferretti

"The pizza bases are perfect: in the rise, the consistency,
the digestibility. The toppings are like real dishes
chosen and put together on the basis of a constantly
new harmonic game of colors, flavors, and textures."
—Alessia Gallian

"Every ingredient is scrupulously selected by Simone
Padoan, who leaves nothing to chance."
—Gianpaolo Giacobbo

Before I Tigli's Simone Padoan came along it was multi-starred
chefs and sushi masters who worked with tweezers, not
pizzaioli. Applying impeccable raw materials with meticulous
craftsmanship Padoan transformed pizza into gourmet finger
food. He introduced sashimi to pizza, laying raw red shrimp
(prawns), arugula (rocket), mango, and macadamia nuts over an
airy base. He created a brioche pizza dough as a pizza platform
for foie gras. With his trio of Margheritas—Croccante (crisp),
Soffice (soft), and La Bufala—Padoan donned the true colors
of a pizza pioneer, balancing different dough textures with the
richness of tomatoes (grape or San Marzano plum) and the
utter freshness of unblemished burrata, mozzarella (from
Puglia), or *mozzarella di bufala* (from Paestum).

SAPORÈ

Via Ponte 55A
San Martino Buon Albergo
Verona
Veneto 37036
Italy
+39 0458781791
www.saporeverona.it

Opening hours...Closed Monday
Credit cards.....................................Accepted but not AMEX
Style of pizza..Gourmet
Recommended pizza...........Aria di Pane; Bresaola; Crunch;
Double Crunch Stuffed with Eggplant (aubergine);
Mortadella, Misticanza, and Pistachios; Steamed
Mozzarella di Pane

"Renato Bosco is one of the greatest bread-making
experts in Italy and he transforms anything to do with
water and flour into excellence. It may seem simple
but in reality it is hard to never get it wrong. Renato
Bosco never gets it wrong."—Matteo Aloe

"Bosco has an ability to interpret all styles with
extraordinary technique: from *pizza alla pala*
to the classic round pizza via steamed pizzas. This
is where you can find the widest range of high-
quality doughs in just one restaurant."
—Marco Locatelli

"Saporè distinguishes itself by the absolute quality,
variety, and elaborated creativity of the doughs."
—Pierluigi Portinari

Renato Bosco has taken pizza dough completely apart and
put it back together in six ingenious ways. The great adventure
at Saporè is in trying all six breads-with-toppings and deciding
which ones are truly pizzas. The celebrated Aria di Pane (air
of bread) is a golden fluff of pizza, or bread, with a wholegrain
character. The most elemental version is layered with burrata
cheese and Sant'Ilario 30-month-aged *prosciutto crudo*. The
hot-water bath for Bosco's trademark bagel pizza, so-called
because the dough is simmered first and baked second,
is flavored with pancetta, rosemary, curry, or beer. La Pizza
Tradizionale, round and thin-crusted, with an inflated
cornicione, is positively pizza and undeniably special.

IL CHIOSTRO

Corso Cesare Battisti 72
Sanguinetto
Verona
Veneto
37058
Italy
+39 0442365472
www.ilchiostropizzeria.it

Opening hours..Open 7 days
Credit cards.....................................Accepted but not AMEX
Style of pizza...Classic
Recommended pizza...Margherita

OTTOCENTO SIMPLY FOOD

Contrà San Giorgio 2
Bassano del Grappa
Vicenza
Veneto 36061
Italy
+39 0424503510
www.800simplyfood.com

Opening hours..Open 7 days
Credit cards.....................................Accepted but not AMEX
Style of pizza...Gourmet
Recommended pizza....................Gorgonzola, Broccoli, and
Walnuts; Margherita

PIZZERIA SAN MARTIN

Via San Martin 36
Cornedo Vicentino
Vicenza
Veneto 36073
Italy
+39 0445951241
www.pizzeriasanmartin.it

Opening hours..Open 7 days
Credit cards..Accepted
Style of pizza..Roman
Recommended pizza...................Pizza Fritta; Radicchio and
Soppressa; Wild Herbs

"*Pizzaiolo* Federico and maitre d' Paolo have come
a long way. The sourcing of local produce and the
study of dough and leavening have given them a well
deserved place among the big names in the 'Made in
Veneto' pizza world. They propose a tasting of various
pizzas with strictly seasonal Slow Food products. Their
passion also shows through in the choice of wines
and beers: this is one of the few restaurants in Italy to
have famous Cantillon beers on its menu."
—Enrico Bonardo

ERIO'S PIZZA

Via Lanzarini 27
Romano d'Ezzelino VI
Vicenza
Veneto 36060
Italy
+39 0424573943

Opening hours..Closed Monday
Credit cards......................................Accepted but not AMEX
Style of pizza...Neapolitan takeout
Recommended pizza..Erio's Pizza

OSTERIA IMBUSA'

Via Gazzo 2
Zovencedo
Vicenza
Veneto 36020
Italy
+39 3890056697

Opening hours........................Closed Monday and Tuesday
Credit cards..Accepted
Style of pizza..Italian
Recommended pizza..Vegan

"ONE OF THE BEST PIZZAS IN NAPLES (AND THEREFORE, IN THE WHOLE WORLD)!"
SABINO BERARDINO P.282

"GO. WAIT IN LINE. EAT. YOU WILL NOT REGRET IT."
JOE DiLIBERTO P.280

NAPLES

"THERE ARE ONLY SIX OR SEVEN PIZZAS ON THE MENU, YOU MUST TRY THEM ALL!"
NICOLA DE SIMONE & MASSIMO CINQUINA P.283

"AWESOME FLAVORS AND SPECIAL PIZZAS."
ORAZIO D'ELIA P.281

"EATING AT DI MATTEO IS SHOCKING— LIKE HAVING PIZZA FOR THE FIRST TIME."
ANDREAS VIESTAD P.284

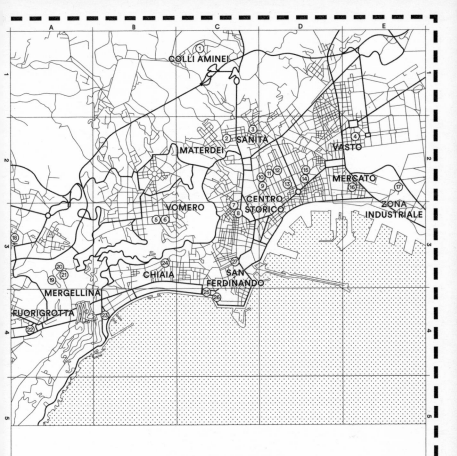

NAPLES

SCALE

0   500   1000   1500 yd.

1. PIZZERIA LUCA CASTELLANO, COLLI AMINEI (P.280)
2. STARITA, MATERDEI (P.281)
3. DA CONCETTINA AI TRE SANTI, SANITÀ (P.284)
4. PIZZERIA PELLONE, VASTO (P.285)
5. PIZZERIA GORIZIA 1916, VOMERO (P.286)
6. ACUNZO, VOMERO (P.285)
7. DA ATTILIO, PIGNASECCA (P.283)
8. MATTOZZI, CENTRO STORICO (P.280)
9. PALAZZO PETRUCCI, CENTRO STORICO (P.280)
10. PIZZERIA GINO SORBILLO, SAN LORENZO (P.285)
11. ANTICA PIZZA FRITTA DA ESTERINA SORBILLO, SAN LORENZO (P.284)
12. PIZZERIA DI MATTEO, SAN LORENZO (P.284)
13. LA FIGLIA DEL PRESIDENTE, SAN LORENZO (P.284)
14. L'ANTICA PIZZERIA DA MICHELE, FORCELLA (P.280)
15. ANTICA PIZZERIA DE' FIGLIOLE, FORCELLA (P.281)
16. LA MASARDONA, MERCATO (P.281)
17. GUGLIELMO VUOLO A ECCELLENZE CAMPANE, ZONA INDUSTRIALE (P.286)
18. PIZZERIA LAMPO 2, SOCCAVO (P.285)
19. PIZZARIA LA NOTIZIA, 94, MERGELLINA (P.283)
20. PIZZARIA LA NOTIZIA, 53, MERGELLINA (P.282)
21. SOLO PIZZA VIA MANZONI, MERGELLINA (P.283)
22. DI NAPOLI, FUORIGROTTA (P.281)
23. 50 KALÒ, MERGELLINA (P.282)
24. PIZZERIA MICHELE, CHIAIA (P.280)
25. LIEVITO MADRE AL MARE, SAN FERDINANDO (P.283)
26. ROSSOPOMODORO, SAN FERDINANDO (P.284)
27. BRANDI, SAN FERDINANDO (P.283)

MATTOZZI

Piazza Carità 2
Centro Storico
Naples
Campania 80134
Italy
+39 0815524322
www.ristorantemattozzi.it

Opening hours	Open 7 days
Credit cards	Accepted
Style of pizza	Neapolitan
Recommended pizza	Margherita

"This pizzeria in the center of historic Naples is managed by Lelo and Paolo Surace. They use only the freshest ingredients from the Campania region. It is also an excellent seafood restaurant."—André Guidón

PALAZZO PETRUCCI

Piazza San Domenico Maggiore 4
Centro Storico
Naples
Campania 80134
Italy
+39 0815512460
www.palazzopetrucci.it

Opening hours	Open 7 days
Credit cards	Accepted
Style of pizza	Gourmet Neapolitan
Recommended pizza	Green Pepper and Provolone Cheese

"Gourmet pizza made by the great expert and researcher Michele Leo."
—Salvatore Salvo & Francesco Salvo

PIZZERIA MICHELE

Via Giuseppe Martucci 93
Chiaia
Naples
Campania 80121
Italy
+39 08119576887

Opening hours	Open 7 days
Credit cards	Accepted but not AMEX
Style of pizza	Neapolitan
Recommended pizza	Margherita

"By far the most authentic Neapolitan pizza."
—Massimo Covone

PIZZERIA LUCA CASTELLANO

Viale dei Pini 25
Colli Aminei
Naples
Campania 80131
Italy
+39 0817418243
www.castellanopizzeria.it

Opening hours	Open 7 days
Credit cards	Accepted
Style of pizza	Neapolitan
Recommended pizza	Napul'è

L'ANTICA PIZZERIA DA MICHELE

Via Cesare Sersale 1–3
Forcella
Naples
Campania 80139
Italy
+39 0815539204
www.damichele.net

Opening hours	Open 7 days
Credit cards	Not accepted
Style of pizza	Neapolitan
Recommended pizza	Margherita; Marinara

"Pizza pared down to the basics, but perfect. Great crust, great sauce, great cheese. No add-ons, no choices. Go. Wait in line. Eat. You will not regret it."
—Joe Diliberto

"The Margherita is out-of-this world good, but it's the simplicity of the original Marinara pizza that wins here...sauce, garlic, herbs, extra virgin olive oil...and that's it!"—Ingrid Langtry

"You could come to Naples and only eat pizza from here and you could leave with no regrets."
—Andrew Levins

Da Michele is part pizza temple and part pizza time-machine. Free-form pizzas with more black spots than a Dalmatian are perfect in their rustic imperfection. The smells and sounds can transport you back to 1870, the year Salvatore Condurro received his license to make pizza, or to 1906, the year his son Michele opened the family's first pizzeria. The Da Michele mystique rests on the resolve of the succeeding generations of Condurros to limit their selection of food to two classic pizzas, the Marinara and the Margherita. They don't count the Margherita Doppio Mozzarella, which has repercussions: this double-cheese Margherita arouses envy in those who only learn of its existence by spotting one on a nearby table.

ANTICA PIZZERIA DE' FIGLIOLE

Via Giudecca Vecchia 39
Forcella
Naples
Campania 80139
Italy
+39 081286721

Opening hours	Closed Sunday
Credit cards	Not accepted
Style of pizza	Deep-fried
Recommended pizza	Chicchinese

"The best deep-fried pizza in Naples according to many."—Luca Iaccarino

DI NAPOLI

Via Marc'Antonio 31
Fuorigrotta
Naples
Campania 80125
Italy
+39 0812396942
www.pizzeriadinapoli.it

Opening hours	Closed Tuesday
Credit cards	Accepted
Style of pizza	Neapolitan
Recommended pizza	Margherita; Mushroom

"The pizza differs from the traditional Neapolitan-style pizza but it's just as delicious."—Emidio Mansi

STARITA

Via Materdei 27–28
Materdei
Naples
Campania 80136
Italy
+39 0815441485
www.pizzeriestarita.it

Opening hours	Closed Sunday morning
Credit cards	Accepted
Style of pizza	Neapolitan
Recommended pizza	Angioletti; Diavola; Margherita; Marinara; Montanara

"Owner Antonio Starita is one of the pioneers of Neapolitan pizza in Naples. The pizzeria is in the style of the late twentieth century, adorned with Pucinella (Punch) puppets and Neapolitan objets d'art."
—Ivo Virgilio

"Awesome flavors and special pizzas."—Orazio d'Elia

"This is the first place I go for a meal when I arrive in Naples. Starita does an excellent pizza Montanara."
—Leandro Caffarena

The legend of Starita will be forever linked with two idols: Sophia Loren, who portrayed a *pizzaiola* selling fried pizza in the 1954 film classic *The Gold of Naples*, and Antonio Starita, the third-generation *pizzaiolo* venerated by the many he's mentored, inspired, or fed. Don Antonio's signature pizza is the Montanara Starita, a street food classic made by deep-frying a small disk of dough, topping it with tomato, smoked scamorza cheese, Pecorino Romano cheese, and fresh basil and finishing it off in the oven. His Porta a Porta, a rectangular pizza pouch stuffed with ricotta cheese, broccoli raab, cherry tomatoes, and *mozzarella di bufala*, is baked both on the Via Materdei, a Naples street long synonymous with Loren and Starita, and at Don Antonio by Starita, the New York outpost he opened with protégé Roberto Caporuscio.

LA MASARDONA

Via Giulio Cesare Capaccio 27
Mercato
Naples
Campania 80142
Italy
+39 081281057

Opening hours	Closed Monday morning
Credit cards	Accepted
Style of pizza	*Pizza fritta*
Recommended pizza	Battilocchio; Provola and Tomato; Senza Pomodoro

"Enzo Piccirillo only offers deep-fried pizza, and his deep-fried pizza is a form of art."—Alba Pezone

"The best deep-fried pizza in Naples, crispy and dry, with excellent stuffing."—Emidio Mansi

50 KALÒ

Piazza Sannazaro 201B
Mergellina
Naples
Campania 80122
Italy
+39 08119204667
www.50kalo.it

Opening hours...Open 7 days
Credit cards.............................Accepted but not AMEX
Style of pizza...Neapolitan
Recommended pizza..............50 Kalò; Calzone; Margherita;
Marinara; 'Nduja di Spilinga; Pizza dell'Alleanza;
Pizza Fritta

"It is the classic Neapolitan pizza, large and with beautiful, pronounced edges, a spongy and soft base with flawless air pockets and a real fresh flavor."
—Carmelita Cianci

"Ciro Salvo combines lightness, digestibility, and creativity of toppings. One of the best pizzas in Naples (and therefore, in the whole world)!"
—Sabino Berardino

"This is the pizzeria I recommend to all my friends who come to Naples for the first time. When you eat pizza at 50 Kalò and then take a walk along the seafront you get the taste of Naples."—Valentina Scotti

The excitement and glamor permeating 50 Kalò reflects the freshly elevated status of pizza in Naples. A message taped to the *banco* (bench), as the baker's work counter is known, tells its own story: ingredienti: *acqua, farina, lievito, sale* (ingredients: water, flour, yeast, salt). In an obscure dialect, "50" means "dough" and "kalò" means "good." When he's not pressed into posing for selfies, *pizzaiolo* Ciro Salvo can be seen at the *banco*, stretching the dough and pushing its invisible bubbles outward. He leaves the business of dressing and cooking pizzas to colleagues. Originals like the Pizza dell'Alleanza, with mozzarella, Cipolla di Montoro (a sweet, fragrant onion), Lardo di Colonnata (cured fatback from Tuscan pigs), and Conciato Romano cheese, show off 50 Kalò's sophistication and sourcing but, as Salvo concedes, they can dominate the dough. To best appreciate his incomparably light crust with deep pockets of air around the *cornicione*, he recommends the simpler Margherita or Marinara.

PIZZARIA LA NOTIZIA, 53

Via Michelangelo da Caravaggio 53A
Mergellina
Naples
Campania 80126
Italy
+39 0817142155
www.pizzarialanotizia.com

Opening hours...Closed Monday
Credit cards.............................Accepted but not AMEX
Style of pizza...Neapolitan
Recommended pizza....................Ciropedia; Del Contadino;
Margherita DOP; Marinara; Napoletana

"This small authentic pizzeria is rightly considered to be one of the best in the world."
—Anna Laura Mattesini

"The choice of the basic ingredients is extraordinary and, above all, the *pizzaiolo* Enzo Coccia is a master of the leavening process. Even on a traditional level the so-called 'innovative' pizzas with non-classic ingredients and combinations are excellent."
—Simone Nicòtina

"Authentic flavors and masterful production."
—Donatella Bernabò Silurata

Revered at home and around the world for his scholarly command of Neapolitan pizza, maestro *pizzaiolo* Enzo Coccia was trained on the streets of Naples. He worked at his family's pizza stand near the central train station and retains the glee of a boy clasping a folded, paper-wrapped, hot pizza. He can lecture on dough hydration or rhapsodize over the stretchy, stringy mozzarella clinging to a pizza as a slice of it is pulled away. It is this delicious paradox that makes Pizzaria La Notizia remarkable: you can order an inventive pizza with stunning ingredients and know the recipe was conceived by a learned *pizzaiolo* or choose a classic Margherita and appreciate it was designed for, and by, a kid. The one Coccia constant is the peerless dough. A second location is at Via Caravaggio 94.

PIZZARIA LA NOTIZIA, 94

Via Michelangelo da Caravaggio 94
Mergellina
Naples
Campania 80100
Italy
+39 08119531937
www.pizzarialanotizia.com

Opening hours	Closed Sunday
Credit cards	Accepted but not AMEX
Style of pizza	Neapolitan
Recommended pizza	Ciropedia; Margherita

"Enzo Coccia is one of the masters of the Neapolitan pizza."—Dora Sorrentino

"The pizza is simply excellent."—Loredana Pietroniro

SOLO PIZZA VIA MANZONI

Via Alessandro Manzoni 26
Mergellina
Naples
Campania 80123
Italy
+39 0817146634
www.solopizzaviamanzoni.it

Opening hours	Closed Monday
Credit cards	Accepted
Style of pizza	Neapolitan
Recommended pizza	Don Egidio

"The pizzeria is very welcoming and adorned with products that are exclusively from the region of Campania."—Ivo Virgilio

DA ATTILIO

Via Pignasecca 17
Pignasecca
Naples
Campania 80134
Italy
+39 0815520479

Opening hours	Closed Sunday
Credit cards	Accepted but not AMEX
Style of pizza	Neapolitan
Recommended pizza	Broccoli Raab and Sausage; Carnevale; Endive; Sole nel Piatto

"To me, eating a pizza here is like going back in time. So definitely the century-old tradition."
—Enzo Coccia

"Attilio's pizza are the best I ever had in Naples. It is still a mystery how he can make that dough so soft and stretchy and unique."—Pasquale Chionchio

The old-school warmth of this pizzeria is preserved by Maria Francesca Mariniello, the daughter-in-law of the Attilio Bachetti who opened it and the mother of the Attilio Bachetti who runs it now. Every inch of wall space is covered with celebrity photos, press clippings, and napkin doodles preserved in picture frames. The homespun authenticity hasn't made Da Attilio famous but it does keep it on the shortlists of some very respected pizza people. The airy crusts Attilio Bachetti the younger tailors to each pizza are superbly thin and digestible, none more so than the one supporting the *pizza cosacca*, a cross between a Marinara and a Margherita with mozzarella out and grated cheese in. The sun-shaped Carnevale pizza, the eight points around its *cornicione* filled with ricotta, is a Da Attilio trademark and a Naples landmark.

BRANDI

Salita Sant'Anna di Palazzo 2
San Ferdinando
Naples
Campania 80132
Italy
+39 081416928
www.brandi.it

Opening hours	Closed Monday
Credit cards	Accepted
Style of pizza	Neapolitan
Recommended pizza	Margherita

"Gold-standard pizza Napoletana."—Bill McCaig

LIEVITO MADRE AL MARE

Via Partenope 1
San Ferdinando
Naples
Campania 80100
Italy
+39 08119331280
www.sorbillo.it

Opening hours	Open 7 days
Credit cards	Accepted
Style of pizza	Neapolitan

"There are only six or seven pizzas on the menu, you must try them all!"
—Nicola de Simone & Massimo Cinquina

ROSSOPOMODORO

Via Partenope 11
San Ferdinando
Naples
Campania 80121
Italy
+39 0817646012
www.rossopomodoro.it

Opening hours..Open 7 days
Credit cards..Accepted
Style of pizza...Neapolitan
Recommended pizza...Verace

"The double rise, the long proofing time, and the addition of wholewheat flour all help to make these pizzas of the winner of the World Championship light and easy to digest. You eat them with a view on Capri."—Vincenzo Pagano

DA CONCETTINA AI TRE SANTI

Via Arena alla Sanità 7B
Sanità
Naples
Campania 80137
Italy
+39 081290037
www.pizzeriaoliva.it

Opening hours..Open 7 days
Credit cards..Accepted
Style of pizza...Neapolitan
Recommended pizza...........Costiera; Frezzella; Pizza Fritta

"In one of the most fascinating working-class areas of Naples, the Oliva family have been *pizzaioli* for four generations. In addition to classic pizzas, they serve what they call *pizze eccellenti* with a seasonal rotation and a curated selection of ingredients from Campania."—Lydia Capasso

ANTICA PIZZA FRITTA DA ESTERINA SORBILLO

Via dei Tribunali 35
San Lorenzo
Naples
Campania 80138
Italy
+39 0814421364

Opening hours..Open 7 days
Credit cards..Not accepted
Style of pizza...*Pizza fritta*
Recommended pizza...Completa

LA FIGLIA DEL PRESIDENTE

Via del Grande Archivio 23
San Lorenzo
Naples
Campania 80100
Italy
+39 081286738
www.ernestocacialli.altervista.org

Opening hours..Closed Sunday
Credit cards...................................Accepted but not AMEX
Style of pizza...Neapolitan
Recommended pizza..Pizza Fritta

PIZZERIA DI MATTEO

Via dei Tribunali 94
San Lorenzo
Naples
Campania 80139
Italy
+39 081455262
www.pizzeriadimatteo.com

Opening hours..Open 7 days
Credit cards..Accepted
Style of pizza...Neapolitan
Recommended pizza...................Bufalina DOP; Pizza Fritta

"Eating at Di Matteo is shocking—like having pizza for the first time. It's so simple, just a few variations around the Margherita served in the simplest surroundings imaginable."—Andreas Viestad

"In this temple of Neapolitan street food, with its counter overflowing with mini-omelettes, fried rice balls, potato croquettes, and battered vegetables, Salvatore Di Matteo offers a big choice of classic pizzas, all of which are large and excellent. An experience to try absolutely."—Enrico Di Roberti

At Di Matteo, on the Via dei Tribunali in the old historic center of Naples, the dining rooms are upstairs but the action is on the street. *Pizza fritta* (fried pizza) and *pizza a portafoglia* (folded "wallet" style) are sold from the takeout counter, befitting a pizzeria that doubles as a *friggatoria* (fried-food shop). The baked pizzas are prepared in rapid succession by the two *pizzaioli* who shape them and a third who works the turquoise-tiled, wood-fired oven. The fried pizzas are often assembled by Salvatore Di Matteo himself. He seals cheese, tomato, ham, and other fillings between two flattened rounds of pizza dough and lowers the package into a vat of hot oil. Out comes *pizza fritta ripieno* (fried stuffed pizza)—a fluffy, delicately crisp saucer of golden goodness.

PIZZERIA GINO SORBILLO

Via dei Tribunali 32
San Lorenzo
Naples
Campania 80138
Italy
+39 081446643
www.sorbillo.it

Opening hours	Open 7 days
Credit cards	Accepted
Style of pizza	Neapolitan
Recommended pizza	Bufalina; Margherita; Margherita Gialla; Marinara; Napoletana; 'Nduja

"One of the best, cheapest, and most authentic pizzas you will find in Naples (and in the world)."
—Fabio Gándara Pumar & Susana López-Urrutia

When the city is Naples, the district is Spaccanapoli, the street is Via dei Tribunali, and the pizzeria and *pizzaiolo* share the name Gino Sorbillo, you've hit the epicenter of the Neapolitan pizza earthquake shaking the world. Those invariably waiting outside for their first Sorbillo pizza may be in for a few surprises: first, when Sorbillo is in the kitchen he is not grinning, as he always seems to be on Italian television or Facebook. He works with intensity, speed, and purpose. Second, this is a paper-cup establishment with low prices, its fame notwithstanding. Lastly, the beautifully balanced Margherita ceases to be the customary red, white, and green: when the red sea of tomato commingles with the clustered white dots of molten mozzarella a pink perfection is achieved.

PIZZERIA LAMPO 2

Via Cornelia Gracchi 27
Soccavo
Naples
Campania 80126
Italy
+39 08119519954
www.pizzerialampo2.it

Opening hours	Open 7 days
Credit cards	Not accepted
Style of pizza	Neapolitan
Recommended pizza	Quattro Formaggi

"This pizzeria was founded on the passion and the experience of owner Errico Porzio who is always looking for the best produce to fulfill the demands of his customers."—Ivo Virgilio

PIZZERIA PELLONE

Via Nazionale 93
Vasto
Naples
Campania 80143
Italy
+39 0815538614

Opening hours	Closed Sunday
Credit cards	Accepted but not AMEX
Style of pizza	Neapolitan
Recommended pizza	Margherita

"I've eaten at dozens of pizzerias in Naples and this one may be my favorite. Its pizzas feature bright, fruity tomato and silky mozzarella atop a lightly blistered flat-edged crust."—Scott Wiener

"One of Naples' pizzeria institutions. Extra large pizzas are its forte."—Orazio d'Elia

ACUNZO

Via Cimarosa 60–62
Vomero
Naples
Campania 80127
Italy
+39 0815785362

Opening hours	Closed Sunday
Credit cards	Accepted but not AMEX
Style of pizza	Neapolitan

PIZZERIA GORIZIA 1916
Via Gianlorenzo Bernini 29–31
Vomero
Naples
Campania 80129
Italy
+39 0815782248
www.gorizia1916.com

Opening hours..Open 7 days
Credit cards..Accepted
Style of pizza..Neapolitan
Recommended pizza...Margherita

GUGLIELMO VUOLO
A ECCELLENZE CAMPANE
Via Benedetto Brin 49
Zona Industriale
Naples
Campania 80142
Italy
+39 081203657
www.eccellenzecampane.it

Opening hours..Open 7 days
Credit cards..Accepted
Style of pizza..Neapolitan
Recommended pizza...Marinara

"I ATE THE BEST PIZZA OF MY LIFE AMID THE TOURIST BUSTLE OF PIAZZA NAVONA."

BARBARA GOERLICH P.291

"THE MARGHERITA PIZZA IS A RICH, FLAVORFUL, PERFECTLY SALTY MASTERPIECE."

LISA PEPIN P.294

ROME

"GABRIELE BONCI HAS BEEN CHRISTENED 'THE MICHELANGELO OF PIZZA' AND WITH GOOD REASON."

ORLANDO BORTOLAMI P.292

"AN EXCELLENT SPOT FOR TRADITIONAL ROMAN *PIZZA AL TAGLIO*.'

MARK BELLO P.292

"ARTENIO FANELLA EXCELS AT MAKING DEEPLY SATISFYING AND SHOCKINGLY SIMPLE PIZZETTE AT HIS STALL IN THE 'NEW' TESTACCIO MARKET." KATIE PARLA P.295

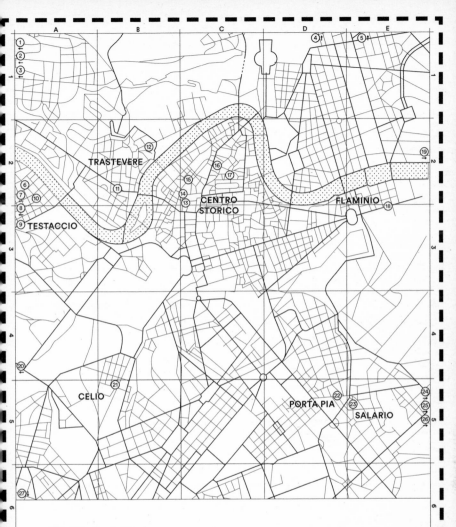

TRASTEVERE

CENTRO STORICO

FLAMINIO

TESTACCIO

CELIO

PORTA PIA

SALARIO

ROME

SCALE

0   300   600   900
                        yd.

1. LA GATTA MANGIONA, MONTEVERDE VECCHIO (P.293)
2. PRELIBATO, MONTEVERDE VECCHIO (P.293)
3. IN FUCINA, PORTUENSE (P.295)
4. PIZZARIUM, CIPRO - OTTAVIANO (P.292)
5. PANIFICIO BONCI, TRIONFALE (P.297)
6. TRAPIZZINO, TESTACCIO (P.296)
7. DA ARTENIO, TESTACCIO (P.295)
8. PIZZERIA OSTIENSE, OSTIENSE (P.294)
9. VOLPETTI, TESTACCIO (P.296)
10. DA REMO, TESTACCIO (P.296)
11. PIZZERIA AI MARMI, TRASTEVERE (P.297)
12. DAR POETA, TRASTEVERE (P.297)
13. EMMA, CENTRO STORICO (P.290)
14. ANTICO FORNO ROSCIOLI, CENTRO STORICO (P.290)
15. FORNO CAMPO DE' FIORI, CENTRO STORICO (P.290)
16. LA MONTECARLO, CENTRO STORICO (P.291)
17. NAVONA NOTTE, CENTRO STORICO (P.291)
18. PIZZA RUSTICA, FLAMINIO (P.292)
19. TRAPIZZINO, PONTE MILVIO (P.294)
20. IL FUNGO - PIANO ZERO, EUR (P.292)
21. LI RIONI, CELIO (P.290)
22. AL FORNO DELLA SOFFITTA, PORTA PIA (P.294)
23. PRO LOCO PINCIANO, SALARIO (P.295)
24. FIORE DI ZUCCA, PARIOLI (P.294)
25. PIZZERIA ANGELO E SIMONETTA, NOMENTANO (P.293)
26. TONDA, MONTESACRO (P.292)
27. SFORNO, CINECITTÀ (P.291)

LI RIONI

Via Dei SS. Quattro 24
Celio
Rome
Lazio 00184
Italy
+39 0670450605
www.lirioni.it

Opening hours	Closed Tuesday
Credit cards	Accepted
Style of pizza	Roman thin-crust
Recommended pizza	Artichoke

"Li Rioni serves very good standard-style *supplì* (Roman rice croquettes) and classic thin-crust Roman pizza, which is getting harder and harder to find, with rather better wines than one might expect, and it doesn't put on airs. Service is brisk but friendly and efficient. Reservations are a good idea (same day is usually fine)."—Maureen B. Fant

ANTICO FORNO ROSCIOLI

Via dei Chiavari 34
Centro Storico
Rome
Lazio 00186
Italy
+39 066864045
www.anticofornoroscioli.it

Opening hours	Closed Sunday
Credit cards	Accepted but not AMEX
Style of pizza	*Pizza al taglio*
Recommended pizza	Margherita; Tomato

"Roscioli's Margherita is thinly crusted with a perfectly balanced tomato sauce, and it is, of course, topped with mozzarella cheese. It has to be eaten burning hot out of the oven."—Sofie Wochner

EMMA

Via Monte della Farina 28–29
Centro Storico
Rome
Lazio 00186
Italy
+39 0664760475
www.emmapizzeria.com

Opening hours	Open 7 days
Credit cards	Accepted
Style of pizza	Gourmet Roman
Recommended pizza	Tuscan Kale and Pancetta; SuperBio

"Emma's central location near Largo Argentina means you can go there after sightseeing or shopping, and it's a couple of degrees spiffier than the average Roman pizzeria. The pizza is thin-crusted Roman style, only better, with buffalo mozzarella from Paestum, tomatoes from Vesuvius, garlic from Sulmona, and even anchovies from the Cantabrian Sea and smoked salmon from Loch Fyne."
—Maureen B. Fant

FORNO CAMPO DE' FIORI

Piazza Campo de' Fiori 22
Centro Storico
Rome
Lazio 00186
Italy
+39 0668806662
www.fornocampodefiori.com

Opening hours	Closed Sunday
Credit cards	Not accepted
Style of pizza	Roman
Recommended pizza	Bianca; Potato; Prosciutto with Mortadella and Mozzarella; Tomato; Zucchini (courgette)

"This is one of the best pizzerias in Rome, a perfect demonstration of the Italian philosophy of combining a few high-quality and extremely fresh ingredients for a fantastic result. The pizzas come out of the oven a meter or two in length and you indicate how much you want, with your section being weighed to determine price."—Julian Rea

"Grab a few slices and go eat it on the street while you watch the market vendors, the nuns strolling, the tourists, the locals. Then drop into a wine bar and have a glass of Frascati—you cannot go wrong."
—Jerry Corso & Angelina Tolentino

Forno Campo de' Fiori is a bakery in much the way St. Peter's is a church. Its holy bread is Roman *pizza bianca*, a leavened flatbread with a rough, crisp, golden terrain protecting a softer core. Olive oil is used to bake in texture and can also be redeployed for dipping. The purist and most worshipped version is virtually plain, with only coarse salt and rosemary for flavor. But popular variations like the one topped with thinly sliced zucchini (courgette) and potato are sacred, too. And tomato-coated *pizza rossa* makes this pizza look more like, well, pizza. The toppings are exquisite. Forno Campo de' Fiori is closed from 2:30 p.m. to 4:40 p.m., as scores of broken-hearted pilgrims discover every day.

LA MONTECARLO

Vicolo Savelli 13
Centro Storico
Rome
Lazio 00186
Italy
+39 066861877
www.lamontecarlo.it

Opening hours	Closed Monday
Credit cards	Not accepted
Style of pizza	Roman
Recommended pizza	Mushroom and Onion; Zucchini (courgette) Flowers

"The pizza is excellent and the prices are good. Do not let the long line of people waiting to enter scare you, because it moves very quickly."
—Federica Caccamo

"La Montecarlo is the whole package—the food, the people passing by outside, the music, the air. There's a huge choice of pizzas to indulge in. It's a must if you're visiting Rome."
—Carolina Carriel

NAVONA NOTTE

Via del Teatro Pace 44
Centro Storico
Rome
Lazio 00186
Italy
+39 066869278

Opening hours	Open 7 days
Credit cards	Accepted but not AMEX
Style of pizza	Roman
Recommended pizza	Mushroom

"I ate the best pizza of my life amid the tourist bustle of Piazza Navona. The pizza at Navona Notte had a thin and crispy base and just the right amount of fresh porcini mushrooms. It was delicious."
—Barbara Goerlich

SFORNO

Via Statilio Ottato 110–116
Cinecittà
Rome
Lazio 00175
Italy
+39 0671546118
www.sforno.it

Opening hours	Open 7 days
Credit cards	Accepted but not AMEX
Style of pizza	Neapolitan-Roman
Recommended pizza	Calzone alla Napoletana; Cheese and Black Pepper

"Fantastic ingredients and creativity built on a solid Neapolitan pizza structure. Try the cheese and black pepper pizza an homage to the great Roman pasta dish."—Dino Joannides

There are pizzerias and even pizzas that are worth a detour. Entire journeys are planned around either of two Stefano Callegari triumphs: the pizza Cacio e Pepe, true to Rome's minimalist pasta classic of "cheese and pepper," is a white pizza densely dusted with grated Pecorino Romano cheese and sprinkled with black pepper. The Greenwich is crowned with a blanket of mozzarella, dabs of Blue Stilton cheese, and a spiral of Port reduction. The bubbly *cornicione* framing both is bloated, blackened, and blistered in grand Neapolitan style.

PIZZARIUM

Via della Meloria 43
Cipro - Ottaviano
Rome
Lazio 00136
Italy
+39 0639745416

Opening hours..Open 7 days
Credit cards...Accepted
Style of pizza..*Pizza al taglio*
Recommended pizza...................Foie Gras, Mozzarella, and
Lemon; Margherita with Buffalo Mozzarella; Mortadella
and Stracchino; Potato; Pumpkin and Parma Ham;
Romanesco and Caciocavallo Cheese; Sautéed
Chicory and Anchovies; Zucchini (courgette) Flowers,
Mozzarella, and Anchovies

"This is not a sit-down place; step up to the counter,
point out your selection, and they'll heat it for you.
It's very easy to order (even with limited use of the
Italian language)—a 'must-stop' when in Rome!"
—George Formaro

"Gabriele Bonci has been christened 'the
Michelangelo of pizza' and with good reason."
—Orlando Bortolami

Gabriele Bonci is Rome's undisputed master of *pizza al taglio*,
the rectangular, "by-the-cut," ready-to-go style of pizza
baked in rectangular pans in electric ovens and displayed in
bakery-like window cases throughout Rome. At Pizzarium
the pizza selection is so vast and so impressive there is almost
a risk of it distracting from the singular experience of Bonci's
crust and its compression to the chew. Long slabs of pizza,
generously draped with such rotated toppings as potato,
artichoke, *mozzarella di bufala*, ricotta, lardo, and smoked
Cantabrico anchovies, are sliced to order, priced by the weight,
and reheated upon request. At Pizzarium, as at most *pizza al
taglio* joints, there is no stigma attached to electric pizza ovens
or reheats. There is only joy.

IL FUNGO - PIANO ZERO

Piazza Pakistan 1A
EUR
Rome
Lazio 00144
Italy
+39 065921433
www.ristoranteilfungo.it

Opening hours..Open 7 days
Credit cards...Accepted
Style of pizza...Round

PIZZA RUSTICA

Via Flaminia 24
Flaminio
Rome
Lazio 00196
Italy
+39 063227956

Opening hours..Open 7 days
Credit cards..Not accepted
Style of pizza..*Pizza al taglio*
Recommended pizza...Potato

"An excellent spot for traditional Roman *pizza al
taglio*. No English is spoken, but the staff are super-
friendly and hand gestures are all you need to sample
the spectrum of great ingredients atop perfectly
chewy/crispy crusts. Pizza Rustica was packed with
locals and it was the best pizza we had in the city."
—Mark Bello

TONDA

Via Valle Corteno 31
Montesacro
Rome
Lazio 00141
Italy
+39 068180960
www.tondatonda.com

Opening hours..Open 7 days
Credit cards...Accepted
Style of pizza...Neapolitan
Recommended pizza...................Cheese and Black Pepper;
Margheritissima

"The dough developed by Stefano Callegari is fluffy,
with delicately risen edges, tasty, and easy to digest.
The toppings are delicious, whether in the classic
versions, in the original ones, or in the ones inspired
by Roman culinary traditions."—Luciana Squadrilli

"In addition to pizza the venue also offers sensational
fritters and a good selection of artisanal beers."
—John Regefalk

LA GATTA MANGIONA

Via Federico Ozanam 30–32
Monteverde Vecchio
Rome
Lazio 00152
Italy
+39 065346702
www.lagattamangiona.com

Opening hours..Open 7 days
Credit cards...............................Accepted but not AMEX
Style of pizza..........................Gourmet Neapolitan-Roman
Recommended pizza.............................Capricciosa; Cherry;
    Margherita Flavored with Riesling Kabinett; Marinara;
    Seasonal specials

"La Gatta Mangiona was the first pizzeria in Rome
to offer a high-quality pizza with a wine list and a
large range of spirits."—Gabriele Bonci

"The most Neapolitan pizza to be found in Rome,
and an excellent example of how to fulfill the taste
demands of one's clientele. The pizzas have a great
selection of ingredients and a base that is just a little
crispier than the classic Neapolitan base, just how
the Romans like it."—Monica Piscitelli

"The pizzas are—with occasional exceptions—terrific.
The range of drinks is equally good. An extensive and
well-chosen wine list. Which other pizzeria in Italy
would recommend a German Riesling (Schloss Lieser)
with a pizza Margherita?"—Torsten Goffin

Pizza master Giancarlo Casa responded to the Roman
preference for crisp pizza by giving more firmness and less
droop to his Naples-styled pizzas. But when it came to the
ingredients that went in and atop his long-leavened dough
there was no bending. La Gatta Mangiona (the gluttonous cat)
puts sensational pizza in a cozy dining room with paintings and
statuettes of cats, thus appealing to two groups of social-media
obsessives. Casa and his wife Cecilia Capitani are not ones
for brevity: they offer nearly 200 wines, 60 beers, and 30-plus
pizzas, from seasonal originals like the Aromatica, with Asiago
cheese, asparagus, duck speck, and pink peppercorns to
classics paired with wines—a white Riesling Kabinett for the
Margherita and a red Montepulciano d'Abruzzo Cerasuolo for
the Marinara.

PRELIBATO

Viale di Villa Pamphili 214–216
Monteverde Vecchio
Rome
Lazio 00152
Italy
+39 0693577165

Opening hours..Closed Sunday
Credit cards.............................Accepted but not AMEX
Style of pizza...Pizza al taglio
Recommended pizza..Amatriciana

"There are literally hundreds of pizza-by-the-slice
joints in Rome but few invest in quality ingredients or
create dough that is properly leavened. At Prelibato
in Monteverde Vecchio, former chef Stefano Preli has
mastered the art of fermentation and creates light
and highly digestible bases with seasonal toppings."
—Katie Parla

PIZZERIA ANGELO E SIMONETTA

Via Nomentana 581
Nomentano
Rome
Lazio 00141
Italy
+39 0687188853

Opening hours..Open 7 days
Credit cards...Not accepted
Style of pizza...Pizza al taglio
Recommended pizza..............Buffalo Mozzarella; Crostino;
    Focaccia with Mortadella

"Angelo Lezzi makes the best Roman pizza; from the
dough to the toppings it is the number one place
for pizza al taglio lovers."—Dario Mulino

"My hands-down favorite is the pizza with hand-
pulled pieces of cloud-white buffalo mozzarella
(added post-bake), tomato sauce, basil leaves,
and olive oil."—Michael Berman

"A real pioneer of the dough, Angelo offers pan-baked
pizza that is the result of his 30 years of research. The
pizza is fluffy, crispy, dry, and delicious at the same
time."—Stefano Callegari

PIZZERIA OSTIENSE

Via Ostiense 56B
Ostiense
Rome
Lazio 00154
Italy
+39 0657305081
www.pizzeriaostiense.com

Opening hours	Open 7 days
Credit cards	Accepted but not AMEX
Style of pizza	Roman
Recommended pizza	Margherita with Mozzarella 'al Piove' (it's not on the menu, you have to ask for it); Ostiense

"As a New Jersey native, the pizza I miss the most is the greasy slice from my neighborhood spot. This place fills that need. It's a solid, quick pizza that you order on a card with check boxes. It's not the kind of place that you linger for hours: order, eat, and leave."
—Christopher Behr

FIORE DI ZUCCA

Via Gaetano Donizetti 16
Parioli
Rome
Lazio 00198
Italy
+39 0684242417
www.ristorantefioredizucca.com

Opening hours	Closed Saturday morning
Credit cards	Accepted
Style of pizza	Italian brick-oven
Recommended pizza	Margherita

"This out-of-the-way pizzeria is worth the detour. It's in a residential area where you will be elbow-to-elbow with the locals from the surrounding upscale neighborhood. Everything on the menu is excellent and served with friendly professionalism, but the Margherita pizza is a rich, flavorful, perfectly salty masterpiece."—Lisa Pepin

TRAPIZZINO

Piazzale Ponte Milvio 13
Ponte Milvio
Rome
Lazio 00135
Italy
+39 0633221964
www.trapizzino.it

Opening hours	Open 7 days
Credit cards	Accepted but not AMEX
Style of pizza	Stuffed
Recommended pizza	Tongue in Salsa Verde

"It is a 'pocket' of white pizza, soft inside and crispy outside, filled with traditional Roman condiments. Perfect for those who go to the football Olympic stadium to watch a match."—Vincenzo Pagano

AL FORNO DELLA SOFFITTA

Via Piave 62–64
Porta Pia
Rome
Lazio 00187
Italy
+39 0642011164
www.alfornodellasoffitta.it

Opening hours	Open 7 days
Credit cards	Accepted
Style of pizza	Neapolitan
Recommended pizza	Cheese and Black Pepper

"This place is very cozy. It serves Neapolitan-style pizzas with light, soft dough and thick crusts. In addition to the traditional toppings, there is a range of pizzas dedicated to *nuovi gusti* (new tastes), which includes some very creative and tasty options."
—Silvana Azevedo

IN FUCINA

Via Giuseppe Lunati 25–31
Portuense
Rome
Lazio 00149
Italy
+39 065593368
www.infucina.com

Opening hours...Closed Tuesday
Credit cards...Accepted
Style of pizza...Gourmet
Recommended pizza......................Alaskan Smoked Salmon,
    Ricotta, and Buffalo Mozzarella; Margherita al Rum

"The pizza is simple and delicious but there are the wild topping combinations. Trust the owner on this. People are shocked by the prices because they seem to be double what other locals charge. But these pizzas are more shareable than the usual Roman individual pies."—Victoria Pesce Elliot

"This pizza with its outstanding dough shows off Chef Edoardo Papa's culinary skills."—Maurizio Valeriani

PRO LOCO PINCIANO

Via Bergamo 18
Salario
Rome
Lazio 00198
Italy
+39 068414136
www.prolocopinciano.it

Opening hours...................................Closed Sunday morning
Credit cards.....................................Accepted but not AMEX
Style of pizza...Neapolitan-Roman
Recommended pizza.................................Smoked Margherita

"Both white and red pizzas are fragrant and tasty and they don't need a lot of toppings. The best might be the unsophisticated focaccia with rosemary, which is simply spectacular—the crust is lovely and the center is fluffy and airy."—John Regefalk

DA ARTENIO

Box 90, Mercato Coperto di Testaccio, Via Galvani
Testaccio
Rome
Lazio 00153
Italy
+39 3479941575
www.daartenio.it

Opening hours...Closed Sunday
Credit cards..Not accepted
Style of pizza..Pizzetta
Recommended pizza..Pizzetta Rossa

"Artenio Fanella excels at making deeply satisfying and shockingly simple pizzette at his stall in the 'new' Testaccio Market. There are plenty of bakeries in the market and the surrounding area, but few invest in quality flours and toppings. Artenio sells breads that have been baked in wood-fired ovens in his home village of Lariano as well as pizzette, hand-shaped snack-sized pizza, which he makes hourly in the oven on his stall to ensure maximum freshness. The slightly sour dough is topped with a bit of tangy and sweet tomato sauce or sliced potatoes for an exquisitely balanced result."—Katie Parla

DA REMO

Piazza di Santa Maria Liberatrice 44
Testaccio
Rome
Lazio 00153
Italy
+39 065746270

Opening hours...Closed Sunday
Credit cards...Accepted
Style of pizza...Roman
Recommended pizza...............Bianca; Diavola; Margherita;
Marinara

"Da Remo's pizza is, in my estimation, the quintessential Roman pizza: perfectly thin, perfectly crisp, perfectly minimal, and unbelievably fragrant."
—Jonathan Gold

"Da Remo is in the heart of Rome and you may have to wait up to an hour so go early...or late. Waiters are cheeky and the hustle and bustle is great to watch."
—Ingrid Langtry

Those who describe Da Remo as the pizzeria near the Piazza di Santa Maria Liberatrice in Testaccio may have their priorities backward. The lovely square is triangular in shape, like a slice hastily cut from Da Remo's truly devilish pizza Diavola, with spicy Ventricina (a salami from Abruzzo) tomato, mozzarella, and Parmigiano. Tourists and locals alike put up with the boisterous confusion outside and inside the pizzeria for a crack at the crunch or, to say it the Roman way, scrocchiarella. That sensation is delivered by the extremely thin, thoroughly crisp crust that is typical of round pizza Romana. Da Remo's verson is lightly charred around the *cornicione*, where the scrocchiarella of its Margherita, Marinara, and *pizza bianca* is most acute.

TRAPIZZINO

Via Giovanni Branca 88
Testaccio
Rome
Lazio 00153
Italy
+39 0643419624
www.trapizzino.it

Opening hours...Closed Monday
Credit cards.....................................Accepted but not AMEX
Style of pizza...Stuffed
Recommended pizza.......................Hunter's Chicken; Oxtail

"Pizza chef Stefano Callegari of Tonda and Sforno fame invented the trapizzino at his former pizza-by-the-slice joint 00100 in Testaccio. The invention took off and now there are two dedicated Trapizzino locations that serve this delectable, creative, and portable snack. A trapizzino is a triangular slice of long-leavened *pizza bianca*, which is sliced open and filled with Roman specialties like chicken with bell peppers, tongue with salsa verde, and oxtail simmered with tomato and celery."
—Katie Parla

VOLPETTI

Via Marmorata 47
Testaccio
Rome
Lazio 00153
Italy
+39 065742352
www.volpetti.com

Opening hours...Closed Sunday
Credit cards...Accepted
Style of pizza..*Pizza al taglio*
Recommended pizza...Potato

"This pizzeria is just a counter inside the door of this gourmet shop (although the pizza is also available at Volpetti Più, its snack bar around the corner). This is the other kind of Roman pizza—yeasty rectangles cut into slices and sold by weight. You can buy slices topped with fresh tiny tomatoes, or zucchini (courgette) flowers and anchovies, or (yes!) sliced potatoes and mozzarella. But it's about the taste of the pizza, not the toppings. Try the *pizza bianca*—no topping, just golden brown on both sides. Or have it split so you can make a sandwich (super prosciutto, salami, and cheese are sold at the next counter). Or, in summer, buy fresh ripe figs at the nearby Testaccio market, peel them, and stuff them inside your *pizza bianca* with some slices of *Prosciutto di Parma*."
—Maureen B. Fant

DAR POETA

Vicolo del Bologna 45
Trastevere
Rome
Lazio 00153
Italy
+39 065880516
www.darpoeta.com

Opening hours...Open 7 days
Credit cards...Accepted
Style of pizza...Unique
Recommended pizza...Burrata

"I have been to many restaurants in Rome over the years, and this one really stands out for its immaculate pizza. Dar Poeta describes its pizza as 'not Roman or Neapolitan...it is unique!'—and it is true. You can eat very well in Rome, and particularly well at Dar Poeta."—Joe Diliberto

PIZZERIA AI MARMI

Viale Trastevere 53
Trastevere
Rome
Lazio 00153
Italy
+39 065800919

Opening hours...Closed Wednesday
Credit cards...................................Accepted but not AMEX
Style of pizza..Roman

"Pizzeria Ai Marmi, also known as L'Obitorio, is a crowded place with immense marble tables. There's such a racket you cannot hear a thing, and a white light radiates through the room. The pizza crust is so thin and perfect, so accurate in its balance and its flavors. It's an absolute delight, a real experience. Enjoy the pizza with a draft beer as it quenches one's thirst in the heat of the room and encourages one to eat pizza in abundance."—Boris Beaucarne

PANIFICIO BONCI

Via Trionfale 36
Trionfale
Rome
Lazio 00136
Italy
+39 0639734457

Opening hours...Closed Sunday
Credit cards.....................................Accepted but not AMEX
Style of pizza...*Pizza al taglio*

"THE FOCACCIA IS EXCELLENT AS AN APERITIF ALONGSIDE ONE OF THE OUTSTANDING COCKTAILS."

MARCO LOCATELLI P.301

"THIS IS A MINIMALIST VENUE WITH A MODERN RATHER THAN TRADITIONAL TOUCH."

PAVE' LUCA SCANNI P.301

MILAN

"YOU WOULDN'T NOTICE THIS PIZZERIA IN PORTA ROMANA IF IT WASN'T FOR THE LINE THAT VERY OFTEN FORMS AT THE ENTRANCE."

LYDIA CAPASSO P.301

"IT HAS A NEAPOLITAN MENU WITH DEEP-FRIED APPETIZERS AND NEAPOLITAN FIRST COURSES."

PAOLA SUCATO P.300

"GINO SORBILLO HAS BROUGHT THE NEAPOLITAN PIZZA TO MILAN."

DORA SORRENTINO P.300

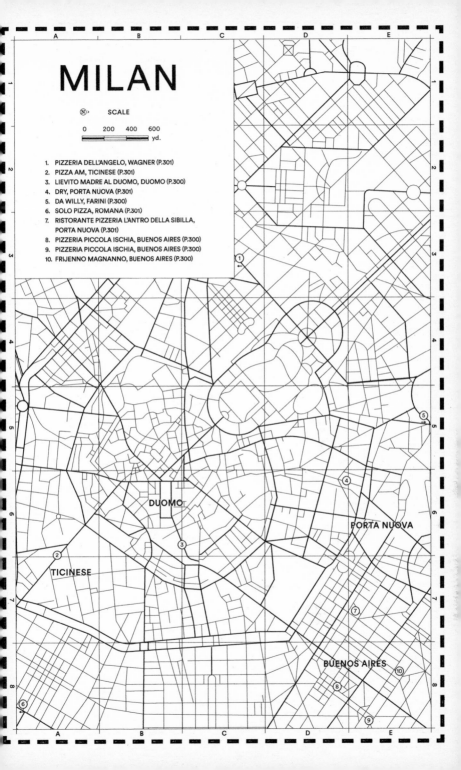

MILAN

SCALE

0   200   400   600
yd.

1. PIZZERIA DELL'ANGELO, WAGNER (P.301)
2. PIZZA AM, TICINESE (P.301)
3. LIEVITO MADRE AL DUOMO, DUOMO (P.300)
4. DRY, PORTA NUOVA (P.301)
5. DA WILLY, FARINI (P.300)
6. SOLO PIZZA, ROMANA (P.301)
7. RISTORANTE PIZZERIA L'ANTRO DELLA SIBILLA, PORTA NUOVA (P.301)
8. PIZZERIA PICCOLA ISCHIA, BUENOS AIRES (P.300)
9. PIZZERIA PICCOLA ISCHIA, BUENOS AIRES (P.300)
10. FRIJENNO MAGNANNO, BUENOS AIRES (P.300)

DUOMO

PORTA NUOVA

TICINESE

BUENOS AIRES

FRIJENNO MAGNANNO

Via Benedetto Marcello 93
Buenos Aires
Milan
Lombardy 20124
Italy
+39 0229403654
www.frijennomagnanno.it

Opening hours	Closed Sunday
Credit cards	Accepted but not AMEX
Style of pizza	Neapolitan
Recommended pizza	Margherita; Sausage and Broccoli Raab

"A real Neapolitan pizza in the heart of Milan."
—Federica Caccamo

"It has a Neapolitan menu with deep-fried appetizers and Neapolitan first courses."—Paola Sucato

PIZZERIA PICCOLA ISCHIA

Via Giovanni Battista Morgagni 7
Buenos Aires
Milan
Lombardy 20129
Italy
+39 022047613
www.piccolaischia.it

Opening hours	Closed Wednesday
Credit cards	Accepted but not AMEX
Style of pizza	Neapolitan
Recommended pizza	Margherita

"In addition to the classic Margherita, one of the house specials is the fried pizza, which is perfect as an appetizer."—Pave' Luca Scanni

PIZZERIA PICCOLA ISCHIA

Viale Abruzzi 62
Buenos Aires
Milan
Lombardy 20131
Italy
+39 0229412420
www.piccolaischia.it

Opening hours	Closed Tuesday
Credit cards	Accepted but not AMEX
Style of pizza	Neapolitan
Recommended pizza	Regina Margherita; Rustica Casatiello

"A great place to go to eat Neapolitan pizza outside of Naples."—Maria Romano

LIEVITO MADRE AL DUOMO

Largo Corsia dei Servi 11
Duomo
Milan
Lombardy 20122
Italy
+39 0245375930
www.sorbillo.it

Opening hours	Open 7 days
Credit cards	Accepted
Style of pizza	Neapolitan
Recommended pizza	Margherita Bufala DOP; Margherita Gialla; Filetto Fresco di Pomodoro; Pizza dell'Alleanza Slow Food

"Gino Sorbillo has brought the Neapolitan pizza to Milan. With Lievito Madre al Duomo he follows the same style as his pizzeria in Naples on the seafront. The pizzas are made with high-quality ingredients and the dough with organic flour."—Dora Sorrentino

DA WILLY

Via Carlo Farini 78–80
Farini
Milan
Lombardy 20159
Italy
+39 0269016126

Opening hours	Closed Sunday
Credit cards	Accepted but not AMEX
Style of pizza	Classic
Recommended pizza	Margherita

"Light well-cooked pizza, with good toppings at a great price."—Francisco Carreño

DRY

Via Solferino 33
Porta Nuova
Milan
Lombardy 20121
Italy
+39 0263793414
www.drymilano.it

Opening hours..Open 7 days
Credit cards..Accepted
Style of pizza..............................Gourmet Neapolitan
Recommended pizza.............Focaccia with Squacquerone
Cheese, Mortadella, and Watercress; Focaccia with
Veal and Tuna; Sausage and Broccoli Raab

"The focaccia is excellent as an aperitif alongside
one of the outstanding cocktails."—Marco Locatelli

"At the heart of the Milan food trend, Dry specializes
in pizza and cocktails but its main strength is focaccia:
fluffy and light, made of the same dough as pizza but
let to rest for 72 hours, and cooked in a small pan."
—Lydia Capasso

RISTORANTE PIZZERIA L'ANTRO DELLA SIBILLA

Via San Gregorio 37
Porta Nuova
Milan
Lombardy 20124
Italy
+39 0267481054
www.antrodellasibilla.com

Opening hours..Open 7 days
Credit cards..Accepted
Style of pizza..Neapolitan
Recommended pizza..............................Margherita; Siciliana

"This is a minimalist venue with a modern rather than
traditional touch, but the pizzas are in a perfect
Neapolitan style. It gets extremely crowded at
lunchtime during the week because of the office
workers who rush there."—Pave' Luca Scanni

SOLO PIZZA

Viale Umbria 25
Romana
Milan
Lombardy 20135
Italy
+39 0259900990
www.solopizza.com

Opening hours..Open 7 days
Credit cards........................Accepted but not AMEX
Style of pizza..Neapolitan
Recommended pizza..Margherita

"You can enjoy real Neapolitan pizza in this minimalist
venue, where the realness of the ingredients is the
uncontested protagonist."
—Pietro & Francesca Singer

PIZZA AM

Corso di Porta Romana 83
Ticinese
Milan
Lombardy 20122
Italy
+39 025510579
www.pizzaam.it

Opening hours...Closed Monday
Credit cards........................Accepted but not AMEX
Style of pizza..Neapolitan
Recommended pizza...........Margherita; Pometto Pasquale

"You wouldn't notice this pizzeria in Porta Romana
if it wasn't for the line that very often forms at the
entrance. Don't be intimidated by the crowd as the
staff, always very accommodating, supplies slices
of pizza to the people waiting."—Lydia Capasso

PIZZERIA DELL'ANGELO

Via Belfiore 7
Wagner
Milan
Lombardy 20145
Italy
+39 0248005367

Opening hours..Open 7 days
Credit cards..Not accepted
Style of pizza..Pizza by the slice

"Pizzeria dell'Angelo hasn't changed the recipe nor
the quality of the slices it sells in 40 years."
—Pave' Luca Scanni

"CLASSIC PIZZA WITH OOMPH."
ALESSANDRA TINOZZI P.304

"WHEN IN PIEDMONT DON'T OVERLOOK THE REAL TURIN-STYLE PIZZA MADE IN A DISH."
LUCA IACCARINO P.305

TURIN

"CIT MA BON IS GOOD VALUE FOR MONEY. IT IS ALWAYS FULL."
LAURA RANGONI P.304

"THE PIZZA IS CRISPY, SOFT, AND VERY DELICIOUS."
LUISA PANDOLFI P.304

"THE CHOICE OF PIZZA RANGES FROM ONES THAT ARE ALWAYS ON THE MENU TO THE 'SURPRISES' THAT ARE SEASONAL AND CONTINUALLY CHANGING."
ENRICO BONARDO P.304

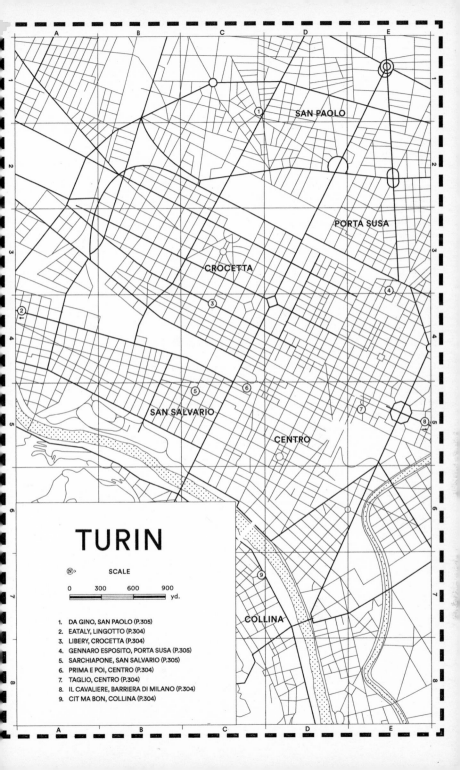

TURIN

SCALE

0   300   600   900   yd.

1. DA GINO, SAN PAOLO (P.305)
2. EATALY, LINGOTTO (P.304)
3. LIBERY, CROCETTA (P.304)
4. GENNARO ESPOSITO, PORTA SUSA (P.305)
5. SARCHIAPONE, SAN SALVARIO (P.305)
6. PRIMA E POI, CENTRO (P.304)
7. TAGLIO, CENTRO (P.304)
8. IL CAVALIERE, BARRIERA DI MILANO (P.304)
9. CIT MA BON, COLLINA (P.304)

SAN PAOLO

PORTA SUSA

CROCETTA

SAN SALVARIO

CENTRO

COLLINA

IL CAVALIERE

Corso Vercelli 79
Barriera di Milano
Turin
Piedmont 10155
Italy
+39 011852657
www.pizzeriailcavalieretorino.com

Opening hours...Closed Tuesday
Credit cards.......................................Accepted but not AMEX
Style of pizza...Deep-pan

"The pizza is crispy, soft, and very delicious.
The farinata is also excellent."—Luisa Pandolfi

PRIMA E POI

Via Lagrange 43
Centro
Turin
Piedmont 10123
Italy
+39 0115178698
www.primaepoi.com

Opening hours...Closed Monday
Credit cards...Accepted
Style of pizza...Neapolitan
Recommended pizza..Napoletana

TAGLIO

Largo IV Marzo 17C
Centro
Turin
Piedmont 10122
Italy
+39 0115215575
www.taglioperfetta.com

Opening hours...Closed Tuesday
Credit cards.......................................Accepted but not AMEX
Style of pizza...*Pizza al taglio*
Recommended pizza..Punto F

"The choice of pizza ranges from ones that are always
on the menu to the 'surprises' that are seasonal and
continually changing."—Enrico Bonardo

CIT MA BON

Corso Casale 34
Collina
Turin
Piedmont 10131
Italy
+39 0118196845

Opening hours...Closed Sunday
Credit cards.......................................Accepted but not AMEX
Style of pizza...Deep-dish
Recommended pizza..................Sausage and Broccoli Raab

"Cit Ma Bon is good value for money. It is always full."
—Laura Rangoni

LIBERY

Via Legnano 14
Crocetta
Turin
Piedmont 10128
Italy
+39 0114546040

Opening hours...Closed Monday
Credit cards...Accepted
Style of pizza...Italian
Recommended pizza...Vegetable

"Classic pizza with oomph."—Alessandra Tinozzi

EATALY

Via Nizza 230
Lingotto
Turin
Piedmont 10126
Italy
+39 01119506801
www.eataly.net/it_it/negozi/torino-lingotto/

Opening hours...Open 7 days
Credit cards...Accepted
Style of pizza...Neapolitan
Recommended pizza...Margherita

GENNARO ESPOSITO

Via Giuseppe Luigi Passalacqua 1G
Porta Susa
Turin
Piedmont 10122
Italy
+39 011535905

Opening hours	Closed Saturday and Sunday
Credit cards	Accepted
Style of pizza	Neapolitan
Recommended pizza	Santa Anastasia; Sausage and Broccoli Raab

DA GINO

Via Monginevro 46
San Paolo
Turin
Piedmont 10141
Italy
+39 0113854335
www.ginopizzeria.it

Opening hours	Closed Wednesday
Credit cards	Accepted but not AMEX
Style of pizza	Deep-dish
Recommended pizza	Farinata; Napoletana

"When in Piedmont don't overlook the real Turin-style pizza made in a dish. Soft dough is cooked in a single-portion tin giving a deep, soft pizza that is small but delicious. Gino has been one of the great pioneers of this type of pizza since 1935. Da Gino is an old-fashioned local pizzeria with yellow walls, a marble floor, a few pictures hanging on the wall, and not much else. It is particularly loved by workers and students."
—Luca Iaccarino

SARCHIAPONE

Via Claudio Luigi Berthollet 17
San Salvario
Turin
Piedmont 10125
Italy
+39 0116503055
www.sarchiaponepizzeria.it

Opening hours	Closed Wednesday
Credit cards	Accepted
Style of pizza	Neapolitan
Recommended pizza	Sausage and Broccoli Raab

"Sarchiapone is a top-quality pizzeria in the heart of the buzzing San Salvario neighborhood. It has a lively atmosphere, polite service, large colorful paintings, and is, above all, one of the best Neapolitan pizzerias in the city. The dough, cooking, and toppings come together to produce an excellent pizza."
—Luca Iaccarino

"THE PIZZA CRUST HAD A PERFECT CHEW, AND THE FRESH TOMATO SAUCE WITH FRESH MOZZARELLA CHEESE TRANSPORTED ME TO ANOTHER PLANET." AMANDA CLARK P.310

"THIS IS NO SIMPLE PIZZA BY THE SLICE."
STEFANIA PIANIGIANI P.309

"AN INTERESTING PIZZERIA WITH TRADITIONAL TASTY PIZZA."
LEONARDO ROMANELLI P.309

FLORENCE

"THE RICOTTA-STUFFED-CRUST PIZZA IS UNIQUE AND INCREDIBLY DELICIOUS."
TONY MANTUANO P.309

"THE PLACE IS ALWAYS PACKED WITH LOUD AND HUNGRY LOCALS."
NOMI ABELIOVICH P.308

FLORENCE

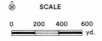

SCALE

0   200   400   600
▬▬▬▬▬▬ yd.

1. SUD, SANTA MARIA NOVELLA (P.310)
2. TRATTORIA DA GARIBARDI, SANTA MARIA NOVELLA (P.310)
3. MAMMA NAPOLI, SANTA MARIA NOVELLA (P.310)
4. CIRO AND SONS, SANTA MARIA NOVELLA (P.310)
5. YELLOW BAR, SAN GIOVANNI (P.308)
6. CUCINA TORCICODA, SANTA CROCE (P.309)
7. OSTERIA CAFFÈ ITALIANO, SANTA CROCE (P.309)
8. LA DIVINA PIZZA, SANTA CROCE (P.309)
9. IL PIZZAIUOLO, SANTA CROCE (P.309)
10. ACCÀ RISTOPIZZAPERITIVO, SAN FREDIANO (P.308)
11. BERBERÈ FIRENZE, OLTRARNO (P.308)
12. DA GHERARDO, OLTRARNO (P.308)
13. GUSTA PIZZA, OLTRARNO (P.308)

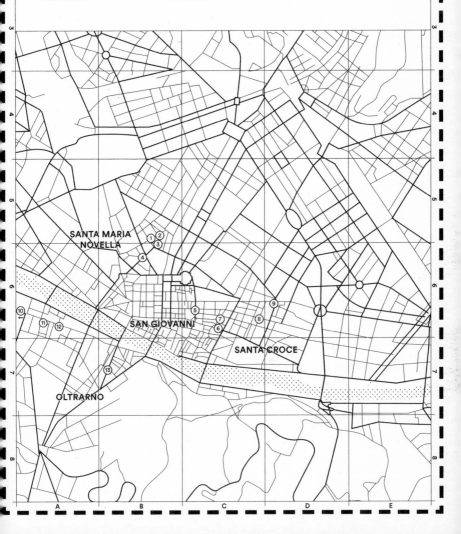

BERBERÈ FIRENZE

Piazza De' Nerli 1
Oltrarno
Florence
Tuscany 50124
Italy
+39 0552382946
www.berberepizza.it

Opening hours	Open 7 days
Credit cards	Accepted
Style of pizza	Gourmet
Recommended pizza	Margherita; Marinara

"An easily digestible pizza with a very springy, long-rise dough produced with flour from the Molino Quaglia and the Molino Marino mills."
—Stefano Degli Innocenti

"It's not Neapolitan pizza, but neither is it Roman or Florentine. If you want to understand what it is, pop in and try it."—Giovanni Santarpia

DA GHERARDO

Borgo San Frediano 57R
Oltrarno
Florence
Tuscany 50124
Italy
+39 055282921
www.gherardopizzeria.com

Opening hours	Open 7 days
Credit cards	Not accepted
Style of pizza	Neapolitan
Recommended pizza	Margherita

"Da Gherardo is a typical restaurant on the Florentine Oltrarno: small and inviting with authentic pizza."
—Aldo Fiordelli

GUSTA PIZZA

Via Maggio 46R
Oltrarno
Florence
Tuscany 50125
Italy
+39 055285068

Opening hours	Closed Monday
Credit cards	Not accepted
Style of pizza	Neapolitan
Recommended pizza	Calabrese

"The place is always packed with loud and hungry locals despite the fact the variety of pizzas is limited to a few. The pizzas are baked to order in a wood-fired oven and best consumed immediately. There's an interesting ordering system with tickets and numbers but the pizza is worth the wait."
—Nomi Abeliovich

ACCÀ RISTOPIZZAPERITIVO

Via Pisana 120R
San Frediano
Florence
Tuscany 50124
Italy
+39 0555308920
www.hristopizzaperitivo.com

Opening hours	Closed Monday
Credit cards	Accepted
Style of pizza	Traditional
Recommended pizza	Napoli DOP

"Accà Ristopizzaperitivo has a Neapolitan atmosphere and excellent pizzas."—Paolo Pellegrini

YELLOW BAR

Via del Proconsolo 39R
San Giovanni
Florence
Tuscany 50122
Italy
+39 055211766
www.yellowbar.it

Opening hours	Closed Monday
Credit cards	Accepted but not AMEX
Style of pizza	Wood-fired
Recommended pizza	Tuna

"This pizzeria is an absolute classic in Florence. One of the few places where Japanese, Americans, and genuine Florentine locals of all ages can enjoy eating pizza side by side. A very democratic, lively, and colorful place."—Michaela Bogner

CUCINA TORCICODA

Via Torta 5R
Santa Croce
Florence
Tuscany 50122
Italy
+39 0552654329
www.cucinatorcicoda.com

Opening hours..Open 7 days
Credit cards..Accepted
Style of pizza...Neapolitan
Recommended pizza............Napoli with Cetara Anchovies

"The ricotta-stuffed-crust pizza is unique and incredibly delicious."—Tony Mantuano

LA DIVINA PIZZA

Via Borgo Allegri 50R
Santa Croce
Florence
Tuscany 50122
Italy
+39 0552347498
www.ladivinapizza.it

Opening hours...Closed Sunday
Credit cards................................Accepted but not AMEX
Style of pizza...Gourmet
Recommended pizza...............Bianca with Barilla Plant and
Parmesan Flakes; Gorgonzola and Certaldo Onions
Braised in Wine; Margherita; Vegetariana

"This is no simple pizza by the slice. Here they use select stone-ground flour and natural leaven to make the dough. The pizza is garnished either in a classic way or more usually with anchovies and cheese."
—Stefania Pianigiani

"Come here not only for the classic Margherita but also for the gourmet focaccias with excellent ingredients such as Cantabrico anchovies, Parmigiano-Reggiano, or Tarese Valdarno pancetta."—Aldo Fiordelli

OSTERIA CAFFÈ ITALIANO

Via dell'Isola delle Stinche 11–13R
Santa Croce
Florence
Tuscany 50122
Italy
+39 055289368
www.osteriacaffeitaliano.com

Opening hours..Closed Monday
Credit cards...Not accepted
Style of pizza...Neapolitan
Recommended pizza...............Margherita; Marinara; Napoli

"The pizzeria is part of the osteria and does not take reservations, you write your name on a piece of paper and then wait outside for your turn. The choice is limited to three flavors: Margherita, Marinara, and Napoli."—Stefano Degli Innocenti

IL PIZZAIUOLO

Via de' Macci 113
Santa Croce
Florence
Tuscany 50122
Italy
+39 055241171

Opening hours...Closed Sunday
Credit cards..Accepted
Style of pizza...Neapolitan
Recommended pizza...Napoletana

"An interesting pizzeria with traditional tasty pizza."
—Leonardo Romanelli

CIRO AND SONS

Via del Giglio 28R
Santa Maria Novella
Florence
Tuscany 50123
Italy
+39 055289694
www.ciroandsons.com

Opening hours	Closed Sunday
Credit cards	Accepted
Style of pizza	Neapolitan with gluten-free options
Recommended pizza	Margherita

"With its sophisticated atmosphere, this is no simple pizzeria but rather it is somewhere you can spend an evening thanks also to its high-level kitchen. The pizza is light with an excellent rise. It is pleasingly tasty without going overboard on flavors."
—Leonardo Romanelli

MAMMA NAPOLI

Piazza del Mercato Centrale 17–18R
Santa Maria Novella
Florence
Tuscany 50123
Italy
+39 055211131
www.mammanapolibycellini.com

Opening hours	Open 7 days
Credit cards	Accepted but not AMEX
Style of pizza	Neapolitan
Recommended pizza	Mamma Napoli; Margherita; Marinara

"When I enter this pizzeria I feel instantly at home."
—Giovanni Santarpia

SUD

Piazza del Mercato Centrale
Santa Maria Novella
Florence
Tuscany 50123
Italy
+39 0552741150
www.mercatocentrale.it

Opening hours	Open 7 days
Credit cards	Accepted but not AMEX
Style of pizza	Neapolitan
Recommended pizza	Margherita; Marinara; Napoli; Pizza Fritta

"Romualdo Rizzuti has undertaken a new challenge on the first floor of the Mercato Centrale to make traditional pizzas as they should be: Margherita, Napoli, and Marinara. Every so often you may come across a seasonal pizza not on the short menu."
—Stefania Pianigiani

Considering its spectacular, if somewhat commercialized, setting in Florence's soaring Mercato Centrale you expect Sud, the food market's polished pizzeria, to have more of a gourmet edge, more flash. But *pizzaiolo* Romualdo Rizzuti, a native of the Sud, or south, specifically Camerota, in Campania, keeps to the basics of his home region. As for his low profile, Florence just isn't that into the *pizzaiolo*-mania thing yet. The selection is limited to four classics: Margherita, Marinara, Napoli (with anchovies added at the last moment), and Fritti (deep-fried). The Margherita bears all the true Neapolitan trademarks, most notably the rounded, airy, black-speckled border hugging unblemished, soft ponds of tomato and mozzarella.

TRATTORIA DA GARIBARDI

Piazza del Mercato Centrale 38R
Santa Maria Novella
Florence
Tuscany 50123
Italy
+39 055212267
www.garibardi.it

Opening hours	Open 7 days
Credit cards	Accepted but not AMEX
Style of pizza	Neapolitan
Recommended pizza	Olives and Eggplant (aubergine)

"This was the best pizza I had during my vacation in Italy. Heck, it's the best pizza I've had in my life. The restaurant sits on a corner of a piazza, and the inside is dimly lit, yet welcoming. The pizza crust had a perfect chew, and the fresh tomato sauce with fresh mozzarella cheese transported me to another planet."
—Amanda Clark

IN ROME AND NEW YORK, SOME LIKE IT CRISP

In 1492 Christopher Columbus convinced us the world was round, not flat. In 2014 Francesco Roscino and Nick Anderer tried to convince us the world was round *and* flat. With soft, doughy, Neapolitan pizza sweeping their respective cities, these two nonconformists opened high-profile restaurants with upgraded interpretations of pizza Romana—the ultra-thin, cracker-crisp, round pizza of Rome. Fond as they were of this pizza style, neither was swayed by sentimentality. "In Rome this pizza was not taken with a whole lot of seriousness," notes Anderer, the chef both at Maialino, a New York trattoria, and Marta, its pizzeria spin-off. "It was more of a quick, easy meal."

Pizzeria Emma, in the historic center of Rome, was conceived for an era when pizza could be something more elevated. Roscino saw Romans were already paying more for superior ingredients and craftsmanship at Neapolitan pizzerias like Sforno, La Gatta Mangiona, and PizzaRé. He and Ilaria Roscino, his sister and business partner, reasoned they could achieve comparable results serving pizza Romana made, for a change, with the best raw materials. "Emma came from a desire to give a new dignity to a type of pizza long appreciated in Rome," says Roscino. To accomplish this goal he convinced his best friend, the baking legend Pier Luigi Roscioli of the renowned Antico Forno Roscioli, to develop the dough.

To put pizza Romana on Rome's culinary map, Roscino and Roscioli put everything down on Emma's menu. "We wanted to communicate the attention to every single ingredient," says Roscino. "Nothing was left to chance." It wasn't enough to note a particular pizza contained tomato, mozzarella, ham, or extra virgin olive oil. With different varieties and producers of these ingredients hand-picked to suit each pizza's composition their provenance had to be specified as well. In a description of the dough mix stretching beyond 40 words, diners were informed it contained wholegrain and white flours from Molino Iacquone in Lazio, organic spelt flour from Molino Fornovecchino in Lazio, gray sea salt from La Guérandaise in Brittany, 0.6 g of fresh yeast (per 2.2 lb/1 kg of flour), and *acqua di Roma*—tap water, locally sourced. In the interest of brevity there was no mention of the 40-hour maturation process consisting of three leavening phases at separate temperatures.

Anderer's focus on sourcing at Marta was every bit as fanatical. His aim, beyond an exceedingly thin, exceptionally digestible version of *pizza tonda* ("round pizza"), as pizza Romana is also known, was a balance of crack, or what the Romans call *scrocchiarella*, and chew. More crack than chew around the *cornicione*. More chew than crack at the nucleus. Taking inspiration from a Roman pasta classic, he introduced his now signature Patate alla Carbonara, a white pizza topped with potato, *guanciale* (cured pork jowl), black pepper, Pecorino Romano cheese, and egg.

The critical success of Emma and Marta proved pizza did not need to be Neapolitan to be taken seriously.

NEAPOLITAN PIZZA OVENS:
AS HOT AS EVER

Paul Giannone brandished photos of his spanking new Stefano Ferrara pizza oven with such glee you'd have thought the owner of the new Paulie Gee's pizzeria in Miami had just taken delivery of a Ferrari, not a Ferrara. But describing Neapolitan brick ovens as the Italian sports cars of the pizza world won't impress *pizzaioli* all over the world who covet something hot and fast from the revered oven craftsmen Gianni Acunto, Michele Strazzullo, Ernesto Agliarulo, or Stefano Ferrara more than they do a Lamborghini or a Maserati. "For me the one fired with wood will not be the end of me," says Gino Sorbillo of the famous pizzeria by that name in Naples. "The oven gives life through pizza."

In the hands of its Neapolitan masters the wood-fired oven is a primordial throwback to ancient baking. It is constructed of firebricks made with local clay valued since the days of the Roman Empire for its resistance to high temperatures. Were the ovens found amid the ruins of Pompeii not damaged in 79 AD by the eruption of Mount Vesuvius, you could imagine Sorbillo baking a pretty mean Margherita in one, maneuvering the pizza with a long-handled peel extended through the arched opening, as he does with his more advanced, but similarly low-tech, Strazzullo model. In little over a minute he would be drawing the bubbling, steaming, leopard-spotted, animate pie from the oven, reenacting the miracle of pizza.

The traditional Neapolitan pizza oven in the form of a cupola is constructed by hand in artisan workshops. Its baking chamber incorporates all three means of transferring heat: conduction, convection, and radiation. The round cooking floor is composed of *biscotto di Sorrento*, a rough, porous brick that's ideal for browning the crust by conduction (direct contact). The curved shape of the dome's inner wall helps carry the currents of hot convection air to every spot in the oven. Heat trapped by the masonry radiates evenly across the round chamber.

The cupola may be sheathed in custom ceramic or marble tiling, a decorative flourish with the power to wow. A clever design can transform the hearth of a pizzeria into the centerpiece of a branding strategy. When Giannone commissioned his first Stefano Ferrara oven for his original pizzeria in Brooklyn he wanted the design of its mosaic cladding to symbolize the centuries-old traditions of two Neapolitan crafts: pizza and pizza ovens. Rather than have "PAULIE GEE'S" spelled out in mosaic he asked that "NAPOLI" be inscribed on the hood of the oven, just above the arched opening. Every pizza would have to pass under "Napoli" twice—going in and out—before it was served.

What no oven can do, not even a Ferrara with a shiny black finish on its 5,000-lb (2,268-kg) body, is ensure a great pizza. Expecting that, says Anthony Mangieri, who bakes in a Ferrara oven at Una Pizza Napoletana in San Francisco, "would be like buying a Fender Stratocaster electric guitar and thinking you can play like Hendrix."

"TRATTORIA AMICI, TUCKED AWAY IN PEACEFUL AND SHELTERED PART OF KARADJODJEV PARK, IS THE PLACE FOR LOVERS OF ITALIAN FOOD."

UROS UROSEVIC P.322

"PIZZA BAR IS THE ONLY PIZZERIA IN BELGRADE THAT SERVES DEEP-PAN PIZZA."

NIKOLA BIĆ P.321

"THE CHEESIEST MARGHERITAS IN CROATIA."

PURVA MEHRA P.318

CROATIA, SERBIA & GREECE

"PIZZERIA UNO HAS BOTH LOCAL SLAVONIAN PIZZAS AND REAL ITALIAN PIZZAS."

ZLATKO SEDLANIĆ P.318

"IT'S REALLY WORTH A TRIP TO CACIO E PEPE IF YOU'RE VISITING SANTORINI."

NASOS KOUZELIS P.323

"THIS PIZZA IS DELECTABLE."

DIMITRIS KOPARANIS P.323

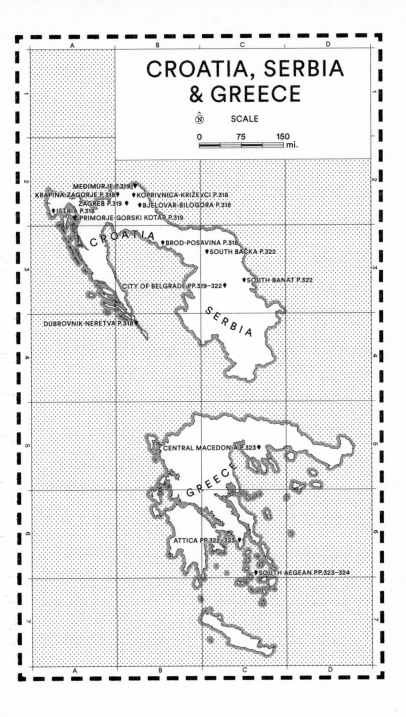

CROATIA, SERBIA & GREECE

$\hat{N}$ SCALE

0   75   150 mi.

MEĐIMURJE P.319
KRAPINA-ZAGORJE P.318   KOPRIVNICA-KRIŽEVCI P.318
ZAGREB P.319   BJELOVAR-BILOGORA P.318
ISTRIA P.318
PRIMORJE-GORSKI KOTAR P.319

CROATIA

BROD-POSAVINA P.318
SOUTH BAČKA P.322

SOUTH BANAT P.322

CITY OF BELGRADE PP.319–322

SERBIA

DUBROVNIK-NERETVA P.318

CENTRAL MACEDONIA P.323

GREECE

ATTICA PP.322–323

SOUTH AEGEAN PP.323–324

PIZZERIA PALMA

Ulica Ivana Mažuranića 6
Bjelovar
Bjelovar-Bilogora 43000
Croatia
+385 43241230

Opening hours	Open 7 days
Credit cards	Accepted but not AMEX
Style of pizza	Classic
Recommended pizza	Capricciosa

"This is a well-known place for good pizza. You can ask the *pizzaiolo* to make a custom pizza for you according to what you like."—Dejan Stanković

PIZZERIA UNO

Ulica Nikole Zrinskog 7
Slavonski Brod
Brod-Posavina 35000
Croatia
+385 35442107

Opening hours	Open 7 days
Credit cards	Accepted
Style of pizza	Slavonian and Italian
Recommended pizza	Slavonian

"Pizzeria Uno has both local Slavonian pizzas and real Italian pizzas."—Zlatko Sedlanić

KONOBA BONACA

Sustjepanska Obala 23
Dubrovnik
Dubrovnik-Neretva 20000
Croatia
+385 20450000
www.konoba-bonaca.info

Opening hours	Open 7 days
Credit cards	Accepted
Style of pizza	Thin-crust
Recommended pizza	Cheese; Margherita

"The cheesiest Margheritas in Croatia. The pies are generously portioned, loaded with cheese, and the ultimate in comfort."—Purva Mehra

PIZZERIA BARKUN

Krležina 15
Pula
Istria 52100
Croatia
+385 52391212

Opening hours	Open 7 days
Credit cards	Accepted but not AMEX
Style of pizza	Roman
Recommended pizza	Istrian; Tartuffe

"The dough is neither too thin nor too thick, so pizza lovers can be happy."—Loreena Meda

KALIMERO

Starogradska 50
Starigrad
Koprivnica
Koprivnica-Križevci 48000
Croatia
+385 48634200
www.kalimero.hr

Opening hours	Open 7 days
Credit cards	Accepted
Style of pizza	Classic
Recommended pizza	Goricka

PIZZERIA ORO-GORO

Marije Jurić Zagorke 25
Oroslavje
Krapina-Zagorje 49243
Croatia
+385 49284785
www.orogoro.hr

Opening hours	Open 7 days
Credit cards	Not accepted
Style of pizza	Italian
Recommended pizza	Zagorska

"This is the only place in the Zagorje region of Croatia that bakes pizzas in a rotating wood-fired oven. This new style of baking ensures even heat distribution and creates exquisite-tasting pizzas."
—Zlatko Sedlanić

PIZZERIJA PANORAMA

Matije Gupca 102
Prelog
Međimurje 40323
Croatia
+385 40648090
www.dg-sport.com/pizzerija

Opening hours	Open 7 days
Credit cards	Accepted
Style of pizza	Neapolitan
Recommended pizza	Maestro

KOKOLO

Zametska Ulica 58
Rijeka
Primorje-Gorski Kotar 51000
Croatia
+385 51263394
www.kokolo.hr

Opening hours	Open 7 days
Credit cards	Accepted
Style of pizza	Multiple

KARIJOLA

Kranjčevićeva 16A
Zagreb
Zagreb 10000
Croatia
+385 13667044
www.pizzeria-karijola.com

Opening hours	Open 7 days
Credit cards	Accepted
Style of pizza	Thin-crust
Recommended pizza	Mushroom; Pancetta; Prosciutto and Arugula (rocket)

MUNDOAKA STREET FOOD

Petrinjska 2
Zagreb
Zagreb 10000
Croatia
+385 17888777

Opening hours	Closed Sunday
Credit cards	Accepted but not AMEX
Style of pizza	Classic

O'HARA

Ivane Brlić Mažuranić 1B
Zagreb
Zagreb 10000
Croatia
+385 13792112
www.oharazagreb.com/pizza

Opening hours	Closed Monday
Credit cards	Accepted
Style of pizza	Multiple
Recommended pizza	Napoletana; O'Hara

"O'Hara has about 20 pizzas on the menu and the best Fiorentina steak in Zagreb. The owner makes the pizza dough without yeast so expect a small one."
—Loreena Meda

BOTAKO

Nevesinjska 6
Belgrade
City of Belgrade 11000
Serbia
+381 113446770
www.pizzabotako.rs

Opening hours	Open 7 days
Credit cards	Accepted but not AMEX
Style of pizza	Italian
Recommended pizza	Mediterraneo

"Botako combines traditional Italian cuisine with local tradition. The pizzas have abundant sauce, ingredients are fresh, and service is fast."
—Danijela Pantić Vlahović

CASA RESTAURANT

Mekenzijeva 24
Belgrade
City of Belgrade 11000
Serbia
+381 112421554
www.casarestoran.com

Opening hours	Open 7 days
Credit cards	Accepted
Style of pizza	Neapolitan
Recommended pizza	Pizza Casa

"Casa Restaurant is decorated in a Tuscan style. Its dishes are of moderate size and always fresh."
—Ivo Andric

CEZAR

Dušana Vukasovića 61A
Belgrade
City of Belgrade 11070
Serbia
+381 658338003

Opening hours	Open 7 days
Credit cards	Not accepted
Style of pizza	Italian
Recommended pizza	Margherita

"Located in New Belgrade's high-rise neighborhood, Cezar offers excellent service, superior food, and pleasant and professional staff."—Dejan Stanković

CUOCO

Bulevar Kralja Aleksandra 250
Belgrade
City of Belgrade 11000
Serbia
+381 112444440
www.cuocorestoran.com

Opening hours	Open 7 days
Credit cards	Not accepted
Style of pizza	Italian
Recommended pizza	Contadina

"The pizza is excellent."—Jovica Jovicic

DRUGA LA PIAZZA

Karadjordjeva 2–4
Belgrade
City of Belgrade 11000
Serbia
+381 113398333

Opening hours	Open 7 days
Credit cards	Accepted
Style of pizza	Roman and Neapolitan
Recommended pizza	Capricciosa; Pancetta

"Druga's handmade wood-burning oven makes all the difference and gives its pizzas a crispy thin crust that is difficult to achieve. When I close my eyes and think of pizza, this is what comes to mind first."
—Vanja Puskar

DUOMO

Strahinjića Bana 66A
Belgrade
City of Belgrade 11000
Serbia
+381 113036076
www.duomo.rs

Opening hours	Open 7 days
Credit cards	Accepted
Style of pizza	Italian
Recommended pizza	Artichoke

LAVINA

Đorđa Stanojevića 9V
Belgrade
City of Belgrade 11070
Serbia
+381 116302112
www.restoranlavina.rs

Opening hours	Open 7 days
Credit cards	Accepted
Style of pizza	Italian
Recommended pizza	Four Cheese with Prosciutto, Arugula (rocket), and Cherry Tomato

"The restaurant is located in the Belville neighborhood of New Belgrade. It has a very interesting interior and a large selection of Italian food and wine."
—Nikola Bić

LA PIAZZA

Milesevska 54
Belgrade
City of Belgrade 11000
Serbia
+381 113836634

Opening hours	Open 7 days
Credit cards	Accepted
Style of pizza	Ligurian
Recommended pizza	Dassi

PICERIJA ATOS

Bulevar Arsenija Carnojevica 95
Belgrade
City of Belgrade 1070
Serbia
+381 1131131091
www.picerija-atos.com

Opening hours	Closed Sunday
Credit cards	Accepted
Style of pizza	Italian
Recommended pizza	Parma

PIZZA BAR

Bulevar Mihajla Pupina 165
Belgrade
City of Belgrade 11070
Serbia
+381 112225467
www.pizzabar.rs

Opening hours	Open 7 days
Credit cards	Accepted but not AMEX
Style of pizza	Chicago deep-dish
Recommended pizza	Black Delight; Inverno; Pepperoni; Verona Nero

"Pizza Bar is the only pizzeria in Belgrade that serves deep-pan pizza."—Nikola Bić

Chicago design inspires this New Belgrade pizza emporium, in the shape of its golden deep-dish pizzas and its modern architecture. The plate-glass facade encloses a soaring space with a playful mix of fixtures and fittings. Like all deep-dish options, the Inverno, with ham, bell peppers, barbecue sauce, olives, mushrooms, and two Serbian cheeses, is baked in a conveyer oven. Thin-crusted pizzas are cooked in a stone oven at a higher temperature, if not *that* hot: two distinctive varieties, Verona Nero and Black Delight, are blackened, not from charring, but through the addition of squid ink to the dough.

PIZZERIA OLA-LA

Vidikovacki Venac 3
Belgrade
City of Belgrade 11090
Serbia
+381 631110120

Opening hours	Open 7 days
Credit cards	Not accepted
Style of pizza	Italian
Recommended pizza	Capricciosa

POMODORO

Hilandarska 32
Belgrade
City of Belgrade 11000
Serbia
+381 113345405
www.pomodoro.rs

Opening hours	Open 7 days
Credit cards	Accepted
Style of pizza	Italian
Recommended pizza	Mafiosa

"Whoever designed the Mafiosa pizza (mozzarella, tomato sauce, ham, pepperoni, chiles, garlic, olives, and oregano) did it with lots of emotion."
—Dejan Stanković

RESTORAN PICERIJA GULI

Skadarska 13
Belgrade
City of Belgrade 11000
Serbia
+381 117237204
www.guli.rs

Opening hours	Open 7 days
Credit cards	Accepted
Style of pizza	Italian
Recommended pizza	Artichoke; Prosciutto Crudo

"Modern cuisine, quality ingredients, and kind staff—those are the main characteristics of this restaurant in Skadarlia. Its pizzas are among the best in town."—Danijela Pantić Vlahović

TERMINAL

Bore Stankovića 17
Belgrade
City of Belgrade 11000
Serbia
+381 0628002017
www.terminalgastrobar.rs

Opening hours	Open 7 days
Credit cards	Accepted but not AMEX
Style of pizza	Roman
Recommended pizza	Truffle; White

"Terminal has an open kitchen, which makes it possible to watch the food being prepared."—Nikola Bić

TRATTORIA AMICI

Nebojsina 8
Belgrade
City of Belgrade 11000
Serbia
+381 113863999
www.restoranamici.rs

Opening hours	Open 7 days
Credit cards	Accepted but not AMEX
Style of pizza	Roman
Recommended pizza	Caprino

"Trattoria Amici, tucked away in a peaceful and sheltered part of Karadjodjev Park, is the place for lovers of Italian food. The restaurant has a patio overlooking the park and offers a large selection of pizzas *alla romana*, prepared in the beech-wood oven."—Uros Urosevic

PIZZERIA CAIO

Braće Jovandić 1
Novi Sad
South Bačka 21000
Serbia
+381 216612654
www.pizzeriacaio.rs

Opening hours	Open 7 days
Credit cards	Accepted
Style of pizza	Italian
Recommended pizza	Calzone with Smoked Ham, Mushrooms, Kackavalj Cheese, Sour Cream, and Horseradish

PIZZERIA MASTERS

Mate Matejića 6A
Vršac
South Banat 26300
Serbia
+381 13837000
www.pizzeria-masters.rs

Opening hours	Open 7 days
Credit cards	Accepted but not AMEX
Style of pizza	Italian
Recommended pizza	White

"Situated in a beautiful location in Vršac, Pizzeria Masters has a large and varied selection of Italian food. The ingredients are fresh and the toppings are generous and tasty."
—Danijela Pantić Vlahović

MARGHERITA PIZZA ARTIGIANALE

Kifisias Avenue 363
Athens
Attica 14671
Greece
+30 2114081132
www.pizzamargherita.gr

Opening hours	Open 7 days
Credit cards	Not accepted
Style of pizza	Italian
Recommended pizza	Egeo; Orientale

"This small, cute pizza joint is ideal for delivery and takeout, but you can also stop by, grab a seat on a bench, and try one of the Neapolitan-style pizzas, which are baked in a wood-fired oven. Classic yet original pizzas combine Italian and Greek ingredients, creating an everyday gourmet effect that is approachable and interesting."
—Angela Stamatiadou

VEZENE

Vrasida 11
Athens
Attica 11528
Greece
+30 2107232002
www.vezene.gr

Opening hours	Closed Sunday
Credit cards	Accepted
Style of pizza	Italian
Recommended pizza	Aubergine and Smoked Metsovone Cheese; Baby Lamb

"Vezene is more of a restaurant than a pizzeria.
Meat is a strong point and the pasta is also good,
but the three or four choices of pizza offered, baked
in a wood-fired oven, are some of the best to be
found in Athens. The crust is fluffy and crisp, the
topping ingredients are excellent, and the flavor
combinations are balanced and unusual."
—Angela Stamatiadou

DA LEONARDO

Filippou 50
Thessaloniki
Central Macedonia 55535
Greece
+30 2310323377
www.daleonardo.gr

Opening hours	Open 7 days
Credit cards	Accepted but not AMEX
Style of pizza	Italian thin-crust
Recommended pizza	Margherita (with extra fresh arugula/rocket on the side and drizzled with spicy oil)

"With a thin crust and Da Leonardo's wonderful
signature tomato sauce, this pizza is delectable."
—Dimitris Koparanis

PIZZA PLEASE

Georgiou Stavrou 9
Thessaloniki
Central Macedonia 56423
Greece
+30 2310278777

Opening hours	Closed Sunday
Credit cards	Not accepted
Style of pizza	Neapolitan
Recommended pizza	Contadina; Marinara

"The dough is aged for 12 hours and then baked
at high temperature. It is crisp with large bubbles—
heaven."—Dimitris Koparanis

PIZZA POSELLI

2 Vilara and Siggrou Street
Thessaloniki
Central Macedonia 54625
Greece
+30 2314019687

Opening hours	Closed Sunday
Credit cards	Not accepted
Style of pizza	Italian
Recommended pizza	Artichoke; Truffle Oil and Buffalo Mozzarella

"Pizza Poselli is opposite La Doze, one of the city's
best bars, and it is open till the early hours."
—Dimitris Koparanis

CACIO E PEPE

Via 25 Marzo
Fira
Santorini
South Aegean 84700
Greece
+30 2286024971
www.cacioepepe.gr

Opening hours	Open 7 days
Credit cards	Accepted
Style of pizza	Italian
Recommended pizza	Basil, Mozzarella, and Tomato

"Although this restaurant's location isn't the best,
it's really worth a trip to Cacio e Pepe if you're visiting
Santorini."—Nasos Kouzelis

LA OPERA DI COSTA

Agios Georgios Beach
Perivolos
Santorini
South Aegean 84700
Greece
+30 2286083439
www.laoperadicosta.com

Opening hours...Open 7 days
Credit cards......................................Accepted but not AMEX
Style of pizza..Italian
Recommended pizza...Seafood

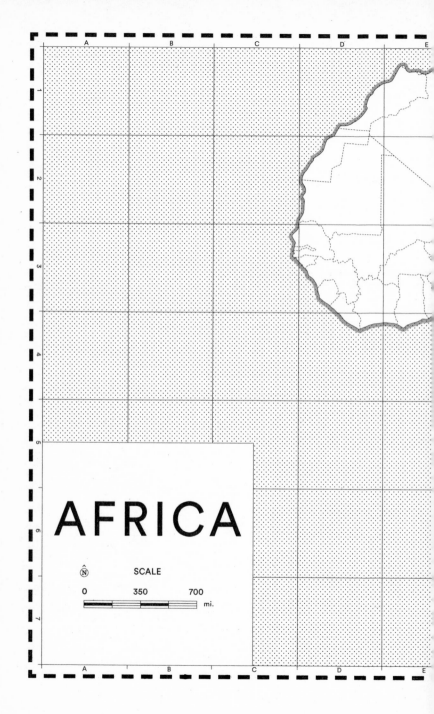

AFRICA

N̂

SCALE

0   350   700

mi.

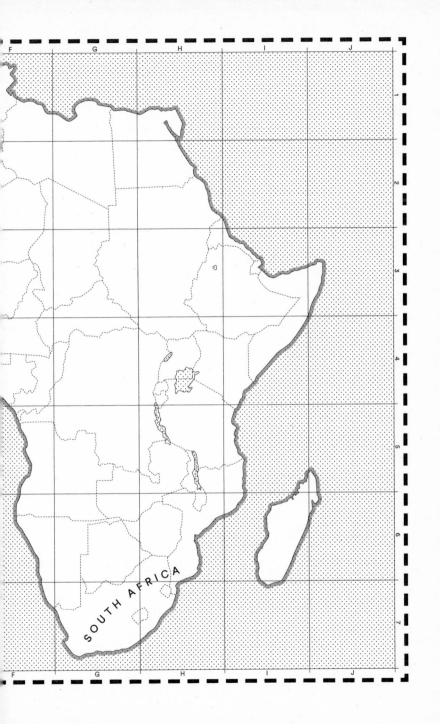

SOUTH AFRICA

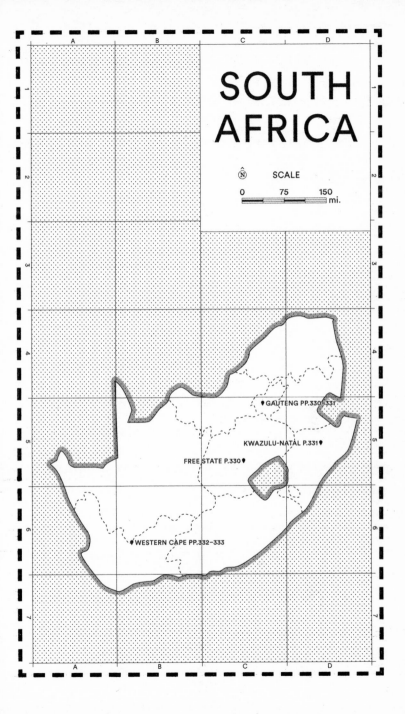

SOUTH AFRICA

N

SCALE

0   75   150 mi.

GAUTENG PP.330–331

KWAZULU-NATAL P.331

FREE STATE P.330

WESTERN CAPE PP.332–333

MOSAIC PIZZERIA

Van Zyl Street
Clarens
Free State 9707
South Africa
+27 582561884

Opening hours...Closed Monday
Credit cards...................................Accepted but not AMEX
Style of pizza...Neapolitan

"It is hard to find good food in the superbly pretty mountain village of Clarens in the Eastern Free State. Mosaic Pizzeria is an exception to the rule. It serves cracklingly crisp thin-based wood-fired pizzas. Pizza toppings range from traditional (artichokes, olives, salami) to wacky (cranberry, halloumi, marshmallow)."
—Anna Trapido

CNR CAFÉ

Corner Buckingham and Rothesay Avenues
Johannesburg
Gauteng 2196
South Africa
+27 118802244
www.cnrcafe.co.za

Opening hours..Open 7 days
Credit cards..Accepted
Style of pizza...Wood-fired
Recommended pizza.................Cream-dipped Buffalo-milk
Mozzarella, Zucchini (courgette), and Prosciutto on a
Tomato Base

"A giant pizza oven occupies part of the restaurant and is a work of art, covered in mosaics with pieces of vintage crockery and cutlery worked into the pattern. What comes out of the oven is just as beautiful: thin-crust pizza dough is made in the traditional northern Italian way with toppings that do not smother or dominate but add to the perfect pizza experience."
—Sue de Groot

COL'CACCHIO PIZZARIA

Shop 6A, Phase 6, Northgate Shopping Centre
Johannesburg
Gauteng 2169
South Africa
+27 117944422
www.colcacchio.co.za

Opening hours..Open 7 days
Credit cards..Accepted
Style of pizza...Wood-fired
Recommended pizza...Carpe Funghi

"Toppings are not only creative and original but ingredients are always fresh and pizzas are not buried under cheese, so the toppings can be fully appreciated. The option to order pizzas 'half and half' is great for those who can't choose one."—Adele Stiehler

FRANCO'S PIZZERIA AND TRATTORIA

54 Tyrone Avenue
Johannesburg
Gauteng 2193
South Africa
+27 116465449
www.francoforleo.co.za

Opening hours...Closed Monday
Credit cards...................................Accepted but not AMEX
Style of pizza............................Sturdy wood-fired crust and
traditional toppings
Recommended pizza...Dall'Orto

"Franco Forleo and his family are pillars of the Italian community in Johannesburg. Since it opened in 1987, Franco's has become known as 'the dining room of Parkview' for its warm atmosphere and excellent food. It feels like you are eating in the home of a big, happy Italian family. It does a roaring trade in both sit-down and takeout pizza."—Sue de Groot

LUCA'S RISTORANTE ITALIANO

Rivonia Crossing Phase 2
3 Achter Road
Johannesburg
Gauteng 2191
South Africa
+27 112341085
www.lucasristorante.co.za

Opening hours...Closed Monday
Credit cards..Accepted
Style of pizza...Traditional
Recommended pizza...................................Margherita; Regina

"Great pizzas and great service from a true Italian."
—George Dalla Cia

TRABELLA

Illovo Junction
Corner Oxford Road and Corlett Drive
Johannesburg
Gauteng 2196
South Africa
+27 114420413

Opening hours	Open 7 days
Credit cards	Accepted
Style of pizza	Wood-fired with modern fusion toppings
Recommended pizza	Tre Colori

"A restaurant on the junction of two traffic-heavy Johannesburg roads might not be everyone's first choice of location, but Trabella is calm inside and constantly full because of the exceptionally good food. Twelve inventive pizza toppings range from plain Margherita, to brie and cranberries, to shrimp (prawns) in honey teriyaki with fresh cilantro (coriander), and chile."—Sue de Groot

FUMO

Groenkloof Plaza
43 Bronkhorst Street
Pretoria
Gauteng 0181
South Africa
+27 123460916
www.fumo.co.za

Opening hours	Open 7 days
Credit cards	Accepted
Style of pizza	Neapolitan wood-fired
Recommended pizza	Capricciosa; Diavolo

"This is as close to a Neapolitan-style pizza that you will find in this part of the world. A bready-but-light base, slightly charred and deliciously smoky, topped with quality ingredients and just enough cheese that rest of the ingredients can be appreciated. The restaurant actually caters for a more upmarket crowd, but its pizzas are the best comfort food."
—Adele Stiehler

RITROVO RISTORANTE

103 Club Avenue
Pretoria
Gauteng 0065
South Africa
+27 124605173
www.ritrovoristorante.com

Opening hours	Closed Monday
Credit cards	Accepted
Style of pizza	Neapolitan
Recommended pizza	Napoletana

"Ritrovo comprises an informal salumeria with a curved picture window overlooking undulating hills, and a smarter dining room much favored by the rich and famous. The scope of the clientele is mind-blowing—somehow Giovanni and Fortunato Mazzone manage to simultaneously feed the mayor, the minister, and a family with toddlers without anyone feeling short-changed. Everyone feels loved and attended to but never smothered or intruded upon. The Neapolitan-style pizzas are like great ancient flatbreads, wood-fired and slightly blistered on the bottom, with buffalo mozzarella and classic toppings—anchovies, olives (grown at the chef's own farm), salami etc.—none of this cilantro (coriander) and Thai chicken nonsense."—Anna Trapido

AL FIRENZE

21 Ray Paul Drive
Durban
KwaZulu-Natal 4019
South Africa
+27 315725559
www.alfirenze.co.za

Opening hours	Closed Monday
Credit cards	Accepted
Style of pizza	Authentic
Recommended pizza	Seafood

"Old-fashioned but charming."—Marc Kent

BOCCA

Corner Bree and Wale Streets
Cape Town
Western Cape 8000
South Africa
+27 214220188
www.bocca.co.za

Opening hours...Closed Sunday
Credit cards.................................Accepted but not AMEX
Style of pizza..Authentic
Recommended pizza...Lady Zaza

"Bocca is a small modern space offering an authentic pizza base that's made using proper flour. I love the soft thin base that's airy and elastic."
—Abigail Donnelly

BURRATA

The Old Biscuit Mill
375 Albert Road
Cape Town
Western Cape 7925
South Africa
+27 214476505
www.burrata.co.za

Opening hours...Closed Sunday
Credit cards..Accepted
Style of pizza....................................Neapolitan wood-fired
Recommended pizza...................Diavolo; Ham and Arugula
(rocket); Sausage

"The owners imported a hand-built pizza oven made by a family business in Naples. This reaches higher temperatures than the average pizza oven, which is evident in the fresh, crispy base and bubbling topping. The location is trendy and relaxed, conducive to long lunches or dinners. Pizzas are topped with a few simple, fresh ingredients that combine intense flavors (a welcome change from those that try to stuff a global smorgasbord on top of the poor pizza)."
—Sue de Groot

"The Neapolitan-style base and technique is (almost) unique to Burrata in the Cape Town scene."
—Marc Kent

COL'CACCHIO PIZZARIA

Shop 2, Redefine North Wharf
42 Hans Strijdom Avenue
Cape Town
Western Cape 8001
South Africa
+27 214194848
www.colcacchio.co.za

Opening hours...Open 7 days
Credit cards..Accepted
Style of pizza...Wood-fired thin-crust
Recommended pizza..........................Margherita; Stagionata

"The pizzas are always delicious and perfect."
—Abigail Donnelly

MAGICA ROMA

8 Central Square
Cape Town
Western Cape 7405
South Africa
+27 215311489

Opening hours..........................Closed Sunday and Monday
Credit cards..Accepted
Style of pizza..Roman
Recommended pizza...Romana

"The pizzas are extra crispy with good toppings. It's easy to eat a whole pizza for lunch or share one as a delightful snack."—Jean-Pierre Rossouw

MASSIMO'S

Oakhurst Farm Park
Main Road
Cape Town
Western Cape 7806
South Africa
+27 217905648
www.pizzaclub.co.za

Opening hours..Closed Monday
Credit cards..Accepted but not AMEX
Style of pizza......................................Neapolitan wood-fired
Recommended pizza...............Chorizo; Mafiosa; Piemonte;
Trota

"The setting is beautiful, the owners are super-friendly, and the pizza is sublime. Mozzarella and other Italian cheeses (including cacio and Taleggio) are joined by gourmet cured meats and other locally sourced ingredients to create the gamut of traditional toppings, with a few surprises thrown in. You can also order cheese-stuffed Ligurian-style focaccia."
—Sue de Groot

"The 'pizza feast' is a pizza-tasting journey for groups, from delicate *bianco* to really spicy."
—Jean-Pierre Rossouw

PIZZA VESUVIO

Canal Edge Walkway
Carl Cronje Drive
Cape Town
Western Cape 7530
South Africa
+27 219141414

Opening hours...Closed Sunday
Credit cards..Accepted but not AMEX
Style of pizza...Authentic
Recommended pizza...La Bufala

"Pizza Vesuvio has a relaxed, child-friendly environment."—Marc Kent

GINO'S AT DE KELDER

63 Dorp Street
Stellenbosch
Western Cape 7600
South Africa
+27 218879786
www.ginos.co.za

Opening hours..Closed Monday
Credit cards...Accepted
Style of pizza...Traditional
Recommended pizza..Margherita

"It has a variety of traditional and non-traditional pizzas to choose from. You can choose between a thick base or a thin base."—George Dalla Cia

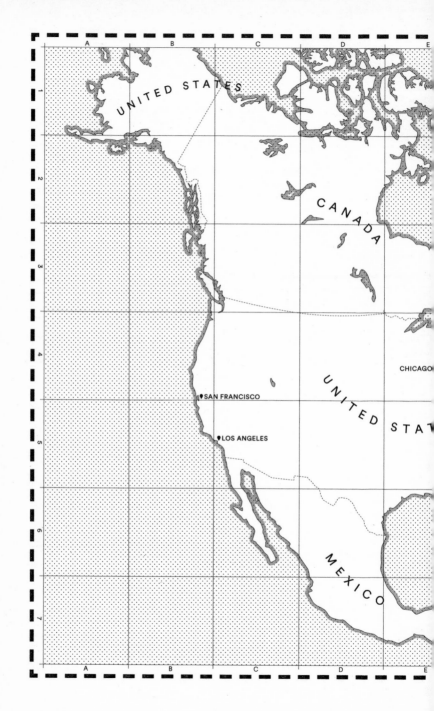

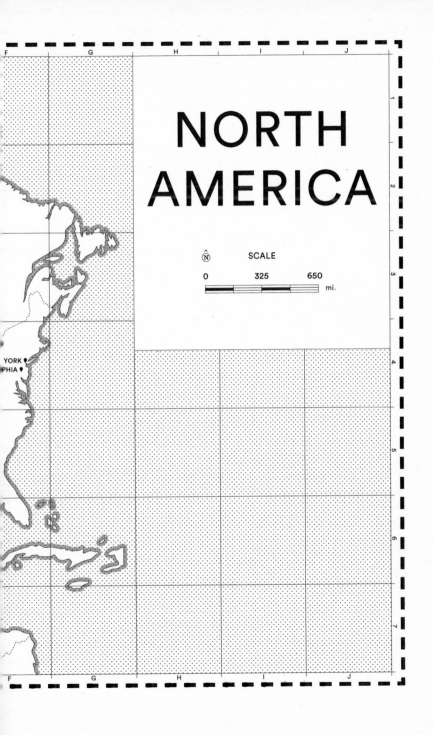

NORTH
AMERICA

N   SCALE

0   325   650
⊢━━━━━━━┿━━━━━━━┥ mi.

YORK ●
PHIA ●

F G H I J

1

2

3

4

5

6

7

"BEER REVOLUTION KEEPS ITS PIZZA TOPPINGS ÜBER CREATIVE AND ITS CRUSTS THIN AND, MOST IMPORTANTLY, EXTRA CRISPY AROUND THE EDGES!"
DAN CLAPSON P.338

"THE ATMOSPHERE IS LIKE A FULL-TILT ITALIAN HOUSE PARTY."
JOHN GILCHRIST P.338

CANADA

"THIS PIZZERIA IS CONSISTENTLY CONSIDERED ONE OF THE BEST IN VANCOUVER."
BILL McCAIG P.342

"YOU CAN TELL THAT EVERYTHING IS SOURCED LOCALLY AND MADE WITH LOVE!"
TERESA SPINELLI P.340

"THE LEMON PIZZA IS RENOWNED IN EDMONTON, THE ONE ITEM PACKRAT LOUIE STAFF SAY THEY COULD NEVER REMOVE FROM THE MENU."
LIANE FAULDER P.340

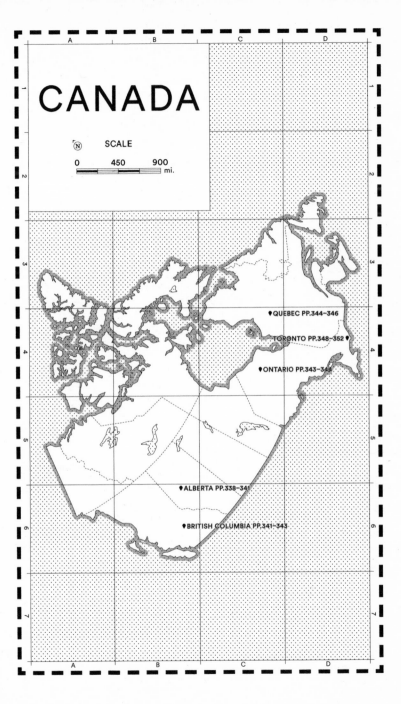

CANADA

N SCALE

0   450   900 mi.

QUEBEC PP.344–346

TORONTO PP.348–352

ONTARIO PP.343–344

ALBERTA PP.338–341

BRITISH COLUMBIA PP.341–343

4TH SPOT KITCHEN & BAR
2620 4th Street Northwest
Calgary
Alberta T2M 3A3
Canada
+1 4039843474
www.4thspot.com

Opening hours	Open 7 days
Credit cards	Accepted
Style of pizza	Thick-crust
Recommended pizza	Ring of Fire; Three Little Pigs

"It uses an old family recipe for the pizza dough."
—Wanda Baker

BEER REVOLUTION
1080 8th Street Southwest
Calgary
Alberta TR2 0E5
Canada
+1 4032642739
www.beerrevolution.ca

Opening hours	Open 7 days
Credit cards	Accepted
Style of pizza	Non-traditional thin-crust
Recommended pizza	Junior Boy

"Beer Revolution keeps its pizza toppings über creative and its crusts thin and, most importantly, extra crispy around the edges! Couple a pizza like that with a delicious microbrew beer and I'm pretty much in heaven."—Dan Clapson

IL CENTRO
6036 3rd Street Southwest, #106
Calgary
Alberta T2H 0H9
Canada
+1 4032582294
www.ilcentropizzeria.ca

Opening hours	Closed Sunday
Credit cards	Accepted but not AMEX
Style of pizza	Roman
Recommended pizza	Gilchrist

"Classic Roman-style pizza is tossed by Calgary's primo *pizzaiolo* Fedele Ricioppo. The sauce is tangy, the toppings top notch, and the crust is perfectly dense and chewy—in a good way. The atmosphere is like a full-tilt Italian house party."—John Gilchrist

FAMOSO
105-2303 4th Street Southwest
Calgary
Alberta T2S 2S7
Canada
+1 4034553839
www.famoso.ca

Opening hours	Open 7 days
Credit cards	Accepted
Style of pizza	Neapolitan
Recommended pizza	Spicy Thai

"You write out your order on the provided form and take it to the counter to pay and place the order. This is a great open, friendly, and airy environment."
—Wanda Baker

POSTO
1014 8th Street Southwest
Calgary
Alberta T2R 1K2
Canada
+1 4032634876
www.posto.ca

Opening hours	Open 7 days
Credit cards	Accepted
Style of pizza	Contemporary Neapolitan
Recommended pizza	Gorgonzola, Figs, Potato, Radicchio, and Rosemary; Potato, Crème Fraîche, Leek, and Smoked Pancetta

"Posto is still very much an Italian restaurant, but it isn't afraid to step away from the traditional and predictable when it comes to its pizzas. The service is fantastic and the wine list is also worth noting."
—Dan Clapson

PULCINELLA

1147 Kensington Crescent Northwest
Calgary
Alberta T2N 1X7
Canada
+1 4032831166
www.pulcinella.ca

Opening hours	Open 7 days
Credit cards	Accepted
Style of pizza	Neapolitan
Recommended pizza	Diavola

"As classic Neapolitan as you can get outside Naples
—they are VPN certified—Pulcinella pulls thin pies
cooked in seconds. Very tasty all around."
—John Gilchrist

SAVINO PIZZERIA

Food truck—check website, Facebook, and Twitter for
upcoming locations
Calgary
Alberta
Canada
www.savinopizzeria.com

Opening hours	Variable
Credit cards	Not accepted
Style of pizza	Neapolitan

"It's hard to believe that such proper pizza can come
out of a truck. Made using its hand-built brick oven
imported from Italy, Savino's pizzas are simple and
done quickly to satisfy the needs of food-truck fans,
but done to restaurant quality."—Diana Ng

SCOPA

2220 Centre Street North
Calgary
Alberta T2E 2T5
Canada
+1 4032762030
www.scopacalgary.com

Opening hours	Open 7 days
Credit cards	Accepted
Style of pizza	Neapolitan
Recommended pizza	Salumi

"A lively, fun, and family-friendly restaurant."
—Wanda Baker

UNA PIZZA & WINE

618 17th Avenue Southwest
Calgary
Alberta T2S OB4
Canada
+1 4034531183
www.unapizzeria.com

Opening hours	Open 7 days
Credit cards	Accepted
Style of pizza	Thin-crust
Recommended pizza	Beltline; Tiki

"I've never had a pizza at UNA that I haven't liked.
In fact, I've never had anything at UNA that I haven't
liked. Great food, always. I frequently take leftover
pieces of UNA pizza home for dinner, and it heats up
perfectly on a pizza stone, crust and all. Now, that's
a perfect pizza!"—Kathy Richardier

WITHOUT PAPERS

1216 9th Avenue Southeast
Calgary
Alberta T2G 0T1
Canada
+1 4034571154
www.wopizza.ca

Opening hours	Open 7 days
Credit cards	Accepted
Style of pizza	Neapolitan
Recommended pizza	Shrooom

"Its Shrooom pizza is unlike any other mushroom
pizza. Sure, some might complain that the pizzas
are slightly burnt, but the chewiness of the crust,
the smokiness of the charred blisters, and the high
quality of the local ingredients—like the garlic truffle
panna and wild mushrooms—make this vegetarian
pizza especially hearty."—Diana Ng

FAMOSO
1951-8882 170th Street Northwest
Edmonton
Alberta T5T 4M2
Canada
+1 7804870046
www.famoso.ca

Opening hours..Open 7 days
Credit cards...Accepted
Style of pizza...Neaopolitan
Recommended pizza...Nutella

ITALIAN CENTRE SHOP
17010 90th Avenue Northwest
Edmonton
Alberta T5T 1L6
Canada
+1 7804544869
www.italiancentre.ca

Opening hours..Open 7 days
Credit cards.................................Accepted but not AMEX
Style of pizza...................................Authentic Italian
Recommended pizza...................................Calabrese

"You can tell that everything is sourced locally and
made with love!"—Teresa Spinelli

LEVA
11053 86th Avenue Northwest
Edmonton
Alberta T6G 0X1
Canada
+1 7804795382
www.cafeleva.com

Opening hours..Open 7 days
Credit cards.................................Accepted but not AMEX
Style of pizza...Thin-crust
Recommended pizza...................................Quattro Formaggi

"Leva is situated in the beautiful neighborhood of
Garneau. It always has a great atmosphere, full
of university students, families, coffee aficionados,
and, of course, pizza lovers."—Blair Lebsack

PACKRAT LOUIE
10335 83rd Avenue Northwest
Edmonton
Alberta T6E 5C3
Canada
+1 7804330123
www.packratlouie.com

Opening hours..Open 7 days
Credit cards...Accepted
Style of pizza...Wood-fired
Recommended pizza...Lemon

"The lemon pizza is renowned in Edmonton, the one
item Packrat Louie staff say they could never remove
from the menu. It's layered with fontina cheese, and
served with fresh lemon slices perfect for squeezing."
—Liane Faulder

RAGAZZI BISTRO ITALIANO
8110 82nd Avenue Northwest
Edmonton
Alberta T6C 0Y4
Canada
+1 7804140500
www.ragazzibistro.ca

Opening hours...Closed Sunday
Credit cards.................................Accepted but not AMEX
Style of pizza...New York
Recommended pizza.......................The Godfather's Choice

ROSEBOWL PIZZA AND ROUGE LOUNGE
10111 117th Street Northwest
Edmonton
Alberta T5K 1X5
Canada
+1 7804825152
www.rougelounge.ca

Opening hours..Open 7 days
Credit cards...Accepted
Style of pizza...Classic Western
Recommended pizza...................Mushroom and Pepperoni

"RoseBowl has been in Edmonton forever, attached
to a lounge called Rouge. But it's the pizza parlor,
found to the back of the joint, that draws the crowds,
particularly for takeout."—Liane Faulder

TONY'S PIZZA PALACE

9605 111th Avenue Northwest
Edmonton
Alberta T5G 0A7
Canada
+1 7804248777
www.tonyspizzapalace.com

Opening hours	Open 7 days
Credit cards	Accepted
Style of pizza	New York
Recommended pizza	Bianca; Classic

"It's a family-run establishment, with a fair bit of show in the open kitchen, so patrons can watch the pizzas being stretched and twirled."—Liane Faulder

BUFALA

5395 West Boulevard
Vancouver
British Columbia V6M 3W4
Canada
+1 6042677499
www.bufala.ca

Opening hours	Open 7 days
Credit cards	Accepted
Style of pizza	Neapolitan-inspired
Recommended pizza	Finocchiona; Green Peas and Ham

"A sourdough starter gives the crust a lovely tang and chew. The pies are (mostly) thoughtful twists on the classics made with top-notch ingredients."
—Neil Ingram

CAMPAGNOLO ROMA

2297 Hastings Street East
Vancouver
British Columbia V5L 1V3
Canada
+1 6045690456
www.campagnoloroma.com

Opening hours	Open 7 days
Credit cards	Accepted but not AMEX
Style of pizza	Hybrid
Recommended pizza	Girasole

NICLI ANTICA PIZZERIA

62 East Cordova Street
Vancouver
British Columbia V6A 1K2
Canada
+1 6046696985
www.niclipizzeria.ca

Opening hours	Open 7 days
Credit cards	Accepted
Style of pizza	Neapolitan
Recommended pizza	Bianca; Margherita; The secret pizza (look on the back of the menu!)

"Nicli Antica Pizzeria has unwavering dedication to the best ingredients mixed with a super-authentic Naples technique (they don't even cut the pizza!), and a healthy dash of creativity."—Mark Busse

"Authentic pizza, fun location and restaurant, delicious sauce."—Wanda Baker

PIZZA FABRIKA

1680 Robson Street
Vancouver
British Columbia V6G 1C7
Canada
+1 6045591680
www.pizzafabrika.ca

Opening hours	Open 7 days
Credit cards	Accepted
Style of pizza	Thin-crust
Recommended pizza	Flammkuchen

"Fun and vibrant."—Wanda Baker

PIZZERIA BARBARELLA

654 East Broadway
Vancouver
British Columbia V5T 1X7
Canada
+1 6042106111
www.pizzeriabarbarella.com

Opening hours	Open 7 days
Credit cards	Accepted but not AMEX
Style of pizza	Neapolitan
Recommended pizza	Filetti; Il Pero

"The classics are great but the alternatives are terrific."—Neil Ingram

PIZZERIA FARINA

915 Main Street
Vancouver
British Columbia V6A 2V8
Canada
+1 6046819334
www.pizzeriafarina.com

Opening hours	Open 7 days
Credit cards	Accepted
Style of pizza	Neapolitan
Recommended pizza	Calabrese; Finocchiona; Margherita; Mushroom; Pistachio

"As good and honest as it gets with the pizza being really the sole focus. Absolutely delicious crust and consistently perfect execution."—James Iranzad

"This pizzeria is consistently considered one of the best in Vancouver. It only makes 100 dough balls per day and serves until it runs out."—Bill McCaig

"Simple, unpretentious, delicious. If you want a quick bite or takeout, this is solid pizza."—Mark Busse

A stylishly crafted communal table running down the center of this whitewashed pizza shop makes it possible to eat on the premises but the long-legged workshop chairs, with their hard-as-steel seats, discourage any sitting around. The pizza crusts are built for takeout, too: chef J-C Poirier uses classic Neapolitan dough as his starting point but gives his lovely pizzas a crisper, firmer core that travels better in those irresistibly cool, red-and-white pizza boxes. The selection shifts from classics, like the Margherita and the Marinara, to creatives like the Pistachio, with mortadella, Parmesan sauce, aged mozzarella, pistachios, and olive oil.

VIA TEVERE

1190 Victoria Drive
Vancouver
British Columbia V5L 4G5
Canada
+1 6043361803
www.viateverepizzeria.com

Opening hours	Closed Monday
Credit cards	Accepted
Style of pizza	Neapolitan
Recommended pizza	Margherita; Marinara; Sausage and Broccoli Raab; Vesuvio

"A family-style pizzeria serving top-notch pizza in an established neighborhood, great for groups and kids."—Bill McCaig

"It's cozy as can be, and while it serves its neighborhood well, many drive from afar to enjoy it too."
—James Iranzad

Vancouver's quest for authentic Italian pizza evolved from an objective into an obsession and Frank Morra was in the middle of it. In 2003 he launched Ragazzi Pizza, taking pride in hand-stretched, stone-baked pizza while bending a bit to Canadian tastes. At Via Tevere, which he opened with his brother Dominic in 2011, everything is strictly Neapolitan, from the centerpiece wood-fired oven to the leopard spots it leaves on the fluffy edges of the supple pizza. Naming the pizzeria after the road in Naples where their father lived didn't go far enough; Via Tevere had to have Naples street cred, too.

ZACCARY'S PIZZA

3150 Oak Street
Vancouver
British Columbia V6H 2L1
Canada
+1 6047371933
www.zaccaryspizza.com

Opening hours	Variable
Credit cards	Not accepted
Style of pizza	Classic Western
Recommended pizza	Oak Street Special

"The proprietor, Leo, the only guy in the joint, takes an interest in each and every customer who comes through his modest door."—Liane Faulder

PIZZERIA PRIMA STRADA

2960 Bridge Street
Victoria
British Columbia V8T4T3
Canada
+1 2505904380
www.pizzeriaprimastrada.com

Opening hours	Closed Sunday and Monday
Credit cards	Accepted but not AMEX
Style of pizza	Neapolitan
Recommended pizza	Broccoli Raab and Sausage; Diavola

"It's some of the best wood-fired pizza I've had in Canada. Always fantastic service, too, and it's always fun to sit right up at the bar by the big oven to watch the cooks do their thing!"—Dan Clapson

"A very warm, unpretentious, family-style restaurant with top- quality pies."—J-C Poirier

ZAMBRI'S
820 Yates Street
Victoria
British Columbia V8W 1L8
Canada
+1 2503601171
www.zambris.ca

Opening hours	Open 7 days
Credit cards	Accepted
Style of pizza	Classic
Recommended pizza	The chef's special

"Amazing flavor and dense, chewy crust. One of Canada's best cooks puts together some of the best-tasting combinations—chanterelle and Tallegio with potatoes, garlic and chile, broccoli raab, squash blossom, and young garlic. Drool."
—Jonathan Chovancek

BREAD HEADS
16 Duke Street East
Kitchener
Ontario N2H 1A3
Canada
www.breadheads.ca

Opening hours	Closed Saturday and Sunday
Credit cards	Accepted but not AMEX
Style of pizza	Neapolitan
Recommended pizza	Margherita

"It is artisanal pizza but not fussy pizza. It's delicious and comforting; well balanced in texture, acidity, and seasonings."—Andrew Coppolino

CITY CAFÉ BAKERY
175 West Avenue
Kitchener
Ontario N2G 1R9
Canada

Opening hours	Open 7 days
Credit cards	Not accepted
Style of pizza	Cracker-crust
Recommended pizza	Veggie

"The wood-burning pizza oven, shipped from California, burns at a nice high temperature for this very thin, almost cracker-like, crust. The bakery-cafe itself is quirky: place an order verbally at the front or grab an existing slice and then you pay on your honor."—Andrew Coppolino

DELS
2980 King Street East
Kitchener
Ontario N2A 1A9
Canada
+1 5198932911
www.delsenoteca.ca

Opening hours	Open 7 days
Credit cards	Accepted
Style of pizza	Neapolitan
Recommended pizza	Lorenzo

"Dels uses a gas-fired stone-hearth oven and hand-stretched dough to make pizza that approaches the Neapolitan style. Slow-simmered Ontario tomatoes make the sauce; 00 flour is the base for the dough. The base of the cooked pizza is crispy and firm, and you can get that bit of blackening and char on the dough's edges that adds depth of rich flavor and texture."—Andrew Coppolino

MARCONI PIZZA
3635 Cawthra Road
Mississauga
Ontario L5A 2Y5
Canada
+1 9052790151
www.marconipizza.com

Opening hours	Open 7 days
Credit cards	Accepted but not AMEX
Style of pizza	American
Recommended pizza	Super

"The quintessential delivery pizza. Quality ingredients, excellent pepperoni, fantastic sauce—the best pizza in the western suburbs."—Frank Kocis

7 ENOTECA

16 Lakeshore Road East
Oakville
Ontario L6J 1H
Canada
+1 9058424777
www.the7.ca

Opening hours	Closed Monday
Credit cards	Accepted
Style of pizza	Neapolitan
Recommended pizza	Margherita

"The crust is not super-thin but has a good resistance/chew, which is what I like most about this pizza. My favorite is the Margherita with San Marzano tomato sauce, Bufala mozzarella, fresh basil leaves, and a drizzle of olive oil at the table plus a few grains of added salt."—John Placko

CIAO ROMA

28 Roytec Road
Woodbridge
Ontario L4L 8E4
Canada
+1 9052642121
www.crpizza.ca

Opening hours	Open 7 days
Credit cards	Not accepted
Style of pizza	Roman *pizza al taglio*
Recommended pizza	Bianca with Potatoes

"Dough is the base to any great pizza and it has a great one."—Roberto Manderino

BOTTEGA PIZZERIA

2059 Saint-Martin Ouest
Laval
Quebec H7S 1N3
Canada
+1 4506881100
www.bottega.ca

Opening hours	Closed Monday
Credit cards	Accepted
Style of pizza	Neapolitan
Recommended pizza	Diavola

BOTTEGA PIZZERIA

65 Rue Saint-Zotique Est
Montreal
Quebec H2S 1K6
Canada
+1 5142778104
www.bottega.ca

Opening hours	Closed Monday
Credit cards	Accepted
Style of pizza	Neapolitan
Recommended pizza	La Caprese; Margherita; Panozzo; Porcini Mushrooms; Tronchetto

"A pizzeria that is so authentic you can easily feel that you're in Naples, Rome, or Milan."
—Jean-Philippe Tastet

"The atmosphere is friendly with highly professional service and great attention to detail."
—Riccardo Michele Bertolino

When, in 2006, Fabrizio and Massimo Covone opened Bottega they were hardly the first to serve wood-fired Neapolitan pizza in Montreal's Petite Italie. That distinction belonged to Pizzeria Napoletana, an iconic joint that's been around since 1948. The Covones did, however, lead a wave of crafty, ingredient-driven places that would change the pizza game in this city, as they had, or would, in so many others. Fabrizio trained at several pizzerias in Naples and then brought home something so old and beautiful it was new: the rustic, San Marzano-sauced Margherita with charred spots all over its airy, rounded rim. In 2010, the Covones opened a second Bottega north of Montreal in Laval.

GEMA

6827 Rue Saint Dominique
Montreal
Quebec H2S 3B1
Canada
+1 5144194448
www.pizzeriagema.com

Opening hours	Closed Monday
Credit cards	Accepted but not AMEX
Style of pizza	Roman
Recommended pizza	1889; The monthly special

"Thin pizzas vary according to the chef's mood, and come laden with market produce. Always fresh and delicious."—Gildas Meneu

NO. 900

1248 Avenue Bernard Ouest
Montreal
Quebec H2V 1V6
Canada
+1 4383860900
www.no900.com

Opening hours	Open 7 days
Credit cards	Accepted
Style of pizza	Neapolitan
Recommended pizza	Prosciutto; Sausage

"On the ground floor of the Outremont theater, in a rather cramped space, a handful of jolly fellows decided to open a pizzeria. They installed a perfect oven, put a delivery tricycle in front of the door, and serve very pretty little dishes to go with their pizzas. The design company Blazysgérard miraculously managed to create an elegant spot in which clients rush to obtain one of the 20 seats. You snack and feel like you're in Milan or in Naples in a little place kept secret by the locals."
—Jean-Philippe Tastet

PIZZERIA MAGPIE

16 Rue Maguire
Montreal
Quebec H2T 1B8
Canada
+1 5145072900
www.pizzeriamagpie.com

Opening hours	Closed Monday
Credit cards	Accepted but not AMEX
Style of pizza	Artisanal wood-fired
Recommended pizza	Magpie Margherita

"Impeccable bases, deliciously cooked in a wood-fired oven, with fresh first-class ingredients."
—Gildas Meneu

SAN GENNARO

69 Saint-Zotique Est
Montreal
Quebec H2S 1K7
Canada
+1 5142736868
www.sangennaro.ca

Opening hours	Open 7 days
Credit cards	Accepted
Style of pizza	*Pizza al taglio*
Recommended pizza	Potatoes and 'Nduja

CHIC ALORS!

927 Rue Jean-Gauvin
Quebec
Quebec G1X 4M4
Canada
+1 4188774747
www.chic-alors.com

Opening hours	Open 7 days
Credit cards	Accepted
Style of pizza	Hybrid
Recommended pizza	Italian Sausage

"Chic alors! plainly intends to go one step beyond basic pizza without falling for the 'bung-it-all-on' option. Conventional pizzas share the menu with bolder ones, like the Prosciutto (with figs) or the explosive Caliente (with jalapeños, lemon, and cilantro/coriander). As a bonus, the homemade desserts are gorgeous."—Stéphanie Bois-Houde

NINA PIZZA NAPOLITAINE

410 Rue Saint-Anselme
Quebec
Quebec G1K 5T2
Canada
+1 5817422012
www.ninapizzanapolitaine.ca

Opening hours..Closed Tuesday
Credit cards......................................Accepted but not AMEX
Style of pizza..Neapolitan
Recommended pizza........................Greenpoint; Prosciutto -
La Luca

"Proper Neapolitan-style pizza. The base at Nina's is
thin without being dry. Best of all, these golden-edged
disks are crowned with ingredients that set off
fireworks in your mouth. Why? Because they have
a respect for the base. The Margherita is divine, but
treat yourself to one of the bolder pizzas, like the the
Piselli e Pancetta (peas and pancetta scattered with
mint and quenelles of mascarpone)."
—Stéphanie Bois-Houde

"This pizzeria is owned and run by two ladies who
went to New York to do a real Neapolitan pizza
course. They were the first to bring the pizza tradition
to Quebec. Bravissimi!"—Paolo Macchi

PIZZA MAG

1465 Avenue Maguire
Quebec
Quebec G1T 1Z2
Canada
+1 4186831561
www.pizzamag.com

Opening hours..Open 7 days
Credit cards......................................Accepted but not AMEX
Style of pizza..Classic
Recommended pizza..Parmesan

"The combinations of toppings don't reinvent
the wheel, but never fail to please, from the
Parmentière (laden with fine slices of potato and
Calabrese sausage) to the Suisse (oozing with
Emmental, Swiss cheese and mozzarella)."
—Stéphanie Bois-Houde

"WELL EXECUTED, AUTHENTIC, AND GREAT SERVICE."

SHAHIR MASSOUD P.351

"NO-FRILLS GOOEY CHEESE AND PEPPERONI PIZZAS."

ROSSY EARLE P.351

"UNCOMPROMISING QUALITY EVERY TIME—ONE OF THE LEADERS IN CRAFT PIZZA IN CANADA."

JONATHAN CHOVANCEK P.352

TORONTO

"I'M CONTINUALLY IMPRESSED WITH WHAT THESE GENTS CAN TURN OUT WITH A FEW SIMPLE INGREDIENTS."

JASON FINESTONE P.350

"THE BEST-TASTING PIZZA-BY-THE-SLICE AVAILABLE IN TORONTO."

ROBERTO MANDERINO P.352

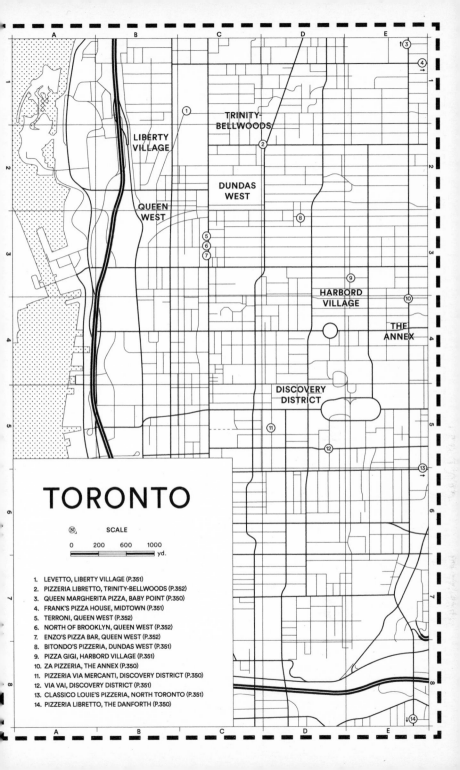

TORONTO

1. LEVETTO, LIBERTY VILLAGE (P.351)
2. PIZZERIA LIBRETTO, TRINITY-BELLWOODS (P.352)
3. QUEEN MARGHERITA PIZZA, BABY POINT (P.350)
4. FRANK'S PIZZA HOUSE, MIDTOWN (P.351)
5. TERRONI, QUEEN WEST (P.352)
6. NORTH OF BROOKLYN, QUEEN WEST (P.352)
7. ENZO'S PIZZA BAR, QUEEN WEST (P.352)
8. BITONDO'S PIZZERIA, DUNDAS WEST (P.351)
9. PIZZA GIGI, HARBORD VILLAGE (P.351)
10. ZA PIZZERIA, THE ANNEX (P.350)
11. PIZZERIA VIA MERCANTI, DISCOVERY DISTRICT (P.350)
12. VIA VAI, DISCOVERY DISTRICT (P.351)
13. CLASSICO LOUIE'S PIZZERIA, NORTH TORONTO (P.351)
14. PIZZERIA LIBRETTO, THE DANFORTH (P.350)

BESTIA

Food truck—check website, Facebook, and Twitter for
upcoming locations
Toronto
Ontario
Canada
+1 4162712790
www.bestianera.com

Opening hours	Variable
Credit cards	Not accepted
Style of pizza	Neapolitan
Recommended pizza	Biancaneve

ZA PIZZERIA

402 Bloor Street West
The Annex
Toronto
Ontario M5S 1X5
Canada
+1 6473459292
www.za-pizzeria.com

Opening hours	Closed Monday
Credit cards	Accepted
Style of pizza	Barbecue
Recommended pizza	Duck and Grapes; Oh Canada

"Jason Costantini has designed pizzas based on
deconstructed restaurant dishes like French onion
soup, souvlaki, and duck confit and grapes, and
cooks toppings before they hit the oven. It really
stands out."—Jason Finestone

QUEEN MARGHERITA PIZZA

785 Annette Street
Baby Point
Toronto
Ontario M6S 2E4
Canada
+1 6473454466
www.qmpizza.com

Opening hours	Open 7 days
Credit cards	Accepted
Style of pizza	Neapolitan
Recommended pizza	Margherita

"I almost always order the Margherita pizza. A true
test of the basic ingredients prepared and cooked the
old-fashioned way. The dough for the pizzas here is
made with Caputo Tipo 00 flour. The sauce is made
with San Marzano tomatoes DOP and mozzarella
crowns the pizza along with the fresh leaves of basil.
Baked in a wood-fired oven, the crust has some
pockets of air and some blisters but not many. The
crust is very thin and delicious with just the right
amount of chew to it."—John Placko

PIZZERIA LIBRETTO

550 Danforth Avenue
The Danforth
Toronto
Ontario M4K 1P8
Canada
+1 4164660400
www.pizzerialibretto.com

Opening hours	Open 7 days
Credit cards	Accepted but not AMEX
Style of pizza	Neapolitan
Recommended pizza	Margherita

PIZZERIA VIA MERCANTI

87 Elm Street
Discovery District
Toronto
Ontario M5G 0A8
Canada
+1 4169011899
www.pizzeriaviamercanti.ca

Opening hours	Open 7 days
Credit cards	Accepted
Style of pizza	Neapolitan
Recommended pizza	Scarpariello

"I'm not one for simple Margherita pizza—I love
my toppings—but I'm continually impressed with
what these gents can turn out with a few simple
ingredients. If you really want to go wild, they have
a two-layer pizza (Via Mercanti) which includes a
Margherita on top and a bottom of ricotta, *prosciutto
cotto*, hot soppressata, and mushrooms."
—Jason Finestone

VIA VAI

832 Bay Street
Discovery District
Toronto
Ontario M5S 1Z6
Canada
+1 4163620123
www.viavai.ca

Opening hours	Open 7 days
Credit cards	Accepted
Style of pizza	Neapolitan
Recommended pizza	Margherita

"Well executed, authentic, and great service."
—Shahir Massoud

BITONDO'S PIZZERIA

11 Clinton Street
Dundas West
Toronto
Ontario M6J 2N7
Canada
+1 4165334101

Opening hours	Open 7 days
Credit cards	Not accepted
Style of pizza	Old-school
Recommended pizza	Pepperoni

"Quick and dirty. As in good dirty! No-frills gooey cheese and pepperoni pizzas. The place is not much to look at, pizzas are cheap, and its panzerotti is the best."—Rossy Earle

PIZZA GIGI

189 Harbord Street
Harbord Village
Toronto
Ontario M5S 1H5
Canada
+1 4165354444
www.pizzagigi.ca

Opening hours	Open 7 days
Credit cards	Not accepted
Style of pizza	Takeout and delivery
Recommended pizza	Tomato, Cheese, Bacon, Onion, Sausage, and Banana Peppers

"I love the salivating sensation when you open the box and the smell hits your nose."—Rocco Agostino

LEVETTO

68 Sudbury Street
Liberty Village
Toronto
Ontario M6J 0B7
Canada
+1 6373503933
www.levetto.com

Opening hours	Open 7 days
Credit cards	Accepted
Style of pizza	Roman
Recommended pizza	Mushroom

FRANK'S PIZZA HOUSE

1352 St. Clair Avenue West
Midtown
Toronto
Ontario M6E 1C4
Canada
+1 4166546554
www.frankspizzahouse.com

Opening hours	Closed Monday
Credit cards	Accepted
Style of pizza	Delivery
Recommended pizza	Diavola

CLASSICO LOUIE'S PIZZERIA

2549 Yonge Street
North Toronto
Toronto
Ontario M4P 2H9
Canada
+1 4163223267
www.classicolouiespizza.ca

Opening hours	Open 7 days
Credit cards	Accepted
Style of pizza	Thin-crust
Recommended pizza	Specialty Pizza #11

"Classico's received Best Pizza in North Toronto accolades for over a decade. The crust is made from durum semolina and then rolled in cornmeal, which gives it an audible crunch and a thin, toothsome base that holds up to whatever toppings you pile on."
—Jason Finestone

ENZO'S PIZZA BAR

646 Queen Street West
Queen West
Toronto
Ontario M6J 1E4
Canada
+1 4163660009
www.getenzo.com

Opening hours	Closed Monday
Credit cards	Accepted
Style of pizza	Neapolitan-Roman
Recommended pizza	Americano

"Traditional red or white pizzas offer classic combinations of ingredients, but most special of all is the Americano on the secret menu. It's essentially a Big Mac pizza loaded with ground beef, American cheese, pickles, and secret sauce."—Liora Ipsum

NORTH OF BROOKLYN

650.5 Queen Street West
Queen West
Toronto
Ontario M6J 1E4
Canada
+1 6473525700
www.northofbrooklyn.com

Opening hours	Open 7 days
Credit cards	Accepted but not AMEX
Style of pizza	New York
Recommended pizza	Kale and Bacon; Pepperoni; Puttanesca

"This a pizza that you can walk in and have at any time of the day and keep going back to have more."
—Rocco Agostino

"The best-tasting pizza-by-the-slice available in Toronto."—Roberto Manderino

TERRONI

720 Queen Street West
Queen West
Toronto
Ontario M6J 1E8
Canada
+1 4165040320
www.queen.terroni.com

Opening hours	Open 7 days
Credit cards	Accepted
Style of pizza	South Italian thin-crust
Recommended pizza	Capricciosa; Marinara; Quattro Stagioni

"Terroni has grown into an all-round Italian restaurant brand, yet the pizzas maintain a high standard. You can count on a thin pizza crust, crisp like a biscuit, with a good amount of toppings. Having the right proportion between crust and topping makes Terroni's pizzas one of the best in the city."—Wilson Fok

PIZZERIA LIBRETTO

221 Ossington Avenue
Trinity-Bellwoods
Toronto
Ontario M6J 2Z8
Canada
+1 4165328000
www.pizzerialibretto.com

Opening hours	Open 7 days
Credit cards	Accepted
Style of pizza	Neapolitan
Recommended pizza	Duck Confit; Margherita; 'Nduja; White Anchovy

"Uncompromising quality every time—one of the leaders in craft pizza in Canada."
—Jonathan Chovancek

"The best wood-fired pizza I've had anywhere. Perfectly executed, completely authentic Neapolitan-style pizza."—Donnie Burtless

The now unmistakable char, chew, airy rim, and saggy middle of by-the-book Neapolitan pizza was completely new to Toronto when Rocco Agostino and Max Rimaldi opened this, the snazzy original location of Libretto, in 2008. Now the city has three pizzerias with VPN certification, plus three additional Libretto locations. The duck confit, bosc pea, and mozzarella pizza proves Libretto's fidelity to tradition does have limits. Plus, nowhere in Italy will you find a pizza topped with prosciutto, buffalo mozzarella, and mozzarella from producers in the Canadian province of Ontario.

"THE MOOSE'S TOOTH IS A SACRED COW IN ANCHORAGE."

MARA SEVERIN P.356

"THE CRUST IS PHENOMENAL!"

JERRY CORSO & ANGELINA TOLENTINO P.374

USA WEST

"JACKPOT! JUST OFF THE OLD STRIP, PIZZA ROCK IS THE ONE PLACE IN VEGAS YOU JUST CAN'T LOSE."

SEAN TAYLOR P.369

"LOCATED ON THE CLASSIC ROUTE 66, IN THE HIGH DESERT OF ALBUQUERQUE, NEW MEXICO, IS THE CULINARY OASIS KNOWN AS FARINA."

MATT RATTIGAN P.367

"J. J. DOLAN'S IS ONE OF DOWNTOWN HONOLULU'S FAVORITE *PAU HANA* (AFTER WORK) SPOTS: WHERE THE ATMOSPHERE IS WARM, THE BEER IS COLD, AND THE PIZZA SO GOOD THAT THE FIRST TWO THINGS HARDLY MATTER." MARTHA CHENG P.365

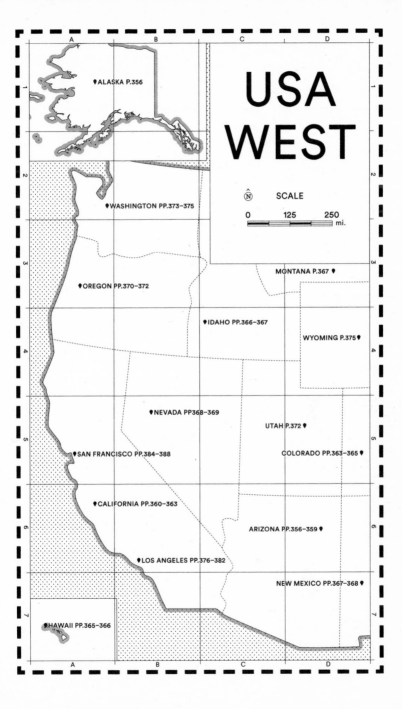

USA
WEST

ALASKA P.356

WASHINGTON PP.373–375

SCALE

0   125   250
mi.

MONTANA P.367

OREGON PP.370–372

IDAHO PP.366–367

WYOMING P.375

NEVADA PP368–369

UTAH P.372

SAN FRANCISCO PP.384–388

COLORADO PP.363–365

CALIFORNIA PP.360–363

ARIZONA PP.356–359

LOS ANGELES PP.376–382

NEW MEXICO PP.367–368

HAWAII PP.365–366

FIORI D'ITALIA

2502 McRae Road
Anchorage
Alaska 99517
United States
+1 9072439990
www.fioriak.com

Opening hours	Open 7 days (Closed August)
Credit cards	Accepted
Style of pizza	Old-School American
Recommended pizza	Pizza Alla Siciliana

"Fiori d'Italia doesn't so much transport you to Italy as it transports you back in time. Old-school Italian-American food, stained glass, Chianti bottles, and plastic grapes lend the perfect atmosphere to someone missing East Coast American-Italian cuisine."—Mara Severin

MOOSE'S TOOTH PUB & PIZZERIA

3300 Old Seward Highway
Anchorage
Alaska 99503
United States
+1 9072582537
www.moosestooth.net

Opening hours	Open 7 days
Credit cards	Accepted
Style of pizza	Gourmet
Recommended pizza	Avalanche; Santa's Little Helper; Wild Mushroom

"When rock-climbing friends Rod Hancock and Matt Jones abandoned their corporate world trajectory to start a pizza and beer company in 1996, they had no idea it would turn into a mini Anchorage empire. Their adventurous pizzas range from classics to more inspired combinations of gourmet toppings."
—Elissa Brown

"The Moose's Tooth is a sacred cow in Anchorage. A social, culinary, and musical hub that seems to be packed all day every day. Considering the volume of pizza it turns out, it's consistently delicious and offers a wide variety from well-executed classics to creative, sometimes over-the-top 'specialty' pies."
—Mara Severin

MOUNTAIN HIGH PIZZA PIE

Downtown Talkeetna
Talkeetna
Alaska 99676
United States
+1 9077331234
www.pizzapietalkeetna.com

Opening hours	Open 7 days
Credit cards	Accepted but not AMEX
Style of pizza	American
Recommended pizza	Game On

"Ask most Alaskans and they'll agree: everything tastes better in Talkeetna. A tiny, funky town at the base of Denali, Talkeetna feels both remote and tuned in. Also, it's a town with a surprising amount of good food including a great pizzeria that serves hearty pies with culinary confidence."
—Mara Severin

PIZZICLETTA

203 West Phoenix Avenue
Flagstaff
Arizona 86001
United States
+1 9287743242
www.pizzicletta.com

Opening hours	Open 7 days
Credit cards	Accepted
Style of pizza	Neapolitan wood-fired
Recommended pizza	Amore oi Mari

LA PIAZZA AL FORNO

5803 West Glendale Avenue
Glendale
Arizona 85301
United States
+1 6238473301
www.lapiazzaalforno.com

Opening hours..........................Closed Sunday and Monday
Credit cards...Accepted
Style of pizza...Neapolitan
Recommended pizza.....................................Salvatore

"In Arizona, you can have an authentic Neapolitan pizza without ever traveling to Naples, Italy. All you have to do is visit La Piazza Al Forno in Old Town Glendale. Pizzas here are VPN-approved, meaning they meet artisanal standards set by Italy's VPN Association. From ingredients used to the baking temperature, the entire process is strictly controlled."
—Jennifer McClellan

PANE BIANCO

4404 North Central Avenue
Phoenix
Arizona 85012
United States
+1 6022342100
www.pizzeriabianco.com

Opening hours..Open 7 days
Credit cards...Accepted
Style of pizza...American
Recommended pizza............................Rosa; Wiseguy

"Chris Bianco has a true love for pizza and all delicious food and you can feel it when you eat at Pane Bianco, even if he's not at the pizzeria at the time. The pizzas are straightforward and perfectly balanced with a superior crust."—Sarah Minnick

"It has a cult following. I am part of the cult!"
—Peter Danis

ISA'S PIZZA

777 East Thunderbird Road
Phoenix
Arizona 85022
United States
+1 6029387492
www.isaspizza.com

Opening hours..Open 7 days
Credit cards...Accepted
Style of pizza...New York
Recommended pizza............Classic Pepperoni and Cheese

"Old-school done right, foldable, and yes, perfectly greasy. Isa's Pizza serves inexpensive, classic, well-made New York-style pizzas you can't find within a very wide radius."—Justin Lee

THE PARLOR

1916 East Camelback Road
Phoenix
Arizona 85016
United States
+1 6022482480
www.theparlor.us

Opening hours..Closed Sunday
Credit cards...Accepted
Style of pizza...Wood-fired
Recommended pizza......................................Mushroom

"The Parlor offers inventive ingredients for the appetizers and pizzas and has plenty of seating. Its wine list goes well with the food and it is open for lunch."—Caleb Schiff

PIZZERIA BIANCO

623 East Adams Street
Phoenix
Arizona 85004
United States
+1 6022588300
www.pizzeriabianco.com

Opening hours..Open 7 days
Credit cards...Accepted
Style of pizza..Neapolitan wood-fired
Recommended pizza......................Biancoverde; Margherita;
Marinara; Rosa; Sonny Boy; Wiseguy

"A pizza like no other. Biting into any of its pizze will
make you reconsider everything you thought
you knew about pizza. Eating at Pizzeria Bianco
is for many a memorable transformative experience.
It certainly was for me."—Roxana Jullapat

"Arguably the best pizza in America."
—Sheri Castle

"Pizzeria Bianco is quite possibly the best pizza
in the world. I flew to Phoenix once for a day just
to eat every one of the pizzas at the original spot and
I'd gladly do it again tomorrow."—David Dadekian

Chris Bianco is the pizza pioneer who transformed Phoenix,
Arizona into Margheritaville, USA. Nowadays young American
do-it-yourself pizza geeks with wood-fired ovens seem to grow
on trees. But there was no such animal in 1988, when Bianco
began making pizzas in a grocery store. With the know-how
he developed in New York and Italy, the supplies he sourced
from trusted local farmers and producers, and the mozzarella
he made himself, he crafted the touchstone for artisanal pizza.
His Pizza Rosa, with Parmigiano-Reggiano, onion, rosemary,
and pistachios, sounds trendy even today. But it, like the Wiseguy, with wood-roasted onions, house-smoked mozzarella, and
fennel sausage, is an established classic that foreshadowed a
new genre of pizza and won Bianco the James Beard Award
in 2003 for Best Chef in the American Southwest.

PIZZERIA BIANCO

4743 North 20th Street
Phoenix
Arizona 85016
United States
+1 6023683273
www.pizzeriabianco.com

Opening hours..Open 7 days
Credit cards...Accepted
Style of pizza..Neapolitan wood-fired
Recommended pizza...Wiseguy

"The quality of Chris Bianco's pizzas is incredible.
This is his second location, and the one he seems to
oversee most often himself. It's not as difficult to get
into as his downtown location but has a charming
homey atmosphere and great patio."
—Cheryl Alters Jamison

POMO PIZZERIA NAPOLETANA

705 North 1st Street, Suite 120
Phoenix
Arizona 85004
United States
+1 6027952555
www.pomopizzeria.com

Opening hours..Closed Monday
Credit cards...Accepted
Style of pizza..Neapolitan
Recommended pizza..Bufala Verace

"Pomo Pizzeria is everything you want in a truly
orthodox, textbook Neapolitan pizza. Superior
imported ingredients and a chewy, thin and just-
blistered crust, with wonderfully wet center,
it's exactly the way the pizza gods intended."
—Justin Lee

LAMP WOOD OVEN PIZZERIA

8900 East Pinnacle Peak Road
Scottsdale
Arizona 85255
United States
+1 4802928773
www.lamppizza.com

Opening hours	Closed Monday
Credit cards	Accepted
Style of pizza	Wood-fired
Recommended pizza	Kicker

"The pizza has a wonderful puffy, blistered crust with the perfect chew and high-quality ingredients such as Sicilian sausage, Calabrian salami, and wood-roasted mushrooms. Tip: ask for a side order of Calabrian chile oil."—Christina Barrueta

POMO PIZZERIA NAPOLETANA

8977 North Scottsdale Road
Scottsdale
Arizona 85253
United States
+1 4809981366
www.pomopizzeria.com

Opening hours	Closed Sunday
Credit cards	Accepted
Style of pizza	Neapolitan
Recommended pizza	Bufala Verace

"Pomo's pizza is certified by the VPN Association and the Associazione Pizzaiuoli Napoletani (Neapolitan Association of Pizza Makers) so you're guaranteed to get an authentic Neapolitan pizza. It's made with a sourdough that takes 24 hours to rise, baked for 90 seconds at 905°F (485°C)+ in a wood-burning brick oven, and topped with imported ingredients such as a sauce made with San Marzano DOP tomatoes, mozzarella, and *Mozzarella di Bufala* Campana DOP. All this contributes to the traditional soft crust that is slightly charred but retains its soft center— a hallmark of a true Neapolitan pie."
—Christina Barrueta

PIZZERIA BIANCO

272 East Congress Street
Tucson
Arizona 85701
United States
+1 5208380818
www.pizzeriabianco.com

Opening hours	Closed Sunday
Credit cards	Accepted
Style of pizza	Neapolitan wood-fired
Recommended pizza	Rosa

"Chris Bianco is a national and international legend of pizza. He pioneered a movement in food and his commitment to locally sourced grains and produce is phenomenal. The menu is simple but well thought out and always well executed."—Tyler Fenton

REILLY CRAFT PIZZA & DRINK

101 East Pennington Street
Tucson
Arizona 85701
United States
+1 5208825550
www.reillypizza.com

Opening hours	Open 7 days
Credit cards	Accepted
Style of pizza	Artisan
Recommended pizza	Speck and Egg

SCORDATOS PIZZERIA

4280 North Campbell Avenue
Tucson
Arizona 85718
United States
+1 5205292700
www.scordatospizzeria.com

Opening hours	Open 7 days
Credit cards	Accepted
Style of pizza	Artisan
Recommended pizza	Chicken Meatball and Ricotta Cheese; Mortadella, Pepperoni, and Soppressata

"Owned by local legend Daniel Scordato, from a family of local restaurateurs. Danny was the first person to bring true artisan pizza to Tucson, putting time into developing a delicious dough and always sourcing the highest-quality ingredients."—Tyler Fenton

CHEESE BOARD COLLECTIVE

1504 Shattuck Avenue
Berkeley
California 94709
United States
+1 5105493183
www.cheeseboardcollective.coop

Opening hours...Closed Sunday
Credit cards.....................................Accepted but not AMEX
Style of pizza..California
Recommended pizza...............Fresh Corn, Red Bell Pepper,
Red Onion, Mozzarella, Corsican Feta Cheeses,
Garlic Olive Oil, and Cilantro (coriander)

"This vegetarian neighborhood pizzeria makes one
kind of pizza per day and it's available by the slice,
half, or whole pie. Patrons eat pizza on the grassy
median in the middle of Shattuck Avenue while a live
band plays inside the restaurant. The sourdough crust
and massive piling of vegetables makes this pizza the
ultimate hippy pie, in a good way."
—Sarah Minnick

"Incredibly cool—you line up, then eat on the street.
Definitely worth the trip."—Konstantin Filippou

CHEZ PANISSE CAFÉ

1517 Shattuck Avenue
Berkeley
California 94709
United States
+1 5105485525
www.chezpanisse.com

Opening hours...Closed Sunday
Credit cards...Accepted
Style of pizza..California
Recommended pizza..........Broccoli di Ciccio, Roasted Red
Onions, and Black Olives

"Along with Wolfgang Puck, Alice Waters brought
the idea of pizza cooked in a wood-burning oven
to California. And when Chez Panisse opened over
40 years ago, those pizzas were a revelation. They
still are delicious today, especially the smaller
pizzette with various toppings. I think this is the
first place I saw put squash blossoms on a pizza."
—S. Irene Virbila

EMILIA'S PIZZERIA

2995 Shattuck Avenue
Berkeley
California 94705
United States
+1 5107041794
www.emiliaspizzeria.com

Opening hours.................................Closed Sunday–Tuesday
Credit cards..Not accepted
Style of pizza.......................................New York coal-fired
Recommended pizza.....................Gina Calabrese; Standard

"Keith Freilich is a one-man show making pizzas
out of a space that seems only slightly larger than
a shoebox, and those pies happen to be the very
best New York-style pizza on the West Coast. Using
a blend of fresh and aged cheeses, it's a completely
unique hybrid between the old-school coal-oven pies
he grew up eating (and making) in New York and a
new school Neo-Neapolitan. There's a fixed number
of pizzas going out each night, and only two tables
available for those who want it fresh, but it's worth
the work, and the wait. Just make sure you call ahead
an hour before he opens at 5 to get a reservation—
even if you want takeout."—Lance Roberts

GIOIA

1586 Hopkins Street
Berkeley
California 94707
United States
+1 5105284692
www.gioiapizzeria.com

Opening hours...Open 7 days
Credit cards...Accepted
Style of pizza..New York
Recommended pizza............................Accuighe; Mushroom;
The Julian

"The best by-the-slice pizza in the East Bay!"
—Samin Nosrat

ZACHARY'S CHICAGO PIZZA

1853 Solano Avenue
Berkeley
California 94707
United States
+1 5105255950
www.zacharys.com/locations/berkeley

Opening hours..Open 7 days
Credit cards.............................Accepted but not AMEX
Style of pizza...Chicago
Recommended pizza...Carne

BLUE RIBBON ARTISAN PIZZA

897 South Coast Highway 101, Suite F102
Encinitas
California 92024
United States
+1 7606347671
www.blueribbonpizzeria.com

Opening hours..Open 7 days
Credit cards...Accepted
Style of pizza..Neapolitan
Recommended pizza....................................Staff's Favorite

"San Diegans were taken aback when noted chef
Wade Hageman decided to open a pizza place but
they quickly realized that being a *pizzaiolo* was his
calling. Hageman's three-day fermented dough has
a pleasingly sour bite and the texture is inexplicably
crisp on the outside and doughy on the inside.
Simplicity here is key. Nothing is over-adorned
and everything is seasonal."—Michele Parente

NEAPOLITAN PIZZERIA & BIRRERIA

31542 South Coast Highway
Laguna Beach
California 92651
United States
+1 9494994531
www.nealaguna.com

Opening hours..Open 7 days
Credit cards...Accepted
Style of pizza..Neapolitan
Recommended pizza...Blackberry

MICHAEL'S PIZZERIA

5616 East 2nd Street
Naples Island
Long Beach
California 90803
United States
+1 5629874000
www.michaelspizzeria.com

Opening hours..Open 7 days
Credit cards...Accepted
Style of pizza..Neapolitan
Recommended pizza...........Prosciutto and Arugula (rocket)

"Sometimes, simplicity is perfection. Michael's offers
straightforward wood-fired pizza with a bubbly, airy,
perfectly charred crust. They don't need any bells or
whistles here; only crust, sauce, and cheese for one
of the best pizzas you'll ever eat!"
—George Formaro

"The crust is is amazing: flavorful, perfectly cooked,
a great consistency, very thin in the middle and
doughy and chewy on the outer edge but crispy
on the outside. The cheese is made fresh in-house
and you can tell. The sauce is really tasty, packed
with flavor, not too sweet but not too spiced, but
a perfect balance. This place is DOP certified—
so its authenticity is a given."—John Berardi

LOVE & SALT

317 Manhattan Beach Boulevard
Manhattan Beach
California 920266
United States
+1 3105455252
www.loveandsaltla.com

Opening hours..Open 7 days
Credit cards...Accepted
Style of pizza.................................California wood-fired
Recommended pizza...Duck Egg

"Its pizze are always playful, almost intriguing. You
can tell a chef with a less traditional point of view
is behind their selection. The crust is baked to a crisp
with just the right amount of chew."
—Roxana Jullapat

OENOTRI

1425 1st Street
Napa
California 94559
United States
+1 7072521022
www.oenotri.com

Opening hours..Open 7 days
Credit cards..Accepted
Style of pizza..Neapolitan
Recommended pizza..Margherita

"This full-service restaurant is amazing from the wine program to the entrees and pizza."—Tony Gemignani

PIZZAIOLO

5008 Telegraph Avenue
Oakland
California 94609
United States
+1 5106524888
www.pizzaiolooakland.com

Opening hours..Closed Sunday
Credit cards..Accepted
Style of pizza..California-Neapolitan
Recommended pizza..........Broccoli Raab and House-made
Sausage; Potato, Pancetta, Fontina, and Rosemary;
Squid and Aioli; Wild Nettles and Pecorino

"Great crust, great ingredients, and most of all a great atmosphere—especially after dark."—Paulie Gee

"The vibe is warm and raucous, kids are welcome, the clientele is diverse, and the service is great. It's the ideal neighborhood restaurant."—Samin Nosrat

Charlie Hallowell gave new meaning to the notion of a local pizzeria when he launched Pizzaiolo in 2005—it is his ingredients and not necessarily his patrons that travel a short distance. Hallowell worked for eight years in the kitchen of groundbreaking restaurant Chez Panisse and developed a commitment to local, conscientious, seasonal sourcing. For the pizzeria's meats he procures whole animals from trusted ranchers. The pizza crust may be wood-fired Neapolitan in shape, texture, and color but its flour is milled in Oakland. The market-driven menu changes daily, which has its frustrations: you can't be sure such original compositions as Broccoli Raab and House-made Sausage or Wild Nettles and Pecorino will be featured. Sometimes they don't even last through the day.

PATXI'S

441 Emerson Street
Palo Alto
California 94301
United States
+1 6504739999
www.patxispizza.com

Opening hours..Open 7 days
Credit cards..Accepted
Style of pizza..Chicago
Recommended pizza..Spinach Pesto

"Nothing beats the serious amount of cheese and the chunky, thick, oregano-ed sauce on top. Delicious!" —Geoff Trenholme

SETTEBELLO

625 East Colorado Boulevard
Pasadena
California 91101
United States
+1 6267659550
www.settebello.net

Opening hours..Open 7 days
Credit cards..Accepted
Style of pizza..Neapolitan
Recommended pizza..Margherita DOC

"I didn't realize how good Settebello's pizza was until I spent time in Campania and realized how impeccably it adhered to the standard."—Jonathan Gold

BUONA FORCHETTA

3001 Beech Street
San Diego
California 92102
United States
+1 6193814844
www.buonaforchettasd.com

Opening hours..Open 7 days
Credit cards..Accepted
Style of pizza..Neapolitan
Recommended pizza..Margherita

"Buona Forchetta imported its handmade, gold-domed pizza oven halfway around the world from Naples and even gave it a name (Sofia). That's how serious it is about its pizza. Pies have that supremely crispy, blistered crust that you can only get from being flash-baked at 1,000°F (538°C)."—Michele Parente

CUCINA URBANA

505 Laurel Street
San Diego
California 92101
United States
+1 6192392222
www.urbankitchengroup.com

Opening hours..Open 7 days
Credit cards..Accepted
Style of pizza..California
Recommended pizza.................Hen of the Woods, Cremini
(chestnut) and Oyster Mushrooms, Goat Cheese,
Fried Onion, and Truffle Oil

"Let the purists scoff, Cucina Urbana's creative,
sometimes quirky, topping combinations make for a
slice of pure California farm-to-pizza-oven sensibility.
Roasted grape and Gorgonzola with scallion (spring
onion), morel, and vincotto on a pizza? Why not,
when it's this delicious."—Michele Parente

BANTAM

1010 Fair Avenue, Suite J
Santa Cruz
California 95060
United States
+1 8314200101
www.bantam1010.com

Opening hours..Closed Sunday
Credit cards...............................Accepted but not AMEX
Style of pizza..Neapolitan

"Bantam is down home and perfect after a good surf."
—Charlie Hallowell

BAR BOCCE

1250 Bridgeway
Sausalito
California 94965
United States
+1 4153310555
www.barbocce.com

Opening hours..Open 7 days
Credit cards...............................Accepted but not AMEX
Style of pizza..Wood-fired
Recommended pizza.........................Monterey Bay Calimari

"The ocean views are awesome."—Tony Gemignani

REDD WOOD

6755 Washington Street
Yountville
California 94599
United States
+1 7072995030
www.redd-wood.com

Opening hours..Open 7 days
Credit cards..Accepted
Style of pizza..California
Recommended pizza.......................................White Anchovy

"This pizzeria from lauded Napa Valley chef is worth
a special trip."—Robert Alexander

BASTA

3601 Arapahoe Avenue
Boulder
Colorado 80303
United States
+1 3039978775
www.bastaboulder.com

Opening hours..Open 7 days
Credit cards..Accepted
Style of pizza.........................Neapolitan wood-fired
Recommended pizza..Clam

PIZZERIA LOCALE

1730 Pearl Street
Boulder
Colorado 80301
United States
+1 3034423003
www.localeboulder.com

Opening hours..Open 7 days
Credit cards..Accepted
Style of pizza..Neapolitan
Recommended pizza...............Mais Mozzarella with Sweet
Corn, Prosciutto Cotto, Crème Fraîche, Garlic,
and Chive

"The wood-fired oven is what makes this original
location of Pizzeria Locale special. It also has an
outrageous wine list, compliments of the shared wine
cellar with Frasca Food and Wine."—Andra Zeppelin

CART-DRIVER

2500 Larimer Street, #100
Denver
Colorado 80205
United States
+1 3032923553
www.cart-driver.com

Opening hours	Open 7 days
Credit cards	Accepted
Style of pizza	Neapolitan wood-fired
Recommended pizza	Cart-Driver

"The crust is thin and not overcooked but not soupy either, and the toppings are always carefully balanced with strong savory elements and just the right amount of spice."—Andra Zeppelin

ERNIE'S BAR & PIZZA

2915 West 44th Avenue
Denver
Colorado 80211
United States
+1 3039555580
www.erniesdenver.com

Opening hours	Open 7 days
Credit cards	Accepted
Style of pizza	New York
Recommended pizza	Pineapple Express

"The huge, misshapen pizzas at this longtime Sunnyside joint are works of art, lovingly slathered with cheese and homemade sauce, thick-crusted and chewy, with big, fat crust handles."—Kyle Wagner

HOPS & PIE

3920 Tennyson Street
Denver
Colorado 80212
United States
+1 3034777000
www.hopsandpie.com

Opening hours	Closed Monday
Credit cards	Accepted
Style of pizza	New York and California
Recommended pizza	Artisan Pie of the Month

"Unique toppings—dollops of mashed potatoes, beer-braised brisket, black mission fig compote, to name a few—and an unparalleled and rotating craft beer roster make this a pizzeria worth seeking out."
—Kyle Wagner

"This great neighborhood spot serves up a variety of pizzas and quality ingredients to satisfy the New York-style fans as well as the vegan, gluten-free guests who crave novel, decidedly less traditional combinations of California-style pizzas."
—Tricia Cornish

MARCO'S COAL-FIRED PIZZA

2129 Larimer Street
Denver
Colorado 80205
United States
+1 3032967000
www.marcoscoalfiredpizza.com

Opening hours	Open 7 days
Credit cards	Accepted
Style of pizza	Neapolitan and New York
Recommended pizza	Abruzzo; Campania

"The coal-fired ovens turn out superior pies with toothsome thin crusts and the proper little char spots on the bottom."—William Porter

"Authentic Neapolitan is hard to come by and usually falls short, but this is the real deal. The sloppy-slurpy New York-style pizzas are terrific, too."
—Kyle Wagner

OSTERIA MARCO

1453 Larimer Street
Denver
Colorado 80202
United States
+1 3035345855
www.osteriamarco.com

Opening hours	Open 7 days
Credit cards	Accepted
Style of pizza	Wood-fired
Recommended pizza	Carbonara

"Osteria Marco has great pizzas and small shared dishes."—Randall Layman

PAXTI'S PIZZA

1598 East 17th Avenue
Denver
Colorado 80218
United States
+1 3038328000
www.paxtispizza.com

Opening hours	Open 7 days
Credit cards	Accepted
Style of pizza	Deep-dish and thin-crust
Recommended pizza	Spinach

"Sheer attention to detail sets this place apart.
Friendly staffers, an excellent beverage list, and
enough variety to please straight-up cheese-and-
pepperoni purists and diners with more arcane
tastes."—William Porter

PIZZERIA LOCALE

550 Broadway, Unit C
Denver
Colorado 80203
United States
+1 7205088828
www.pizzerialocale.com

Opening hours	Open 7 days
Credit cards	Accepted
Style of pizza	Neapolitan
Recommended pizza	Bianca

"The folks behind Pizzeria Locale have long operated
a high-end restaurant in Boulder, Colorado, that's one
of the best fine-dining establishments in the region,
and they bring the same meticulous eye for detail to
their pizza place."—William Porter

SEXY PIZZA

1018 East 11th Avenue
Denver
Colorado 80218
United States
+1 3038308111
www.sexypizzaonline.com

Opening hours	Open 7 days
Credit cards	Accepted
Style of pizza	New York
Recommended pizza	Regular Cheese

"Whether you want takeout, delivery, or to buy a slice
from the counter and then be on your way, Sexy Pizza
is the way to go."—Tricia Cornish

WAZEE STREET SUPPER CLUB

1600 15th Street
Denver
Colorado 80202
United States
+1 3036239518
www.wazeesupperclub.com

Opening hours	Open 7 days
Credit cards	Accepted
Style of pizza	Colorado
Recommended pizza	Prosciutto and Arugula (rocket)

EDGEWATER INN PIZZA

5302 West 25th Avenue
Edgewater
Colorado 80214
United States
+1 3032373524
www.edgeinn9.wix.com

Opening hours	Closed Monday
Credit cards	Accepted but not AMEX
Style of pizza	Southwestern American
Recommended pizza	Howdy Special

J. J. DOLAN'S

1147 Bethel Street
Honolulu
Hawaii 96813
United States
+1 8085374992
www.jjdolans.com

Opening hours	Closed Sunday
Credit cards	Accepted
Style of pizza	New York
Recommended pizza	Spinach and Garlic Pie

"J. J. Dolan's is one of downtown Honolulu's favorite
pau hana (after work) spots: where the atmosphere
is warm, the beer is cold, and the pizza so good that
the first two things hardly matter."—Martha Cheng

PRIMA

108 Hekili Street, #107
Kailua
Hawaii 96734
United States
+1 8088888933
www.primahawaii.com

Opening hours	Open 7 days
Credit cards	Accepted but not AMEX
Style of pizza	Neapolitan
Recommended pizza	Boquerones

"Pizzas here come out of a blazing hot kiawe-wood-fired oven. The crust makes it: puffy edges, thin in the middle, just the right amount of char, a slight tang from fermentation. Then there's the sauce, simple and bright with San Marzano tomatoes as the base. And fresh mozzarella. Prima makes some of my favorite pizzas ever in the country."—Martha Cheng

FLYING PIE PIZZARIA

6508 West Fairview Avenue
Boise
Idaho 83704
United States
+1 2083450000
www.flyingpie.com

Opening hours	Open 7 days
Credit cards	Accepted
Style of pizza	Non-traditional American
Recommended pizza	Zambini

"Flying Pie Pizzaria has a lively atmosphere and excellent rotating beer selection. It's a Boise original."
—Michael Runsvold

GUIDO'S PIZZERIA

235 North 5th Street
Boise
Idaho 83702
United States
+1 2083459011
www.guidosdowntown.com

Opening hours	Open 7 days
Credit cards	Accepted but not AMEX
Style of pizza	New York
Recommended pizza	Cheese and Basil; Cheese and Pepperoni

"No-frills pizza by the slice. A great lunch when you have 10 minutes and 5 dollars."—Michael Runsvold

"Quick, cheap, hot, and filling—Guido's nails it on all fronts."—Tara Morgan

PIZZALCHIK

7330 West State Street
Boise
Idaho 83714
United States
+1 2088537757
www.pizzalchik.com

Opening hours	Open 7 days
Credit cards	Accepted
Style of pizza	New York
Recommended pizza	Cheese and Anchovy; Wild Forest Mist

"Short for 'pizza, salad, chicken,' this eclectic Boise eatery specializes in crisp. thin-crust pies cooked in a stone hearth oven. The spot also serves elaborate salads loaded with veggies and hearth-roasted whole chickens. Servers are decked out in tie-dye shirts, there's a great selection of rotating micros on draft, and the owner's band jams out on weekends."—Tara Morgan

TONY'S PIZZERIA TEATRO

105 North Capitol Boulevard
Boise
Idaho 83702
United States
+1 2083431052
www.tonyspizzeriateatro.com

Opening hours	Closed Sunday
Credit cards	Accepted
Style of pizza	Neapolitan
Recommended pizza	Puttanesca; Quattro Stagioni

"Located next to Boise's historic Egyptian Theatre, this charmingly tiny red-brick pizzeria is perennially packed with folks enjoying Tony's Neapolitan-style brick-oven pies, calzones, and homemade tiramisu. Snag a seat on the patio, grab a glass of wine, and watch the city drift by."—Tara Morgan

VU VILLA

521 West Park Street
Butte
Montana 59701
United States
+1 4067239885
www.vuvillabutte.com

Opening hours	Open 7 days
Credit cards	Accepted
Style of pizza	Thin-crust
Recommended pizza	Copper King

"It's neighborhood college bar that is well known for its pizza. I love the Copper King. It's just damn delicious pizza."—Lynn Donaldson

BIGA PIZZA

241 West Main Street
Missoula
Montana 59802
United States
+1 4067282579
www.bigapizza.com

Opening hours	Closed Sunday
Credit cards	Accepted
Style of pizza	Brick-oven
Recommended pizza	Flathead Cherry

"It's simply delicious...especially the Flathead Cherry pizza. I order it every time I'm in Missoula."
—Lynn Donaldson

AMORE NEAPOLITAN PIZZERIA

2929 Monte Vista Boulevard Northeast
Albuquerque
New Mexico 87106
United States
+1 5055541967
www.amoreabq.com

Opening hours	Closed Monday
Credit cards	Accepted
Style of pizza	Neapolitan
Recommended pizza	Chile P; Zia

"When a pie goes into the wood-burning oven, it doesn't stay there for very long. Your pie will be ready in 60 to 90 seconds. The high heat renders the crust crispy, but not overly so. The *cornicione*, an Italian term for the 'lip' or puffy outer edge of the pizza, is soft and chewy. Best of all, the pizza has the flavor and aroma of just baked bread."—Gil Garduno

FARINA

510 Central Avenue Southeast
Albuquerque
New Mexico 87102
United States
+1 5052430130
www.farinapizzeria.com

Opening hours	Open 7 days
Credit cards	Accepted
Style of pizza	Artisan
Recommended pizza	Mushroom

"Located on the classic Route 66, in the high desert of Albuquerque, New Mexico, is the culinary oasis known as Farina. This place hangs the paintings of great local artists on the walls and has the local Marble Brewery on tap. Farina is a prime example of what every city should have: a place to eat good pizza, drink good beer, and enjoy great artwork."
—Matt Rattigan

GIOVANNI'S PIZZERIA

921 San Pedro Drive Southeast
Albuquerque
New Mexico 87108
United States
+1 5052551233
www.giovannispizzaalbuquerque.com

Opening hours	Open 7 days
Credit cards	Accepted but not AMEX
Style of pizza	New York thin-crust
Recommended pizza	Green Chile; White Pie

"Giovanni's is as close to an authentic New York-style pizzeria as you'll find in the desert hamlet of Albuquerque, a practitioner of pizzeria perfection considered by many to be the best of its genre in the city."—Gil Garduno

PIZZA CENTRO

Santa Fe Design Center
418 Cerrillos Road
Santa Fe
New Mexico 87501
United States
+1 5059888825
www.pizzacentronys.com

Opening hours	Open 7 days
Credit cards	Accepted but not AMEX
Style of pizza	New York
Recommended pizza	Hell's Kitchen

ROOFTOP PIZZERIA

600 East San Francisco Street
Santa Fe
New Mexico 87501
United States
+1 5059840008
www.rooftoppizzeria.com

Opening hours	Open 7 days
Credit cards	Accepted
Style of pizza	Contemporary
Recommended pizza	Smoked Duck, Roasted Garlic Spread, Spinach, Basil, and Peppercorns; Four Cheeses

"The Rooftop Pizzeria features 11 house specialty pizzas as well as 'build-your-own' options served on either of two premium homemade pizza doughs—a traditional artisan crust and a locally inspired blue corn crust. The gourmet ingredients topping the specialty pies will have you doing a double-take. If the air wasn't so crispy and clean, you might think you're in Los Angeles where pizza toppings range from the sublime to the frou-frou. Of course, to gastronomes such ingredients as lobster, shrimp (prawns), apple-smoked bacon, and smoked duck fall under the category of sublime."—Gil Garduno

IL VICINO

321 West San Francisco Street
Santa Fe
New Mexico 87501
United States
+1 5059868700
www.santafe.ilvicino.com

Opening hours	Open 7 days
Credit cards	Accepted
Style of pizza	Wood-fired thin-crust
Recommended pizza	Margherita

CUGINO'S ITALIAN DELI & PIZZA

4550 Maryland Parkway
Las Vegas
Nevada 89119
United States
+1 7028957561
www.cuginositalian.com

Opening hours	Closed Monday
Credit cards	Accepted
Style of pizza	New York and Sicilian
Recommended pizza	Clam

"Cugino's is a great place for a New York transplant in Las Vegas. Everything about it screams NY deli and pizzeria. The food is authentic and made by hand, the entire family works there, and you get a sense of being 'home' when you are there."
—Christopher Palmeri

METRO PIZZA

395 East Tropicana Avenue
Las Vegas
Nevada 89119
United States
+1 7027361955
www.metropizza.com

Opening hours	Open 7 days
Credit cards	Accepted
Style of pizza	Most American styles
Recommended pizza	Mott Street; Spring Street

"Metro Pizza is owned by John Arena who is one of the great students of pizza. His pizzeria pays homage to some of the great pizzerias across the country. You can order white pizza with clams as if you were at Frank Pepe's or a Chicago-style as if you were at Home Run Inn. Metro is a true treasure of a pizzeria and there is no better place to have a pizza party at."
—Jonathan Porter

METRO PIZZA

4178 Koval Lane
Las Vegas
Nevada 89109
United States
+1 7023125888
www.metropizza.com

Opening hours	Open 7 days
Credit cards	Accepted
Style of pizza	Most American styles
Recommended pizza	Sicilian

"Metro is a true pizza chameleon. It reproduces pizza styles from most major American cities, a concept born out of the complex makeup of Las Vegas residents."—Scott Wiener

NAKED CITY PIZZA

4608 Paradise Road
Las Vegas
Nevada 89169
United States
+1 7027222241
www.nakedcitylv.com

Opening hours	Open 7 days
Credit cards	Accepted
Style of pizza	Buffalo, New York
Recommended pizza	Guinea Pie

"The unique combinations of ingredients on the specialty pizzas and a homage to the food of Buffalo, New York, is what I feel sets Naked City Pizza apart from other restaurants."—Christopher Palmeri

PIZZA ROCK

201 North 3rd Street
Las Vegas
Nevada 89101
United States
+1 7023850838
www.pizzarocklasvegas.com

Opening hours	Open 7 days
Credit cards	Accepted
Style of pizza	Multiple
Recommended pizza	Margherita (Neapolitan); Sam Giancana (Chicago)

"Jackpot! Just off the old strip, Pizza Rock is the one place in Vegas you just can't lose. Co-owner and founder and international Pizza Cup Champion Tony Gemignani teamed up with nightclub experts George Karpaty and Trevor Hewitt to create a pizzeria that rocks in every sense of the word. From the stones in the ovens to the dynamic sound system to the taste of the pies, you will be rocked!"—Sean Taylor

"Pizza Rock has a bunch of different ovens to properly cook the crusts as needed, from Neapolitan-style pies that only get 90 seconds in there, to Chicago-style cracker-thin crust, to big floppy slices of New York-style pizza and the doughy rectangles known as Roman-style. And they're all good!"—Grace Bascos

RADIO CITY PIZZA

508 East Fremont Street
Las Vegas
Nevada 89101
United States
+1 7029825055

Opening hours	Open 7 days
Credit cards	Accepted
Style of pizza	Free-form pies
Recommended pizza	Pork Pie

"Radio City Pizza is on the busiest stretch of street downtown, and it has a walk-up window where they sling slices of pepperoni and cheese all night, but I just want to tell these drunken fools that there's WAY better pizza inside—topped with *guanciale* chorizo or duck confit or squash."—Grace Bascos

SETTEBELLO

140 South Green Valley Parkway
Henderson
Las Vegas
Nevada 89012
United States
+1 7022223556
www.settebello.net

Opening hours	Open 7 days
Credit cards	Accepted
Style of pizza	Neapolitan
Recommended pizza	Capricciosa; Settebello

"Old-country pizza that you can tear apart with your hands."—Susan Stapleton

OAK & RYE

303 North Santa Cruz Avenue
Los Gatos
Oregon 95030
United States
+1 4083954441
www.oakandryepizza.com

Opening hours..Open 7 days
Credit cards...Accepted
Style of pizza...Brooklyn
Recommended pizza...........................Commissioner Gordon

"The pizza combinations are refreshing and the pizzas
are very well executed."—Gary Okazaki

APIZZA SCHOLLS

4741 Southeast Hawthorne Boulevard
Portland
Oregon 97215
United States
+1 5032331286
www.apizzascholls.com

Opening hours..Open 7 days
Credit cards...Accepted
Style of pizza.....................................New York-New Haven
Recommended pizza..............Apizza Amore; Bacon Bianca;
Margherita with Anchovies; Margherita with Capicola
(cured pork shoulder); Margherita with Sausage

"Brian Spangler's East Coast-inspired *apizza* most
closely resemble the crisp-crusted beauties of New
Haven, Connecticut, though tradition diverges in
both shape (perfectly round pies instead of oblong
or roundish) and heat source (electric instead of
coal)."—Adam Lindsley

"Bold, expertly baked, cheesy, New York classic-style
pizzas with attitude."—Ken Forkish

Brian Spangler and his wife Kim Nyland will let you build
your own pizza over their plain pie, basically an 18-inch
(45-cm) Margherita. But, like parents setting boundaries, they
won't let you add more than three extra ingredients. It's a
developmental concern: too many toppings can weigh down
the pie as it bakes and hinder the crust's crispy, flaky, crackly,
chewy, airy structure. One extra, *capicola*, is all that many
ask for. That cured pork shoulder, from the local charcuterie
producer Olympia Provisions, is integral to the Apizza Amore,
along with tomato, fresh mozzarella, Pecorino Romano,
Parmigiano-Reggiano, garlic, extra virgin olive oil, and basil.
"*Apizza*" is a New Haven-Neapolitan corruption of *la pizza*
or *una pizza*, "Scholls" is the rural community in the state of
Oregon where Spangler and Nyland started out.

DOVE VIVI

2727 Northeast Glisan Street
Portland
Oregon 97232
United States
+1 5032934444
www.dovevivipizza.com

Opening hours..Open 7 days
Credit cards...Accepted
Style of pizza...Chicago
Recommended pizza....................................Sausage Classico

"Dove Vivi's pizza is very similar to Chicago deep-dish
pizza but not quite. It has a very unusual cornmeal
crust. I love it because it is different."—Gary Okazaki

ESCAPE FROM NEW YORK

622 Northwest 23rd Avenue
Portland
Oregon 97210
United States
+1 5032275423
www.efnypizza.net

Opening hours..Open 7 days
Credit cards...Accepted
Style of pizza...East Coast American

"Escape from New York always delivers a
satisfying slice. The slices are big and perfectly
greasy enough to absorb lots of shaken Parmesan
and chili flakes."—Sarah Minnick

HANDSOME PIZZA

1603 Northeast Killingsworth Street
Portland
Oregon 97211
United States
+1 5032477499
www.handsomepizza.com

Opening hours..Closed Wednesday
Credit cards...Accepted
Style of pizza...New York-Neapolitan
Recommended pizza..Rico Suave

"Owner-*pizzaiolo* Will Fain brings a deep-seated
passion for pizza to his business, and it shows in
every pie emerging from the blistering hot oven.
As with any pizzeria worth talking about, quality
ingredients and honed craftsmanship are the name
of the game here, but what really sets Handsome
Pizza apart is the utter lack of pretension. This isn't

a 'go-to-be-seen' destination, it's the kind of place you go when you want hot pizza that, despite its greatness, still manages to fly under the radar in a city known for ravenous enthusiasm."
—Adam Lindsley

KEN'S ARTISAN PIZZA
304 Southeast 28th Avenue
Portland
Oregon 97214
United States
+1 5035179951
www.kensartisan.com

Opening hours...Open 7 days
Credit cards...Accepted
Style of pizza...Neapolitan
Recommended pizza..................Arrabbiata; Fennel Sausage and Onions; Margherita with Arugula (rocket)

"Co-founders Ken Forkish and Alan Maniscalco built their delicious crust on the strength of Forkish's prowess with flour, water, salt, and yeast, then topped it with impeccable ingredients judiciously apportioned. If you're dining alone, grab a stool at the bar and plan to put away an entire 12-inch (30-cm) pie yourself, but if you're with company you'd be clinically insane not to add the seasonal roasted vegetable plate to your order."—Adam Lindsley

"Crispy, chewy wood-fired crusts so compelling that the line for a table starts at least 15 minutes before opening and never seems to let up."—Jen Stevenson

"The restaurant is totally unassuming and unerringly consistent—just pie after perfect pie of blistered crusts, enviable tomato sauce, and restrained toppings."
—Marnie Hanel

Ken Forkish is the master of his massive wood-fired oven, not the other way around. The 12-inch (30-cm) pizzas pulled from the 900°F (482°C) heat may look ravaged by it, so charred, blistered, and bubbly are their rims. But the crumb of the crust is as chewy and tender as its surface is crisp, and the glistening toppings come out unscathed. The harmony of sensations, aromas, and flavors in—to take one prime example—the fennel sausage, caramelized onion, and Calabrian chile pizza is crafted by a baker in complete control of the elements. Ken's Artisan Pizza grew out of Ken's Artisan Bakery and its successful Monday pizza nights. Forkish and chef/co-owner Alan Maniscalco opened this rustic pizzeria with the large, wood-framed picture windows in 2006. The corner of Pine and 28th in southeast Portland has not stopped buzzing since.

LOVELY'S FIFTY FIFTY
4039 North Mississippi Avenue
Portland
Oregon 97217
United States
+1 5032814060
www.lovelysfiftyfifty.wordpress.com

Opening hours...Closed Monday
Credit cards.................................Accepted but not AMEX
Style of pizza...California wood-fired
Recommended pizza..........................Morel Mushrooms with Pecorino Tartufo, Reggiano, and Gremolata; New Potatoes, Chives, Brussels Sprouts, Roasted Onions, Glacier Blue, and Sunflower Sprouts; New Potatoes with Snap Peas, Pancetta, Taleggio, and Dill Yogurt; Salami with Mama Lil's Sweet Hot Peppers, Oil, Cured Olives, and Oregano

"This might just be the happiest place in Portland. It's always teeming with regulars, especially families, and the booths are packed with people having a good time. You go here once, and then you quickly begin going all the time. It makes the most delicious homemade ice cream, which is a draw on par with the pizza. And the pizza! Let me tell you about it. It's bubbly-crusted pizza and generous, and sprinkled with some amazing combination of seasonal ingredients."—Marnie Hanel

"Lovely's wood-fired pizza crusts are built on a fermented dough that uses a wild-yeast starter, which adds delicious depth of flavor."—Danielle Centoni

"Lovely's turns out the most relentlessly seasonal pizzas in town—if something looked particularly good at the farmers' market that morning, it's on your pizza...or in one of the homemade ice creams."
—Jen Stevenson

NOSTRANA
1401 Southeast Morrison Street
Portland
Oregon 97214
United States
+1 5032342427
www.nostrana.com

Opening hours...Open 7 days
Credit cards...Accepted
Style of pizza..Neapolitan
Recommended pizza.......................................Margherita

"My idea of great pizza is a naturally leavened crust with seasonal toppings and Nostrana delivers both."
—Sarah Minnick

"A pure representation of Neapolitan-style pizza made with great ingredients."—Ken Forkish

TASTEBUD
Food truck—check website, Facebook, and Instagram for upcoming locations'
Portland
Oregon
United States
+1 5032340330
www.tastebudfarm.com

Opening hours...Variable
Credit cards...Accepted
Style of pizza...American market
Recommended pizza..Peach-za

"Tastebud is a roving pizza truck that sets up at farmers' markets and caters special events. The pizzas are big, beautiful, and perfectly cooked. The crust is thick and the toppings are inventive. The owner Mark Doxtader shops for pizza ingredients at the farmers' markets where he slings the pies."—Sarah Minnick

PIZZERIA 712
320 South State Street, #185
Orem
Utah 84058
United States
+1 8016236712
www.pizzeria712.com

Opening hours...Closed Sunday
Credit cards...Accepted
Style of pizza...Utah
Recommended pizza..Mushroom

"This isn't Neapolitan, it's not deep-dish, New York, or American pizza parlor pizza—it's Utah pizza. Pizzeria 712 is committed to sourcing food from local family farms whenever possible. Pizzas are cooked in a wood-fired oven at 712°F (378°C). The culmination of all this care is irresistible, crisp, chewy-crusted pizza."—Mary Brown Malouf

VINTO
900 Main Street
Park City
Utah 84060
United States
+1 4356159990
www.vinto.com

Opening hours...Open 7 days
Credit cards...Accepted
Style of pizza..American

SETTEBELLO
260 South 200 West
Salt Lake City
Utah 84101
United States
+1 8013223556
www.settebello.net

Opening hours...Open 7 days
Credit cards...Accepted
Style of pizza..Neapolitan
Recommended pizza...Vico

VINTO
418 East 200 South
Salt Lake City
Utah 84111
United States
+1 8015399999
www.vinto.com

Opening hours..........................Closed Sunday and Monday
Credit cards...Accepted
Style of pizza..American
Recommended pizza...Potato

"The original consulting chef worked to create her own unique dough for the pizza crust here. It's sturdy but not heavy and is cooked at a temperature that ensures lovely blistering without charring."
—Mary Brown Malouf

HOGSTONE WOOD OVEN

460 Main Street
Orcas Island
Washington 98245
United States
+1 3603764647
www.hogstone.com

Opening hours	Open 7 days
Credit cards	Accepted but not AMEX
Style of pizza	Artisan wood-fired
Recommended pizza	Nettle

"Serious farm-to-table fare and four-star quality. Hogstone raises its own pigs, grows its own greens, and produces pretty much everything piled on its pies."—Rebekah Denn

BAR COTTO

1546 15th Avenue
Seattle
Washington 98122
United States
+1 2068388081
www.ethanstowellrestaurants.com

Opening hours	Open 7 days
Credit cards	Accepted
Style of pizza	Italian wood-fired
Recommended pizza	Calabrese

"It's crazy how good the pizza is, and the toppings are equally well sourced. I love that there's a simplicity about the place but that all the details are carefully looked after."—Allison Scheff

BAR DEL CORSO

3057 Beacon Avenue South
Seattle
Washington 98144
United States
+1 2063952069
www.bardelcorso.com

Opening hours	Closed Sunday and Monday
Credit cards	Accepted
Style of pizza	Neapolitan
Recommended pizza	Broccoli Raab; Ortolana

"The rotund, blue-tiled beehive oven, an Italian import, is one of coolest around, and the pizzas Jerry Corso pulls from it—variously topped with salami, anchovies, broccoli raab, or clams—truly taste of Naples."—Providence Cicero

DELANCEY

1415 Northwest 70th Street
Seattle
Washington 98117
United States
+1 2068381960
www.delanceyseattle.com

Opening hours	Closed Monday
Credit cards	Accepted but not AMEX
Style of pizza	Wood-fired
Recommended pizza	Margherita; Sausage

"Brandon Pettit is a pizza savant who knows the differences between every single square inch of his oven and how to use them."—Francis Lam

"The crust is artisanal and incredibly delicious. Fantastic pizza."—Luisa Weiss

The form and fame of this mom-and-pop pizzeria from chef Brandon Pettit and writer Molly Wizenberg, of the food blog Orangette, stretch coast to coast. The name comes from a street on New York's Lower East Side; the inspiration from the charred and chewy pizza of Brooklyn. The sourcing is primarily West Coast: fresh mozzarella from LA. Bacon, pepperoni, and spicy salami from Zoe's Meats in Santa Rosa, California. Flour from a Washington State mill. Wizenberg detailed it all in *Delancey*, her bestselling memoir. The ensuing excitement set expectations the Sausage pizza easily fulfilled. A thin crust that—under the weight of tomato, fresh and aged mozzarella, grated Grana Padano cheese, and house-made sausage—can take the heat of a fully cranked wood-fired oven can handle a little hype, too.

THE INDEPENDENT PIZZERIA

4235 East Madison Street
Seattle
Washington 98112
United States
+1 2068606110
www.theindiepizzeria.com

Opening hours	Closed Monday and Tuesday
Credit cards	Accepted
Style of pizza	New York-Neapolitan
Recommended pizza	The Farmer; The Stevedore

"The Independent Pizzeria is a cozy little dig lying on the edge of Lake Washington's Madison Beach."
—Thomas Siegel

PIZZERIA GABBIANO

240 2nd Avenue South, Suite 102
Seattle
Washington 98104
United States
+1 2062092231
www.pizzeriagabbiano.com

Opening hours..........................Closed Saturday and Sunday
Credit cards......................................Accepted but not AMEX
Style of pizza...Roman
Recommended pizza...............................Eggplant (aubergine)
Parmigiano

"The crust is phenomenal! It's made in the morning and has the most amazing chew and slightly sour flavor, making it the perfect vehicle for any number of toppings. The toppings are high quality and unbelievably good—the mortadella, homemade mozzarella, and stuffed zucchini (courgette) blossoms (when you can get them) are especially good. Best of all, since you order by weight, you can try a couple different pizza's at one time."
—Jerry Corso & Angelina Tolentino

SERIOUS PIE

1124 Pike Street
Seattle
Washington 98101
United States
+1 2069238012
www.seriouspieseattle.com

Opening hours..Open 7 days
Credit cards..Accepted
Style of pizza...Artisan thin-crust
Recommended pizza..........................Sweet Fennel Sausage,
Roasted Peppers, and Provolone

"Serious Pie always makes great pizzas with beautiful toppings and great produce."—Zvonko Sokcic

SERIOUS PIE

316 Virginia Street
Seattle
Washington 98121
United States
+1 2068387388
www.seriouspieseattle.com

Opening hours..Open 7 days
Credit cards..Accepted
Style of pizza...Artisan thin-crust
Recommended pizza.................Penn Cove Clams, Pancetta
Tesa, and Lemon Thyme; Roasted Seasonal
Mushrooms, and Truffle Cheese; Yukon Gold Potato,
Rosemary, and Pecorino Romano

"Tom Douglas has created a fun, communal pizzeria that delivers some of the best pizza in the country. His technique of adding cheese just before the pizza is finished, so the cheese just barely melts and remains luxurious instead of overcooked and separated, is a game changer."—Tyler Fenton

"It has a decidedly laid-back Seattle vibe."
—Sharon Ardiana

VIA TRIBUNALI

913 East Pike Street
Seattle
Washington 98122
United States
+1 2063229234
www.viatribunali.com

Opening hours..Open 7 days
Credit cards..Accepted
Style of pizza..Neapolitan
Recommended pizza...................Misto Salumi; Puttanesca;
Via Tribunali

"A funky joint with a church-like feel. The pizza has a great crust and the tomatoes just melt and create bubbling pockets of oozy cheese."—Daniel Gray

WORLD PIZZA

672 South King Street
Seattle
Washington 98104
United States
+1 2066824161
www.worldpizza.tumblr.com

Opening hours	Open 7 days
Credit cards	Accepted
Style of pizza	New York thin-crust
Recommended pizza	Roasted Red Potato, Garlic, Rosemary, and Gorgonzola Cheese

"I love World Pizza for its sturdy crust and great toppings and groovy atmosphere. It's a vegetarian pizza parlor in the heart of Seattle's Chinatown. It kicks ass!"—Allison Scheff

GANNETT GRILL IN THE LANDER BAR

126 Main Street
Lander
Wyoming 82520
United States
+1 3073328228
www.landerbar.com/gannett-grill

Opening hours	Open 7 days
Credit cards	Accepted
Style of pizza	New York
Recommended pizza	Oregano Trail; Veg Head

"The Gannett Grill is located inside the Lander Bar in Lander, Wyoming, which is a small town full of ranchers and rock climbers at the base of the Wind River Mountains. You may eat your pizza at the bar, in the rustic dining room, or outside on the deck in the shade of a stately old tree. Stick around after dark and you may see live country western music."
—Seonaid B. Campbell

GRAND AVENUE PIZZA

301 Grand Avenue
Laramie
Wyoming 82070
United States
+1 3077212909
www.grandavenuepizza.com

Opening hours	Closed Monday
Credit cards	Accepted
Style of pizza	Gourmet
Recommended pizza	Apple Sage; New Orleans Chicken

"Locals, students, and travelers on holiday all enjoy Grand Avenue Pizza. From the simple (La Blanca or Mediterranean) to the strange (Thai Pizza or Philly Beef), the chef uses ingredients in combinations that are simply delicious and not overly complicated."—Seonaid B. Campbell

CALICO

2650 Moose Wilson Road
Teton Village Road
Wilson
Wyoming 83025
United States
+1 3077332460
www.calicorestaurant.com

Opening hours	Open 7 days
Credit cards	Accepted
Style of pizza	Neapolitan
Recommended pizza	Tom's Bomber

"For decades Calico has been making stupendous pizzas from scratch with herbs grown in its organic garden. Not only is its classic, thin-crust, made-to-order pizza delicious, but eating it on the deck during summer is sublime."—Seonaid B. Campbell

"THE BLISTERED CRUST AT THIS NEW FAIRFAX HOT SPOT IS PERFECTLY DELICIOUS BY ITSELF, BUT JON & VINNY'S ALSO OFFERS DIPPING SAUCES."

JO MAXWELL STOUGAARD P.380

LOS ANGELES

"MOZZA'S UNIQUE BREADY CRUST AND UNCOMPROMISING TOPPINGS REIGN SUPREME IN LOS ANGELES."

LANCE ROBERTS P.381

"THE BEST NEW YORK-STYLE PIE YOU'LL FIND IN LOS ANGELES."

LESLEY SUTER P.381

"GJELINA MAKES THE ULTIMATE PIZZA."

SOFIE WOCHNER P.380

"THE PURISTS' CHOICE."

S. IRENE VIRBILA P.379

LOS ANGELES

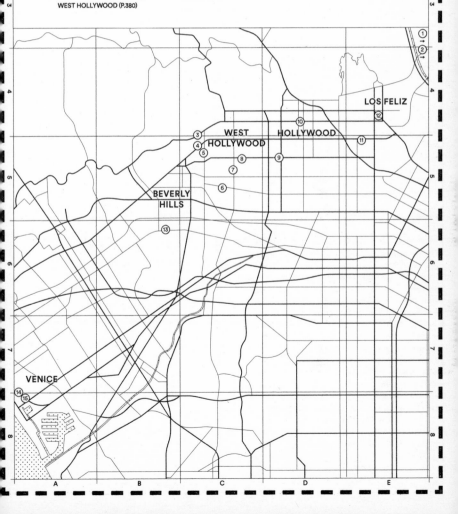

N   SCALE

0   1500   3000   4500
                                yd.

1. CASA BIANCA PIZZA PIE, EAGLE ROCK (P.378)
2. ALL' ACQUA, ATWATER VILLAGE (P.378)
3. JOE'S PIZZA, WEST HOLLYWOOD (P.380)
4. PROVA PIZZERIA, WEST HOLLYWOOD (P.381)
5. VITO'S, WEST HOLLYWOOD (P.382)
6. OLIO WOOD FIRED PIZZERIA, WEST HOLLYWOOD (P.380)
7. JON & VINNY'S, WEST HOLLYWOOD (P.380)
8. TOMATO PIE, WEST HOLLYWOOD (P.381)
9. PIZZERIA MOZZA, WEST HOLLYWOOD (P.381)
10. STELLA BARRA, HOLLYWOOD (P.379)
11. DESANO PIZZA BAKERY, HOLLYWOOD (P.379)
12. MOTHER DOUGH, LOS FELIZ (P.379)
13. SOTTO, BEVERLY HILLS (P.378)
14. GJELINA, VENICE (P.380)
15. ABBOT'S PIZZA COMPANY, VENICE (P.379)

LOS FELIZ

WEST HOLLYWOOD

HOLLYWOOD

BEVERLY HILLS

VENICE

ALL' ACQUA

3280 Glendale Boulevard
Atwater Village
Los Angeles
California 90039
United States
+1 3236633280
www.allacquarestaurant.com

Opening hours	Open 7 days
Credit cards	Accepted
Style of pizza	Neapolitan
Recommended pizza	Diavolo; Mushroom; Puttanesca

"Chef Don Dickman's pizzas just keep getting better and better as he learns to work the Neapolitan wood-burning oven at this newish restaurant in Atwater Village. He's currently going for a crisper crust than Neapolitan pizza usually has. It has an excellent California and Italian wine list, too."
—S. Irene Virbila

SOTTO

9575 West Pico Boulevard
Beverly Hills
Los Angeles
California 90035
United States
+1 3102770210
www.sottorestaurant.com

Opening hours	Open 7 days
Credit cards	Accepted
Style of pizza	Neapolitan
Recommended pizza	Guanciale; Margherita

"Sotto has Neapolitan pizza that pushes the envelope. First there's the big, soft, bulbous crust bursting with a cranked-up sourdough funky flavor. Then there's the best charred leopard spots in the city, if not the state (or the country). And finally there's the southern Italian toppings, all savory and in your face. Once in a while it's a little too much for some people, but Zach Pollack and Steve Samson don't mind—they're in it for the flavor. Sotto definitely isn't the delicate Neapolitan that purists are used to, but anyone looking for big, unique flavors in pizza is going to be happy."—Lance Roberts

"Where do I start? The leoparding on the crust, the gooey center, the staunchly northern Italian ingredients? The petite pies are the city's best, simple as that."—Lesley Suter

Sotto can mean "under," befitting a basement Neapolitan pizza act, or "south of," for the restaurant's southern Italian credentials. Chefs Steve Samson and Zach Pollack developed their pizza dough, a slow-leavened mix of flour, water, salt, and natural starter yeast, at Pizzeria Ortica in Costa Mesa, California. Its success inspired Sotto, near LA's Century City. The classically light and humid template, with deceptively indiscriminate puffing and charring on the border, accommodates California flavors and local sourcing. You typically don't see much buckwheat honey, Bloomsdale spinach, or Maitake mushroom in Naples. The Guanciale pizza, Sotto's biggest hit, is composed of house-cured pork jowl, ricotta, scallions (spring onions), and fennel pollen.

CASA BIANCA PIZZA PIE

1650 Colorado Boulevard
Eagle Rock
Los Angeles
California 90041
United States
+1 3232569617
www.casabiancapizza.com

Opening hours	Closed Sunday
Credit cards	Not accepted
Style of pizza	Chicago
Recommended pizza	Sausage and Fried Eggplant (aubergine)

"To my mind, the best of the old-time pizzerias in Los Angeles. The pizza is often thought to be New York-style, but in retrospect it is probably closer to a crisp, thin-crust bar pie from the South Side of Chicago, birthplace of the founder Sal Martorana."
—Jonathan Gold

DESANO PIZZA BAKERY

4959 Santa Monica Boulevard
Hollywood
Los Angeles
California 90029
United States
+1 3239137000
www.desanopizza.it

Opening hours	Open 7 days
Credit cards	Accepted
Style of pizza	Neapolitan
Recommended pizza	Margherita DOP

"The attention to detail and ingredients is what makes this place special. Its wood-burning ovens are heated with volcanic rock from Mount Vesuvius, which cooks the pizzas in 60 seconds. Folding a slice and eating it will take you straight to Naples."
—Jenn Harris

STELLA BARRA

6372 West Sunset Boulevard
Hollywood
Los Angeles
California 90028
United States
+1 3233014001
www.stellabarra.com

Opening hours	Open 7 days
Credit cards	Accepted
Style of pizza	Artisan California
Recommended pizza	Bloomsdale Spinach and Kale; Rossa

"Chef Jeff Mahin honed his craft under The Fat Duck's Heston Blumenthal, including the dough Mahin uses in his pizzerias. His pizza piled high with kale was pleasing palates before the superfood became a trend."—Jo Maxwell Stougaard

MOTHER DOUGH

4648 Hollywood Boulevard
Los Feliz
Los Angeles
California 90027
United States
+1 3236442885
www.motherdoughpizza.com

Opening hours	Closed Monday
Credit cards	Accepted
Style of pizza	Neapolitan
Recommended pizza	Margherita; Napoletana; Oven-roasted Vine Tomatoes; Zucchini (courgette)

"The purists' choice. Bez Compani is so devoted to his dough that he doesn't let anybody else touch it—or the sourdough mother he saves back to feed the next day's dough. Compani, an Iranian who was raised in London and trained in pizza in Naples, turns out classic Neapolitan pizza from a massive wood-burning oven at the back of this bare-bones Los Feliz space. The oven works at such a high temperature that pizzas—just a half dozen are on offer—cook in about a minute."—S. Irene Virbila

"This is true artisan pizza. The owner makes it every night of the week."—Enrico Nicoletta

ABBOT'S PIZZA COMPANY

1407 Abbot Kinney Boulevard
Venice
Los Angeles
California 90291
United States
+1 3103967334
www.abbotspizzaco.com

Opening hours	Open 7 days
Credit cards	Accepted
Style of pizza	Classic
Recommended pizza	Margherita

"Abbot Kinney Boulevard is now full of great restaurants packed with stylish people, but when I first visited 15 years ago it was a much less salubrious area. I went because I had heard that it is 'the kind of pizza you could eat every day.' The simple Margheritas are particularly delicious, and it is really special to eat freshly made pizza in these surroundings."
—Yuri Nomura

GJELINA

1429 Abbot Kinney Boulevard
Venice
Los Angeles
California 90291
United States
+1 3104501429
www.gjelina.com

Opening hours..Open 7 days
Credit cards..Accepted
Style of pizza..Neapolitan
Recommended pizza.................Four Onion; Lamb Sausage,
Confit Tomato, Broccoli Raab, Pecorino, and Asiago;
Nettles, Raclette, Mozzarella, Parmesan, Fresno Chile,
Confit Garlic, and Oregano

"As you wait in line crammed into a tiny space your eyes flick over every inch of display counter and blackboard to try to make a decision. It isn't easy here. Travis Lett knows how to cook and he knows what his customers want. Strong flavors and local ingredients combine to seduce. The dough is charred in a wood fire with a good chew. Toppings are seasonal."
—Evan Kleiman

"Gjelina makes the ultimate pizza."—Sofie Wochner

"The pizza is the star of a restaurant that's excellent on every level."—Michalene Busico

JOE'S PIZZA

8539 Sunset Boulevard
West Hollywood
Los Angeles
California 90069
United States
+1 3103580900
www.joespizza.it

Opening hours..Open 7 days
Credit cards..Accepted
Style of pizza..New York thin-crust

"Classic thin and crispy pizza with an amazing sweet tomato sauce."—John Berardi

JON & VINNY'S

412 North Fairfax Avenue
West Hollywood
Los Angeles
California 90036
United States
+1 3233343369
www.jonandvinnys.com

Opening hours..Open 7 days
Credit cards..Accepted
Style of pizza..Artisan New York
Recommended pizza....................................Sonny's Favorite

"The blistered crust at this new Fairfax hot spot is perfectly delicious by itself, but Jon & Vinny's also offers dipping sauces. You don't have to be a kid to enjoy swirling those final crusty pieces into marinara or ranch dressing. It is indeed a family-friendly spot but so very hip too."—Jo Maxwell Stougaard

OLIO WOOD FIRED PIZZERIA

8075 West 3rd Street, #100
West Hollywood
Los Angeles
California 90048
United States
+1 3239309490
www.oliowfp.com

Opening hours..Open 7 days
Credit cards..Accepted
Style of pizza................................Neapolitan wood-fired
Recommended pizza............................Margherita Plus; Wild
Mushroom and Prosciutto

"Olio's pizza is a quintessential pizza. The dough is very straightforward without any bells and whistles, but it performs magically in the wood-burning oven."
—Roxana Jullapat

PIZZERIA MOZZA

641 North Highland Avenue
West Hollywood
Los Angeles
California 90036
United States
+1 3232970101
www.pizzeriamozza.com

Opening hours	Open 7 days
Credit cards	Accepted
Style of pizza	Ecelectic
Recommended pizza	Bianca; Egg, Bacon, Yukon Gold Potato, and Bermuda Onions; Fennel Sausage, Panna, Mozzarella, Red Onions, and Scallions (spring onions); Funghi Misti, Fontina, Taleggio, and Thyme; Napolitana; Pizzetta; Squash Blossoms, Tomato, and Burrata

"Nancy Silverton spent years developing her pizza dough and learning how to use the wood-fired oven. The crust is billowy, more bready than some, caramelized and chewy on the rim. The choices are vast, and do change from time to time. At the bottom is a section of purists' pizzas (that's not what she calls it) made with the tomatoes Chris Bianco is growing in California. Mozza is the only pizzeria I know where you can get great antipasti, wonderful desserts, and a beautiful little list of all-Italian wines. Excellent service, too, so it's the complete package."
—S. Irene Virbila

"Every aspect of its menu is bang-on and I've never had a dish that I didn't love, and the wine list is frustratingly packed with perfect pizza pairings."
—James Iranzad

"Mozza's unique bready crust and uncompromising toppings reign supreme in Los Angeles."
—Lance Roberts

LA's award-winning baker Nancy Silverton opened Pizzeria Mozza in 2006 with two stars of the New York food world, chef Mario Batali and restaurateur Joe Bastianich. The contributions of the New Yorkers are less immediately apparent than the bulbous rim on Silverton's crisp, chewy, charred sourdough pizza crust. It embraces the base layers of boutique meats, produce, and cheese with some initial resistance and then only tenderness. When the burrata cheese, squash blossom, and tomato pizza was introduced in 2006, it broke new ground, the only widely familiar ingredient being tomato. The pizza alla Benno, with speck, pineapple, jalapeño, mozzarella, and tomato, exhibits expert sourcing and a sophisticated chef's approach to pizza composition. Pizzeria Mozza has expanded to Newport Beach and Singapore.

PROVA PIZZERIA

8729 Santa Monica Boulevard
West Hollywood
Los Angeles
California 90069
United States
+1 3108557285
www.pizzaprova.com

Opening hours	Open 7 days
Credit cards	Accepted
Style of pizza	Neapolitan
Recommended pizza	La Vito

"The crust is like you're in Naples. It's bubbly, thin, and chewy, and perfect every time. Consistency is key. I've had the pizza multiple times and the crust is always on point and the toppings always fresh."
—Jenn Harris

TOMATO PIE

7751 Melrose Avenue
West Hollywood
Los Angeles
California 90046
United States
+1 3236539993
www.tomatopiepizzajoint.com

Opening hours	Open 7 days
Credit cards	Accepted
Style of pizza	New York delivery
Recommended pizza	Grandma

"The best New York-style pie you'll find in Los Angeles."
—Lesley Suter

VITO'S

846 North La Cienega Boulevard
West Hollywood
Los Angeles
California 90069
United States
+1 3106526859
www.vitopizza.com

Opening hours..Open 7 days
Credit cards...Accepted
Style of pizza..New York
Recommended pizza..Cheese Pie

"Vito's has everything you want from a neighborhood pizza joint. It's in a shopping center and has no frills—just a couple of seats, good customer service, Parmesan cheese and chili flakes on the tables, and great pizza. The dough is paper-thin and chewy, and the pies only come in one size—big."—Jenn Harris

"THERE ARE FEW PEOPLE IN THE WORLD WHO TAKE PIZZA AS SERIOUSLY AS UNA PIZZA NAPOLETANA'S OWNER, ANTHONY MANGIERI. IN A WORLD OF FAUX ARTISANS, THIS GUY IS THE REAL DEAL, AND PIZZA IS HIS LIFE."

JESSICA BATTILANA P.388

SAN FRANCISCO

"BETTER DEEP DISH THAN ANYTHING I'VE HAD IN CHICAGO... BRING ON THE HATERS!"

JON CHIRI P.388

"TONY GEMIGNANI IS A PIZZA SCHOLAR AND A SHAMELESS SHOWMAN."

JONATHAN KAUFFMAN P.387

"THE CRUST IS PERFECT, THE PIES ARE SIMPLE AND SEASONAL, AND THE PEOPLE-WATCHING IS EXCELLENT."

JEN STEVENSON P.387

SAN FRANCISCO

SCALE

0   450   900   1350
yd.

1. PIZZETTA 211, RICHMOND (P.388)
2. RAGAZZA, HAIGHT-ASHBURY (P.386)
3. LITTLE STAR PIZZA, WESTERN ADDITION (P.388)
4. A16, MARINA (P.386)
5. GIALINA, GLEN PARK (P.386)
6. PIZZA HACKER, BERNAL HEIGHTS (P.386)
7. PIZZERIA DELFINA, THE MISSION (P.387)
8. LITTLE STAR PIZZA, THE MISSION (P.387)
9. UNA PIZZA NAPOLETANA, SOMA (P.388)
10. COTOGNA, EMBARCADERO (P.386)
11. TONY'S PIZZA NAPOLETANA, NORTH BEACH (P.387)

DEL POPOLO

Food truck—check website, Facebook, and Twitter for
upcoming locations
San Francisco
California
United States
www.delpopolosf.com

Opening hours	Closed Saturday–Monday
Credit cards	Accepted
Style of pizza	Neapolitan
Recommended pizza	Sausage Pie

"Jon Darsky keeps his pizza evolving."
—Chad Roberston

"The best 'leopard' out there. Del Popolo masters the
temperatures of the oven like no other and manages
to do it in a food truck. The offerings of pizzas are cut
to the bone, so everything offered is fresh and of the
highest quality."—Christian Puglisi

PIZZA HACKER

3229 Mission Street
Bernal Heights
San Francisco
California 94110
United States
+1 4158745585
www.pizzahacker.com

Opening hours	Closed Monday
Credit cards	Accepted
Style of pizza	Neapolitan-San Francisco sourdough
Recommended pizza	Heavy Nettle (add an egg if available)

COTOGNA

490 Pacific Avenue
Embarcadero
San Francisco
California 94133
United States
+1 4157758508
www.cotognasf.com

Opening hours	Open 7 days
Credit cards	Accepted
Style of pizza	Neapolitan

GIALINA

2842 Diamond Street
Glen Park
San Francisco
California 94131
United States
+1 4152398500
www.gialina.com

Opening hours	Open 7 days
Credit cards	Accepted but not AMEX
Style of pizza	Neapolitan
Recommended pizza	Amatriciana

"The huge black-and-white photographs of the
owner's family on ruby-colored walls make you
immediately feel right at home. The pizzas are
made with ingredients from local farms and
change according to the seasons."—Sharon Ardiana

RAGAZZA

311 Divisadero Street
Haight-Ashbury
San Francisco
California 94117
United States
+1 4152551133
www.ragazzasf.com

Opening hours	Open 7 days
Credit cards	Accepted but not AMEX
Style of pizza	Neapolitan
Recommended pizza	Moto

"These are nouveau pies, topped with whatever is
fresh and in season, with no slavish commitment to
tradition. So you can get a pizza topped with nettles,
pancetta, mushrooms, red onions, and provolone,
or one that pairs pulled pork with Taleggio and
Calabrian chiles. They're all good, never gimmicky,
built on a chewy, bready crust."—Jessica Battilana

A16

2355 Chestnut Street
Marina
San Francisco
California 94123
United States
+1 4157712216
www.a16sf.com

Opening hours	Open 7 days
Credit cards	Accepted
Style of pizza	Neapolitan

LITTLE STAR PIZZA

400 Valencia Street
The Mission
San Francisco
California 94103
United States
+1 4155517827
www.littlestarpizza.com

Opening hours..Open 7 days
Credit cards..Accepted
Style of pizza...Chicago deep-dish
Recommended pizza..Little Star

"Delicious ingredients, perfect tomato sauce,
and really good dough prepared in an American
deep-dish style, with a perfect crust."
—Fabio Gándara Pumar & Susana López-Urrutia

PIZZERIA DELFINA

3621 18th Street
The Mission
San Francisco
California 94110
United States
+1 4154376800
www.pizzeriadelfina.com

Opening hours..Open 7 days
Credit cards..Accepted
Style of pizza...Neapolitan
Recommended pizza...............Amatriciana; Broccoli Raab;
Clam Pie; Margherita; Napoletana

"There's just something about this always slammed
little Mission district pizzeria that keeps you coming
back time after time, year after year. The crust is
perfect, the pies are simple and seasonal, and the
people-watching is excellent."—Jen Stevenson

"If you can imagine taking the best parts of a
Neapolitan-style pizza and combining them with
the best parts of a New York-style pizza you are likely
imagining a pie made by Pizzeria Delfina. The pies
are personal-sized, in the tradition of Naples, yet
superbly cooked to provide a solid underside that
New Yorkers call 'foldable.' Just about everyone calls
it 'delicious.' The demand for these gas-oven crusted
masterpieces far exceeds the seating capacity of the
quaint pizzeria but, trust me, it's worth the wait."
—Sean Taylor

This snug pizzeria grew out of Delfina, the Italian restaurant
next door, also called Delfina, and the dream of chef Craig Stoll
and his wife Annie to bring the Naples pizza experience to San
Francisco's Mission district. The shape and lightness of the
12-inch (30-cm) pizza, with blackened bubbles around its puffy
rim, are unmistakably Neapolitan, only with less sag and sogginess toward the middle. The Clam Pie, with Cherrystone clams,
tomato, oregano, Pecorino, and hot peppers, is San Francisco's
answer to the New Haven classic. The source material for the
Broccoli Raab, with Caciocavallo cheese, mozzarella, olives, hot
peppers, and Star Root Farms broccoli raab, is closer to home.
The opening of new locations (Pacific Heights, Burlingame,
Palo Alto) has reduced neither affection nor demand for the
600-square-foot (56-square-meter) original.

TONY'S PIZZA NAPOLETANA

1570 Stockton Street
North Beach
San Francisco
California 94133
United States
+1 4158359888
www.tonyspizzanapoletana.com

Opening hours...Closed Tuesday
Credit cards..Accepted
Style of pizza...Multiple
Recommended pizza...........................Detroit; Margherita;
Napoletana; Romana

"This is a fantastic place, quite possibly the best
pizzeria in the world, with friendly service, great
drinks, and those pizzas—I've never eaten better,
not even in Naples or Rome."—Mikko Takala

"Tony Gemignani is a pizza scholar and a shameless
showman. He has studied regional pizzas all over
the country and recreates them—with sausages and
mozzarella from scratch—in a host of ovens set to
different temperatures."—Jonathan Kauffman

Champion *pizzaiolo* Tony Gemignani is the ultimate pizza
showman and Tony's Pizza Napoletana is his fantasy showplace.
In order to prepare credibly authentic versions of up to a
dozen regional pizzas he installed seven pizza ovens. He has
a 550°F (290°C) gas oven for Sicilian, classic American and
Detroit- styles; a 700°F (370°C) electric for Roman slabs; a
900°F (482°C) wood-fired *forno* for Neapolitan, and a blistering
1,000°F (538°C) coal chamber for New York and New Haven
pizza. Tony's serving this many pizza styles under one roof at
one time doesn't make it any easier to choose. For those
resigned to ordering just one, there's a hint of a suggestion
in the pizzeria's name: Gemignani recommends grabbing one
of the 73 Neapolitan-style Margheritas prepared every day.

PIZZETTA 211

211 23rd Street
Richmond
San Francisco
California 94121
United States
+1 4153799880
www.pizzetta211.com

Opening hours..Closed Tuesday
Credit cards...Accepted
Style of pizza...Thin-crust
Recommended pizza..........Rosemary, Fiore Sardo Cheese,
and Pine Nuts

"Pizzetta 211 is small, warm, and cozy and has a very personal vision that permeates the entire restaurant."
—Sharon Ardiana

UNA PIZZA NAPOLETANA

210 11th Street
SoMa
San Francisco
California 94103
United States
+1 4158613444
www.unapizza.com

Opening hours...................................Closed Sunday–Tuesday
Credit cards.......................................Accepted but not AMEX
Style of pizza...Neapolitan
Recommended pizza....................Bianca; Filetti; Margherita

"This is the best pizza I have ever eaten. Anthony Mangieri is admired by pizza makers worldwide for his devotion to tradition and commitment to his craft. The dough is naturally leavened and Anthony makes every pizza they serve."—Leonardo Bresolin

"There are few people in the world who take pizza as seriously as Una Pizza Napoletana's owner, Anthony Mangieri. In a world of faux artisans, this guy is the real deal, and pizza is his life."—Jessica Battilana

"The pizzas are nothing like the mannered certified Neapolitans most places serve. They're wildly bubbly and smoky and ephemeral."—Jonathan Kauffman

At Una Pizza Napoletana, San Francisco's hard-core home of soft-cored pizza, it's not the customer who's always right. It's Anthony Mangieri, the uncompromising owner. Little gets between this single-minded *pizzaiolo* and his pursuit of a Neapolitan pizza ideal. Some of his handcrafted Margheritas, Marinaras and Biancas (buffalo mozzarella, extra virgin olive oil, fresh garlic, fresh basil, and sea salt) are more perfect than others. This is either by design or according to the very nature of a naturally leavened dough sensitive to the slightest changes in atmospheric conditions. Mangieri's bad days, if he in fact has them, are better than nearly everyone else's good ones, which is why people endure the long lines, limited selection, high prices, and strange hours. The pizzeria is open four nights a week, from 5 p.m. until Mangieri runs out of dough.

LITTLE STAR PIZZA

846 Divisadero Street
Western Addition
San Francisco
California 94117
United States
+1 4154411118
www.littlestarpizza.com

Opening hours...Open 7 days
Credit cards...Accepted
Style of pizza...Chicago deep-dish
Recommended pizza....................................Classic; Little Star

"I'm a fan of Little Star's deep-dish cornmeal crust and crushed tomatoes—hardy, almost cakelike, delicious. It does thin-crust too, but it's the deep dish that's worthy of a nod."—Rachel Levin

"Better deep dish than anything I've had in Chicago… bring on the haters!"—Jon Chiri

THE ART OF THE PIZZA BOX

In optimum conditions all pizza would be served within 30 seconds and 30 feet (9 meters) of its point of departure from the pizza oven. Fresh is best. But most people live in houses and apartments, not ideal worlds. Many wish to receive their pizza within 10 seconds and 10 feet (3 meters) of their living-room couch. That's why the real world needs pizza boxes. They've facilitated the great luxury of warm pizza in your home, at work, or parked outside a packed pizzeria with too long a wait for a table. "If you're going to do pizza you have to have boxes," says chef-restaurateur Jon Shook, one half of Jon & Vinny's pizza restaurant in Los Angeles.

By most accounts the corrugated pizza box was developed in the early 1960s by the American pizza chain Domino's. Then, as now, they were flatpacked and foldable, with air vents to release steam. Hot pizza transported in them can still suffer from sogginess over time, as moisture and cardboardy flavor are slowly absorbed. Even so, their value as conveyors of convenience is undeniable. What's maybe more difficult to swallow are claims that pizza boxes are works of art. "The surface of a pizza box is perhaps the most overlooked artistic medium of the past century," insists Scott Weiner, who, besides serving as this guide's regional expert for New York, is author of *Viva La Pizza!: The Art of the Pizza Box*.

To back his words Weiner turns to his personal collection of 975 unique pizza boxes from over 50 countries. None has the remains of pizzas sitting in them, thankfully. One of his favorites is a caricature by Italian illustrator Luca Ciancio of the Neapolitan screen legends Sophia Loren and Totò in a sort of "Adoration of the Pizza" pose. The most common pizza-box motif, apart from a pizzeria's telephone number, is of a man with toque on head and mustache under nose, holding a pizza. A version of this proud chef figures prominently in a recent photographic essay on the pizza box by British photographer Luke Stephenson. He was fascinated by the triteness of the illustration and graphic, with its Italian red, white, and green. As the box's lid kept the pizza warm, the kitsch kept the box's lid frozen in time. "I do like these little overlooked things that people take for granted," says Stephenson.

As cool as such pizza-box classics look in Stephenson's photos, or on hipster t-shirts, more style-conscious pizzerias are looking to stamp, print, or even hand draw their brand identity on boxes. Jon Shook and Vinny Dotolo, the hotshot chefs behind the LA restaurants Animal and Son of a Gun, turned to artist Ben Jones to design the box for their pizzeria. They wanted something iconic but not over the top. No illustration, no website URL, no Instagram, no phone number. Only their names would go on the box's white surface: "JON&" stacked over "VINNY's" in big, slightly uneven, green letters. "Our boxes go to meetings, homes," says Shook. "There are guys who will think about us all day!"

USA MIDWEST

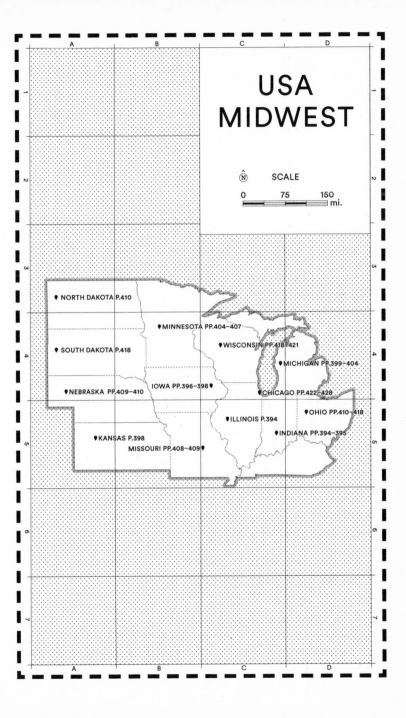

USA
MIDWEST

N̂   SCALE

0   75   150
▬▬▬▬▬▬ mi.

♦ NORTH DAKOTA P.410

♦ MINNESOTA PP.404–407

♦ SOUTH DAKOTA P.418

♦ WISCONSIN PP.418–421

♦ MICHIGAN PP.399–404

♦ NEBRASKA PP.409–410   IOWA PP.396–398 ♦

♦ CHICAGO PP.422–428

♦ OHIO PP.410–418

♦ ILLINOIS P.394

♦ KANSAS P.398   ♦ INDIANA PP.394–395

MISSOURI PP.408–409 ♦

CANNOVA'S PIZZERIA

247 North Main Street
Galena
Illinois 61036
United States
+1 8157773735

Opening hours	Open 7 days
Credit cards	Accepted
Style of pizza	Thin-crust
Recommended pizza	Venetian

"This small storefront Italian restaurant is perfect for romance or a pizza for the whole family."
—Amy Boynton

LOU MALNATI'S PIZZERIA

6649 North Lincoln Avenue
Lincolnwood
Illinois 60712
United States
+1 8476730800
www.loumalnatis.com

Opening hours	Open 7 days
Credit cards	Accepted
Style of pizza	Chicago deep-dish
Recommended pizza	Malnati Chicago Classic; Sausage

"The Lincolnwood location is the original Lou Malnati's, and there's a reason people get Lou's shipped to them all around the world. It is simply the best deep-dish pizza in the world. That sausage patty is legendary. The flaky, buttery crust. Oh my. The tomato sauce is so fresh and so ripe and so bright."
—Jason DeRusha

"It's classic Chicago pizza."—Rich Melman

BURT'S PLACE

8541 Ferris Avenue
Morton Grove
Illinois 60053
United States
+1 8479657997

Opening hours	Closed Monday and Tuesday
Credit cards	Not accepted
Style of pizza	Chicago deep-dish
Recommended pizza	Sausage with Onions, Mushrooms, and Green Bell Peppers

"There's deep-dish pizza in Chicago, and then there's Burt's. He's an old dude with a scraggly beard and the restaurant is an old house with all sort of vintage knicknacks strewn about. Burt improved on Chicago-style pizza by caramelizing the deep, already flaky crust. The result is a deeply flavored, chewy from the burnt cheese but still flaky crust. He does the dough himself each day, and when he's out, he's out. Burt's in such high demand that you have to call and order your pizza ahead of time even if you want to eat it there."—Grace Bascos

GIORDANO'S

1115 West Chicago Avenue
Oak Park
Illinois 60302
United States
+1 7083862223
www.giordanos.com

Opening hours	Open 7 days
Credit cards	Accepted
Style of pizza	Deep-dish
Recommended pizza	Meat and More Meat

"Cakey. Thick. Messy. Magical."—Jason Finestone

800 DEGREES THREE FIRES

5215 Illinois Road, Suite 101
Fort Wayne
Indiana 46804
United States
+1 2604160005
www.800degrees.net

Opening hours	Open 7 days
Credit cards	Accepted
Style of pizza	Neapolitan
Recommended pizza	800°

"Its attention to detail is unmatched in the Fort Wayne area. Local ingredients, great beer selection, family-friendly, and great service make this the best pizzeria in the area."—Aaron Butts

800 DEGREES WOOD FIRED PIZZA

10020 Lima Road, Suite F
Fort Wayne
Indiana 46818
United States
+1 2604900111
www.800degrees.net

Opening hours	Open 7 days
Credit cards	Accepted
Style of pizza	Neapolitan
Recommended pizza	Sausage

"Special care is taken to source the right ingredients and they are treated with care. The dough is started using a *biga* (naturally leavened starter) and allowed to ferment for three days. The meats are hand-butchered from heirloom pigs, and all the sausages are made in house."—Thomas England

OLEY'S PIZZA

10910 US Highway 24 West
Fort Wayne
Indiana 46814
United States
+1 2604326996
www.oleys.net

Opening hours	Closed Sunday
Credit cards	Accepted
Style of pizza	Deep-dish
Recommended pizza	Godfather

"Oley's Pizza is famous for its double-crust stuffed pizzas."—Aaron Butts

BAZBEAUX

811 East Westfield Boulevard
Indianapolis
Indiana 46220
United States
+1 3172555711
www.bazbeaux.com

Opening hours	Open 7 days
Credit cards	Accepted
Style of pizza	Gourmet
Recommended pizza	Bazbeaux Special

"This eclectic gourmet pizzeria opened in the art district of Broad Ripple in 1986. Its pizza is off-the-charts with interesting toppings."—Brad Rocco

NAPOLESE

114 East 49th Street
Indianapolis
Indiana 46205
United States
+1 3179250765
www.napolesepizzeria.com

Opening hours	Open 7 days
Credit cards	Accepted
Style of pizza	Neapolitan
Recommended pizza	Asparagus, Shaved Fennel, Tomato, and Fleur de Terre Cheese; Hamaker's Corner

"An intimate atmosphere, thoughtfully sourced local ingredients, and creative combinations make this my go-to place when visiting Indianapolis."—Aaron Butts

PIZZOLOGY CRAFT PIZZA & PUB

608 Massachusetts Avenue
Indianapolis
Indiana 46204
United States
+1 3176852550
www.pizzologyindy.com

Opening hours	Open 7 days
Credit cards	Accepted
Style of pizza	Neapolitan
Recommended pizza	Margherita

"The wood-fired brick ovens kept near 905°F (485°C) produce pizza with the perfect texture."
—Thomas England

CENTRO

1003 Locust Street
Des Moines
Iowa 50309
United States
+1 5152481780
www.centrodesmoines.com

Opening hours..Open 7 days
Credit cards...Not accepted
Style of pizza...Brooklyn coal-fired
Recommended pizza..Margherita

"The pizzas have a super-thin, charred crust with nice bubbles. Subtle tomato sauce is lightly applied so it doesn't weigh down the pizza and there's plenty of fresh mozzarella."—Jennifer Miller

CHUCK'S RESTAURANT

3610 6th Avenue
Des Moines
Iowa 50310
United States
+1 5152444104
www.chucksdsm.com

Opening hours..........................Closed Sunday and Monday
Credit cards..Accepted
Style of pizza...Midwestern thin-crust
Recommended pizza..................Chuck's Homemade Italian
Sausage; Margherita

"Opened in 1956, this Italian-American restaurant has an old-world feel that appeals to my nostalgic tastes. The crust is thin, crispy, and flavorful—you can tell the dough is nicely matured because of how it colors in the oven. The sauce is fresh, zesty, and pleasantly tart. The restaurant's front window peers into the pizza prep area, allowing hungry guests to get a sneak peek as they arrive. A truly magical place!"
—George Formaro

EATERY A

2932 Ingersoll Avenue
Des Moines
Iowa 50312
United States
+1 5152828085
www.eateryadsm.com

Opening hours..Open 7 days
Credit cards..Accepted
Style of pizza...Wood-fired
Recommended pizza.........................Italian Sausage, Braised
Fennel, and Mushroom; Margherita

"Eatery A has interesting combinations of ingredients like vegetables with sumac."—Jennifer Miller

FELIX & OSCAR'S

4050 Merle Hay Road
Des Moines
Iowa 50310
United States
+1 5152788887
www.felixandoscars.com

Opening hours..Open 7 days
Credit cards..Accepted
Style of pizza...Deep-dish
Recommended pizza..............Cheese Topper with Alfredo,
Sausage, and Pepperoni

"Felix & Oscar's specializes in Chicago-style deep dish in Des Moines, Iowa. Its Cheese Topper is its riff on the classic, featuring a blend of cheeses on the base topped with meats, sauce, and another blend of cheeses to cap it all off. Felix & Oscar's offers an Alfredo sauce option as well that is quite possibly the most decadent pizza on Earth."—George Formaro

FONG'S PIZZA

223 4th Street
Des Moines
Iowa 50309
United States
+1 5153233333
www.fongspizza.com

Opening hours	Open 7 days
Credit cards	Accepted
Style of pizza	Traditional
Recommended pizza	Crab Rangoon

"The building that once housed Iowa's oldest Chinese restaurant, King Ying Low, now is home to the state's funkiest pizza joint. The inspired location birthed a Chinese-Italian cuisine: Crab Rangoon pizza, kung pao and teriyaki sauces on your crust and pizza rolls served with egg roll wrappers. Somehow it all works, and this has become a more trendy spot than the century-old Chinese restaurant that preceded it. Admire the decorative elements salvaged from the previous restaurant and pass the sweet and sour sauce."—John Naughton

GUSTO PIZZA CO.

1905 Ingersoll Avenue
Des Moines
Iowa 50309
United States
+1 5152448786
www.gustopizzaco.com

Opening hours	Open 7 days
Credit cards	Accepted
Style of pizza	Traditional thin-crust
Recommended pizza	Deburgo

"This relative newcomer puts a twist on traditional family recipes. Cajun bacon on your pizza? Sure. Breaded eggplant (aubergine)? Yep. Vegan mozzarella? Check. Locally sourced ingredients are featured: Graziano's brand sausage, La Quercia prosciutto, and bacon from a small-town Iowa meat locker."
—John Naughton

NOAH'S ARK

2400 Ingersoll Avenue
Des Moines
Iowa 50312
United States
+1 5152882246
www.noahsarkdesmoines.com

Opening hours	Closed Sunday
Credit cards	Accepted
Style of pizza	Des Moines-Neapolitan
Recommended pizza	Green Olive and Onion

"Noah's is one of the oldest restaurants in town and the interior exists in a kind of time warp. The pizza is very thin-crust and classic Des Moines-style Italian with stringy yellow mozzarella."—Jennifer Miller

LA PIZZA HOUSE

1440 Maury Street
Des Moines
Iowa 50317
United States
+1 5152882211

Opening hours	Closed Sunday and Monday
Credit cards	Accepted but not AMEX
Style of pizza	Midwestern tavern
Recommended pizza	Sausage

"This is one of Des Moines' original pizza places, and it's still slinging pies on the south side. Its pizza is famous for what I call a Midwestern tavern-style crust—thin and cracker-like with a yeasty bread flavor. This style can be found in many of the old-school bars and restaurants in town. La Pizza House's pizzas are assembled a bit differently, with sauce, sausage, and other meats topped with mozzarella cheese and even more sauce. The homemade sausage has a nice fennel kick."—George Formaro

L. MAY EATERY

1072 Main Street
Dubuque
Iowa 52001
United States
+1 5635560505
www.lmayeatery.com

Opening hours	Closed Tuesday and Wednesday
Credit cards	Accepted
Style of pizza	Wood-fired thin-crust
Recommended pizza	"You're in Dubuque"

"L. May Eatery is a lovely urban bistro with a great ambience and delicious food."—Amy Boynton

SHOT TOWER INN

390 Locust Street
Dubuque
Iowa 52001
United States
+1 5635561061
www.shottowerinn.net

Opening hours	Open 7 days
Credit cards	Accepted
Style of pizza	Deep-dish and thin-crust
Recommended pizza	Bianco

"A local classic—very casual and kid-friendly with great pizza."—Amy Boynton

LINCOLN WINEBAR

125 1st Street West
Mount Vernon
Iowa 52314
United States
+1 3198959463
www.foodisimportant.com

Opening hours	Closed Sunday and Monday
Credit cards	Accepted but not AMEX
Style of pizza	Wood-fired

"Lincoln Winebar uses ingredients that are fresh from the farm."—Jim Duncan

LIMESTONE

814 Massachusetts Street
Lawrence
Kansas 66044
United States
+1 7858562825
www.limestonepkb.com

Opening hours	Open 7 days
Credit cards	Accepted
Style of pizza	Neapolitan
Recommended pizza	Mushroom; Sausage; Spud

"Limestone is located on bustling, eclectic Massachusetts Street, not far from the University of Kansas, in a building with limestone walls, high ceilings, and an exhibition-style pizza. The owners know what they're doing, and do it well, with locally sourced Kansas ingredients, modest prices, and a carefully curated menu that includes bar bites, salads, sandwiches, snacks, and plates. But first and foremost, Limestone is a pizzeria."
—Kimberly Winter Stern

SPIN! NEAPOLITAN PIZZA

6541 West 119th Street
Overland Park
Kansas 66209
United States
+1 9134517746
www.spinpizza.com

Opening hours	Open 7 days
Credit cards	Accepted
Style of pizza	Neapolitan
Recommended pizza	Goat Cheese and Fresh Arugula (rocket); Roasted Potato; SPIN! Margherita

"This Kansas City homegrown restaurant serves authentic, hand-tossed, swoony pizza (and the option of a fabulous gluten-free crust and flatbread), along with salads and gelato. I love SPIN! not only for its perfect pies, but also for its community karma— weekly bike rides, live music during the summer on its patios, even a fund-raising event where you can dine with your pooch. Mmm...but it's the pizza that keeps me coming back."—Kimberly Winter Stern

ANTHONY'S GOURMET PIZZA

621 South Main Street
Ann Arbor
Michigan 48104
United States
+1 7349713555
www.anthonysgourmet.com

Opening hours..Open 7 days
Credit cards...Accepted
Style of pizza..Chicago stuffed
Recommended pizza...............................Carnivorous Delight

"Anthony's Gourmet Pizza delivers in Ann Arbor and the Carnivorous Delight has always been a favorite among my friends and relatives."—Frank Carollo

BIGALORA WOOD FIRED CUCINA

3050 Washtenaw Avenue, Suite 112
Ann Arbor
Michigan 48104
United States
+1 7349712442
www.bigalora.com

Opening hours..Open 7 days
Credit cards...Accepted
Style of pizza...Neapolitan
Recommended pizza.............Capricciosa; Margherita DOP

"Everything on the menu has an unmistakable Italian authenticity, and ingredients are either homemade, locally produced, or imported from Italy. The pizzas bake (and many other items also roast) in the domed, wood-fired Italian-made ovens. Chef-owner Luciano DelSignore's dough uses a homemade, naturally leavened starter that Italian bakers call 'biga,' so the crusts are light but wonderfully chewy and contain no commercial yeasts or added sugars. The choice of pizza toppings is huge."—Sylvia Rector

JET'S PIZZA

1749 Plymouth Road
Ann Arbor
Michigan 48105
United States
+1 7343321300
www.jetspizza.com

Opening hours..Open 7 days
Credit cards...Accepted
Style of pizza...Deep-dish
Recommended pizza...........................8 Corner BBQ Chicken

"The deep-dish BBQ Chicken pizza is my go-to chain pizza. It is never too bready, it always has a good balance of cheese, toppings, and crust, and the corners are always perfectly caramelized and crunchy."
—Adam Baru

MANI OSTERIA & BAR

341 East Liberty Street
Ann Arbor
Michigan 48104
United States
+1 7347696700
www.maniosteria.com

Opening hours..Closed Monday
Credit cards...Accepted
Style of pizza.............................Neapolitan wood-fired
Recommended pizza........................Arugula and Prosciutto;
  Market; Pepperoni; Red Onion and Pistachio; Sausage
  and Peppers; Tartufo

"Mani Osteria & Bar's wood-fired Neapolitan-style pizzas were a sensation in Ann Arbor when owner Adam Baru opened the restaurant in 2011, and it's still one of the college town's hot spots. The pizzas are excellent with thin, crisp, blistered crusts and sophisticated toppings that range from smoked scamorza cheese to truffles and Calabrian chiles."
—Sylvia Rector

"I love the Market pizza as it uses the ingredients that are in season at the time—this past summer the Peach and Prosciutto was delicious."—Tommy York

NEOPAPALIS

500 East Williams Street
Ann Arbor
Michigan 48104
United States
+1 7349292227
www.neopapalis.com

Opening hours..Open 7 days
Credit cards...Accepted
Style of pizza..........................New York-Neapolitan
Recommended pizza...............Bianca; Classica; Margherita

"The Margherita is at the top of the menu and the top of my list at NeoPapalis."—Tommy York

NEW YORK PIZZA DEPOT (NYPD)

605 East Williams Street
Ann Arbor
Michigan 48104
United States
+1 7346696973
www.newyorkpizza-annarbor.com

Opening hours	Open 7 days
Credit cards	Accepted
Style of pizza	New York
Recommended pizza	Baked Ziti; Mixed Mushroom; White

"This is the place to go for a quick slice. It has 5–15 pizzas made and ready for a quick reheat in the oven. The slices are huge and the variety is great."
—Tommy York

FLO'S PIZZERIA RISTORANTE & SPORTS BAR

1259 Post Drive Northeast
Belmont
Michigan 49306
United States
+1 6167845555
www.flossportsbar.com

Opening hours	Open 7 days
Credit cards	Accepted
Style of pizza	Chicago grilled
Recommended pizza	Flo's Signature Pizza

"Excellent pizza, good Italian or Mexican entrees, and a fun sports atmosphere."
—Joe Borrello

AMICI'S

3249 West 12 Mile Road
Berkley
Michigan 48072
United States
+1 2485444100
www.amicispizza.com

Opening hours	Open 7 days
Credit cards	Accepted
Style of pizza	Round
Recommended pizza	Asparagus

"Cool flavor combinations with tons of fresh ingredients, including a really herby, fresh tomato sauce."
—Steve Byrne

CRISPELLI'S BAKERY & PIZZERIA

28939 Woodward Avenue
Berkley
Michigan 48072
United States
+1 2485913300
www.crispellis.com

Opening hours	Open 7 days
Credit cards	Accepted
Style of pizza	Neapolitan and Detroit
Recommended pizza	Prosciutto

"You can taste the freshness and quality in everything Crispelli's makes."—Sylvia Rector

J. BALDWIN'S

16981 18 Mile Road
Clinton Township
Michigan 48038
United States
+1 5864163500
www.jbaldwins.com

Opening hours	Open 7 days
Credit cards	Accepted
Style of pizza	Flatbread

RANDAZZO FRESH MARKET

36800 Garfield Road
Clinton Township
Michigan 48035
United States
+1 5862933500
www.randazzofreshmarket.com

Opening hours	Open 7 days
Credit cards	Accepted
Style of pizza	Neapolitan
Recommended pizza	Broccoli and Garlic

"Covered with a high-quality cheese and topped with many exclusive ingredients, these pizzas are unique and delicious."—Tony Tocco

DIMAGGIO'S PIZZA

6410 North M 63
Coloma
Michigan 49038
United States
+1 2698491521
www.dimaggiospizzaandburgers.com

Opening hours	Open 7 days
Credit cards	Not accepted
Style of pizza	Midwestern
Recommended pizza	Cheese, Sausage, and Mushroom

"This family-owned restaurant, which opened almost 60 years ago, is so crowded on Saturday nights that there's a line to get in."—Jane Simon Ammeson

BUDDY'S PIZZA

17125 Conant Street
Detroit
Michigan 48212
United States
+1 3138929001
www.buddyspizza.com

Opening hours	Open 7 days
Credit cards	Accepted
Style of pizza	Detroit deep-dish
Recommended pizza	Cheese; Detroiter

"Buddy's has nine metro Detroit locations but the original old-school pizzeria on Conant Street in a working-class Detroit neighborhood is where the first 'Detroit-style' pizza was made in 1946. The thick pies are square (actually, rectangular) with a thick but crisp and airy crust; a heavy layer of cheese (often, Wisconsin brick) on top of the dough, and other toppings and dollops of thick, dark red, long-simmered sauce on top. In the high heat of the oven, the cheese caramelizes against the sides of the blackened steel pans, forming a chewy, dark golden edge and corners—the best part of the pie. Buddy's is the standard for Detroit-style pizza, and this atmospheric old joint on Conant is where it all began."—Sylvia Rector

NIKI'S

735 Beaubien Street
Detroit
Michigan 48226
United States
+1 3139614303
www.nikisdetroit.com

Opening hours	Open 7 days
Credit cards	Accepted
Style of pizza	Deep-dish
Recommended pizza	Pepperoni or Sausage with Olive and Banana Peppers

"Niki's is open late so it always has a bit of a buzz. The pizza sauce is rich and zesty and fills your belly with just enough grease to cure the hangover I don't have yet."—Sharon Juergens

SUPINO PIZZERIA

2457 Russell Street
Detroit
Michigan 48207
United States
+1 3135677879
www.supinopizzeria.com

Opening hours	Closed Sunday and Monday
Credit cards	Accepted
Style of pizza	New York
Recommended pizza	Bismarck; Cheese; Supino; Vegetables and Mushrooms

"Owner Dave Mancini became obsessed with pizza after visiting Supino, Italy, where his family is from. After returning home, he spent more than a year perfecting his own recipe before opening his tiny, hole-in-the-wall shop in Detroit's Eastern Market district in 2008. His big, wide, thin-crust pies became a sensation with their crisp but chewy crusts, sublimely simple tomato sauce and locally sourced fresh toppings. I can't explain why they're so simple and yet so different and flavorful, but people wait an hour or more to get theirs fresh from the old-fashioned deck oven. Supino made a tremendous impact on pizza tastes in Detroit. It not only kick-started the thin-crust trend here, it also set the standard."—Sylvia Rector

When David Mancini set up his pizza shop on Russell Street, beside Eastern Market, in 2008, Detroit was feared and vilified. Its status as a haven for hipsters was years away. Supino's breakout success with a thin and round pizza, as opposed to Detroit's beloved deep-dish square, was the shape of things to come. Well thought out combinations of high-quality ingredients never descend into crazy pileups. You feel each hit of garlic and chili oil on the Supino pizza, with ricotta and mozzarella, but the one–two punch doesn't quite knock you off your feet. Mancini, a cherished champion of Detroit's burgeoning band of indie shopkeepers and DIY entrepreneurs, can be spotted wearing their t-shirts but never his.

BUDDY'S PIZZA

31646 Northwestern Highway
Farmington Hills
Michigan 48334
United States
+1 2488554600
www.buddyspizza.com

Opening hours	Open 7 days
Credit cards	Accepted
Style of pizza	Detroit deep-dish
Recommended pizza	Detroiter

"When people talk Detroit-style pizza, this is what they mean."—Steve Byrne

FRICANO'S PIZZA TAVERN

1400 Fulton Street
Grand Haven
Michigan 49417
United States
+1 6168428640
www.fricanospizzatavern.com

Opening hours	Closed Sunday
Credit cards	Not accepted
Style of pizza	Thin-crust
Recommended pizza	Fricano's EBA (Everything But Anchovies)

"The place is an institution for thin-crust pizza in West Michigan—since 1949. Lively spices in the sauce and crispy, burnt cheese edges on the pizza make these pies unique and longtime favorites." —Joe Borrello

BISTRO BELLA VITA

44 Grandville Avenue Southwest
Grand Rapids
Michigan 49503
United States
+1 6162224600
www.bistrobellavita.com

Opening hours	Open 7 days
Credit cards	Accepted
Style of pizza	Neapolitan
Recommended pizza	Rustica

"The pizzas are full of great flavor."—Tony Tocco

THE B.O.B.

20 Monroe Avenue
Grand Rapids
Michigan 49503
United States
+1 6163562000
www.thebob.com

Opening hours	Closed Sunday
Credit cards	Accepted
Style of pizza	Wood-fired
Recommended pizza	Pepperoni

"The pizzas are coated with a unique selection of ingredients and high-quality, delicious cheese." —Tony Tocco

LICARI'S SICILIAN PIZZA KITCHEN

2869 Knapp Street, Suite B
Grand Rapids
Michigan 49525
United States
+1 6166086912
www.licarispizzakitchen.com

Opening hours..Open 7 days
Credit cards...Accepted
Style of pizza..Sicilian
Recommended pizza...Rosso

"Fantastic service."—Tony Tocco

VITALE'S PIZZA

834 Leonard Street Northeast
Grand Rapids
Michigan 49503
United States
+1 6164583766
www.vitalespizza.com

Opening hours..Open 7 days
Credit cards...Accepted
Style of pizza..........................Chicago regular or deep-dish
Recommended pizza...................Regular Crust with Sliced
Meatballs, Sausage, and Black Olives

"An old-world Sicilian restaurant with noteworthy
food."—Joe Borrello

LUIGI'S

36691 Jefferson Avenue
Harrison Township
Michigan 48045
United States
+1 5864687711
www.luigisoriginal.com

Opening hours..Open 7 days
Credit cards...Accepted
Style of pizza...Classic
Recommended pizza.......................................Margherita

"Luigi's pizzas have a soft and chewy sesame seed
crust. It is well balanced and very flavorful."
—Wesley Pikula

LOUI'S PIZZA

23141 Dequindre Road
Hazel Park
Michigan 48030
United States
+1 2485471711
www.louispizza.net

Opening hours........................Closed Monday and Tuesday
Credit cards..............................Accepted but not AMEX
Style of pizza...Detroit
Recommended pizza...................Cheese and Tomato Sauce

"If you haven't had Detroit-style pizza, you should,
and Loui's might be the best place to start. More
Sicilian than pan pizza, this thick-crust beast is baked
in an oiled aluminum pan until the cheesy corners get
charred into magic. You're not going to find a fancy
pizzeria using brick cheese and dollops of canned
sauce in large amounts, but there's probably no
regionally specific pizza style more indicative of
a place than the hard-charging Detroit style, and
there's very little more satisfying."—Lance Roberts

ERBELLI'S

6214 Stadium Drive
Kalamazoo
Michigan 49009
United States
+1 2693750408
www.erbellis.com

Opening hours..Open 7 days
Credit cards...Accepted
Style of pizza...Classic

"I had a fantastic pizza here during a trip to the USA.
The pizza was covered in arugula (rocket) and the
dough was sumptuous—it was very, very tasty.
Erbelli's really was remarkable."—Philippe Genion

PIZZA E VINO

849 Penniman Avenue
Plymouth
Michigan 48170
United States
+1 7342540275
www.cellar849.com

Opening hours..........................Closed Sunday and Monday
Credit cards..Accepted
Style of pizza..Neapolitan
Recommended pizza...............................Three Cheese White

"Pizza e Vino uses a variety of unique ingredients, with high-quality fine cheese and with the perfect texture of dough."—Tony Tocco

BIGALORA WOOD FIRED CUCINA

711 South Main Street
Royal Oak
Michigan 48067
United States
+1 2485442442
www.bigalora.com

Opening hours..Open 7 days
Credit cards..Accepted
Style of pizza..Neapolitan
Recommended pizza...Bacco Sausage

"Bigalora is delicious with a cool vibe, good music, and a great wine list and drinks."—Sharon Juergens

"Even a cheese-less vegan pizza was stellar, with toppings chopped finely so that all the flavors dance on your tongue rather than only a large hunk of onion or pepper overwhelming everything else. It's beautifully balanced."—Mary Bilyeu

BIGALORA WOOD FIRED CUCINA

29110 Franklin Road
Southfield
Michigan 48034
United States
+1 2487502442
www.bigalora.com

Opening hours..Open 7 days
Credit cards..Accepted
Style of pizza..Neapolitan
Recommended pizza...Duck Prosciutto

SANTANIELLO'S RESTAURANT AND BANQUET FACILITY

2262 West Glenlord Road
Stevensville
Michigan 49127
United States
+1 2694293966

Opening hours..Closed Monday
Credit cards..Accepted
Style of pizza..Pizza parlor
Recommended pizza...............................Meatball; Mushroom

"Santaniello's is a neighborhood favorite."
—Jane Simon Ammeson

TOSI'S RESTAURANT

4337 Ridge Road
Stevensville
Michigan 49127
United States
+1 2694293689
www.tosis.com

Opening hours..Closed Sunday
Credit cards..Accepted
Style of pizza..Neapolitan
Recommended pizza...Mediterranean

"This Italian restaurant first opened in the 1940s as a resort for Italians from the Chicago area who wanted to escape the summer heat. Many of Mama Tosi's original recipes are used here but the pizza is more typical of what you'd find in a trendy northern Italian restaurant in a big city."—Jane Simon Ammeson

SAMMY'S PIZZA & RESTAURANT

103 West 1st Street
Duluth
Minnesota 55802
United States
+1 2187278551
www.mysammys.com

Opening hours..Open 7 days
Credit cards..Accepted
Style of pizza....................................Midwestern square-cut
Recommended pizza.....................................Sammy's Special

"This family-owned restaurant chain stretches across the Iron Range, but the original Duluth location is the place to sample a Sammy's pie. It's utterly addictive."—Joy Summers

HELLO PIZZA

3904 Sunnyside Road
Edina
Minnesota 55424
United States
+1 9523034514
www.hellopizza.com

Opening hours	Open 7 days
Credit cards	Accepted
Style of pizza	New York and Sicilian
Recommended pizza	Sicilian Pan Pie

PIZZA LUCÉ

210 North Blake Road
Hopkins
Minnesota 55343
United States
+1 9527670854
www.pizzaluce.com

Opening hours	Open 7 days
Credit cards	Accepted
Style of pizza	Minnesota hand-tossed
Recommended pizza	Ruby Rae; Wild Mushroom and Arugula (rocket)

"A heavy hand with spice and flavor combinations makes Pizza Lucé one of my favorites. It is consistently awesome."—Heather Manley

BLACK SHEEP COAL FIRED PIZZA

600 Washington Avenue North
Minneapolis
Minnesota 55408
United States
+1 6123422625
www.blacksheeppizza.com

Opening hours	Open 7 days
Credit cards	Accepted
Style of pizza	Coal-fired thin-crust
Recommended pizza	Oyster Mushroom, Smoked Mozzarella, Rosemary, and Garlic; Tomato and Oregano

"Located in the hottest neighborhood in the Twin Cities—the North Loop on the outskirts of downtown Minneapolis, Black Sheep is a great stop for lunch and takeout. The room is simple and the emphasis is on the pizza, as they serve only a handful of additional side items. The crisp, thin, burnt crust is my favorite in town and goes well with any toppings."
—Dave Ostlund

BRODERS' CUCINA ITALIANA

2308 West 50th Street
Minneapolis
Minnesota 55410
United States
+1 6129253113
www.broders.com

Opening hours	Open 7 days
Credit cards	Accepted but not AMEX
Style of pizza	New York
Recommended pizza	Sausage

"A neighborhood gourmet Italian deli that's been an institution in South Minneapolis for more than three decades. A small space with only a half-dozen tables, it is the perfect place to swing by fast and pick up a slice to go."—Dave Ostlund

BURCH PIZZA

1933 Colfax Avenue South
Minneapolis
Minnesota 55403
United States
+1 6128431500
www.burchrestaurant.com

Opening hours	Open 7 days
Credit cards	Accepted
Style of pizza	Chef-driven
Recommended pizza	Sausage and Fennel

"This is what you get when a James Beard Award-winning chef (Isaac Becker) creates a pizza joint. The wood-fired pizza in Burch's cozy cave-like confines isn't just perfectly executed, it's perfectly creative with topping options that include lamp, raw tuna, or more traditional fare."—Drew Wood

PARKWAY PIZZA

4359 Minnehaha Avenue
Minneapolis
Minnesota 55406
United States
+1 6127299090
www.parkwaypizzamn.com

Opening hours	Open 7 days
Credit cards	Accepted but not AMEX
Style of pizza	Traditional oven-baked
Recommended pizza	Farmers Market

"Parkway Pizza make good solid neighborhood pizza with a tangy sauce."—Molly Hermann

PIZZA NEA

306 East Hennepin Avenue
Minneapolis
Minnesota 55414
United States
+1 6123319298
www.pizzanea.com

Opening hours	Open 7 days
Credit cards	Accepted
Style of pizza	Neapolitan
Recommended pizza	Capricciosa; The monthly special

"Pizza Nea is without peer not only in the Twin Cities, but also on the national scene."—Jason DeRusha

PIZZERIA LOLA

5557 South Xerxes Avenue
Minneapolis
Minnesota 55410
United States
+1 6124248338
www.pizzerialola.com

Opening hours	Open 7 days
Credit cards	Accepted
Style of pizza	Artisan wood-fired
Recommended pizza	Forager; Korean BBQ; Lady ZaZa; Sunnyside

"Chef Ann Kim is wrapped up in a love affair with pizza and she wields the peel with deft and charm. Her pizzas have zip and whimsy, but also class: she never forgets that someone hungry for pizza is usually really ready to eat. Those pies are substantial and not the least bit frilly, using the best ingredients to achieve pizza in it's highest form."—Stephanie March

"When it first launched in 2010, Lola was an under-the-radar upstart that I was glad was just a block from my house. But it didn't take long for the harpy song of its warm neighborhood vibe and fresh, clean, crispy artisanal pies to be heard by pizza scavengers far and wide. Sure, Pizzeria Lola's success ruined parking in my old neighborhood forever, but I don't begrudge it of that because it's pizza perfection." —Drew Wood

"Chef Ann Kim brings an insane level of creativity to her pizza selections. She uses fresh ingredients and her Korean influence to combine ingredients that are a splendid experience for your taste buds." —Todd Walker

The Lady ZaZa pizza is the showstopper Ann Kim—Lola's Korean co-owner, chef, and *pizzaiola*—outfits with tomato sauce, kimchi, Korean sausage, Serrano peppers, scallions (spring onions), and a sesame and soy chili glaze. Its spicy style is backed by the substance of the thin, crisp crust Kim maneuvers in her copper-clad, Le Panyol wood-fired oven. For lightness and depth of flavor she ferments her dough for 48 hours with a poolish starter. The same care goes into the selection and assembly of ingredients for classic Italian pizzas and Lola originals alike. The Sunnyside, a *pizza alla carbonara*, takes its *guanciale* from the Iowa producer La Quercia and its name from the yolks-up position of its two eggs.

RED WAGON PIZZA COMPANY

5416 Penn Avenue South
Minneapolis
Minnesota 55419
United States
+1 6122597147
www.redwagon-mpls.com

Opening hours	Open 7 days
Credit cards	Accepted
Style of pizza	Wood-fired
Recommended pizza	Banh Mi

"This place takes a unique approach to its toppings, often using slow-braised meats. It also has a seasonal rotation of ingredients resulting in delicious pizzas." —Keane Amdahl

PIG ATE MY PIZZA

4154 Broadway Avenue
Robbinsdale
Minnesota 55422
United States
+1 7635377267

Opening hours...........................Closed Sunday and Monday
Credit cards...Accepted
Style of pizza...Experimental
Recommended pizza...........................Big Cheeser; Piggy Pie

"A fun, novel environment and a solid beer list bolster its extraordinary pies."—Drew Wood

"As the brainchild of the Travail boys, expect some wildly inventive toppings and unusual delivery of your pizza!"—Molly Hermann

THE ITALIAN PIE SHOPPE

1670 Grand Avenue
St. Paul
Minnesota 55105
United States
+1 6512210093
www.italianpieshoppe.com

Opening hours...Open 7 days
Credit cards...Accepted
Style of pizza..Chicago stuffed
Recommended pizza...........................Sausage and Pepperoni

"The Italian Pie Shop has mastered the art of making a pizza pie. The crust is filled with fresh ingredients and then covered with the final layer of crust."
—Todd Walker

THE ORIGINAL RED'S SAVOY PIZZA

421 7th Street East
St. Paul
Minnesota 55101
United States
+1 6512271437
www.savoypizza.com

Opening hours...Open 7 days
Credit cards...Accepted
Style of pizza.......................................Minnesota thin-crust
Recommended pizza...........................Savoy House Special,
        Pepperoni and Sausage; Sausage and Sauerkraut

"There is nothing fancy about Red's Savoy Pizza. It simply takes the original concept of a pizza and somehow sprinkles fairy dust on the pie, making

every bite feel as if the ingredients have been intensified with mind-blowing flavor."—Todd Walker

"These guys are the high priests of Minnesota-style pizza: a giant round pie with a thin cracker crust, thickly laden with a savory bright red sauce, covered with a mantle of whole-milk Wisconsin cheese, and cut into squares. Simple, satisfying, elegant in its humility, trashy in it's seductive charms."
—Stephanie March

PUNCH PIZZA

704 Cleveland Avenue South
St. Paul
Minnesota 55116
United States
+1 6516961066
www.punchpizza.com

Opening hours...Open 7 days
Credit cards...Accepted
Style of pizza.......................................Wood-fired Neapolitan
Recommended pizza...................Margherita; Toto; Vesuvio

"These thin, chewy crusts spawned a local chain that has rigorous standards. Not only are they VPN-certified, you'll also find no Buffalo chicken or pineapple in their *mise en place*, only traditional ingredients befitting a Naples pie."
—Stephanie March

PIZZERIA PEZZO

2143 4th Street
White Bear Lake
Minnesota 55110
United States
+1 6517887844
www.pizzeriapezzo.com

Opening hours...Closed Monday
Credit cards...Accepted
Style of pizza.................Coal-fired and Chicago deep-dish

"Pizzeria Pezzo makes the most amazing deep-dish pizza."—Eliesa Johnson

PASTARIA

7734 Forsyth Boulevard
Clayton
Missouri 63105
United States
+1 3148626603
www.pastariastl.com

Opening hours	Open 7 days
Credit cards	Accepted
Style of pizza	Wood-fired Neapolitan
Recommended pizza	Brussels Sprouts; Pastaria Hawaiian; Quattro Formaggi; "The Roman"

"Fabulous, fabulous crust. One of the best-executed pizzas in town."—Ligaya Figueras

IL LAZZARONE

412 Delaware Street
Kansas City
Missouri 64105
United States
+1 8165413695
www.illazzarone.org

Opening hours	Open 7 days
Credit cards	Accepted
Style of pizza	Neapolitan
Recommended pizza	Bruxelles; Uovo

"Erik Borger adheres to the strict standards set forth by the Italian association that oversees authentic Neapolitan pizza: the dough is four ingredients only—sea salt, Caputo 00 pizzeria flour, water, and yeast, combined in a spiral fork mixer, and rolled out by hand."—Kimberly Winter Stern

MARTIN CITY BREWING COMPANY PIZZA & TAPROOM

410 East 135th Street
Kansas City
Missouri 64145
United States
+1 8162682222
www.martincitybrewingcompany.com

Opening hours	Open 7 days
Credit cards	Accepted
Style of pizza	Neapolitan wood-fired
Recommended pizza	Margherita; Wild Mushroom

"Martin City Brewing Company Pizza & Taproom serves up big-flavored appetizers, salads, sandwiches, and inventive Neapolitan-style pies from a postage-stamp-sized kitchen."—Kimberly Winter Stern

BLACK THORN PUB & PIZZA

3735 Wyoming Street
St. Louis
Missouri 63116
United States
+1 3147760534

Opening hours	Open 7 days
Credit cards	Accepted
Style of pizza	Chicago deep-dish

"This South City St. Louis dive bar is known for pitchers of cheap American light lager and a St. Louis take on Chicago deep dish that layers striations of spicy tomato sauce, copious amounts of toppings, and a overly generous application of cheese into a pizza that fans gladly wait up to two hours to be pulled from a waiting deck oven."
—Andrew Mark Veety

LA PIZZA

8137 Delmar Boulevard
St. Louis
Missouri 63130
United States
+1 3147251230
www.lapizzamenu.com

Opening hours	Open 7 days
Credit cards	Accepted
Style of pizza	New York thin-crust
Recommended pizza	Cheese; Pepperoni, Mushrooms, and Jalapeños

"La Pizza is the one and only place in St. Louis to find honest-to-goodness East Coast pizza in town."
—Andrew Mark Veety

PIZZEOLI

1928 South 12th Street
St. Louis
Missouri 63104
United States
+1 3144491111
www.pizzeoli.com

Opening hours	Closed Sunday and Monday
Credit cards	Accepted
Style of pizza	Neapolitan
Recommended pizza	Bianca

"Owner and chef Scott Sandler left a career in real estate to pursue his passion for Neapolitan pizza, but the crust is so perfect you'd think he'd been running this place for decades. The restaurant is meat-free, but you won't mind."—Ian Froeb

PIZZERIA TIVOLI

5859 South Kingshighway Boulevard
St. Louis
Missouri 63109
United States
+1 3148323222

Opening hours	Open 7 days
Credit cards	Accepted
Style of pizza	Neapolitan-Roman wood-fired
Recommended pizza	Castel Madama

"Perhaps the most hidden of hidden pizza gems in St. Louis, this unassuming neighborhood spot sports a handmade brick oven in the back, and turns out lightly topped pies that strike a welcome balance between wood-oven char and crisp crusts that give way to chewy, bread cores."
—Andrew Mark Veety

LA CASA PIZZARIA

4432 Leavenworth Street
Omaha
Nebraska 68105
United States
+1 4025566464
www.lacasapizzaria.net

Opening hours	Closed Monday
Credit cards	Accepted
Style of pizza	Neapolitan grilled
Recommended pizza	Hamburger Onion with Mozzarella and Romano

"The crust is unique and delicious. It is well-stretched dough that is still very tender."—Brian O'Malley

DANTE RISTORANTE PIZZERIA

The Shops of Legacy
16901 Wright Plaza
Omaha
Nebraska 68130
United States
+1 4029323078
www.dantepizzeria.com

Opening hours	Open 7 days
Credit cards	Accepted
Style of pizza	Neapolitan
Recommended pizza	Daviolo; Margherita

FRANK'S PIZZERIA

Linden Market
711 North 132nd Street
Omaha
Nebraska 68154
United States
+1 4024930404
www.franksnewyorkpizza.com

Opening hours	Closed Sunday
Credit cards	Accepted
Style of pizza	New York
Recommended pizza	Pepperoni and Mushroom

"It's got that thin, foldable crust a good New York-style pizza needs with just the right mix of crust, sauce, and toppings combined with a no frills, bring-the-softball-team type atmosphere."
—Tre Brashear

THE ORIGINAL RED'S SAVOY PIZZA

3510 North 167th Circle
Omaha
Nebraska 68116
United States
+1 4022892929
www.savoypizza.com

Opening hours	Open 7 days
Credit cards	Accepted
Style of pizza	Traditional
Recommended pizza	The Hammer

"Great homemade sausage combined with a spicy sauce."—Tre Brashear

PITCH COAL-FIRED PIZZERIA

5021 Underwood Avenue
Omaha
Nebraska 68132
United States
+1 4025902625
www.pitchpizzeria.com

Opening hours	Open 7 days
Credit cards	Accepted
Style of pizza	Contemporary coal-fired
Recommended pizza	Shrooms

"The atmosphere is fun and modern, the pizza is
unique, and the staff are friendly and informed."
—Tre Brashear

FIREFLOUR

111 North 5th Street
Bismarck
North Dakota 58501
United States
+1 7013239000
www.fireflourpizza.com

Opening hours	Closed Sunday
Credit cards	Accepted
Style of pizza	Neapolitan

"The crust kills it! It's tasty and chewy, just how
a Neapolitan crust should be. Fireflour also has local
offerings as toppings, like pulled Venison."—Molly Yeh

BLACKBIRD WOODFIRE

206 Broadway North
Fargo
North Dakota 58102
United States
+1 7014781968
www.blackbirdwoodfire.com

Opening hours	Closed Sunday
Credit cards	Accepted
Style of pizza	Neapolitan
Recommended pizza	BLT

"The pizzas here are kind of what would happen if
a sandwich and a pizza made a baby. They're made
with a great chewy wood-fired pizza crust but topped
with things like bacon, mixed greens, aioli, and
roasted Brussels sprouts."—Molly Yeh

RHOMBUS GUYS

312 Kittson Avenue
Grand Forks
North Dakota 58201
United States
+1 7017877317
www.rhombuspizza.com

Opening hours	Open 7 days
Credit cards	Accepted
Style of pizza	Midwestern
Recommended pizza	Happy Pig; T-Rex; Tater-Tot

"The charm of Rhombus Guys is the variation of
toppings offered here. Things like tater tots, mustard
sauce, and Thai chicken make it onto its pizzas
in crazy combinations that work. It has also got a
secret menu option where you can order any pizza as
nachos. It's bonkers. All of the pizza toppings come
melted onto a bed of nacho chips. It's SO good."
—Molly Yeh

LUIGI'S RESTAURANT

105 North Main Street
Akron
Ohio 44308
United States
+1 3302532999
www.luigisrestaurant.com

Opening hours	Open 7 days
Credit cards	Not accepted
Style of pizza	Italian-American Classic
Recommended pizza	Number Three

"An Akron, Ohio, favorite since 1949, prepare to
wait in line for a seat at this iconic pizza parlor that
is operated by the Ciriello family. The pizza is oh-so
cheesy with a soft, chewy crust."—Lisa Abraham

"A great, funky, old-school shop with a line out the
door and really satisfying pizzas."—Joe Crea

RENDINO'S PIZZA

5197 Manchester Road
Akron
Ohio 44319
United States
+1 3306447521
www.rendinospizza.com

Opening hours	Closed Monday
Credit cards	Accepted but not AMEX
Style of pizza	Traditional
Recommended pizza	Pepperoni

"Owner Patty Rendino has been making pizza at this Portage Lakes location for 40 years, following in the footsteps of her mother who operated pizza shops in the area beginning in 1960."—Lisa Abraham

BEXLEY PIZZA PLUS

2651 East Main Street
Bexley
Ohio 43209
United States
+1 6142373305
www.bexleypizzaplus.com

Opening hours	Open 7 days
Credit cards	Accepted
Style of pizza	Columbus
Recommended pizza	Ultimate

"Bexley Pizza Plus creates the perfect pizza. Its medium-thick crust is hearty and supports the huge amount of toppings that go on it. While its pizza borders on gourmet, the best thing it does is a simple traditional pizza."—Brad Rocco

RUBINO'S PIZZA

2643 East Main Street
Bexley
Ohio 43209
United States
+1 6142351700

Opening hours	Closed Monday
Credit cards	Not accepted
Style of pizza	Columbus
Recommended pizza	Pepperoni; Sausage

"This vintage pizza parlor serves the best old-school Columbus-style pizza. The crust is cracker-thin and cut into rectangles, and the classic pepperoni curls up around the edges when it cooks."—Shelley Mann

"Rubino's eschews modern contraptions like the pizza box and instead to-go pies are wrapped in a tall wax paper bag."—Samuel Peterson

NOCE GOURMET PIZZERIA

125 Main Street
Chardon
Ohio 44024
United States
+1 4402790303
www.nocegourmetpizza.com

Opening hours	Closed Sunday and Monday
Credit cards	Accepted but not AMEX
Style of pizza	Refined and inventive
Recommended pizza	Rustic Roma; Thai Chicken

"The pizza has a hard-to-find style of crust with a baguette's crispy finish."—Joe Crea

ADRIATICO'S PIZZA

113 West McMillan Street
Cincinnati
Ohio 45219
United States
+1 5132814344
www.adriaticosuc.com

Opening hours	Open 7 days
Credit cards	Accepted
Style of pizza	New York
Recommended pizza	Sicilian with Cheese

"Adriatico's square slice packs a mean punch with a low-moisture mozzarella and provolone cheese blend, oregano, and a spicy sauce. Most notably, Adriatico's sell an enormous pie on the campuses of Ohio State and the University of Cincinnati called the Buckeye and the Bearcat. I fly a large pie back to NYC every year."—Miriam Weiskind

A TAVOLA

1220 Vine Street
Cincinnati
Ohio 45202
United States
+1 5132460192
www.atavolapizza.com

Opening hours..Open 7 days
Credit cards...Accepted
Style of pizza...Neapolitan wood-fired
Recommended pizza....................................Fig and Prosciutto;
Brussels Sprout

"A Tavola's handmade traditional wood-fired pizza is about as close to taking a trip to a Neapolitan trattoria as you can get. The cocktails are fabulous and the homemade gelato is a must-have ending."—Ilene Ross

MIO'S

3703 Paxton Avenue
Cincinnati
Ohio 45209
United States
+1 5135314200
www.miospizza.com

Opening hours..Open 7 days
Credit cards...Accepted
Style of pizza..Cincinnati
Recommended pizza................Cheese with Sesame Crust

"A great pizza made memorable by the sesame crust, perfect color, and chew. Don't forget to order the sesame crust."—Mike Randolph

BAR CENTO

1948 West 25th Street
Cleveland
Ohio 44113
United States
+1 2162741010
www.barcento.com

Opening hours..Open 7 days
Credit cards...Accepted
Style of pizza...Neapolitan wood-fired
Recommended pizza....................................Potato; Sunnyside

"A staple of the Ohio City neighborhood—just across the street from the venerable West Side Market—Bar Cento excels at crisp and delicious thin-crust pizzas that are available late into the night every day of the year."—Douglas Trattner

"Consistently voted one of the best pizzas in Cleveland."—Laura Adiletta

"Every pie just has that perfect balance of acid, fat and sweetness that makes pizza a meal in a bite." —Beth Stallings

MAROTTA'S

2289 Lee Road
Cleveland
Ohio 44118
United States
+1 2169329264
www.marottas.com

Opening hours..Closed Sunday
Credit cards...Accepted
Style of pizza..New York
Recommended pizza..Traditionale

"Big pies, fresh ingredients, and a good ratio of cheese to sauce to crust."—Laura Adiletta

VALENTINO'S PIZZA

2197 Murray Hill Road
Cleveland
Ohio 44106
United States
+1 2167950463
www.valentinospizzacleveland.com

Opening hours..Open 7 days
Credit cards...Accepted
Style of pizza..New York
Recommended pizza..Pepperoni

"Sometimes you don't want anything fancy or twee; just a big, floppy New York-style pie with tangy-sweet sauce, great cheese, and quality toppings." —Douglas Trattner

VERO PIZZA NAPOLETANA

12421 Cedar Road
Cleveland Heights
Ohio 44106
United States
+1 2162298383
www.verocleveland.com

Opening hours..........................Closed Sunday and Monday
Credit cards...............................Accepted but not AMEX
Style of pizza..Neapolitan brick-oven
Recommended pizza....................................Farm Egg; Salumi

"Boasting one of the few all wood-burning ovens in town, Vero turns out some of the most authentic Neapolitan-style pizza around. An airy, chewy outer crust blistered with char gives way to a thin, crisp inner crust supporting a few choice ingredients."
—Douglas Trattner

ADRIATICO'S PIZZA

265 West 11th Avenue
Columbus
Ohio 43210
United States
+1 6144212300
www.adriaticososu.com

Opening hours	Open 7 days
Credit cards	Accepted
Style of pizza	New York
Recommended pizza	Sicilian

"The garlic-infused crust is wonderful."
—Jim Ellison

BONO PIZZA

1420 Presidential Drive
Columbus
Ohio 43212
United States
+1 6149068646
www.bonopizzacolumbus.com

Opening hours	Open 7 days
Credit cards	Accepted but not AMEX
Style of pizza	Neapolitan wood-fired
Recommended pizza	Hulk; San Rolando; TonnoBono

"This tiny pizza operation with a big soul has survived through multiple moves, and continues to build a near-fanatic following. No matter the location, at the heart is always a wood-fired brick oven where pizzas are lovingly cooked one at a time. The pies have airy, charred crusts and are loaded with top-quality meats and mounds of fresh vegetables."—Shelley Mann

"This place is an eccentric riot located in a dive bar... but the pizzas are spectacular."—G. A. Benton

The uninitiated are more impressed with the fixings on Bono thin-crusted, wood-fired pizzas than those decorating its current digs. Combinations of zippy ingredients, like the Hulk, with fresh pesto, fresh mozzarella, and a changing assortment of green things—zucchini (courgette), artichokes, olives, arugula (rocket), bell pepper—are more distinctive than the room's red-checkered tablecloths and Dali prints. The regulars, though, are mad about the quirky design, right down to the last twinkle light. After enduring various discomforts at Bono's prior locations, they're thrilled just to have a satisfactory place to sit and spend quality time with their beloved San Rolando and its tomato sauce, pepperoni, crumbled sausage, and mozzarella.

BORGATA PIZZA CAFE

5701 Parkville Street
Columbus
Ohio 43229
United States
+1 6148912345
www.borgatapizzacafe.com

Opening hours	Closed Sunday
Credit cards	Accepted
Style of pizza	New York
Recommended pizza	Pepperoni; Sausage

"A New York-style pizza doesn't call for anything special: just pepperoni or sausage. At Borgata they're both fantastic."—Samuel Peterson

DONATOS PIZZA

3489 North High Street
Columbus
Ohio 43214
United States
+1 6142689559

Opening hours	Open 7 days
Credit cards	Accepted
Style of pizza	Traditional
Recommended pizza	Mushroom; Pepperoni

FIGLIO WOOD FIRED PIZZA

1369 Grandview Avenue
Columbus
Ohio 43212
United States
+1 6144818850
www.figliopizza.com

Opening hours	Closed Sunday
Credit cards	Accepted
Style of pizza	Gourmet wood-fired
Recommended pizza	Pear and Brie

GATTO'S PIZZA

2928 North High Street
Columbus
Ohio 43202
United States
+1 6142633737

Opening hours	Open 7 days
Credit cards	Not accepted
Style of pizza	Columbus
Recommended pizza	Sausage, Meatball, and Hot Peppers

"Gatto's makes great pizzas—and has done so for about half a century. As is customary in many square-shaped Midwestern states, its thin to medium-thin crispy crusts are 'party cut' into little rectangles."
—G. A. Benton

HARVEST PIZZERIA

2885 North High Street
Columbus
Ohio 43202
United States
+1 6149477133
www.harvestpizzeria.com

Opening hours	Closed Sunday
Credit cards	Accepted
Style of pizza	Italian thin-crust
Recommended pizza	Fennel Sausage; Ohio Double Bacon; Spicy Yuma

"Harvest is a relaxed but sophisticated pizzeria with great wines, craft beers, fancy cocktails, impressive appetizers, salads made with 'live,' local greens, intense desserts, and the proverbial rustic-chic ambience. The lovely and toothsome pies are crackly on their toasty edges, delicate in the center, and topped with local cheeses and meats and produce from the owner's farm."—G. A. Benton

HARVEST PIZZERIA

495 South 4th Street
Columbus
Ohio 43206
United States
+1 6148241769
www.harvestpizzeria.com

Opening hours	Closed Sunday
Credit cards	Accepted
Style of pizza	Neapolitan
Recommended pizza	Fennel Sausage; Mushroom; Spicy Yuma

"It's great pie that's got the flavor of Ohio."
—Beth Stallings

"Every detail is perfect, from the charred and crispy crust to the herb-flecked sauce to the artfully arranged toppings."—Shelley Mann

"The best crust I have ever had."—Chris Crader

A great champion of everything local—farmers, dairies, meat producers, pizza lovers—Harvest's Chris Crader reveals Ohio as pizza heartland. The menu's geography is wide, from the American Southwest-inspired Spicy Yuma pizza, with Gouda, chorizo, jalapeño, corn, roasted red bell pepper, and chipotle-corrupted tomato, to the Pietmonte (sic) pizza, named for its Piedmontese salami. But much of its cheese, produce, and meats are produced in the state. The artisan, stone-baked crust is crisp on entry, with a wonderful sinking feeling to follow. The original location, in the historic German Village neighborhood, is a modern-casual twist on farmhouse chic. A second Harvest is in the Clintonville neighborhood.

HOUNDDOGS THREE DEGREE PIZZA

2657 North High Street
Columbus
Ohio 43202
United States
+1 6142614686

Opening hours	Open 7 days
Credit cards	Accepted
Style of pizza	Multiple
Recommended pizza	Russell

"Hounddogs has been an old North Columbus icon for years and still is. The tagline for the company is 'pizza for the people.'"—Jim Ellison

MATT THE MILLER'S TAVERN

1400 Grandview Avenue
Columbus
Ohio 43212
United States
+1 6147541026
www.mtmtavern.com

Opening hours..Open 7 days
Credit cards..Accepted
Style of pizza..Flatbread
Recommended pizza....................................Ahi Tuna

MEISTERS' PIZZA

1168 Chambers Road
Columbus
Ohio 43212
United States
+1 6144813050

Opening hours..Open 7 days
Credit cards..Accepted
Style of pizza..Chicago
Recommended pizza................................Meat Feast

PIZZA HOUSE OF COLUMBUS OHIO

747 East Lincoln Avenue
Columbus
Ohio 43229
United States
+1 6148853121
www.pizzahousecolumbus.com

Opening hours..Open 7 days
Credit cards..Accepted
Style of pizza..Columbus
Recommended pizza....................Pepperoni, Sausage, and
Mushroom

"This pizzeria has been around for over 50 years. Even
though it is one of the busiest pizzerias in the city,
it never let its product suffer. Medium-thick-crust
pizzas are baked perfectly to order."—Brad Rocco

PLANK'S CAFE & PIZZERIA

743 Parsons Avenue
Columbus
Ohio 43206
United States
+1 6144457221
www.plankscafe.com

Opening hours..Closed Sunday
Credit cards..Accepted
Style of pizza..Columbus thin-crust
Recommended pizza....................Cajun Chicken; Sausage
and Pepperoni

"I have probably eaten more pizza from Plank's Cafe
(not to be confused with the similarly named Plank's
Bier Garten) than from any other single location. Like
other pizza places in Columbus, the pizza features
a thin crust with square-cut slices. But, that crust
stands out for one reason: it's sweet. Not quite as
sweet as a cookie, but close. And that sweetness
works perfectly with a combination of tomato sauce
and spicy pepperoni."—Samuel Peterson

ROTOLO'S ITALIAN PIZZERIA

1749 West 5th Avenue
Columbus
Ohio 43212
United States
+1 6144887934
www.rotolospizza.com

Opening hours..Open 7 days
Credit cards..Accepted
Style of pizza..Classic
Recommended pizza................................Italian Sausage

MARION'S PIAZZA

711 Shroyer Road
Dayton
Ohio 45419
United States
+1 9372936991
www.marionspiazza.com

Opening hours..Open 7 days
Credit cards..Accepted but not AMEX
Style of pizza..Dayton square-cut
Recommended pizza....................Mushroom and Anchovy

"Marion's is the finest example of one of the nation's
most regionally specific pizzas, complete with salty
cheese and canned mushrooms."—Hanna Raskin

MARION'S PIAZZA

Country Square Shopping Center
404 West National Road
Englewood
Ohio 45322
United States
+1 9378320333
www.marionspiazza.com

Opening hours..Open 7 days
Credit cards......................................Accepted but not AMEX
Style of pizza...Tavern
Recommended pizza...Cheese

"Tavern-style pizza that is thin, crispy, and cut into squares. Heavy on the oregano, this is a pie that is very sweet and salty at first bite."—Miriam Weiskind

TRISTANO'S PIZZERIA

3306 Columbus Street
Grove City
Ohio 43123
United States
+1 6148755509
www.tristanospizza.com

Opening hours..Open 7 days
Credit cards......................................Accepted but not AMEX
Style of pizza.............................Chicago and traditional
Recommended pizza.............................Screamin' Tristano

"It is difficult to find true Chicago-style deep dish outside of the Windy City but Lou does the style justice. Everything on the menu is good and it is worth the effort to find this place."—Jim Ellison

ANGELO'S

13715 Madison Avenue
Lakewood
Ohio 44107
United States
+1 2162210440
www.angelosonline.com

Opening hours..Open 7 days
Credit cards..Accepted
Style of pizza...Deep-dish
Recommended pizza.........................Angelo's Meat Lovers;
Margherita; Mediterranean

"One of the most notable pizza shops in Cleveland. It makes everything in-house, from the dough to the sauce, and it nails classic and creative combinations alike."—Beth Stallings

SOL PIE PIZZA

3159 Whitewood Street Northwest
North Canton
Ohio 44720
United States
+1 3304943131
www.solpiepizza.com

Opening hours..Open 7 days
Credit cards..Accepted
Style of pizza............................Neapolitan and California
Recommended pizza.................................Daydreamer

"Sol Pie Pizza owners Alan and Lisa Frank work directly with local farmers to obtain the best produce for their restaurant. Alan walks through high tunnels and windswept fields to hand-select the best basil, tomatoes, and other ingredients that end up on hand-tossed crust and specialty salads."—Barbara Abbott

THE ELMTON

584 5th Street
Struthers
Ohio 44471
United States
+1 3307558511

Opening hours..Closed Sunday
Credit cards......................................Accepted but not AMEX
Style of pizza..Traditional
Recommended pizza...................Italian Sausage; Pepperoni

"It's the blend of three cheeses—mozzarella, provolone, and Swiss—that gives this pie its special taste. Locals will wait in line for hours on weekends for a seat at The Elmton. Consider ordering the pie 'extra crispy' so the bottom crust is crunchy as well as chewy."—Lisa Abraham

PARK ST. PIZZA

215R Dover Road Northwest
Sugarcreek
Ohio 44681
United States
+1 3308522993
www.parkstreetpizza.com

Opening hours..Open 7 days
Credit cards......................................Accepted but not AMEX
Style of pizza..California
Recommended pizza...Christo's Greek

"Top notch."—Barbara Abbott

JO-JO'S ORIGINAL PIZZERIA

4336 Monroe Street
Toledo
Ohio 43606
United States
+1 4194731223
www.theoriginaljojospizzeria.com

Opening hours..Closed Sunday
Credit cards..Accepted
Style of pizza...Thin-crust
Recommended pizza..Pepperoni

"A family-owned business that's very casual and very friendly. The pizza is always excellent."—Mary Bilyeu

ROSIE'S ITALIAN GRILLE

606 North McCord Road
Toledo
Ohio 43615
United States
+1 4198665007
www.rosiesitaliangrille.com

Opening hours..Open 7 days
Credit cards..Accepted
Style of pizza...Tuscan thin-crust
Recommended pizza..............Grilled Chicken, Bacon, and
Roasted Cherry Pepper

"Phil Barone, the owner, is the second generation serving true Italian cuisine in Toledo. He greets customers and chats with them as though he's welcoming them to his home. The pizza has a crisp crust, lots of flavor, and old world character."
—Mary Bilyeu

SAMOSKY'S HOMESTYLE PIZZERIA

6738 Center Road
Valley City
Ohio 44280
United States
+1 3304832000

Opening hours..Closed Sunday
Credit cards..Accepted
Style of pizza.................................Old-fashioned American
Recommended pizza..............................Philly Cheese Steak

"A good marriage of traditional chewy-crust pies with imaginative toppings."—Joe Crea

THE SUNRISE INN

510 East Market Street
Warren
Ohio 44481
United States
+1 3303925176
www.sunriseinnofwarren.com

Opening hours..Open 7 days
Credit cards..Accepted
Style of pizza...Old World
Recommended pizza..................Greek; Red with Pepperoni

"The pizza has a thick crust and flavorful sauce; it's made in the old world tradition of pizza shops in Ohio's Mahoning Valley—which means no mozzarella. Instead, the sauce is topped with a generous sprinkling of grated Romano cheese. The locals call this style of pizza 'Brier Hill' after the Youngstown, Ohio, neighborhood settled by Italian immigrants, where the style became popular."—Lisa Abraham

MASSEY'S PIZZA

5310 East Main Street
Whitehall
Ohio 43213
United States
+1 6148660700
www.masseyspizza.com

Opening hours..Open 7 days
Credit cards..Accepted
Style of pizza...Columbus
Recommended pizza..Pepperoni

"Massey's pizzas have a medium crust and a sweet, tangy red sauce. The cheese and toppings are loaded up—so there's no need to order extra pepperoni here. The pizzas are baked on a hearth-stone six-shelf rotating gas bagel oven—awesome!"—Brad Rocco

COCCIA HOUSE PIZZA

764 Pittsburgh Avenue
Wooster
Ohio 44691
United States
+1 3302627136
www.cocciahouse.com

Opening hours..Closed Tuesday
Credit cards..Accepted
Style of pizza..Abruzzi
Recommended pizza.........................Anything with crumbly
sausage; Grandma Coccia's

"Coccia House has a long-standing tradition of exceptional pizza, and this is single-handedly attributed to its crust. This unusual biscuit- and pastry-like creation adds unexpected flavor and complexity, and clearly stands out from traditional pizza."—Barbara Abbott

"Regulars know the way to order the pizza—'bricked' if you want it super crispy on the bottom, 'light' or 'no grass' if you don't want the extra oregano-heavy seasoning."—Beth Stallings

NATALIE'S COAL-FIRED PIZZA

5601 North High Street
Worthington
Ohio 43085
United States
+1 6144362625
www.nataliescoalfiredpizza.com

Opening hours...Closed Monday
Credit cards..Accepted
Style of pizza..Coal-fired
Recommended pizza...Venetian Jail

"It's rare to find pies cooked in a coal-fired oven. This extreme heat produces blistery, bubbly old-world New York-style pizzas. Sourcing is taken seriously here: veggies come from nearby farmers' markets and cheeses are imported from Italy."—Beth Stallings

BREADICO

201 North Weber Avenue
Sioux Falls
South Dakota 57103
United States
+1 6053321202
www.breadico.com

Opening hours.........................Closed Sunday and Monday
Credit cards..Accepted
Style of pizza...Artisan sourdough
Recommended pizza.................Mushroom and Cambozola

REDROSSA PIZZERIA

3412 South Western Avenue
Sioux Falls
South Dakota 57105
United States
+1 6053393675
www.redrossa.com

Opening hours..Open 7 days
Credit cards..Accepted
Style of pizza...Neapolitan
Recommended pizza...Gabagool

"Redrossa makes its wood-fired pizza right in front of you. The pizzas are always great and it has great salads to choose from to complement any meal."
—David Napolitano

BLAZE PIZZA

5734 North Bayshore Drive
Glendale
Wisconsin 53217
United States
+1 4149678805
www.blazepizza.com

Opening hours..Open 7 days
Credit cards..Accepted
Style of pizza...Wood-fired

MANGIA WINE BAR

5717 Sheridan Road
Kenosha
Wisconsin 53140
United States
+1 2626524285
www.kenoshamangia.com

Opening hours	Closed Monday
Credit cards	Accepted
Style of pizza	Wood-fired
Recommended pizza	Smoke and Cure

PIZZA BRUTTA

1805 Monroe Street
Madison
Wisconsin 53711
United States
+1 6082572120
www.pizzabrutta.com

Opening hours	Open 7 days
Credit cards	Accepted
Style of pizza	Wood-fired Neapolitan
Recommended pizza	Marinara

"An unassuming and humble little pizza place, Pizza Brutta is second to none. The pizzas have a beautiful crust that's incredibly consistent, and all done with domestic organic flour. Everything is locally sourced (except the San Marzano tomatoes)."
—Lacee Perry & Matthew McClutchy

ANODYNE BAY VIEW CAFE & PIZZA

2920 South Kinnickinnic Avenue
Milwaukee
Wisconsin 53207
United States
+1 4144890765
www.anodynecoffee.com

Opening hours	Closed Monday
Credit cards	Accepted
Style of pizza	Wood-fired Neapolitan
Recommended pizza	Beet (beetroot); Margherita; Mr Potato; The seasonal special

BALISTRERI'S BLUEMOUND INN

6501 West Bluemound Road
Milwaukee
Wisconsin 53213
United States
+1 4142589881
www.balistreris.com

Opening hours	Open 7 days
Credit cards	Accepted
Style of pizza	Regular and thin-crust
Recommended pizza	White

"The place just smells wonderful when you walk in. Its an all-fashion supper club. Where else can you get a pizza with aged Cheddar, charbroiled (chargrilled) bratwurst, and caramelized sauerkraut?"
—Susan Laughlin

CALDERONE CLUB

842 North Old World 3rd Street
Milwaukee
Wisconsin 53203
United States
+1 4142733236
www.calderoneclub.net

Opening hours	Open 7 days
Credit cards	Accepted
Style of pizza	Neapolitan thin-crust
Recommended pizza	Margherita; Pepperoni

"I would recommend the Margherita pizza, but I don't believe you can make a bad choice here."
—Rick Rodriguez

GLORIOSO'S ITALIAN MARKET / TRIO'S PIZZA

101 1 East Brady Street
Milwaukee
Wisconsin 53202
United States
+1 4142720540
www.gloriosos.com

Opening hours	Open 7 days
Credit cards	Accepted
Style of pizza	Thin-crust
Recommended pizza	Black Olive, Mushroom, Artichoke, and Onion; Pepperoni; Sausage, Green Pepper, and Onion

MARIA'S PIZZARIA

5025 West Forest Home Avenue
Milwaukee
Wisconsin 53219
United States
+1 4145434606

Opening hours	Closed Monday
Credit cards	Not accepted
Style of pizza	Midwestern thin-crust
Recommended pizza	Sausage, Mushrooms, and Onions

"Thin- and flaky-crusted, these pizzas are loaded with toppings until they can take no more, then served on trays far too small for their cheesy, delicious bounty. But the pizza's only part of it. You have to eat at Maria's. The place is the outward manifestation of the original generation's unique vision—Christmas lights, red-checkered tablecloths, and paint-by-number religious iconography fill the place. It's one of the vanishingly unique places America has to offer."
—Adam Kuban

WOLF PEACH

1818 North Hubbard Street
Milwaukee
Wisconsin 53212
United States
+1 4143748480
www.wolf-peach.com

Opening hours	Open 7 days
Credit cards	Accepted
Style of pizza	Wood-fired
Recommended pizza	Margherita

"The pizza has a light airy yet flavorful crust with the big bubbles from a fast and hot bake. The sauce is balanced—not too sweet or salty or spicy."
—Geoff Trenholme

ZAFFIRO'S PIZZA

1724 North Farwell Avenue
Milwaukee
Wisconsin 53202
United States
+1 4142898776
www.zaffirospizza.com

Opening hours	Open 7 days
Credit cards	Accepted
Style of pizza	Thin-crust
Recommended pizza	Veggie

"The thinnest crust pizza I ever had, almost like cracker bread."—Michael A. Glorioso

WELLS BROTHERS ITALIAN RESTAURANT & BAR

2148 Mead Street
Racine
Wisconsin 53403
United States
+1 2626324408
www.wellsbrosracine.com

Opening hours	Closed Sunday and Monday
Credit cards	Accepted
Style of pizza	Thin-crust
Recommended pizza	Fresh Basil; Onions and Garlic

"This place delightfully eschews the handcrafted artisan style of the day and rolls its dough—through rollers!—into a super-thin foundation for any combo of super-fresh toppings that you choose from the list. Family run and family-friendly, you know that if you lived in Racine you would be a regular."
—Penny Pollack

IL RITROVO

515 South 8th Street
Sheboygan
Wisconsin 53081
United States
+1 9208037516
www.ilritrovopizza.com

Opening hours	Closed Sunday
Credit cards	Accepted
Style of pizza	Wood-fired Neapolitan
Recommended pizza	Giuseppe; Mushroom

"One of just a handful of pizzerias in Wisconsin carrying the VPN certification. The crust is crisp on the outside and perfectly charred from the wood-burning oven. It's truly a Wisconsin treasure."—Rick Rodriguez

"The sauce is the star at Il Ritrovo. While deep and rich in flavor it still holds a brightness that delights. And the service is always top notch."
—Lacee Perry & Matthew McClutchy

ALPHONSO'S THE ORIGINAL

1119 South 108th Street
West Allis
Wisconsin 53214
United States
+1 4147550341
www.alphonsostheoriginal.com

Opening hours	Closed Monday
Credit cards	Accepted
Style of pizza	Hand-tossed thin-crust
Recommended pizza	Cheese, Sausage, and Pepperoni; Super Special

"Alphonso's has several crust options including honey, red pepper flake, and scorpion pepper. I prefer the thin cracker crust with the delicious spicy sauce and large chunks of Italian sausage."—Rick Rodriguez

"I'M 110 PERCENT COMFORTABLE CROWNING THIS PLACE THE KING OF NEAPOLITAN PIZZA IN CHICAGO." PENNY POLLACK P.428

CHICAGO

"THE BEST PAN PIZZA I HAVE EVER EATEN."
NELLA GRASSANO P.425

"NOT GIMMICKY OR TRYING TO IMPRESS, IT JUST OFFERS UP A STELLAR HUNK OF PIE."
STEPHANIE MARCH P.424

"OLD-SCHOOL SQUARE-CUT JUNKED-UP PIES WITH ALL THE TRIMMINGS."
KEN MILLER & GREG O'NEILL P.424

"FOR THOSE WHO LOVE CHICAGO-STYLE DEEP-DISH PIZZA, WATCHING THE FIRST SLICE OF ONE OF LOU MALNATI'S PIZZAS BEING LIFTED OUT OF THE PAN IS ALMOST A RELIGIOUS EXPERIENCE." JANE SIMON AMMESON P.425

CHICAGO

N   SCALE

0   1000   2000   3000
                          yd.

1. RANALLI'S, ANDERSONVILLE (P.424)
2. SPACCA NAPOLI PIZZERIA, UPTOWN (P.428)
3. DANTE'S PIZZERIA, LOGAN SQUARE (P.426)
4. JOHN'S PIZZERIA RISTORANTE AND LOUNGE, BUCKTOWN (P.424)
5. MY PI, BUCKTOWN (P.424)
6. PIECE BREWERY AND PIZZERIA, WICKER PARK (P.428)
7. PIZZERIA DA NELLA, LINCOLN PARK (P.426)

8. PEQUOD'S PIZZA, LINCOLN PARK (P.425)
9. STELLA BARRA, OLD TOWN (P.426)
10. BALENA, OLD TOWN (P.426)
11. COALFIRE PIZZA, WEST LOOP (P.428)
12. EDWARDO'S NATURAL PIZZA, GOLD COAST (P.425)
13. LOU MALNATI'S PIZZERIA, RIVER NORTH (P.427)
14. PIZANO'S PIZZA & PASTA, RIVER NORTH (P.427)

15. GINO'S EAST, RIVER NORTH (P.427)
16. PIZZERIA UNO, RIVER NORTH (P.427)
17. PIZANO'S PIZZA & PASTA, THE LOOP (P.426)
18. LOU MALNATI'S PIZZERIA, GOLD COAST (P.425)
19. VITO & NICK'S PIZZERIA, BURBANK (P.424)
20. FREDDIES, BRIDGEPORT (P.424)
21. CONNIE'S PIZZA, CHINATOWN (P.425)

CHICAGO PIZZA BOSS

Mobile pizzeria—check website, Facebook, Twitter,
and Instagram for upcoming locations
Chicago
Illinois
United States
+1 6309150063
www.chicagopizzaboss.com

Opening hours	Variable
Credit cards	Accepted
Style of pizza	Neapolitan
Recommended pizza	Fig and Prosciutto; Hellfire's Kiss; Salami and Pickled Giardiniera

"Chicago Pizza Boss is known for its high-end
ingredients: 24-hour proofed dough, award-winning
Caputo fresh mozzarella, imported grated Parmesan
cheese, imported crushed San Marzano tomatoes;
with an extra virgin olive oil drizzle."
—Jane Simon Ammeson

RANALLI'S

1512 West Berwyn Avenue
Andersonville
Chicago
Illinois 60640
United States
+1 7733341300
www.ranallisandersonville.com

Opening hours	Open 7 days
Credit cards	Accepted
Style of pizza	Chicago
Recommended pizza	Pepperoni

FREDDIES

701 West 31st Street
Bridgeport
Chicago
Illinois 60616
United States
+1 3128080147
www.freddieson31st.com

Opening hours	Open 7 days
Credit cards	Accepted
Style of pizza	Thin-crust
Recommended pizza	Sausage

"It uses great homemade sausage on the pizza."
—Nella Grassano

JOHN'S PIZZERIA RISTORANTE AND LOUNGE

2104 North Western Avenue
Bucktown
Chicago
Illinois 60647
United States
www.johnspizzachicago.com

Opening hours	Open 7 days
Credit cards	Accepted but not AMEX
Style of pizza	Chicago tavern
Recommended pizza	Meat-zza

"Old-school square-cut junked-up pies with all the
trimmings."—Ken Miller & Greg O'Neill

MY PI

2010 North Damen Avenue
Bucktown
Chicago
Illinois 60647
United States
+1 7733946900
www.mypiepizza.com

Opening hours	Open 7 days
Credit cards	Accepted
Style of pizza	Deep-dish

"This is the only legit deep-dish pizza in Chicago.
Not gimmicky or trying to impress, it just offers
up a stellar hunk of pie."—Stephanie March

VITO & NICK'S PIZZERIA

8433 South Pulaski Road
Burbank
Chicago
Illinois 60652
United States
+1 7737352050
www.vitoandnicks.com

Opening hours	Open 7 days
Credit cards	Not accepted
Style of pizza	Chicago tavern
Recommended pizza	Pepperoni and Egg; Sausage; Sausage, Beef, and Giardiniera; Vito and Nick's House Special

"Like most places it all starts with the atmosphere.
As you enter Vito & Nick's you'll see the local patrons
bellied up to the bar drinking Old Style on tap, and

like every good south side joint, a clear shot of the prep area and ovens. Vito & Nick's is one of the oldest pizzerias in Chicago and it has survived simply because it is one of the best. The thinnest thin crust you'll ever taste, it's a circular pizza cut into squares that keeps the outer pieces crisp as a cracker and the inner squares soft and foldable."
—Jonathan Porter

CONNIE'S PIZZA

2373 South Archer Avenue
Chinatown
Chicago
Illinois 60616
United States
+1 3123263443
www.conniespizza.com

Opening hours	Open 7 days
Credit cards	Accepted
Style of pizza	Pan
Recommended pizza	Pepperoni

"The best pan pizza I have ever eaten."
—Nella Grassano

EDWARDO'S NATURAL PIZZA

1212 North Dearborn Street
Gold Coast
Chicago
Illinois 60610
United States
+1 3123374490
www.edwardos.com

Opening hours	Open 7 days
Credit cards	Accepted
Style of pizza	Chicago deep-dish stuffed
Recommended pizza	Fresh Spinach

"Edwardo's is a stuffed, deep-dish pizza. That's a cornmeal-type crust stuffed with toppings and cheese, then another layer of crust and then sauce on top! You have to have one to believe it, very filling and delicious!"—Brad Rocco

LOU MALNATI'S PIZZERIA

805 South State Street
Gold Coast
Chicago
Illinois 60605
United States
+1 3127861000
www.loumalnatis.com

Opening hours	Open 7 days
Credit cards	Accepted
Style of pizza	Chicago deep-dish
Recommended pizza	The "Lou"

"For those who love Chicago-style deep-dish pizza, watching the first slice of one of Lou Malnati's pizzas being lifted out of the pan is almost a religious experience."—Jane Simon Ammeson

PEQUOD'S PIZZA

2207 North Clybourn Avenue
Lincoln Park
Chicago
Illinois 60614
United States
+1 7733271512
www.pequodspizza.com

Opening hours	Open 7 days
Credit cards	Accepted
Style of pizza	Pan
Recommended pizza	Sausage and Giardiniera; Sausage, Onion, Garlic, and Spinach

"The pan pizza at Pequod's does everything I wish deep dish did. Sure, it's enormously thick, but it also has a flavorful crust that does more than act as a platform for other ingredients. The best part is the Parmesan cheese sprinkled on the edge, which transforms into a blackened ring of darkly caramelized cheese."—Nick Kindelsperger

"The pizza's kind of grungy in a super-authentic way."
—Michael Muser

PIZZERIA DA NELLA

1443 West Fullerton
Lincoln Park
Chicago
Illinois 60614
United States
+1 7732816600
www.pizzeriadanella.com

Opening hours	Open 7 days
Credit cards	Accepted
Style of pizza	Neapolitan
Recommended pizza	Margherita

"Uncompromising in its authenticity."—Mike Sula

DANTE'S PIZZERIA

3028 West Armitage Avenue
Logan Square
Chicago
Illinois 60647
United States
+1 7733420002
www.dantespizzeriachicago.com

Opening hours	Open 7 days
Credit cards	Accepted but not AMEX
Style of pizza	New York
Recommended pizza	Plain cheese

"This is foldable New York-style pizza. The ratio of cheese to sauce is perfect."
—Ken Miller & Greg O'Neill

PIZANO'S PIZZA & PASTA

Mallers Building, 61 East Madison Street
The Loop
Chicago
Illinois 60603
United States
+1 3122361777
www.pizanoschicago.com

Opening hours	Open 7 days
Credit cards	Accepted
Style of pizza	Deep-dish and tavern
Recommended pizza	Mark's Special; Rudy's Special

"Pizano's is a classic Chicago pizza joint. Starting with the atmosphere, you have the red checkered tablecloths and the smell of bubbling tomatoes and garlic as you enter. As you pass through the front door, you are immediately set for Chicago-style pizza. The ingredients Pizano's uses are perfect for the style of pizza it creates. From the Wisconsin mozzarella to the California-grown tomatoes, the pies are simply the result of the best ingredients melding together in a place that lets you know you are in sweet home Chicago." —Jonathan Porter

BALENA

1633 North Halsted Street
Old Town
Chicago
Illinois 60614
United States
+1 3128673888
www.balenachicago.com

Opening hours	Open 7 days
Credit cards	Accepted
Style of pizza	Artisan New York-Neapolitan
Recommended pizza	Mortadella and Pistachio Pesto; Rhubarb

"The crust is really just exceptional bread, which is crisp and delicate on the outside, and soft and chewy inside."—Nick Kindelsperger

STELLA BARRA

1954 North Halsted Street
Old Town
Chicago
Illinois 60614
United States
+1 7736344101
www.stellabarra.com

Opening hours	Open 7 days
Credit cards	Accepted
Style of pizza	Roman
Recommended pizza	Bloomsdale Spinach and Kale

"The Stella Barra pizza is homemade with a crisp crust and chewy center. You can also order a Thin Sin pizza with an extra-thin crust."—Rich Melman

GINO'S EAST

162 East Superior Street
River North
Chicago
Illinois 60611
United States
+1 3122663337
www.ginoseast.com

Opening hours	Open 7 days
Credit cards	Accepted
Style of pizza	Deep-dish
Recommended pizza	Chicago Fire; Gino's Supreme

"Since 1966, Gino's East has been spreading the gospel of deep-dish pies. The city has become so attached to this variety that it is popularly identified as 'Chicago style.' Some critics may argue that this thick-crusted behemoth is cake, not pizza. You can order thin-crust, but in the presence of thick-pie Nirvana, why bother?"—John Naughton

LOU MALNATI'S PIZZERIA

1120 North State Street
River North
Chicago
Illinois 60610
United States
+1 3127257777
www.loumalnatis.com

Opening hours	Open 7 days
Credit cards	Accepted
Style of pizza	Chicago deep-dish
Recommended pizza	Malnati Chicago Classic; The "Lou"

"This is the true Chicago pizza with cornmeal crunch and thick heavy slices."—Thomas England

PIZANO'S PIZZA & PASTA

864 North State Street
River North
Chicago
Illinois 60610
United States
+1 3127511766
www.pizanoschicago.com

Opening hours	Open 7 days
Credit cards	Accepted
Style of pizza	Chicago medium-crust
Recommended pizza	Cheese

"What makes this pizzeria special? The crust, the crust, the crust and its caramelized edges. It is dusted with cornmeal and the perfect cross between deep-dish thick and cracker-crisp thin. The crust never sogs out from sauce, so even 'middle' pieces of this party-cut pie bring crusty pleasure."—Penny Pollack

PIZZERIA UNO

29 East Ohio Street
River North
Chicago
Illinois 60611
United States
+1 3123211000
www.unos.com

Opening hours	Open 7 days
Credit cards	Accepted
Style of pizza	Chicago deep-dish
Recommended pizza	Sausage and Cheese

"Uno's is the birthplace of deep-dish pizza, and visiting takes you on a nostalgic trip to old Chicago. The crust is pastry-like with an almost nutty crunch. The pizzas are baked in seasoned black steel pans and layered with cheese, then meat, followed by the sauce, Parmesan cheese, and oregano. Uno's is the original and still an all-time favorite of mine."
—George Formaro

SPACCA NAPOLI PIZZERIA

1769 West Sunnyside Avenue
Uptown
Chicago
Illinois 60640
United States
+1 7738782420
www.spaccanapolipizzeria.com

Opening hours..Open 7 days
Credit cards..Accepted
Style of pizza...Neapolitan
Recommended pizza..............Bufalina; Diavola; Margherita;
Marinara DOP; Puttanesca; Quatro Formaggi; The
Chef's Special

"I'm 110 percent comfortable crowning this place the
king of Neapolitan pizza in Chicago."
—Penny Pollack

"Not everyone has the opportunity to visit Naples
and sample the varieties of pies from the most
historic pizza place on Earth. Fortunately, Jonathan
Goldsmith from Spacca Napoli takes the time to, and
gets every last detail correct. With such delicious
authentic pizza, there is no more relaxing meal in
Chicago."—Jonathan Porter

"Everything the owner sources is from Campania:
flour, cheese, olive oil, tomatoes, even the wine."
—Tony Mantuano

Jonathan Goldsmith returns with regularity to Naples to eat
pizza so Chicagoans don't have to. Any pleasure he gets from
these research trips is incidental to the goal of ensuring the
Neapolitan pizza at Spacca Napoli is as authentic and as good
as it can be. If Goldsmith takes a liking to Piennolo or Corborino
tomatoes, two prized varieties from the Campania region, no
sooner are they on the menu in Chicago. If he admires the work
of a *pizzaiolo* he'll bring him to Chicago, too, if only for a guest
appearance. Goldsmith splits his pizzas into two categories,
verace and tradizione. This means that some are real and
genuine while others are made according to tradition.

COALFIRE PIZZA

1321 West Grand Avenue
West Loop
Chicago
Illinois 60642
United States
+1 3122262625
www.coalfirechicago.com

Opening hours..Closed Monday
Credit cards...Not accepted
Style of pizza...Coal-fired thin-crust
Recommended pizza........................Margherita; 'Nduja and
Béchamel; Pepperoni and Whipped Ricotta

"Coalfire Pizza uses top-quality ingredients and
simple presentations with a crust that has the perfect
balance of chewy and crisp."
—Ken Miller & Greg O'Neill

"Chicago's only coal-fired pizza."—Mike Sula

PIECE BREWERY AND PIZZERIA

1927 West North Avenue
Wicker Park
Chicago
Illinois 60622
United States
+1 7737724422
www.piecechicago.com

Opening hours..Open 7 days
Credit cards..Accepted
Style of pizza...New Haven thin-crust
Recommended pizza...................Pepperoni and Mushroom;
White Pizza with Bacon, Clams, and Artichokes

"Whether or not it stands up to the best New
Haven-style pizza, I'm not sure. But it's the most
consistently exceptional thin-crust in Chicago. The
crust looks remarkably thin, but it also has great hole
structure and development, with a pleasantly tangy
aroma."—Nick Kindelsperger

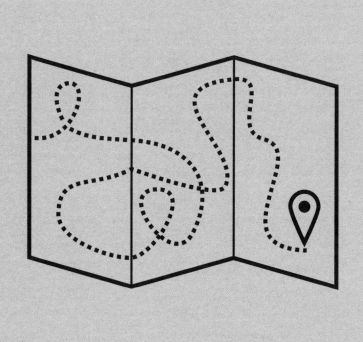

PIZZA TOURS

If the benefit of going on a guided tour is to discover a city's main points of interest, there should be nothing peculiar about a city tour dedicated to its landmarks of pizza. Yet those closest to Jon Porter questioned his sanity when he quit his day and night jobs to lead pizza tours of Chicago. His friends thought he was joking, up until the time he bought a bus. His wife told him he was crazy, but, letting her guard down, conceded it was the greatest idea she'd ever heard.

In 2010 Porter launched Chicago Pizza Tours to nourish existing pizza passions and inspire new ones. His bus tours are a lesson in local pizza, with an insider's look and taste of four of the city's top pizzerias in three hours. Porter invites locals to experience a first-rate version of their preferred type of Chicago pizza and reassess alternate styles. Tourists discover that Chicago is not exclusively a deep-dish town.

Diversity is also a key component of pizza tours in cities as near to Chicago as Milwaukee or as far as Rome. The Pizza Bus Tour run by Theresa Nemetz of Milwaukee Food stops first for a tavern-cut (square) slice of Milwaukee-style SMO (sausage, mushroom, onion) pizza at the city's oldest licensed pizzeria, Caradaro Club. Then it rolls on for Neapolitan pizza, New York-style pizza, and traditional wood-fired pizza with a modern twist. The Rome Pizza Food Tour, a walking tour of the Monti district organized by Italy Food Tours, explores three resident pizza styles: *pizza al taglio* (thick, square-cut), *pizza tonda* (round, thin, and crisp), and Neapolitan.

There is but a single pizza style on the Pizza and Pints Bike Tour mapped out by Taste of New Haven's Colin Caplan. The route stops at five pizzerias all serving crisp, thin-crusted New Haven pizza or *apizza* (pronounced "ah-beetz"), according to the Neapolitan immigrants' dialect. The basic version, by Caplan's description, is topped with crushed plum tomatoes, grated Romano cheese, and olive oil, and baked to a char, often in a coal-fired oven. Mozzarella or "muzzarelli," as it is written on an old wall menu at Modern Apizza, is optional.

Scott's Pizza Tours merges both approaches. Its walking tours of Manhattan and Brooklyn neighborhoods and bus tours of the outer New York City boroughs examine different variations of New York-style pizza, both whole and by the slice, as well as different interpretations within those variations. "You really start to notice the nuances when you try multiple pizzerias in a row," says Scott Wiener, who launched the company in April 2008, at the age of 26. He and his team of guides have led over 30,000 people on over 2,000 tours since. With stops for slices at three, and sometimes four, pizzerias on each tour that amounts to a heck of a lot of pizza.

So are these pizza tours merely excuses to eat too much pizza? Wiener, the granddaddy of pizza tour guides, naturally says no. "People sometimes assume the tour is all about gorging on pizza, but it's really a deep education on the science and history of the dish."

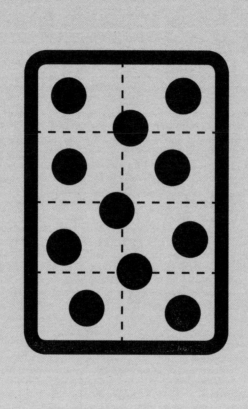

THE SECRET OF DETROIT PIZZA GETS OUT

The uninitiated may spot some peculiarities when they see a Detroit-style square pizza for the first time. For starters there's the shape. It's a rectangle, not a square. Next, the toppings are upside down. The pepperoni is pressed into the dough and then topped with cheese and tomato sauce. Still, this pizza's oddest characteristic must be how long it's taken people outside Detroit to take notice.

Detroit-style pizza was created in 1946 at Buddy's, a neighborhood tavern at the corner of Conant and Six Mile Roads in Detroit. Then owner Gus Guerra, working with his wife Anna, whose mother was Sicilian, brought visionary thinking to his search for a high-sided pizza pan. While others looked at the blue steel utility trays used at the Motor City's auto assembly plants and saw only nuts, bolts, and thingamajigs, Guerra envisioned a Sicilian-like deep-dish pizza.

The crux of what became known locally as square pizza is the crust baked in those repurposed pans. It's light and yielding, not dense, as deep-dish varieties can be. Crisp resistance at bottom and borders challenges you, theoretically, to eat a slice with knife and fork. "It's the sort of crust someone might want to cut through with a knife," says Wesley Pikula, vice president of operations at Buddy's. "I'm not that person." If you press a corner of the pizza between thumb and forefinger, as Pikula suggests, it cracks. The golden-brown walls that meet at the corners are encrusted in caramelized cheese, delivering a sweet, slightly burnt crunch. The cheese of choice is Wisconsin brick (a semihard white cheese), a slower melter than mozzarella.

Buddy's expanded to 11 locations as far as Auburn Hills, Michigan, 30 miles (50 km) north. But as an exporter of a Detroit original, Buddy's was no Ford Motor Company or Motown Records. "Growing up I didn't make it out of the area," says Shawn Randazzo of Detroit Style Pizza Co., among the newest of Buddy's many local rivals. "I thought this type of pizza was everywhere. I didn't know this regional culinary masterpiece had been a secret for 60 years."

Randazzo, who started out as a pizza delivery driver, left home in 2012, for a week, to compete in the International Pizza Challenge at Pizza Expo in Las Vegas. He won first prize in two categories, Best American Pan Pizza and Pizza Maker of the Year, enthralling judges with the brand-newness of his specialty. The taste of victory made a pizza ambassador of him: he helped Detroit pizza joints get started in California, Colorado, and Kentucky. He supplied pans to Zane and Brandon Hunt, brothers from Detroit who named their Austin, Texas, pizza trailer Via 313 after their hometown area code. Their success in the heart of hipster Texas quickly surpassed that which Randazzo had achieved at the Detroit-area pizzeria he opened at roughly the same time. "I've worked with people in areas where no one has heard of this style and it's a new thing and it does so great," he says with the bittersweetness of caramelized Brick cheese. "I'm here where it's everywhere on every corner."

"IT'S A TASTE OF NEW YORK IN THE HEART OF DC."

NEVIN MARTELL P.437

"THIS QUIRKY HIPSTER HANGOUT SERVES SOME OF THE FINEST PIES IN MIAMI."

VICTORIA PESCE ELLIOT P.439

USA SOUTH

"IT DOES A CRAB-TOPPED PIZZA THAT IS OUT OF THIS WORLD!"

MICHELLE FLISEK P.444

"YOU CAN FEEL THE ATTENTION TO DETAIL IN EVERY PIE."

LIZ BARRETT P.440

"THE KING BEE IS A DARK CRAFT COCKTAIL LOUNGE WHERE MIXOLOGIST BILLY HANKEY MAKES THE DRINKS AND PARTNER COLETTE DEIN JUST HAPPENS TO MAKE SOME OF THE BEST PIZZA IN AUSTIN." RACHEL FORREST P.454

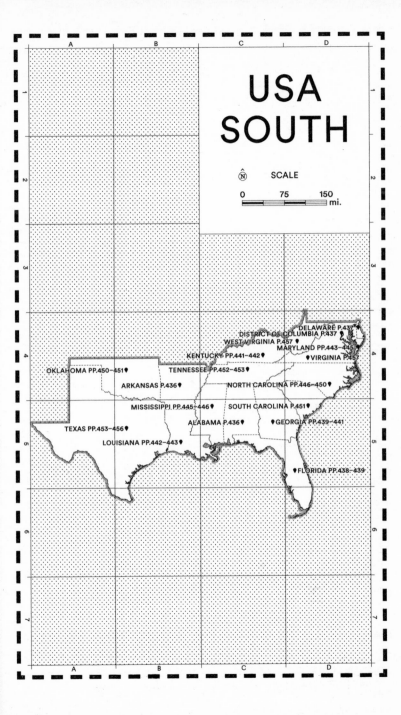

USA
SOUTH

SCALE

0   75   150 mi.

DELAWARE P.437
DISTRICT OF COLUMBIA P.437
WEST VIRGINIA P.457
MARYLAND PP.443–445
KENTUCKY PP.441–442
VIRGINIA P.457
OKLAHOMA PP.450–451
TENNESSEE PP.452–453
ARKANSAS P.436
NORTH CAROLINA PP.446–450
MISSISSIPPI PP.445–446
SOUTH CAROLINA P.451
TEXAS PP.453–456
ALABAMA P.436
GEORGIA PP.439–441
LOUISIANA PP.442–443
FLORIDA PP.438–439

POST OFFICE PIES

209 41st Street South
Birmingham
Alabama 35222
United States
+1 2055999900
www.postofficepies.com

Opening hours	Open 7 days
Credit cards	Accepted
Style of pizza	Wood-fired
Recommended pizza	Swine Pie

"Good flavors, good technique, great ingredients, and soul."—Austin Hu

ZAZA FINE SALAD & WOOD OVEN PIZZA CO.

1050 Ellis Avenue, Suite 110
Conway
Arkansas 72032
United States
+1 5013369292
www.zazapizzaandsalad.com

Opening hours	Open 7 days
Credit cards	Accepted
Style of pizza	South Italian thin-crust
Recommended pizza	Classic Pepperoni; Forager

"This order-at-the-counter, then seat-yourself restaurant uses local produce and ingredients when possible, and there are family-friendly options for other dishes, including made-to-order salads and an authentic gelato bar. The vibe is modern and casual."—Jay Jennings

DAMGOODE PIES

500 President Clinton Avenue
Little Rock
Arkansas 72201
United States
+1 5016642239
www.damgoodepies.com

Opening hours	Open 7 days
Credit cards	Accepted
Style of pizza	Classic American
Recommended pizza	BBQ Chicken

"A perpetual poll-winner of local best-pizza votes, Damgoode lays it on thick, whether it's the cheese, sauce, or the irreverent menu descriptions."
—Jay Jennings

THE PIZZERIA @ TERRY'S FINER FOODS

5018 Kavanaugh Boulevard
Little Rock
Arkansas 72207
United States
+1 5015511388
www.pizzeria-santalucia.com

Opening hours	Closed Monday
Credit cards	Accepted
Style of pizza	Neapolitan
Recommended pizza	Shrimp (prawn) Scampi; Margherita

"Attached to a longtime neighborhood gourmet grocery, the space is as narrow as a sailboat's galley but warm and homey, with a wall of wine bottles soaring to a wood-slat ceiling. Near the entrance sits the engine of the place, a wood-fired oven from Acunto Mario in Naples that gives the crust a dark char. The single size available, the approximate size of a dinner plate, can be consumed by a diner alone without leaving you feeling too gluttonous or shared with another when combined with a salad. There's also a full bar and a generous selection of draft beers, from regional and local microbrews."—Jay Jennings

ZAZA FINE SALAD & WOOD OVEN PIZZA CO.

5600 Kavanaugh Boulevard, Suite 100
Little Rock
Arkansas 72207
United States
+1 5016619292
www.zazapizzaandsalad.com

Opening hours	Open 7 days
Credit cards	Accepted
Style of pizza	South Italian thin-crust
Recommended pizza	Classic Pepperoni; Forager

GROTTO PIZZERIA

36 Rehoboth Avenue
Rehoboth Beach
Delaware 19971
United States
+1 3022273278
www.grottopizza.com

Opening hours	Open 7 days
Credit cards	Accepted
Style of pizza	Classic
Recommended pizza	Plain Pie

"What makes the pizza unique is a distinctively sweeter sauce, that's applied over the rich cheese in concentric rings."—Leah Mennies

2 AMYS

3715 Macomb Street Northwest
Washington
District of Columbia 20016
United States
+1 2028855700
www.development.ginatolentino.com/2amys

Opening hours	Open 7 days
Credit cards	Accepted but not AMEX
Style of pizza	Neapolitan
Recommended pizza	Margherita Extra; Santa Brigida Vongole

"Neapolitan pizza is prolific in Washington, but 2 Amys stands out in two important ways: the restaurant was the first to serve DOC pizza in the area, and it's still the best to this day."—Anna Spiegel

"2 Amys nails the Neapolitan style of pizza, but also has some lovely small plates that will transport you directly to Italy. The room is light and airy and filled with people—it's bustling in a good way."
—Jerry Corso & Angelina Tolentino

DISTRICT OF PI

910 F Street Northwest
Washington
District of Columbia 20004
United States
+1 2023935484
www.pi-pizza.com

Opening hours	Open 7 days
Credit cards	Accepted
Style of pizza	St. Louis deep-dish
Recommended pizza	Berkeley

GHIBELLINA

1610 14th Street Northwest
Washington
District of Columbia 20009
United States
+1 2028032389
www.ghibellina.com

Opening hours	Open 7 days
Credit cards	Accepted
Style of pizza	Neapolitan
Recommended pizza	Olive and Artichoke

PIZZERIA PARADISO

3282 Main Street Northwest
Washington
District of Columbia 20007
United States
+1 2023371245
www.eatyourpizza.com

Opening hours	Open 7 days
Credit cards	Accepted but not AMEX
Style of pizza	Classic American
Recommended pizza	Bianca

VACE ITALIAN DELICATESSEN

3315 Connecticut Avenue Northwest
Washington
District of Columbia 20008
United States
+1 2023631999
www.vaceitaliandeli.com

Opening hours	Open 7 days
Credit cards	Accepted
Style of pizza	Italian

WISEGUY NY PIZZA

300 Massachusetts Avenue Northwest, #1
Washington
District of Columbia 20001
United States
+1 2024087800
www.wiseguynypizza.com

Opening hours	Open 7 days
Credit cards	Accepted
Style of pizza	New York
Recommended pizza	Brooklyn Bridge

"It's a taste of New York in the heart of DC."
—Nevin Martell

SCUOLA VECCHIA PIZZERIA

522 East Atlantic Avenue
Delray Beach
Florida 33483
United States
+1 5618655923
www.scuolavecchiapizzeria.com

Opening hours	Closed Tuesday
Credit cards	Accepted
Style of pizza	Neapolitan
Recommended pizza	Regina Margherita

"A tiny spot with huge pizza creds, this place imports its flour from Italy, handmakes some cheeses and imports others, and puts out some of the most stellar pizza this side of Naples, and, frankly, anywhere."—Lesley Abravanel

HARRY'S PIZZERIA

3918 North Miami Avenue
Miami
Florida 33127
United States
+1 7862754963
www.harryspizzeria.com

Opening hours	Open 7 days
Credit cards	Accepted
Style of pizza	Neapolitan
Recommended pizza	Short Rib, Gruyère, Caramelized Onion, and Arugula (rocket)

"Michael Schwartz's neighborhood pizzeria menu is chef-driven, marrying carefully selected ingredients to the melty cheese and crust. Don't go expecting your classic Margherita, go with the knowledge that you'll be blown away by stepping outside the pizza box."—Lee Brian Schrager

PROOF PIZZA & PASTA

3328 North Miami Avenue
Miami
Florida 33127
United States
+1 7865369562
www.proofpizza.com

Opening hours	Closed Monday
Credit cards	Accepted
Style of pizza	Neapolitan
Recommended pizza	White

"Proof's pizzas have the right balance of dough, cheese, and ingredients to enjoy a perfect bite each time."—Lee Brian Schrager

VA PIANO PIZZA MIAMI

1221 Brickel Avenue
Miami
Florida 33131
United States
+1 3053740311
www.vapiano.com

Opening hours	Open 7 days
Credit cards	Accepted
Style of pizza	Italian-American
Recommended pizza	Diavolo

"You can really taste the handmade dough and the freshness of the tomato. It is a high-quality chain restaurant."—Mickaël & Gaël Tourteaux

DOLCE ITALIAN

1690 Collins Avenue
Miami Beach
Florida 33139
United States
+1 7869752550
www.dolceitalianrestaurant.com

Opening hours	Open 7 days
Credit cards	Accepted
Style of pizza	Neapolitan
Recommended pizza	Broccoli Raab and Italian Sausage

"Dolce's incredibly fresh toppings give a burst of happiness to your taste buds every time."
—Lee Brian Schrager

FRATELLI LA BUFALA

437 Washington Avenue
Miami Beach
Florida 33139
United States
+1 3055320700
www.flbmiami.com

Opening hours	Open 7 days
Credit cards	Accepted
Style of pizza	Neapolitan
Recommended pizza	Margherita

"This is a classic pizzeria with pies that are always perfect."—Victoria Pesce Elliot

LUCALI

1930 Bay Road
Miami Beach
Florida 33139
United States
+1 3056954441
www.lucali.com

Opening hours	Open 7 days
Credit cards	Accepted
Style of pizza	Brooklyn-Neapolitan brick-oven
Recommended pizza	House-cured Artichoke Hearts and Mushrooms

"A Brooklyn import, this quirky hipster hangout serves some of the finest pies in Miami. They are monstrously huge—enough for two or three people to share with a crust that is light, airy, and full of bubbles that get a nice black scorching from the brick oven. What makes it best is the quality of ingredients for the sauce and the cheese as well as the toppings."—Victoria Pesce Elliot

EVIO'S PIZZA & GRILL

12600 Biscayne Boulevard
North Miami
Florida 33181
United States
+1 3058997699
www.eviospizza.com

Opening hours	Open 7 days
Credit cards	Accepted
Style of pizza	New York and Sicilian
Recommended pizza	Gyro

"If you're in the mood for something a little different, the Gyro pizza with gyro meat, tzatziki sauce, tomatoes, and onions is amazing."—Jen Karetnick

COWGIRL KITCHEN

54 Main Street
Rosemary Beach
Florida 32413
United States
+1 8502130058
www.cowgirlkitchen.com

Opening hours	Open 7 days
Credit cards	Accepted
Style of pizza	American
Recommended pizza	30A Special; Drunken Cowgirl

"This little hole-in-the-wall pumps out so many pizzas during its busy summer season. The pizzas are incredible because they are made from scratch with amazing toppings and sauces."—Melanie M. Ward

AUTOMATIC PIZZA

1397 Prince Avenue
Athens
Georgia 30606
United States
+1 7068502037

Opening hours	Open 7 days
Credit cards	Accepted
Style of pizza	New York

"This renovated filling station makes great use of a small footprint. Its pizza is simple but tasty, with good ingredients like high-quality anchovies. You get a plastic animal with your order to let the waitstaff find your table."—Hillary Brown

LITTLE ITALY

125 North Lumpkin Street
Athens
Georgia 30601
United States
+1 7066137100

Opening hours	Closed Sunday
Credit cards	Accepted
Style of pizza	New York

TED'S MOST BEST

254 West Washington Street
Athens
Georgia 30601
United States
+1 7065431523
www.tedsmostbest.com

Opening hours..Open 7 days
Credit cards.................................Accepted but not AMEX
Style of pizza...Thin-crust
Recommended pizza...Bacon and Egg

"Located in a renovated tire shop, Ted's Most Best makes light unsoggy pizzas with great refinement but absolutely no pretension."—Hillary Brown

ANTICO PIZZA

1093 Hemphill Avenue
Atlanta
Georgia 30318
United States
+1 4047242333
www.littleitalia.com

Opening hours...Closed Sunday
Credit cards...Accepted
Style of pizza...Neapolitan
Recommended pizza......................Margherita; Pomodorini;
San Gennaro

"Antico Pizza is probably the most famous Neapolitan pizza in Atlanta; the 'rugged' locale and the way pizzas are served makes this spot unique in the Atlanta region."—Pietro Gianni

FRITTI

309 North Highland Avenue Northeast
Atlanta
Georgia 30307
United States
+1 4048809559
www.frittirestaurant.com

Opening hours..Open 7 days
Credit cards...Accepted
Style of pizza...Neapolitan
Recommended pizza...........Regina Margherita (ask for the
buffalo mozzarella variation)

"Fritti's pizza chef Massimo is a true pizza maker from Napoli and is responsible for all the pizza creations, and he is fantastic!"—Pietro Gianni

OLD FOURTH WARD PIZZA

660 Irwin Street Northeast
Atlanta
Georgia 30312
United States
+1 6785153388

Opening hours..Closed Monday
Credit cards...Accepted
Style of pizza...New Jersey
Recommended pizza...Grandma Pie

"It is a small place with great grandma pies—a rectangular style of pizza from New York and New Jersey."—Jennifer Zyman

VARASANO'S PIZZERIA

2171 Peachtree Road
Atlanta
Georgia 30309
United States
+1 4043528216
www.varasanos.com

Opening hours..Open 7 days
Credit cards...Accepted
Style of pizza...New York-Neapolitan
Recommended pizza...................Chica Bella; Dessert Pizza;
Nana's; Nucci

"The owner spent years attempting to perfect a pizza from his hometown, creating a huge audience of online followers who read about his processes. His battle for perfection lead him to open Varasano's, and you can feel the attention to detail in every pie."—Liz Barrett

"The careful, consistent execution yields a house style that is found only at Varasano's. Fans of traditional Neapolitan would in some cases cry blasphemy over the pizzas but that's in part why I find them so special."—Robert Alexander

Usually people try your pizzeria first and then seek out your pizza recipe. With Jeff Varasano they tried his recipe first and then sought out his pizzeria. Varasano opened his namesake pizza place on the strength of his 20,000-word online pizza treatise and its top-ranked position for pizza recipe searches on Google. His pizza incorporates elements of the classic New York and Naples styles. The dough, made with a sourdough starter, is aged for three or four days, creating a crust that's light, soft, and moist, if not to Neapolitan extremes. The inspiration for the unique specialty pizzas is all his own. The Nucci, with garlic, Kalamata olives, and Emmental cheese, is garnished with arugula (rocket), *capicola*, and herbs.

VARUNI NAPOLI

1540 Monroe Drive Northeast
Atlanta
Georgia 30324
United States
+1 4047092690
www.varuni.us

Opening hours...Closed Monday
Credit cards...Accepted
Style of pizza...Neapolitan
Recommended pizza...................Chiattona; King of Napoli

"The expertise of Luca Varuni and his family make
this the best experience for Neapolitan pizza in
Atlanta."—Pietro Gianni

"Tender, generous, fresh, and fragrant."
—Christiane Lauterbach

LABELLA'S PIZZERIA

2635 Sandy Plains Road, Suite A7
Marietta
Georgia 30066
United States
+1 7709730052
www.labellaspizzeria.net

Opening hours...Open 7 days
Credit cards...Accepted
Style of pizza..New York
Recommended pizza...Plain Cheese

"This is the only place in Atlanta to get a 'real' New
York slice. The place is nothing fancy, but the pizza
is legit."—Jeff Varasano

THE FLORENCE

1 B West Victory Drive
Savannah
Georgia 31405
United States
+1 9122345522
www.theflorencesavannah.com

Opening hours...Closed Monday
Credit cards...Accepted
Style of pizza...Neapolitan
Recommended pizza..Lorraine

"So much Neapolitan praise is heaped on how
the crust is cooked, but it's the flavor of the dough
that distinguishes the graceful pies at The
Florence."—Hanna Raskin

VINNIE VAN GO GO'S PIZZA

317 West Bryan Street
Savannah
Georgia 31401
United States
+1 9122336394
www.vinnievangogo.com

Opening hours...Open 7 days
Credit cards...Not accepted
Style of pizza..New York
Recommended pizza..Pepperoni

"Vinnie Van Go Go's is punk rock, with cute but tough
waitresses, cheap beer, and a cash-only policy. It also
makes a delicious big slice of pizza."—Hillary Brown

STEVE O'S ITALIAN KITCHEN

4205 West Highway 146
Lagrange
Kentucky 40031
United States
+1 5022220300
www.steveositaliankitchen.com

Opening hours...Closed Sunday
Credit cards...Accepted
Style of pizza..New York
Recommended pizza...Plain Cheese

"This pizzeria offers delicious pies utilizing top-notch
ingredients. The owner's interactions with all of his
guests make this pizza joint extra special."
—Tony Palombino

JOE BOLOGNA'S

120 West Maxwell Street
Lexington
Kentucky 40508
United States
+1 8592590495
www.joebolognas.com

Opening hours...Open 7 days
Credit cards...Accepted
Style of pizza..New York
Recommended pizza..Beef Meatball

"This pizza parlor has a casual vibe, with the added
bonus of being housed in a former church with
beautiful stained-glass windows."—Tony Palombino

BOOMBOZZ CRAFT PIZZA & TAPHOUSE

3939 Shelbyville Road, #103
Louisville
Kentucky 40207
United States
+1 5028969090
www.boombozz.com

Opening hours	Open 7 days
Credit cards	Accepted
Style of pizza	Multiple
Recommended pizza	Pollotate

"The success of two-big ideas—first delivering gourmet pizzas in the late 1990s, and then recognizing the synergy between craft beer and upscale pizza—has made this 16-year-old brand very popular with the locals."—Tony Palombino

COALS ARTISAN PIZZA

3730 Frankfort Avenue
Louisville
Kentucky 40207
United States
+1 5027428200
www.coalsartisanpizza.com

Opening hours	Open 7 days
Credit cards	Accepted
Style of pizza	American-Neapolitan
Recommended pizza	Waverly

GARAGE BAR

700 East Market Street
Louisville
Kentucky 40202
United States
+1 5027497100
www.garageonmarket.com

Opening hours	Open 7 days
Credit cards	Accepted
Style of pizza	Neapolitan
Recommended pizza	Sweet Corn and Bacon Pie

"Set in an old garage, you can get a wonderful Neapolitan pizza from the Garage Bar wood-burning oven. It's a very happening place, with a huge outdoor patio that offers lighted ping-pong tables."
—Madeline Peters & Mark Peters

R&O'S RESTAURANT

216 Metairie-Hammond Highway
Metaire
Louisiana 70005
United States
+1 5048311248

Opening hours	Open 7 days
Credit cards	Accepted
Style of pizza	American tavern
Recommended pizza	Meatball

"There is a time and a place for fancy brick-oven pizzas with locally sourced ingredients, heirloom flour, and fancy toppings. Then there is a time for taking the little league team out for pizza after a game for saucy, cheesy, bready sustenance on plastic tablecloths and R&O's fulfills that role to perfection."—Brett Martin

DOLCE VITA

1205 Saint Charles Avenue
New Orleans
Louisiana 70130
United States
+1 5043247674
www.dvpizzeria.com

Opening hours	Open 7 days
Credit cards	Accepted
Style of pizza	Wood-fired
Recommended pizza	Margherita

DOMENICA

123 Baronne Street
New Orleans
Louisiana 70112
United States
+1 5046486020
www.domenicarestaurant.com

Opening hours	Open 7 days
Credit cards	Accepted
Style of pizza	New York wood-fired
Recommended pizza	Calabrese; Gorgonzola

"Domenica uses house-cured meats on its pizzas, which really sets it apart."—Chris Shepherd

PIZZA DELICIOUS

617 Piety Street
New Orleans
Louisiana 70117
United States
+1 5046768482
www.pizzadelicious.com

Opening hours...Closed Monday
Credit cards..Accepted
Style of pizza..New York
Recommended pizza.............Cheese; Eggplant (aubergine)
Parmesan; Half Cheese and Half Pepperoni; Margherita

"It isn't easy to make the leap from pop-up to excellent
restaurant, but Pizza Delicious did it splendidly,
serving the best New York-style pie south of Staten
Island."—Brett Martin

The trajectory of Pizza D's from Sunday pop-up to cinderblock
warehouse pizzeria fits the hipster success story, right down to
the denial that invariably surrounds it: a hipster in the Bywater
neighborhood of New Orleans is pretty much anyone who
protests he isn't one. Transplanted New Yorkers Greg Augarten
and Michael Friedman did rewrite the wood-fired Neapolitan
pizza script by featuring New York by-the-slice pizza cooked in
a gas-fired deck oven instead. These self-taught pizza geeks got
it right, from the greasy surface sheen through to the crisp,
close-knit crust with just enough bend and give. New York style
doesn't depend on NYC H2O, apparently. Three daily
pizzas—cheese, pepperoni, and Margherita—are augmented
by specials like the White Pie—with spinach, ricotta, and
cherry tomatoes—and the excellent Eggplant (aubergine)
Parmesan pie.

PIZZA DOMENICA

4933 Magazine Street
New Orleans
Louisiana 70115
United States
+1 5043014978
www.pizzadomenica.com

Opening hours...Open 7 days
Credit cards..Accepted
Style of pizza..Neapolitan
Recommended pizza...........................Clam; Roasted Carrot;
Smoked Pork

"It's the best example of wood-fired Neapolitan-style
pizza in New Orleans, with the char-marked crust
of good character and an approach to toppings that
goes outside of strict tradition."—Ian McNulty

VENEZIA

134 North Carrollton Avenue
New Orleans
Louisiana 70119
United States
+1 5044887991
www.venezianeworleans.net

Opening hours.......................Closed Monday and Tuesday
Credit cards..Accepted
Style of pizza...Italian
Recommended pizza...House Special

"Venezia is a 1950s-vintage Italian restaurant that
comes to life on Sunday nights (and other nights) and
draws people from across the area. It has the feel of a
neighborhood institution without any hype. The pizza
has a chew to the crust, tang to the cheese, and good
grease balance."—Ian McNulty

WOOD

404 Andrew Higgins Drive
New Orleans
Louisiana 70130
United States
+1 5042814893

Opening hours...Open 7 days
Credit cards..Accepted
Style of pizza...Wood-fired
Recommended pizza...................Mushroom, Garlic Cream,
Red Onions, and Egg

VIN 909

909 Bay Ridge Avenue
Annapolis
Maryland 21403
United States
+1 4109901846
www.vin909.com

Opening hours...Closed Monday
Credit cards..Accepted
Style of pizza...Wood-fired
Recommended pizza...........................Charcuterie; No-skimp
Margherita

"Most pizzerias offer 'custom' combinations with
unusual ingredients, but where plenty of others fail,
Vin 909 pulls it off beautifully. Case in point: the
Spotted Pig with spicy soppressata, wild boar
meatballs, mozzarella, and basil."—Anna Spiegel

BAGBY PIZZA COMPANY

1006 Fleet Street
Baltimore
Maryland 21202
United States
+1 4106050444
www.bagbypizza.com

Opening hours	Open 7 days
Credit cards	Accepted
Style of pizza	Gourmet thin-crust
Recommended pizza	BBQ Chicken; Gourmet Vegetable; Spicy Shrimp (prawns); Sweet and Spicy

"There's always the right amount of sweet and salty elements, and the perfect amount of cheese. Crusts are super thin and crackly textured, yet sturdy and flavorful."—Kathy Patterson

BIRROTECA

1520 Clipper Road
Baltimore
Maryland 21211
United States
+1 4437081934
www.bmorebirroteca.com

Opening hours	Open 7 days
Credit cards	Accepted
Style of pizza	Artisan Italian thin-crust
Recommended pizza	Double D; Duck Duck Goose; Spicy Fennel Sausage

"I like Birroteca's creativity but also its respect for the pizza. It crosses the line but gets the basics right before it does."—Cyrus Keefer

"The pizzas are all delicious."—Diane Macklin

EARTH, WOOD, AND FIRE

1407 Clarkview Road
Baltimore
Maryland 21209
United States
+1 4108253473
www.earthwoodfire.com

Opening hours	Open 7 days
Credit cards	Accepted
Style of pizza	Coal-fired thin-crust
Recommended pizza	Scampi

"The pizzas at Earth, Wood, and Fire are cooked at a very high heat, which makes for a delicious char on the crust. Crusts are thin and crispy, and while toppings are generous, it's not enough to make the crust sag in the middle."—Kathy Patterson

IGGIES

818 North Calvert Street
Baltimore
Maryland 21202
United States
+1 4105280818
www.iggiespizza.com

Opening hours	Closed Monday
Credit cards	Accepted
Style of pizza	Thin-crust
Recommended pizza	Alice; Pistachio

JOHNNY RADS

2108 Eastern Avenue
Baltimore
Maryland 21231
United States
+1 4437596464
www.johnnyrads.com

Opening hours	Open 7 days
Credit cards	Accepted
Style of pizza	Neapolitan
Recommended pizza	A1 Meats

MATTHEW'S PIZZA

3131 Eastern Avenue
Baltimore
Maryland 21224
United States
+1 4102768755
www.matthewspizza.com

Opening hours	Open 7 days
Credit cards	Accepted
Style of pizza	Greek
Recommended pizza	Both Cheese; Crab

"It does a crab-topped pizza that is out of this world!"—Michelle Flisek

"Matthew's is such a special Charm City institution, beloved by tourists and locals alike. Its pie style is so distinctive, with a crunchy outer crust and focaccia-like crumb."—Drew Lazor

OUR HOUSE
1121 Hull Street
Baltimore
Maryland 21230
United States
+1 4107276797
www.ourhousebaltimore.com

Opening hours	Closed Monday
Credit cards	Accepted
Style of pizza	Thick-crust
Recommended pizza	Both Cheese; Breakfast Pizza with Fried Eggs

"It has amazing breakfast pizzas!"—Diane Macklin

SQUIRE'S
6723 Holabird Avenue
Baltimore
Maryland 21222
United States
+1 4102880081
www.squirescatering.com

Opening hours	Open 7 days
Credit cards	Accepted
Style of pizza	Italian
Recommended pizza	Everything

"This is the pizza I've been eating since I was a kid, and it's still one of the best in town. The crust is sturdy, neither thin nor thick, and always perfectly browned. The *cornicione* is crunchy like a breadstick, rather than doughy, which is my preference. Its pizza sauce is amazing, very herby and just sweet enough, and the toppings are more than generous."
—Kathy Patterson

VERDE
641 South Montford Avenue
Baltimore
Maryland 21224
United States
+1 4105221000
www.verdepizza.com

Opening hours	Open 7 days
Credit cards	Accepted
Style of pizza	Neapolitan
Recommended pizza	Pistachio and Sausage; Prosciutto and Fig

"The dough has intense chew and great flavor; Verde uses quality ingredients and it shows."—Cyrus Keefer

VIVO
7793 Arundel Mills Boulevard
Hanover
Maryland 21076
United States
+1 4107997440
www.vivotrattoria.com

Opening hours	Open 7 days
Credit cards	Accepted
Style of pizza	Brick-oven
Recommended pizza	Margherita; Prosciutto and Arugula (rocket)

"Excellent pizza, sauce, and crust...all perfectly prepared."—Diane Macklin

TABELLA
3720-A Hardy Street
Midtown Market
Hattiesburg
Mississippi 39402
United States
+1 6012555488
www.tabellapronto.com

Opening hours	Open 7 days
Credit cards	Accepted
Style of pizza	Tuscan
Recommended pizza	Classic Margherita

BRAVO!
I-55 North, Exit 100, Northside Drive
Highland Village Shopping Center, South Plaza
Jackson
Mississippi 39211
United States
+1 6019828111
www.bravobuzz.com

Opening hours	Closed Monday
Credit cards	Accepted
Style of pizza	Italian wood-fired
Recommended pizza	Bianca; Milano; Verdúre

"My favorite pizza is the Bianca and I eat it at least once a week. It isn't on the menu but old-timers know you can still order it. It's a chicken prosciutto with a béchamel sauce. I crave it."—Melanie M. Ward

SAL AND MOOKIES NEW YORK PIZZA AND ICE CREAM JOINT

565 Taylor Street
Jackson
Mississippi 39216
United States
+1 6012926548
www.salandmookies.com

Opening hours	Closed Monday
Credit cards	Accepted
Style of pizza	New York
Recommended pizza	Empire State

TOM'S EXTREME PIZZERIA

1006 Robinson Avenue
Ocean Springs
Mississippi 39564
United States
+1 2288724340
www.tomsextremepizzeria.com

Opening hours	Open 7 days
Credit cards	Accepted
Style of pizza	Multiple
Recommended pizza	Biloxi Shrimp (prawns)

"Tom's can get the crust thin and crisp and make a classic Italian pizza or several alternative (a food snob would say bastardized) versions of the classic Italian pie."—Robert St. John

SOULSHINE PIZZA FACTORY

1111 Highland Colony Parkway
Ridgeland
Mississippi 39157
United States
+1 6018568646
www.soulshinepizza.com

Opening hours	Open 7 days
Credit cards	Accepted
Style of pizza	Specialty
Recommended pizza	Jacksonian

"It's the array of combinations that make these thin-crust pizzas special, like the Bob Marley featuring Jamaican jerk seasoning, mozzarella, smoked pulled chicken, grilled chicken, and sun-dried tomatoes."—Melanie M. Ward

TRIBECCA ALLIE

216 South Main Street
Sardis
Mississippi 38666
United States
+1 6624872233
www.tribeccaallie.com

Opening hours	Closed Monday and Tuesday
Credit cards	Accepted
Style of pizza	Neapolitan
Recommended pizza	Magnolia Rosa; Potato

"In addition to fantastic pizza every time I visit, the owners welcome everyone like family. It's not unusual to be greeted with a hug and a kiss on the cheek. When it's not crazy busy, the owners will sit down at your table for a chat during the meal. I always feel like I'm going to visit family here."—Liz Barrett

STOMBOLI'S

408 University Drive
Starkville
Mississippi 39759
United States
+1 6626154080
www.strombolismsu.com

Opening hours	Closed Sunday
Credit cards	Accepted
Style of pizza	Thick-crust
Recommended pizza	Chicken Ranchero

ALL SOULS PIZZA

175 Clingman Avenue
Asheville
North Carolina 28801
United States
+1 8282540169
www.allsoulspizza.com

Opening hours	Closed Monday
Credit cards	Accepted but not AMEX
Style of pizza	Wood-fired
Recommended pizza	Salted Turnips, Garlic, Cream, and Taleggio

"Chef Brendan Reusing and baker David Bauer own the place and their commitment to using local, seasonal produce is evident on every menu item. The polenta 'pizza' is an interesting addition to the menu, focusing on the most traditional grain in the region but it is the natural leaven fresh-milled wheat pizzas that are worth the trip here."—Evan Kleiman

"David Bauer mills all of his own flour by hand, which makes for an outstanding crust. Beyond that, the local sourcing is impeccable. Definitely a unique pizza experience."—Mackensy Lunsford

FAVILLA'S NEW YORK PIZZA
1093 Patton Avenue
Asheville
North Carolina 28806
United States
+1 8282253032
www.favillasnewyorkpizza.com

Opening hours	Open 7 hours
Credit cards	Accepted but not AMEX
Style of pizza	New York

"Fantastic New York-style pizza in western North Carolina. Favilla's is legit."—Mackensy Lunsford

MARCO'S PIZZERIA
946 Merrimon Avenue
Asheville
North Carolina 28804
United States
+1 8282850709
www.marcos-pizzeria.com

Opening hours	Closed Monday
Credit cards	Accepted
Style of pizza	New York
Recommended pizza	Kale Pie

INTERMEZZO PIZZERIA AND CAFÉ
1427 East 10th Street
Charlotte
North Carolina 28204
United States
+1 7043472626
www.intermezzopizzeria.com

Opening hours	Open 7 days
Credit cards	Accepted
Style of pizza	Neapolitan wood-fired
Recommended pizza	Grilled Mushroom

"Brothers Branko and Djordje Avramovic hail from Serbia, but the pizzas they have been crafting at Intermezzo since 2007 are some of the best Neapolitan-style dishes in the region. Perennially perfect crust can be ordered with hearty traditional toppings of Italian sausage and pepperoni, or kept simple with homemade mozzarella, tomatoes, herbs, and oil."—Amy Rogers

LUISA'S BRICK OVEN PIZZA
1730 Abbey Place
Charlotte
North Carolina 28209
United States
+1 7045228782
www.luisasbrickovenpizza.com

Opening hours	Open 7 days
Credit cards	Accepted
Style of pizza	Neapolitan wood-fired
Recommended pizza	Fiorentina

"In the 1990s Luisa Land became one of the first restaurateurs in the region to import a wood-fired oven from her home country of Italy. With that, she changed the entire city's perception of pizza, and Luisa's became a mainstay as word spread. Current owner Jeff Russell helps assure the restaurant by carrying on Luisa's tradition of using homemade ingredients that guarantee a consistently great pizza."—Amy Rogers

PORTOFINO'S RISTORANTE ITALIANO E PIZZERIA
3124 Eastway Drive, #500
Charlotte
North Carolina 28205
United States
+1 7045687933
www.portofinos-us.com

Opening hours	Open 7 days
Credit cards	Accepted
Style of pizza	New York
Recommended pizza	Cheese; Pepperoni

"Ex-pat New Yorkers living in Charlotte who long for their hometown's signature style of pizza will feel right at home at Portofino's, where diners in the know forgo the knife and fork and instead fold the giant slices to eat them by hand, street-style."
—Amy Rogers

PIZZERIA TORO
105 East Chapel Hill Street
Durham
North Carolina 27701
United States
+1 9199086936
www.pizzeriatoro.com

Opening hours..Open 7 days
Credit cards...Accepted
Style of pizza....................................... Neapolitan wood-fired
Recommended pizza.................Spicy Lamb Meatball, Kale,
and Rustico BP

"It keeps the toppings light or, better yet, zeroes in on
the specials, which highlight the best in North Carolina
produce and charcuterie."—Andrew Mark Veety

GIA – DRINK EAT LISTEN
1941 New Garden Road, #208
Greensboro
North Carolina 27410
United States
+1 3369077536
www.drinkeatlisten.com

Opening hours..Open 7 days
Credit cards...Accepted
Style of pizza..Sicilian flatbread
Recommended pizza......................Pineapple and Cranberry
Sausage

"Gia's atmosphere is upscale, like a swanky lounge
or nightclub with live music and small plates. The
best thing on its menu is its extensive list of Sicilian
flatbreads."—Amanda Clark

NEW YORK PIZZA
337 Tate Street
Greensboro
North Carolina 27403
United States
+1 3362728953
www.nyp-gboro.com

Opening hours..Open 7 days
Credit cards.................................Accepted but not AMEX
Style of pizza..New York
Recommended pizza...................Ham, Pineapple, and Fresh
Jalapeños; Pepperoni and Sausage

"The thin-crust New York-style pizza is sensational.
The flavor of the sauce and cheese is the bomb."
—Amanda Clark

PIEWORKS PIZZA BY DESIGN
1941 New Garden Road
Greensboro
North Carolina 27410
United States
+1 3362829003
www.pieworks.com

Opening hours..Open 7 days
Credit cards...Accepted
Style of pizza...Gourmet
Recommended pizza............................FruitWorks; Seahorse

"The variety of pizza toppings and combinations stand
above any I've seen in the area. My favorite is the
Seahorse pizza, with shrimp (prawn) scampi on an olive
oil-based crust, topped with scallions (spring onions) and
provolone cheese. Lemony, garlicky shrimp on a pizza—
why isn't this offered everywhere as a standard pizza
topping? It's absolutely heavenly."—Amanda Clark

PIZZERIA L'ITALIANO
219b South Elm Street
Greensboro
North Carolina 27401
United States
+1 3362744810
www.pizzerialitaliano.net

Opening hours...Closed Sunday
Credit cards...Accepted
Style of pizza..New York
Recommended pizza..Caprese

STICKS & STONES CLAY OVEN PIZZA
2200 Walker Avenue
Greensboro
North Carolina 27403
United States
+1 3362750220
www.sticksandstonesclayoven.com

Opening hours..Open 7 days
Credit cards...Accepted
Style of pizza...Wood-fired
Recommended pizza............A Kiss Before I Go; Let It Ride;
Sweet Carolina

"Sticks & Stones is part of a trend of more inventive,
upscale pizzerias that don't even fall in the same
category as common US pizza joints. The ambience,
locally sourced ingredients, attention to detail, and
variety of options are just some of the factors that set
this pizzeria apart."—Eric Ginsburg

WOLFGANG PUCK'S PIZZA BAR

607 Green Valley Road
Greensboro
North Carolina 27408
United States
+1 3368540301
www.wolfgangpuck.com

Opening hours	Open 7 days
Credit cards	Accepted
Style of pizza	Italian
Recommended pizza	Roasted Mushroom; Sweet Fennel Sausage; Wolfgang's Smoked Salmon

"Located on the edge of the Friendly Shopping Center, Wolfgang Puck Pizza Bar offers an array of personal pizzas and a comprehensive wine list to round out the meal. It is quieter, more intimate, and more romantic than the other best pizzerias in the area, and has a slightly older clientele to match. Plus, the service is impeccable."—Eric Ginsburg

WEST FIRST WOOD-FIRED PIZZA

101B 1st Avenue West
Hendersonville
North Carolina 28792
United States
+1 8286931080
www.flatrockwoodfired.com

Opening hours	Closed Sunday
Credit cards	Accepted
Style of pizza	Wood-fired thin-crust
Recommended pizza	Southwestern

"The high-quality ingredients are thoughtful and locally sourced when possible."—Sheri Castle

DOMINIC'S PIZZA

5911 Poyner Village Parkway, #105
Poyner Place Shopping Center
Raleigh
North Carolina 27616
United States
+1 9198787782
www.dominicspizza.com

Opening hours	Open 7 days
Credit cards	Accepted but not AMEX
Style of pizza	New York
Recommended pizza	Meatball

"This is a great New York-style joint—no frills, just a great chewy crust."—Steve McQuaid

LILLY'S PIZZA

1813 Glenwood Avenue
Raleigh
North Carolina 27608
United States
+1 9198330226
www.lillyspizza.com

Opening hours	Open 7 days
Credit cards	Accepted
Style of pizza	Muliple
Recommended pizza	Big Star; Dante's Inferno; The Aristocrat

"Enjoy a pie made just the way you want! Every pie is made to order and baked on a stone hearth."
—Sheri Castle

"Located in a former biker bar and named after a canine companion, Lilly's offers most everything a modern-day pizza customer could desire. The menu boasts more than 70 toppings, thick or thin crusts, and includes gluten-free options. Creative combinations are nearly limitless."—Amy Rogers

"Some people would tell you that BBQ defines North Carolina food. But for me, when I think of eating in North Carolina, the only thing that comes to mind is Lilly's. It's worth the trip to Raleigh for a pizza alone. Or even just a slice."—Samuel Peterson

TROPHY BREWING AND PIZZA CO.

827 West Morgan Street
Raleigh
North Carolina 27603
United States
+1 9198034849
www.trophybrewing.com

Opening hours	Open 7 days
Credit cards	Accepted
Style of pizza	American thick-crust
Recommended pizza	Best Dressed; Local Celebrity

"Trophy thrives at the edge of downtown Raleigh and it's because it makes fresh, creative pizzas and great beers to go with them."—Steve McQuaid

"In the Triangle, there is no finer location for pairing delicious beer and expertly crafted pies. Toppings range from the traditional (typically with a devious twist) to daily and weekly pizza specials that are downright inspired."—Andrew Mark Veety

BROOKLYN PIZZA

6932 Market Street
Wilmington
North Carolina 28411
United States
+1 9103955558
www.brooklynpizzaconc.com

Opening hours	Open 7 days
Credit cards	Accepted
Style of pizza	New York
Recommended pizza	Meats-Only

"This Big Apple transplant has been serving its adopted hometown for decades. Fun pizza variants like the pepperoni pinwheels assure this spot will never get boring, and a full menu of Italian-American staples make it a sit-down destination for some."
—Paul Stephen

I LOVE NY PIZZA

28 North Front Street
Wilmington
North Carolina 28401
United States
+1 9107627628
www.ilovenypizzailm.com

Opening hours	Open 7 days
Credit cards	Not accepted
Style of pizza	New York
Recommended pizza	Cheese; Roma Spinach

"In addition to remarkable pies, this outfit brings big-city attitude to this sleepy southern town it now calls home."—Paul Stephen

PIZZETTA'S PIZZA

4107 Oleander Drive
Wilmington
North Carolina 28401
United States
+1 9107994300

Opening hours	Open 7 days
Credit cards	Accepted
Style of pizza	New York
Recommended pizza	Nonna's Pizza

"This establishment brings a refined approach to pizza, rounding out the experience with a menu that makes the restaurant a date-night-worthy destination."—Paul Stephen

MISSION PIZZA NAPOLETANA

707 North Trade Street
Winston-Salem
North Carolina 27101
United States
+1 3368938217

Opening hours	Closed Sunday
Credit cards	Accepted
Style of pizza	Neapolitan
Recommended pizza	Pancetta; Sopressata

"Mission Pizza is the only Neapolitan-style pizza place in the state, and you can taste the difference."
—Eric Ginsburg

EMPIRE SLICE HOUSE

1734 Northwest 16th Street
Oklahoma City
Oklahoma 73106
United States
+1 4055571760
www.empireslicehouse.com

Opening hours	Open 7 days
Credit cards	Accepted
Style of pizza	New York
Recommended pizza	Brussell Westbrook

"The Empire Slice House has great decor, a rotating menu, and top-notch beer selection, plus a solid crust with fun names and better flavors."—Greg Elwell

PIZZERIA GUSTO

2415 North Walker Avenue
Oklahoma City
Oklahoma 73103
United States
+1 4054374992
www.pizzeria-gusto.com

Opening hours	Open 7 days
Credit cards	Accepted
Style of pizza	Neapolitan
Recommended pizza	Cherry Tomato (minus the Kalamata olives)

"Pizzeria Gusto is more than just a pizzeria, but it makes excellent pies."—Greg Elwell

THE SAUCEE SICILIAN

Food truck—check website, Facebook, and Twitter for
upcoming locations
Oklahoma City
Oklahoma
United States
+1 4054120789
www.thesauceesicilian.com

Opening hours	Variable
Credit cards	Accepted but not AMEX
Style of pizza	Neapolitan
Recommended pizza	Tusa

HIDEAWAY PIZZA

230 South Knoblock
Stillwater
Oklahoma 74074
United States
+1 4053724777
www.hideawaypizza.com

Opening hours	Open 7 days
Credit cards	Accepted
Style of pizza	Traditional mid-American

"The pizza probably wouldn't win an award, but it is
a staple of Oklahoma. No survey of American pizza
would be complete without Hideaway Pizza."
—Renee Wilmeth

CRUST

1956 B Maybank Highway
Terence Plaza
Charleston
South Carolina 29412
United States
+1 8437625500
www.crustwoodfirepizza.com

Opening hours	Open 7 days
Credit cards	Accepted
Style of pizza	Neapolitan
Recommended pizza	Bianca

"There's a great selection of super-flavorful pizzas on
the menu here and they are consistent and stunning."
—Matt Lee & Ted Lee

HEART WOODFIRE KITCHEN

1622 Highland Avenue
Charleston
South Carolina 29412
United States
+1 8437181539
www.heartkitchenji.com

Opening hours	Closed Monday
Credit cards	Accepted
Style of pizza	Mediterranean flatbread
Recommended pizza	Acorn Squash with Goat Cheese and Arugula (rocket) Pesto

"It's not technically a pizzeria. It's a restaurant with
a focus on wood-fired food that happens to feature
a knockout pizza (they call it a 'flatbread') on the
menu every night."—Matt Lee & Ted Lee

EXTRA VIRGIN OVEN WOOD-FIRED PIZZA

1075 East Montague Avenue
North Charleston
South Carolina 29405
United States
+1 8432251796
www.evopizza.com

Opening hours	Closed Sunday
Credit cards	Accepted
Style of pizza	Neapolitan wood-fired
Recommended pizza	Pistachio Pesto

"EVO was the game-changer—the first pizzeria
in Charleston with Slow Food values. It also has
a superb selection of craft beers and a friendly
neighborhood vibe."—Matt Lee & Ted Lee

COMMUNITY PIE

850 Market Street
Chattanooga
Tennessee 37402
United States
+1 4234861743
www.communitypie.com

Opening hours	Open 7 days
Credit cards	Accepted
Style of pizza	New York and Neapolitan
Recommended pizza	Hot Hawaiian; Little Italy

"This is a pizzeria for locals, business types, families, and, of course, die-hard traditionalists. When the weather is good the windows open into the plaza where there are occasionally free concerts."
—Robert Alexander

"The vibe at Community Pie is my kind of pizza joint. It's family-friendly, yet the large bar invites singles and young people. The draft beer list is extensive, and the drinking vinegars piqued my interest (they're amazing.)"—Amanda Clark

BELLA NAPOLI

1200 Villa Place, Suite 206
Nashville
Tennessee 37212
United States
+1 6158911387
www.bellanapolipizzeria.com

Opening hours	Closed Sunday
Credit cards	Accepted
Style of pizza	Neapolitan
Recommended pizza	Capricciosa

"The pizza is perfectly cooked, fresh and hot right out of the oven and to your table."—Andy Nelson

BELLA NASHVILLE

900 Rosa L Parks Boulevard
Nashville
Tennessee 37208
United States
+1 6154573863

Opening hours	Closed Monday
Credit cards	Accepted
Style of pizza	Wood-fired
Recommended pizza	Amaro Scuro

"This pizza shop is located inside the Nashville Farmers' Market, and I appreciate the creative way it showcases local ingredients from farmers. For example, when strawberries are in season, you might find them sliced onto pizza along with thinly shaved country ham, blue cheese, and balsamic reduction."—Jennifer Justus

CITY HOUSE

1222 4th Avenue North
Nashville
Tennessee 37208
United States
+1 6157365838
www.cityhousenashville.com

Opening hours	Closed Tuesday
Credit cards	Accepted
Style of pizza	Wood-fired
Recommended pizza	Belly Ham with Egg

"I appreciate the simplicity of the pizza. Chef Tandy Wilson lets the wood-fired oven and quality ingredients do the work with options such as a Margherita or a pie with chard, mayo, Pecorino, garlic, lemon, and chiles."—Jennifer Justus

DESANO PIZZA BAKERY

115 16th Avenue South
Nashville
Tennessee 37203
United States
+1 6159531168
www.desanopizza.it

Opening hours	Open 7 days
Credit cards	Accepted
Style of pizza	Neapolitan
Recommended pizza	San Gennaro

"Three pizza ovens imported from Italy ensure the best VPN-certified pizza in town comes out quickly and perfectly (slightly) charred from the inferno."
—Chris Chamberlain

"Cafeteria-style seating makes for a great atmosphere and the big ovens are right in front of you. Pizzas come out fast and throwing the pies around is a show for the crowd!"—Andy Nelson

JOEY'S HOUSE OF PIZZA

897 Elm Hill Pike
Nashville
Tennessee 37210
United States
+1 6152545639
www.joeyshouseofpizza.com

Opening hours..........................Closed Saturday and Sunday
Credit cards...Accepted
Style of pizza...New York
Recommended pizza.................................The Gladiator

"By the large slice or full pie, these pizzas are quite reminiscent of the best of Manhattan. A food bar of other Italian pasta classics is a nice extra for patrons who aren't feeling the pizza craving that day."
—Chris Chamberlain

LOCKELAND TABLE COMMUNITY KITCHEN AND BAR

1520 Woodland Street
Nashville
Tennessee 37206
United States
+1 6152284864
www.lockelandtable.com

Opening hours..Closed Sunday
Credit cards...Accepted
Style of pizza..Wood-fired
Recommended pizza...Margherita

"Though the menu at this restaurant includes steak, fish, and an always excellent list of appetizers, chef Hal Holden-Bache says he built the restaurant around the wood-fired pizza oven and bar where you'll sometimes find him filling in at that station to carefully construct his pies and talk with guests."
—Jennifer Justus

MANNY'S HOUSE OF PIZZA

15 Arcade Building
Nashville
Tennessee 37219
United States
+1 6152427144
www.mannyshouseofpizza.com

Opening hours...Closed Sunday
Credit cards...Accepted
Style of pizza...New York
Recommended pizza..........................Spinach and Tomato

"All the traditional techniques and attitude of a great New York pizzeria. Huge slices with just enough grease to remind you that you're treating yourself."
—Chris Chamberlain

PORTA VIA

21 White Bridge Road, #104
Nashville
Tennessee 37205
United States
+1 6153560001
www.eatatportavia.com

Opening hours..Open 7 days
Credit cards...Accepted
Style of pizza..Neapolitan
Recommended pizza...Diavola

"These perfect-sized pies are just so dang good! The crust is fantastic and the sauce is pretty amazing too."—Andy Nelson

THE BACKSPACE

507 San Jacinto Boulevard
Austin
Texas 78701
United States
+1 5124749899
www.thebackspace-austin.com

Opening hours..Open 7 days
Credit cards...Accepted
Style of pizza..Neapolitan

BUFALINA PIZZA
1519 East Cesar Chavez
Austin
Texas 78702
United States
+1 5125242523
www.bufalinapizza.com

Opening hours........................Closed Monday and Tuesday
Credit cards..Accepted
Style of pizza.. Neapolitan
Recommended pizza...........................Calabrese; Greenbelt;
Margherita; Marinara; Taleggio

"In a town where we wait in line to get into ramen bars and BBQ joints, I happily wait in line to get into Bufalina. Well, I plan ahead and get there right when it opens. The pizza menu changes daily and the selection offers perfect examples of crispy and crusty, lightly smoky and charred pies with scant ingredients. The key is in the simplicity of the toppings. Nothing is overdone here, not a topping is out of place."—Rachel Forrest

"Bufalina makes its own mozzarella, and a plate of it alone is among my favorite dishes. But it's even better on Bufalina's outstanding crust, which bubbles and cracks where it should."—Hanna Raskin

"Well-made pizza with an outstanding wine selection."—Michael Fojtasek

EAST SIDE PIES
1401 Rosewood Avenue
Austin
Texas 78702
United States
+1 5125240933
www.eastsidepies.com

Opening hours..Open 7 days
Credit cards..Accepted
Style of pizza..Thin-crust
Recommended pizza..Guiche; Old 97S

"East Side Pies sources from local farms and makes all its own sausage and meatballs and even chimichurri sauce. It also does odd sauces like spinach curry and black bean sauce. It's sort of the old hippie pizzeria, except it hasn't been around as long as the old Austin freaks."—Rachel Forrest

HOME SLICE PIZZA
1415 South Congress Avenue
Austin
Texas 78704
United States
+1 5124447437
www.homeslicepizza.com

Opening hours..Open 7 days
Credit cards..Accepted
Style of pizza..New York
Recommended pizza...............Sausage, Pepper, and Ricotta

"Great caramelized, tender, and yeasty dough and the right proportions of cheese and toppings. Overall an intensely flavored pie."—Julian Barsotti

KING BEE LOUNGE
1906 East 12th Street
Austin
Texas 78721
United States
+1 5126006956

Opening hours..Open 7 days
Credit cards....................................Accepted but not AMEX
Style of pizza..New American
Recommended pizza.......................Green and White Grocer

"The King Bee is a dark craft cocktail lounge where mixologist Billy Hankey makes the drinks and partner Colette Dein just happens to make some of the best pizza in Austin. And that's basically all she makes. Get a frozen Bee's Knees or a smoky sip or two of fine mezcal and order a thin-crust pie that's cut into squares, not slices. It's a cozy vibe in a soon to be hot section of town."—Rachel Forrest

VIA 313
6705 Highway 290, Suite 503
Austin
Texas 78735
United States
+1 5125848084
www.via313.com

Opening hours..Open 7 days
Credit cards..Accepted
Style of pizza..Detroit
Recommended pizza...The Detroiter

"These pizza obsessives are known for their attention to detail and consistently delicious Detroit-style pizzas."—Steven Dilley

IL CANE ROSSO

2612 Commerce Street
Dallas
Texas 75226
United States
+1 2147411188
www.canerosso.com

Opening hours	Open 7 days
Credit cards	Accepted
Style of pizza	Neapolitan
Recommended pizza	Honey Bastard

"The crust of an Il Cane Rosso pie is perfectly swollen and charred beneath its zesty sauce, but owner Jay Jerrier doesn't take much else too seriously: he famously put a side of ranch dressing on the menu, priced at $1,000."—Hanna Raskin

ZOLI'S NY PIZZA TAVERN

202 West Davis Street
Dallas
Texas 75208
United States
+1 2149429654
www.zolispizza.com

Opening hours	Closed Monday and Tuesday
Credit cards	Accepted
Style of pizza	New York
Recommended pizza	Grandma; Sicilian with Hot Soppressatta

"A great neighborhood pizza joint with very friendly staff."—David Uygur

PIZZA SNOB

3051 South University Drive
Fort Worth
Texas 76109
United States
+1 8174627662
www.pizzasnob.com

Opening hours	Open 7 days
Credit cards	Accepted
Style of pizza	Build-your-own
Recommended pizza	Cheddar Baked Potato Pizza with Candied Jalapeños

"A fast, casual 'Chipotle-style' pizzeria with really top-notch ingredients."—Jay Jerrier

CIAO BELLO

5161 San Felipe Street
Sage Plaza Shopping Centre
Houston
Texas 77056
United States
+1 7139600333
www.ciaobellohouston.com

Opening hours	Open 7 days
Credit cards	Accepted
Style of pizza	Roman
Recommended pizza	Margherita

"Arguably, the best tomato sauce in the city."
—Jeremy Parzen

COLTIVARE

3320 White Oak Drive
Houston
Texas 77007
United States
+1 7136374095
www.coltivarehouston.com

Opening hours	Closed Tuesday
Credit cards	Accepted
Style of pizza	Focaccia
Recommended pizza	Gulf Shrimp (prawns), Sungold Tomato, Eggplant (aubergine), Basil, and Smoked Paprika; Lemon Pizza with Goat Cheese, Olives, and Rosemary

"The distinctive focaccia-style crust here is proofed over two days and then brushed with sorghum glaze before it goes in the wood-fired oven, which gives it a lightly caramelized finish that sets off the char. Seasonal toppings come right out of the on-site garden or from local Gulf Coast farmers, and the salumi are made at a sister market right down the street."—Alison Cook

DOLCE VITA PIZZERIA ENOTECA

500 Westheimer Road
Houston
Texas 77006
United States
+1 7135208222
www.dolcevitahouston.com

Opening hours...Closed Monday
Credit cards..Accepted
Style of pizza...Neapolitan
Recommended pizza..............................Margherita; Robiola

"Great ingredient combos by chef Marco Wiles,
a noted Houston food figure."—Alison Cook

LUIGI'S

4505 Bissonnet Street
Houston
Texas 77401
United States
+1 7136650811
www.luigipizzamidtown.com

Opening hours..Open 7 days
Credit cards..Accepted
Style of pizza..New York
Recommended pizza...Pepperoni

"The closest thing to New York-style pizza in
Houston. Nostalgic and delicious."—Jeremy Parzen

LUNA PIZZERIA

3435 Kirby Drive
Houston
Texas 77098
United States
+1 8327676338
www.lunapizzeria.com

Opening hours..Open 7 days
Credit cards..Accepted
Style of pizza..Thick-crust
Recommended pizza.................Mushroom; Spicy Andouille

"A warm and inviting restaurant off the beaten path."
—Wanda Baker

PIZARO'S PIZZA NAPOLETANA

1000 West Gray Street
Houston
Texas 77019
United States
+1 8327425200
www.pizarospizza.com

Opening hours...Closed Monday
Credit cards..Accepted
Style of pizza...Neapolitan
Recommended pizza..............Arugula (rocket); Margherita;
Polpette

"Serious Italian-grade ingredients blasted in a
wood-fired Neapolitan oven. It's family-owned
(paterfamilias Bill Hutchinson has VPN *pizzaiolo*
credentials from Naples), and everything from the
house salad to the polpette show an individual touch.
The stretchy, charry crusts have a high and mighty
crown."—Alison Cook

PROVISIONS

807 Taft Street
Houston
Texas 77019
United States
+1 7136289020
www.passandprovisions.com

Opening hours..Closed Sunday
Credit cards..Accepted
Style of pizza...Wood-fired
Recommended pizza...........Scamorza, Caramelized Onion,
and Guanciale

"The temperature they cook the pizza at gives it a
nice charred crust."—Chris Shepherd

PUPATELLA

5104 Wilson Boulevard
Arlington
Virginia 22205
United States
+1 5713127230
www.pupatella.com

Opening hours	Closed Monday
Credit cards	Accepted
Style of pizza	Neapolitan
Recommended pizza	Burrata; Diavola; Margherita

"Owner-*pizzaiolo* Enzo Algarme forges top-notch DOC certified pizzas using a massive red-tiled, oak-fueled oven burning at 1,000°F (538°C). This allows the crust to stay elastic without crisping up, creating a perfect pie. Whether you go with a simple Margherita or one of the house specialties, you're sure to leave pleased."—Nevin Martell

"Pupatella is another VPN-certified spot, but it lacks all pretense and maintains the relaxed vibe of a true hole-in-the-wall. The pies are delicious, as are the 'friggitoria' items, fried dishes such as sausage-stuffed arancini and panzerotti (potato croquettes)."—Anna Spiegel

BOTTOMS UP PIZZA

1700 Dock Street
Historic Shockoe Bottom
Richmond
Virginia 23223
United States
+1 8046444400
www.bottomsuppizza.com

Opening hours	Open 7 days
Credit cards	Accepted
Style of pizza	Sourdough
Recommended pizza	Bottoms Up Loaded

"It's a fun atmosphere with a great beer list, and a really unique spot to grab some quality pizza."
—Steve McQuaid

PIES AND PINTS

219 West Maple Avenue
Fayetteville
West Virginia 25840
United States
+1 3045742200
www.piesandpints.net

Opening hours	Open 7 days
Credit cards	Accepted
Style of pizza	Italian
Recommended pizza	Chicken Gouda; Cuban Pork; Grape and Gorgonzola

"What started as a small pizzeria in the white-water rafting capital of West Virginia has expanded to other parts of the state and into Ohio. The freshly made hand-tossed crust is topped with eclectic combinations of fresh ingredients, like grape and Gorgonzola, chicken Gouda, and Sriracha shrimp (prawns)."—Nikki Bowman

DICARLO'S PIZZA

1311 Main Street
Wheeling
West Virginia 26003
United States
+1 3042421490
www.dicarlospizza.com

Opening hours	Open 7 days
Credit cards	Accepted
Style of pizza	Italian
Recommended pizza	Basic Pizza with Provolone Cheese

"DiCarlo's Pizza is an institution in the northern Panhandle of West Virginia. Its distinctive square-shaped crispy crust along with its signature sauce and fresh provolone cheese—which is placed on top after the pizza comes out of the oven—makes this a special culinary experience."—Nikki Bowman

SMALL-BATCH PIZZA
IN SMALL TOWN, USA

Caleb Schiff of Pizzicletta and David Bauer of All Souls Pizza make great pizza out of the limelight. They and many others have helped spread the craft-food craze from New York, London, and Tokyo to places with calmer lifestyles and cheaper rents. Small-batch pizza in small town USA has become a big thing, even if hipster cred was the last thing its pioneers were pursuing. Schiff craves only some recognition from the national food media. Bauer is glad to escape the hype machinery. "I was unaware of the whole pizza scene around the country," says Bauer. "It doesn't involve us. We're just doing our thing."

Schiff picked up an itch for Italian cooking, wood-fired ovens, and Neapolitan pizza on a solo bike tour of Italy in 2006. Back home in Flagstaff, Arizona, population 70,000, he started making bread and pizza for "Little Italy" parties in his backyard. The baking sideline grew first into an obsession and finally into Pizzicletta, a Flagstaff pizzeria funded by family, friends, and locals.

Bauer, a baker who builds wood-fired brick ovens, moved from Minnesota to San Francisco in 2006 but didn't endure the madnesses of that food metropolis for long. He accepted an invitation to fix up a bakery 2,500 miles (4,023 km) east in Asheville, North Carolina. That city in the foothills of the Blue Ridge Mountains was not yet a happening enclave for hipster refugees from Portland, Brooklyn, and Atlanta. All Souls Pizza, which he launched with chef Brendan Reusing in 2013, grew out of Farm & Sparrow, his wood-fired bakery.

Bauer sources a variety of heirloom wheats—NuEast, Turkey, Hard White, Yadkin Wheat—he mills himself. The wheat blend for pizza varies by season: in summer he makes a dough with a higher proportion of white wheat, yielding a light crust well suited to pizzas covered with fresh greens. In winter he mills darker flours to back up pizzas topped with soppressata and pepperoni from a local butcher, or house-made fennel sausage, *guanciale* (cured pork jowl), and *bresaola* (air-dried beef). In all seasons the crust is crisp on top, chewy within.

Schiff wants his crust to be as soft as it can without making it impossible to pick up a slice in your hands. His inspiration comes from Naples. The concise menu features a classic Marinara and a Margherita with the mozzarella he makes himself. With his Neapolitan pizza Schiff is not following any outside guidelines, least of all those dictated by the VPN Association. "I really hate VPN shit," says the self-taught baker. "When I say I want our pizza to be distinctive I am saying that if you saw a picture of our pizzas you'd know it was Pizzicletta. The pizza we make is entirely our own."

Bauer dismisses the Neapolitan certification process as a marketing gimmick. He finds it odd that wheat cultivated in other countries is sent to Italy for milling and then shipped to North America for a true Italian experience. "If there was a founder of Neapolitan pizza, a Jesus figure," says Bauer, "he would probably just work with whatever was around him."

"THE PIZZAS ARE LISTED BY THE YEARS THEY WERE POPULAR...THIS PLACE IS LIKE A PIZZA TIME MACHINE."

SCOTT WIENER P.470

"THIS PIZZA HAUNTS MY DREAMS."

JOSEPH HAFNER P.480

USA NORTHEAST

"THE PIZZA IS SOMETHING SPECIAL, AS IF A SICILIAN PIZZA HAD MADE LOVE TO A FLUFFY PILLOWY FOCACCIA."

DAMIAN SANSONETTI P.465

"YOU GO HERE WHEN YOU WANT TO FEEL, AND TASTE, HISTORY."

LIZ BARRETT P.463

"THE LOCATION OF THIS PLACE IS SPECTACULAR. IT'S WORTH THE TRIP TO RURAL VERMONT."

ANDREW VOLK P.483

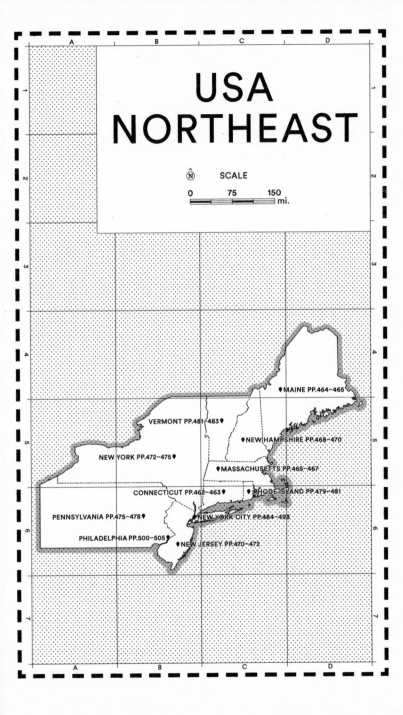

USA
NORTHEAST

N̂   SCALE

0   75   150
                mi.

MAINE PP.464–465

VERMONT PP.481–483

NEW HAMPSHIRE PP.468–470

NEW YORK PP.472–475

MASSACHUSETTS PP.465–467

CONNECTICUT PP.462–463   RHODE ISLAND PP.479–481

PENNSYLVANIA PP.475–478   NEW YORK CITY PP.484–498

PHILADELPHIA PP.500–505   NEW JERSEY PP.470–472

GLENVILLE PIZZERIA

243 Glenville Road
Greenwich
Connecticut 06831
United States
+1 2035319852

Opening hours	Open 7 days
Credit cards	Not accepted
Style of pizza	New York and Sicilian
Recommended pizza	Sicilian

"New Haven may get all the attention when it comes to Connecticut pizza, but this hole-in-the-wall serves hand-tossed New York-style perfection."
—Alice Levitt

ANASTASIO'S

127 Wooster Street
New Haven
Connecticut 06511
United States
+1 2037764825
www.anastasiosnewhaven.com

Opening hours	Open 7 days
Credit cards	Accepted
Style of pizza	Neapolitan
Recommended pizza	White Pie with Bacon and Onion

BAR

254 Crown Street
New Haven
Connecticut 06511
United States
+1 2034958924
www.barnightclub.com

Opening hours	Open 7 days
Credit cards	Accepted
Style of pizza	New Haven thin-crust
Recommended pizza	White Mozzarella with Mashed Potato and Bacon; Tuesday BarCaseus Collaboration

"There are so many reasons to love Bar: the atmosphere, the energetic hip young staff, the house-brewed beer, the music, and, of course, the super-thin-crust pizza."—Jason Sobocinski

FRANK PEPE PIZZERIA NAPOLETANA

157 Wooster Street
New Haven
Connecticut 06511
United States
+1 2038655762
www.pepespizzeria.com

Opening hours	Open 7 days
Credit cards	Not accepted
Style of pizza	New Haven
Recommended pizza	White Clam

"The White Clam pizza is one of the best pies on the planet."—Joseph Hafner

"If you want to discuss the loaded topic of America's best pizza with any authority, you have to embark on a pilgrimage to this legendary New Haven pizzeria."
—Arthur Bovino

The expansion of Frank Pepe's is eyed with suspicion by devotees of this great New Haven pizza institution: will the firm, chewy, coal-baked pizza travel well? Will quality at home be compromised? One thing is certain: the lines outside the original are not getting any shorter. Pepe, an immigrant from the town of Maiori, on the Amalfi Coast, began making *apizza* on Wooster Street in 1925. His then-signature pizza is still a force now—the aptly named Frank Pepe's Original Tomato Pie, with crushed Italian tomatoes, ample olive oil, and grated cheese. But it's the first hot slice of the White Clam Pizza, with freshly shucked clams, grated cheese, oregano, and plenty of fresh garlic, that forever haunts your pizza dreams. The second slice isn't too bad either.

FRANK PEPE PIZZERIA NAPOLETANA

163 Wooster Street
New Haven
Connecticut 06511
United States
+1 2038655762
www.pepespizzeria.com

Opening hours	Closed Monday–Thursday
Credit cards	Accepted
Style of pizza	New Haven
Recommended pizza	White Clam

"I had the White Clam pizza almost 20 years ago and still think about it. Nothing about it should work. The abundant chunks of garlic should overwhelm it. The juicy clams should make it soggy, or just weird. Yet somehow all the pieces meld perfectly into a delicious, unforgettable pie."—Michalene Busico

MODERN APIZZA

874 State Street
New Haven
Connecticut 06511
United States
+1 2037765306
www.modernapizza.com

Opening hours...Closed Monday
Credit cards...Accepted but not AMEX
Style of pizza..Neapolitan
Recommended pizza.........................Bacon, Onion, Sausage,
 Mushroom, and Bell Pepper; Mozzarella and Eggplant
 (aubergine); Veggie Bomb

"Established in 1934, Modern is one of the oldest pizzerias in the country. While most of the attention lavished on New Haven pizza goes to Pepe's (1925) and Sally's (1938), which sit next to each other on Wooster Square, Modern is actually my favorite."—Jeff Varasano

**"New Haven is the unsung pizza capital of America, the tomato pie is the undisputed king of the New Haven pizza canon, and Modern Apizza, also unsung, makes the best tomato pie in New Haven."
—Nathan Winkler-Rhoades & Jonah Fliegelman**

At some point between 1934 and now Modern Apizza stopped being modern. The woodwork and prices may have been periodically updated but the pizza—sorry, *apizza*—is as old school as it gets. Mozzarella melts into puddles over a sea of tomato and olive oil. When you pull apart two slices the cheese stretched between them doesn't know which way to go. The Eggplant (aubergine) pizza, topped with thin slices of fried, breaded eggplant, is only one of several house specialties. Indeed, when you ask a waitress to recommend one pizza she's prone to falter. Maybe she'll mumble something about bacon, which accompanies clams, bell peppers or, in the Italian Bomb, sausage, pepperoni, mushroom, onion, bell pepper, and garlic. The resolutely crisp crust can handle the load.

SALLY'S APIZZA

237 Wooster Street
New Haven
Connecticut 06511
United States
+1 2036245271
www.sallysapizza.com

Opening hours.........................Closed Monday and Tuesday
Credit cards...Not accepted
Style of pizza..New Haven
Recommended pizza.............Clam; Pepperoni; Plain Italian
 Tomato Pie

**"This is classic New Haven. You go here when you want to feel, and taste, history. The pizzas are unlike any you will find in the rest of the country."
—Liz Barrett**

**"This is the most perfect pizza I've ever tasted. I've waited close to three hours for it, and I'd do it again. From the delightful asymmetry to the amazing char, it's got everything a great pizza should."
—Rachel Leah Blumenthal**

"Sally's is still family run, using the original coal-fired brick oven, and it only accepts cash. It was Frank Sinatra's favorite pizza, specifically the mozz. and pepperoni pie."—Colin M. Caplan

At Sally's the perfectly round pizza is an abnormality. A fearless and patient regular might send it back to the kitchen. The rustic, old-world, handmade authenticity of this coal-oven-baked New Haven classic is defined by the irregular geometry of its crusty, blackened rim. "Sally's" is for Salvatore "Sal" Consiglio, who left his uncle Frank Pepe's neighboring pizzeria in 1938 to open one of his own. His sons Bob and Rick run the show now. "*Apizza*," pronounced "ah-beetz" in Neapolitan dialect, is what New Havenites call their thoroughly crisp pizza. Sally's first-rate selection of toppings—mozzarella, anchovies, clams, meatballs—is ignored by purists who can't see beyond the incomparable Plain Italian Tomato Pie. On the odd visit when they're feeling really adventurous, they might order a plain with garlic.

OLDE WORLD BRICK OVEN APIZZA

1957 Whitney Avenue
North Haven
Connecticut 06473
United States
+1 2032878820
www.oldeworldapizza.com

Opening hours..Closed Monday
Credit cards...Not accepted
Style of pizza..Neapolitan
Recommended pizza..............................Eggplant (aubergine)

PIZZA BY ALEX

93 Alfred Street
Biddeford
Maine 04005
United States
+1 2072830002
www.pizzabyalexmaine.com

Opening hours	Open 7 days
Credit cards	Not accepted
Style of pizza	Thin-crust pan
Recommended pizza	Yaya's Greek

"Pizza by Alex (also known as Alex's Pizza) has been a local icon since 1960. It serves just one pizza, a 10-inch (25-cm) Greek-style personal pan-sized pie with a crispy crust, homemade tomato sauce, and Cheddar cheese. There's a long list of toppings but the only other kind of cheese you can get is feta."
—Susan Axelrod

BONOBO

46 Pine Street
Portland
Maine 04102
United States
+1 2073478267
www.bonobopizza.com

Opening hours	Open 7 days
Credit cards	Accepted
Style of pizza	Wood-fired thin-crust
Recommended pizza	Taleggio

"I like the slightly smoky crust from the wood-fired pizza oven and the fresh, unusual, and all-natural toppings."—Susan Axelrod

FLATBREAD COMPANY

72 Commercial Street, #5
Portland
Maine 04101
United States
+1 2077728777
www.flatbreadcompany.com

Opening hours	Open 7 days
Credit cards	Accepted
Style of pizza	Flatbread
Recommended pizza	Casco Bay

"This is an unmissable stop-off in Portland! At once a hipster destination and a child-friendly restaurant, this huge pizza place with a terrace by the port deals in organic local produce. Although there's a bit of a chilled-out vibe and 'coolness,' it takes its pizza very seriously, rebranding it as the best healthy eating option, not to mention a great way to support local farms."—Stéphanie Bois-Houde

LEONARDO'S PIZZA

415 Forest Avenue
Portland
Maine 04102
United States
+1 2077754444
www.leonardosonline.com

Opening hours	Open 7 days
Credit cards	Accepted
Style of pizza	Traditional American

"Wonderfully solid American-style takeout pizza. Nothing fancy, just delicious."—Andrew Volk

MICUCCI GROCERY

45 India Street
Portland
Maine 04101
United States
+1 2077751854
www.micuccigrocery.com

Opening hours	Closed Sunday
Credit cards	Accepted
Style of pizza	Sicilian

OTTO

576 Congress Street
Portland
Maine 04101
United States
+1 2073587090
www.ottoportland.com

Opening hours	Open 7 days
Credit cards	Accepted
Style of pizza	Thin-crust
Recommended pizza	Mashed Potato, Bacon, and Scallion (spring onion)

PIZZA VILLA

940 Congress Street
Portland
Maine 04102
United States
+1 2077741777

Opening hours	Open 7 days
Credit cards	Accepted but not AMEX
Style of pizza	Neapolitan
Recommended pizza	Anchovy and Pepperoni

"Pizza Villa is a cool old-school little place."
—Damian Sansonetti

SLAB

25 Preble Street
Portland
Maine 04101
United States
+1 2072453088
www.slabportland.com

Opening hours	Closed Sunday
Credit cards	Accepted
Style of pizza	Sicilian
Recommended pizza	Hand Slab; Spicy Meat Wedge

"The pizza is something special, as if a Sicilian pizza had made love to a fluffy pillowy focaccia."
—Damian Sansonetti

CORSETTI'S

443 Gray Road
Windham
Maine 04062
United States
+1 2078926291
www.corsettiswindham.com

Opening hours	Open 7 days
Credit cards	Accepted
Style of pizza	Neapolitan
Recommended pizza	Meat Lovers; Veggie Lovers

PRIDES PICCOLA NAPOLETANA

202 Rantoul Street
Beverly
Massachusetts 01915
United States
+1 9789696142
www.pridespiccola.com

Opening hours	Closed Monday
Credit cards	Accepted
Style of pizza	Neapolitan
Recommended pizza	Margherita

COPPA

253 Shawmut Avenue
Boston
Massachusetts 02118
United States
+1 6173910902
www.coppaboston.com

Opening hours	Open 7 days
Credit cards	Accepted
Style of pizza	Wood-fired
Recommended pizza	Bone Marrow; 'Nduja

"Coppa's pizza is the perfect size to crush an entire pie, and then some. It's crispy, chewy, and tasty...everything you want in a good pizza."—Kevin O'Donnell

"Coppa is a petite Italian enoteca, but pizza takes up some significant real estate on the menu. The crust here is nicely charred, but it's really all about the super-creative toppings, such as beef heart, bone marrow, and horseradish; pork sausage and fennel pollen; sweet onion and crescenza cheese."—Leah Mennies

GALLERIA UMBERTO

289 Hanover Street
Boston
Massachusetts 02113
United States
+1 6172275709

Opening hours	Closed Sunday
Credit cards	Not accepted
Style of pizza	Sicilian
Recommended pizza	Plain Sicilian Pie

"This is a long-standing spot with a ton of character—and only a few things on the menu. There are long lines each day for the thick square Sicilian slices, which are always pooled with the kind of grease you want to eat. When they run out, they run out."—Leah Mennies

PICCO

513 Tremont Street
Boston
Massachusetts 02116
United States
+1 6179270066
www.piccorestuarant.com

Opening hours	Open 7 days
Credit cards	Accepted but not AMEX
Style of pizza	Wood-fired
Recommended pizza	Alsatian

"Rick Katz, proprietor of Picco, has a background as a pastry chef, and this skill shows with Picco's crusts, which are blistered and very (purposefully) charred yet super spongy and flavorful within. The place as a whole just does simple things but does them very well—excellent pies, homemade pastas, and, for dessert, epic ice cream sundaes."—Leah Mennies

REGINA PIZZERIA

11½ Thacher Street
Boston
Massachusetts 02113
United States
+1 6172270765
www.reginapizzeria.com

Opening hours	Open 7 days
Credit cards	Accepted
Style of pizza	Brick-oven
Recommended pizza	Cheese; Napoletana

"Opened in 1926, and located in the North End of Boston, Regina Pizzeria is small and cozy with historical, old-school atmosphere. The thin-crust pizza is made with a mild sauce and aged mozzarella, and locals know to order the pizza well done."
—Christina Barrueta

AREA FOUR

500 Technology Square
Cambridge
Massachusetts 02139
United States
+1 6177584444
www.areafour.com

Opening hours	Open 7 days
Credit cards	Accepted
Style of pizza	Wood-fired
Recommended pizza	Soppressata

"Both the chef-owner Michael Leviton and chef de cuisine Jeff Pond are super talented and make some really good pizza. They make their own mozzarella, get great char in the wood-fired oven, and use great ingredients."—Kevin O'Donnell

ARMANDO'S

163 Huron Avenue
Cambridge
Massachusetts 02138
United States
+1 6173548275

Opening hours	Open 7 days
Credit cards	Not accepted
Style of pizza	New York
Recommended pizza	Pepperoni

"This is the quintessential cheap slice shop in the Boston area, serving up pizza that is definitely comparable to a great New York City slice."—Rachel Leah Blumenthal

TONY AND ANN'S

11 Broadway Road
Dracut
Massachusetts 01826
United States
+1 9782513311
www.tonyandannspizza.com

Opening hours	Closed Sunday–Wednesday
Credit cards	Accepted
Style of pizza	Italian
Recommended pizza	Plain Cheese

"This place is worth flying to from anywhere in the world. Tony and Ann's sweet sauce is like nothing you have ever had."—Keith Sarasin

SANTARPIO'S

111 Chelsea Street
East Boston
Massachusetts 02128
United States
+1 6175679871
www.santarpiospizza.com

Opening hours	Open 7 days
Credit cards	Not accepted
Style of pizza	New York
Recommended pizza	Italian Cheese; Sausage and Garlic; Shrimp (prawn) Scampi

"Santarpio's is the perfect place to enjoy hot, cheesy pizzas that come straight from the oven to your table. Served over a bed of cornmeal, the crust is perfectly bubbly, slightly burnt, and deliciously buttery."
—Steve Holt

SHORT AND MAIN

36 Main Street
Gloucester
Massachusetts 01234
United States
+1 9782810044
www.shortandmain.com

Opening hours	Closed Wednesday
Credit cards	Accepted
Style of pizza	Neapolitan
Recommended pizza	Margherita

PINOCCHIO'S PIZZERIA

122 Main Street, #3
Northampton
Massachusetts 01060
United States
+1 4135868275

Opening hours	Open 7 days
Credit cards	Not accepted
Style of pizza	New York
Recommended pizza	Pepperoni

"The pizzas are made ahead and you choose a slice or two to be reheated. I love the pepperoni as my first slice as it is crunchy and full of delicious pepperoni. For my the second slice I look to see what strikes me...trust me you will have a hard time choosing as they put out great combinations!"—Tommy York

SPIRITUS PIZZA

190 Commercial Street
Provincetown
Massachusetts 02657
United States
+1 5084872808
www.spirituspizza.com

Opening hours	Open 7 days
Credit cards	Not accepted
Style of pizza	New York

"This fun place is a total local institution—and the taste is pretty damn good! Late nights are bonkers and there's even a bocce court in the back. It's not Patsy's Pizzeria of NYC, but who cares? It's Spiritus."—Jeff Orlick

AREA FOUR

445 Somerville Avenue
Somerville
Massachusetts 02143
United States
+1 6177644190
www.areafour.com

Opening hours	Open 7 days
Credit cards	Accepted
Style of pizza	Wood-fired
Recommended pizza	Carnivore; Sausage

"For Bostonians who want New Haven pizza without the two-hour drive, this will satisfy the craving, although it's not quite the same style. It's not charcoal-fired, but it's perfectly charred in all the right places. The crust bubbles up and takes up a large percentage of the slice; the remainder is topped with excellent meats and vegetables. Plus, the restaurant's vibe is welcoming and it's easy to feel like a regular on your first visit. Don't miss the Hoodsie Cups for dessert."—Rachel Leah Blumenthal

LA FESTA BRICK & BREW PIZZERIA

300 Central Avenue
Dover
New Hampshire 03820
United States
+1 6037434100
www.lafestabrickandbrew.com

Opening hours	Open 7 days
Credit cards	Accepted
Style of pizza	New York, Sicilian
Recommended pizza	Garlic Knot

900 DEGREES

1 Brickyard Square
Epping
New Hampshire 03042
United States
+1 6037342656
www.900degrees.com

Opening hours	Open 7 days
Credit cards	Accepted
Style of pizza	Thin-crust
Recommended pizza	Basa Nova; Saltimbocca; Tuscan Sun

SHOOTERS SPORTS PUB

6 Columbus Avenue
Exeter
New Hampshire 03833
United States
+1 6037723856
www.shooterssportspub.com

Opening hours	Open 7 days
Credit cards	Not accepted
Style of pizza	Thick-crust
Recommended pizza	All Meat

"Its meat-lovers All Meat pie is the best I've ever had. The 18-inch (45-cm) bad boy is piled high with tons of ham, pepperoni, sausage, hamburger, and full slices of bacon layered across the top. You can't ask for anything better."—Keith J. Lemerise

FREMONT PIZZERIA

431 Main Street
Fremont
New Hampshire 03044
United States
+1 6038956313
www.fremontpizzeria.com

Opening hours	Open 7 days
Credit cards	Accepted
Style of pizza	Thick-crust
Recommended pizza	BBQ Chicken; Pepperoni

"I love the pepperoni with extra cheese and the BBQ Chicken is lip-smacking tangy, tender, and sweet." —Keith J. Lemerise

MOUNTAIN FIRE PIZZA

245 Main Street
Gorham
New Hampshire 03581
United States
+1 6039159009
www.mtfire.biz

Opening hours	Open 7 days
Credit cards	Accepted
Style of pizza	New York wood-fired
Recommended pizza	Plain Cheese

"The crust is chewy, flavorful, and cooked over an open hard-wood fire."—Keith Sarasin

900 DEGREES

50 Dow Street
Manchester
New Hampshire 03101
United States
+1 6036410900
www.900degrees.com

Opening hours	Open 7 days
Credit cards	Accepted
Style of pizza	Wood-fired
Recommended pizza	Margherita

"Cooked at 900°F (482°C), this pizza is flavorful and has a bit of that char-crust flavor that you dream about."—Keith Sarasin

TANO'S PIZZERIA

372 Kelley Street
Manchester
New Hampshire 03102
United States
+1 6036228200
www.tanospizzeria.com

Opening hours	Closed Sunday
Credit cards	Accepted
Style of pizza	Italian-Sicilian
Recommended pizza	Original Margherita

"Tano's is a place we just happened to stumble upon and we are so glad we did! It was the first time we had really good Sicilian-style pizza in New Hampshire. Since that first visit, we've tried many of its specialty pies and calzones and have never been disappointed."—Andrew Toland & Deidre Ashe

MT'S LOCAL KITCHEN & WINE BAR

212 Main Street
Nashua
New Hampshire 03060
United States
+1 6035959334
www.mtslocal.com

Opening hours	Open 7 days
Credit cards	Accepted
Style of pizza	Grilled
Recommended pizza	Marinated Mushrooms and Spinach with Four-cheese Blend; San Marzano Tomatoes and Vermont Goat Cheese

"The dough is rolled out to fit on an oval plate, then grilled on top of a wood-fired grill, and just finished in the oven for a minute. Toppings are creative, including one with MT's four-cheese blend, local sausage, grilled onions, tomato jam, basil, and home-made ricotta."—Susan Laughlin

SOPRANOS PIZZERIA

23 Main Street
Nashua
New Hampshire 03064
United States
+1 6038800443
www.sopranosnashua.com

Opening hours	Open 7 days
Credit cards	Accepted
Style of pizza	New York
Recommended pizza	Plain Cheese

"It's hard to find people who get how amazing New York-style pizza is and this place is as close to New York-style as you can get."—Keith Sarasin

WOODSTOCK INN STATION & BREWERY

135 Main Street
North Woodstock
New Hampshire 03262
United States
+1 6037453951
www.woodstockinnnh.com

Opening hours	Open 7 days
Credit cards	Accepted
Style of pizza	Flatbread
Recommended pizza	BBQ Pork

"Located in New Hampshire's White Mountains, this is a super-popular location for tourists up north. Not only does it make its own great beer, but it uses the spent grain to make the pizza crust."
—Andrew Toland & Deidre Ashe

FLATBREAD COMPANY

138 Congress Street
Portsmouth
New Hampshire 03801
United States
+1 6034367888
www.flatbreadcompany.com

Opening hours	Open 7 days
Credit cards	Accepted
Style of pizza	American Flatbread
Recommended pizza	Punctuated Equilibrium

"The menu at Flatbread Company is simple—salads, flatbreads, desserts, and great beer and wine to go with them. The pies are cooked in a big open hearth, which is constantly stoked, where the little kids love to sit to watch their pizzas come out of the oven."—Rachel Forrest

SAVARIO'S
238 State Street
Portsmouth
New Hampshire 03801
United States
+1 6034272919

Opening hours	Open 7 days
Credit cards	Not accepted
Style of pizza	New York
Recommended pizza	Spicy Pepperoni and Fresh Spinach

"Frank Catalino has had Savario's, named for his godfather, for 25 years. He has a huge following and very short hours—just 3 hours a day—so if you can get there for lunch Monday through Wednesday or on Saturday and Sunday only from 5–8 p.m. you'll be very happy. It's just plain, fold it in half and let the grease drip down your arm pizza, which is rare in New Hampshire, but with fresh ingredients."
—Rachel Forrest

SANTILLO'S BRICK OVEN PIZZA
639 South Broad Street
Elizabeth
New Jersey 07022
United States
+1 9083541887
www.santillopizza.com

Opening hours	Open 7 days
Credit cards	Not accepted
Style of pizza	New Jersey
Recommended pizza	1957; 1964; 2011

"This place is a true hole-in-the-wall. To enter, you have to walk down an alley. Al Santillo bakes in the same oven his grandfather used to bake bread, but it has been converted from coal to natural gas. The pizzas are listed by the years they were popular...this place is like a pizza time machine."
—Scott Wiener

"Al is like H. G. Wells with an oven for a time machine, constantly bringing past pizzas back to the future. The oldest are the 1940 Genuine Tomato Pie (no cheese) and the 1948 Tomato Pie (with grated Parmesan), both a nod of respect to their southern New Jersey pizza brethren in Trenton."
—Richard Frazer

DOZZINO
534 Adams Street
Hoboken
New Jersey 07030
United States
+1 2016566561
www.dozzino.com

Opening hours	Closed Monday
Credit cards	Accepted
Style of pizza	Artisanal
Recommended pizza	Diavolo

"Dozzino's pizza features amazingly fresh ingredients atop a crispy yet soft crust cooked to perfection in a wood-burning oven. Its mozzarella is made in-house with curds from Caputo Brother's Creamery—known for producing America's only naturally cultured mozzarella curd. The quality and freshness in every bite are something that can't be ignored, which makes just about any of its creative combinations drool-inducing."—Brittany Temple

RAZZA PIZZA ARTIGIANALE
275 Grove Street
Jersey City
New Jersey 07302
United States
+1 2013569348
www.razzanj.com

Opening hours	Closed Sunday
Credit cards	Accepted
Style of pizza	Neapolitan
Recommended pizza	La Rossa; Margherita; Pork Pie; Santo

"Razza, the second pizzeria by *pizzaiolo* Dan Richer, is doing something special in Jersey City. People frequently ask what the most important element in a pizza is, and the answer is the dough. If Richer is a religious man, he must be praying to the god of flour and yeast, because his crust and homemade sourdough bread loaves are nothing short of divine."
—Brooks Jones

"Dan Richer works closely with local farmers to grow and mill the wheat for his exceptionally light bases, while seasonal produce abounds in the form of heirloom vegetable and tomato toppings."
—Katie Parla

BIVIO PIZZA NAPOLETANA

7A Paterson Avenue
Little Falls
New Jersey 07424
United States
+1 9732560050
www.biviopizza.com

Opening hours	Closed Sunday–Tuesday
Credit cards	Accepted but not AMEX
Style of pizza	Neapolitan
Recommended pizza	Bianca; Filetti; Margherita

"An authentic wood-burning oven from Italy and super-fresh ingredients transport you to Naples with every bite of this incredible pizza."—Liz George

"The owner is obsessed with his yeast and his fermentation process. Rightfully so, it yields an unbeatable crust!"—Melody Kettle

AH' PIZZ

7 North Willow Street
Montclair
New Jersey 07042
United States
+1 9737839200
www.ahpizz.com

Opening hours	Open 7 days
Credit cards	Accepted
Style of pizza	Neapolitan
Recommended pizza	Margherita

"A very flavorful crust."—Melody Kettle

MANCINNI'S COAL OVEN PIZZA

438 Bloomfield Avenue
Montclair
New Jersey 07042
United States
+1 9737444391
www.mancinnis.net

Opening hours	Open 7 days
Credit cards	Accepted
Style of pizza	Coal-fired thin-crust
Recommended pizza	Pancetta; Prosciutto

"Pancettas, fresh chiles, artichokes, and lemon zest are among the toppings that make these thin, crispy-crusted pies sing!"—Liz George

RUTHIE'S BAR-B-Q AND PIZZA

64½ Chestnut Street
Montclair
New Jersey 07042
United States
+1 9735091134
www.ruthiesbbq.com

Opening hours	Closed Sunday
Credit cards	Accepted
Style of pizza	Neapolitan
Recommended pizza	Texas Sausage

PETE & ELDA'S

96 Woodland Avenue
Neptune City
New Jersey 07753
United States
+1 7327746010
www.peteandeldas.com

Opening hours	Open 7 days
Credit cards	Accepted
Style of pizza	Thin-crust
Recommended pizza	Hot Peppers

"I love the cracker-like crust."—Melissa McCart

TRATTORIA LA SORRENTINA

7831 Bergenline Avenue
Corner of 79th Street
North Bergen
New Jersey 07047
United States
+1 2018698100
www.sorrentinanb.com

Opening hours	Open 7 days
Credit cards	Accepted
Style of pizza	Wood-fired
Recommended pizza	Margherita; Sorrentina

"La Sorrentina takes thin-crust to the next level when it fires it in its large wood-burning oven. The pizza has an amazing crisp to it with just the right amount of smoky flavor. Believe it or not, the pizza is arguably better as leftovers as the crust reaches maximum crisp potential in the reheating process."
—Brittany Temple

STAR TAVERN

400 High Street
Orange
New Jersey 07050
United States
+1 9736753336
www.startavern.net

Opening hours	Open 7 days
Credit cards	Accepted
Style of pizza	New York tavern
Recommended pizza	Regular; Sicilian Tomato; White Clam

"People come from miles around to this typical neighborhood tavern with an awesome atmosphere and food."—Ken Miller & Greg O'Neill

THE FOUNTAIN RESTAURANT

283 New Scotland Avenue
Albany
New York 12208
United States
+1 5184829898
www.sites.google.com/site/thefountainrestaurant/home

Opening hours	Open 7 days
Credit cards	Accepted
Style of pizza	Bar pie
Recommended pizza	Meatball

"The classic bar pizza has a thick, sweet, slightly burnt crust with hot, lightly melted cheese and soft red sauce. Happiness comes eight slices to a pie."—Jeff Orlick

RALPH AND ROSIE DELICATESSEN

19 North Lake Avenue
Bergen
New York 14416
United States
+1 5854942049

Opening hours	Open 7 days
Credit cards	Accepted
Style of pizza	Upstate New York
Recommended pizza	Pepperoni with Sweet Sauce

"It uses a sweet tomato sauce that when combined with pepperoni and the almost biscuit-like crust is one of the most uniquely delicious flavors I've never come across anywhere else."—Sean O'Donnell

PICASSO'S PIZZA

4154 McKinley Parkway, #1000
Blasdell
New York 14219
United States
+1 7162021313
www.picassospizza.net

Opening hours	Open 7 days
Credit cards	Accepted
Style of pizza	Buffalo
Recommended pizza	Cheese and Pepperoni

IMPERIAL PIZZA

1035 Abbott Road
Buffalo
New York 14220
United States
+1 7168253636

Opening hours	Open 7 days
Credit cards	Accepted
Style of pizza	Buffalo
Recommended pizza	Pepperoni

"This takeout-only pizzeria in South Buffalo has a cult following thanks to its unique style."
—Donnie Burtless

LOVEJOY PIZZA

1244 East Lovejoy Street
Buffalo
New York 14202
United States
+1 7168919233
www.lovejoypizza.com

Opening hours	Open 7 days
Credit cards	Not accepted
Style of pizza	Traditional
Recommended pizza	Pepperoni

"Lovejoy Pizza makes the quintessential Buffalo-style pizza. It's a little greasy, sloppy, and has semisweet sauce."—Donnie Burtless

ROMEO & JULIET'S BAKERY & CAFFE

1292 Hertel Avenue
Buffalo
New York 14216
United States
+1 7168735730
www.rjcaffe.com

Opening hours	Closed Sunday and Monday
Credit cards	Accepted
Style of pizza	Roman thin-crust
Recommended pizza	Quattro Formaggi

"Romeo & Juliet's is managed by Italians from Brindisi, Milan, Rome, and Florence. Not surprisingly, the pizza is of a style seen in Italy—thin-crust with a small amount of yeast flavor, nicely charred bottom and edges, and served in a size that's almost a single portion."—Michael Chelus

ANGELINA'S PIZZA

43 Chestnut Street
Cold Spring
New York 10516
United States
+1 8452657078
www.angelinascoldspring.com

Opening hours	Open 7 days
Credit cards	Accepted
Style of pizza	New York
Recommended pizza	Pizza from Mars

"The Pizza from Mars has quite the reputation and it looks just as amazing as it tastes. It has mascarpone cheese, truffle oil, spinach, mushrooms, and sun-dried tomatoes. In all truth, the pizza should be renamed Pizza from Heaven because it's just that."—Jamie Miles

ELM STREET BAKERY

72 Elm Street
East Aurora
New York 14052
United States
+1 7166524720
www.elmstreetbakery.com

Opening hours	Closed Monday
Credit cards	Accepted
Style of pizza	Wood-fired thin-crust
Recommended pizza	Wood-Roasted Brussels Sprout and Pancetta; The seasonal option

"In a city known for pizza with heavy dough, lots of sauce, and excessive toppings, Elm Street Bakery is a standout for not only being different, but for quality and consistency. The dough is light, crispy, and consistently charred perfectly from the wood-fired oven. While there is always a pepperoni pizza on the menu, the options are every changing and thrive on local ingredients."—Michael Chelus

NICK & TONI'S

136 North Main Street
East Hampton
New York 11937
United States
+1 6313243550
www.nickandtonis.com

Opening hours	Open 7 days
Credit cards	Accepted
Style of pizza	Wood-fired thin-crust

JOHNNY'S PIZZERIA

30 West Lincoln Avenue
Mount Vernon
New York 10550
United States
+1 9146681957

Opening hours	Closed Sunday and Monday
Credit cards	Not accepted
Style of pizza	New York
Recommended pizza	Plain Cheese; Plain Cheese with Garlic; Plain Cheese with Sausage

"This is the pizza I crave the most. Super-thin. Very crispy. Very bright sweet sauce. Buttery cheese. Just everything a pizza should be. Make sure you check the hours if you make the pilgrimage, as they have a tendency to close certain days and go off on vacation."—Jeff Varasano

BRIDGE STREET PIZZA

45 West Bridge Street
Oswego
New York 13126
United States
+1 3153136600
www.bridgestreetpizzaoswego.com

Opening hours..Open 7 days
Credit cards................................Accepted but not AMEX
Style of pizza.....................................New York thin-crust
Recommended pizza...Italian Sausage

"Most places that claim to have New York-style thin-crust pizza come pretty close but end up lacking somehow. Not this place. It nails it right on the head. They even slice the sausage lengthwise on the deli slicer so it crisps and caramelizes in the oven."
—Sean O'Donnell

ACME BAR AND PIZZA

495 Monroe Avenue
Rochester
New York 14607
United States
+1 5852712263

Opening hours..Open 7 days
Credit cards...Accepted
Style of pizza.....................................Upstate New York
Recommended pizza..Pepperoni

"This is my neighborhood pizza joint. It serves pizza until the bars close and it offers a huge selection of craft beers. You order pizza by the slice, which is roughly an eighth of an extra-large pizza. It has a nice thin, crispy crust and the perfect sauce to cheese ratio."—Sean O'Donnell

FIAMMA PIZZA E VINO

1308 Buffalo Road
Rochester
New York 14624
United States
+1 5852704683
www.fiammarochester.com

Opening hours..Open 7 days
Credit cards................................Accepted but not AMEX
Style of pizza...Neapolitan
Recommended pizza..Margherita

"Fiamma consistently makes a solid pie that I go back for again and again."—Chris Lindstrom

JOE'S BROOKLYN PIZZA

1100 Jefferson Road, #23B
Rochester
New York 14623
United States
+1 5854245637
www.joesbrooklynpizza.com

Opening hours..Open 7 days
Credit cards...Accepted
Style of pizza...New York
Recommended pizza..Cheese

"This is my favorite New York-style pizza in the area. With a crispy, chewy *cornicione* and a pleasantly herbed red sauce, this is an oasis for decent pizza in the middle of a suburban mall."—Chris Lindstrom

NINO'S PIZZERIA

1330 Culver Road
Rochester
New York 14609
United States
+1 5854822264
www.ninospizzeriarochester.com

Opening hours..Open 7 days
Credit cards...Accepted
Style of pizza...Focaccia
Recommended pizza...................Foccaccia with Portobello Mushrooms and Sausage

"The crusty, crunchy, and slightly oily crust is addictive and helps to create the best takeout pizza in the city."—Chris Lindstrom

LA HACIENDA BRIGHTON

900 Brighton Road
Tonawanda
New York 14150
United States
+1 7168323026
www.lahaciendabrighton.com

Opening hours..Open 7 days
Credit cards...Accepted
Style of pizza..Buffalo
Recommended pizza...Chicken Finger

"Continually voted as one of the top pizzerias in the area."—Christopher Palmeri

PALISADE PIZZA & PASTA

783 Palisade Avenue
Yonkers
New York 10703
United States
+1 9149630127
www.palisadepizzapasta.com

Opening hours	Open 7 days
Credit cards	Accepted
Style of pizza	New York
Recommended pizza	White

"This is iconic New York from the point you walk in the door. From the truly American-Italian owner with thick New York accent to the cross-cultural clientele. The pizza has the perfect bite and the ingredients never overpower the dough."—Thomas England

FRANZONE'S

5th and DeKalb Streets
Bridgeport
Pennsylvania 19405
United States
+1 6102750114
www.franzonespizza.com

Opening hours	Open 7 days
Credit cards	Accepted
Style of pizza	Classic thin-crust
Recommended pizza	Pepperoni; Plain

"Franzone's uses a blend of mozzarella and Cheddar for its cheese, and it has a notably sweet sauce that is applied with a signature bull's-eye swirl. The crust is buttery and almost cracker-like. There's nothing else quite like it, and that's why I love it."
—Drew Lazor

ROSARIO'S PIZZERIA & RISTORANTE

100 Highland Avenue
Clarks Summit
Pennsylvania 18411
United States
+1 5705862899
www.myrosarios.com

Opening hours	Open 7 days
Credit cards	Accepted
Style of pizza	Grandma
Recommended pizza	Grandma Style Square

BASILICO'S PIZZERIA

608 Commerce Boulevard
Dickson City
Pennsylvania 18519
United States
+1 5703410422
www.basilicospizzeriaonline.com

Opening hours	Open 7 days
Credit cards	Accepted
Style of pizza	Neapolitan and Sicilian
Recommended pizza	Buffalo Chicken; Grandma; Montanaro

"With a unique variety of true gourmet pizzas from the grandma, to the Sicilian, to the deep-fried pizza, there's something for everyone."—James Mirabelli

PIZZA L'OVEN

1259 Wyoming Avenue
Exeter
Pennsylvania 18643
United States
+1 5706555544
www.pizzalovenexeter.com

Opening hours	Closed Monday
Credit cards	Accepted but not AMEX
Style of pizza	Pan-fried Sicilian

"The Luzerne County region of northeast Pennsylvania features a unique pizza we call pan-fried Sicilian. It is typically square and thick like a traditional Sicilian, but it's fried in peanut (groundnut) oil. Pizza L'Oven utilizes a wonderful sauce composed of crushed tomatoes, and covers it with a blend of cheeses. Of all the pan-fried Sicilian in this area, Pizza L'Oven does it best!"
—James Mirabelli

SABATINI'S PIZZA

1925 Wyoming Avenue
Exeter
Pennsylvania 18643
United States
+1 5706932270
www.sabatinis.com

Opening hours	Open 7 days
Credit cards	Not accepted
Style of pizza	Round
Recommended pizza	Pepperoni, Green Peppers, Mushroom, and Crushed Garlic

GROTTO PIZZA

3445 Lakeside Drive
Harvey's Lake
Pennsylvania 18618
United States
+1 5706393278
www.grottopizzapa.com

Opening hours	Open 7 days
Credit cards	Accepted
Style of pizza	Round
Recommended pizza	Pineapple, Ham, Jalapeños, and Blue Cheese

"Pineapple and blue cheese sounds a little strange but on a Grotto slice makes the perfect combination of flavors. People need to lighten up and step outside of the pizza box a little bit, you know, you only live once. Try some pineapple on your next pie!"
—Matt Rattigan

NORMA'S PIZZA AT ROOT'S COUNTRY MARKET AND AUCTION

705 Graystone Road
Manheim
Pennsylvania 17545
United States
+1 7173418940
www.rootsmarket.com

Opening hours	Open Tuesday
Credit cards	Not accepted
Style of pizza	Kitchen-sink

"Norma is the darling of the pizza world. When I first started my quest for the perfect dough, Norma was a constant resource for me through her blog and forums. She is famous for experimenting in all sort of techniques, ferments, and ingredients. She's a self-taught baker with a passion for what she does. Find her booth in the Root's Country Market and Auction in Lancaster County, Pennsylvania. She is an American treasure!"
—Madeline Peters & Mark Peters

IL PIZZAIOLO

703 Washington Road
Mount Lebanon
Pennsylvania 15228
United States
+1 4123444123
www.ilpizzaiolo.com

Opening hours	Open 7 days
Credit cards	Accepted
Style of pizza	Neapolitan
Recommended pizza	Margherita

"High-quality ingredients, impeccable technique, and a screaming hot oven help make this location the best Neapolitan pizza destination in the region (and the best by a wide margin, too)."—Hal B. Klein

ARCARO & GENELL RESTAURANT

443 South Main Street
Old Forge
Pennsylvania 18518
United States
+1 5704575555
www.arcaroandgenell.com

Opening hours	Closed Sunday
Credit cards	Accepted
Style of pizza	Old Forge
Recommended pizza	Red; Red with Clams and Sausage; Spinach White with Double Crust; White with Double Crust

"Old Forge, Pennsylvania, is the self-proclaimed pizza capital of the world. The tiny town has gained national recognition for its rectangular 'trays' (as the locals call it) of pizza. The crust is thick and doughy, the sauce is hearty, and it's generally covered with a blend of cheeses that includes American. The best Old Forge pizza can be found at Arcaro & Genell's as it uses the freshest ingredients, the secret recipe is superb, and the pizza is consistent."—James Mirabelli

ARMENTI'S PIZZERIA

1454 East Lackawanna Avenue
Olyphant
Pennsylvania 18447
United States
+1 5703832424
www.armentispizzeria.com

Opening hours	Closed Sunday
Credit cards	Accepted but not AMEX
Style of pizza	New York

VECCHIA PIZZERIA

249 Bridge Street
Phoenixville
Pennsylvania 19460
United States
+1 6109331355

Opening hours..................................Open 7 days
Credit cards.....................................Accepted
Style of pizza....................................Neapolitan
Recommended pizza........................Margherita

"This pizza has melt-in-your-mouth mozzarella, bright tomato sauce that pops, and good crust integrity."
—Michael Klein

BREAD AND SALT BAKERY

330 Pearl Street
Pittsburgh
Pennsylvania 15224
United States
www.breadandsaltbakery.com

Opening hours.........................Closed Sunday–Wednesday
Credit cards....................................Not accepted
Style of pizza...........................Roman *pizza al taglio*
Recommended pizza.....................Heirloom Yellow Tomato,
Fresh Anchovies, and Capers; Marinara; Potato, Wild
Horseradish Greens, and Burrata

"This is the first Roman-style pizza served by the cut in Pittsburgh. Rick is an artisan bread maker first and foremost, so he takes extra time and care with his pizza dough. He also uses the best possible local and imported ingredients available for his toppings. Keeping it simple and delicious."
—Domenic Branduzzi

MINEO'S PIZZA HOUSE

2128 Murray Avenue
Pittsburgh
Pennsylvania 15217
United States
+1 4125219864
www.mineospizza.com

Opening hours..................................Open 7 days
Credit cards....................................Not accepted
Style of pizza......................Neapolitan and Sicilian
Recommended pizza........................Pepperoni; White

PICCOLO FORNO

3801 Butler Street
Pittsburgh
Pennsylvania 15201
United States
+1 4126220111
www.piccolo-forno.com

Opening hours.........................Closed Sunday and Monday
Credit cards....................................Accepted
Style of pizza.........................Tuscan wood-fired
Recommended pizza.................Speck and Mascarpone

"My first visit to Piccolo Forno included a long chat with the pizza maker that night. For the entirety of our conversation, it never came up that Dominic Branduzzi (the pizza maker) was also the owner. It's a humble restaurant in only the way a family-run Italian restaurant can be. Dominic's mother still cooks in the kitchen and the menu tastes of love. The pizza and pastas transport diners out of Pittsburgh."
—Justin Steel

PIZZA ITALIA

5412 Liberty Avenue
Pittsburgh
Pennsylvania 15224
United States
+1 4216218960

Opening hours..................................Open 7 days
Credit cards.........................Accepted but not AMEX
Style of pizza....................................Neapolitan

IL PIZZAIOLO

8 Market Square
Pittsburgh
Pennsylvania 15222
United States
+1 4125755858
www.ilpizzaiolo.com

Opening hours..................................Open 7 days
Credit cards....................................Accepted
Style of pizza....................................Neapolitan

"Great Neapolitan pizza in the United-States."
—Salvatore Salvo & Francesco Salvo

BROWNIE'S

401 South 9th Street
Scranton
Pennsylvania 18504
United States
+1 5709618111
www.browniespizzeria.com

Opening hours..Open 7 days
Credit cards...............................Accepted but not AMEX
Style of pizza...Square

MARONI'S PIZZA

1345 St. Ann Street
Scranton
Pennsylvania 18504
United States
+1 5709619531
www.maronispizza.com

Opening hours...Closed Monday
Credit cards..Not accepted
Style of pizza...Square and round

"The pizza has a very fluffy crust with a great cheese blend and a good tomato sauce."
—Christopher Mullarkey

PIZZA BY PAPPAS

303 North Washington Avenue
Scranton
Pennsylvania 18503
United States
+1 5703462290
www.pizzabypappas.com

Opening hours..Open 7 days
Credit cards...Accepted
Style of pizza...Pan
Recommended pizza.............................Plain with Bacon and Mushrooms; Plain with Sausage and Pepperoni; Plain with Black Olive and Salami

"A unique take on pizza in downtown Scranton, Pennsylvania. Pappas makes 10-inch (25-cm) round pies baked in special pans. A fresh fluffy dough has a combination texture: lightly fried at the crust and soft in the middle. The smell of cheese baking on the pizzas perfumes the air around the restaurant."
—Jim Babinski

ROBERTO'S

635 Luzerne Street
Scranton
Pennsylvania 18504
United States
+1 5703481904

Opening hours..Closed Tuesday
Credit cards...............................Accepted but not AMEX
Style of pizza..New York
Recommended pizza...Plain

"I grew up eating this pizza. It is very well balanced with a nice crisp crust, a delicious homemade tomato sauce, and the perfect amount of mozzarella cheese. I think it's the best pizza in the Scranton, Pennsylvania, area, and I've been eating it for more than 25 years."
—Christopher Mullarkey

VINCENZO'S PIZZERIA & CATERING

131 North Main Avenue
Scranton
Pennsylvania 18504
United States
+1 5703471060
www.vincenzosscranton.com

Opening hours..Closed Sunday
Credit cards...............................Accepted but not AMEX
Style of pizza..New York
Recommended pizza......................Eggplant (aubergine) and Sweet Peppers; Hot Wing with Chicken and Buffalo Wing Sauce

"A great New York pizza without the 120-mile (193-km) trip into the city."—Jim Babinski

THE WAVE

400 Metacom Avenue
Bristol
Rhode Island 02809
United States
+1 4012538811
www.pizzawavebristol.com

Opening hours..Open 7 days
Credit cards..Accepted
Style of pizza...Thin-crust
Recommended pizza..................Fig and Prosciutto

K&S PIZZA

469 Carolina Back Road
Charlestown
Rhode Island 02813
United States
+1 4013640040
www.kandspizza.com

Opening hours..Open 7 days
Credit cards..Accepted
Style of pizza...Thick-crust
Recommended pizza..........................Farmers Harvest

CATANZARO'S

1283 Park Avenue
Cranston
Rhode Island 02910
United States
+1 4019468880
www.catanzarospizzeriacranston.com

Opening hours..Closed Monday
Credit cards..Accepted
Style of pizza...Thick-crust
Recommended pizza...Pepperoni

BRAVO WOOD FIRED PIZZA RESTAURANT

6689 Post Road
North Kingstown
Rhode Island 02852
United States
+1 4013982500
www.bravowoodfiredpizza.com

Opening hours..Closed Monday
Credit cards..Accepted
Style of pizza.............................Neapolitan wood-fired
Recommended pizza..Parma

"This unique pizzeria is located in a former donut shop that has been transformed inside to include a warm casual dining room. It even offers a quick service at lunch and easy takeout with a drive-through window. Anyone who appreciates really well-made Neapolitan-style pizza should visit this restaurant and don't let the exterior appearance fool you, this is the real deal."—Gregg O'Neill

FAMOUS PIZZA

92 Hartford Pike
North Scituate
Rhode Island 02857
United States
+1 4019340278

Opening hours..Open 7 days
Credit cards..Accepted
Style of pizza...New York
Recommended pizza...........Mushroom, Onion, and Pepper

"Sometimes you just want a New York-style pizza from your local neighborhood pizza joint. Famous is particularly good. The crust is thicker and it's always perfectly cooked, crunchy but doughy."
—Cindy Salvato

BACARO

262 South Water Street
Providence
Rhode Island 02903
United States
+1 4017513700
www.bacarorestaurant.net

Opening hours.........................Closed Sunday and Monday
Credit cards..Accepted
Style of pizza.............................Italian wood-fired
Recommended pizza..Pumpkin

"I would crawl for the Pumpkin pizza! Bacaro grows a lot of its own vegetables and when the pumpkins are ready, the pizza is on the menu. It's a little spicy and is perfect with the sweet pumpkin."—Cindy Salvato

BOB & TIMMY'S

32 Spruce Street
Providence
Rhode Island 02903
United States
+1 4014532221
www.bobandtimmys.com

Opening hours	Open 7 days
Credit cards	Accepted
Style of pizza	Grilled
Recommended pizza	Margarita; Trio Of Wild Mushroom

CONSTANTINO'S VENDA BAR & RISTORANTE

275 Atwells Avenue
Providence
Rhode Island 02903
United States
+1 4015281100
www.costantinosristorante.com

Opening hours	Open 7 days
Credit cards	Accepted
Style of pizza	Neapolitan
Recommended pizza	Arugula (rocket) and Prosciutto; Margherita

"The pizza is perfectly thin and cooks in 90 seconds in the 800°F (427°C) oven. The toppings are minimal so the crust does not get soggy."—Cindy Salvato

FIGIDINI WOOD FIRE EATERY

67 Washington Street
Providence
Rhode Island 02903
United States
+1 4018086886
www.figidini.com

Opening hours	Closed Monday
Credit cards	Accepted
Style of pizza	Neapolitan
Recommended pizza	Arugula (rocket); Cremini; Fresh Ricotta

"This is by far the best traditional Neapolitan pizza in the area. The dough is chewy and delicious, everything that's put on the pizza, from local to imported cheese and meats and the outstanding olive oil, is top quality, and then it's expertly cooked in a beautiful wood-fired oven with perfect attention to rapid doneness."
—David Dadekian

The charred *cornicione* embracing Frankie Ceccinelli's Neapolitan pizza is a beautifully thing. It balloons in the wood-fired oven to a size so large you almost think the dough's been leavened with steroids, not starter yeast. But the interior is filled with hot air, not brawn, compressing effortlessly to the chew. Perhaps to remind diners they're in downtown Providence, Rhode Island, not Naples, Italy, most pizzas carry the scent of something grown locally—oregano on the Marinara or chives on the popular Cremini, with mushrooms, truffle oil, black olives, and smoked mozzarella. All pizzas are served uncut. The floppy softness of the classic Margherita is meant to be managed with knife and fork, or finger-folded into pouches of goodness.

AL FORNO

577 South Water Street
Providence
Rhode Island 02903
United States
+1 4012739760
www.alforno.com

Opening hours	Closed Sunday and Monday
Credit cards	Accepted
Style of pizza	Grilled
Recommended pizza	Margarita; Spicy Oil

"The chefs at Al Forno pretty much invented grilled pizza. A good part of the menu is cooked over a wood grill and they discovered that grilling pizza dough with fresh ingredients was unique and delicious. The toppings are not overloaded and kept simple and harmonious."—Gregg O'Neill

"Al Forno found the right formula to make an excellent crisp, thin pizza and has stuck to it. The key to the fantastic flavor is great ingredients, but also cooking it on a custom-made, high-heat grill."
—David Dadekian

"This pizza haunts my dreams."—Joseph Hafner

Al Forno is not a pizzeria. The pizzas are grilled over hardwood charcoal in a flash and sent out as light entertainment before the table is turned over to baked pastas and wood-grilled chops. But if chef-owners Johanne Killeen and George Germon can't prevent people from ordering pizza as a main course, they have only themselves to blame: they accepted credit some 30 years ago for inventing grilled pizza and no one has seriously challenged their claim—or supremacy—since. They color a rectangle of oiled dough on the grill, flip it, top it, and let it smoke. The grill-marked Margarita (sic), with San Marzano tomatoes, two grated cheeses, fresh herbs, and olive oil, has the sure crunch of flatbread and the rustic character of wood-fired pizza.

NAPOLITANO'S BROOKLYN PIZZA

380 Atwells Avenue
Providence
Rhode Island 02909
United States
+1 4012732400
www.napolitanosbrooklynpizza.com

Opening hours	Open 7 days
Credit cards	Accepted
Style of pizza	New York
Recommended pizza	Margherita

"The big slices have a crispy crust that maintains its chewiness, fresh mozzarella, and plenty of prosciutto and fresh basil."—Grace Lentini

NICE SLICE

267 Thayer Street
Providence
Rhode Island 02906
United States
+1 4014536423
www.niceslice.cloudaccess.net

Opening hours	Open 7 days
Credit cards	Accepted but not AMEX
Style of pizza	Thin-crust
Recommended pizza	Margherita

"The mozzarella is fresh, the basil fragrant, and the crust thin and crispy. Every time I walk, in there are different options and I like how creative this pizza joint is."—Grace Lentini

FEDERAL HILL PIZZA

495 Main Street
Warren
Rhode Island 02885
United States
+1 4012450045
www.federalhillpizza.com

Opening hours	Open 7 days
Credit cards	Accepted
Style of pizza	Neapolitan
Recommended pizza	BBQ Chicken; Margherita

"This pizza is more about the dough than anything else in Rhode Island. Good toppings, yes. Nicely cooked in a brick oven, yes. But the dough really shines through here. They've even perfected a good gluten-free dough if that's your thing."
—David Dadekian

SIMONE'S

275 Child Street
Warren
Rhode Island 02885
United States
+1 4012471200
www.simonesri.com

Opening hours	Closed Monday
Credit cards	Accepted
Style of pizza	Thin-crust
Recommended pizza	Margherita; Mushroom with Crème Fraîche and Leeks

"The toppings marry with the crust to make a delicious crunchy and tender experience. Delicious."
—Joe Simone

AMERICAN FLATBREAD

115 Saint Paul Street
Burlington
Vermont 05401
United States
+1 8028612999
www.americanflatbread.com

Opening hours	Open 7 days
Credit cards	Accepted
Style of pizza	Flatbread
Recommended pizza	New Vermont Sausage; Punctuated Equilibrium

"American Flatbread has a great mix of go-to pies worth ordering ever time, plus different specials every night that are worth taking a chance on. Excellent beer is brewed on site."—Zach Minot

PIZZERIA VERITA

156 Saint Paul Street
Burlington
Vermont 05401
United States
+1 8024895644
www.pizzeriaverita.com

Opening hours	Open 7 days
Credit cards	Accepted
Style of pizza	Neapolitan
Recommended pizza	Cherry Amore; Mais; Margherita

"This is the home of beautifully prepared Neapolitan pies made using primarily local ingredients, including homemade mozzarella. The owners studied in New York and Italy, perfecting classic Neapolitan techniques, unavailable anywhere else in Vermont."
—Alice Levitt

WOODBELLY PIZZA

Food truck—check website, Facebook, and Instagram for upcoming locations
Cabot
Vermont
United States
+1 8025523476
www.woodbellypizza.com

Opening hours	Variable
Credit cards	Accepted
Style of pizza	Wood-fired

"The pizzas are unique with delicious cheese toppings— especially the Parmigiano-Reggiano. They are all delicious!"—Nancy Gilman

PIZZA ON EARTH

1510 Hinesburg Road
Charlotte
Vermont 05445
United States
+1 8024252152
www.pizzaonearth.com

Opening hours	Open Thursday and Friday
Credit cards	Not accepted
Style of pizza	Rustic wood-fired

"The pizzas are perfect. The setting is perfect. Everything else to eat there is also perfect."
—Zach Minot

"Pizza on Earth is a tiny little place. The man who farms the fields makes the dough and very rustic, wood-fired pies in the evenings."
—Andrew Volk

PIZZA PAPILLO

Mobile pizzeria—check website, Facebook, Instagram, and Twitter for upcoming locations
Colchester
Vermont
United States
+1 8025982744
www.pizzapapillo.com

Opening hours	Variable
Credit cards	Not accepted
Style of pizza	Italian-Vermont
Recommended pizza	Mac and Sausage

"Local radio host Charlie Papillo uses a mobile oven, custom-made in Italy, to turn out personal-sized pies. Usually, the oven parks at farms, where the pizzas are topped with ingredients grown on-site."
—Alice Levitt

AMERICAN FLATBREAD

137 Maple Street, Suite 29 F
Middlebury
Vermont 05753
United States
+1 8023883300
www.americanflatbread.com

Opening hours	Closed Monday
Credit cards	Accepted
Style of pizza	Flatbread
Recommended pizza	Pepperoni

"Delicious hot flatbreads made with locally sourced ingredients."—Nancy Gilman

OSTERIA CHIARA AL FORNO

1011 Route 5 North
Norwich
Vermont 05055
United States
+1 8026495136
www.osteriachiaraalforno.blogspot.com

Opening hours...Variable
Credit cards..Not accepted
Style of pizza...Wood-fired
Recommended pizza..Margherita

"Steve Ferraris fires up his home-built clay oven at his
monthly underground restaurant. Pizza is served outside,
around a bonfire before guests move inside for a
multi-course Italian dinner served on plates made
at the in-house pottery studio."—Alice Levitt

AMERICAN FLATBREAD

46 Lareau Road
Waitsfield
Vermont 05673
United States
+1 8024968856
www.americanflatbread.com

Opening hours.........................Closed Monday–Wednesday
Credit cards...Accepted
Style of pizza...Flatbread
Recommended pizza................Medicine Wheel; Pepperoni

"The location of this place is spectacular. It's worth
the trip to rural Vermont."—Andrew Volk

THE PARKER PIE CO.

161 County Road
West Glover
Vermont 05875
United States
+1 8025253366
www.parkerpie.com

Opening hours...Open 7 days
Credit cards...Accepted
Style of pizza...American
Recommended pizza...Scott's Revenge

"At the back of a country store, it is a classic pub with
an incredible atmosphere of conviviality, an amazing
beer offering on tap, and some of the most delicious
red sauce on a pie you have ever had."—Mara Welton

"THE TAKEOUT WINDOW IS MY FAVORITE STOP AFTER A YANKEE GAME IN THE BRONX."

RICHARD FRAZER P.487

"IT'S EVERYTHING YOU THINK ABOUT WHEN YOU THINK OF NEW YORK PIZZA."

ANNA BELKINA P.488

NEW YORK CITY

"PRINCE STREET PIZZA MAY BE MAKING THE BEST NEW YORK SQUARE PIZZA IN THE CITY RIGHT NOW."

ADAM KUBAN P.491

"ONE OF THE BEST-KEPT SECRETS IN BROOKLYN."

DOLORES TAY P.493

"THE CRUST IS THIN AND CRACKERY WITH A SLIGHTLY SWEET SAUCE AND JUST ENOUGH TANGY AGED MOZZARELLA CHEESE NOT TO OVERWHELM THE SAUCE."

PAULIE GEE P.498

NEW YORK CITY

MANHATTAN UPTOWN AND CHELSEA

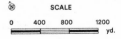

SCALE

0   400   800   1200
yd.

1. SAL AND CARMINE PIZZA, UPPER WEST SIDE (P.488)
2. PATSY'S PIZZERIA, EAST HARLEM (P.487)
3. DELIZIA 73, UPPER EAST SIDE (P.488)
4. PATSY'S PIZZERIA, UPPER WEST SIDE (P.488)
5. DON ANTONIO, HELL'S KITCHEN (P.487)
6. NY PIZZA SUPREMA, CHELSEA (P.486)

7. MARTA, NOMAD (P.487)
8. CO., CHELSEA (P.486)
9. TAPPO THIN CRUST PIZZA, CHELSEA (P.487)
10. ARTICHOKE BASILLE'S PIZZA, CHELSEA (P.486)
11. PROVA, CHELSEA (P.486)

ARTICHOKE BASILLE'S PIZZA

114 Tenth Avenue
Chelsea
Manhattan
New York 10011
United States
+1 2127929200
www.artichokepizza.com

Opening hours	Open 7 days
Credit cards	Accepted
Style of pizza	Unique
Recommended pizza	Artichoke

"It's unlike any other pizza you'll have in NYC. It's a monstrous slice smothered in mozzarella cheese and a spinach and artichoke dip-like sauce. It's super filling, and a good bang for your buck."—Marta

CO.

230 Ninth Avenue
Chelsea
Manhattan
New York 10001
United States
+1 2122431105
www.co-pane.com

Opening hours	Open 7 days
Credit cards	Accepted
Style of pizza	Eclectic Neapolitan
Recommended pizza	Boscaiola; Popeye

"Jim Lahey is one of the premier bread bakers in the country and when he turned to pizza, he created some knockout pies. His crust is superb, the toppings inventive."—S. Irene Virbila

NY PIZZA SUPREMA

413 Eighth Avenue
Chelsea
Manhattan
New York 10001
United States
+1 2125948939
www.nypizzasuprema.com

Opening hours	Open 7 days
Credit cards	Not accepted
Style of pizza	New York
Recommended pizza	Cheese; Regular

"Suprema is special because it looks and feels like any other typical New York pizzeria, but there's way more going on behind the scenes. These guys make four different sauces, one for each pie. It's hidden in plain sight, right next to Madison Square Garden. It's like an oasis in a food desert."—Scott Wiener

"It's the best slice in the city. During lunch, the line of folks trying to get a slice of Suprema stretches almost across the street into Penn Station. It moves quickly thanks to the fast-handed *pizzaioli* behind the counter."—Sean Taylor

PROVA

184 Eighth Avenue
Chelsea
Manhattan
New York 10011
United States
+1 2126410977
www.provanyc.com

Opening hours	Open 7 days
Credit cards	Accepted
Style of pizza	Neapolitan
Recommended pizza	Margherita; Marinara; Truffle; Uni-ca

"Everything is excellent, from the setting, to the master pizza chef Pascuale, to the different types of pizza and the ingredients they use to make them."—Leandro Caffarena

"The *pizzaiolo* is not afraid to experiment and fuse cuisines together in a way I've never seen done before—hence the popular uni-topped pie. Prova serves up both classic and new pies."—Emily Giove

TAPPO THIN CRUST PIZZA

49 West 24th Street
Chelsea
Manhattan
New York 10010
United States
+1 2128079200
www.tappothincrust.com

Opening hours...Open 7 days
Credit cards...Accepted
Style of pizza...Thin-crust
Recommended pizza..Classica

PATSY'S PIZZERIA

2287 First Avenue
East Harlem
Manhattan
New York 10035
United States
+1 2125349783
www.thepatsyspizza.com

Opening hours.........................Closed Monday and Tuesday
Credit cards...Not accepted
Style of pizza..New York coal-fired
Recommended pizza.......................Garlic and Cheese; Plain

"This is the cheapest and only coal-oven slice to be found in NYC. The takeout window is my favorite stop after a Yankee game in the Bronx. The restaurant itself was a favorite of Frank Sinatra's and you can soak in the history of Harlem with a glass of red wine and an entire cheese pizza pie with enough fresh garlic to keep away the vampires."—Richard Frazer

DON ANTONIO

309 West 50th Street
Hell's Kitchen
Manhattan
New York 10019
United States
+1 6467191043
www.donantoniopizza.com

Opening hours...Open 7 days
Credit cards...Accepted
Style of pizza..Neapolitan
Recommended pizza...Montanara

"Don Antonio is one of the best pizza makers in the world. Amazing pizza."—Tony Gemignani

"Absolutely one of the best pizza tastes that I have had, especially the Montanara. Unique and tasty in every aspect."—Rocco Agostino

MARTA

29 East 29th Street
NoMad
Manhattan
New York 10016
United States
+1 2126513800
www.martamanhattan.com

Opening hours...Open 7 days
Credit cards...Accepted
Style of pizza...Roman
Recommended pizza.....................Amatriciana; Margherita;
Mushroom; Patate alla Carbonara; Puttanesca;
Sausage; Seasonal specials

"I never thought I would love a crust thinner than Neapolitan style, but Marta's super-thin, wood-fired Roman-style pizzas have won me over. There's just enough chewy dough to support the toppings and really let them shine."—Danielle Centoni

"Marta's offerings, and surroundings, are richer and more sophisticated than its spiritual counterparts in Rome. The pizzas are restrainedly New Yorkified on top, and pretty faithfully Roman in the crust. The fritti and other antipasti are terrific, and there's a very un-pizzeria-like menu of grilled meat and fish."
—Maureen B. Fant

The pizza at Marta is making noise in New York by virtue of what it is and isn't: the crust is ultra-thin and crunchy, in the Roman style known as *scrocchiarella*, rather than pillowy, in the manner of true and trendy Neapolitan pizza. If restaurateur Danny Meyer of the Union Square Hospitality Group took a creative risk when he installed twin black-brick, wood-fired ovens in the Martha Washington Hotel's made-over lobby it proved to be a measured one. First, New Yorkers have a long history with crispy pizza. Second, if they liked chef Nick Anderer's Bucatini all'Amatriciana at Maialino, the group's Roman trattoria, the chances were good they'd take to his Amatriciana pizza, with Pecorino, onion, and chile, too.

DELIZIA 73

1374 First Avenue
Upper East Side
Manhattan
New York 10021
United States
+1 2125178888
www.delizia73.com

Opening hours	Open 7 days
Credit cards	Accepted
Style of pizza	New York
Recommended pizza	Cheese; Margherita

"The best classic New York-style pizza (which, as everyone knows, is the best pizza in the world) I had in my seven years in NYC. It's everything you think about when you think of New York pizza. Fresh, hot, hearty."—Anna Belkina

PATSY'S PIZZERIA

61 West 74th Street
Upper West Side
Manhattan
New York 10023
United States
+1 2125793000
www.patsyspizzeria.us

Opening hours	Open 7 days
Credit cards	Accepted
Style of pizza	New York
Recommended pizza	Margherita

"Patsy's is the essence of New York pizza with Italian flair. It was definitely my go-to when I lived in the city, and it's one of the best pizzas I have ever tasted."
—Sarah Wali

SAL AND CARMINE PIZZA

2671 Broadway
Upper West Side
Manhattan
New York 10025
United States
+1 2126637651
www.salandcarminepizzanyc.com

Opening hours	Open 7 days
Credit cards	Not accepted
Style of pizza	New York
Recommended pizza	Plain; Sausage

"Sal and Carmine's was about 20 blocks from the apartment I grew up in. I knew, even at a young age, that this place was the real deal. The quality of its pizza, and its adventure-length distance from home, gave Sal and Carmine's an almost mythical aura. As an adult, I love that I can go back and nothing has changed: the pizza is still great, the place looks exactly the same, and there are still kids sitting in the back happily eating their allowance in pizza."
—Tim Reitzes

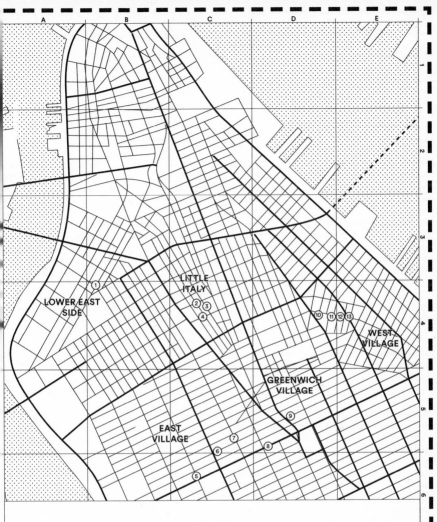

NEW YORK CITY

MANHATTAN DOWNTOWN

SCALE

0   400   800   1200
yd.

1. MISSION CHINESE FOOD, LOWER EAST SIDE (P.491)
2. LOMBARDI'S PIZZA, LITTLE ITALY (P.490)
3. RUBIROSA RISTORANTE, LITTLE ITALY (P.491)
4. PRINCE STREET PIZZA, LITTLE ITALY (P.491)
5. MUZZARELLA PIZZA, EAST VILLAGE (P.490)
6. MOTORINO, EAST VILLAGE (P.490)
7. NUMERO 28, EAST VILLAGE (P.490)

8. JOE'S PIZZA, GREENWICH VILLAGE (P.490)
9. RIBALTA, GREENWICH VILLAGE (P.490)
10. JOE'S PIZZA, WEST VILLAGE (P.492)
11. KESTÉ PIZZA & VINO, WEST VILLAGE (P.492)
12. JOHN'S OF BLEECKER STREET, WEST VILLAGE (P.492)
13. BLEECKER STREET PIZZA, WEST VILLAGE (P.491)

MOTORINO
349 East 12th Street
East Village
Manhattan
New York 10003
United States
+1 2127772644
www.motorinopizza.com

Opening hours..Open 7 days
Credit cards..Accepted
Style of pizza..Neo-Neapolitan
Recommended pizza..Brussels Sprout

"Simple food, executed perfectly."—Don Dickman

MUZZARELLA PIZZA
221 Avenue A
East Village
Manhattan
New York 10009
United States
+1 2126140905

Opening hours..Open 7 days
Credit cards..Not accepted
Style of pizza..New York
Recommended pizza..Lasagna

"Whether it's late at night or the middle of the day,
this slice spot always satisfies. The foldable triangles
are heartily sized and hefty—no skimping here. Get
the lasagna-style pizza, which is almost as filling as
its namesake."—Nevin Martell

NUMERO 28
176 Second Avenue
East Village
Manhattan
New York 10003
United States
+1 2127771555
www.numero28.com

Opening hours..Open 7 days
Credit cards..Not accepted
Style of pizza..*Pizza al metro*
Recommended pizza..Numero 28

"Delicious pizza by the meter. You can choose
2–3 different toppings on the same cut."
—Riccardo Michele Bertolino

JOE'S PIZZA
150 East 14th Street
Greenwich Village
Manhattan
New York 10003
United States
+1 2123889474
www.joespizzanyc.com

Opening hours..Open 7 days
Credit cards..Accepted
Style of pizza..New York
Recommended pizza..Cheese

"Simple street food that's easy to eat."
—Paola Miglio Rossi

RIBALTA
48 East 12th Street
Greenwich Village
Manhattan
New York 10003
United States
+1 2127777781
www.ribaltapizzarestaurant.com

Opening hours..Open 7 days
Credit cards..Accepted
Style of pizza..Neapolitan
Recommended pizza................................Margherita; Porcini
Mushrooms and Pancetta

LOMBARDI'S PIZZA
32 Spring Street
Little Italy
Manhattan
New York 10012
United States
+1 2129417994
www.firstpizza.com

Opening hours..Open 7 days
Credit cards..Not accepted
Style of pizza..Neapolitan
Recommended pizza..Pepperoni

"Big, crispy pizzas in a simple but lively restaurant."
—David Schnapp

PRINCE STREET PIZZA

27 Prince Street
Little Italy
Manhattan
New York 10012
United States
+1 2129664100

Opening hours	Open 7 days
Credit cards	Accepted
Style of pizza	New York-Sicilian
Recommended pizza	Pepperoni: Spicy Spring

"If you're lucky, you can snag a stool and smother your slice in red pepper flakes while people-watching on Prince Street."—Jamie Miles

"Prince Street Pizza may be making the best New York square pizza in the city right now. It's crisp with an airy crumb and just the right amount of melty, gooey cheese and sauce. The round pies there are good, too, but you're doing it wrong if you don't get a square."—Adam Kuban

"The best Sicilian slice in the entire United States."
—Jay Jerrier

Prince Street's charismatic owner Frank Morano hates it when a customer blots a slice of his pizza with a napkin. That's not grease, he protests, it's olive oil. This is only partly true. The crime, if there's one, is in wanting to remove the good grease filling up the curled cups of pepperoni atop the Spicy Spring pizza. With superior sauces and cheeses Prince Street excels at both types of pizza traditionally found at New York slice shops: classic round (thin) and square "Sicilian" (thick). The latter is typically stodgy. Not so Prince Street's superbly light version. The bottom and edges of the so-called Soho Squares, including the Spicy Spring, are beautifully crisped in a well-greased— sorry, Frank—well-oiled pan.

RUBIROSA RISTORANTE

235 Mulberry Street
Little Italy
Manhattan
New York 10012
United States
+1 2129650500
www.rubirosanyc.com

Opening hours	Open 7 days
Credit cards	Accepted
Style of pizza	New York thin-crust
Recommended pizza	Cheese

"The slice at Rubirosa is the kind that inspires cross-section marveling and sets the stage for game-changing pizza paradigm shifts."
—Arthur Bovino

MISSION CHINESE FOOD

171 East Broadway
Lower East Side
Manhattan
New York 10002
United States
+1 2124320300
www.mcfny.com

Opening hours	Closed Monday
Credit cards	Accepted
Style of pizza	San Francisco-Neapolitan
Recommended pizza	Hot Cheese

"The pizza's made with a San Francisco sourdough starter and Italian DOP tomatoes and it's served in a Chinese restaurant with a Filipina chef and a chef-owner who is a Korean-born orphan raised in Oklahoma. Only in America!"—Francis Lam

BLEECKER STREET PIZZA

69 Seventh Avenue South
West Village
Manhattan
New York 10014
United States
+1 2129244466
www.bleeckerstreetpizza.com

Opening hours	Open 7 days
Credit cards	Accepted
Style of pizza	American
Recommended pizza	Margherita; Pepperoni

"This is just good old-fashioned American pizza: large greasy slices, lots of cheese, and a crunchy crust. It may not be gourmet, but I love it and I wouldn't trade a bubbling slice of Margherita at 2 a.m. for (almost) anything in the world."—Rebecca Thandi Norman

JOE'S PIZZA

7 Carmine Street
West Village
Manhattan
New York 10014
United States
+1 2123661182
www.joespizzanyc.com

Opening hours	Open 7 days
Credit cards	Accepted
Style of pizza	New York
Recommended pizza	Plain Cheese; Sicilian Square

"The key to Joe's success is its traditional New York City-style pizza with thin crust, great sauce, and just the right ratio of cheese, sauce, and crust (just a bit less of the first two). Since 1975, Joe's has served tourists and residents alike, making it a truly iconic New York landmark."—Arthur Bovino

JOHN'S OF BLEECKER STREET

278 Bleecker Street
West Village
Manhattan
New York 10014
United States
+1 2122431680
www.johnsbrickovenpizza.com

Opening hours	Open 7 days
Credit cards	Not accepted
Style of pizza	New York coal-fired
Recommended pizza	Cheese; Cheese, Sausage, and Garlic; Sausage; Sausage and Mushroom

"Absolutely classic New York brick-oven pizza, with a thin, crisp crust that's sooty from the coal fire."
—Alison Cook

As pizza lovers scratch their initials into one of John's old booths, the hardwood shreds like cheese, so weakened is it by decades of amorous carvings. The pizza, however, maintains its crisp, charred barrier to entry. The corny Bay of Naples wall murals were painted in homesick blues but the thin, stiff pizza crust embodies a magnificent gulf between the ways of old country and new. Italian immigrant John Sasso put his name over a door on Sullivan Street in 1929 and then moved his coal-fired oven to Bleecker Street in 1934. The mozzarella and tomato pizza is classic New York pizza at its most basic. Adding a potent topping, like crumbled fennel sausage from Faicco's Pork Store, is more rule of thumb than law of the house. At John's the one unbreakable tenet is "no slices."

KESTÉ PIZZA & VINO

271 Bleecker Street
West Village
Manhattan
New York 10014
United States
+1 2122431500
www.kestepizzeria.com

Opening hours	Open 7 days
Credit cards	Accepted
Style of pizza	Neapolitan wood-fired
Recommended pizza	Burrata Roberto; Margherita; Pistachio and Sausage; Regina Margherita

"Rustic and simple, pizzas here are cooked in a wood-fired oven and stand out for their raw ingredients, depth and intensity of flavor, quantity of toppings, and an obsession with cheese—the chef worked for many years as a cheesemaker in Italy."—Daniel Greve

"The pizza is incredibly fresh, savory, and makes my heart flutter with every bite."—Miriam Weiskind

"You can't get much more true to Italy than an Italian family making Neapolitan pizza. I first met the owner during a pizza competition (which he won), and I've been returning for award-winning pizza ever since."—Liz Barrett

As president of the American chapter of the Associazione Pizzaiuoli Napoletani, Roberto Caporuscio leads 10-day courses in Neapolitan pizza making. But since opening Kesté, as in *questo e* (this is it), in 2009 he is perhaps best known for his impromptu, 10-minute classes in Neapolitan pizza eating. With patience and passion he's converted New Yorkers to a softer, soggier crust than the one they were accustomed to. He melted all residual resistance by arranging homemade mozzarella on his definitive Margherita and signature Pizza del Re, with mushroom, Prosciutto di Parma, truffle spread, and olive oil. His second Manhattan pizzeria bears the name of Don Antonio Starita, his mentor and now partner.

LOUIE & ERNIE'S
1300 Crosby Avenue
Bronx
New York 10461
United States
+1 7188296230

Opening hours	Open 7 days
Credit cards	Not accepted
Style of pizza	New York
Recommended pizza	Plain Cheese; Plain Cheese with Sausage; Sausage

"Louie & Ernie's is a little pizza shop almost hidden in the bottom floor of a row house on the corner. It's no frills—serving just pizza and calzones—no pretense, and always filled with locals. If you're looking for the slice that all other slices should emulate, this is it."—Tim Reitzes

"An absolutely classic neighborhood slice shop. The sauce gets seasoned on the spot when each pie is made."—Scott Wiener

BEST PIZZA
33 Havemeyer Street
Brooklyn
New York 11211
United States
+1 7185992210
www.best.piz.za.com

Opening hours	Open 7 days
Credit cards	Accepted
Style of pizza	Neapolitan-American
Recommended pizza	White

"I love the old-school feel of this place. There are paper plates all around the restaurant listing both the menu and showcasing customers' drawings. The beverages are self-serve in a fridge next to the counter and the slices are so good."—Marta

DELMAR PIZZERIA
1668 Sheepshead Bay Road
Brooklyn
New York 11235
United States
+1 7187697766
www.delmarpizzabk.com

Opening hours	Open 7 days
Credit cards	Accepted
Style of pizza	New York
Recommended pizza	Regular

"With a crisp, salty crust, powerful cheese, and integrated sauce, this pizza is six levels better than a standard slice. It goes beyond what a pizza should be. I just can't help but smile while sitting in the orange booths eating a slice. Love is out there."—Jeff Orlick

ELEGANTE PIZZERIA
6922 Fifth Avenue
Brooklyn
New York 11209
United States
+1 7187459715
www.elegantepizzany.com

Opening hours	Open 7 days
Credit cards	Accepted
Style of pizza	New York
Recommended pizza	Margherita

"One of the best-kept secrets in Brooklyn."
—Dolores Tay

EMILY VS. PIZZA LOVES EMILY
919 Fulton Street
Brooklyn
New York 11238
United States
+1 3478449588
www.pizzalovesemily.com

Opening hours	Open 7 days
Credit cards	Accepted
Style of pizza	New York thin-crust
Recommended pizza	Baby D; Colony; Emily

"Each pie has a highly eclectic pairing that leaves you in a pizza universe like none other. With a more well-done wood-fired bake, the crusts still punch an incredible, pillowy bite. This is a pizzeria I keep on reserve for only lovers and friends."
—Miriam Weiskind

DI FARA PIZZA

1424 Avenue J
Brooklyn
New York 11230
United States
+1 7182581367
www.difara.com

Opening hours	Closed Monday and Tuesday
Credit cards	Not accepted
Style of pizza	New York and Sicilian
Recommended pizza	Cheese with Artichoke; Classic Round; Plain; Square Pie with Pepperoni; Tomato and Basil Sicilian Slice

"Di Fara makes a classic Sicilian-style, square slice of pizza with a beautifully crunchy and caramelized crust. The ingredients are top notch and the owner lovingly tops each slice with leafy cut basil and olive oil drizzle."—Adam Baru

"Dom DeMarco has made every pizza at this iconic shop since 1959. The crust is full-bodied with a crispy lightly blistered bottom and amply chewy texture. The dough is complex, the tomato sauce is bright and fresh, and the cheese is creamy with perfect elasticity. It's well worth any wait. The overall experience is ethereal."—Thomas Siegel

The first of many to underestimate Domenico DeMarco may have been the farmer-turned-*pizzaiolo* himself. Instead of lending his name to the Brooklyn pizzeria he opened in 1964, as proud Neapolitan immigrants did before him, he shared billing by settling for "Di Fara," a vague hybrid of DeMarco and Farina, a long forgotten partner. Working solo he crafted his pizza in this corner slice-shop for 35 years before becoming an overnight legend. Now the world waits for him, up to two hours, enduring a line that meanders into a free-for-all as it approaches the counter. The DeMarco pizza, either round or equally prized Sicilian square, is a flowing portmanteau of homemade tomato sauce and up to four cheeses (three mozzarellas and grated Parmigiano or Grana Padano). The crust is browned to a solid crisp and forgiving chew.

FRANNY'S

348 Flatbush Avenue
Brooklyn
New York 11238
United States
+1 7182300221
www.frannysbrooklyn.com

Opening hours	Open 7 days
Credit cards	Accepted
Style of pizza	Italian-American
Recommended pizza	Clams, Chiles, and Parsley; Ramps, 'Nduja, Capers, and Pecorino

"Creative topping combinations raise this pizzeria above the rest of the excellent options in Brooklyn."
—Chris Chamberlain

"The pizzas are divine."—Elizabeth Falkner

L&B SPUMONI GARDENS

2725 86th Street
Brooklyn
New York 11223
United States
+1 7184491230
www.spumonigardens.com

Opening hours	Open 7 days
Credit cards	Accepted
Style of pizza	Sicilian
Recommended pizza	Sicilian (Square) Pie

"The Sicilian slice, or square, at L&B is unrivaled. The rectangular pizza is baked in a pan in one of the 15 gas deck ovens, which allows them to constantly crank out pies to meet the seemingly never-ending demand. The olive oil in the pan creates a crispy, fried undercrust layer before giving way to an airy, sponge-like bread that feels as light as a cloud. A layer of low-moisture mozzarella is added, followed by a heavy dose of bright, sweet crushed tomatoes. Ultimately, it's finished with a heavy coating of Parmesan cheese. The resulting product is a pizza that hits all the right notes in both texture and flavor."—Brooks Jones

LUCALI

575 Henry Street
Brooklyn
New York 11231
United States
+1 7188584086
www.lucali.com

Opening hours	Closed Tuesday
Credit cards	Not accepted
Style of pizza	Brooklyn brick-oven
Recommended pizza	Cheese and Basil; Pepperoni and Garlic; Plain Cheese

"Lucali chef-owner Mark Iacono has cracked the code on the perfect pizza and, fortunately, shares it with others on every single pie that exits his wood-fired brick oven."—Sean Taylor

LUIGI'S PIZZA

686 Fifth Avenue
Brooklyn
New York 11215
United States
+1 7184993857
www.luigispizzabrooklyn.com

Opening hours	Closed Sunday
Credit cards	Not accepted
Style of pizza	New York
Recommended pizza	Fresh Mozzarella; Luigi's Pizza Supreme; Regular

"The regular slice at Luigi's exemplifies what a New York slice should be: it's got crunch, it's got chew, when you fold it the dough within the crack stretches and shows heart, and the sauce and the cheese used are very good quality and not over- or under-employed."—Michael Berman

PAULIE GEE'S

60 Greenpoint Avenue
Brooklyn
New York 11222
United States
+1 3479873747
www.pauliegee.com

Opening hours	Open 7 days
Credit cards	Accepted
Style of pizza	Neapolitan-inspired
Recommended pizza	Anise and Anephew; Cherry Jones; Daniela Spinaci; Delboy; Grapeful Dead; Greenpointer; Hellboy; Monte Cristo; Regina

"Great dough and eccentric toppings, including some pies drizzled with a chili-laced honey. Paulie Gee's makes oddball combinations like prosciutto with Gorgonzola and dried bing cherries work. The place also has a half dozen vegan pizzas on the menu. In summer you can take out a pizza and have it at the pocket park at the end of the street with a view of Manhattan across the water."—S. Irene Virbila

"Paulie's dizzying menu of pizza fare may seem daunting at first glance (and that doesn't even include the secret menu), but every pizza listed has earned its right to be there. What Paulie does best is balance—sure his crust and his secretly sourced tomatoes are divine, but Mr Gee's application of non-traditional toppings (anisette cream, dried cherries, and bacon marmalade to name a few) is expertly augmented by supporting flavors that bring everything into something beyond pizza: it's an experience." —Brooks Jones

Who honors Neapolitan pizza tradition by engraving "NAPOLI" on the face of his wood-burning brick oven, only to garnish the pizzas baked and charred in it with such un-Italian ingredients as pure maple syrup, barbecued beef brisket, and house-pickled pineapple? Paul Giannone—the friendliest frontman in Brooklyn pizza history—is who. A stickler for quality, but not always authenticity, Paulie Gee frees his pizza chefs to take creative leaps, with the understanding that the crust is sacrosanct. The Brian Di Palma pizza, a minimalist classic with only tomatoes and Parmigiano-Reggiano, proves they can do old school with the best. But it's well-balanced pizza originals such as the Hellboy, with fresh mozzarella, Italian tomatoes, Berkshire Sopressata Piccante, Parmigiano-Reggiano, and Mike's hot honey, that bring people from all over to Greenpoint.

ROBERTA'S

261 Moore Street
Brooklyn
New York 11206
United States
+1 7184171118
www.robertaspizza.com

Opening hours..Open 7 days
Credit cards...Accepted
Style of pizza...Brooklyn-Neapolitan
Recommended pizza.........................Beastmaster; Bee Sting;
Famous Original; Margherita; Millennium Falco; RPS;
Tanya Charding

"In a very Bushwick-style atmosphere, behind the
spray-painted door of a street lined with charmless
warehouses is hidden Roberta's, one of the most
sought after addresses in Brooklyn. People come
from Manhattan to mix with the riffraff in this
fantastic restaurant with an industrial decor. Long
tables and picnic benches, rock'n'roll music, and
a young and trendy clientele, the atmosphere at
Roberta's is irresistible!"—Laura Centrella

"I love the aggressively seasoned sauce, the equally
bold char on the puffy crust, and the gorgeous
toppings. The sauce is slightly sweet with a bit of
oregano and a hit of spicy red chili."
—Victoria Pesce Elliot

The utter excitement of finding something new, edgy, and
special in the grimmest outreaches of the city is a part of every
Bohemian counterculture. What's unique about Roberta's rise
from the cinderblocks of Bushwick, Brooklyn, as compared to
other hipster breakthroughs, is that its fame came not from
painting, poetry, or punk rock but from pizza. The singed
markings of Neapolitan inspiration show on the bubbly,
leopard-spotted *cornicione* of every pizza emerging from the
wood-fired oven. The house bias is toward sharp, spicy flavors
applied to traditional tomato and cheese foundations. The
Famous Original consists of tomato, mozzarella, oregano,
Caciocavallo cheese for bite, and chili for heat. The
Beastmaster, with tomato, mozzarella, Gorgonzola, pork
sausage, onion, capers, and jalapeños, is a pizza that stays with
you long after the delicious shock of discovery has worn off.

SAM'S RESTAURANT

238 Court Street
Brooklyn
New York 11201
United States
+1 7185963458

Opening hours...Closed Tuesday
Credit cards..Not accepted
Style of pizza...Brooklyn
Recommended pizza...Regular

"Sam's looks like a diner from the outside and a set
from *The Sopranos* on the inside. The pizza is as
simple as it gets, but it's perfect just the way it is.
A sauce with a raw blend of five different tomatoes
and a simple low-moisture mozzarella cheese blend
perfectly with no unnecessary seasoning."
—Scott Wiener

SPEEDY ROMEO

376 Classon Avenue
Brooklyn
New York 11238
United States
+1 7812300061
www.speedyromeo.com

Opening hours..Open 7 days
Credit cards...Accepted
Style of pizza...Wood-fired
Recommended pizza..Marinara

"A black-painted brick oven infuses the pizza bases
with a great hint of smoke."—René Sépul

TOTONNO'S

1524 Neptune Avenue
Brooklyn
New York 11224
United States
+1 7183728606
www.totonnosconeyisland.com

Opening hours........................Closed Monday—Wednesday
Credit cards..Not accepted
Style of pizza...New York coal-fired
Recommended pizza................................Bianca; Margherita

"The mozzarella and Romano cheese have a delicious
flavor that makes both the plain pie and the white pie
more tasty than any other coal-fired pie I have had."
—Paulie Gee

"Unlike most white pizza in NYC (which is usually made with ricotta), Totonno's makes it with fresh mozzarella, freshly minced garlic, and olive oil. It's sublime."—Michael Berman

"The experience at Totonno's is like stepping into a delicious time capsule, where each ingredient and technique has been carefully preserved."
—Sean Taylor

Italian immigrant Anthony "Totonno" Pero made two momentous crossings in his life. The first brought him from Naples to New York's Little Italy and to employ at Lombardi's, the first licensed pizza shop in the USA. The second, completed in 1924, took the *pizzaiolo* to the Brooklyn side of the East River and this relished relic in Coney Island. With his legacy preserved by his three grandchildren, especially the vigilant Louise "Cookie" Ciminieri, Totonno's recalls a time when the world was as simple as red and white—with tomato sauce or without. In either color the hallmarks of this classic New York-Neapolitan coal-oven pizza are the evenly browned crust, offering just the right resistance to Cookie's expert pinch, and the salty tang of Pecorino Romano cheese sprinkled over the handmade fresh mozzarella.

VINNY'S PIZZA

445 Court Street
Brooklyn
New York 11231
United States
+1 7185969342
www.vinnysbrooklyn.com

Opening hours	Open 7 days
Credit cards	Not accepted
Style of pizza	New York-Sicilian
Recommended pizza	Sfincione

"Sicilian sfincione is a doughy square, loaded down with breadcrumbs, olive oil, Caciocavallo, and caramelized onions. A holiday tradition in Sicily, sfincione is rightly served daily at Vinny's."
—Michele Parente

WILLIAMSBURG PIZZA

265 Union Avenue
Brooklyn
New York 11211
United States
+1 7188558729
www.williamsburgpizza.com

Opening hours	Open 7 days
Credit cards	Accepted
Style of pizza	New York
Recommended pizza	Plain

"One of the best New York–style slices going right now. The crust is thin and crisp yet still flexible enough to fold, as great NY-style should be. Williamsburg Pizza gets the basics right, and then puts some fairly impressive topping combos on there."
—Adam Kuban

AMORE PIZZERIA

3027 Stratton Street
Queens
New York 11354
United States
+1 7184450579

Opening hours	Open 7 days
Credit cards	Not accepted
Style of pizza	New York
Recommended pizza	Cheese; Regular

"The pinnacle of the New York City gas-oven slice pizza."—Hal B. Klein

MARGHERITA PIZZA

16304 Jamaica Avenue
Queens
New York 11432
United States
+1 7186575780

Opening hours	Open 7 days
Credit cards	Not accepted
Style of pizza	New York
Recommended pizza	Plain

"A great old-school place that's immensely popular with locals. This slice is sweet, salty, crispy, and even a bit chewy. It's kind of an extreme slice."
—Jeff Orlick

NEW PARK PIZZA

15671 Cross Bay Boulevard
Queens
New York 11414
United States
+1 7186413082
www.newparkpizza.com

Opening hours	Open 7 days
Credit cards	Not accepted
Style of pizza	Thin-crust
Recommended pizza	Just order a plain slice, ask for it a little well done

"As opposed to a number of the most famous pizzerias, New Park is in a neighborhood that's still almost entirely Italian and the guys making the pizza are Italians (once they added up the number of years experience they had and for three guys it was 71 years combined). You can go wait in line for an hour with the tourists and the foodies at the famous spots, or you can go to New Park and eat amazing pizza within about 2 minutes of walking through the door."
—Famous Fat Dave

JOE & PAT'S

1758 Victory Boulevard
Staten Island
New York 10314
United States
+1 7189810887
www.joeandpatspizzany.com

Opening hours	Open 7 days
Credit cards	Accepted
Style of pizza	Cracker-crust
Recommended pizza	Plain

"The crust is thin and crackery with a slightly sweet sauce and just enough tangy aged mozzarella cheese not to overwhelm the sauce."—Paulie Gee

"There's nothing else out there like a Joe & Pat's pizza. It is ultra-thin and crisp, with a good smattering of sauce and cheese."—Adam Kuban

'WHEN MOST PEOPLE THINK OF PHILADELPHIA, THEY THINK CHEESESTEAKS. I THINK LORENZO'S ON SOUTH STREET.'

MATT RATTIGAN P.504

'I COULD EAT THREE OF THESE PIZZAS IN A ROW AND NOT EVEN BLINK.'

BRIAN DWYER P.502

PHILADELPHIA

'THE BEST PART ABOUT IN RIVA IS ENJOYING A GLASS OF WINE AND A FANTASTIC PIZZA ON THE RELAXING RIVERSIDE PATIO.'

ADAM BARU P.502

'JOE BEDDIA MAKES EVERY SINGLE PIZZA HIMSELF FROM START TO FINISH.'

DREW LAZOR P.503

'TACCONELLI'S IS A PHILADELPHIA TRADITION.'

STEPHANIE REITANO P.504

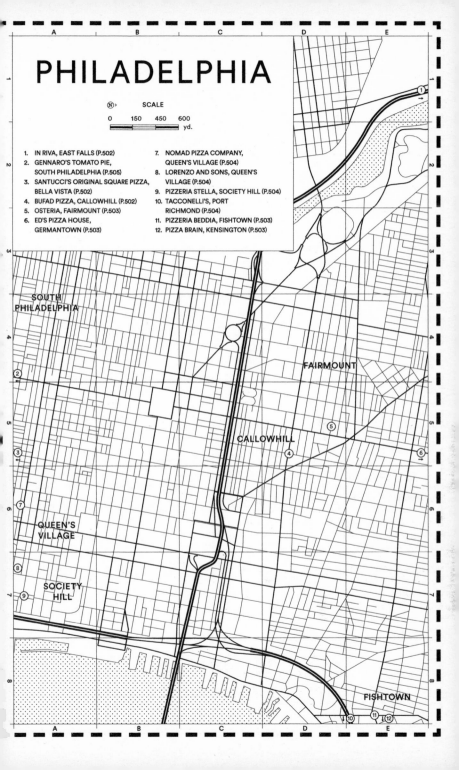

PHILADELPHIA

N↗ SCALE

0   150   450   600
        yd.

1. IN RIVA, EAST FALLS (P.502)
2. GENNARO'S TOMATO PIE, SOUTH PHILADELPHIA (P.505)
3. SANTUCCI'S ORIGINAL SQUARE PIZZA, BELLA VISTA (P.502)
4. BUFAD PIZZA, CALLOWHILL (P.502)
5. OSTERIA, FAIRMOUNT (P.503)
6. ED'S PIZZA HOUSE, GERMANTOWN (P.503)
7. NOMAD PIZZA COMPANY, QUEEN'S VILLAGE (P.504)
8. LORENZO AND SONS, QUEEN'S VILLAGE (P.504)
9. PIZZERIA STELLA, SOCIETY HILL (P.504)
10. TACCONELLI'S, PORT RICHMOND (P.504)
11. PIZZERIA BEDDIA, FISHTOWN (P.503)
12. PIZZA BRAIN, KENSINGTON (P.503)

SOUTH PHILADELPHIA

FAIRMOUNT

CALLOWHILL

QUEEN'S VILLAGE

SOCIETY HILL

FISHTOWN

PITRUCO MOBILE WOOD-FIRED PIZZA

Food truck—check website, Facebook, Instagram, and
Twitter for upcoming locations
Philadelphia
Pennsylvania
United States
+1 4846025454
www.pitrucopizza.com

Opening hours	Variable
Credit cards	Accepted
Style of pizza	Neapolitan brick-oven
Recommended pizza	Spicy Garlic

"The great char on the crust is what is especially
delicious about this pie."—Emilio Mignucci

SANTUCCI'S ORIGINAL SQUARE PIZZA

901 South 10th Street
Bella Vista
Philadelphia
Pennsylvania 19147
United States
+1 2158255304
www.santuccispizza.com

Opening hours	Open 7 days
Credit cards	Not accepted
Style of pizza	Square pan
Recommended pizza	Original Square

"The most delicious, cravable square-pan pizza.
A beautiful mixture of a soft dough protected by a
layer of mozzarella, topped with a tangy, flavorful
sauce and a sprinkle of aged grated cheese. You
remember when your Nonna made you pizza on
Sundays? No? Well, you can pretend you have a
Nonna and she makes kick-ass pizza that makes you
happy and loved. You need this nostalgia."
—Stephanie Reitano

"It's upside down. It's baked in cake pans. I could eat
three of these pizzas in a row and not even blink."
—Brian Dwyer

BUFAD PIZZA

1240 Spring Garden Street
Callowhill
Philadelphia
Pennsylvania 19123
United States
+1 2152389311
www.bufadpizza.com

Opening hours	Closed Monday
Credit cards	Accepted
Style of pizza	Neapolitan
Recommended pizza	Sausage

"The pizza is always perfectly cooked and the rest of
the menu is really enticing. I never just get a pizza."
—Emilio Mignucci

IN RIVA

4116 Ridge Avenue
East Falls
Philadelphia
Pennsylvania 19129
United States
+1 2154384848
www.in-riva.com

Opening hours	Closed Monday
Credit cards	Accepted
Style of pizza	Neapolitan
Recommended pizza	Polpette Diavolo

"A fantastic, industrial space that is beautifully
situated on the Schuylkill River in Philadelphia.
All the pizzas are imaginative, the ingredients fresh,
and the sauce made with 100 percent San Marzano
tomatoes is a great backdrop to many of my favorite
pies. The best part about In Riva is enjoying a glass
of wine and a fantastic pizza on the relaxing riverside
patio."—Adam Baru

OSTERIA

640 North Broad Street
Fairmount
Philadelphia
Pennsylvania 19130
United States
+1 2157630920
www.osteriaphilly.com

Opening hours	Open 7 days
Credit cards	Accepted
Style of pizza	Traditional and Neapolitan
Recommended pizza	Anything with scallions (spring onions) or pistachio pesto

"The pliant crust crackles with just the right amount of crispiness, and the delicately applied toppings can be revelatory."—Trey Popp

PIZZERIA BEDDIA

115 East Girard Avenue
Fishtown
Philadelphia
Pennsylvania 19125
United States
www.pizzeriabeddia.wordpress.com

Opening hours	Closed Sunday–Tuesday
Credit cards	Not accepted
Style of pizza	New Haven-New York
Recommended pizza	Arrabbiata; Plain; White

"Joe Beddia makes every single pizza himself from start to finish and is extremely uncompromising when it comes to ingredients and the process as a whole. This means you wait much longer for your order than the average pizzeria, but I'll prioritize quality over convenience any day."—Drew Lazor

"What makes the pizzeria special? In eight words: no slices, no seating, no phone, no problem."
—Brian Dwyer

"Joe is very specific about the ingredients he uses and it makes for a one-of-a-kind pizza experience. I could eat his pizzas every day and writing this makes me wish I was eating one right now."
—Michelle Flisek

Joseph Beddia is famous in Philadelphia for two things: making one extraordinary pizza and making it extraordinarily difficult to get one. He bakes 40 pizzas four nights a week, one by one, in a single-deck oven. There's no phone, no public restroom, no guarantees. You get in line and take your chances. Time it right and your wait for a 16-inch (40-cm) beauty blessed with Jersey tomatoes, Brooklyn mozzarella, Pennsylvania Old Gold aged cheese (like Gouda), and a crisp base can be as short as 20 minutes. Time it wrong and you suffer in pizza limbo, staring at some dude's back for a couple of hours and hoping beyond hope he doesn't claim the last takeout order of the night.

ED'S PIZZA HOUSE

5022 Wayne Avenue
Germantown
Philadelphia
Pennsylvania 19144
United States
+1 2158495588

Opening hours	Open 7 days
Credit cards	Accepted
Style of pizza	American
Recommended pizza	Sausage and Sweet Pepper

PIZZA BRAIN

2313 Frankford Avenue
Kensington
Philadelphia
Pennsylvania 19125
United States
+1 2152912965
www.pizzabrain.org

Opening hours	Open 7 days
Credit cards	Not accepted
Style of pizza	New York
Recommended pizza	Forbes Waggensense; Granny Divjack

"When Brian Dwyer realized that there was no museum on Earth dedicated to one of the world's most ubiquitous cuisines, he decided to take action. Opening in 2012 in the unassuming Philadelphia neighborhood of Fishtown, Brian and his friends created not only the first pizza museum chronicling Dwyer's Guinness award-winning collection of pizza memorabilia, but a smashing pizzeria to boot."
—Brooks Jones

TACCONELLI'S

2604 East Somerset Street
Port Richmond
Philadelphia
Pennsylvania 19134
United States
+1 2154254983
www.tacconellispizzeria.com

Opening hours	Closed Monday and Tuesday (and Sundays in August)
Credit cards	Not accepted
Style of pizza	New York thin-crust
Recommended pizza	White with Spinach, Tomato, Mozzarella, and Garlic

"Tacconelli's is a Philadelphia tradition and you must reserve your dough before coming. A longer cook time with live fire results in a very crisp dough with a beautiful char. I crave this pizza."—Stephanie Reitano

LORENZO AND SONS

305 South Street
Queen's Village
Philadelphia
Pennsylvania 19147
United States
+1 2158001942
www.lorenzoandsons.com

Opening hours	Open 7 days
Credit cards	Not accepted
Style of pizza	Classic Philadelphia
Recommended pizza	Plain Cheese

"When most people think of Philadelphia, they think cheesesteaks. I think Lorenzo's on South Street. For $3.50 you get the biggest slice of pizza you could ever imagine was possible. There are special 'folds' and techniques that you acquire after a few bouts with this beast of a slice, though masters and amateurs alike are bound to get a few grease stains on their shirt, no matter what."—Matt Rattigan

"My absolute to-die-for pizza anywhere."
—Cyrus Keefer

NOMAD PIZZA COMPANY

611 South 7th Street
Queen's Village
Philadelphia
Pennsylvania 19147
United States
+1 2152380900
www.nomadpizzaco.com

Opening hours	Closed Monday
Credit cards	Accepted
Style of pizza	Neapolitan
Recommended pizza	Arugula (rocket) with Prosciutto; Margherita di Bufala; Quattro Formaggio; Spicy Soppressata

"The extremely thin, very flavorful crust is the first thing that stands out (no doubt the most important also) but the use of very fresh, very local ingredients in such a manner as to have them accentuate each other is the ultimate genius."—Emilio Mignucci

"The Spicy Soppressata pie here is positively Platonic in its balance between the spicy cured pork and a touch of honeyed sweetness."—Trey Popp

PIZZERIA STELLA

420 South 2nd Street
Society Hill
Philadelphia
Pennsylvania 19103
United States
+1 2153208000
www.pizzeriastella.net

Opening hours	Open 7 days
Credit cards	Accepted
Style of pizza	Neapolitan
Recommended pizza	Tartufo

"Stella is the best example of Neapolitan-style pizza in Philadelphia."—Michelle Flisek

GENNARO'S TOMATO PIE

1429 Jackson Street
South Philadelphia
Philadelphia
Pennsylvania 19145
United States
+1 2154635070

Opening hours	Closed Monday and Tuesday
Credit cards	Not accepted
Style of pizza	New York thin-crust
Recommended pizza	Plain; Tomato

"This is old-school New York-style pizza at it's finest."
—Michelle Flisek

"The coal oven produces an intoxicating char and texture that's unlike anything else in Philly. The space itself, with its nostalgic Second World War-era decor and sweet servers in Rosie the Riveter kerchiefs, is also super-charming."—Drew Lazor

THE WAYS
OF THE PIZZA FOLD

With no metal utensils allowed past security checkpoints at Atlanta airport, many passengers try to cut slices from Varasano's Pizzeria with the side of a plastic fork, like a wedge of birthday cake. This drives transplanted New Yorker Jeff Varasano nuts. "Once I told a customer it's better folded," he recalls, "so he rolled it up like a cigar from the tip to the crust, then turned it to the side and bit down. The sauce shot out all over him."

To initiate neophytes into the ways of the pizza fold, Jen Strickland, the co-owner of Home Slice Pizza, a New York-style joint in Austin, Texas, drew up a three-step instructional diagram: 1) Grab the slice by the crust with your thumb and middle finger from points A and B [the corners of the rounded side]. 2) Squeeze to fold in half. 3) Take a bite. "In New York," says Strickland, "if you didn't eat it this way you could be mistaken for a tourist."

When Craig Stoll of Delfina Pizzeria in San Francisco folds a slice of pizza back in New York, his hometown, he wedges a knuckle against the crease to keep the two sides from touching. He seeks the mouthfeel of a thin pizza and not, heaven forbid, a double-layered pizza wad. "You might as well eat that monstrosity known as Chicago-style," says Stoll. "The entire obsession with folding is really a New York conceit. It's because the pies are so much larger than their Neapolitan or West Coast brethren."

Even so, California does have its pizza-folding fanatics. Mishandle your pizza at one of Tony Gemignani's San Francisco pizza joints and you're liable to bend the 11-time World Pizza Champion out of shape, too. "Hey, what are you doing?" Gemignani asked an out-of-towner dissecting a pizza at Slice House SF. "You're picking it apart. You're ruining the whole f***ing slice."

Thin, ultra-crisp crusts, like those in Rome and St. Louis, are too brittle for folding. You don't have to. The slices are self-sustaining. New York pizza is more pliable. It's crisp enough to crack when folded but it won't break. When you pinch a slice and tilt it slightly up to eat, as Gemignani does, there are no cracks through which the cheesy, buttery oil can escape. When you bite the tip the grease streams down the fold and your forearm. "There is nothing better!" says Gemignani.

The droopy pizza of Naples poses special challenges to the eater who isn't too, as the Italians say, *schizzinoso* (squeamish) to eat with his hands. He may flip the tip back over the folded slice to secure its runny tomato and mozzarella. Or, following the rules of the street, he may order a smaller pizza and fold it *a portafolgio* or *a libretto* (like a wallet or a booklet), first in half and then in four, to eat on the go, its fluids enveloped in its folds, to a point. "If you're a real Neapolitan," says Luciano Furia, a Naples food photographer who trained as a bioengineer, "you must get a drip of oil down your wrist."

"THE PIZZA DE COMBINACION HAS EVERYTHING YOU COULD THINK OF ON IT, BUT MY FAVORITE IS EITHER THE CLAM PIZZA OR THE SEAFOOD COMBO PIZZA."

ROSSY EARLE P.511

"BELLARIA IS A HAVEN FOR THE CITY'S ITALIAN COMMUNITY."

JUDITH SERVÍN P.510

CENTRAL AMERICA

"THE PIZZAS ARE EXCEPTIONAL."

SASHA CORREA P.510

"EVERY ONE OF EDUARDO 'LALO' GARCIA'S RESTAURANTS HAS STANDOUT QUALITY...HIS MOST RECENT VENTURE, LALO, SERVES VERY GOOD PIZZAS."

SASHA CORREA P.510

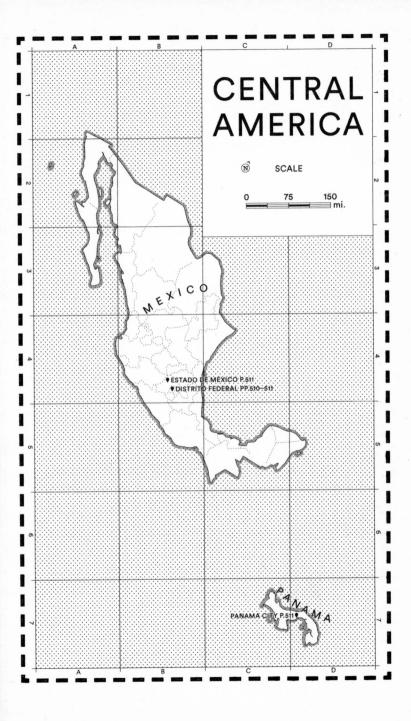

CENTRAL
AMERICA

SCALE

0   75   150
mi.

M E X I C O

▼ESTADO DE MÉXICO P.511
▼DISTRITO FEDERAL PP.510–511

P A N A M A

PANAMA CITY P.511▼

BELLARIA

Presidente Masarik 514
Local A
Mexico City
Distrito Federal 11550
Mexico
+52 5552820413
www.bellaria.com.mx

Opening hours	Open 7 days
Credit cards	Accepted
Style of pizza	Rustic Italian
Recommended pizza	Calabrese

"Bellaria is a haven for the city's Italian community."
—Judith Servín

CRANKER

Vía Santa Fe
Avenida Vasco de Quiroga 3850
Mexico City
Distrito Federal 05109
Mexico
+52 5521678595
www.alboa.com.mx

Opening hours	Open 7 days
Credit cards	Accepted
Style of pizza	Stone-baked
Recommended pizza	Fontina Cheese and Fig

FLIPPIN PIZZA

Avenida De La Paz 57, Locales 21–22
Mexico City
Distrito Federal 01000
Mexico
+52 5562688015
www.flippinpizza.mx

Opening hours	Open 7 days
Credit cards	Accepted
Style of pizza	New York
Recommended pizza	Bronx

LALO!

Calle Zacatecas 173
Mexico City
Distrito Federal 06700
Mexico
+52 5555643388
www.eat-lalo.com

Opening hours	Closed Monday
Credit cards	Accepted
Style of pizza	Neapolitan

"Every one of Eduardo 'Lalo' García's restaurants has standout quality. The chef takes care to offer his diners dishes that are simple yet complex, with seasonal ingredients taking center stage. His most recent venture, Lalo, serves very good pizzas."
—Sasha Correa

LA LOGGIA

Emilio Castelar 44
Mexico City
Distrito Federal 11550
Mexico
+52 5552804807
www.laloggia.mx

Opening hours	Open 7 days
Credit cards	Accepted
Style of pizza	Italian
Recommended pizza	Bella Napoli

"Traditional Italian pizza made by an Italian chef from Naples."—Judith Servín

OSTERIA 8

Sinaloa 252, between Veracruz and Tampico
Mexico City
Distrito Federal 06700
Mexico
+52 5552122008
www.osteria8.amawebs.com

Opening hours	Open 7 days
Credit cards	Accepted but not AMEX
Style of pizza	Neapolitan
Recommended pizza	Serrano Ham

"This is one of those places I go without a second thought because of the quality of the pizzas it serves. The pizzas are exceptional."—Sasha Correa

ROCCO & SIMONA

Virgilio 8
Mexico City
Distrito Federal 11560
Mexico
+52 5552814716
www.roccoysimona.com

Opening hours	Closed Monday
Credit cards	Accepted
Style of pizza	Italian
Recommended pizza	Baked

ARTIGIANO PIZZA RÚSTICA

Calzada de los Jinetes 203
Local 5
Atizapán de Zaragoza
Estado de México 52950
Mexico
+52 5553706825
www.artigiano.com.mx

Opening hours	Open 7 days
Credit cards	Accepted
Style of pizza	Rustic Neapolitan
Recommended pizza	Margherita

NAPOLI

Calle 57 Este Obarrio
Panama City
Panama
+507 2638800
www.napoliobarrio.com

Opening hours	Closed Monday
Credit cards	Accepted
Style of pizza	Neapolitan thin-crust
Recommended pizza	Clam

"Napoli is the go-to place for my family in Panama and I grew up eating its pizzas. The Pizza de Combinacion has everything you could think of on it, but my favorite is either the clam pizza or the seafood combo pizza."—Rossy Earle

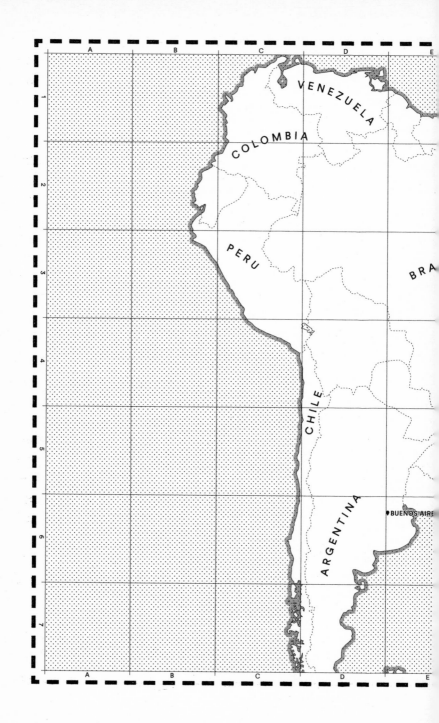

SOUTH

AMERICA

SCALE

0   300   600
mi.

♦RIO DE JANEIRO

"SAN CEFERINO IS ONE OF THE GO-TO PLACES FOR ITALIAN FOOD IN LIMA."

NORA SUGOBONO P.518

"FOR DESSERT, THE NUTELLA PIZZA IS A MUST."

MARISSA CHIAPPE LANATTA P.516

SOUTH AMERICA NORTH

"EVIO'S PIZZA IS A SMALL, WELCOMING SPOT IN CARACAS. AFTER THE HUSTLE AND BUSTLE OF THE CITY, ITS TERRACE OFFERS A MOMENT OF CALM."

SASHA CORREA P.518

"THE BEST PIZZA I FOUND IN LATIN AMERICA."

PAOLA MIGLIO ROSSI P.516

"THE PIZZA IS LIGHT, CRISP, AND VERY FLAVORSOME."

IGNACIO BARRIOS JACOBS P.516

SOUTH
AMERICA
NORTH

MIRANDA P.518

CUNDINAMARCA P.516

VENEZUELA

COLOMBIA

PERU

LIMA PP.516–518.

CUSCO P.516

SCALE

0   225   450 mi.

JULIA

Carrera 5 #69 A-19
Bogotá
Cundinamarca
Colombia
+57 13482835
www.juliapizzeria.com

Opening hours..Open 7 days
Credit cards..Accepted
Style of pizza...Traditional thin-crust
Recommended pizza................Mushroom; Romana; Salumi

"The best pizza I found in Latin America. Precise
cooking and fresh flavors."—Paola Miglio Rossi

LA BODEGA 138

Calle Herrajes 138
Cusco
Cusco 0008
Peru
+51 84260272

Opening hours..Open 7 days
Credit cards..Not accepted
Style of pizza...New York wood-fired
Recommended pizza................La Pituca; Norma; Prosciutto
and Arugula (rocket); Red Hot Chile Peppers

"La Bodega 138 is very attractive and welcoming.
It's got a homely atmosphere and the staff take
good care of you. The pizza is light, crisp, and very
flavorsome. The restaurant is very popular, so it's
a good idea to arrive early or book a table."
—Ignacio Barrios Jacobs

"A hearty, satisfying, and purse-friendly experience."
—Nora Sugobono

"There are no superfluous ingredients—everything
is perfectly balanced. You can choose your own
toppings, but the combinations on offer are
excellent."—Cinzia Repetto

ANTICA

Avenida Prolongación San Martín 201
Barranco
Lima 15063
Peru
+51 14227939
www.anticapizzeria.com.pe

Opening hours..Open 7 days
Credit cards..Accepted
Style of pizza...Wood-fired
Recommended pizza..Isabella; Nutella

"For dessert, the Nutella pizza is a must."
—Marissa Chiappe Lanatta

VEGGIE PIZZA

Jr. Colina 112
Barranco
Lima 15063
Peru
+51 12410590
www.veggiepizza.pe

Opening hours..Open 7 days
Credit cards..Accepted
Style of pizza..Organic
Recommended pizza..Dalia del Bosque

"The pizza has unique ingredients and good flavor
combinations."—Marissa Chiappe Lanatta

VILLA PIZZA

Alameda La Encantada
Chorrillos
Lima 15067
Peru
+51 12540165
www.villapizza.com.pe

Opening hours..Open 7 days
Credit cards..Accepted
Style of pizza...Thin and crispy
Recommended pizza..Europea

"This pizzeria is located inside a private complex at
a beach resort a few kilometers south of Lima. It is
a favorite with residents of the resort, but people
from Lima also come here especially to eat pizza.
It is small, with a welcoming atmosphere, and is just
a stone's throw from the beach."
—Ignacio Barrios Jacobs

PIZZERIA BELLA PACHACAMAC

Avenida Manuel Valle Mz G Lot 719
Lurín
Lima 15823
Peru
+51 13674194

Opening hours	Closed Monday
Credit cards	Accepted but not AMEX
Style of pizza	Artisan wood-fired
Recommended pizza	Anchovy; Margherita

"Master pizza chef Elbert prepares spectacular dough, leaving it to proof under controlled conditions for two days. His pizzas are well balanced, they don't have excessive cheese, so each individual flavor comes through. He cooks his pizzas in a wood-fired oven, giving them a rustic style and distinctive taste."
—Cinzia Repetto

LOS BACHICHE

Avenida La Paz 1025
Miraflores
Lima 15074
Peru
+51 12219283

Opening hours	Open 7 days
Credit cards	Accepted
Style of pizza	Artisan thin-crust
Recommended pizza	Babiche; Eggplant (aubergine)

"The pizza is light and easy to eat, with an extremely thin base given just the right blast of heat to make it crisp. It holds its shape and the toppings don't make it go soggy quickly."—Paola Miglio Rossi

MORELIA

Calle Atahualpa 196
Miraflores
Lima 15074
Peru
+51 12427730
www.morelia.pe

Opening hours	Open 7 days
Credit cards	Accepted
Style of pizza	Grilled
Recommended pizza	Caprese; De La Chacra; Mediterranean; Montecatini; Olivia; Wild Mushroom

"Cooked on the grill, in traditional Argentinian style, the bases of these pizzas take on a distinctive smoky flavor. They are ultra-thin, ultra-crispy, and square.

The combinations of toppings are unusual, but very well balanced and tasty."—Nora Sugobono

"You can order two toppings on a single pizza, allowing you to try more than one combination."
—Cinzia Repetto

VEGGIE PIZZA

Avenida Santa Cruz 825, 3rd Floor
Miraflores
Lima 15074
Peru
+51 12820524

Opening hours	Open 7 days
Credit cards	Accepted
Style of pizza	Vegetarian
Recommended pizza	Veggie

"Highly creative vegetarian pizzas."—Hirka Roca-Rey

LA PIZZERIA DEL TÍO RICHI

Juan Valler 1118 La Planicie
Punta Hermosa
Lima 15846
Peru
+51 12308357

Opening hours	Closed Monday and Tuesday
Credit cards	Accepted
Style of pizza	Wood-fired
Recommended pizza	Lomo Saltado

"These pizzas have light bases and are creative without compromising the balance of flavors. Perfect for a day at the beach."—Nora Sugobono

LA LINTERNA

Calle Los Libertadores 311
San Isidro
Lima 15073
Peru
+51 14403636
www.pizzerialalinterna.com

Opening hours	Open 7 days
Credit cards	Accepted
Style of pizza	New York-Italian
Recommended pizza	Four Seasons; Margherita

"La Linterna has been serving the best pizzas in Lima 'round the clock for 20 years. It never disappoints."
—Marissa Chiappe Lanatta

SAN CEFERINO
Avenida Dos de Mayo 793
San Isidro
Lima 15073
Peru
+51 14221959
www.restaurantsanceferino.com

Opening hours	Open 7 days
Credit cards	Accepted
Style of pizza	Wood-fired
Recommended pizza	Caprese Special; Ceferino Special

"San Ceferino is one of the go-to places for Italian food in Lima. Its menu still features dishes and recipes from the classic school of Italian cuisine, but it has managed to incorporate new ideas to suit the local taste. A meal here never disappoints, especially if you also try one of its great artisan pasta dishes." —Nora Sugobono

SPIZZA
Avenida Dos de Mayo 455
San Isidro
Lima 15073
Peru
+51 12222228
www.spizza.pe

Opening hours	Open 7 days
Credit cards	Accepted
Style of pizza	Neapolitan
Recommended pizza	Don Peppe; Margherita

"Authentic Neapolitan pizza cooked in a wood-fired oven."—Hirka Roca-Rey

"The pizzas have thin bases, with a crispy crust and fresh toppings."—Paola Miglio Rossi

LA PICCOLINA
Simón Salguero #625
Surco
Lima 15048
Peru
+51 12736005
www.trattorialapiccolina.com

Opening hours	Open 7 days
Credit cards	Accepted
Style of pizza	Thin-crust
Recommended pizza	Hawaiian

"La Piccolina offers thin-crust pizzas that are, perhaps, slightly on the thick side, but not too much." —Paola Miglio Rossi

EVIO'S PIZZA
4A Avenida, between 2A and 3A Transversals
Caracas
Miranda 1070
Venezuela
+58 2122836608

Opening hours	Open 7 days
Credit cards	Accepted
Style of pizza	Neapolitan
Recommended pizza	Four Seasons

"Evio's Pizza is a small, welcoming spot in Caracas. After the hustle and bustle of the city, its terrace offers a moment of calm. The pizzas stand out for the attention given to every detail."—Sasha Correa

"ITALIAN-STYLE PIZZA WITH A BRAZILIAN TWIST."

ANTONELLO MONARDO P.524

"THIS IS ONE OF THE NEWEST PIZZERIAS IN SANTIAGO, BUT IT IS RAPIDLY MAKING A NAME FOR ITSELF."

CONSUELO GOEPPINGER P.541

SOUTH AMERICA SOUTH

"A VERY GOOD TRADITIONAL PIZZERIA IN THE MIDDLE OF ONE OF THE MOST BEAUTIFUL BEACHES IN THE WORLD."

SADY HOMRICH P.525

"PIZZA DO PÃO IS THE BEST PLACE FOR TAKEOUT PIZZA."

TATIANA TAVARES P.526

CEARÁ P.522

PERNAMBUCO PP.524-525

BRAZIL

MATO GROSSO P.524

DISTRITO FEDERAL PP.522-524

RIO DE JANEIRO PP.525, 530-534

SÃO PAULO PP.536-540

CHILE

SANTA CATARINA PP.527-528

SANTA FE P.544

RIO GRANDE DO SUL PP.525-527

CÓRDOBA P.543

VALPARAÍSO P.543

SANTIAGO PP.541-543

MENDOZA P.544

BUENOS AIRES PP.543, 546-551

ARGENTINA

SOUTH AMERICA SOUTH

N

SCALE

0   350   700
                    mi.

LA BELLA ITALIA

Rua Almirante Barroso 812
Fortaleza
Ceará 60060-440
Brazil
+55 8532192166
www.labellaitaliafortaleza.com.br

Opening hours..Open 7 days
Credit cards..Accepted
Style of pizza..Italian
Recommended pizza..Calabresa

BUONI AMICI'S

Rua Dragão do Mar 80
Fortaleza
Ceará 60060-195
Brazil
+55 8532195454
www.buoniamicis.com.br

Opening hours..Open 7 days
Credit cards..Accepted
Style of pizza..Traditional
Recommended pizza..Verde

ITÁLIA DA GABRIELE

Avenida Historiador Raimundo Girão 36
Fortaleza
Ceará 60060-570
Brazil
+55 8532194993

Opening hours..Open 7 days
Credit cards...Accepted but not AMEX
Style of pizza..Thin-crust
Recommended pizza............................Half Four Cheese and
Half Napoletana

"I like the very simple surroundings and the service provided by Gabriele, an Italian, and I love the Half Four Cheese and Half Napoletana pizza."
—Marcos Tardin

PIZZA VIGNOLI

Rua Silva Jatahy 529
Fortaleza
Ceará 60160-140
Brazil
+55 8532679450
www.pizzavignoli.com.br/2014/fortaleza

Opening hours..Open 7 days
Credit cards..Accepted
Style of pizza..Thin-crust
Recommended pizza..............................Shiitake; Vignoli

"The bases are so thin that these almost can't be called pizzas, but they use high-quality ingredients, the surroundings are very pleasant, and there is the added charm of eating with plastic gloves."
—Marcos Tardin

VILA MOSQUITO

Rua Antonio Augusto 786
Fortaleza
Ceará 60110-370
Brazil
+55 8532267422
www.vilamosquito.com.br

Opening hours..Closed Monday
Credit cards..Accepted
Style of pizza..Thin-crust
Recommended pizza......................................Four Cheese

"Juicy pizza with generous toppings is served on plates that look like pieces of pizza."
—Liége Xavier da Cruz

BACO PIZZARIA

408 Sul, Bloco C, Loja 35
Brasilia
Distrito Federal 70257-530
Brazil
+55 6132442292
www.bacopizzaria.com.br

Opening hours..Open 7 days
Credit cards..Accepted
Style of pizza..Neapolitan
Recommended pizza......................Caprina with Rosemary;
Vera Pizza Margherita

"The pizzas are well baked and made with high-quality ingredients. It also has a range of pizzas certified by the VPN Association that are beautifully prepared by the pizza chefs."—Ricardo Castanho

The retro look, from the checkerboard mosaic floor to the photographic wall murals, was inspired by early twentieth-century Italy. You can say that about the classic wood-fired pizzas, too. Baco was the first pizzeria in Brasilia to meet the demanding specs of the VPN Association. Baco's leopard-spotted Margherita and Marinara are substantial by Naples standards, wispy by Brazilian ones. All pizzas come in two shapes: Napoletana (thin with a pronounced edge) and Romana (very thin with a thin edge). The Margherita Premium, with mozzarella, peeled grape (baby plum) and plum tomatoes, basil, and cream-gushing burrata, is available in two sizes: individual (four slices) and grande (eight slices). The second Baco is at 309 Norte, Bloco A, Loja 30/40.

LA FORNACELLA

312 Norte, Bloco B, Loja 43
Brasilia
Distrito Federal 70765-520
Brazil
+55 6130332345
www.lafornacella.com.br

Opening hours	Closed Monday
Credit cards	Accepted
Style of pizza	Roman
Recommended pizza	Neapolitan; Parma Ham

FRATELLO UNO

103 Sul, Bloco A, Loja 36
Brasilia
Distrito Federal 70342-510
Brazil
+55 6133213213
www.fratellounopizzaria.com.br

Opening hours	Open 7 days
Credit cards	Accepted
Style of pizza	Italian-Brazilian thin-crust
Recommended pizza	Americana; Maçarico; Mozzarella

"This pizzeria shows exceptional creativity in its use of ingredients, without overdoing it with extravagant combinations. When you taste one of the chef-inspired pizzas, you feel like the ingredients were made for each other. A classic example is the Maçarico pizza, which features the chef's own black olive pesto and raisins as 'seasoning' for a pizza topped with peeled tomatoes, spicy sausage, buffalo mozzarella, and sliced zucchini (courgette). It tastes incredible."
—Rodrigo Caetano

PIZZA DOM BOSCO

CLS 107, Bloco D, Loja 20
Brasilia
Distrito Federal 7034-6540
Brazil
+55 6134437579

Opening hours	Open 7 days
Credit cards	Not accepted
Style of pizza	By the slice
Recommended pizza	Mozzarella with Special Tomato Sauce

"This pizzeria is iconic in Brasilia. It has a few branches around the city and sells slices of just one type of pizza: Mozzarella with Special Tomato Sauce. The slices are sold at a counter and there are no tables. It is one of the oldest establishments in the city and was first launched in the 1960s. Dom Bosco's pizzas are thin-crust with tomato sauce and generous amounts of cheese."—Ana Rosa

PIZZERIA DON GIOVANNI

QI 11, Lago Sul - Brasília, Bloco H, Lojas 12/16
Brasilia
Distrito Federal 71625-570
Brazil
+55 6132484018

Opening hours	Open 7 days
Credit cards	Accepted
Style of pizza	Sicilian
Recommended pizza	Brasilia; Rolled Eggplant (aubergine)

"The owner, Giovanni Spatola, introduced authentic Sicilian-inspired pizza to Brasilia. All the Italians who live in Brasilia eat here!"—Antonello Monardo

SANTA PIZZA
CLS 207, Bloco B, Loja 05
Brasilia
Distrito Federal 70253-520
Brazil
+55 6132441415
www.stapizza.com.br

Opening hours	Open 7 days
Credit cards	Accepted
Style of pizza	Roman
Recommended pizza	Parma Ham and Mushroom

"Italian-style pizza with a Brazilian twist."
—Antonello Monardo

VALENTINA PIZZARIA
214 Norte, Bloco A, Lojas 9/11
Brasilia
Distrito Federal 70873-510
Brazil
+55 6133409898
www.valentinapizzaria.com.br

Opening hours	Open 7 days
Credit cards	Accepted but not AMEX
Style of pizza	Italian-Brazilian
Recommended pizza	Artichoke; Caprina; Leek and Mascarpone; Sun-dried Tomato

"This is among the top three pizzerias in Brasilia and is better than most of the others in the city. However, the quality and presentation of the pizzas is not quite that of Fratello Uno and Baco, despite having a very similar menu."—Rodrigo Caetano

The mosaic-tiled open kitchen of Valentina, with its long, white marble counter and copper-plated wood-fired ovens as staging ground, is great Brazilian pizza theater. The adroit *pizzaioli* roll out balls of dough in seconds and then rapidly assemble medium-thick pizzas in 60 creative but not too crazy ways— 54 Salgadas (salts, meaning savory pizzas) and six Doces (sweets, or dessert pizzas). The choreography is complicated by the fact that many orders are for half-and-half pizzas: one side might get a Caprina, a house favorite with tomato, spicy Calabresa sausage, goat cheese, zucchini (courgette), and oregano; the other, an Alcachofrinha, with artichoke, tomato, oregano, and blankets of mozzarella and Emmental cheese. A second Valentina is at 310 Sul, Bloco A, Lojas 6 e 8.

SPECIALI
Rua Fernandes Tourinho 805
Belo Horizonte
Mato Grosso 30112-000
Brazil
+55 3132847060
www.specialipizzabar.wordpress.com

Opening hours	Open 7 days
Credit cards	Accepted
Style of pizza	Brazilian
Recommended pizza	Salt Cod

"Speciali has a cosmopolitan vibe. It is warm and welcoming, and has an excellent wine list. Innovative pizzas are made with a wide variety of Brazilian produce."
—Luís Américo Aguiar de Moura Rodrigues Teixeira

BOTECO BARAZZONE
Avenida Bernardo Vieira de Melo 1250
Jaboatão dos Guararapes
Pernambuco 54400-000
Brazil
+55 8134621088
www.pizzariabarazzone.com.br

Opening hours	Open 7 days
Credit cards	Accepted
Style of pizza	Wood-fired
Recommended pizza	Barazzone

"It has a variety of well-made pizzas with top-quality ingredients."—Maria Maranhão Chaves

ANTICA ROMA
Estrada Real do Poço 177
Recife
Pernambuco 52061-200
Brazil
+55 8132049086

Opening hours	Closed Tuesday
Credit cards	Accepted
Style of pizza	Thin-crust
Recommended pizza	Cassia

"Although Antica Roma is a traditional Italian pizzeria, its has a relaxed Brazilian attitude to serving pizza. The pizzas are tasty and varied, and the prices are good too."—Maria Maranhão Chaves

RESTAURANTE LIBÓRIO PRAIA
Rua Setúbal 1586
Recife
Pernambuco 51030-010
Brazil
+55 8133437211

Opening hours	Closed Monday
Credit cards	Accepted
Style of pizza	Thin-crust
Recommended pizza	Four Cheese

RISTORANTE E PIZZARIA TOMASELLI
Rua Conselheiro Portela 536
Recife
Pernambuco 52020-030
Brazil
+55 8134273710
www.restaurantetomaselli.com.br

Opening hours	Open 7 days
Credit cards	Accepted
Style of pizza	Thin-crust
Recommended pizza	Margherita; Marinara

RISTORANTE E PIZZARIA TOMASELLI
Rua Frei Leandro 50
Recife
Pernambuco 51011-600
Brazil
+55 8134273710
www.restaurantetomaselli.com.br

Opening hours	Open 7 days
Credit cards	Accepted
Style of pizza	Thin-crust
Recommended pizza	Margherita

"I like the pizzas a lot—they have thin crusts and are made with homemade tomato sauce and tasty ingredients."—Maria Raquel Matos de Carvalho

PIZZA GOOL
Rua Manoel Turíbio de Farias 2, Lojas 10 e 11
Armação dos Buzios
Rio de Janeiro 28950-000
Brazil
+55 2226234643

Opening hours	Open 7 days
Credit cards	Not accepted
Style of pizza	Traditional
Recommended pizza	Brazilian Pesto

"A very good traditional pizzeria in the middle of one of the most beautiful beaches in the world."
—Sady Homrich

PIZZA ENTRE VINHOS
Estrada RS 444 – KM 18,9
Vale des Vinhedos
Bento Gonçalves
Rio Grande do Sul 95700-000
Brazil
+55 5434591392

Opening hours	Closed Sunday and Monday
Credit cards	Accepted
Style of pizza	Brazilian
Recommended pizza	San Daniele

CHU RESTAURANTE
Rua Andrade Neves 3880
Pelotas
Rio Grande do Sul 96020-080
Brazil
+55 5332250250
www.churestaurante.com

Opening hours	Closed Monday
Credit cards	Accepted
Style of pizza	Gourmet thin-crust
Recommended pizza	Pizzalino

"The Italian flour, the perfect oven, and the excellent surroundings make CHU Restaurante very popular in southernmost Brazil."—Sady Homrich

BAZKARIA

Rua Comendador Caminha 324
Porto Alegre
Rio Grande do Sul 90430-030
Brazil
+55 5130616262
www.bazkaria.com.br

Opening hours...Open 7 days
Credit cards...Accepted
Style of pizza...Brazilian
Recommended pizza...Guapa

"The use of regional ingredients makes these pizzas much more interesting."—Tatiana Tavares

FORNELLONE

Avenida Nova York 93
Porto Alegre
Rio Grande do Sul 90550-070
Brazil
+55 5130287575
www.fornellone.com.br

Opening hours...Open 7 days
Credit cards...Accepted
Style of pizza...Brazilian
Recommended pizza...Charque; Geremia

"Fornellone mixes traditional ingredients with local ones, creating beautiful and flavorsome pizzas. It is one of the oldest pizzerias in town."
—Diego Fabris

OLIVOS 657

Rua da República 657
Porto Alegre
Rio Grande do Sul 90050-321
Brazil
+55 5133726256

Opening hours...Closed Monday
Credit cards...Accepted
Style of pizza...Thin-crust
Recommended pizza...Pastrami and Arugula (rocket)

"Olivos 657 pizzas are made with the best ingredients and the artisan touch of the up-and-coming chef, Marcelo."—Sady Homrich

PIZZA DO PÃO

Rua Irmão José Otão 588
Porto Alegre
Rio Grande do Sul 90035-060
Brazil
+55 5137378439
www.pizzadopao.com.br

Opening hours...Open 7 days
Credit cards...Accepted
Style of pizza...Crispy
Recommended pizza...Santo Babado

"Pizza do Pão is the best place for takeout pizza."
—Tatiana Tavares

POT. POURRÍ

Rua Pedro Chaves Barcelos 845
Porto Alegre
Rio Grande do Sul 90450-010
Brazil
+55 5184314981

Opening hours...Closed Monday
Credit cards...Accepted
Style of pizza...Thin-crust
Recommended pizza...Pepper and Lemon

"It's a cozy place, perfect for couples. It doesn't have many tables, but the ones it does have are surrounded by candles and flowers."
—Tatiana Tavares

PUPPI BAGGIO

Rua Dinarte Ribeiro 155
Porto Alegre
Rio Grande do Sul 90570-000
Brazil
+55 5133463630
www.puppibaggio.com.br

Opening hours...Closed Monday
Credit cards...Accepted
Style of pizza...Italian
Recommended pizza...Bianca; Carbonara; Margherita

"Traditional Italian-style pizza prepared with tasty ingredients and a thin crust. It serves an amazing Carbonara pizza, with pancetta and eggs, that is really unusual and delicious."—Diego Fabris

SALVIA PIZZA
Rua Comendador Caminha 338
Porto Alegre
Rio Grande do Sul 90570-060
Brazil
+55 5132646001

Opening hours	Open 7 days
Credit cards	Accepted
Style of pizza	Traditional
Recommended pizza	Predilecta

"A very creative, traditional pizza chef who finds original ways to use ordinary ingredients."
—Sady Homrich

BASÍLICO
Rua Laurindo Januário da Silveira 647
Florianópolis
Santa Catarina 88062-200
Brazil
+55 4832321129
www.pizzariabasilico.com.br

Opening hours	Open 7 days
Credit cards	Accepted
Style of pizza	California
Recommended pizza	Basilica

FORNERIA CATARINA
Avenida Madre Benvenuta 1248
Florianópolis
Santa Catarina 88036-500
Brazil
+55 4832360633
www.forneriacatarina.com.br

Opening hours	Open 7 days
Credit cards	Accepted
Style of pizza	Thin-crust
Recommended pizza	Santa Monica; Trio de Cogumelos

"This pizzeria has a good family atmosphere and it's a great place to go in groups."—Renata Diem

FORNERIA CATARINA
Rua Esteves Junior 604
Florianópolis
Santa Catarina 88015-130
Brazil
+55 4833330707
www.forneriacatarina.com.br

Opening hours	Open 7 days
Credit cards	Accepted
Style of pizza	Thin-crust
Recommended pizza	Filomena

"The service is second to none due to the polite, well-trained, and attentive waiters. Pizzas are prepared in a wood-fired oven with thick crusts but thin bases, making them unique in the region. There is also a lactose-free menu for allergy sufferers, featuring delicious pizza prepared with lactose-free mozzarella and Pecorino Romano cheese."
—Priscila Prudêncio

LENHA E OLIVA
Rua Vera Linhares de Andrade 1870
Florianópolis
Santa Catarina 88037-395
Brazil
+55 4832063242
www.lenhaoliva.com.br

Opening hours	Open 7 days
Credit cards	Accepted
Style of pizza	California
Recommended pizza	Firenze

PIZZERIA ELBA D'ITALIA
Avenida Luiz Boiteux Piazza 3481
Florianópolis
Santa Catarina 88056-000
Brazil
+55 4833691901
www.pizzeriaelba.com.br

Opening hours	Closed Monday–Thursday
Credit cards	Accepted but not AMEX
Style of pizza	Thin-crust
Recommended pizza	Napoletana

"Pizzeria Elba d'Italia upholds traditional recipes and customs with individual, thin-crust pizzas prepared in a wood-fired oven. Its attention to detail includes cutlery wrapped in individual disposable pouches and delicious Herdade do Esporão olive oil on each table."—Priscila Prudêncio

PIZZERIA MILANO

Rua Bocaiúva 2226
Florianópolis
Santa Catarina 88015-530
Brazil
+55 4830240034
www.pizzeriamilano.com.br

Opening hours	Open 7 days
Credit cards	Accepted
Style of pizza	Thin-crust
Recommended pizza	Tartufina

"The Italian owner, Maria Grazia Fraschini, has perfected her technique to create unforgettable pizzas. I don't know if it's the organic ingredients she uses, the imported flour, the high-quality olive oil, or her own yeast....Perhaps the secret ingredient is just love."
—Priscila Prudêncio

VINIL PIZZAS E CLÁSSICOS

Rua Senador Ivo D'Aquino 51
Florianópolis
Santa Catarina 88062-050
Brazil
+55 4832323301

Opening hours	Open 7 days
Credit cards	Accepted
Style of pizza	Thin-crust
Recommended pizza	Leek and Cream Cheese

"This is a small, alternative place that is great for happy hour. It serves thin and crispy pizzas that you can eat with your hands, and it has a record player that anyone is free to play records on."—Renata Diem

"TRADITIONAL NEAPOLITAN-STYLE PIZZA MADE WITH THE FRESHEST INGREDIENTS AND ORIGINAL FLAVOR COMBINATIONS."
JUAREZ BECOZA P.533

"BRÁZ ALWAYS USES EXCEPTIONAL INGREDIENTS. I PARTICULARLY LIKE THE CALABRESA PIZZA, MAINLY BECAUSE OF THE QUALITY OF THE HANDMADE SAUSAGES USED." LUCIANA FRÓES P.532

RIO DE JANEIRO

"THIS IS NOT A PIZZERIA, IT IS, IN FACT, THE CITY'S OLDEST PASTRY SHOP, ESTABLISHED IN 1860 IN THE BELLE ÉPOQUE. ITS PIZZAS PLUNGE YOU INTO THE CITY'S HISTORY AND TAKE YOU BACK TO YOUR CHILDHOOD."
BERG SILVA P.533

"IT HAS A GREAT ATMOSPHERE AND IS LOCATED IN ONE OF THE MOST BOHEMIAN PARTS OF BOTAFOGO."
ERICK NAKO P.532

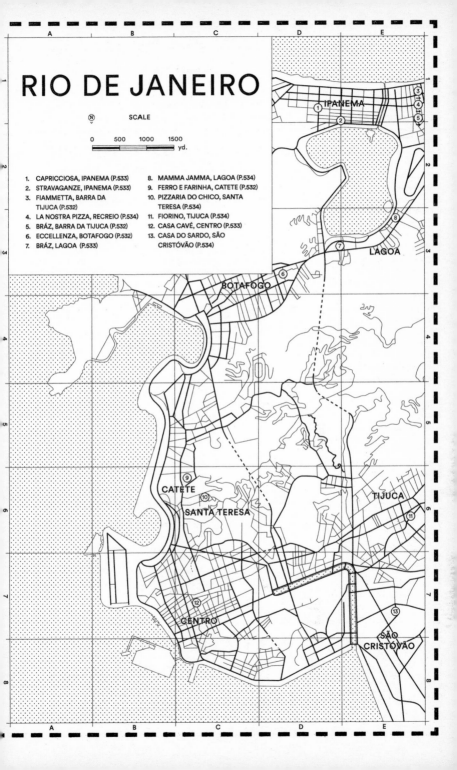

RIO DE JANEIRO

SCALE

0 500 1000 1500
yd.

1. CAPRICCIOSA, IPANEMA (P.533)
2. STRAVAGANZE, IPANEMA (P.533)
3. FIAMMETTA, BARRA DA TIJUCA (P.532)
4. LA NOSTRA PIZZA, RECREIO (P.534)
5. BRÁZ, BARRA DA TIJUCA (P.532)
6. ECCELLENZA, BOTAFOGO (P.532)
7. BRÁZ, LAGOA (P.533)
8. MAMMA JAMMA, LAGOA (P.534)
9. FERRO E FARINHA, CATETE (P.532)
10. PIZZARIA DO CHICO, SANTA TERESA (P.534)
11. FIORINO, TIJUCA (P.534)
12. CASA CAVÉ, CENTRO (P.533)
13. CASA DO SARDO, SÃO CRISTÓVÃO (P.534)

IPANEMA

LAGOA

BOTAFOGO

CATETE

SANTA TERESA

TIJUCA

CENTRO

SÃO CRISTÓVÃO

BRÁZ

Avenida Érico Veríssimo 46
Barra da Tijuca
Rio de Janeiro
Rio de Janeiro 22621-180
Brazil
+55 2124917170
www.brazpizzaria.com.br

Opening hours	Open 7 days
Credit cards	Accepted
Style of pizza	Neapolitan
Recommended pizza	Calabresa

"Bráz always uses exceptional ingredients. I particularly like the Calabresa pizza, mainly because of the quality of the handmade sausages used."—Luciana Fróes

FIAMMETTA

Rio Design Barra, Avenida das Américas 7777
Barra da Tijuca
Rio de Janeiro
Rio de Janeiro 22793-011
Brazil
+55 2124387500
www.fiammetta.com.br

Opening hours	Open 7 days
Credit cards	Accepted
Style of pizza	Thin-crust
Recommended pizza	Toscana

"Traditional thin and crispy pizza dough with creative and original toppings."—Berg Silva

ECCELLENZA

Rua Visconde de Caravelas 121
Botafogo
Rio de Janeiro
Rio de Janeiro 22271-030
Brazil
+55 2122665774
www.eccellenza.com.br

Opening hours	Open 7 days
Credit cards	Accepted
Style of pizza	Neapolitan-Brazilian thin-crust
Recommended pizza	Margherita di Capra; Calabrese Tradizionale

"Eccellenza's pizza bases are lovely and thin, with a creative array of toppings. Many of its recipes are created exclusively by well-known Brazilian chefs. It has several mozzarella-free pizza options (served with other types of cheese, such as feta and goat cheese), which I like a lot."—Juarez Becoza

"It has a great atmosphere and is located in one of the most bohemian parts of Botafogo."—Erick Nako

FERRO E FARINHA

Rua Andrade Pertence 42D
Catete
Rio de Janeiro
Rio de Janeiro 22220-010
Brazil

Opening hours	Closed Monday and Tuesday
Credit cards	Accepted
Style of pizza	Neapolitan
Recommended pizza	Margherita

"Despite the slightly sparse surroundings, Ferro e Farinha's pizzas are entirely faithful to Neapolitan tradition, with light but thick pizza crusts, not too much cheese, and very fresh ingredients. There are no frills, nothing is over the top. It's very basic, in fact, but the pizzas make up for it."—Erick Nako

CASA CAVÉ

Rua Sete de Setembro 133
Centro
Rio de Janeiro
Rio de Janeiro 20050-006
Brazil
+55 2122242520
www.casacave.com.br

Opening hours	Closed Sunday
Credit cards	Not accepted
Style of pizza	Portuguese deep-pan
Recommended pizza	Sardine

"This is not a pizzeria, it is, in fact, the city's oldest pastry shop, established in 1860 in the Belle Époque. Its pizzas plunge you into the city's history and take you back to your childhood."—Berg Silva

CAPRICCIOSA

Rua Vinícius de Moraes 134
Ipanema
Rio de Janeiro
Rio de Janeiro 22411-010
Brazil
+55 2125233394
www.capricciosa.com.br

Opening hours	Closed Sunday
Credit cards	Accepted
Style of pizza	Italian thin-crust
Recommended pizza	Marinara; Tomato and Basil

"Capricciosa has always maintained a consistently high Italian standard."—Salvatore Loi

STRAVAGANZE

Rua Maria Quitéria 132
Ipanema
Rio de Janeiro
Rio de Janeiro 22410-040
Brazil
+55 2125232391
www.stravaganze.com.br

Opening hours	Open 7 days
Credit cards	Accepted
Style of pizza	Neapolitan-Brazilian
Recommended pizza	Fratello; Itália; Maratea

"The ingredients are always light and carefully chosen—often imported. The pizzas do not rely on large quantities of mozzarella and the recipes are extremely creative and unusual. They often feature vegetables such as eggplant (aubergine) and zucchini (courgette)."—Juarez Becoza

"I like the creativity and flavor of the toppings, which are far from conventional. There are some very unusual combinations—they even created an octopus and banana pizza, which is no longer on the menu." —Guilherme Guimaraes Studart

BRÁZ

Rua Maria Angelica 129
Lagoa
Rio de Janeiro
Rio de Janeiro 22461-000
Brazil
+55 2125350687
www.brazpizzaria.com.br

Opening hours	Open 7 days
Credit cards	Accepted
Style of pizza	Neapolitan
Recommended pizza	Calabresa; Caprese; Maçarico

"Traditional Neapolitan-style pizza made with the freshest ingredients and original flavor combinations. The pizzeria has a canteen feel and is always cozy, festive, and very pleasant. The service is also excellent, which is unusual for a large restaurant in Rio de Janeiro."—Juarez Becoza

"This São Paulo pizzeria goes by the name of the city's main Italian neighborhood and makes the best pizza in town. Amazing antipasto and delicious sausage bread!"—Ricardo Amaral

Planted in the Jardim Botânico neighborhood this outpost of São Paulo's celebrated Bráz—its white tiles and dark woods evoking the old cantinas in the original Italian quarter of São Paulo, from which the name Bráz comes—is cherished for something not expected in a Rio pizzeria: obliging service. Waiters in white jackets glide from kitchen to table, presenting the charred, puffy-rimmed, wood-fired Margherita whole and then deftly serving it one slice at a time, somehow managing to keep its thick coat of liquified mozzarella from running off the sides. Though fanatical about the prized ingredients imported from Italy, no Brazilian pizzeria, not even Bráz, can resist such domestic classics as spicy Calabresa sausage and Catupiry, a creamy curd cheese as viscous as condensed milk. Both were developed in Brazil by Italian immigrants.

MAMMA JAMMA

Rua Saturnino de Brito 50
Lagoa
Rio de Janeiro
Rio de Janeiro 22470-030
Brazil
+55 2138751223
www.mammajamma.com.br

Opening hours	Open 7 days
Credit cards	Accepted
Style of pizza	Rustic
Recommended pizza	Mamma Jamma, Eggplant (aubergine) and Pesto

"This pizzeria calls on renowned chefs to create signature toppings. It also provides a wonderful selection of olive oils."—Luciana Fróes

"The pizzas are not entirely true to Italian tradition but they are perfect for Brazilian tastes, with plenty of toppings and cheese."—Erick Nako

LA NOSTRA PIZZA

Rua Almirante Ary Rongel 445
Recreio
Rio de Janeiro
Rio de Janeiro 22790-430
Brazil
+55 2132286783
www.lanostrapizza.com.br

Opening hours	Closed Monday
Credit cards	Accepted
Style of pizza	Thin-crust
Recommended pizza	Ktama

PIZZARIA DO CHICO

Rua Santa Cristina 21
Santa Teresa
Rio de Janeiro
Rio de Janeiro 22441-250
Brazil
+55 2125087180

Opening hours	Closed Sunday
Credit cards	Accepted
Style of pizza	Thin-crust
Recommended pizza	Pepperonata; Toscana

"Pizzaria Chico's simplicity and informality make it more of a bar that serves pizza than a pizzeria. There are no plates, only cutlery, and the pizzas are served and eaten off baking sheets. It's a small space with only a few tables and it is always packed. It's the best alternative pizza place in the city, in my opinion."
—Guilherme Guimaraes Studart

CASA DO SARDO

Rua São Cristóvão 405
São Cristóvão
Rio de Janeiro
Rio de Janeiro 20940-001
Brazil
+55 2125019848
www.restaurantecasadosardo.com.br

Opening hours	Open 7 days
Credit cards	Accepted
Style of pizza	Italian
Recommended pizza	Sardine

"These are pizzas made to traditional Italian standards, prioritizing the flavor of the dough. The fresh toppings transport you to Sardinia, where chef Silvio Phodda was born. He is both the owner and creator of the menu at this simple but wonderful restaurant."
—Berg Silva

FIORINO

Avenida Heitor Beltrão 126
Tijuca
Rio de Janeiro
Rio de Janeiro 20550-000
Brazil
+55 2125674476
www.ristorantefiorino.com.br

Opening hours	7 days
Credit cards	Not accepted
Style of pizza	Italian thin-crust
Recommended pizza	Margherita

"Fiorino is a member of the Italian Food Academy, based in Bologna, and it follows the typical culinary traditions of Emilia-Romagna. The pizza bases are light and topped with high-quality ingredients."
—Berg Silva

SÃO PAULO

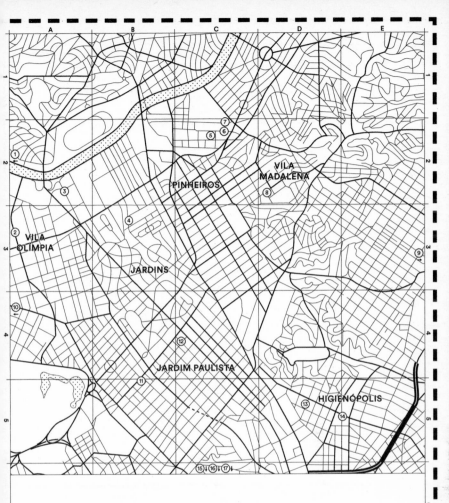

SÃO PAULO

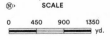 SCALE

| 0 | 450 | 900 | 1350 |

yd.

1. BRÁZ TRATTORIA, MORUMBI (P.539)
2. ROSSOPOMODORO, VILA
   OLÍMPIA (P.540)
3. CRISTAL PIZZA, JARDINS (P.539)
4. PRIMO BASÍLICO, JARDINS (P.539)
5. I VITELLONI, PINHEIROS (P.540)
6. BRÁZ, PINHEIROS (P.540)
7. FORQUILHA, PINHEIROS (P.540)

8. CARLOS PIZZA, VILA
   MADALENA (P.540)
9. LEGGERA PIZZA NAPOLETANA,
   PERDIZES (P.540)
10. BRÁZ, MOEMA (P.539)
11. CAMELO, JARDIM PAULISTA (P.538)
12. PIZZARIA MAREMONTI, JARDIM
    PAULISTA (P.539)

13. BRÁZ, HIGIENÓPOLIS (P.538)
14. JARDIM DE NAPOLI,
    HIGIENÓPOLIS (P.538)
15. SPERANZA 13 DE MAIO,
    BELA VISTA (P.538)
16. A PIZZA DA MOOCA, MOOCA (P.539)
17. CANTINA CASTELÕES PIZZARIA,
    BRÁS (P.538)

DIVINA INCRENCA FOOD TRUCK

Food truck—check Facebook for upcoming locations
São Paulo
Brazil
+55 11961655575

Opening hours	Closed Monday
Credit cards	Accepted
Style of pizza	Traditional
Recommended pizza	Dolce Diavolo

"The pizzas have a delicate, light, and soft crust, with thick rims and crispy bases. There is no fixed menu as the flavors change on a daily basis, but the combinations always feature high-quality ingredients. Being a food truck, Divina Increnca travels around the city but you can track its route on Facebook."
—Silvana Azevedo

SPERANZA 13 DE MAIO

Rua 13 de Maio 1004
Bela Vista
São Paulo
São Paulo 01327-000
Brazil
+55 1132888502
www.pizzaria.com.br

Opening hours	Open 7 days
Credit cards	Accepted
Style of pizza	Deep-pan
Recommended pizza	Margherita

"It makes a perfect Margherita with a light tomato sauce and a thick crust…delicious."
—Andre Lima de Luca

CANTINA CASTELÕES PIZZARIA

Rua Jairo Gois 126
Brás
São Paulo
São Paulo 03004-010
Brazil
+55 1132290542
www.casteloes.com.br

Opening hours	Open 7 days
Credit cards	Not accepted
Style of pizza	Rustic
Recommended pizza	Castelões

"This is the oldest pizzeria in São Paulo (supposedly opened in 1924) and one of the best in a city that loves pizza. It has a very traditional canteen feel that has changed very little over the years."
—Guilherme Guimaraes Studart

BRÁZ

Rua Sergipe 406
Higienópolis
São Paulo
São Paulo 01243-000
Brazil
+55 1132558090
www.brazpizzaria.com.br

Opening hours	Open 7 days
Credit cards	Accepted
Style of pizza	Neapolitan
Recommended pizza	Toscana

"I like the special ingredients that Bráz uses, such as wild boar sausage with rosemary, and its extensive use of vegetables."
—José Bonifácio de Oliveira Sobrino

JARDIM DE NAPOLI

Rua Martinico Prado 463
Higienópolis
São Paulo
São Paulo 01224-010
Brazil
+55 1136663022
www.jardimdenapoli.com.br

Opening hours	Open 7 days
Credit cards	Accepted
Style of pizza	Deep-pan
Recommended pizza	Garlic

"It has a traditional family atmosphere that captures the essence of trattorias around the world."
—Ricardo Amaral

CAMELO

Rua Pamplona 1873
Jardim Paulista
São Paulo
São Paulo 04543-010
Brazil
+55 1138878764
www.pizzariacamelo.com.br

Opening hours	Closed Sunday
Credit cards	Accepted
Style of pizza	Thin-crust
Recommended pizza	Siciliana

PIZZARIA MAREMONTI

Rua Padre Joao Manoel 1160
Jardim Paulista
São Paulo
São Paulo 01411-000
Brazil
+55 1130881160
www.maremonti.com.br

Opening hours	Open 7 days
Credit cards	Accepted
Style of pizza	Traditional
Recommended pizza	Riviera

"Cozy and rustic, this pizzeria uses top-quality ingredients and meticulous care to produce its pizzas."—Guilherme Guimaraes Studart

CRISTAL PIZZA

Rua Professor Arthur Ramos 551
Jardins
São Paulo
São Paulo 01454-011
Brazil
+55 1130310828
www.cristalpizza.com.br

Opening hours	Open 7 days
Credit cards	Accepted
Style of pizza	Thin-crust
Recommended pizza	Portuguesa

"Cristal was one of the first pizzerias in the world to produce thin-crust pizza and it has been going for 32 years. It's a stylish place."—Ricardo Amaral

PRIMO BASÍLICO

Alameda Gabriel Monteiro da Silva 1864
Jardins
São Paulo
São Paulo 01441-001
Brazil
+55 1130828027
www.primobasilico.com.br

Opening hours	Open 7 days
Credit cards	Accepted
Style of pizza	São Paulo
Recommended pizza	Basílica

"These pizzas are ideal for sharing and are delicious with a drizzle of good olive oil."—Erick Nako

BRÁZ

Rua Graúna 125
Moema
São Paulo
São Paulo 04514-000
Brazil
+55 1155611736
www.brazpizzaria.com.br

Opening hours	Open 7 days
Credit cards	Accepted
Style of pizza	Neapolitan
Recommended pizza	Anchovy

"I really like the thin pizza bases encircled in a thick but crispy crust."—Salvatore Loi

A PIZZA DA MOOCA

Rua Guaimbe 439
Mooca
São Paulo
São Paulo 03118-030
Brazil
+55 1126014653
www.apizzadamooca.com.br

Opening hours	Closed Monday
Credit cards	Accepted
Style of pizza	Wood-fired
Recommended pizza	Calabresa; Margherita

"The owner, Felipe, uses high-end ingredients and flour sprinkled with cheese. He is extremely talented and you always eat very well at A Pizza da Mooca."
—Andre Lima de Luca

BRÁZ TRATTORIA

Avenida Magalhães de Castro 12,000
Morumbi
São Paulo
São Paulo 05676-120
Brazil
+55 1131989435
www.braztrattoria.com.br

Opening hours	Open 7 days
Credit cards	Accepted
Style of pizza	Neapolitan
Recommended pizza	Castelões

LEGGERA PIZZA NAPOLETANA
Rua Diana 80
Perdizes
São Paulo
São Paulo 05019-000
Brazil
+55 1138622581
www.pizzerialeggera.com.br

Opening hours	Closed Sunday and Monday
Credit cards	Accepted
Style of pizza	Neapolitan
Recommended pizza	Margherita; Marinara

"André Guidón has previously been voted the best foreign pizza chef in the world. His pizzeria is one of the few certified by the VPN Association and it lives up to that standard. If you want to try real Neapolitan pizza, go to Leggera Pizza Napoletana."—Erick Nako

BRÁZ
Rua Vupabussu 271
Pinheiros
São Paulo
São Paulo 05429-040
Brazil
+55 1130377975
www.brazpizzaria.com.br

Opening hours	Open 7 days
Credit cards	Accepted
Style of pizza	Neapolitan
Recommended pizza	Carbonara

"Bráz is a very pleasant place and it serves great beer!"—Silvana Azevedo

FORQUILHA
Rua Vupabussu 347
Pinheiros
São Paulo
São Paulo 05429-040
Brazil
+55 1123717981
www.forquilhaforneria.com.br

Opening hours	Closed Monday
Credit cards	Accepted
Style of pizza	Rustic
Recommended pizza	Caprese

"The rectangular pizzas are light and very rustic, made with high-quality ingredients and plenty of toppings."—André Guidón

I VITELLONI
Rua Conde Silvio Álvares Penteado 31
Pinheiros
São Paulo
São Paulo 05427-020
Brazil
+55 1138163071
www.ivitellonipizzeria.com.br

Opening hours	Closed Monday
Credit cards	Accepted
Style of pizza	Traditional
Recommended pizza	Calabresa

CARLOS PIZZA
Rua Harmonia 501
Vila Madalena
São Paulo
São Paulo 05435-000
Brazil
+55 1138132017
www.carlospizza.com.br

Opening hours	Closed Monday
Credit cards	Accepted
Style of pizza	Thin-crust
Recommended pizza	Anchovy

ROSSOPOMODORO
Avenida Presidente Juscelino Kubitschek 1489
Vila Olimpia
São Paulo
São Paulo 04543-011
Brazil
+55 1132793300
www.eataly.com.br

Opening hours	Open 7 days
Credit cards	Accepted
Style of pizza	Neapolitan
Recommended pizza	Margherita STG

"It makes authentic Neapolitan-style pizzas—light and topped with high-quality ingredients."
—André Guidón

BRUNAPOLI

Avenida José Alcalde Délano 10.545, Local 1.062
Santiago
Metropolitana de Santiago 7691231
Chile
+56 232033468
www.brunapoli.cl

Opening hours..Open 7 days
Credit cards...Accepted
Style of pizza...Neapolitan
Recommended pizza.................Diavolo; Marinara; Raffaele

"Brunapoli creates great pizzas, which are in a class of their own thanks to the Italian tomato sauce and excellent dough—you could almost be in Naples. It also serves great rum babas for dessert."
—Araceli Paz

"This is one of the newest pizzerias in Santiago, but it is rapidly making a name for itself, thanks to its excellent Italian pizzas, made by a *pizzaiolo* from Naples."
—Consuelo Goeppinger

LA FABBRICA

Avenida Ossa 123
Santiago
Metropolitana de Santiago 7870151
Chile
+56 228306208

Opening hours..Open 7 days
Credit cards...Accepted
Style of pizza...Neapolitan
Recommended pizza...Estate; Regina

"The restaurant is situated in a tastefully renovated historic house, with *pizzaioli* working in an open kitchen and live jazz every night."—Jérôme Reynes

"Pizzas at Fabbrica are both rustic and refined, with well-risen dough baked in a convection oven imported from Verona."—Daniel Greve

LA FINESTRA

Irarrázabal 3465
Santiago
Metropolitana de Santiago 7760050
Chile
+56 222054502
www.lafinestra.cl

Opening hours...........................Closed Monday–Thursday
Credit cards...Accepted
Style of pizza...Neapolitan
Recommended pizza...Margherita

"La Finestra has a great, laid-back atmosphere and a lovely terrace. Its pasta dishes are also amazing."
—Araceli Paz

GREEN PIZZA

Avenida La Dehesa 3265, Local 1
Santiago
Metropolitana de Santiago 7700239
Chile
+56 222418248
www.greenpizza.cl

Opening hours..Closed Tuesday
Credit cards...Not accepted
Style of pizza...Neapolitan
Recommended pizza...Bufala

"Green Pizza honors the Neapolitan tradition, making its dough using Italian flour and leaving it to rest overnight, and it also has a refractory pizza oven. The mozzarella is Italian too, and it is served baked (melted), just how I like it, rather than cold."—Araceli Paz

OLIMPIA
Providencia 2033
Santiago
Metropolitana de Santiago 7510148
Chile
+56 222331330

Opening hours	Closed Sunday
Credit cards	Accepted
Style of pizza	Stone-baked
Recommended pizza	Palta

"I like the high-quality ingredients used in the pizzas, appetizers, and juices that are served here. The combinations of pizza toppings are interesting and incorporate popular elements of the local cuisine, such as *carne mechada* (shredded beef) and *ají en escabeche* (pickled green chiles)."—Carolina Carriel

RESTAURANT CAPPERI
Avenida Italia 1463
Santiago
Metropolitana de Santiago 7501464
Chile
+56 23419105
www.capperi.cl

Opening hours	Closed Monday
Credit cards	Accepted
Style of pizza	Chilean-Italian
Recommended pizza	Margherita

ROMAMOR
Antonio Varas 1362
Torre 1, Local 1, Corner of Bilbao
Santiago
Metropolitana de Santiago 7501042
Chile
+56 228953314
www.romamor.cl

Opening hours	Closed Sunday
Credit cards	Accepted
Style of pizza	Roman
Recommended pizza	Pear and Roquefort Cheese

"The best thing about Romanor is the counter serving pizza by the slice, where, for a great price, they offer over 15 different pizzas with toppings including shrimp (prawn), salmon, potato and rosemary, pear and blue cheese, anchovies, zucchini (courgette), and more. The pizzas are rustic, with crunchy 1-inch (2-cm) thick bases, and, of course, a lot of flavor. Excellent value for money."—Consuelo Goeppinger

SIGNORE
Avenida Vitacura 2615
Santiago
Metropolitana de Santiago 7550191
Chile
+56 227176985
www.signore.cl

Opening hours	Open 7 days
Credit cards	Accepted
Style of pizza	Thin and crispy
Recommended pizza	Farellones; Magallánica; Signore

"The dough is handmade using Italian flour, with each ball individually kneaded and cold-fermented for 48 hours, making this the best crust around. When combined with the finest Italian ingredients and fresh Chilean produce, the result is a high-quality, light, and tasty pizza. This is the best pizza in Chile according to food critics and the local Italian community."
—Francisco Carreño

"The pizzas are made by one of Chile's best Italian *pizzaioli*—Renato Baccin."—Consuelo Goeppinger

TAN TANO
Avenida Tobalaba 2055
Santiago
Metropolitana de Santiago 7510708
Chile
+56 229847078
www.tantano.com

Opening hours	Open 7 days
Credit cards	Accepted
Style of pizza	Italian-Genovese
Recommended pizza	Artichoke and Olive

"A deep, spongy pizza that turns into a sandwich if folded in half. Very tasty and special for Chile, it is made using olive oil and fresh toppings."
—Francisco Carreño

WALLO'S PIZZA

Calle Simón Bolívar 3761
Santiago
Metropolitana de Santiago 7790575
Chile
+56 222230393
www.wallospizza.cl

Opening hours..Closed Monday
Credit cards...Accepted
Style of pizza...Brazilian
Recommended pizza...Ají verde

"Wallo's Pizza is one of my favorite pizzerias. It has
over 50 varieties of savory pizza, as well as sweet
pizzas to finish. The bases are very tasty and there
is the option of a cream-cheese-stuffed crust, which
never hurts."—Carolina Carriel

PIZZERÍA MALANDRINO

Calle Almirante Montt 532
Cerro Alegre
Valparaíso
Valparaíso 2340000
Chile
+56 323184827
www.malandrino.cl

Opening hours........................Closed Monday and Tuesday
Credit cards...Accepted
Style of pizza...Thin-crust
Recommended pizza...Margherita

"This little pizzeria is considered by many to be one
of the best in Valparaíso. Located in a renovated
1920s mansion, pizzas are cooked in a wood-fired
clay oven built by owner Paolo Caorsi. They are tasty
and uncompromising, with a thin and crispy base and
excellent raw materials, including many organic
ingredients. The restaurant itself is cute and welcoming."
—Consuelo Goeppinger

EL MUNDO DE LA PIZZA

Dorrego 55
Bahía Blanca
Buenos Aires 8000
Argentina
+54 2914500050
www.elmundodelapizza.com.ar

Opening hours...Open 7 days
Credit cards...Accepted
Style of pizza...Argentinian
Recommended pizza...........................Arugula (rocket)

PIZZERIA ITALIA

Juan Antonio Lavalleja 1388
Córdoba
Córdoba 5008
Argentina
+54 3514710606
www.pizzaitaliaweb.com.ar

Opening hours...Open 7 days
Credit cards...Accepted
Style of pizza...Medium-crust
Recommended pizza...................Arugula (rocket) and Ham;
Puttanesca; Special

DI SOLITO

Santa Rosa 826
Córdoba
Córdoba 5000
Argentina
+54 3514254321

Opening hours...Closed Sunday
Credit cards...Not accepted
Style of pizza.......................Italian-Argentinian stone-baked
Recommended pizza...........Artichoke Heart; Blue Cheese,
Pear, and Brown Sugar; Capricciosa; Pink Salmon
and Mozzarella

"Some of the unusual toppings are really special."
—Andrés Javier Chaijale

QUATTRO STAGIONI

Avenida San Martín 8075
Chacras de Coria
Mendoza 5505
Argentina
+54 2614364246

Opening hours	Open 7 days
Credit cards	Not accepted
Style of pizza	Italian-Argentinian stone-baked
Recommended pizza	Vegetarian

DOPPIO ZERO

Tucumán 1281
Rosario
Santa Fe 2000
Argentina
+54 3414240236
www.doppio-zero.com

Opening hours	Open 7 days
Credit cards	Accepted
Style of pizza	Stone-baked
Recommended pizza	Margherita

SANTA MARIA

Corner of Avenida San Martin and Garay 970
Rosario
Santa Fe 2000
Argentina
+54 3414815044
www.pizzeria-santamaria.com.ar

Opening hours	Closed Monday
Credit cards	Not accepted
Style of pizza	Argentinian thick-crust
Recommended pizza	Clásica Especial

> **"PIZZAS ARE COOKED ON AN ARGENTINIAN GRILL, WHICH GIVES THEM A SMOKY FLAVOR."**
> MAURIZIO DeROSA P.548

> **"GÜERRIN IS FAMOUS THROUGHOUT BUENOS AIRES."**
> FABIAN COUTO P.551

BUENOS AIRES

> **"THERE ARE JUST TWO PLACES TO TRY *FAINÁ* (CHICKPEA FLATBREAD) IN ARGENTINA, AND THE NUMBER ONE BEST *FAINÁ* IS FOUND IN EL FORTÍN."** JOSÉ ANTONIO CARROZZI P.548

> **"LA ESQUINA HAS A GOOD OVEN AND THE THICK-CRUST PIZZA IS DELICIOUS AND CRISP."**
> LEANDRO CAFFARENA P.548

> **"THIS IS NEAPOLITAN PIZZA MADE BY THE RULES. PARTÉNOPE USES EXCELLENT INGREDIENTS AND TOPPINGS ARE NEVER EXCESSIVE."**
> RAQUEL ROSEMBERG P.549

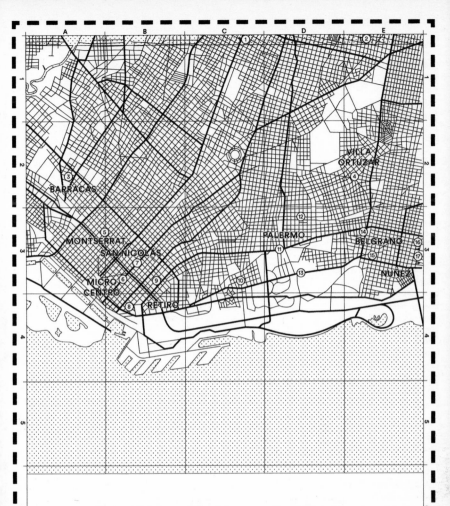

BUENOS AIRES

SCALE

0   500   1000   1500

yd.

1. LA POSTA DE ACHAVAL,
    CABALLITO (P.548)
2. EL FORTÍN, MONTE CASTRO (P.548)
3. LA ESQUINA, BARRACAS (P.548)
4. LA MEZZETTA, VILLA ORTÚZAR (P.551)
5. EL MAZACOTE, MONTSERRAT (P.549)
6. EL PALACIO DE LA PIZZA, MICRO
    CENTRO (P.548)
7. GÜERRIN, SAN NICOLÁS (P.551)

8. FILO, RETIRO (P.551)
9. EL CUARTITO, RETIRO (P.550)
10. LA STAMPA, PALERMO (P.549)
11. KENTUCKY, PALERMO
    VIEJO (P.550)
12. SIAMO NEL FORNO, PALERMO
    VIEJO (P.550)
13. PARTÉNOPE, PALERMO (P.549)
14. DELIVERY URBANO, BELGRANO (P.548)

15. LA MAS QUERIDA, BELGRANO (P.548)
16. LA GUITARRITA, NUÑEZ (P.549)
17. ASTRAL PIZZERIA, MUNRO (P.549)

LA ESQUINA

Dr Enrique Finochietto 1701
Barracas
Buenos Aires
Ciudad de Buenos Aires 1275
Argentina
+54 1143045560

Opening hours	Open 7 days
Credit cards	Not accepted
Style of pizza	Argentinian thick-crust
Recommended pizza	Napolitana

"La Esquina has a good oven and the thick-crust pizza is delicious and crisp."—Leandro Caffarena

DELIVERY URBANO

Virrey del Pino 2328
Belgrano
Buenos Aires
Ciudad de Buenos Aires 1426
Argentina
+54 1147800020

Opening hours	Closed Monday
Credit cards	Accepted
Style of pizza	Artisan
Recommended pizza	Burrata

"The dough is fermented very slowly, for up to a week, giving results that are both flavorsome and light."—Maurizio DeRosa

LA MAS QUERIDA

Echeverría 1618
Belgrano
Buenos Aires
Ciudad de Buenos Aires 1428
Argentina
+54 1147881455

Opening hours	Closed Monday
Credit cards	Not accepted
Style of pizza	Grilled
Recommended pizza	Arugula (rocket) and Pancetta

"Pizzas are cooked on an Argentinian grill, which gives them a smoky flavor."—Maurizio DeRosa

LA POSTA DE ACHAVAL

Avenida Directorio 1497
Caballito
Buenos Aires
Ciudad de Buenos Aires 1406
Argentina
+54 1144320170

Opening hours	Closed Sunday
Credit cards	Not accepted
Style of pizza	Classic

EL PALACIO DE LA PIZZA

Avenida Corrientes 751
Micro Centro
Buenos Aires
Ciudad de Buenos Aires 1108
Argentina
+54 1143229762

Opening hours	Closed Sunday
Credit cards	Not accepted
Style of pizza	Argentinian
Recommended pizza	Fugazetta; Muzzarella

"El Palacio de la Pizza scores top marks for the two most popular pizza styles in present-day Argentina—Muzzarella pizza and Fugazzeta."
—José Antonio Carrozzi

EL FORTÍN

Avenida Alvarez Jonte 5299
Monte Castro
Buenos Aires
Ciudad de Buenos Aires 1407
Argentina
+54 1145668279

Opening hours	Open 7 days
Credit cards	Not accepted
Style of pizza	Argentinian
Recommended pizza	Fainá; Mozzarella

"When you feel the urge to satiate your desire for Argentinian pizza, your heart will skip a beat at the sight of this street-corner spot in the Monte Castro neighborhood. The dough is a marvel: thick, light, yet satisfying, its undercarriage always crisp. Also, there are just two places to try *fainá* (chickpea flatbread) in Argentina, and the number one best *fainá* is found in El Fortín."—José Antonio Carrozzi

EL MAZACOTE

Calle Chile 1400
Montserrat
Buenos Aires
Ciudad de Buenos Aires 1098
Argentina
+54 1143814649

Opening hours..........................Closed Sunday and Monday
Credit cards..Not accepted
Style of pizza..Classic

ASTRAL PIZZERIA

Velez Sarsfield 4646
Munro
Buenos Aires
Ciudad de Buenos Aires 1605
Argentina
+54 1147625910

Opening hours...Open 7 days
Credit cards..Not accepted
Style of pizza..Argentinian
Recommended pizza..........Fugazetta; Mozzarella; Spinach

"Pizzas are served alongside other traditional
working-class dishes. As Munro locals always say,
'In Astral, it's all good.'"—José Antonio Carrozzi

LA GUITARRITA

Calle Cuba 3300
Nuñez
Buenos Aires
Ciudad de Buenos Aires 1429
Argentina
+54 1147040756
www.laguitarrita.com.ar

Opening hours...Open 7 days
Credit cards..Accepted
Style of pizza..Classic

PARTÉNOPE

Avenida del Libertador 4004
Palermo
Buenos Aires
Ciudad de Buenos Aires 1636
Argentina
+54 1147991050
www.partenopepizza.com

Opening hours...Open 7 days
Credit cards..Accepted
Style of pizza...Neapolitan
Recommended pizza.........................Marinara; Mastunicola;
Puttanesca

"The pizza here is so perfect, golden, and light, that
it's easy to eat the whole thing. The dough is handmade and hand-stretched, the result being just a little
smaller than a standard large pizza. The underside
has a very slight crunch, and the crust provides a
delicious conclusion to each slice."—Fabian Couto

"This is Neapolitan pizza made by the rules.
Parténope uses excellent ingredients and toppings
are never excessive."—Raquel Rosemberg

LA STAMPA

Jerónimo Salguero 2741
Palermo
Buenos Aires
Ciudad de Buenos Aires 1426
Argentina
+54 1148011711
www.lastamparistorante.com

Opening hours...Open 7 days
Credit cards..Accepted
Style of pizza..Italian
Recommended pizza..Onion

KENTUCKY

Santa Fe 4602
Palermo Viejo
Buenos Aires
Ciudad de Buenos Aires 1425
Argentina
+54 1147737869
www.pizzeriaskentucky.com

Opening hours	Open 7 days
Credit cards	Accepted
Style of pizza	Argentinian
Recommended pizza	Fugazzeta

"You'll never need to order double cheese in this
pizzeria—its generous servings of homemade
mozzarella will satisfy any dairy lover."
—Carolina Carriel

SIAMO NEL FORNO

Costa Rica 5886
Palermo Viejo
Buenos Aires
Ciudad de Buenos Aires 1414
Argentina
+55 1147750337

Opening hours	Closed Monday
Credit cards	Accepted
Style of pizza	Neapolitan
Recommended pizza	Bianco e Rosso; Margherita; Potato; Spinach

"The wood-fired oven was shipped over from Italy,
and can reach extremely high temperatures,
cooking pizzas almost instantly, in just one and
a half minutes. This means that both the base and
the crust take on an incredible flavor."
—Fabian Couto

"Siamo Nel Forno is one of the few places in the
city that makes true Neapolitan pizza, certified for
authenticity. Regardless of cost, it only uses the best
ingredients, and owner Nestor Gattorna pays the
utmost attention to every detail. I could eat several of
these pizzas, one is not enough."—Raquel Rosemberg

If there was one great pizza capital that could defy the true-
Neapolitan revolution it had to be Buenos Aires. Porteños
believe Argentinian pizza is second to none. But now their
conviction gets a severe test from Nestor Gattorna, a renegade
who took off to Naples for a year, studied pizza, and then
returned to open Siamo Nel Forno. His place is the first in
Argentina to win certification from the arbiters of authenticity
at the VPN Association. The exceptionally soft, steaming,

light-as-air Margherita passes a stricter test than theirs: it's won
the approval of even chauvinistic Argentines, possibly because
it's so different to what they're used to and yet familiar, too.
The Patate pizza, with new potatoes, Pecorino cheese, black
pepper, and sea salt, possesses the simple elegance of the
pizzeria itself.

EL CUARTITO

Talcahuano 937
Retiro
Buenos Aires
Ciudad de Buenos Aires 1013
Argentina
+54 1148161758

Opening hours	Open 7 days
Credit cards	Not accepted
Style of pizza	Buenos Aires
Recommended pizza	Fugazzeta

"El Cuartito is popular with locals, who have now
been joined by tourists, so you have to be patient.
It's always busy, but is well worth the wait."
—Raquel Rosemberg

"Pizza that demands to be sliced and eaten quickly.
Deep-pan with toppings that are simple and
unpretentious, just like the restaurant. Delicious
and crowd-pleasing."—Juarez Becoza

The old wood chairs at El Cuartito feel snug when you sit down
and only get smaller as the minutes pass. Or maybe it seems
so on account of the *pizza al molde*, the deep-dish pizza of
Argentina. Laden with weighty toppings and baked in a cast-
iron pan each beauty comes out spongy, chewy, saucy, cheesy,
and altogether too much of an irresistible thing. The Fugazzeta
is a stuffed pizza with dreamy white cheese oozing from its
pores. Every inch of wall space in the noisy, always bustling El
Cuartito is covered with photos of Argentine soccer heroes and
movie memorabilia. There may be less touristy places in Buenos
Aires to go for pizza and beer than this enduring 1934 classic
but no one here is giving up their seat.

FILO

San Martín 975
Retiro
Buenos Aires
Ciudad de Buenos Aires 1004
Argentina
+54 1143110312
www.filo-ristorante.com

Opening hours	Open 7 days
Credit cards	Accepted
Style of pizza	Classic
Recommended pizza	Margherita

"Filo serves authentic Italian-style pizza. As the years have gone by, the high quality of the dishes and ingredients has always remained."
—Daniel López Roca

GÜERRIN

Avenida Corrientes 1368
San Nicolás
Buenos Aires
Ciudad de Buenos Aires 1043
Argentina
+54 1143718141
www.pizzeriaguerrin.com

Opening hours	Open 7 days
Credit cards	Not accepted
Style of pizza	Argentinian
Recommended pizza	Fainá; Mixta; Mozzarella

"Güerrin is famous throughout Buenos Aires. Mention Güerrin and what comes to mind is one of the best wood-fired deep-dish pizzas around. My advice is to find a space at one of the counters and sample the various different specialties fresh from the oven."
—Fabian Couto

"Güerrin is one of the most successful pizzerias in Buenos Aires, and rightly so. It works hard by day, and is packed to the rafters every evening."
—José Antonio Carrozzi

LA MEZZETTA

Avenida Álvarez Thomas 1321
Villa Ortúzar
Buenos Aires
Ciudad de Buenos Aires 1427
Argentina
+54 1145547585

Opening hours	Closed on Monday
Credit cards	Not accepted
Style of pizza	Buenos Aires
Recommended pizza	Fugazzeta

"A great example of the hybrid Buenos Aires pizza culture, where Neapolitan and Genoan styles have come together in a single pie."—Maurizio DeRosa

"This traditional pizza spot has stood the test of time. Customers eat standing up, and it's a favorite with workers, taxi drivers, and young people."
—Pablo Giudice

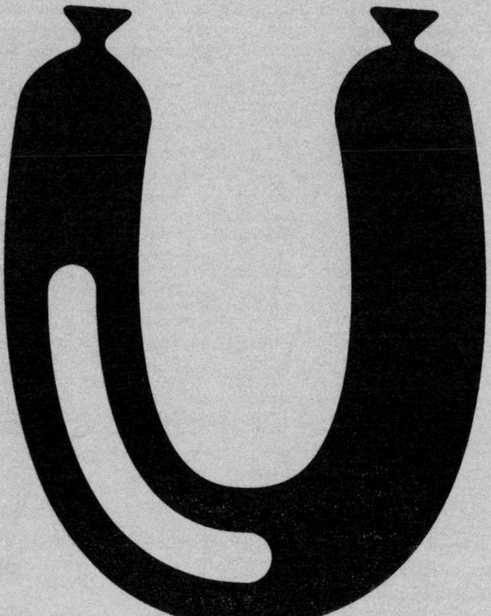

A VISIT TO CASTELÕES

To eat at Castelões is to visit a São Paulo that now lives in black-and-white photos. A time when warehouses sat alongside homes and cars didn't clog the streets—horses and trams were responsible for the chaos. A city where every corner hid gastronomic specialties produced by the hands of immigrants who came from Italy, Japan, Lebanon, Portugal, and Germany, fleeing from misery and war to find in Brazil a welcoming place.

To eat in São Paulo's oldest pizzeria, founded in 1924, is to travel to the origins of "São Paulo pizza," a mix of influences from Rome and Naples, sprinkled with Brazilian generosity. Served in a large size, to be shared by up to four people, this pizza has puffed and lightly toasted edges, elastic dough, and often incorporates Brazilian ingredients—such as Catupiry cheese, pulled chicken, and corn—in its topping, along with toppings as Italian as Italy itself—basil, burrata, salami. It's this fusion that encapsulates the city.

São Paulo is so deeply Italian that of its twelve million people, six million are of Italian descent and were born here or are at least third-generation descendants*. The 4,500 pizzerias in this metropolis produce one million pizzas a day, almost 700 per minute. We are more familiar with bruschetta, basil, and *maiale* than *jambu*, *umbu*, or *tucupi*, ingredients from the Brazilian Amazon region. And, yes, we "talk" with our hands. We wave them in the air to get the waiter's attention over the buzz of conversation and sound of noisy families' cutlery, a typical scene at pizzerias and canteens.

The old pizzeria is no longer "fashionable," does not appear in trendy guides, and is now away from the busiest axis of restaurants and bars. It ended up squeezed in a dilapidated, dark (and a bit scary in silent nights) corner of town. But it's still there, with its green and red neon lights, framed sun-bleached pictures of dishes, food cans and wine bottles stacked on dusty shelves.

Castelões continues entertaining its many loyal customers with the lasting empathy of the waiters who have been working there for 30, 35 years. It continues selling the pizza variety that bears its name and was created decades ago—tomato sauce, mozzarella, thin-sliced Calabresa sausage, and oregano. It is loved by *"paulistanos"* and is considered a city treasure.

Today, Castelões serves not only pizza, but nostalgia.

AILIN ALEIXO
* Data: São Paulo State Government

THE CONTRIBUTORS

ARGENTINA
Leandro Caffarena, José Antonio Carrozzi, Andrés Javier Chaijale, Fabian Couto, Maurizio DeRosa, Antonello Grandolfo, Dante Liporace, Daniel López Roca, Guillermo Megna, Raquel Rosemberg, Pietro Sorba.

AUSTRALIA
Marco Balestrini, Max Brearley, Sophie Budd, Lara Caraturo, Flavio Carnevale, Michael Dalton, Orazio d'Elia, Ben Devlin, Johnny Di Francesco, Pete Dillon, Fiona Donnelly, Larissa Dubecki, Liz Egan, Tristram Fini, Sharlee Gibb, Veda Gilbert, Jocelyn Hancock, Darren Haunold, Theo Kalogeracos, Cordell Khoury, Morag Kobez, Ingrid Langtry, Andrew Levins, Catherine Natale, Pat Nourse, Elizabeth Rodriguez, Cav. Alessandro Sorbello, Dan Stock, Nic Trimboli, Dani Valent, Gail Williams, Nino Zoccali.

AUSTRIA
Severin Corti, Antonino Crupi, Alessandro d'Ambrosio, Georges Desrues, Konstantin Filippou, Roberto Pavlovic-Hariwijadi, Joseph Weghaupt.

BELGIUM
Boris Beaucarne, Stéphanie Candidoflore, Laura Centrella, Massimo Cinquina, Jehan Delbruyère, Nicola de Simone, Philippe Genion, Kim Rothuys, René Sépul.

BRAZIL
Ailin Aleixo, Ricardo Amaral, Silvana Azevedo, Juarez Becoza, Rodrigo Caetano, Ricardo Castanho, Maria Maranhão Chaves, Dudu Cunha, Liége Xavier da Cruz, Maria Raquel Matos de Carvalho, Andre Lima de Luca, José Bonifácio de Oliveira Sobrino, Renata Diem, Rafaela Enes, Diego Fabris, Maíra Ferraz, Luciana Fróes, André Guidón, Sady Homrich, Alberto La Bella, Alexandre Lalas, Pedro Landim, Salvatore Loi, Sebastián Luis, Moacyr Luz, Antonello Monardo, Erick Nako, Parasole, Ville Della Penna, Per Paolo Picchi, Priscila Prudêncio, Ana Rosa, Berg Silva, Guilherme Guimaraes Studart, Marcos Tardin, Tatiana Tavares, Rosario Tessier.

CANADA
Rocco Agostino, Wanda Baker, Robert Belcham, Riccardo Michele Bertolino, Stéphanie Bois-Houde, Mark Busse, Jonathan Chovancek, Dan Clapson, Andrew Coppolino, Massimo Covone, Suresh Doss, Rossy Earle, Liane Faulder, Jason Finestone, Jeffrey Finkelstein, John Gilchrist, Ian Harrison, Neil Ingram, Liora Ipsum, James Iranzad, Frank Kocis, Blair Lebsack, Paolo Macchi, Roberto Manderino, Shahir Massoud, Bill McCaig, Gildas Meneu, Dom Morra, Diana Ng, Josh Pape, John Placko, J-C Poirier, Kathy Richardier, Joel Solish, Teresa Spinelli, Jean-Philippe Tastet.

CHILE
Francisco Carreño, Carolina Carriel, Darío Córdova, Isidora Díaz, Consuelo Goeppinger, Daniel Greve, Araceli Paz, Jérôme Reynes.

CHINA
Jamie Barys, Marino D'Antonio, Jenny Gao, Camden Hauge, Austin Hu, Cat Nelson, Iain Shaw.

CROATIA
Darko Baretić, Dragica Domjanić, Časlav Matijević, Loreena Meda, Silvija Munda, Zlatko Sedlanić, Saša Špiranec, Tomislav Stiplošek, Morana Zibar.

CZECH REPUBLIC
Antonio Barba, Andrea Crippa, Fiona Gaze, Martin Kuciel, Radek Pecko, Taste of Prague.

DENMARK
Jonas Astrup, Katherine Bont, Nana Hagel, Ditte Ingemann, Claus Meyer, Rebecca Thandi Norman, Christian Puglisi.

FINLAND
Tony Ilmoni, Arto Koskelo, Antto Melasniemi, Kenneth Nars, Mariaana Nelimarkka, Alex Nieminen, Luca Platania, Sikke Sumari, Mikko Takala, Saku Tuominen.

FRANCE

Isabelle Battarel, Florence Bianchi, Michel Blanc, Jon Chiri, Romain Clavel-Millo, Mauro Colagreco, Stephen Cronk, Myriam Darmoni, Priscilla Davigny, Vincent Delmas, Kristin Espinasse, Stephanie Fray, Julie Gerbet, Kevin Hin, David Lanher, Alexander Lobrano, Daniel Luperini, Julie Mautner, Alexandre Mazzia, Tina Meyer, Colette Monsat, Stefano Palombari, Estérelle Payany, Lisa Pepin, Emmanuel Perrodin, Alba Pezone, Alessandra Pierini, Pierre Psaltis, Gilles Pudlowski, Clotilde Roux, Julia Sammut, Gaël Tourteaux, Mickaël Tourteaux, Ludovic Turac, Elodie Van Zele, Georgiana Viou, Ken Wallace, Ezéchiel Zérah.

GERMANY

Giuseppe Abbate, Niklas Bichinger, Michaela Bogner, Torben Bonhöft, Sebastian Bordthäuser, Cathrin Brandes, Joe Diliberto, Beatrix Eichbaum, Claudia Eilers, Koral Elci, Malin Elmlid, Sebastian Enste, Wolfgang Fassbender, Rabea Ganz, Sebastian Georgi, Hans Gerlach, Barbara Goerlich, Torsten Goffin, Sylee Gore, Kerstin Greiner, Hans-Jürgen Hartauer, Stefan Hettinger, Monika Johannes, Bernd Labetzsch, Andrea Laquinta, Jossi Loibl, Christian Mook, Herwig Niggemann, Antonio Pasqualino, Hans Petersen, Marco Richter, Vijay Sapre, Marius Schöttler, Alfredo Sironi, Tommy Tannock, Andrea Thode, Luisa Weiss, Gisela Williams, Fritz Zickuhr.

GREECE

Denny Kallivoka, Eleonora Kanaki, Dimitris Koparanis, Nasos Kouzelis, Angeliki Sapika, Angela Stamatiadou, Kiki Trintafilli, Thaleia Tsixlaki, Fotis Valatos.

HONG KONG

Rachel Balota, Wilson Fok, Janice Leung Hayes, Dario Mulino, Michelle Ng, Rachel Read, Gary Suen.

INDIA

Saransh Goila, Suresh Hinduja, Nandita Iyer, Purva Mehra, Nikhil Merchant, Vicky Ratnani, Roshini Bajaj Sanghvi, Shilarna Vaze.

IRELAND

Joanne Cronin, Tom Doorley, Niall Harbison, Gillian Nelis.

ISRAEL

Nomi Abeliovich, Barak Aharoni, Shir Halpern, Gil Hovav, Nurit Kariv, Mena Strum, Ofer Vardi.

ITALY

Daniela Acquadro, Giuseppe Aldè, Matteo Aloe, Marco Andreani, Michele Armano, Lucia Bailetti, Paolo Baldelli, Cristina Barbera, Marilena Barbera, Giuseppe Barone, Maria Luisa Basile, Heinz Beck, Christopher Behr, Antonio Benanti, Roberto Bentivegna, Sabino Berardino, Francesco Biasi, Michele Bocci, Enrico Bonardo, Gabriele Bonci, Orlando Bortolami, Renato Bosco, Fabio Bottonelli, Nicola Bove, Cristina Bowerman, Anna Marlena Buscemi, Federica Caccamo, Giuseppe Calabrese, Stefano Callegari, Cinzia Canzian, Lydia Capasso, Carlo Lodovico Cappelletti, Luana Caprino, Valerio Capriotti, Giuseppe Carrus, Martina Caruso, Miriam Caruso, Giustino Catalano, Stefano Cavallito, Bianca Celano, Carmelita Cianci, Leonardo Ciomei, Alfredo Cocchiarella, Enzo Coccia, Marco Colognese, Angelo Concas, Marzio Contessa, Giuseppe Cordioli, Maurizio Cortese, Jacopo Cossater, Luigi Costa, Maria Costanzo, Massimo D'Alma, Arcangelo Dandini, Vincenzo D'Antonio, Ivan De Chiara, Gea De Leonardis, Alessandro Dettori, Giovanni Maria Dettori, Giuseppe Di Martino, Enrico Di Roberti, Concetta Donato, Eliodoro D'Orazio, Fabio D'Uffizi, Rosamaria Esposito, Tommaso Esposito, Giovanni Elce Fabbretti, Maureen B. Fant, Elena Farinelli, Daniele Fava, Lorenzo Ferrari, Anna Ferretti, Annalucia Festa, Aldo Fiordelli, Fabio Fiorillo,

Ettore Franca, Sylvie Franceschini, Luciano Furia, Alessia Gallian, Marco Gallina, Fabrizio Gallino, Laura Gambacorta, Gianpaolo Giacobbo, Danilo Giaffreda, Sonia Gioia, Yves Grange, Catia Gressani, Salvo Gurrieri, Luca Iaccarino, Stefano Degli Innocenti, Michela Iorio, Michele Italiani, Manuela Laiacona, Marco Locatelli, Antonio Lucisano, Tommaso Luongo, Marco Paolo Mangiamele, Emidio Mansi, Domenico Maraglino, Elis Marchetti, Daniela Marfisa, Francesco Martino, Angelo Massaro, Anna Laura Mattesini, Raffaello Maugeri, Paola Mencarelli, Elisia Menduni, Antonella Millarte, Clara Minissale, Federico Molinari, Graziano Monogrammi, Cristina Mosca, Francesca Negri, Simone Nicòtina, Vincenzo Pagano, Luisa Pandolfi, Katie Parla, Paolo Pellegrini, Francesco Pensovecchio, Bruno Petronilli, Roberto Petza, Karen Phillips, Stefania Pianigiani, Massimo Pierini, Loredana Pietroniro, Luciano Pilotto, Oliver Piras, Monica Piscitelli, Pierluigi Portinari, Giampiero Prozzo, Francesco Quercetti, Marco Ramassotto, Martin Rance, Laura Rangoni, Alessandro Reale, John Regefalk, Alessandro Ricci, Patrick Ricci, Davide Ricciardiello, Alberto Rinieri, Leonardo Romanelli, Maria Romano, Mattia Romano, Alessandro Roscioli, Pier Luigi Roscioli, Giuseppe Russo, Margareth Russo, Ciro Salvo, Francesco Salvo, Luigi Salvo, Salvatore Salvo, Giovanni Santarpia, Rocco Saracino, Barbara Scabin, Pave' Luca Scanni, Davide Scapin, Valentina Scotti, Donatella Bernabò Silurata, Francesca Singer, Pietro Singer, Dora Sorrentino, Andrea Sponzilli, Luciana Squadrilli, Paola Sucato, Giovanni Tesauro, Manuel Terzi, Alessandra Tinozzi, Marco Tonelli, Giuseppe Toso, Gianfranco Truglio, Giampiero Valente, Maurizio Valeriani, Federico Valicenti, Valerio Valle, Sofie Wochner, Luca Leone Zampa, Stefania Zolotti.

JAPAN
Sachi Akimoto, Rossella Ceccarini, Luca Fantin, Nao Fukumura, Yumiko Inukai, Ohata Katsutoshi, Michael Kleindl, Tsuguo Konishi, Chikara Kubota, Masayuki Minezaki, Taijiro Mori, Hirofumi Jaffa Morita, Kiyoshi Ciccio Nakamura, Takanori Nakamura, Hitomi Nakano, Akio Nishikawa, Yuri Nomura, Takeshi Ozawa, Yukari Sakamoto, Michiaki Sasamori, Robbie Swinnerton, Ivo Virgilio, Hisanori Yamamoto.

KUWAIT
Alia Al Ramli, Zeyad Alobaid, Amr Alrefai, Noor, Sarah Wali.

LEBANON
Badeeh Abla, Sotiris Ananiadis, Danielle Issa, Bethany Kehdy, Najib Mitri, Anthony Rahayel, Nadim Safieddine.

LUXEMBOURG
Gianfranco Aiello, Roberto Beltramini, Carlotta Benedetti, Giovanni Farinella, Francesco Malvezzi, Ernesto Prosperi, Isabella Sardo, Carlo Sauber.

MEXICO
Sasha Correa, Daniel Ovadía, Alonso Rubalcaba, Judith Servín.

THE NETHERLANDS
Gessica Bordini, Gianni Bordini, Miriam Bunnik, Marjan Ippel, Claudia Krijger, Deborah Mullin, Maurice Pilet, Mick Sonnenfeld, Paul van den Hooven, Jannet van der Ree, Marco Zander.

NEW ZEALAND
Leonardo Bresolin, Jacob Brown, David Burton, Antonio Cacace, Richard Klein, Darren Lovell, Delaney Mes, Kevin Morris, Sarah Nicholson, Bevan Smith, Giulio Sturla.

NORWAY
Tore Gjesteland, Hector G. Guardia, Hilde Gulbrandsen, Eirik Sevaldsen, Andreas Viestad, Craig Whitson.

PERU
Catherine Contreras, Ignacio Barrios Jacobs, Marissa Chiappe Lanatta, Cinzia Repetto, Hirka Roca-Rey, Paola Miglio Rossi, Nora Sugobono.

PORTUGAL
José Avillez, Alexandra Prado Coelho, Luís Américo Aguiar de Moura Rodrigues Teixeira, Fátima Iken, João Luís Oliveira, Suzana Parreira, Miguel Pires, Susana Ribeiro, Ljubomir Stanisic, Tanka Sapkota.

THE RUSSIAN FEDERATION
Irina Avrutskaya, Anna Belkina, Valentino Bontempi, Sarah Crowther, Eva Mala, Gabrio Marchetti, Giuseppe Todisco.

SERBIA
Ivo Andric, Nikola Bić, Nenad Gladic, Jovica Jovicic, Andrea Kusic, Aleksandar Pavlovic, Vanja Puskar, Dejan Stankovič, Zoja Stojanovic, Uros Urosevic, Danijela Pantić Vlahović.

SINGAPORE
Beppe De Vito, Marco Guccio, Desiree Koh, Michel Lu, Sylvester Ng, Bjorn Shen, Sulyn Tan, Dolores Tay, Debbie Yong.

SLOVENIA
Irena Fonda, Tilen Konte, Gregor Lisjak, Martin Mahorčič, Uroš Mencinger, Boštjan Napotnik, Igor Peresson, Tomaz Srsen.

SOUTH AFRICA
Carrie Adams, George Dalla Cia, Sue de Groot, Abigail Donnelly, Marc Kent, Jean-Pierre Rossouw, Adele Stiehler, Anna Trapido.

SOUTH KOREA
Daniel Gray, Eun-jo Kim, Joe McPherson, Tim Mitchell.

SPAIN
Mireia de la Torre, Pablo Giudice, Marta Fernández Guadaño, Mikel López Iturriaga, Susana López-Urrutia, David Maldonado, Javier Marca, Fabio Gándara Pumar.

SWEDEN
Carl Reinholdtzon Belfrage, Olle T. Cellton, Andrea Consonni, Andreas Dahlberg, Björn Frantzén, Lars Peder Hedberg, Mattias Kroon, David Lundin, Rasmus Ragnarsson, Zvonko Sokcic.

SWITZERLAND
Nathalie Chiva, Antonio Colaianni, Max Fisher, Jonell Galloway, Sakura Hori, Gabriele Merlo, Laura Righettoni, David Schnapp.

UNITED ARAB EMIRATES
Sudeshna Ghosh, Maurizio Pelli, Stefano, Samantha Wood.

UNITED KINGDOM
Diane Amesbury, Alessandro Betti, Bruno Breillet, Lee Burns, Tazmin Cane, Richard Carver, Pasquale Chionchio, Ben Davy, Samantha Evans, Ed Gilbert, Helen Graves, Paul Grimwood, Shauna Guinn, Michael Hanson, Stephen Harris, Andy Hayler, Dino Joannides, Peter Ljungquist, Ailbhe Malone, Kirstie McCrum, Isaac McHale, Ellie Michell, Owen Morgan, Laura Nickoll, Michael O'Hare, Julian Rea, Paul Robinshaw, Scott from Bacon on the Beach, Secret Diner, Gaby Soutar, Hilary Sturzaker, Victoria Trott, Fran Villani, Emma Wilcox, Daniel Young.

UNITED STATES OF AMERICA

Barbara Abbott, Lisa Abraham, Lesley Abravanel, Laura Adiletta, Carolyn Alburger, Robert Alexander, Keane Amdahl, Jane Simon Ammeson, Brett Anderson, Sharon Ardiana, Deidre Ashe, Susan Axelrod, Jim Babinski, Liz Barrett, Christina Barrueta, Julian Barsotti, Adam Baru, Grace Bascos, Jessica Battilana, Joe Beddia, Mark Bello, G. A. Benton, John Berardi, Michael Berman, Sunil Bhatt, Vishwesh Bhatt, Mary Bilyeu, Jamie Bissonnette, Chris Blackburn, Dan Blumenthal, Rachel Leah Blumenthal, Joe Borrello, Arthur Bovino, Nikki Bowman, Amy Boynton, Domenic Branduzzi, Tre Brashear, Elissa Brown, Hillary Brown, Dara Bunjon, Donnie Burtless, Michalene Busico, Aaron Butts, Steve Byrne, Seonaid B. Campbell, Colin M. Caplan, Frank Carollo, Sheri Castle, Danielle Centoni, Chris Chamberlain, Michael Chelus, Martha Cheng, Providence Cicero, Amanda Clark, Alison Cook, Tricia Cornish, Jerry Corso, Chris Crader, Joe Crea, John Currence, David Dadekian, Peter Danis, Famous Fat Dave, Massimo Dell'Olio, Luciano DelSignore, Rebekah Denn, Jason DeRusha, Josh Deth, Sara Dickerman, Don Dickman, Steven Dilley, Lynn Donaldson, Jim Duncan, Brian Dwyer, Victoria Pesce Elliot, Jim Ellison, Greg Elwell, Thomas England, Dean Falcone, Elizabeth Falkner, Tyler Fenton, Ligaya Figueras, Jonah Fliegelman, Michelle Flisek, Michael Fojtasek, Ken Forkish, George Formaro, Rachel Forrest, Jeffrey Fox, Richard Frazer, Helen Freund, Ian Froeb, Evan Funke, Gil Garduno, Paulie Gee, Tony Gemignani, Peter Genovese, Liz George, Pietro Gianni, Nancy Gilman, Eric Ginsburg, Emily Giove, Michael A. Glorioso, Jonathan Gold, John Golden, Nella Grassano, Joseph Hafner, Charlie Hallowell, Marnie Hanel, Jenn Harris, Tim Healea, Molly Hermann, Sandra Holl, Steve Holt, Cheryl Alters Jamison, Jay Jennings, Jay Jerrier, Tony Jioio, Robert St. John, Eliesa Johnson, Brooks Jones, Sharon Juergens, Roxana Jullapat, Jennifer Justus, Jen Karetnick, Jonathan Kauffman, Cyrus Keefer, Melody Kettle, Ann Kim, Nick Kindelsperger, Evan Kleiman, Hal B. Klein, Michael Klein, Katie Kleyla, Todd Kliman, Kate Krader, Adam Kuban, Francis Lam, Susan Laughlin, Christiane Lauterbach, Randall Layman, Drew Lazor, Justin Lee, Matt Lee, Ted Lee, Adam Lehrman, Keith J. Lemerise, Grace Lentini, Rachel Levin, Alice Levitt, Adam Lindsley, Chris Lindstrom, Mackensy Lunsford, Joshua Lurie, Diane Macklin, Marc Malnati, Mary Brown Malouf, Heather Manley, Shelley Mann, Tony Mantuano, Stephanie March, Rick Markunas, Marta, Nevin Martell, Brett Martin, Melissa McCart, Jennifer McClellan, Matthew McClutchy, Ian McNulty, Steve McQuaid, Rich Melman, Leah Mennies, Danny Meyer, Emilio Mignucci, Jamie Miles, Jennifer Miller, Ken Miller, Sarah Minnick, Zach Minot, James Mirabelli, Tara Morgan, Christopher Mullarkey, Michael Muser, David Napolitano, Joan Nathan, John Naughton, Andy Nelson, Charlie Nelson, Enrico Nicoletta, Samin Nosrat, Kevin O'Donnell, Sean O'Donnell, Gary Okazaki, Brian O'Malley, Greg O'Neill, Gregg O'Neill, Jeff Orlick, Dave Ostlund, Josh Page, Christopher Palmeri, Tony Palombino, Jason Paluska, Chris Pandel, Michele Parente, Jeremy Parzen, Kathy Patterson, Lacee Perry, Madeline Peters, Mark Peters, Samuel Peterson, Wesley Pikula, Penny Pollack, Trey Popp, Jonathan Porter, William Porter, Steve Quattrucci, Mike Randolph, Hanna Raskin, Matt Rattigan, Sylvia Rector, Stephanie Reitano, Tim Reitzes, Chad Roberston, Kaitlyn Roberts, Lance Roberts, Brad Rocco, Rick Rodriguez, Amy Rogers, Ilene Ross, Michael Runsvold, Cindy Salvato, Damian Sansonetti, Keith Sarasin, Allison Scheff, Caleb Schiff, Lee Brian Schrager, Robbin Seipold, Mara Severin, Patricia Sharpe, Chris Shepherd, Steve Siegel, Thomas Siegel, Joe Simone, Jason Sobocinski, Cedric Warner Sparkman, Anna Spiegel, Beth Stallings, Susan Stapleton, Justin Steel, Paul Stephen, Kimberly Winter Stern, Jen Stevenson, Jo Maxwell Stougaard, Steve Stover, Loubnen Sukkar, Mike Sula, Joy Summers, Lesley Suter, David Sweeney, Sean Taylor, Brittany Temple, Martha Thomas, Tony Tocco, Andrew Toland, Angelina Tolentino, Douglas Trattner, Geoff Trenholme, David Uygur, Jeff Varasano, Andrew Mark Veety, S. Irene Virbila, Andrew Volk, Kyle Wagner, Todd Walker, Melanie M. Ward, Miriam Weiskind, Mara Welton, Merry White, Scott Wiener, Renee Wilmeth, Nathan Winkler-Rhoades, Drew Wood, Bethia Woolf, Molly Yeh, Tommy York, Andra Zeppelin, Jennifer Zyman.

VIETNAM

Mike Ives, Francesco Patella, Le Ha Uyen.

INDEX BY RESTAURANT

Alphabetically by restaurant name

2 Amys 437
Le 3 Piante 259
4th Spot Kitchen & Bar 338
7 Enoteca 344
8E9 240
50 Kalò 282
90 Secondi 47
208 Duecento Otto 99
400 Gradi 46
485 Grad 202
800 Degrees Three Fires 394–5
800 Degrees Wood Fired Pizza 395
800 Grader 126
800 Pizza 70
900 Degrees 468

A
A16 386
Abbot's Pizza Company 379
Abraxes North 71
Accà Ristopizzaperitivo 308
Ace Pizza 54
Acme Bar and Pizza 474
Acqua e Farina 260
Acunzo 285
Addommé Pizzeria and Trattoria 149
Adriatico's Pizza 411, 413
African Queen 173
Ago's Pizzeria 262
Ah'Pizz 471
Alberto Berardi 257
Alce Nero Berberè 245
Da Aldo 126
Alfons' Pizza 132
All Souls Pizza 446–7
All'Acqua 378
Allegra 183
Allegro Pizza 54
Alphonso's The Original 421
Alt. Pizza 84–5
Amalfi 202
American Flatbread 481, 482, 483
Amici's 400
Amore Neapolitan Pizzeria 367
Amore Pizzeria 497
Les Amoreux 178
Anastasio's 462
Anatoni's 150
Anema e Core 214
Angelina's Pizza 473
Angelo Betti 158
Angelo's 416
L'Angolo Della Pizza 206

Anodyne Bay View Café & Pizza 419
Anthony's Gourmet Pizza 399
Antica 516
Antica Osteria Pizzeria Stefano Pepe 241
Antica Pizza Fritta da Esterina Sorbillo 284
L'Antica Pizzeria 148
L'Antica Pizzeria da Michele 280
Antica Pizzeria de' Figliole 281
Antica Roma 524
Antico Baglio 267
Antico Campanile 266
Antico Forno Roscioli 290
Antico Pizza 440
Aperitivo 41
Apizza Scholls 370
Arcaro & Genell Restaurant 476
Area Four 466, 467
Ariele Ristoro e Pizza Bio 274
Armando's 466
Armenti's Pizzeria 476
L'Arnia del Cuciniere 257
L'Arrocco 261
L'Arte 115
L'Arte Pizzeria 165
Da Artenio 295
Artichoke Basille's Pizza 486
Artigiano Pizza Rústica 511
The Artisan 126
The Artisan Cook 153
Astral Pizzeria 549
L'Atelier Pizza 172
Da Attilio 283
Attimi 178
Auberge de Théo 178
Aubergine 273
Aurora Ristorante 242
Automatic Pizza 439
Avalon 234
Avio Pub 223
Azzurro 214

B
Babette 127
Bacaro 479
Los Bachiche 517
The Backspace 453
Baco Pizzaria 522–3
Bæst 128
Bagby Pizza Company 444
Balena 426
Balisteri's Bluemound Inn 419
Baltazar 124
La Bambola 165
Bank Street 36
Bantam 363
Bar 462

Bar Bocce 363
Bar Branduzzi 271
Bar Centro 412
Bar Cotto 373
Bar de Corso 373
Bar Lehem 71
Baravin 151
La Baronne 175
Bashnya 228
Basilico 527
Basilico's Pizzeria 475
Basta 363
Basta Cosi 179
Bazbeaux 395
Bazkaria 526
Beccofino 34
Beer Revolution 338
La Bella Italia 61, 522
Bella Italia Im Kaufland 198
Bella Napoli 167, 253, 452
La Bella Napoli 190
Bella Nashville 452
Bellaria 510
Berberè 246
Berberè Firenze 308
La Bergerie 174
La Bersagliera 271
Bertha's Pizza 138
Best Pizza 493
Bestia 350
Bexley Pizza Plus 411
BH Foz 194
The Big Blu 149
Biga Pizza 367
Bigalora Wood Fired Cucina 399, 404
Bird 158
Birroteca 444
Bistro Bella Vita 402
Bistrot du Pass 254
Le Bistrot Napolitain 183
Bitondo's Pizzeria 351
Bivio Pizza Napoletana 471
The Black Sheep 99
Black Sheep Coal Fired Pizza 405
Black Thorn Pub & Pizza 408
Blackbird Woodfire 410
Blaze Pizza 418
Bleecker Street Pizza 491
Blue Ribbon Artisan Pizza 361
The B.O.B. 402
Bob & Timmy's 480
Bocca 332
In Bocca al Lupo 193
Bocconcino 226
La Bodega 138 516
Bono Pizza 413
Bonobo 464
Boombozz Craft Pizza & Taphouse 442

Borgata Pizza Café 413
Borghetto Santa Caterina 266
Il Borgo 253
Bosco 264
Botako 319
Boteco Barazzone 524
Bottega 92
La Bottega della Pizza 164
Bottega Pizzeria 344
La Bottega Siciliana 226
Bottoms Up Pizza 457
La Braceria 84
Brandi 283
Brandi Pizzeria 70
Bravi Ragazzi 149
Bravo! 445
Bravo Wood Fired Pizza Restaurant 479
Bráz 532, 533, 538, 539, 540
Bráz Trattoria 539
Bread and Salt Bakery 477
Bread Heads 343
Bread of Life 80
Breadico 418
La Briciola 182, 190
Brick Oven New York Pizzeria 100
Bridge Street Pizza 474
Il Brigante 185
Broders' Cucina Italiana 405
Brooklyn Pizza 450
Brownie's 478
Brunapoli 541
Brunello Pizzeria and Ristorante 124
La Buca 273
Bucefalo 261
Il Buco 58
Buddy's Pizza 401, 402
Bufad Pizza 502
Bufala 341
La Bufalaccia 267
Bufalina Pizza 454
Buona Forchetta 362
Buona Sera 201
Buoni Amici's 522
Burch Pizza 405
Burrata 332
Burt's Place 394

C
Cacio e Pepe 323
Café Aroma 198
Café Chokkolatta 226
Café Citta 150
Café du Cours 175
Caffe Roma 42
Calabrisella 151
Calderone Club 419
Calico 375
Cal's Own 141

Calypso Restaurant & Lounge 93
Camelo 538
Le Camion à Pizza du 104 185
Campagnolo Roma 341
Campanello Caffè Delicatessen 72
Campo de' Fiori 154
Il Cane Rosso 455
Cannova's Pizzeria 394
Cantina Castelões Pizzaria 538
Cantinetta Antinori 226
La Capanna 258
Capo 93
Il Caponi 237
Capricciosa 533
Caravanserraglio 269
Cardamomo 254
Carlos Pizza 540
La Carretta 166
Cart-Driver 364
Casa & Gusto "Da Natale" 166
Casa Bianca Pizza Pie 378
Casa Cavé 533
Casa Ciomod 269
La Casa di Totò 235
Casa do Sardo 534
Casa Mia 70
A Casa Mia 141
La Casa Pizzaria 409
Casa Restaurant 319
Casadoro 194
Casanova 192
Cascina Le Noci 259
La Casetta 212
Castellamare 152
Il Castello 247
Catanzaro's 479
La Catapecchia 251
Il Cavaliere 304
Cavallo Bianco 234
Celini 78
Cena Pizzeria 36
Il Centro 338
Centro 396
C'Era Una Volta 258
Cezar 320
Checco Pizza 236
Cheese Board Collective 360
Chelsea Pizza Co. 55
Chez Bartolo 182
Chez Etienne 176
Chez Henri 179
Chez Mariannick 78
Chez Noël 176
Chez Panisse Café 360
Chez Sauveur 176
Chic Alors! 345
Chicago Pizza Boss 424
Les Chineurs 174
Il Chiostro 276
Chu Restaurante 525
Chuck's Restaurant 396
Ciao Bello 455
Ciao Ciao 158
Ciao Roma 344
Cibo 151

Cibus Noster 272
Ciccio Passami L'Olio 267
Cicheti 85
Ciro and Sons 310
Cit Ma Bon 304
City Café Bakery 343
City House 452
Civerinos 149
Classico Louie's Pizzeria 351
CNR Café 330
Co. 486
Coalfire Pizza 428
Coals Artisan Pizza 442
Coccia House Pizza 418
Col'Cacchio Pizzaria 330, 332
Coltivare 455
Come a Roma 172
Community Pie 452
Da Concettina ai Tre Santi 284
Connie's Pizza 425
Constantino's Venda Bar & Ristorante 480
Al Contegrasso 262
Coppa 465
Corsetti's 465
Cotogna 386
The Cow Pizza and Spaghetti House 60
Cowgirl Kitchen 439
Cranker 510
Crispelli's Bakery & Pizzeria 400
Cristal Pizza 539
Crust 451
El Cuartito 550
La Cucina 154
Cucina Torcicoda 309
Cucina Urbana 363
Cucina 1871 59
Cugino's Italian Deli & Pizza 368
Cuoco 320
La Cúpula 191
Cyrano 128

D
Daejangjangi Fabbro 100
Damgoode Pies 436
Dante Ristorante Pizzeria 409
Dante's Pizzeria 426
Dantes Pizzeria Napoletana 58
Dar Poeta 297
La Dea Bendata 243
Dejavu 263
Del Popolo 386
Delancey 373
Delisio 55
Delivery Urbano 548
Delizia 73 488
Le Delizie di Maria 252
Delmar Pizzeria 493
Dels 343
Desano Pizza Bakery 379, 452
Di Fara Pizza 494
Dicarlo's Pizza 457
Dieci al Lago 213
Dietro Le Mura 265

Difontaine's 153
Dimaggio's Pizza 401
Disco Volante 220
La Disfida 41
District of Pi 437
Divina Increnca Food Truck 538
La Divina Pizza 309
Dobra Vila Pizzeria 222
D.O.C. 46, 93
Dolce Italian 438
Dolce Vita 442
Dolce Vita Pizzeria Enoteca 456
Domani 115
Domenica 442
Dominic's Pizza 449
Don Antonio 487
Don Franchino 232
Don Lisander 191
Da Donato 234
Donato's Pizza 413
Doppio 73
Doppio Zero 544
Dough Boys 142
Dove Vivi 370
Dozzino 470
Druga La Piazza 320
Dry 301
Duca di Castelmonte 270
La Duchessa 248
I Due Forni 199
Duomo 320
Dusty Knuckle Pizza Company 151

E
Earth, Wood, and Fire 444
East Mamma 183
East Side Pies 454
Eataly 70, 304
Eatery A 396
L'Eau à la Bouche 176
Eccellenza 532
Eccome No! 164
Edgewater Inn Pizza 365
Ed's Pizza House 503
Edwardo's Natural Pizza 425
Eetwinkel Buurman & Buurman 162
Einstein Bistro 210
Eisenstein 210
Elegante Pizzeria 493
Élite 241
Elm Street Bakery 473
The Elmton 416
Emilia's Pizzeria 360
Emily Vs. Pizza Loves Emily 493
Emma 290
Empire Slice House 450
Enosteria Lipen 255
Enzo's Pizza Bar 352
Erbelli's 403
Erio's Pizza 277
Ernie's Bar & Pizza 364
Escape from New York 370

Escopocodisera 239
Esplanade 59
Esposito 266
La Esquina 548
Euridice 248
Evio's Pizza 518
Evio's Pizza & Grill 439
Extra Virgin Oven Wood-Fired Pizza 451
Extra Virgin Pizza 85

F
Faam 162
Fabbrica 206
La Fabbrica 541
Al Falco Grillaio 237
La Famiglia di Rebellato 182
Family Pizzeria 78
Famoso 338, 340
Famous Pizza 479
Fandango 238
Farina 367
Del Favero 211
Favilla's New York Pizza 447
Favolsa Pizza 174
La Favorita Delivered 150
Federal Hill Pizza 481
Felix & Oscar's 396
Fellini's 78
Ferro e Farinha 532
La Festa Brick & Brew Pizzeria 468
Fiamma Pizza e Vino 474
Fiammetta 532
Figidini Wood Fire Eatery 480
La Figlia del Presidente 284
Figlio Wood Fired Pizza 413
Filo 551
La Finestra 193, 541
Fiore di Zucca 294
Fiori d'Italia 356
Fiorino 534
La Fiorita 129
Fireflour 410
Al Firenze 331
Flatbread Company 464, 469
Flippin Pizza 510
The Florence 441
Flo's Pizzeria Ristorante & Sports Bar 400
Flying Pie Pizzaria 366
Fong's Pizza 397
La Forketta 86
La Fornacella 523
Fornellone 526
Forneria Catarina 527
Forneria de São Pedro 195
Fornetto 226
Fornitaly 132
Al Forno 36 480
Il Forno 227
Forno Auto 127
Forno Campo de' Fiori 290–1
Al Forno Della Soffitta 294
Forno d'Oro 193
Al Forno East Coast 84
Forno Ottaviani 252

Forquilha 540
El Fortín 548
The Fountain Restaurant 472
Francesca's Italian Kitchen 61
Francesco's Pizzeria 79
Franco Manca 146
Franco's Pizzeria and Trattoria 330
Frank Pepe Pizzeria Napoletana 462
Frank's Pizza House 351
Frank's Pizzeria 409
Franny's 494
Franzone's 475
Fratelli 61
Fratelli La Bufala 70, 438
Fratello Uno 523
Freddies 424
Freemans 59
Fremont Pizzeria 468
Fresca 71
Frey's Famous Pizzeria 113
Fricano's Pizza Tavern 402
Frida Pizzeria 268
Friden Gårdskrog 126
Frijenno Magnanno 300
Fritti 440
Fritz K 107
Frizza 142
Di Fronte al Verdi 250
La Fucina 163
In Fucina 295
Fud 265
Fumo 331
Il Fungo Piano Zero 292
Fuoco Vivo 163

G
Gabin 252
Gaia 98
Galeone 112
Il Galeone 247
Galleria Umberto 465
Gannett Grill in the Lander Bar 375
Garage Bar 442
Gasthaus Figl 198
La Gatta Mangiona 293
Gatto's Pizza 414
GB Pizza Co. 141
Gema 344
Genio 184
Gennaro Esposito 305
Gennaro's Tomato Pie 505
Da Gherardo 308
Ghibellina 437
Gia Drink Eat Listen 448
Gialina 386
La Giara 269
Giardini d'Italia 212
Giardino Romano 212
Gigi 42
Gigi Pipa 273
Gigio's 213
Gilles 175
Da Gino 305
Gino's at de Kelder 333

Gino's East 427
Gioia 360
Giordano's 394
Gioroldo's Pizza 251
Giovanni's Pizzeria 367
Giro 127
Gjelina 380
Glenville Pizzeria 462
Glorioso's Italian Market/Trio's Pizza 419
Gorm's 129
Gostilna-Pizzeria Škorpion 223
Gostilna-Pizzerija Ambasador 223
Gotham Café 153
La Goutte Bleue 175
Gradi at Crown 49
Grand Avenue Pizza 375
La Grange 172
Great Leap Brewing #45 Brewpub 92
Green Pizz 184
Green Pizza 541
Grigoris 274
El Gringo 273
Grosvenor Hotel 49
La Grotte 176
Grotto Pizza 476
Grotto Pizzeria 437
Güerrin 551
Guglielmo Vuolo a Eccellenze Campane 286
Guido's Pizzeria 366
La Guitarrita 549
Gusta Pizza 308
Gusto Divino 261
Gusto Pizza Co. 397
La Gustosa 202

H
La Hacienda Brighton 474
Handsome Pizza 370–1
Hapizza 72
Harry's Pizzeria 438
Harvest Pizzeria 414
Heart Woodfire Kitchen 451
The Hearth Pizzeria 139
Hello Pizza 405
Hell's Kitchen 124
Hideaway Pizza 451
Hogstone Wood Oven 373
Home Slice Pizza 454
Homeslice 146–7
Honest Crust 139
Hops & Pie 364
Hounddogs Three Degree Pizza 414
H'ugo's 206

I
I Love NY Pizza 450
Iggies 444
Imperial Pizza 472
In De Wulf 166
In Riva 502
In Un Angolo di Mondo 265
The Independent Pizzeria 373

Indigo Delicatessen 79
Intermezzo Pizzeria and Café 447
Isa's Pizza 357
Italia Al Pezzo 256
Itália da Gabriele 522
De Italiaan 163
Italian Centre Shop 340
The Italian Pie Shoppe 407

J
J. Baldwin's 400
Jardim de Napoli 538
Jet's Pizza 399
J.J. Dolan's 365
Jo-Jo's Original Pizzeria 417
Joe & Pat's 498
Joe Bologna's 441
Joe's Brooklyn Pizza 474
Joey's House of Pizza 453
Joey's Pizza 79
Johnny Rads 444
Johnny's Pizzeria 473
John's of Bleecker Street 492
John's Pizzeria Ristorante and Lounge 424
Jon & Vinny's 380
Julia 516
Julius Pizzeria 34

K
K&S Pizza 479
Kalimero 318
Kaprica 46
Karijola 319
Kebec Micro Bakery 163
Ken's Artisan Pizza 371
Kentucky 550
Kernowforno 138
Kesté Pizza & Vino 492
Kilómetros de Pizza 191
King Bee Lounge 454
The Kitchen Salvatore Cuomo 100
Kokolo 319
Konoba Bonaca 318

L
L&B Spumoni Gardens 494
L. May Eatery 398
Labella's Pizzeria 441
Ladro 47, 49
Lady Green 257
Lagano 129
Lalo! 510
Lamp Wood Oven Pizzeria 359
La Lampara 271
Lardo 147
Lavina 320
Lazerpig 47
Il Lazzarone 408
Das Leben ist Schön 200
Leggera Pizza Napoletana 540
Lenha e Oliva 527
Da Leonardo 323
Leonardo's Pizza 464

Leva 340
Levetto 351
Li Rioni 290
Libero Arbitrio 257
Libery 304
Licari's Sicilian Pizza Kitchen 403
Lievito Madre al Duomo 300
Lievito Madre al Mare 283
Lilly's Pizza 449
Limestone 398
Limoncello 84
Il Limoneto 242
Lincoln Winebar 398
Linguini Fini 98
La Linterna 517
Liquid Laundry 94
Little Caesars Pizzeria 37
Little Creatures 37
Little Italy 439
Little Star Pizza 387, 388
Lo Sfizio 242
Lo Spela 271
La Locanda 240
Locanda Busento 207
Locanda Cervino 233
Lockeland Table Community Kitchen and Bar 453
Lofthus Samvirkelag 124
La Loggia 510
Lombardi's Pizza 490
The Long @ Times Square 81
Lord Morpeth 146
Lorenzo 200
Lorenzo and Sons 504
Loretta 61
Lou Malnati's Pizzeria 394, 425, 427
Louie & Ernie's 493
Loui's Pizza 403
Love & Salt 361
Lovejoy Pizza 472
Lovely's Fifty Fifty 371
Lucali 439, 495
Luca's Ristorante Italiano 330–1
Luccanalu 116
Lucio Pizzeria 41
Luigia 212
Luigi's 403, 456
Luigi's Pizza 495
Luigi's Restaurant 410
Luisa's Brick Oven Pizza 447
Luna Pizzeria 456
Luna Rossa 192
Il Lupone 112
Luppolo & Farina 235

M
Le Macàre 235
Maddux Pizza 100
Magica Roma 332
Le Magnolie 239, 269
La Mamma 173
Mamma Jamma 534
Mamma Mia 210
Mamma Napoli 310

Mamma Rosa 258
Da Mamo 275
Mana Ricco 112
Mancinni's Coal Oven Pizza 471
Mangia Wine Bar 419
Mangiassai 163
Mani Osteria & Bar 399
Manifesto 154
Manny's House of Pizza 453
Manuelina 253
Le Marco Polo 165
Marconi Pizza 343
Marco's Coal-Fired Pizza 364
Marco's Pizzeria 447
Il Mare 220
Margherita 73, 74
Margherita Pizza 497
Margherita Pizza Artigianale 322
Margo's 195
Maria Marì 243
Maria's Pizzaria 420
Da Mario 42
Marion's Piazza 415, 416
Maroni's Pizza 478
Marotta's 412
Marta 487
Martin City Brewing Company Pizza & Taproom 408
La Mas Querida 548
Masaniello 199
La Masardona 281
Le Maschere 232
Maschmanns Matmarked 124
Massey's Pizza 417
Massimo's 333
Massimottavio 116
Matt the Miller's Tavern 415
Matthew's Pizza 444
Da Mattia 223
Al Matto 101
Mattozzi 280
El Mazacote 549
Mediterraneo 253
Das Mehl 210
Meisters' Pizza 415
Menchetti 271
Mercato 94
Metro Pizza 368, 369
Meyers Bageri 129
Meyers Spisehus 131
La Mezzetta 551
Mezzometro 258
Michael's Pizzeria 361
Michelangelo Mamo 173
Da Micione 238
Micucci Grocery 464
Mignemi Mastro Fornaio 265
Milestone Pizzorante 262
Milk and Honey 34
Mineo's Pizza House 477
Mio's 412
Mipi 182
Mission Chinese Food 491
Mission Pizza Napoletana 450

Modern Apizza 463
La Molisana 213
Mòmò 236
I Monelli Pizza & Co 234
Montalto 227
Montana 200
La Montecarlo 291
Moor's Head 49
Moose's Tooth Pub & Pizzeria 356
Morelia 517
Morsi & Rimorsi, Terroni in Pizzeria 241
Mosaic Pizzeria 330
Mother 130
Mother Dough 379
Motorino 99, 490
Mountain Fire Pizza 468
Mountain High Pizza Pie 356
MT's Local Kitchen & Wine Bar 469
Mulino Bianco 165
El Mundo de la Pizza 543
Mundoaka Street Food 319
Muzzarella Pizza 490
My Pi 424

N
Naked City Pizza 369
N.A.P. (Neapolitan Authentic Pizza) 190
Napolese 395
Di Napoli 281
Napoli 511
Napoli's Pizza & Caffé 100
Napolitano's Brooklyn Pizza 481
Napule È 254
N'ata Cosa 240
Natalie's Coal-Fired Pizza 418
Navona Notte 291
Neapolitan Pizzeria & Birreria 361
Neighborhood Pizza 54–5
Neighbourhood 130
Nenu the Artisan Baker 195
Neopapalis 399
Nero Pizza & Grilll 206
Nero's Pizza 212
Neuhauser 207
New Park Pizza 498
New York Pizza 448
New York Pizza Depot (NYPD) 400
Nhà Léo Pizza & Cakes 80
Nice Slice 481
Nick & Toni's 473
Nicli Antica Pizzeria 341
Niki's 401
Nina Pizza Napolitaine 346
Nino's Pizzeria 474
No. 900 345
Noah's Ark 397
Noce Gourmet Pizzeria 411
Nomad Pizza Company 504
Nonno Gino Pizza and Pasta 55

Norma's Pizza at Root's Country Market and Auction 476
North of Brooklyn 352
La Nostra Pizza 534
Nostrana 372
Numero 28 490
NY Pizza Suprema 486

O
'O Fiore Mio 248
Oak & Rye 370
Occy's 36
Oenotri 362
Officine Degli Apuli 245
Da Oggi 115
Oh Julia 206
O'Hara 319
Ol Marì 237
Old Fourth Ward Pizza 440
Old Lira 54
Olde World Brick Oven Apizza 463
Oley's Pizza 395
Olimpia 542
Olio Wood Fired Pizzeria 380
D'Oliva 194
Oliva Pizzamore 238
Oliver Hardy 235
Olivos 657 526
Ombra 46–7
Omnipollos Hatt 127
O'Pazzo 158
La Opera di Costa 324
O'Principe 190
Da Orazio Pizza + Porchetta 40
Origano 150
The Original Red's Savoy Pizza 407, 409
O'Scià 182
Osteria 503
Osteria 8 510
Osteria Caffè Italiano 309
Osteria Chiara al Forno 483
Osteria Della Piazza 256
Osteria il Nido 202
Osteria Imbusa' 277
Osteria Lucio 153
Osteria Marco 364
Osteria O'Pizzaiuolo 259
Osteria Ovo 131
Otto 464
Ottocento Simply Food 276
Ouh Babbo 191
Our House 445
Ovest 50

P
La Pace 260
Packrat Louie 340
Il Padrino 140
La Pagnottella 234
Paisano's Pizzeria 98
El Palacio de la Pizza 548
Palazzo Petrucci 280
Palazzo Vialdo 244
Palisade Pizza & Pasta 475

Pane Bianco 357
Panificio Bonci 297
Paninoteca No.1 200
Da Paolo Westlake 81
Papè Satan 264
Il Paradiso Della Pizza 255
Park St. Pizza 416
The Parker Pie Co. 483
Parkway Pizza 406
The Parlor 357
Parténope 549
Le Parùle 242
Al Passatore 190–1
Pasta I Basta 227
Pastaria 408
Il Patriarca 234
Patsy's Pizzeria 487, 488
Patxi's 362
Pauli Pizza 211
Paulie Gee's 495
Paulie's Pizza 153
Paxti's Pizza 365
Di Penco 126
Pepe in Grani 241
Pepe Nero 221
Peperino Trieste 250
Da Peppe Pizzeria Napoletana 72
Pequod's Pizza 425
Perbacco 261
Perciasacchi 268
Percorsi di Gusto 232
La Pergola 232
La Perla 162
Pete & Elda's 471
Peter's Yard Café 150
La Piazza 320
La Piazza al Forno 357
La Piazzetta 198, 264
Picasso's Pizza 472
Picco 466
Piccola Piedigrotta 249
Piccola Roma 78
La Piccola Tavola 117
La Piccolina 518
Piccolo Forno 477
Il Piccolo Ghetto 238
Piccolo Pizzeria & Bar 99
Picerija Atos 321
Picerija Etna 223
Picsa 192
Pie Squared 92
Piece Brewery and Pizzeria 428
Pies and Pints 457
Pietra d'Oro 239
Pieworks Pizza by Design 448
Pig Ate My Pizza 407
La Pinède 175
Pinocchio's Pizzeria 467
Pinzeria by Bontempi 227
Pistache 162
Pitch Coal-Fired Pizzeria 410
Pitruco Mobile Wood-Fired Pizza 502
Pizano's Pizza & Pasta 427

Pizaro's Pizza Napoletana 456
Pizza+ 93
La Pizza 158, 172, 408
Pizza 4P's 81
Pizza à Pezzi 193
Pizza al Cuadrado 192
Pizza AM 301
Pizza & Babbà 242
Pizza ar Taio 104
Pizza Bande 211
Pizza Bar 321
Pizza Brain 503
Pizza Brun 177
Pizza Brutta 419
Pizza by Alex 464
Pizza by Pappas 478
Pizza Capri 173
Pizza Centro 368
Pizza Coco 178
La Pizza Cresci 174, 178
Pizza da Mimmo 125
A Pizza da Mooca 539
Pizza dei Cioppi 184
La Pizza del Born 191
Pizza Delicious 443
Pizza do Pão 526
Pizza Dom Bosco 523
Pizza Domenica 443
La Pizza d'Or 173
Pizza du Sud 179
Pizza e Vino 404
Pizza on Earth 482
Pizza East 148–9
Pizza Entre Vinhos 525
Pizza Express 98, 100
Pizza Fabrica 86
Pizza Fabrika 341
Pizza Gigi 351
Pizza Gool 525
Pizza Hacker 386
La Pizza House 397
Pizza House of Columbus
    Ohio 415
Pizza Huset 130
Pizza Italia 477
Pizza L'Oven 475
Pizza Lucé 405
Pizza Mag 346
Pizza Margareta 220
Pizza Mari 220
Pizza Mercato 106
Pizza a Metro da Gigino 245
Pizza Metro Pizza 79
Pizza Mongelli 172
La Pizza Napoletana Regalo
    108
La Pizza Napoli 92, 93
Pizza Nea 406
Pizza Nuova 221
Pizza Pala 98–9
Pizza Papillo 482
Pizza Pazza Italiana 107
Pizza Petro 200
Pizza Pierrot 177
Pizza Pilgrims 149
Pizza Please 323
Pizza Pomodoro 62

Pizza Poselli 323
Pizza Pronto 152
Pizza Quartier 220
Pizza Religion 49
Pizza Rock 369
Pizza Rustica 292
Pizza Slice 71
Pizza Snob 455
Pizza Strada 113
Pizza Vesuvio 333
Pizza Vignoli 522
Pizza Villa 465
Pizza World & M 104
Pizzaface 139
Pizzaiolo 362
Il Pizzaiolo 476, 477
Il Pizzaiuolo 309
Pizzalchik 366
Pizzaperta 42
Pizzaria do Bairro 194
Pizzaria do Chico 534
Pizzaria La Notizia, 53 282
Pizzaria La Notizia, 94 283
Pizzaria Lisboa 194
Pizzaria Maremonti 539
Pizzarium 131, 292
Pizzartist 246
Pizzatipi 152
Le Pizze di Frankie 221
Pizz'elia 260
Pizzeoli 408
Pizzeria 712 372
Pizzeria al Marmi 297
Pizzeria al Tiglio 250
Pizzeria al Vesuvio 259
Pizzeria Amami 73
Pizzeria & Birreria Karis 250
Pizzeria Angelo e Simonetta
    293
Pizzeria Apogeo 272
The Pizzeria @ Terry's Finer
    Foods 436
Pizzeria Azzurri 106
Pizzeria Barbarella 341
Pizzeria Barkun 318
Pizzeria Beddia 503
Pizzeria Bella Napoli 233
Pizzeria Bella Pachacamac 517
Pizzeria Bianco 358, 359
Pizzeria Blade Runner 239
Pizzeria Caio 322
Pizzeria Capraro 240
Pizzeria Capri da Nasti 254
Pizzeria Claudio 257
Pizzeria Conte Luna 264
Pizzeria u Cucuncio 266
Pizzeria da Albert 270
Pizzeria da Cimino 201
Pizzeria da Ciruzzo 105
Pizzeria da Fabio 256
Pizzeria da Nella 426
Pizzeria da Peppe Napoli Sta'
    CA" 114
Pizzeria da Sasino 104
Pizzeria da Zio Giacomo 236
Pizzeria d'Auteuil 184
Pizzeria D'Buzza 101

Pizzeria del Nonno 250
La Pizzeria del Tío Richi 517
Pizzeria Delfina 387
Pizzeria Dell'Angelo 301
Pizzeria Desiderio 256
Pizzeria di Matteo 284–5
La Pizzeria di Rebellato 185
Pizzeria Dick & Doof 201
Pizzeria Dino 115
Pizzeria Don Giovanni 523
Pizzeria Elba d'Italia 527
Pizzeria Excelsior 270
Pizzeria Farina 258, 342
Pizzeria Fiat 221
Pizzeria Fratelli Salvo 244
Pizzeria Fratelli Valle 233
Pizzeria Gabbiano 374
Pizzeria Gennaro Esposito 260
Pizzeria GG Kamakura 106
Pizzeria GG Kichijyouji 115
Pizzeria Gino Sorbillo 285
Pizzeria Gorizia 1916 286
Pizzeria Grotta Azzurra 233
Pizzeria Grütli 213
Pizzeria Gusto 450
Pizzeria Il Tamburello 112
Pizzeria Italia 543
Pizzeria Jolly 198
Pizzéria La Bonne Mère 177
Pizzeria La Kambusa 271
Pizzeria La Panca 237
Pizzeria Lampo 2 285
Pizzeria Le Castellar 174
Pizzeria Libretto 350, 352
Pizzeria L'Italiano 448
Pizzeria Locale 363, 365
Pizzeria Lola 406
Pizzeria L'Operetta 86
Pizzeria Luca Castellano 280
Pizzeria Luna Rossa 255
Pizzeria McKenzie 258
Pizzeria Magpie 345
Pizzería Malandrino 543
Pizzeria Massè 244
Pizzeria Masters 322
Pizzeria Michele 280
Pizzeria Milano 528
Pizzeria Montegrigna Tric
    Trac 255
Pizzeria Mozza 85, 381
Pizzeria Napoletana da Yuki
    107
Pizzeria Napoli 62, 131
Pizzeria O' Sole Mio 272
Pizzeria Okay 270
Pizzeria Ola-la 321
Pizzeria Olbia 201
Pizzeria Oro-Goro 318
Pizzeria Orsucci da Armando
    247
Pizzeria Ostiense 294
Pizzeria Palma 318
Pizzeria Paradiso 437
Pizzeria Parma 222
Pizzeria Passaparola Enoteca
    207
Pizzeria Pellone 285

Pizzeria Pezzo 407
Pizzeria Piccola Ischia 300
Pizzeria Piedigrotta 251
Pizzeria Prima Strada 342
Pizzeria Pugliese 166
Pizzeria Pulcinella 194
Pizzeria Reginella 239
Pizzeria Ristorante La Mama
    252
Pizzeria Ristorante L'Aquila 248
Pizzeria Ristorante Piedigrotta
    256
Pizzeria Romana Gianicolo 114
Pizzeria Romana il Pentito 116
Pizzeria Sabatini Aoyama 114
Pizzeria San Martin 277
Pizzeria S'Arzola 263
Pizzeria Solono 107
Pizzeria Stella 213, 504
Pizzeria Stoà Reale 273
Pizzeria That's Amore 259
Pizzeria Tivoli 409
Pizzeria Toro 448
Pizzeria Totò e i Sapori 242
Pizzeria Trattoria Cesari 104
Pizzeria e Trattoria da ISA 113
Pizzeria e Trattoria da
    Masaniello 106
Pizzeria Trattoria Europa 249
Pizzeria Trattoria Napule 114
Pizzeria Trattoria Partenope
    Ebisu 116
Pizzeria Trta 222
Pizzeria Uno 318, 427
Pizzeria Vecchia Malga 246
Pizzeria Verita 482
Pizzeria Vesuvio 152
Pizzeria Via Mercanti 350
Pizzeria Vincere 112
Pizzeria Violetta 34
Pizzeria Yuiciro & A 117
Pizzerija Panorama 319
La Pizzetta 183
Pizzetta 211 388
Pizzetta's Pizza 450
Pizzicletta 356
Il Pizz'ino 260
Pizzology Craft Pizza & Pub
    395
Pjazza 132
Plank's Café & Pizzeria 415
+39 47
Pomo Pizzeria Napoletana
    358, 359
Pomodoro 321
Pomodoro & Basilico 262
Pompei's 40
Porcelli Tavern 272
Il Porcospino 236
Porta Via 453
Portarossa 195
Al Portici 2.0 240
Portofino's Ristorante Italiano
    E Pizzeria 447
Posillipo 140
Post Office Pies 436
La Posta de Achaval 548

Posto 338
Posto al Sole 164
Pot. Pourrí 526
The Pour House 37
Prelibato 293
Premiata Pizzeria 235
Prides Piccola Napoletana 465
Prima 366
Prima e Poi 304
Prima o Poi 249
Primo Basílico 539
Prince Street Pizza 491
Pro Loco Pinciano 295
Proof Pizza & Pasta 438
Prostens Pizza 125
Prova 486
Prova Pizzeria 381
Provisions 456
Pulcinella 339
Punch Pizza 407
Pupatella 457
Puppi Baggio 526
Putte's 132
Pzza.co 74

Q

Quattro Stagioni 544
Queen Margaret 48
Queen Margherita Pizza 350

R

R&O's Restaurant 442
Radio City Pizza 369
Ragazza 386
Ragazzi Bistro Italiano 340
Ralph and Rosie Delicatessen 472
Ranalli's 424
Randazzo Fresh Market 401
Ranzani 13 246
Ray's Café & Pizzeria 80
Razza Pizza Artigianale 470
Red Wagon Pizza Company 406
Redd Wood 363
Redrossa Pizzeria 418
La Regina 259
Regina Pizzeria 466
Reilly Craft Pizza & Drink 359
Da Remo 296
Renaa Xpress 125
Rendino's Pizza 411
Restaurant al Forno 195
Restaurant Beim Abruzzebier 167
Restaurant Capperi 542
Restaurant Giovanni Rana 167
Restaurant Notaro 167
Restaurant San Carlo 222
Restaurante Libório Praia 525
Restoran Picerija Guli 321
Rhombus Guys 410
Ribalta 490
Ricciotti 85
Da Ricknyo 106
Rio Barbaira 253
Ristorante Bellavista 233

Ristorante Cucina 214
Ristorante da Costantino 245
Ristorante da Valentino 84
Ristorante Delfino 269
Ristorante don Leone 214
Ristorante e Pizzeria Tomaselli 525
Ristorante il Giardino 256
Ristorante Le Gourmet 265
Ristorante Lo Scalo 253
Ristorante Mediterraneo 250
Il Ristorante Novecento Dell' Hotel Rovereto 270
Ristorante Pizzeria Chichibio 251
Ristorante Pizzeria La Lucciola 260
Ristorante Pizzeria La Mimosa 239
Ristorante Pizzeria L'Abate 244
Ristorante Pizzeria L'Antro Della Sibilla 301
Ristorante Pizzeria Lo Stroncapane 271
Ristorante Pizzeria Milleluci 238
Ristorante Pizzeria Onesto 168
Ristorante Pizzeria Totò 233
Il Ritrovo 420
Ritrovo Ristorante 331
Riva 220–1
Riva Cafè 254
Riva Schwabing 207
Riva Summer Stage 221
Riva Tal 206
Rivoletto 133
Roberta's 496
Roberto's 478
Rocco & Simona 511
Roco 185
Rojano's in the Square 138
La Roma 201
Romamor 542
La Romantica 272
Romeo & Juliet's Bakery & Caffe 473
Ron Telesky Canadian Pizza 199
Rooftop Pizzeria 368
La Rosa dei Venti 263
La Rosa The Strand 40
Rosario's Pizzeria & Ristorante 475
Rosebowl Pizza and Rouge Lounge 340
Rosie's Italian Grille 417
Rosso 214
Rosso Piccante 236
Rosso Pomodoro 40, 240
Rossopomodoro 146, 257, 284, 540
Rossovivo 70
Rotolo's Italian Pizzeria 415
Rubino's Pizza 411
Rubirosa Ristorante 491
Rubiu 263
Rudy's Neapolitan Pizza 140

Rugantino 222
Rugantino 2 222
Russo's New York Pizzeria 71
Ruthie's Bar-B-Q and Pizza 471

S

Sa Tracca 262
Sa Veranda di Fra Diavolo 263
Sabatini's Pizza 475
Sacraceno d'Oro 245
Sacro Cuore 148
Safari 179
Sakuragumi 105
Sal and Carmine Pizza 488
Sal and Mookies New York Pizza and Ice Cream Joint 446
Sale Pepe Rosmarino 164
Sally's Apizza 463
Salò 207
Salute 203
Salvia Pizza 527
Salvo's 142
Sammy's Pizza & Restaurant 404
Samosky's Homestyle Pizzeria 417
Sam's Restaurant 496
San Ceferino 518
San Gennaro 345
San Michele 211
Sancho 252
Santa Katarina 72
Santa Lucia Oerlikon 214
Santa Maria 147, 544
Santa Pizza 524
Santaniello's Restaurant and Banquet Facility 404
Santarpio's 467
Santillo's Brick Oven Pizza 470
Santucci's Original Square Pizza 502
Saporé 276
Sapore Italiano 148
Sapori a Colori 273
Saporitalia 148
Saporoso 274
Sarchiapone 305
Sardasalata 264
Sasso 60
The Saucee Sicilian 451
Savario's 470
Savino Pizzeria 339
Savò 252
Savoy 115
Sazi e Sani 265
Lo Scarabeo 232
Scoozi 46
Scopa 62, 339
Scordatos Pizzeria 359
Scotts Brewing Co. 60
Scream for Pizza 141
Scuola Vecchia Pizzeria 438
Seirinkan 113
La Serenata 177
Sereno 165
Serious Pie 374

Il Sestante 221
Settebello 58, 362, 369, 372
Seve 94
Sexy Pizza 365
Sforno 291
Shalom 125
Shawcross Pizza 48
Shooters Sports Pub 468
Short and Main 467
Shot Tower Inn 398
Siamo Nel Forno 550
La Sicilia 159
Signore 542
Simone's 481
Sini 178
Sirani 254
Sironi (Il Pane di Milano) 199
Da Sirulicchiu 272
Sisiliya 106
Skiffer 133
Skinflint 153
Skur 33 125
Slab 465
Slice 142
Slim Jims 211
La Smorfia 247
Smorza 270
Söderberg & Sara 126
Söderberg Bakery 150
Sodo 147
Il Sogno 162
Sol Pie Pizza 416
Del Sole 105
Sole Pomodoro 86
Il Sole Ten-3 108
Di Solito 543
Solo Pizza 301
Solo Pizza Napoletana 104
Solo Pizza Napulitana 73
Solo Pizza Via Manzoni 283
Sopranos Pizzeria 469
Sorellina 35
La Sorgente 232
Sotto 163, 378
Soulshine Pizza Factory 446
Spacca Napoli Pizzeria 428
La Spartura 247
Speceriet 127
Speciali 524
Speedy Romeo 496
Speranza 13 de Maio 538
Spin! Neapolitan Pizza 398
Spiritus Pizza 467
Spizza 518
Spizza Mercato 85
Squire's 445
The Stable 138
La Stampa 549
Standard Pizza 199
Star Tavern 472
Starita 281
La Stazione 267
Stefano's 59
Stella Barra 379, 426
Steve O's Italian Kitchen 441

Sticks & Stones Clay Oven Pizza 448
Stomboli's 446
Story 146
Stravaganze 533
Stuzzico 54
Sud 310
Sugo 159
Sugo Mi 35
The Sunrise Inn 417
Supermaxi 48
Supino Pizzeria 402

T
Tabella 445
Tacconelli's 504
Al Taglio 184
Taglio 304
La Talpa Ristorante Pizzeria 238
Tampopo 108
Tan Tano 542
Tano's Pizzeria 469
Tappo Thin Crust Pizza 487
Tartarughino 264
Tartufo 35
Tastebud 372
Taverna Brillo 128
A Tavola 412
Tavola Calda Europa 266
A Tavola! Pizza & Pasta 200
Tavolina 74
Ted's Most Best 440
Terminal 322
Terroni 352
Theo & Co Pizzeria 55
Three Coins 55
I Tigli 275
Al Tiglio 251
Timbre @ The Substation 84
Tinderbox 35
Tintå 131
Da Tita 78
In Tomasin 251
Tomato Pie 381
Tommy Il Cantiere della Pizza 274
Tommy Millions 62
Tom's Extreme Pizzeria 446
Tonda 292
Tondo 268
Tonino's 58
Tony and Ann's 466
Tony Vespa 72–3
Tony's Pizza 86
Tony's Pizza Napoletana 387
Tony's Pizza Palace 341
Tony's Pizzeria Teatro 366–7
La Torre 168
La Toscane 172
Toscanini 203
Tosi's Restaurant 404
Totò 74
Toto Pizza 58
Totonno's 496–7
Trabella 331
Traminer 266

Trapizzino 294, 296
Trattoria 80
Trattoria Alberobello 128
Trattoria Amici 322
Trattoria Caprese 255
Trattoria da Garibardi 310
Trattoria del Parco 166
Trattoria La Sorrentina 471
Trattoria Pizzeria Amore Kiyamachi 107
Trattoria Pizzeria Belle Arti 246
Trattoria Pizzeria a Casa Vecia 275
Trattoria Pizzeria Ciro 105
Trattoria Roma Sparita 210
La Trattoria Sporting Monte-Carlo 179
Tre Leoni La Pizzeria Con Cicchetteria 274
Trevia 101
TriBecca Allie 446
La Tripletta 116
Tristano's Pizzeria 416
Trophy Brewing and Pizza Co. 449
Il Truletto 165
TSC Signature 74
Tutti I Sapori 47

U
U. Giuseppe 228
Una Pizza & Wine 339
Una Pizza Napoletana 388
Upper Crust 73
Uva e Menta 270

V
Va Piano Pizza Miami 438
Vacanza Pizzeria 42
Vace Italian Delicatessen 437
Valentina Pizzaria 524
Valentino's Pizza 412
Vallelunga Beach 167
Varasano's Pizzeria 440
Varuni Napoli 441
Vecchia Pizzeria 477
La Vecchia Scuola 247
Le Vecchie Cantine 237
Il Vecchio Cortile 268
Veggie Pizza 516, 517
La Vela 201
Velona 105
Venezia 443
Verde 445
Verdi's 152
Vero Pizza Napoletana 412–13
Vezene 323
Vezzo Pizza 173
Via Napoli Pizzeria 41
Via Tevere 342
Via Tribunali 374
Via Vai 351
Via Vai Pizza Al Taglio 210
Via 313 454
Il Vicino 368
Vila Mosquito 522
Villa Costanza 268

Villa Fortugno 269
Villa Giovanna 243
Villa Paradiso 125
Villa Pizza 516
Villa Zuccaro 267
Vin 909 443
Vincenzo's Pizzeria & Catering 478
Vinil Pizzas e Clássicos 528
Vinnie Van Go Go's Pizza 441
Vinny's Pizza 497
Vinto 372
Il Violino 166
Vitale's Pizza 403
I Vitelloni 540
Vito & Nick's Pizzeria 424–5
Vito's 382
Vivo 445
Vknow 60
Al Volo 211
Al Volo Pizzeria 59
Volpetti 296
Volpino 36
Vu Villa 367

W
Wackes 203
Wallo's Pizza 543
The Wave 479
Wazee Street Supper Club 365
Wells Brothers Italian Restaurant & Bar 420
West First Wood-Fired Pizza 449
Wildbake 139
Williamsburg Pizza 497
Da Willy 300
Wiseguy NY Pizza 437
Without Papers 339
Wolf Peach 420
Wolfgang Puck's Pizza Bar 449
Wood 443
Woodbelly Pizza 482
Woodside Inn 80
Woodstock 48
Woodstock Inn Station & Brewery 469
World Pizza 375

Y
YamYam 164
Yard Sale Pizza 147
Yellow Bar 308

Z
Za Pizzeria 350
Zaccary's Pizza 342
Zachary's Chicago Pizza 361
Zaffiro's Pizza 420
Zambri's 343
Zaza Fine Salad & Wood Oven Pizza Co. 436
Zia Pina 40
Zingarò 249
Da Zio Peppe 235
Zola 199
Zoli's NY Pizza Tavern 455

INDEX BY COUNTRY

A

Argentina
Ciudad de Buenos Aires
Bahía Blanca: El Mundo de la Pizza 543
Buenos Aires
Astral Pizzeria 549
El Cuartito 550
Delivery Urbano 548
La Esquina 548
Filo 551
El Fortín 548
Güerrin 551
La Guitarrita 549
Kentucky 550
La Mas Querida 548
El Mazacote 549
La Mezzetta 551
El Palacio de la Pizza 548
Parténope 549
La Posta de Achaval 548
Siamo Nel Forno 550
La Stampa 549
Córdoba
Córdoba
Pizzeria Italia 543
Di Solito 543
Mendoza
Chacras de Coria: Quattro Stagioni 544
Santa Fe
Rosario
Doppio Zero 544
Santa Maria 544
Australia
New South Wales
Mullumbimby: Milk and Honey 34
Sydney
Aperitivo 41
Caffe Roma 42
La Disfida 41
Gigi 42
Lucio Pizzeria 41
Da Mario 42
Da Orazio Pizza + Porchetta 40
Pizzaperta 42
Pompei's 40
La Rosa The Strand 40
Rosso Pomodoro 40
Vacanza Pizzeria 42
Via Napoli Pizzeria 41
Zia Pina 40
Queensland
Brisbane
Beccofino 34
Julius Pizzeria 34
Pizzeria Violetta 34
Sorellina 35

Sugo Mi 35
Tartufo 35
Tinderbox 35
Victoria
Avenel: Bank Street 36
Melbourne
90 Secondi 47
400 Gradi 46
D.O.C. 46
Gradi At Crown 49
Grosvenor Hotel 49
Kaprica 46
Ladro 47, 49
Lazerpig 47
Moor's Head 49
Ombra 46–7
Ovest 50
Pizza Religion 49
+39 47
Queen Margaret 48
Scoozi 46
Shawcross Pizza 48
Supermaxi 48
Tutti I Sapori 47
Woodstock 48
Mount Martha: Volpino 36
Western Australia
Busselton
Cena Pizzeria 36
Al Forno 36
Dunsborough
Occy's 36
The Pour House 37
Fremantle: Little Creatures 37
Mundaring: Little Caesars Pizzeria 37
Perth
Ace Pizza 54
Allegro Pizza 54
Chelsea Pizza Co. 55
Delisio 55
Neighborhood Pizza 54–5
Nonno Gino Pizza and Pasta 55
Old Lira 54
Stuzzico 54
Theo & Co Pizzeria 55
Three Coins 55
Austria
Vienna
Vienna
Disco Volante 220
Il Mare 220
Pizza Margareta 220
Pizza Mari 220
Pizza Quartier 220
Riva 220–1
Riva Summer Stage 221
Il Sestante 221

B

Belgium
Brussels-Capital
Brussels
La Bottega della Pizza 164
Sale Pepe Rosmarino 164
Ixelles: Eccome No! 164
Saint-Gilles: Posto al Sole 164
Hainaut
Frameries: Le Marco Polo 165
Marchienne au Pont: Sereno 165
Ransart: Il Truletto 165
Le Roeulx: Mulino Bianco 165
Liège
Ans: L'Arte Pizzeria 165
Liège
La Bambola 165
Pizzeria Pugliese 166
Seraing: Il Violino 166
Soumagne: Casa & Gusto "Da Natale" 166
Luxembourg
Hotton: La Carretta 166
Walloon Brabant
Nivelles: Trattoria del Parco 166
West Flanders
Dranouter: In De Wulf 166
Brazil
Ceará
Fortaleza
La Bella Italia 522
Buoni Amici's 522
Itália da Gabriele 522
Pizza Vignoli 522
Vila Mosquito 522
Distrito Federal
Brasilia
Baco Pizzaria 522–3
La Fornacella 523
Fratello Uno 523
Pizza Dom Bosco 523
Pizzeria Don Giovanni 523
Santa Pizza 524
Valentina Pizzaria 524
Mato Grosso
Belo Horizonte: Speciali 524
Pernambuco
Jaboatão dos Guararapes: Boteco Barazzone 524
Recife
Antica Roma 524
Restaurante Libório Praia 525
Ristorante e Pizzeria Tomaselli 525

Rio de Janeiro
Armação dos Buzios: Pizza Gool 525
Rio de Janeiro
Bráz 532, 533
Capricciosa 533
Casa Cavé 533
Casa do Sardo 534
Eccellenza 532
Ferro e Farinha 532
Fiammetta 532
Fiorino 534
Mamma Jamma 534
La Nostra Pizza 534
Pizzaria do Chico 534
Stravaganze 533
Rio Grande do Sul
Bento Gonçalves: Pizza Entre Vinhos 525
Pelotas: Chu Restaurante 525
Porto Alegre
Bazkaria 526
Fornellone 526
Olivos 657 526
Pizza do Pão 526
Pot. Pourrí 526
Puppi Baggio 526
Salvia Pizza 527
Santa Catarina
Florianópolis
Basílico 527
Forneria Catarina 527
Lenha e Oliva 527
Pizzeria Elba d'Italia 527
Pizzeria Milano 528
Vinil Pizzas e Clássicos 528
São Paulo
São Paulo
Bráz 538, 539, 540
Bráz Trattoria 539
Camelo 538
Cantina Castelöes Pizzaria 538
Carlos Pizza 540
Cristal Pizza 539
Divina Increnca Food Truck 538
Forquilha 540
Jardim de Napoli 538
Leggera Pizza Napoletana 540
A Pizza da Mooca 539
Pizzaria Maremonti 539
Primo Basílico 539
Rossopomodoro 540
Speranza 13 de Maio 538
I Vitelloni 540

C

Canada

Alberta

Calgary
4th Spot Kitchen & Bar 338
Beer Revolution 338
Il Centro 338
Famoso 338
Posto 338
Pulcinella 339
Savino Pizzeria 339
Scopa 339
Una Pizza & Wine 339
Without Papers 339

Edmonton
Famoso 340
Italian Centre Shop 340
Leva 340
Packrat Louie 340
Ragazzi Bistro Italiano 340
Rosebowl Pizza and Rouge Lounge 340
Tony's Pizza Palace 341

British Columbia

Vancouver
Bufala 341
Campagnolo Roma 341
Nicli Antica Pizzeria 341
Pizza Fabrika 341
Pizzeria Barbarella 341
Pizzeria Farina 342
Via Tevere 342
Zaccary's Pizza 342

Victoria
Pizzeria Prima Strada 342
Zambri's 343

Ontario

Kitchener
Bread Heads 343
City Café Bakery 343
Dels 343

Mississauga: Marconi Pizza 343

Oakville: 7 Enoteca 344

Toronto
Bestia 350
Bitondo's Pizzeria 351
Classico Louie's Pizzeria 351
Enzo's Pizza Bar 352
Frank's Pizza House 351
Levetto 351
North of Brooklyn 352
Pizza Gigi 351
Pizzeria Libretto 350, 352
Pizzeria Via Mercanti 350
Queen Margherita Pizza 350
Terroni 352
Via Vai 351
Za Pizzeria 350
Woodbridge: Ciao Roma 344

Quebec

Laval: Bottega Pizzeria 344

Montreal
Bottega Pizzeria 344
Gema 344
No. 900 345

Pizzeria Magpie 345
San Gennaro 345

Quebec
Chic Alors! 345
Nina Pizza Napolitaine 346
Pizza Mag 346

Chile

Metropolitana de Santiago

Santiago
Brunapoli 541
La Fabbrica 541
La Finestra 541
Green Pizza 541
Olimpia 542
Restaurant Capperi 542
Romamor 542
Signore 542
Tan Tano 542
Wallo's Pizza 543

Valparaíso
Valparaíso: Pizzería Malandrino 543

China

Beijing Shi

Beijing
Bottega 92
Great Leap Brewing #45 Brewpub 92
Pie Squared 92
Pizza+ 93
La Pizza Napoli 92, 93

Hong Kong
208 Duecento Otto 99
The Black Sheep 99
Gaia 98
Linguini Fini 98
Motorino 99
Napoli's Pizza & Caffé 100
Paisano's Pizzeria 98
Piccolo Pizzeria & Bar 99
Pizza Express 98, 100
Pizza Pala 98–9

Shanghai Shi

Shanghai
Calypso Restaurant & Lounge 93
Capo 93
D.O.C. 93
Liquid Laundry 94
Mercato 94
Seve 94

Colombia

Cundinamarca
Bogotá: Julia 516

Croatia

Bjelovar-Bilogora
Bjelovar: Pizzeria Palma 318

Brod-Posavina
Slavonski Brod: Pizzeria Uno 318

Dubrovnik-Neretva
Dubrovnik: Konoba Bonaca 318

Istria
Pula: Pizzeria Barkun 318

Koprivnica-Križevci
Koprivnica: Kalimero 318

Krapina-Zagorje
Oroslavje: Pizzeria Oro-Goro 318

Međimurje
Prelog: Pizzerija Panorama 319

Primorje-Gorski Kotar
Rijeka: Kokolo 319

Zagreb

Zagreb
Karijola 319
Mundoaka Street Food 319
O'Hara 319

Czech Republic

Prague

Prague
Pepe Nero 221
Pizza Nuova 221
Le Pizze di Frankie 221
Pizzeria Fiat 221
Restaurant San Carlo 222
Rugantino 222
Rugantino 2 222

D

Denmark

Hovedstaden

Copenhagen
Bæst 128
La Fiorita 129
Gorm's 129
Lagano 129
Meyers Bageri 129
Mother 130
Neighbourhood 130
Pizza Huset 130
Kongens Lyngby: Meyers Spisehus 131

E

England

Bristol: Bertha's Pizza 138

Cornwall
Lostwithiel: Kernowforno 138
Newquay: The Stable 138
Padstow: Rojano's in the Square 138
Wadebridge: Wildbake 139

East Sussex
Brighton: Pizzaface 139
Lewes: The Hearth Pizzeria 139

Greater Manchester
Altrincham: Honest Crust 139
Manchester: Rudy's Neapolitan Pizza 140

Kent
Broadstairs: Posillipo 140
Faversham: Posillipo 140
Gravesend: Il Padrino 140
Herne Bay: A Casa Mia 141
Margate: GB Pizza Co. 141

London
Addommé Pizzeria and Trattoria 149

L'Antica Pizzeria 148
Bravi Ragazzi 149
Franco Manca 146
Homeslice 146–7
Lardo 147
Lord Morpeth 146
Pizza East 148–9
Pizza Pilgrims 149
Rossopomodoro 146
Sacro Cuore 148
Santa Maria 147
Sapore Italiano 148
Saporitalia 148
Sodo 147
Story 146
Yard Sale Pizza 147

Tyne on Wear
Gateshead: Scream for Pizza 141

Newcastle upon Tyne
Cal's Own 141
Slice 142

West Yorkshire

Leeds
Dough Boys 142
Frizza 142
Salvo's 142

F

Finland

Pirkanmaa
Tampere: Pizzeria Napoli 131

Southwest Finland
Turku
Osteria Ovo 131
Pizzarium 131
Tintå 131

Uusimaa
Helsinki
Alfons' Pizza 132
Fornitaly 132
Pjazza 132
Putte's 132
Rivoletto 133
Skiffer 133

France

Alsace
Strasbourg: Come a Roma 172

Île-de-France

Paris
Allegra 183
Le Bistrot Napolitain 183
La Briciola 182
Il Brigante 185
Le Camion à Pizza du 104 185
Chez Bartolo 182
East Mamma 183
La Famiglia di Rebellato 182
Genio 184
Green Pizz 184
Mipi 182
O'Scià 182
Pizza dei Cioppi 184
Pizzeria d'Auteuil 184
La Pizzeria di Rebellato 185

La Pizzetta 183
Roco 185
Al Taglio 184
Saint-Germain-lès-Corbeil:
L'Atelier Pizza 172
Lorraine
Metz: La Toscane 172
Midi-Pyrénées
Tournefeuille: Pizza Mongelli 172
Provence-Alpes-Côte d'Azur
Aix-en-Provence
La Grange 172
La Pizza 172
Pizza Capri 173
Antibes
Michelangelo Mamo 173
La Pizza d'Or 173
Les Arcs sur Argens: La Pinède 175
Arles: La Mamma 173
Avignon: Vezzo Pizza 173
Beaulieu-sur-Mer: African Queen 173
Bédoin: Favolsa Pizza 174
Bonnieux: La Bergerie 174
Cadenet: Pizzeria le Castellar 174
Cannes: La Pizza Cresci 174
Carcès: Les Chineurs 174
Cotignac: Café du Cours 175
Courthézon: La Goutte Bleue 175
Eygalières: Gilles 175
Marseille
Chez Etienne 176
Chez Noël 176
Chez Sauveur 176
L'Eau à la Bouche 176
La Grotte 176
Pizza Pierrot 177
Pizzéria la Bonne Mère 177
La Serenata 177
Maussane: Pizza Brun 177
Menton: Sini 178
Nice
Les Amoreux 178
Attimi 178
Auberge de Théo 178
Pizza Coco 178
La Pizza Cresci 178
Safari 179
Les Pennes-Mirabeau: La Baronne 175
Saint-Cyr-sur-Mer
Chez Henri 179
Pizza du Sud 179
Villeneuve-les-Avignon: Basta Cosi 179

G
Germany
Bavaria
Munich
L'Angolo Della Pizza 206
Fabbrica 206
H'ugo's 206

Locanda Busento 207
Nero Pizza & Grilll 206
Neuhauser 207
Oh Julia 206
Pizzeria Passaparola Enoteca 207
Riva Schwabing 207
Riva Tal 206
Salò 207
Rosenheim: Bella Italia Im Kaufland 198
Schönau am Königssee: Pizzeria Jolly 198
Würzburg: La Piazzetta 198
Berlin
Berlin
Café Aroma 198
I Due Forni 199
Gasthaus Figl 198
Masaniello 199
Ron Telesky Canadian Pizza 199
Sironi (Il Pane di Milano) 199
Standard Pizza 199
Zola 199
Hamburg
Hamburg
La Casetta 212
Einstein Bistro 210
Eisenstein 210
Del Favero 211
Mamma Mia 210
Das Mehl 210
Pauli Pizza 211
Pizza Bande 211
San Michele 211
Slim Jims 211
Trattoria Roma Sparita 210
Via Vai Pizza Al Taglio 210
Al Volo 211
Hesse
Bad Vilbel: Lorenzo 200
Frankfurt
Das Leben ist Schön 200
Montana 200
Paninoteca No.1 200
Pizza Petro 200
Pizzeria da Cimino 201
Pizzeria Dick & Doof 201
Pizzeria Olbia 201
A Tavola! Pizza & Pasta 200
La Vela 201
Lower Saxony
Lüneburg
Buona Sera 201
La Roma 201
North Rhine-Westphalia
Bochum: Amalfi 202
Cologne
485 Grad 202
La Gustosa 202
Osteria il Nido 202
Salute 203
Toscanini 203
Wackes 203

Greece
Attica
Athens
Margherita Pizza Artigianale 322
Vezene 323
Central Macedonia
Thessaloniki
Da Leonardo 323
Pizza Please 323
Pizza Poselli 323
South Aegean
Santorini
Cacio e Pepe 323
La Opera di Costa 324

I
India
Goa
Arambol: Fellini's 78
Majorda: Da Tita 78
Vagator: Piccola Roma 78
Himachal Pradesh: Family Pizzeria 78
Karnataka
Bangalore: Chez Mariannick 78
Maharashtra
Mumbai
Celini 78
Francesco's Pizzeria 79
Indigo Delicatessen 79
Joey's Pizza 79
Pizza Metro Pizza 79
Ray's Café & Pizzeria 80
Trattoria 80
Woodside Inn 80
Israel
North
Jordan Valley: Fresca 71
Tel Aviv
Ramat Hasharon: Pizza Slice 71
Tel Aviv
Abraxes North 71
Bar Lehem 71
Campanello Caffè Delicatessen 72
Hapizza 72
Da Peppe Pizzeria Napoletana 72
Santa Katarina 72
Tony Vespa 72–3
Italy
Abruzzo
L'Aquila
L'Aquila: Percorsi di Gusto 232
Chieti
Cupello: Lo Scarabeo 232
Guardiagrele: La Sorgente 232
Tollo: Le Maschere 232
Vasto: La Pergola 232
Teramo
Castelnuovo Vomano: Don Franchino 232

Giulianova: Ristorante Bellavista 233
Montorio Al Vomano: Ristorante Pizzeria Totò 233
Roseto degli Abruzzi: Pizzeria Fratelli Valle 233
Aosta Valley
Aosta
Aosta
Pizzeria Bella Napoli 233
Pizzeria Grotta Azzurra 233
Chatillon: Locanda Cervino 233
Introd: Avalon 234
Quart: Cavallo Bianco 234
Apulia
Bari
Bari: Da Donato 234
Bitonto: Il Patriarca 234
Carovigno: La Pagnottella 234
Molfetta: I Monelli Pizza & Co 234
Noci: Oliver Hardy 235
Putignano
La Casa di Totò 235
Premiata Pizzeria 235
Brindisi
Ceglie Messapico: Da Zio Peppe 235
Latiano: Luppolo & Farina 235
Lecce
Alezio: Le Macàre 235
Lecce: Checco Pizza 236
Taranto
Martina Franca: Pizzeria da Zio Giacomo 236
Massafra: Il Porcospino 236
Taranto
Mòmò 236
Rosso Piccante 236
Le Vecchie Cantine 237
Basilicata
Matera
Matera
I Caponi 237
Al Falco Grillaio 237
Ol Marì 237
Pizzeria la Panca 237
La Talpa Ristorante Pizzeria 238
Potenza
Maschito: Da Micione 238
Scalera di Filiano: Fandango 238
Calabria
Cosenza
Acri: Oliva Pizzamore 238
Belvedere Marittimo: Ristorante Pizzeria Milleluci 238
Capitano: Il Piccolo Ghetto 238

Castrolibero: Pizzeria Blade
  Runner 239
Corigliano Calabro:
  Ristorante Pizzeria la
  Mimosa 239
Cosenza: Le Magnolie 239
Grisolia: Pietra d'Oro 239
Guardia Piemontese:
  Pizzeria Reginella 239
Praia a Mare:
  Escopocodisera 239
Rende
  8E9 240
  La Locanda 240
  N'ata Cosa 240
  Al Portici 2.0 240
  Rosso Pomodoro 240
Trebisacce: Pizzeria
  Capraro 240
Campania
Caserta
  Alvignano: Élite 241
  Caiazzo
    Antica Osteria Pizzeria
    Stefano Pepe 241
    Pepe in Grani 241
  Caserta: Morsi & Rimorsi,
    Terroni in Pizzeria 241
  Santa Maria Capua Vetere:
    Pizza & Babbà 242
Naples
  Acerra: Pizzeria Totò e i
    Sapori 242
  Capri
    Aurora Ristorante 242
    Lo Sfizio 242
  Ercolano: Le Parùle 242
  Forio: Il Limoneto 242
  Giugliano in Campania:
    Maria Marì 243
  Naples
    50 Kalò 282
    Antica Pizza Fritta da
      Esterina Sorbillo 284
    L'Antica Pizzeria da
      Michele 280
    Antica Pizzeria de' Figliole
      281
    Da Attilio 283
    Brandi 283
    Da Concettina ai Tre Santi
      284
    La Figlia del Presidente
      284
    Guglielmo Vuolo a
      Eccellenze Campane 286
    Lievito Madre al Mare 283
    La Masardona 281
    Mattozzi 280
    Di Napoli 281
    Palazzo Petrucci 280
    Pizzaria La Notizia, 53 282
    Pizzaria La Notizia, 94 283
    Pizzeria di Matteo 284–5
    Pizzeria Gino Sorbillo 285
    Pizzeria Gorizia 1916 286
    Pizzeria Lampo 2 285

Pizzeria Luca Castellano
  280
Pizzeria Michele 280
Pizzeria Pellone 285
Rossopomodoro 284
Solo Pizza Via Manzoni
  283
Starita 281
Ottaviano: Villa Giovanna
  243
Pozzuoli: La Dea Bendata
  243
San Giorgio a Cremano:
  Pizzeria Fratelli Salvo
  244
Sorrento: Ristorante
  Pizzeria l'Abate 244
Torre Annunziata: Pizzeria
  Massè 244
Torre del Greco: Palazzo
  Vialdo 244
Vico Equense: Pizza a Metro
  da Gigino 245
Salerno
  Positano
    Ristorante da Costantino
      245
    Sacraceno d'Oro 245
Emilia-Romagna
Bologna
  Bologna
    Alce Nero Berberè 245
    Officine Degli Apuli 245
    Pizzartist 246
    Pizzeria Vecchia Malga
      246
    Ranzani 13 246
    Trattoria Pizzeria Belle Arti
      246
  Castel Maggiore: Berberè
    246
  San Lazzaro di Savena: Il
    Galeone 247
  Savigno: La Spartura 247
Ferrara
  Ferrara: Pizzeria Orsucci da
    Armando 247
Modena
  Montese: La Vecchia Scuola
    247
  Nonantola: La Smorfia 247
  Vignola: Il Castello 247
  Zocca: Pizzeria Ristorante
    l'Aquila 248
Parma
  Parma
    La Duchessa 248
    Euridice 248
Ravenna
  Faenza
    'O Fiore Mio 248
    Zingarò 249
Reggio Emilia
  Reggio Emilia: Piccola
    Piedigrotta 249
Rimini
  Rimini: Prima O Poi 249

Friuli-Venezia Giulia
Gorizia
  Fogliano-Redipuglia:
    Pizzeria Trattoria Europa
    249
Pordenone
  Tamai di Brugnera:
    Ristorante Mediterraneo
    250
Trieste
  Basovizza: Pizzeria al Tiglio
    250
  San Dorligo della Valle:
    Pizzeria & Birreria Karis
    250
  Trieste
    Di Fronte al Verdi 250
    Peperino Trieste 250
    Pizzeria del Nonno 250
    Pizzeria Piedigrotta 251
Udine
  Cervignano del Friuli:
    Ristorante Pizzeria
    Chichibio 251
  Comeglians: In Tomasin
    251
  Fiumicello: La Catapecchia
    251
  Flambro: Gioroldo's Pizza
    251
  Moruzzo: Al Tiglio 251
  Udine: Gabin 252
Lazio
Frosinone
  Arpino: Le Delizie di Maria
    252
Rome
  Fiumicino: Sancho 252
  Nettuno: Forno Ottaviani
    252
  Rome
    Antico Forno Roscioli 290
    Da Artenio 295
    Dar Poeta 297
    Emma 290
    Fiore di Zucca 294
    Forno Campo de' Fiori
      290–1
    Al Forno Della Soffitta 294
    Il Fungo Piano Zero 292
    La Gatta Mangiona 293
    In Fucina 295
    Li Rioni 290
    La Montecarlo 291
    Navona Notte 291
    Panificio Bonci 297
    Pizza Rustica 292
    Pizzarium 292
    Pizzeria al Marmi 297
    Pizzeria Angelo e
      Simonetta 293
    Pizzeria Ostiense 294
    Prelibato 293
    Pro Loco Pinciano 295
    Da Remo 296
    Sforno 291
    Tonda 292

Trapizzino 294, 296
Volpetti 296
Liguria
Genoa
  Genoa
    Pizzeria Ristorante La
      Mama 252
    Savò 252
  Pieve Ligure: Ristorante Lo
    Scalo 253
  Recco: Manuelina 253
Imperia
  Dolceacqua: Il Borgo 253
  Rocchetta Nervina: Rio
    Barbaira 253
  Sanremo: Mediterraneo 253
Savona
  Savona: Bella Napoli 253
Lombardy
Bergamo
  Bergamo: Pizzeria Capri da
    Nasti 254
Brescia
  Bagnolo Mella: Sirani 254
Como
  Como
    Cardamomo 254
    Napule È 254
    Riva Cafè 254
Lecco
  Vercurago: Bistrot du Pass
    254
Milan
  Cormano: Pizzeria Luna
    Rossa 255
  Legnano: Pizzeria
    Montegrigna Tric Trac 255
  Milan
    Dry 301
    Frijenno Magnanno 300
    Lievito Madre al Duomo
      300
    Pizza AM 301
    Pizzeria Dell'Angelo 301
    Pizzeria Piccola Ischia 300
    Ristorante Pizzeria L'Antro
      Della Sibilla 301
    Solo Pizza 301
    Da Willy 300
  Vimercate: Il Paradiso Della
    Pizza 255
Monza and Brianza
  Canonica Lambro: Enosteria
    Lipen 255
  Monza: Trattoria Caprese
    255
Varese
  Varese: Pizzeria Ristorante
    Piedigrotta 256
Marche
Ancona
  Ancona
    Italia Al Pezzo 256
    Osteria Della Piazza 256
    Pizzeria da Fabio 256
    Pizzeria Desiderio 256
    Ristorante il Giardino 256

Rossopomodoro 257
Chiaravalle: Pizzeria
Claudio 257
Falconara Marittima: L'Arnia
del Cuciniere 257
Maiolati Spontini: Libero
Arbitrio 257
Moie Maiolati Spontini:
Lady Green 257
Montemarciano: Alberto
Berardi 257
Senigallia: Mezzometro
258
Fermo
Ortezzano: Mamma Rosa
258
Pesaro and Urbino
Fano: Pizzeria McKenzie
258
Pesaro
La Capanna 258
C'Era Una Volta 258
Pizzeria Farina 258
Urbino: Le 3 Piante 259
Molise
Campobasso
Campobasso
Pizzeria That's Amore 259
La Regina 259
Isernia
Isernia: Osteria O'Pizzaiuolo
259
Venafro
Cascina Le Noci 259
Pizzeria al Vesuvio 259
Piedmont
Alessandria
Alessandria: Il Pizz'ino 260
Biella
Biella
Acqua e Farina 260
La Pace 260
Ristorante Pizzeria La
Lucciola 260
Cuneo
Bra: Pizzeria Gennaro
Esposito 260
Fossano: Pizz'elia 260
La Morra: Perbacco 261
Saluzzo: Gusto Divino 261
Savigliano: Bucefalo 261
Turin
Rivoli: L'Arrocco 261
San Mauro Torinese:
Pomodoro & Basilico 262
Turin
Il Cavaliere 304
Cit Ma Bon 304
Eataly 304
Gennaro Esposito 305
Da Gino 305
Libery 304
Prima e Poi 304
Sarchiapone 305
Taglio 304
Vinovo: Al Contegrasso
262

Sardinia
Cagliari
Cagliari
Ago's Pizzeria 262
Milestone Pizzorante 262
Sa Tracca 262
Carbonia-Iglesias
Sant'Antioco: Rubiu 263
Medio Campidano
Pauli Arbarei: Sa Veranda di
Fra Diavolo 263
Nuoro
Orotelli: Pizzeria S'Arzola
263
Olbia-Tempio
Olbia: Dejavu 263
Porto Rotondo
La Rosa dei Venti 263
Tartarughino 264
Santa Teresa di Gallura:
Papè Satan 264
Tempio Pausania: Bosco
264
Sicily
Agrigento
Licata: Sardasalata 264
Menfi: La Piazzetta 264
Sciacca
Pizzeria Conte Luna 264
Ristorante Le Gourmet
265
Catania
Aci Castello: Dietro Le
Mura 265
Acireale: In Un Angolo di
Mondo 265
Catania
Fud 265
Mignemi Mastro Fornaio
265
Sazi e Sani 265
Pedara: Borghetto Santa
Caterina 266
Viagrande: Antico
Campanile 266
Enna
Enna: Tavola Calda Europa
266
Messina
Barcellona Pozzo di Gotto:
Traminer 266
Malfa Salina: Pizzeria u
Cucuncio 266
Milazzo: Esposito 266
Taormina: Villa Zuccaro 267
Palermo
Castelbuono: Antico Baglio
267
Cinisi: La Stazione 267
Palermo
La Bufalaccia 267
Ciccio Passami L'Olio 267
Frida Pizzeria 268
Perciasacchi 268
Tondo 268
Il Vecchio Cortile 268
Villa Costanza 268

Ragusa
Frigentini – Modica: Le
Magnolie 269
Modica: Casa Ciomod 269
Pozzallo: Ristorante Delfino
269
Ragusa
Caravanserraglio 269
Villa Fortugno 269
Trapani
Alcamo: La Giara 269
Trapani: Duca di
Castelmonte 270
Trentino-Alto Adige
Trento
Cavalese: Pizzeria Excelsior
270
Romagnano: Smorza 270
Rovereto
Pizzeria Okay 270
Il Ristorante Novecento
Dell' Hotel Rovereto 270
Trento
Pizzeria da Albert 270
Uva e Menta 270
Tuscany
Arezzo
Arezzo: Menchetti 271
Monte San Savino:
Ristorante Pizzeria Lo
Stroncapane 271
Florence
Greve in Chianti: Lo Spela
271
Florence
Accà Ristopizzaperitivo
308
Berberè Firenze 308
Ciro and Sons 310
Cucina Torcicoda 309
La Divina Pizza 309
Da Gherardo 308
Gusta Pizza 308
Mamma Napoli 310
Osteria Caffè Italiano 309
Il Pizzaiuolo 309
Sud 310
Trattoria da Garibardi 310
Yellow Bar 308
Llvorno
Capoliveri: La Lampara 271
Lucca
Borgo a Mozzano: Bar
Branduzzi 271
Lucca: La Bersagliera 271
Massarosa: Pizzeria La
Kambusa 271
Pietrasanta: Pizzeria
Apogeo 272
Viareggio: Pizzeria O' Sole
Mio 272
Umbria
Perugia
Norcia: Da Sirulicchiu 272
Perugia: La Romantica 272
Terni
Amelia: Porcelli Tavern 272

Terni
Cibus Noster 272
Pizzeria Stoà Reale 273
Veneto
Belluno
Belluno: La Buca 273
Calalzo di Cadore: El
Gringo 273
Padua
Abano Terme: Aubergine
273
Este: Gigi Pipa 273
Montegrotto Terme: Sapori
a Colori 273
Selvazzano Dentro: Tommy
Il Cantiere della Pizza 274
Treviso
Conegliano
Ariele Ristoro e Pizza Bio
274
Saporoso 274
Venice
Chirignago: Grigoris 274
Jesolo: Tre Leoni La Pizzeria
Con Cicchetteria 274
Moniego di Noale: Trattoria
Pizzeria a Casa Vecia 275
Venice: Da Mamo 275
Verona
San Bonifacio: I Tigli 275
San Martino Buon Albergo:
Saporé 276
Sanguinetto: Il Chiostro 276
Vicenza
Bassano del Grappa:
Ottocento Simply Food
276
Cornedo Vicentino: Pizzeria
San Martin 277
Romano d'Ezzelino VI: Erio's
Pizza 277
Zovencedo: Osteria Imbusa'
277

J
Japan
Aichi
Nagoya
Pizzeria Trattoria Cesari 104
Solo Pizza Napoletana 104
Aomori
Hirosaki: Pizzeria da Sasino
104
Fukuoka
Fukuoka
Pizza ar Taio 104
Pizza World & M 104
Pizzeria da Ciruzzo 105
Velona 105
Hokkaido
Abuta-gun: Del Sole 105
Hyogo
Akashi: Trattoria Pizzeria
Ciro 105
Ako: Sakuragumi 105
Kobe: Pizzeria Azzurri 106
Nishinomiya: Da Ricknyo 106

Takarazuka: Pizzeria e
  Trattoria da Masaniello 106
Kanagawa
  Kamakura: Pizzeria GG
    Kamakura 106
  Yokohama: Sisiliya 106
Kyoto
  Kyoto
    Pizza Mercato 106
    Pizza Pazza Italiana 107
    Pizzeria Napoletana da Yuki
      107
    Pizzeria Solono 107
    Trattoria Pizzeria Amore
      Kiyamachi 107
  Nakagyo-ku: Fritz K 107
  Souraku-gun: Tampopo 108
Osaka
  Osaka
    La Pizza Napoletana Regalo
      108
    Il Sole Ten-3 108
Tokyo
  L'Arte 115
  Domani 115
  Frey's Famous Pizzeria 113
  Galeone 112
  Luccanali 116
  Il Lupone 112
  Mana Ricco 112
  Massimottavio 116
  Da Oggi 115
  La Piccola Tavola 117
  Pizza Strada 113
  Pizzeria da Peppe Napoli Sta'
    CA" 114
  Pizzeria Dino 115
  Pizzeria GG Kichijyouji 115
  Pizzeria Il Tamburello 112
  Pizzeria Romana Gianicolo
    114
  Pizzeria Romana il Pentito
    116
  Pizzeria Sabatini Aoyama
    114
  Pizzeria e Trattoria da ISA
    113
  Pizzeria Trattoria Napule
    114
  Pizzeria Trattoria Partenope
    Ebisu 116
  Pizzeria Vincere 112
  Pizzeria Yuiciro & A 117
  Savoy 115
  Seirinkan 113
  La Tripletta 116

K
Kuwait
  Abu Hasaneah: Upper Crust
    73
  Kuwait City
    Doppio 73
    Margherita 73
    Solo Pizza Napulitana 73
  Salmiya: Pizzeria Amami 73

L
Lebanon
  Beirut
    Beirut
      Margherita 74
      Pzza.co 74
      Tavolina 74
      Totò 74
      TSC Signature 74
Luxembourg
  Bridel: Vallelunga Beach
    167
  Foetz: Restaurant Giovanni
    Rana 167
  Grosbous: Restaurant Beim
    Abruzzebier 167
  Luxembourg City
    Bella Napoli 167
    Restaurant Notaro 167
    Ristorante Pizzeria Onesto
      168
    La Torre 168

M
Malta
  Valletta
    Margo's 195
    Nenu the Artisan Baker 195
Mexico
  Distrito Federal
    Mexico City
      Bellaria 510
      Cranker 510
      Flippin Pizza 510
      Lalo! 510
      La Loggia 510
      Osteria 8 510
      Rocco & Simona 511
  Estado de México
    Atizipán de Zaragoza:
      Artigiano Pizza Rústica
      511
Monaco
  Monte Carlo: La Trattoria
    Sporting Monte-Carlo
    179

N
Netherlands
  North Holland
    Amsterdam
      Eetwinkel Buurman &
        Buurman 162
      Faam 162
      La Fucina 163
      Fuoco Vivo 163
      De Italiaan 163
      Kebec Micro Bakery 163
      Mangiassai 163
      La Perla 162
      Pistache 162
      Il Sogno 162
      Sotto 163
      YamYam 164
  South Holland
    Rotterdam
      Angelo Betti 158

Bird 158
      Ciao Ciao 158
      O'Pazzo 158
      La Pizza 158
      Sugo 159
    Rozenburg: La Sicilia 159
New Zealand
  Auckland
    Auckland
      Il Buco 58
      Dantes Pizzeria Napoletana
        58
      Settebello 58
      Tonino's 58
      Toto Pizza 58
      Al Volo Pizzeria 59
  Canterbury
    Lyttelton: Freemans 59
  Nelson
    Nelson: Stefano's 59
  Otago
    Dunedin: Esplanade 59
    Oamaru
      Cucina 1871 59
      Scotts Brewing Co. 60
  Queenstown
    The Cow Pizza and
      Spaghetti House 60
    Sasso 60
    Vknow 60
    Wanaka: Francesca's Italian
      Kitchen 61
  Wellington
    Wellington
      La Bella Italia 61
      Fratelli 61
      Loretta 61
      Pizza Pomodoro 62
      Pizzeria Napoli 62
      Scopa 62
      Tommy Millions 62
Norway
  Oslo
    Oslo
      Baltazar 124
      Brunello Pizzeria and
        Ristorante 124
      Hell's Kitchen 124
      Lofthus Samvirkelag 124
      Maschmanns Matmarked
        124
      Pizza da Mimmo 125
      Skur 33 125
      Villa Paradiso 125
  Rogaland
    Stavanger: Renaa Xpress
      125

P
Panama
  Panama City: Napoli 511
Peru
  Cusco
    Cusco: La Bodega 138 516
  Lima
    Barranco
      Antica 516

Veggie Pizza 516
    Chorrillos: Villa Pizza 516
  Lurín
    Lurín: Pizzeria Bella
      Pachacamac 517
  Miraflores
    Los Bachiche 517
    Morelia 517
    Veggie Pizza 517
  Punta Hermosa: La Pizzeria
    del Tío Richi 517
  San Isidro
    La Linterna 517
    San Ceferino 518
    Spizza 518
  Surco: La Piccolina 518
Portugal
  Faro
    Vilamoura: Luna Rossa
      192
  Lisbon
    Lisbon
      In Bocca al Lupo 193
      Casanova 192
      La Finestra 193
      Forno d'Oro 193
      Pizza à Pezzi 193
      Pizzaria do Bairro 194
      Pizzaria Lisboa 194
  Porto
    Porto
      BH Foz 194
      Casadoro 194
      D'Oliva 194
      Pizzeria Pulcinella 194
      Portarossa 195
      Restaurant al Forno
        195
    Vila Nova de Gaia: Forneria
      de São Pedro 195

R
Republic of Ireland
  County Dublin
    Dublin
      Difontaine's 153
      Gotham Café 153
      Manifesto 154
      Osteria Lucio 153
      Paulie's Pizza 153
      Skinflint 153
  County Limerick
    Castletroy: La Cucina 154
  County Wicklow
    Bray: Campo de' Fiori 154
Russia
  Moscow
    Moscow
      Bocconcino 226
      La Bottega Siciliana 226
      Café Chokkolatta 226
      Cantinetta Antinori
        226
      Fornetto 226
      Il Forno 227
      Montalto 227
      Pasta I Basta 227

Pinzeria by Bontempi 227
U. Giuseppe 228
Moscow Oblast
Reutov: Bashnya 228

S
Scotland
East Lothian
Dunbar: The Big Blu 149
Edinburgh
Civerinos 149
La Favorita Delivered 150
Origano 150
Peter's Yard Café 150
Söderberg Bakery 150
Serbia
City of Belgrade
Belgrade
Botako 319
Casa Restaurant 319
Cezar 320
Cuoco 320
Druga La Piazza 320
Duomo 320
Lavina 320
La Piazza 320
Picerija Atos 321
Pizza Bar 321
Pizzeria Ola-la 321
Pomodoro 321
Restoran Picerija Guli 321
Terminal 322
Trattoria Amici 322
South Bačka
Novi Sad: Pizzeria Caio 322
South Banat
Vršac: Pizzeria Masters 322
Singapore
Alt. Pizza 84–5
La Braceria 84
Cicheti 85
Extra Virgin Pizza 85
La Forketta 86
Al Forno East Coast 84
Limoncello 84
Pizza Fabrica 86
Pizzeria L'Operetta 86
Pizzeria Mozza 85
Ricciotti 85
Ristorante da Valentino 84
Sole Pomodoro 86
Spizza Mercato 85
Timbre @ The Substation 84
Tony's Pizza 86
Slovenia
Central Slovenia
Ljubljana
Dobra Vila Pizzeria 222
Pizzeria Parma 222
Pizzeria Trta 222
Coastal-Karst
Divača: Picerija Etna 223
Lokev: Gostilna-Pizzerija Ambasador 223
Littoral-Inner Carniola
Ilirska Bistrica: Gostilna-Pizzeria Škorpion 223

Prestranek: Avio Pub 223
Upper Carniola
Trzin: Da Mattia 223
South Africa
Free State
Clarens: Mosaic Pizzeria 330
Gauteng
Johannesburg
CNR Café 330
Col'Cacchio Pizzaria 330
Franco's Pizzeria and Trattoria 330
Luca's Ristorante Italiano 330–1
Trabella 331
Pretoria
Fumo 331
Ritrovo Ristorante 331
KwaZulu-Natal
Durban: Al Firenze 331
Western Cape
Cape Town
Bocca 332
Burrata 332
Col'Cacchio Pizzaria 332
Magica Roma 332
Massimo's 333
Pizza Vesuvio 333
Stellenbosch: Gino's at de Kelder 333
South Korea
Seoul
Seoul
Brick Oven New York Pizzeria 100
Daejangjangi Fabbro 100
The Kitchen Salvatore Cuomo 100
Maddux Pizza 100
Al Matto 101
Pizzeria D'Buzza 101
Trevia 101
Spain
Barcelona
Barcelona
La Bella Napoli 190
La Briciola 190
N.A.P. (Neapolitan Authentic Pizza) 190
O'Principe 190
Al Passatore 190–1
La Pizza del Born 191
Madrid
Madrid
La Cúpula 191
Don Lisander 191
Kilómetros de Pizza 191
Ouh Babbo 191
Picsa 192
Pizza al Cuadrado 192
Sweden
Halland
Falkenberg: Prostens Pizza 125
Jönköping
Tranås: Shalom 125
Scania
Kivik: Friden Gårdskrog 126

Löderup: Söderberg & Sara 126
Malmö: Di Penco 126
Skanör: Da Aldo 126
Stockholm
Stockholm
800 Grader 126
The Artisan 126
Babette 127
Forno Auto 127
Giro 127
Omnipollos Hatt 127
Speceriet 127
Taverna Brillo 128
Vastra Gotaland
Gothenburg: Cyrano 128
Stenungsund: Trattoria Alberobello 128
Switzerland
Geneva
Geneva
Giardino Romano 212
Luigia 212
Nero's Pizza 212
Lausanne
Lausanne
Giardini d'Italia 212
Gigio's 213
La Molisana 213
St. Gallen
Rapperswil: Dieci al Lago 213
Ticino
Mendrisio
Pizzeria Grütli 213
Pizzeria Stella 213
Viganello: Anema e Core 214
Zurich
Zurich
Azzurro 214
Ristorante Cucina 214
Ristorante don Leone 214
Rosso 214
Santa Lucia Oerlikon 214

U
United Arab Emirates
Dubai
800 Pizza 70
Brandi Pizzeria 70
Casa Mia 70
Eataly 70
Fratelli La Bufala 70
Rossovivo 70
Russo's New York Pizzeria 71
United States
Alabama
Birmingham: Post Office Pies 436
Alaska
Anchorage
Fiori d'Italia 356
Moose's Tooth Pub & Pizzeria 356
Talkeetna: Mountain High Pizza Pie 356
Arizona
Flagstaff: Pizzicletta 356

Glendale: La Piazza al Forno 357
Phoenix
Isa's Pizza 357
Pane Bianco 357
The Parlor 357
Pizzeria Bianco 358
Pomo Pizzeria Napoletana 358
Scottsdale
Lamp Wood Oven Pizzeria 359
Pomo Pizzeria Napoletana 359
Tucson
Pizzeria Bianco 359
Reilly Craft Pizza & Drink 359
Scordatos Pizzeria 359
Arkansas
Conway: Zaza Fine Salad & Wood Oven Pizza Co. 436
Little Rock
Damgoode Pies 436
The Pizzeria @ Terry's Finer Foods 436
Zaza Fine Salad & Wood Oven Pizza Co. 436
California
Berkeley
Cheese Board Collective 360
Chez Panisse Café 360
Emilia's Pizzeria 360
Gioia 360
Zachary's Chicago Pizza 361
Encinitas: Blue Ribbon Artisan Pizza 361
Laguna Beach: Neapolitan Pizzeria & Birreria 361
Long Beach: Michael's Pizzeria 361
Los Angeles
Abbot's Pizza Company 379
All'Acqua 378
Casa Bianca Pizza Pie 378
Desano Pizza Bakery 379
Gjelina 380
Joe's Pizza 380
Jon & Vinny's 380
Mother Dough 379
Olio Wood Fired Pizzeria 380
Pizzeria Mozza 381
Prova Pizzeria 381
Sotto 378
Stella Barra 379
Tomato Pie 381
Vito's 382
Manhattan Beach: Love & Salt 361
Napa: Oenotri 362
Oakland: Pizzaiolo 362
Palo Alto: Patxi's 362
Pasadena: Settebello 362
San Diego
Buona Forchetta 362
Cucina Urbana 363

San Francisco
A16 386
Cotogna 386
Del Popolo 386
Gialina 386
Little Star Pizza 387, 388
Pizza Hacker 386
Pizzeria Delfina 387
Pizzetta 211 388
Ragazza 386
Tony's Pizza Napoletana 387
Una Pizza Napoletana 388
Santa Cruz: Bantam 363
Sausalito: Bar Bocce 363
Yountville: Redd Wood 363
Colorado
Boulder
Basta 363
Pizzeria Locale 363
Denver
Cart-Driver 364
Ernie's Bar & Pizza 364
Hops & Pie 364
Marco's Coal-Fired Pizza 364
Osteria Marco 364
Paxti's Pizza 365
Pizzeria Locale 365
Sexy Pizza 365
Wazee Street Supper Club 365
Edgewater: Edgewater Inn Pizza 365
Connecticut
Greenwich: Glenville Pizzeria 462
New Haven
Anastasio's 462
Bar 462
Frank Pepe Pizzeria Napoletana 462, 462
Modern Apizza 463
Sally's Apizza 463
North Haven: Olde World Brick Oven Apizza 463
Delaware
Rehoboth Beach: Grotto Pizzeria 437
District of Columbia
Washington
2 Amys 437
District of Pi 437
Ghibellina 437
Pizzeria Paradiso 437
Vace Italian Delicatessen 437
Wiseguy NY Pizza 437
Florida
Delray Beach: Scuola Vecchia Pizzeria 438
Miami
Harry's Pizzeria 438
Proof Pizza & Pasta 438
Va Piano Pizza Miami 438
Miami Beach
Dolce Italian 438

Fratelli La Bufala 438
Lucali 439
North Miami: Evio's Pizza & Grill 439
Rosemary Beach: Cowgirl Kitchen 439
Georgia
Athens
Automatic Pizza 439
Little Italy 439
Ted's Most Best 440
Atlanta
Antico Pizza 440
Fritti 440
Old Fourth Ward Pizza 440
Varasano's Pizzeria 440
Varuni Napoli 441
Marietta: Labella's Pizzeria 441
Savannah
The Florence 441
Vinnie Van Go Go's Pizza 441
Hawaii
Honolulu: J.J. Dolan's 365
Kailua: Prima 366
Idaho
Boise
Flying Pie Pizzaria 366
Guido's Pizzeria 366
Pizzalchik 366
Tony's Pizzeria Teatro 366–7
Illinois
Chicago
Balena 426
Chicago Pizza Boss 424
Coalfire Pizza 428
Connie's Pizza 425
Dante's Pizzeria 426
Edwardo's Natural Pizza 425
Freddies 424
Gino's East 427
John's Pizzeria Ristorante and Lounge 424
Lou Malnati's Pizzeria 425, 427
My Pi 424
Pequod's Pizza 425
Piece Brewery and Pizzeria 428
Pizano's Pizza & Pasta 427
Pizzeria da Nella 426
Pizzeria Uno 427
Ranalli's 424
Spacca Napoli Pizzeria 428
Stella Barra 426
Vito & Nick's Pizzeria 424–5
Galena: Cannova's Pizzeria 394
Lincolnwood: Lou Malnati's Pizzeria 394
Morton Grove: Burt's Place 394
Oak Park: Giordano's 394

Indiana
Fort Wayne
800 Degrees Three Fires 394–5
800 Degrees Wood Fired Pizza 395
Oley's Pizza 395
Indianapolis
Bazbeaux 395
Napolese 395
Pizzology Craft Pizza & Pub 395
Iowa
Des Moines
Centro 396
Chuck's Restaurant 396
Eatery A 396
Felix & Oscar's 396
Fong's Pizza 397
Gusto Pizza Co. 397
Noah's Ark 397
La Pizza House 397
Dubuque
L. May Eatery 398
Shot Tower Inn 398
Mount Vernon: Lincoln Winebar 398
Kansas
Lawrence: Limestone 398
Overland Park: Spin! Neapolitan Pizza 398
Kentucky
Lagrange: Steve O's Italian Kitchen 441
Lexington: Joe Bologna's 441
Louisville
Boombozz Craft Pizza & Taphouse 442
Coals Artisan Pizza 442
Garage Bar 442
Louisiana
Metaire: R&O's Restaurant 442
New Orleans
Dolce Vita 442
Domenica 442
Pizza Delicious 443
Pizza Domenica 443
Venezia 443
Wood 443
Maine
Biddeford: Pizza by Alex 464
Portland
Bonobo 464
Flatbread Company 464
Leonardo's Pizza 464
Micucci Grocery 464
Otto 464
Pizza Villa 465
Slab 465
Windham: Corsetti's 465
Maryland
Annapolis: Vin 909 443
Baltimore
Bagby Pizza Company 444
Birroteca 444
Earth, Wood, and Fire 444

Iggies 444
Johnny Rads 444
Matthew's Pizza 444
Our House 445
Squire's 445
Verde 445
Hanover: Vivo 445
Massachusetts
Beverly: Prides Piccola Napoletana 465
Boston
Coppa 465
Galleria Umberto 465
Picco 466
Regina Pizzeria 466
Cambridge
Area Four 466
Armando's 466
Dracut: Tony and Ann's 466
East Boston: Santarpio's 467
Gloucester: Short and Main 467
Northampton: Pinocchio's Pizzeria 467
Provincetown: Spiritus Pizza 467
Somerville: Area Four 467
Michigan
Ann Arbor
Anthony's Gourmet Pizza 399
Bigalora Wood Fired Cucina 399
Jet's Pizza 399
Mani Osteria & Bar 399
Neopapalis 399
New York Pizza Depot (NYPD) 400
Belmont: Flo's Pizzeria Ristorante & Sports Bar 400
Berkley
Amici's 400
Crispelli's Bakery & Pizzeria 400
Clinton Township
J. Baldwin's 400
Randazzo Fresh Market 401
Coloma: Dimaggio's Pizza 401
Detroit
Buddy's Pizza 401
Niki's 401
Supino Pizzeria 402
Farmington Hills: Buddy's Pizza 402
Grand Haven: Fricano's Pizza Tavern 402
Grand Rapids
Bistro Bella Vita 402
The B.O.B. 402
Licari's Sicilian Pizza Kitchen 403
Vitale's Pizza 403
Harrison Township: Luigi's 403

Hazel Park: Loui's Pizza 403
Kalamazoo: Erbelli's 403
Plymouth: Pizza e Vino 404
Royal Oak: Bigalora Wood Fired Cucina 404
Southfield: Bigalora Wood Fired Cucina 404
Stevensville
  Santaniello's Restaurant and Banquet Facility 404
  Tosi's Restaurant 404
Minnesota
  Duluth: Sammy's Pizza & Restaurant 404
  Edina: Hello Pizza 405
  Hopkins: Pizza Lucé 405
  Minneapolis
    Black Sheep Coal Fired Pizza 405
    Broders' Cucina Italiana 405
    Burch Pizza 405
    Parkway Pizza 406
    Pizza Nea 406
    Pizzeria Lola 406
    Red Wagon Pizza Company 406
  Robbinsdale: Pig Ate My Pizza 407
  St. Paul
    The Italian Pie Shoppe 407
    The Original Red's Savoy Pizza 407
    Punch Pizza 407
  White Bear Lake: Pizzeria Pezzo 407
Mississippi
  Hattiesburg: Tabella 445
  Jackson
    Bravo! 445
    Sal and Mookies New York Pizza and Ice Cream Joint 446
  Ocean Springs: Tom's Extreme Pizzeria 446
  Ridgeland: Soulshine Pizza Factory 446
  Sardis: TriBecca Allie 446
  Starkville: Stomboli's 446
Missouri
  Clayton: Pastaria 408
  Kansas City
    Il Lazzarone 408
    Martin City Brewing Company Pizza & Taproom 408
  St. Louis
    Black Thorn Pub & Pizza 408
    La Pizza 408
    Pizzeoli 408
    Pizzeria Tivoli 409
Montana
  Butte: Vu Villa 367
  Missoula: Biga Pizza 367

Nebraska
Omaha
  La Casa Pizzaria 409
  Dante Ristorante Pizzeria 409
  Frank's Pizzeria 409
  The Original Red's Savoy Pizza 409
  Pitch Coal-Fired Pizzeria 410
Nevada
  Las Vegas
    Cugino's Italian Deli & Pizza 368
    Metro Pizza 368, 369
    Naked City Pizza 369
    Pizza Rock 369
    Radio City Pizza 369
    Settebello 369
New Hampshire
  Dover: La Festa Brick & Brew Pizzeria 468
  Epping: 900 Degrees 468
  Exeter: Shooters Sports Pub 468
  Fremont: Fremont Pizzeria 468
  Gorham: Mountain Fire Pizza 468
  Manchester
    900 Degrees 468
    Tano's Pizzeria 469
  Nashua
    MT's Local Kitchen & Wine Bar 469
    Sopranos Pizzeria 469
  North Woodstock: Woodstock Inn Station & Brewery 469
  Portsmouth
    Flatbread Company 469
    Savario's 470
New Jersey
  Albany: The Fountain Restaurant 472
  Elizabeth: Santillo's Brick Oven Pizza 470
  Hoboken: Dozzino 470
  Jersey City: Razza Pizza Artigianale 470
  Little Falls: Bivio Pizza Napoletana 471
  Montclair
    Ah'Pizz 471
    Mancinni's Coal Oven Pizza 471
    Ruthie's Bar-B-Q and Pizza 471
  Neptune City: Pete & Elda's 471
  North Bergen: Trattoria La Sorrentina 471
  Orange: Star Tavern 472
New Mexico
  Albuquerque
    Amore Neapolitan Pizzeria 367

Farina 367
Giovanni's Pizzeria 367
Santa Fe
  Pizza Centro 368
  Rooftop Pizzeria 368
  Il Vicino 368
New York
  Bergen: Ralph and Rosie Delicatessen 472
  Blasdell: Picasso's Pizza 472
  Bronx: Louie & Ernie's 493
  Brooklyn
    Best Pizza 493
    Delmar Pizzeria 493
    Di Fara Pizza 494
    Elegante Pizzeria 493
    Emily Vs. Pizza Loves Emily 493
    Franny's 494
    L&B Spumoni Gardens 494
    Lucali 495
    Luigi's Pizza 495
    Paulie Gee's 495
    Roberta's 496
    Sam's Restaurant 496
    Speedy Romeo 496
    Totonno's 496–7
    Vinny's Pizza 497
    Williamsburg Pizza 497
  Buffalo
    Imperial Pizza 472
    Lovejoy Pizza 472
    Romeo & Juliet's Bakery & Caffe 473
  Cold Spring: Angelina's Pizza 473
  East Aurora: Elm Street Bakery 473
  East Hampton: Nick & Toni's 473
  Manhattan
    Artichoke Basille's Pizza 486
    Bleecker Street Pizza Co. 486
    Delizia 73 488
    Don Antonio 487
    Joe's Pizza 490, 492
    John's of Bleecker Street 492
    Kesté Pizza & Vino 492
    Lombardi's Pizza 490
    Marta 487
    Mission Chinese Food 491
    Motorino 490
    Muzzarella Pizza 490
    Numero 28 490
    NY Pizza Suprema 486
    Patsy's Pizzeria 487, 488
    Prince Street Pizza 491
    Prova 486
    Ribalta 490
    Rubirosa Ristorante 491
    Sal and Carmine Pizza 488
    Tappo Thin Crust Pizza 487
  Mount Vernon: Johnny's Pizzeria 473

Oswego: Bridge Street Pizza 474
Queens
  Amore Pizzeria 497
  Margherita Pizza 497
  New Park Pizza 498
Rochester
  Acme Bar and Pizza 474
  Fiamma Pizza e Vino 474
  Joe's Brooklyn Pizza 474
  Nino's Pizzeria 474
Staten Island: Joe & Pat's 498
Tonawanda: La Hacienda Brighton 474
Yonkers: Palisade Pizza & Pasta 475
North Carolina
  Asheville
    All Souls Pizza 446–7
    Favilla's New York Pizza 447
    Marco's Pizzeria 447
  Charlotte
    Intermezzo Pizzeria and Café 447
    Luisa's Brick Oven Pizza 447
    Portofino's Ristorante Italiano E Pizzeria 447
  Durham: Pizzeria Toro 448
  Greensboro
    Gia Drink Eat Listen 448
    New York Pizza 448
    Pieworks Pizza by Design 448
    Pizzeria L'Italiano 448
    Sticks & Stones Clay Oven Pizza 448
    Wolfgang Puck's Pizza Bar 449
  Hendersonville: West First Wood-Fired Pizza 449
  Rayleigh
    Dominic's Pizza 449
    Lilly's Pizza 449
    Trophy Brewing and Pizza Co. 449
  Wilmington
    Brooklyn Pizza 450
    I Love NY Pizza 450
    Pizzetta's Pizza 450
  Winston-Salem: Mission Pizza Napoletana 450
North Dakota
  Bismarck: Fireflour 410
  Fargo: Blackbird Woodfire 410
  Grand Forks: Rhombus Guys 410
Ohio
  Akron
    Luigi's Restaurant 410
    Rendino's Pizza 411
  Bexley
    Bexley Pizza Plus 411
    Rubino's Pizza 411
  Chardon: Noce Gourmet Pizzeria 411

Cincinnati
  Adriatico's Pizza 411
  Mio's 412
  A Tavola 412
Cleveland
  Bar Centro 412
  Marotta's 412
  Valentino's Pizza 412
Cleveland Heights: Vero
  Pizza Napoletana 412–13
Columbus
  Adriatico's Pizza 413
  Bono Pizza 413
  Borgata Pizza Café 413
  Donato's Pizza 413
  Figlio Wood Fired Pizza 413
  Gatto's Pizza 414
  Harvest Pizzeria 414
  Hounddogs Three Degree
    Pizza 414
  Matt the Miller's Tavern 415
  Meisters' Pizza 415
  Pizza House of Columbus
    Ohio 415
  Plank's Café & Pizzeria 415
  Rotolo's Italian Pizzeria 415
Dayton: Marion's Piazza 415
Englewood: Marion's Piazza
  416
Grove City: Tristano's
  Pizzeria 416
Lakewood: Angelo's 416
North Canton: Sol Pie Pizza
  416
Struthers: The Elmton 416
Sugarcreek: Park St. Pizza
  416
Toledo
  Jo-Jo's Original Pizzeria 417
  Rosie's Italian Grille 417
Valley City: Samosky's
  Homestyle Pizzeria 417
Warren: The Sunrise Inn
  417
Whitehall: Massey's Pizza
  417
Wooster: Coccia House
  Pizza 418
Worthington: Natalie's Coal-
  Fired Pizza 418
Oklahoma
Oklahoma City
  Empire Slice House 450
  Pizzeria Gusto 450
  The Saucee Sicilian 451
Stillwater: Hideaway Pizza
  451
Oregon
Los Gatos: Oak & Rye 370
Portland
  Apizza Scholls 370
  Dove Vivi 370
  Escape from New York 370
  Handsome Pizza 370–1
  Ken's Artisan Pizza 371
  Lovely's Fifty Fifty 371
  Nostrana 372
  Tastebud 372

Pennsylvania
Bridgeport: Franzone's 475
Clarks Summit: Rosario's
  Pizzeria & Ristorante 475
Dickson City: Basilico's
  Pizzeria 475
Exeter
  Pizza L'Oven 475
  Sabatini's Pizza 475
Harvey's Lake: Grotto Pizza
  476
Manheim: Norma's Pizza at
  Root's Country Market and
  Auction 476
Mount Lebanon: Il Pizzaiolo
  476
Old Forge: Arcaro & Genell
  Restaurant 476
Olyphant: Armenti's Pizzeria
  476
Philadelphia
  Bufad Pizza 502
  Ed's Pizza House 503
  Gennaro's Tomato Pie 505
  In Riva 502
  Lorenzo and Sons 504
  Nomad Pizza Company 504
  Osteria 503
  Pitruco Mobile Wood-Fired
    Pizza 502
  Pizza Brain 503
  Pizzeria Beddia 503
  Pizzeria Stella 504
  Santucci's Original Square
    Pizza 502
  Tacconelli's 504
Phoenixville: Vecchia
  Pizzeria 477
Pittsburgh
  Bread and Salt Bakery 477
  Mineo's Pizza House 477
  Piccolo Forno 477
  Pizza Italia 477
  Il Pizzaiolo 477
Scranton
  Brownie's 478
  Maroni's Pizza 478
  Pizza by Pappas 478
  Roberto's 478
  Vincenzo's Pizzeria &
    Catering 478
Rhode Island
Bristol: The Wave 479
Charlestown: K&S Pizza 479
Cranston: Catanzaro's 479
North Kingstown: Bravo
  Wood Fired Pizza
  Restaurant 479
North Scituate: Famous Pizza
  479
Providence
  Bacaro 479
  Bob & Timmy's 480
  Constantino's Venda Bar &
    Ristorante 480
  Figidini Wood Fire Eatery
    480
  Al Forno 480

Napolitano's Brooklyn Pizza
  481
Nice Slice 481
Warren
  Federal Hill Pizza 481
  Simone's 481
South Carolina
Charleston
  Crust 451
  Heart Woodfire Kitchen
    451
North Charleston: Extra
  Virgin Oven Wood-Fired
  Pizza 451
South Dakota
Sioux Falls
  Breadico 418
  Redrossa Pizzeria 418
Tennessee
Chattanooga: Community
  Pie 452
Nashville
  Bella Napoli 452
  Bella Nashville 452
  City House 452
  Desano Pizza Bakery 452
  Joey's House of Pizza 453
  Lockeland Table
    Community Kitchen and
    Bar 453
  Manny's House of Pizza
    453
  Porta Via 453
Texas
Austin
  The Backspace 453
  Bufalina Pizza 454
  East Side Pies 454
  Home Slice Pizza 454
  King Bee Lounge 454
  Via 313 454
Dallas
  Il Cane Rosso 455
  Zoli's NY Pizza Tavern 455
Fort Worth: Pizza Snob 455
Houston
  Ciao Bello 455
  Coltivare 455
  Dolce Vita Pizzeria Enoteca
    456
  Luigi's 456
  Luna Pizzeria 456
  Pizaro's Pizza Napoletana
    456
  Provisions 456
Utah
Orem: Pizzeria 712 372
Park City: Vinto 372
Salt Lake City
  Settebello 372
  Vinto 372
Vermont
Burlington
  American Flatbread 481
  Pizzeria Verita 482
Cabot: Woodbelly Pizza 482
Charlotte
  Pizza on Earth 482

Pizza Papillo 482
Middlebury: American
  Flatbread 482
Norwich: Osteria Chiara al
  Forno 483
Richmond: Bottoms Up Pizza
  457
Waitsfield: American
  Flatbread 483
West Glover: The Parker Pie
  Co. 483
Virginia
Arlington: Pupatella 457
Washington
Orcas Island: Hogstone
  Wood Oven 373
Seattle
  Bar Cotto 373
  Bar de Corso 373
  Delancey 373
  The Independent Pizzeria
    373
  Pizzeria Gabbiano 374
  Serious Pie 374
  Via Tribunali 374
  World Pizza 375
West Virginia
Fayetteville: Pies and Pints
  457
Wheeling: Dicarlo's Pizza
  457
Wisconsin
Glendale: Blaze Pizza 418
Kenosha: Mangia Wine Bar
  419
Madison: Pizza Brutta 419
Milwaukee
  Anodyne Bay View Café &
    Pizza 419
  Balisteri's Bluemound Inn
    419
  Calderone Club 419
  Glorioso's Italian Market/
    Trio's Pizza 419
  Maria's Pizzaria 420
  Wolf Peach 420
  Zaffiro's Pizza 420
Racine: Wells Brothers Italian
  Restaurant & Bar 420
Sheboygan: Il Ritrovo 420
West Allis: Alphonso's The
  Original 421
Wyoming
Lander: Gannett Grill in the
  Lander Bar 375
Laramie: Grand Avenue
  Pizza 375
Wilson: Calico 375

V
Venezuela
Miranda
  Caracas: Evio's Pizza 518
Vietnam
Da Nang
  Bread of Life 80
  Nhà Léo Pizza & Cakes 80
Hanoi: Da Paolo Westlake 81

Ho Chi Minh City
  The Long @ Times Square 81
  Pizza 4P's 81

W

Wales
Cardiff
  Anatoni's 150
  Café Citta 150
  Calabrisella 151
  Cibo 151
  Dusty Knuckle Pizza
    Company 151
Ceredigion
  Aberystwyth: Baravin 151
  Cardigan: Pizzatipi 152
Swansea
  Castellamare 152
  Pizzeria Vesuvio 152
  Verdi's 152
Vale of Glamorgan
  Penarth: Pizza Pronto 152
  Sully: The Artisan Cook 153

Phaidon Press Limited
Regent's Wharf
All Saints Street
London N1 9AP

Phaidon Press Inc.
65 Bleecker Street
New York, NY 10012

phaidon.com

First published in 2016
© 2016 Phaidon Press Limited

ISBN 978 0 7148 7116 5

CIP catalogue records for this book are available from
the British Library and the Library of Congress.

As many restaurants are closed Sunday and/or Monday,
and some change their opening hours in relation to the
seasons or close for extended periods at different times
of the year, it is always advisable to check opening
hours before visiting. All information is correct at the
time of going to print, but is subject to change.

Commissioning Editor: Emilia Terragni
Project Editors: Clare Churly and Ellie Smith
Production Controller: Steve Bryant

Designed by Kobi Benezri and Julia Hasting

Printed in Italy

The publisher would like to thank all the participating
contributors for their generosity, time, and insightful
restaurant recommendations; Daniel Young for his
commitment and enthusiasm; and Ailin Aleixo, Jane Birch,
Vanessa Bird, Rachel Bond, Sophie Chatellier, Clare Churly,
Capucine Conix, Mia Daltas, Jane Ellis, Yuma Gartner,
Sam Gordon, Lena Hall, Anne Heining, Rosamund King,
Fiona Koscak, Justin Lewis, Lucas Liccini, Lesley Malkin,
Aisha Maniar, João Mota, Jo Murray, Tom Powell, Helen
Rutherford, Jennifer Shanmugaratnam, Hannah Sullivan,
Robin Thompson, Giulia Tognon, and Jana Zajicova for
their contributions to the book.

Illustrations from thenounproject.com: pizza by Marcus
Michaels (cover); Japanese flag by Derek Williams Green
(p.118); pizza cutter by Ale Estrada (p.312); pizza oven
by Rafael Farias Leão (p.314); pizza box by Surendra
Jayawardena (p.390); map by Karsten Barnett (p.430);
wheatsheaf by Eva Verbeek (p.458); sausage by Jeroen
Schoonderbeek (p.552). Illustrations on pages 64, 88, 432,
and 506 by Julia Hasting.

About the author
Food critic Daniel Young is the London pop-up pioneer
behind youngandfoodish.com and its BurgerMonday,
PizzaTuesday, and SpagWednesday event series.
He established himself as a pizza authority while
restaurant critic of the *New York Daily News*. "He has,"
wrote Ed Levine, the creator of Serious Eats, "perfect
pizza pitch." He is the author of eight books, including
The Paris Cafe Cookbook and *Made in Marseille*. He
has written about food for the *New York Times*, the
Los Angeles Times, and the *Guardian* and was named
Online Writer of the Year at the Fortnum & Mason Food
and Drink Awards 2013.

Author acknowledgments
It took a lot of great people to create *Where to Eat Pizza* for
a global audience. It was a special privilege to
collaborate with the 120 distinguished colleagues who
served as regional experts. All but seven were new
acquaintances who generously put their confidence in
me and their confidences in the guide. They completed
our survey, disclosing their top pizzeria picks, and enlisted
nearly one thousand trusted insiders to do the same. The
recommendations and commentaries of these astute pizza
informants form the guts of the guide. If only I could take
them all out for a Margherita to thank them in person.

For the essays I drew on the knowledge of Massimo
Bosco, Rossella Ceccarini, Enzo Coccia, Vincenzo
D'Antonio, Stefano Ferrara, Tony Gemignani, Akio
Nishikawa, Franco Pepe, Wesley Pikula, Christian Puglisi,
Sylvia Rector, Francesco Salvo, Gino Sorbillo, Jeff
Varasano, and Scott Weiner.

Every aspect of the survey, from the design,
translation, and implementation of the questions to the
collection, processing, and editing of the responses, was
coordinated by our indefatigable project editor Clare
Churly. Ellie Smith, commissioning editor for food at
Phaidon Press, guided this ambitious undertaking from
inception to conclusion, ensuring standards were never
compromised. Phaidon editorial director Emilia Terragni
and I began discussing a pizza book in 2008. This guide
was made possible by her persistence. I also had the
backing of my agent Alice Martell and her unerring
smarts, class, and loyalty.

This book is dedicated to my mother Mimi Young, my
late father David Young, my brothers Bill Young and Roy
Young, and our family pizza nights at Luigino's.

My wife Vivian Constantinopoulos was *Where to Eat
Pizza*'s secret weapon. She is a perceptive judge of words
and a darn good one of pizza, too. When out with our son
David she insists we order and share one pizza at a time,
never letting it cool.